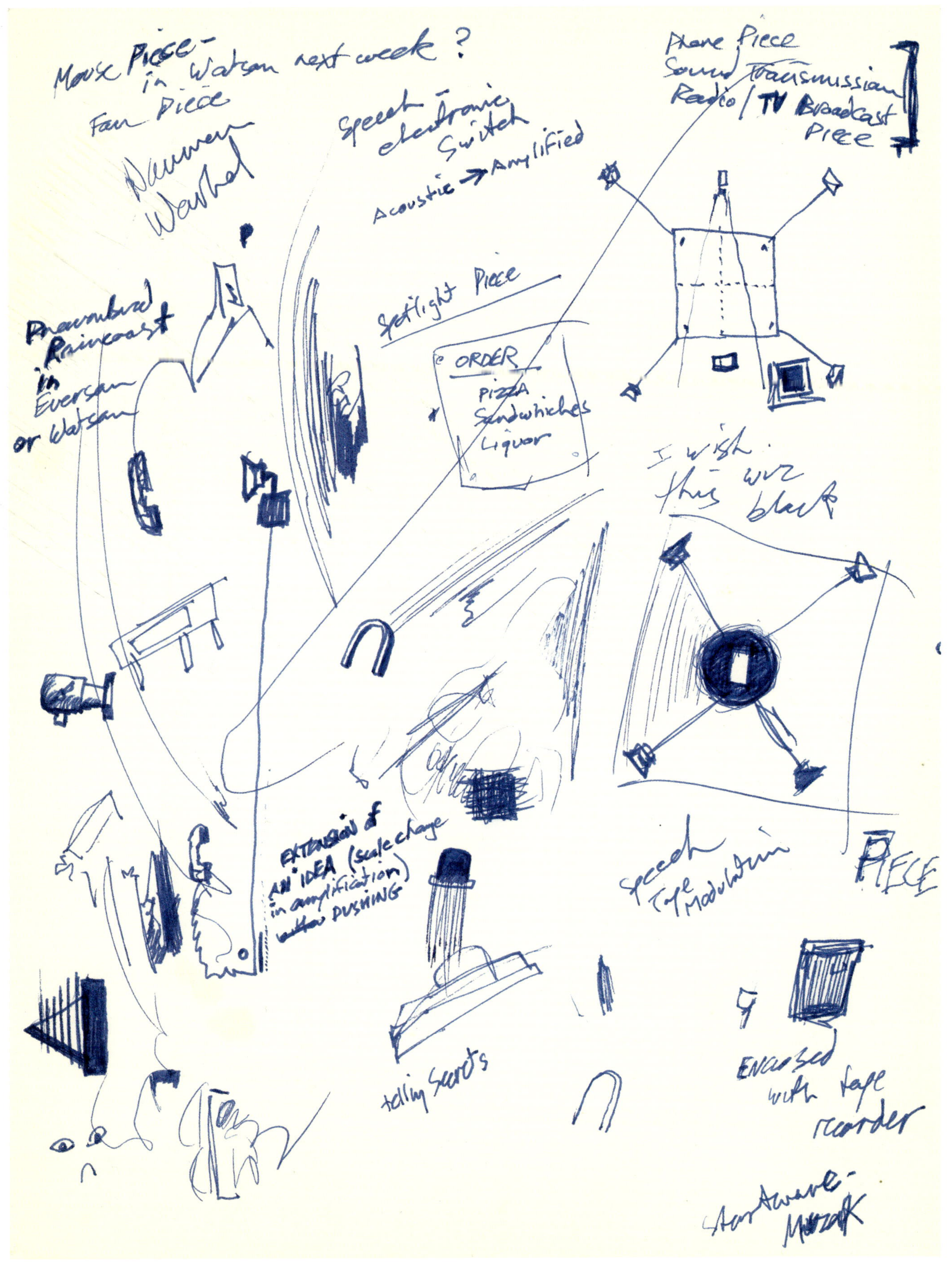

Mouse Piece - in Watson next week ?
Fan Piece
Phone Piece
Sound Transmission
Radio / TV Broadcast Piece
Speech - electronic Switch
Acoustic → Amplified
Spotlight Piece
ORDER
PIZZA
Sandwiches
Liquor
I wish this wuz black
EXTENSION of AN IDEA (scale change in amplification) without PUSHING
Speech Tape Modulation
PIECE
telling secrets
Encased with tape recorder

BILL VIOLA

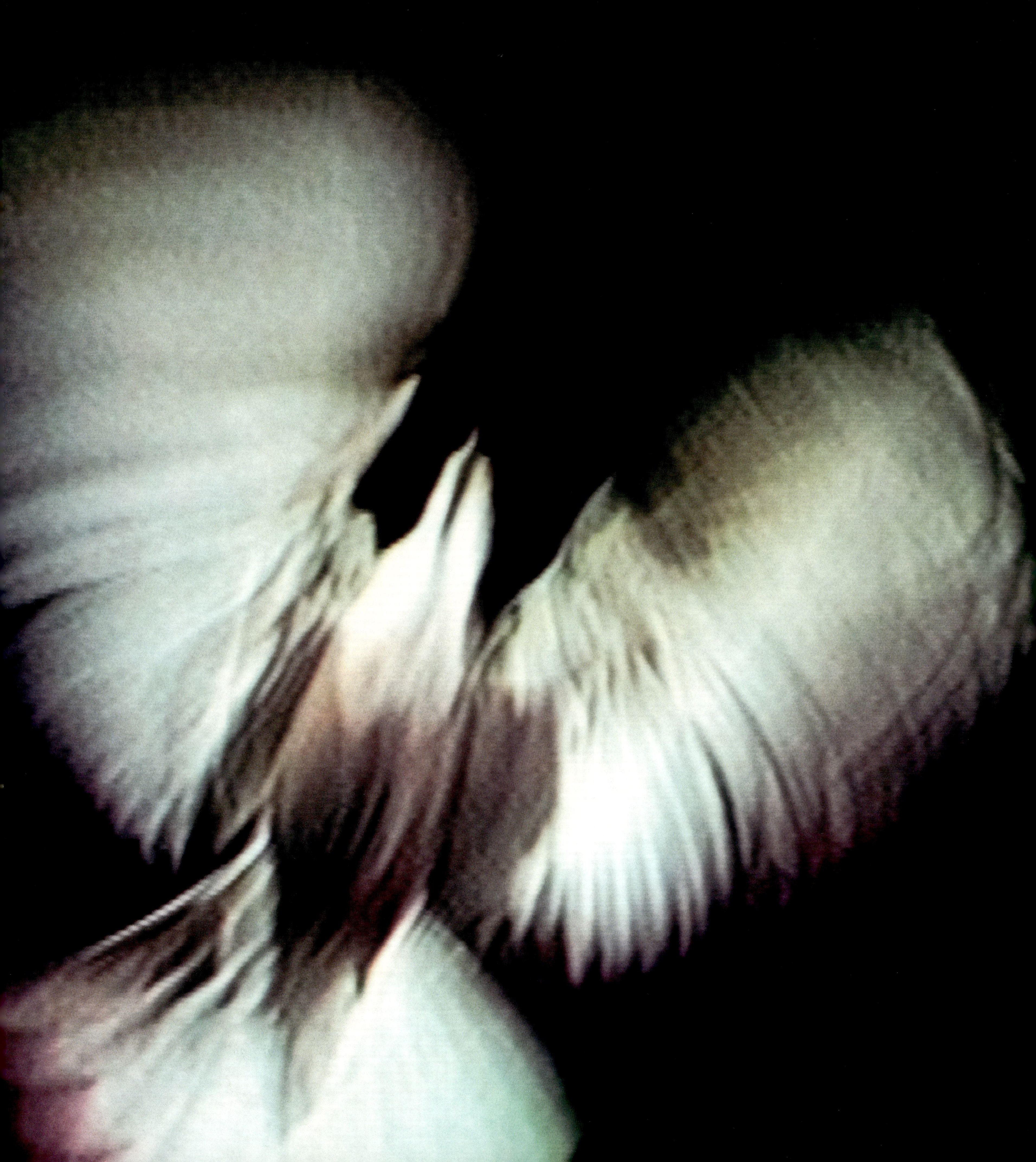

BILL VIOLA

JOHN G. HANHARDT Edited by KIRA PEROV

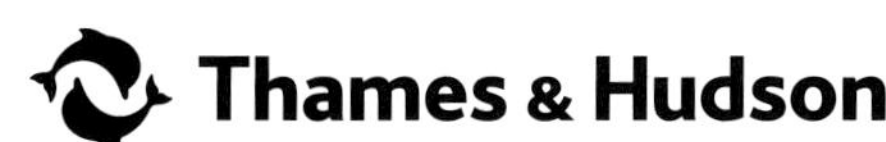

The Middens — the refuse of society.
junk heap of images

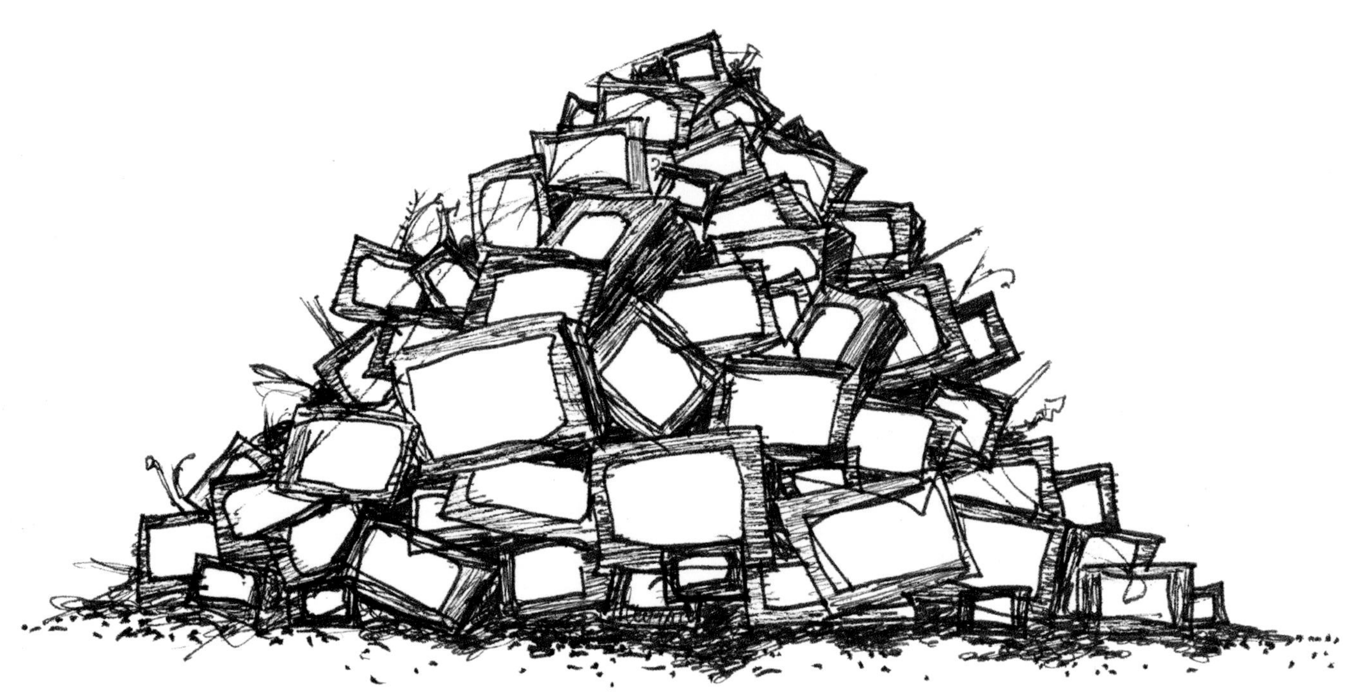

12 ft. high pile of junked televisions
Images flicker across the screens, interspersed with snow and static. The TV's ~~[illegible]~~ seem like they have just been junked a moment ago while still on. The entire pile feels like it could explode. Sound is loud combination of static and actual source video. The images are of mass media clutter as background with images of the refuse of culture poor, homeless, ~~sick~~, and or archival footage

Sequential switching - certain image sources are switched at high speed throughout the monitor matrix. There are several pathways of the images other sets are broken or flicker in snow.

CONTENTS

PREFACE

KIRA PEROV

It has been almost forty years since Bill Viola walked into my office at La Trobe University in Melbourne, Australia, coming at my invitation in 1977 to participate in the first video exhibition on a campus that welcomed cutting-edge forms of creative expression. Bill had not long been immersed in this new medium of video, but the works that he showed at that time already contained the foundation of his exploration of the fundamental themes at the core of our existence—life, death, birth, rebirth, transformation, transfiguration—that would continue to be the basis of his work throughout his creative life. "Birth is not a beginning, death is not an end,"[1] he transcribed into his journal.

1. Chuang Tzu (399–295 BC).

Bill's work resonated deeply in me; it came from a place that was part of the invisible world, a place of inner landscapes that I found easy to inhabit. Landscapes where time is stretched to infinity, where subtle changes of light create an eternity, and where sound is extended beyond hearing. It was a space for meditation, contemplation, and, perhaps, even epiphany.

As we became friends, Bill and I discovered that our life experiences had been taking a similar path, and a year after we met, we decided to journey together. It has been a privilege to be not only a witness but also a participant in the creation of his profound body of work. From the early days of traveling and gathering materials, to the more complicated projects requiring studios and specialized crews, my role grew larger until eventually I found myself managing all aspects of Bill's art commissions, exhibitions, documentation, and catalogues. And always, the goal was to help bring Bill's inner visions into the world.

The invitation from Thames & Hudson to edit a book on the art of Bill Viola offered a wonderful opportunity to realize something I have been thinking about for many years: to create a book that was not focused on an exhibition but was a reflection on Bill's career and the evolution of a large body of work. In addition, this survey would provide insights into the ideas and life experiences that informed that work, and also its unique place in contemporary art.

The first step was to identify the right person to contribute the text for the book. Bill and I looked to John Hanhardt, a respected curator of film and media arts who did so much to bring video art into the museum. John has shown and commissioned a number of Bill's pieces, and his deep familiarity with Bill's work, as well as his scholarship in film and media art, made him the perfect person to write for this book. It has been a pleasure to work with John. His openness to all aspects of Bill's work, his interviews with both of us, and his insights into the contemporary art world make this an invaluable text.

Another goal was to produce a book designed to illustrate both the process of creating the artworks and the way each piece fits into an overall aesthetic. For this reason, I incorporated a selection of photo documentation of individual pieces, a presentation of pages from Bill's notebooks, as well as material drawn from the vast archive of my photographs detailing the production process. I sought to weave all these elements through John's text in order to visually represent Bill's personal and artistic journey.

The design of this book was a wonderful creative collaboration with Lorraine Wild of Green Dragon Office and her associate, Amy Fortunato. I first worked with Lorraine in 2003 on our award-winning catalogue for the J. Paul Getty Museum, *Bill Viola: The Passions*. Her familiarity with and deep understanding of the artwork enabled us to find new ways to represent video pieces on the pages of a book. In addition, Amy's skillful and careful attention to all the details was essential in supporting the book's design. My special thanks go to Elizabeth Steele Basile at Bill Viola Studio, for her diligent research assistance, and to Stephanie Camu for her kind support and helpful advice. Thanks also to Rusty Sena and Rick Legorreta of Echelon Color for their extra care with the reproduction of Bill's original notebooks and drawings. I am grateful to Jacky Klein, formerly with Thames & Hudson, who invited me to edit this book, and I extend thanks to her successor, Roger Thorp, and the members of staff at the press—Johanna Neurath, Ginny Liggitt, Mark Ralph, and Maria Ranauro—who helped make the realization of this book such a smooth process.

This project has been a significant undertaking that has provided me with an opportunity to reflect back as well as look forward. I am indebted to my family, sons Blake and Andrei, for their support, and especially to Bill, whose profound vision has enriched our lives. And finally, I am deeply grateful to my mother, Lucy Perov, who taught me about the eternal lighting of candles at the shrine of Self-Knowledge.

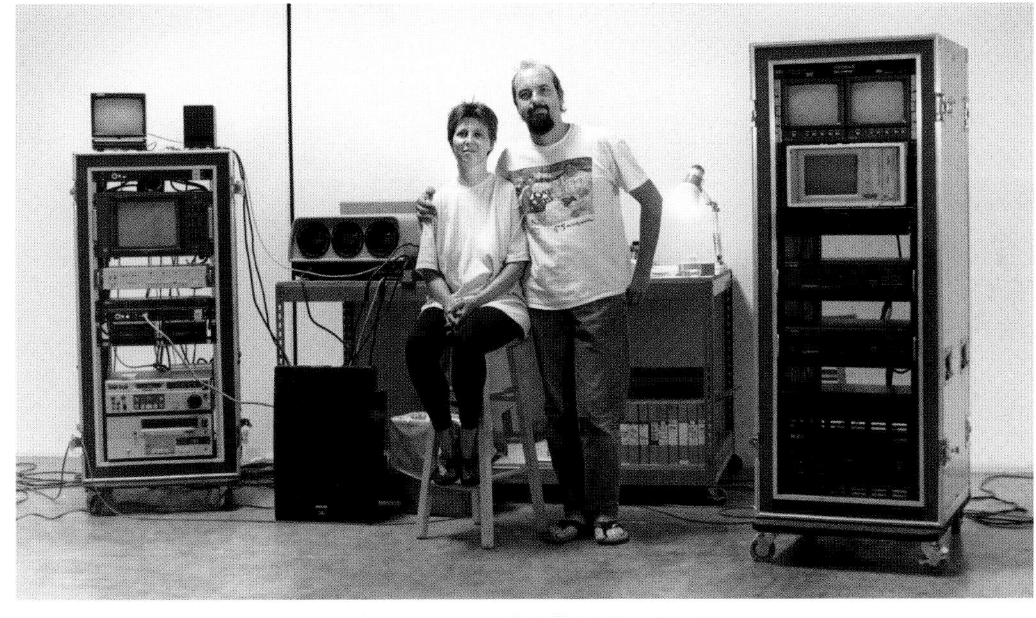

Kira Perov and Bill Viola, Bill Viola Studio, Signal Hill, CA, August 1992

Bill Viola

LET'S DIVORCE the FUTURE FROM TECHNOLOGY AND TALK ABOUT HUMAN VALUES. I SEE the NATURE of THINGS TODAY IN the WORLD AND THERE SEEMS to BE A STRONG FORCE of DISCONTENT AND EVIL. AND I WONDER HOW THERE CANNOT BE SOME COUNTERBALANCING FORCE, SOMETHING THAT CAN APPLY ITSELF to the SPIRIT of MAN? AND I BEGIN to THINK ABOUT WHAT IS the MEANING of the FILM WORK I'M DOING? I BELIEVE IT'S POSSIBLE THAT AN INADVERTENT SPIN-OFF FROM TECHNOLOGY WILL TRANSFORM MAN INTO A TRANSCENDENTAL BEING. THERE ISN'T MUCH WE CAN CONCIEVE NOW THAT CAN GIVE US A CLUE TO HOW IT WILL COME ABOUT. BUT I SUSPECT VISION WILL PLAY AN IMPORTANT ROLE. THE EYE WILL HAVE A LOT TO DO WITH IT. IT COULD CONCIEVABLY BE SOME EXTERNAL THING, WHICH METAPHYSICALLY WILL AFFECT the MIND AND CAUSE SOME TRANSCENDENTAL EXPERIENCE. SO WITH THAT IN MIND I'VE BEEN THINKING of WAYS to INTEGRATE the REALIST IMAGE INTO the NON OBJECTIVE IMAGE SO THAT A SYNTHESIS WILL EVOLVE, A CINEMATIC EXPERIENCE WHICH MIGHT CONTRIBUTE to AN EVOLUTIONARY TRANSFORMATION of MAN'S THOUGHT PROCESSES.

— John Whitney, Jr.

INTRODUCTION

THOUGHT, REFLECTION, BELIEF

If the doors of perception were cleansed, then everything would appear to man as it is, infinite.

—William Blake, as quoted in Bill Viola, Notebook, 1979

Imagination as the link with the infinite.

—Bill Viola, writings, loose sheet, *c.* 1976

. . . all you need to do is look. And that is what we did.

—Kira Perov, 2008

The prevalence of the moving image as an artist's medium in today's art world follows from a long history, beginning with the development of the motion picture in the late nineteenth century and continuing in the mid-twentieth with the growth of the electronic medium of video. Today, the media arts, through the Internet and multiple digital platforms, are influencing the creation and distribution of moving images. Museums, galleries, international art fairs, and collectors are recognizing this long history and the key artists who shaped video into a contemporary art form. Among the pioneering artists who first turned to video and television, none played a more seminal role than the Korean-born Nam June Paik (1932–2006), whose writing and teaching, astonishing body of videotapes, sculptures, installations, and television productions were extraordinarily influential. For the generations of artists who were inspired by Paik's early example, the growth of new-media technologies offered opportunities to expand the moving image's presence in the history of late twentieth-century and contemporary art.

Bill Viola is the major artist in the generation that followed Nam June Paik. His ambitious, exemplary body of work explores the moving image as a way of expanding our understanding of the world around us. Viola has taken inspiration from the history of world art, culture and religions to create a powerful body of work that celebrates beauty, mystery and the spiritual in

Notebook, first page, *c.* January 1973

our lives and the environments we inhabit. He has been honored with commissions, retrospective exhibitions, and one-artist shows, has received numerous grants and honors, and is represented by leading galleries. His work is in major museum and private collections. The realization of his artworks, often ambitious in scale, as well as the many exhibitions and catalogues that have been produced, has been led by his wife and artistic collaborator, Kira Perov. Australian-born Perov joined Viola in New York in 1978, a year after she had invited him to show his work at La Trobe University, Melbourne. Since then, they have traveled and worked together. Viola could not have achieved what he has without her support and creative input. It is one of the great partnerships in contemporary art.

This monograph is an appreciation of Viola's unique and distinctive artistic achievement. It is an achievement that both embodies an exploration of the phenomenology of perception and conveys a powerful sense of feeling and empathy for the human condition. This is reflected, as is so much else in Viola's creative thinking, in his Notebooks. I would cite, for example, Viola's quoting of Rumi, the thirteenth-century poet, theologian, and Sufi mystic: "I AM the SERVANT OF HIM WHO LOOKS INTO HIMSELF."[1] It is this active self-inquiry, together with an ethical dimension of responsibility and openness to the lives of others, that sets Viola's achievement apart.

My reflections follow the arc of a narrative that began to take shape as I looked back at Viola's artwork, had conversations with the artist, reviewed his Notebooks, and viewed his most recent pieces. I came to realize that there was a continuity of thought and an underlying spirituality that informed and shaped his approach to the moving image. In his text "Presence and Absence: Vision and the Invisible in the Media Age," Viola cites the Zen poet Ryokan (1758–1831), who was born into wealth but left that life for a monastery and eventually retreated into a mountainous area where he lived alone in a hut for thirty-five years. In reflecting on his poems, which were written in isolation, Viola notes that "the most special thing about them, and so easily overlooked, is that the inspiration and the action, perception, and reflection are one."[2] Viola's art embodies an intense bringing together of sensory life and experience. A power emanates from his art that emerges through subtle yet dramatic representational imagery that embraces all that exists around him, from his home and personal journals (his Notebooks) and library to the natural world outside.

It became clear to me that Viola's later single-channel videotapes and installations draw on his early work in their constant interplay that create new visions of the world. Viola establishes in his artwork an unfolding process that draws the viewer into a conversation with the moving image. His art reflects the visionary poets and mystics whose writings make up his personal library and who embody a belief in transcendence. At the same time, Viola's art gives time a palpable presence, recalling the shape-shifting

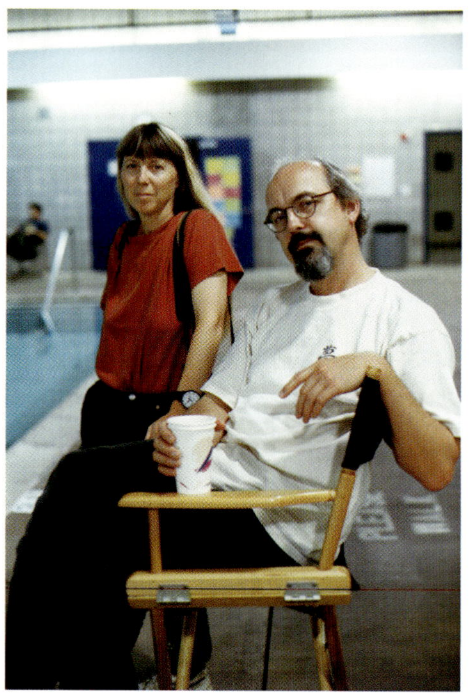

Kira Perov and Bill Viola on the set of *Five Angels for the Millennium* (2001), Martin Luther King Jr. Park Pool, Long Beach, CA, September 1999

The white moon gleams through scudding
clouds in the cold sky of the Ninth
Month. The white frost weighs down the
Leaves and the branches bend low
Over the freezing water.
All alone I sit by my
Window. The crushing burden
of the passing days never
grows lighter for an instant.
I write poems, change and correct them,
and finally throw them away.
Gold chrysanthemums wither
Along the balcony. Hard
cries of migrating storks fall
Heavily from the icy sky.
All alone by my window
Hidden in an empty room,
All alone, I burn incense,
And dream in the smoke, all alone.

Chu Shu-Chen
11th cent. female poet
SUNG DYNASTY
Modern name: Zhu Shuzhen
(1063-1106)

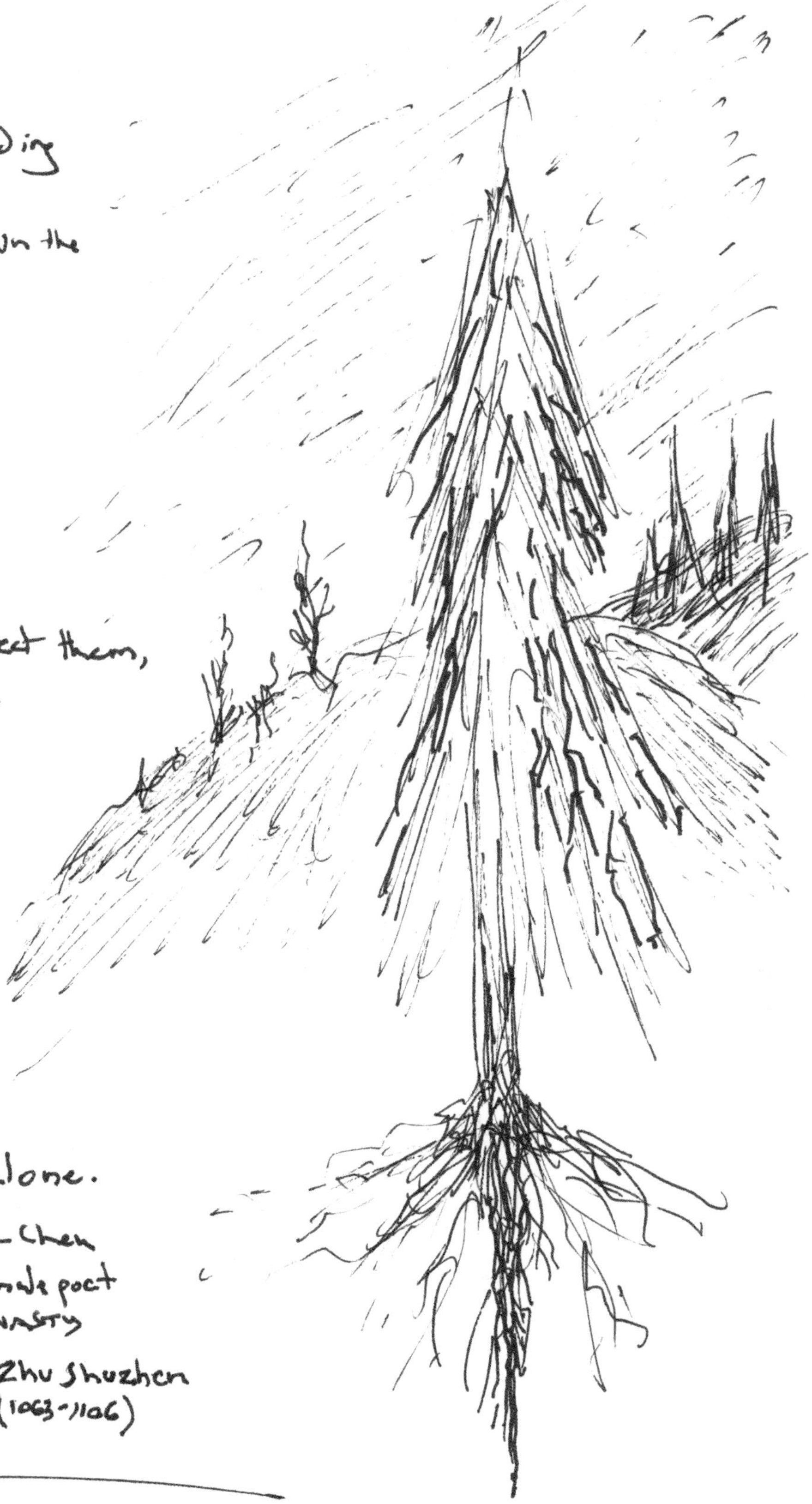

tactics of the stream-of-consciousness literary style that transformed twentieth-century fiction and modernist poetics. Viola's art does not aim to represent the past; rather, his single-channel videotapes and installations represent life as experienced in the present tense.

I have focused this essay on a number of humanistic and theological issues that are important to Viola, and which recur repeatedly in his videos and installations. Rather than following a linear structure, I have organized the essay in a way that spirals through a discussion of his work, incorporating his earliest videos through to his most recent, and returns again and again—as Viola does himself—to a number of large and key ideas. These include the human body, spirituality and transcendence; the forces and cycles of nature, birth, life, death, and memory; and, more generally, the way in which Viola has used these ideas constantly to address the potential of video itself as a medium. The book's coda is devoted to *Martyrs (Earth, Air, Fire, Water)* (2014), a work commissioned for St. Paul's Cathedral in London that explores the redemption of the martyr, achieved through the strength of his or her beliefs and it reminds us of the redemptive power of Viola's own remarkable aesthetics of belief.

Thought, reflection, and belief are terms that I will return to in exploring the artist's desire to forge an aesthetic that speaks across history and generations. "Thought" refers to recovering previous ways of thinking and visualizing, guided by the artist's research into Renaissance art, Paleolithic cave painting, Islamic and Christian mysticism, and Asian poetry and philosophy. This process is framed by "reflection," the creation of art that embodies a self-reflective and spiritual openness. "Belief" underpins both "thought" and "reflection" as the artist searches for a way to express the theological power of what we believe. What has become clear to me is how this process of thought, reflection, and belief gives structure to Viola's emergence as an artist. In conversation with him, he reflected on the river as embodying the flow and continuity of history. Knowledge, he noted, was "like flowing water, we jump into the stream current and go along with it." For Viola, the river is a metaphor for "the life force taking us forward but we don't know where ... [for the] mystery in this process."[3]

Sound is a key element in Viola's installations and single-channel videotapes. The invention of instruments and compositional strategies was, early on, an example of the process of art-making that informed Viola's emergence as a video artist. The development of new techniques and the instrumental means to create and compose sound was an integral part of the work of the American pianist and composer David Tudor (1926–1996), and it informed and inspired Viola's own work as an audio and video artist. In 1973, as an undergraduate at Syracuse University, Viola performed in Tudor's seminal audio installation *Rainforest IV* at the Everson Museum of Art in Syracuse, New York. Along with John Cage, Tudor played a key role in

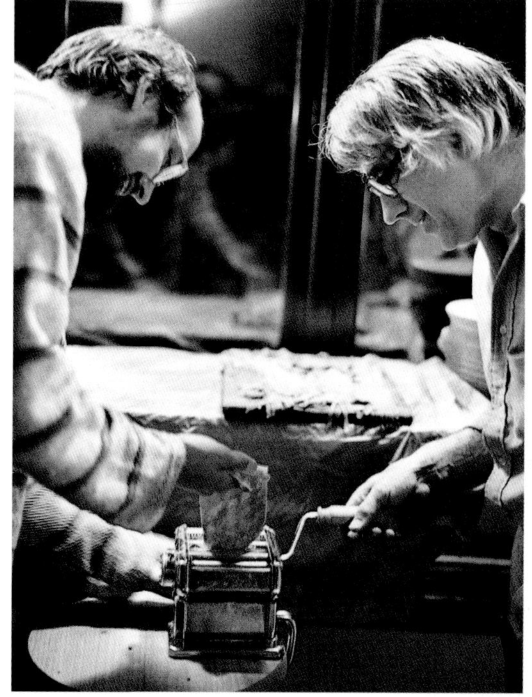

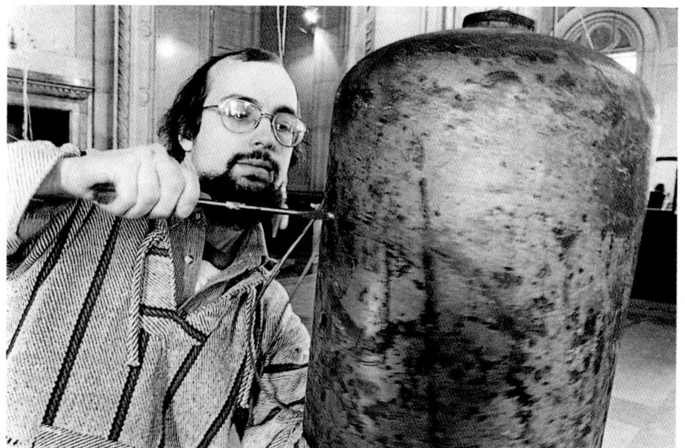

Above
Bill Viola and David Tudor making pasta in Tudor's home, Stony Point, NY, August 20, 1979 (top); adjusting an object for *Rainforest IV* (bottom)

Opposite
David Tudor, *Rainforest IV*. Bill Viola preparing for its first performance, New Music New Hampshire, Chocorua, NH, June 1973 (top); Drexel First National Bank Building, Philadelphia, PA, April 1979 (bottom)

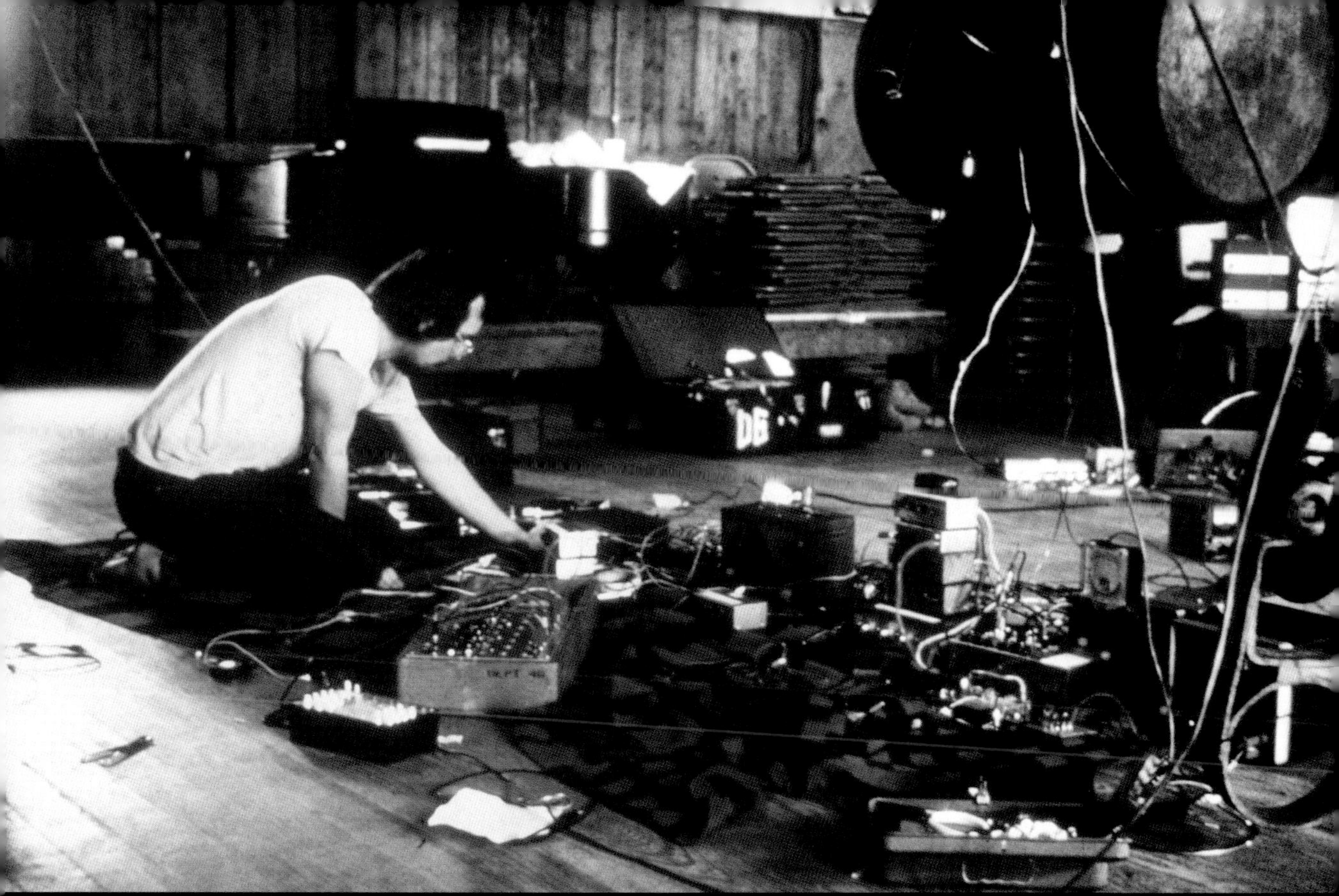

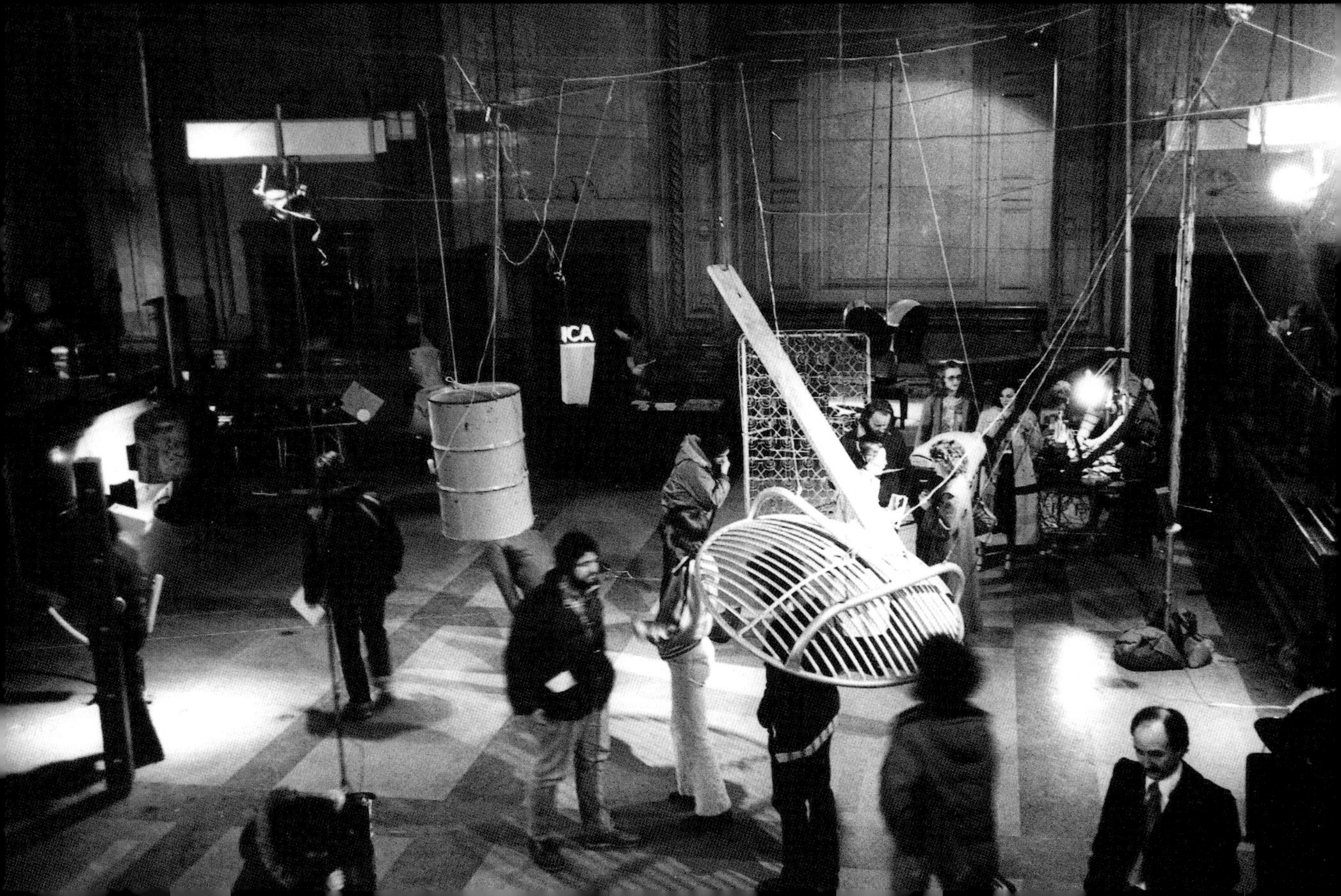

opening up the idea of music by exploring audio in all of its dimensions. The experience of working on *Rainforest IV* was, for Viola, "probably the greatest experience I had in terms of opening up my eyes and ears to the invisible world of sound."[4] Developed in Chocorua '73 in New Hampshire, Tudor's performance/installation consisted of a vast array of handmade audio equipment, from synthesizers and audio analyzers to transmitters and transducers, manipulated by individuals moving between tables and suspended objects. It unfolds and develops as combinations of signals create a "forest" of sounds from the interaction of transducers with the vibrating surface of these objects. After he graduated, Viola toured with *Rainforest IV* and often performed his own sound works at such places as the Festival d'Automne, Paris, and "Für Augen und Ohren," Akademie der Kunst, Berlin. In Kawaji Onsen in Japan he created a sound environment for the Japanese artist Fujiko Nakaya's fog sculpture in a mountain riverbed. *Rainforest IV* became a model for how Viola reworked video as a visual and auditory instrument for recording and manipulating sound and image. It is important to recall *Rainforest IV* not only for its impact on Viola's early engagement with video, but also in terms of his later work with the music of the French composer Edgard Varèse (Viola's *Déserts*, 1994), of Trent Reznor of the American industrial rock band Nine Inch Nails (for Reznor's *Fragility Tour v2.0*, 2000) and of Richard Wagner (Viola's 4-hour video for the opera *Tristan und Isolde*, 2004–05). Viola's interest in classical and modernist

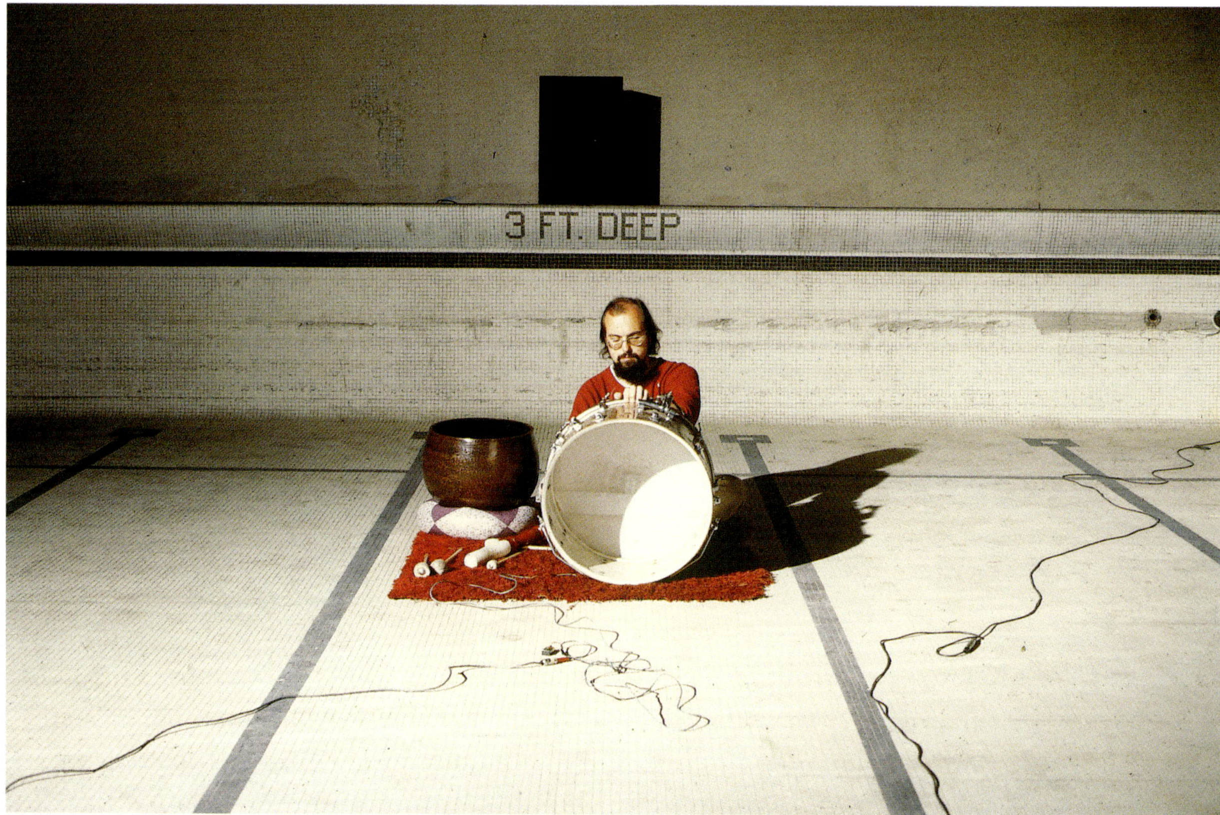

Bill Viola performing *The Talking Drum* (1979), Buffalo, NY, July 1982

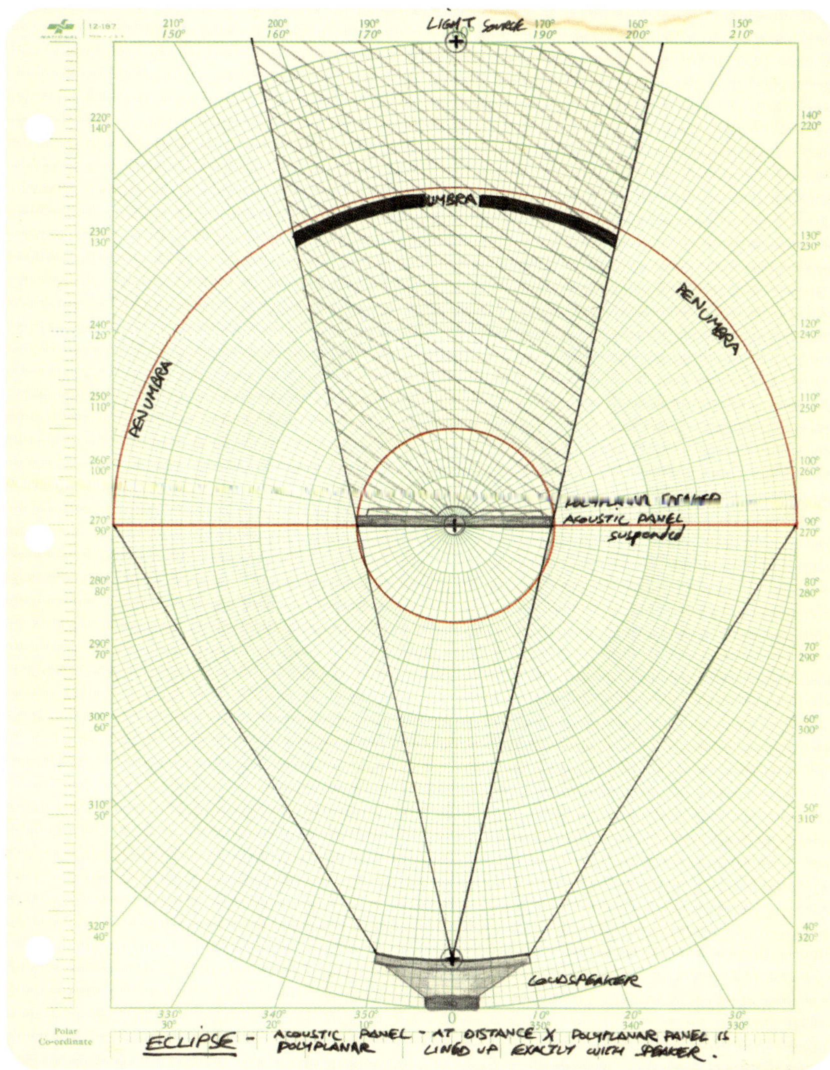

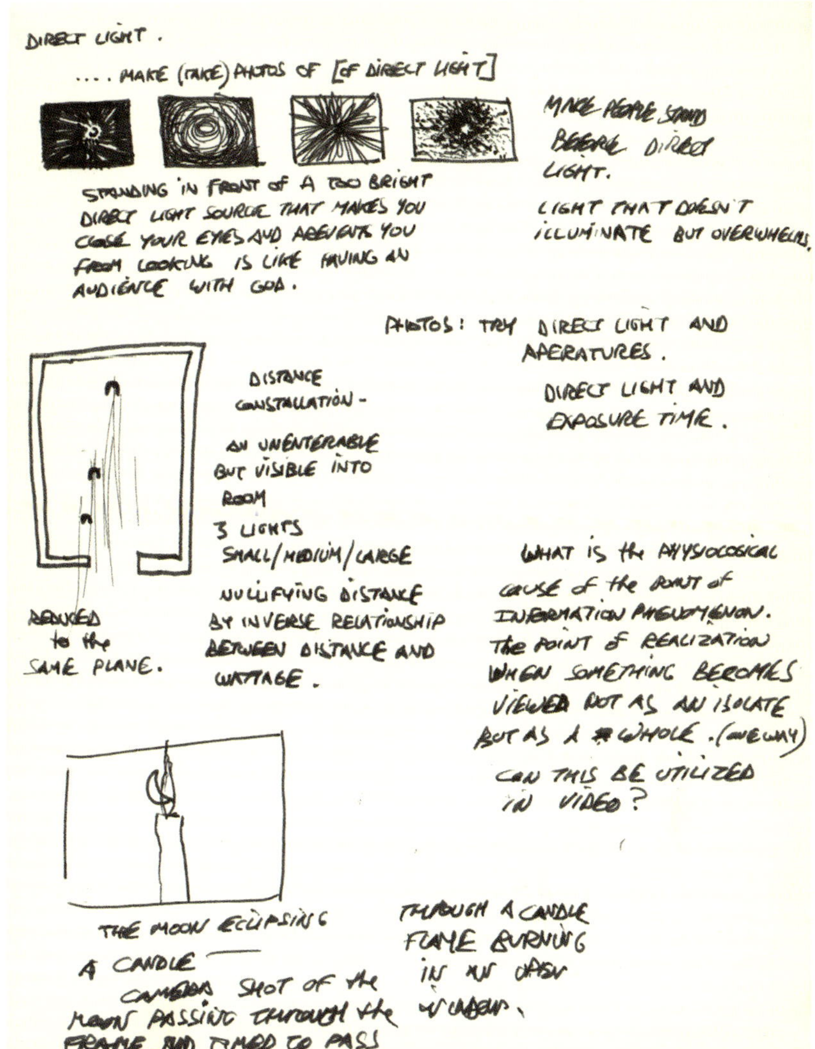

Above, left Drawing for sound installation *Eclipse*, *c.* 1973

Above, right Drawing for videotape *Eclipse*, Florence Notebook, November 1974

music was also informed early on by Kira Perov, and later by Peter Sellars, director of the Wagner production.

Viola's use of the river as a way to visualize the continual flow of time, history, and experience became an extended metaphor for exploring what he called the "backwater of eddies," referring to tributaries and movements outside of the mainstream of religion and culture. This becomes especially clear in his extraordinary Notebooks, Project Books, and Working Books, which he began during his early years in college, and which he continues to fill to this day with technical diagrams alongside quotations from a variety of thinkers and artists who have clearly shaped how he sees the possibilities of the medium. Viola's writings are essential to his creative process and his intellectual engagement with aesthetics and history. Through his writings, we can follow his treatment of the concept of the river and water as visual metaphors for states of mind and the spiritual in such later works as *The Sleepers* (1992), *The Crossing* (1996), and *Five Angels for the Millennium* (2001). The Notebooks offer a map of references and ideas

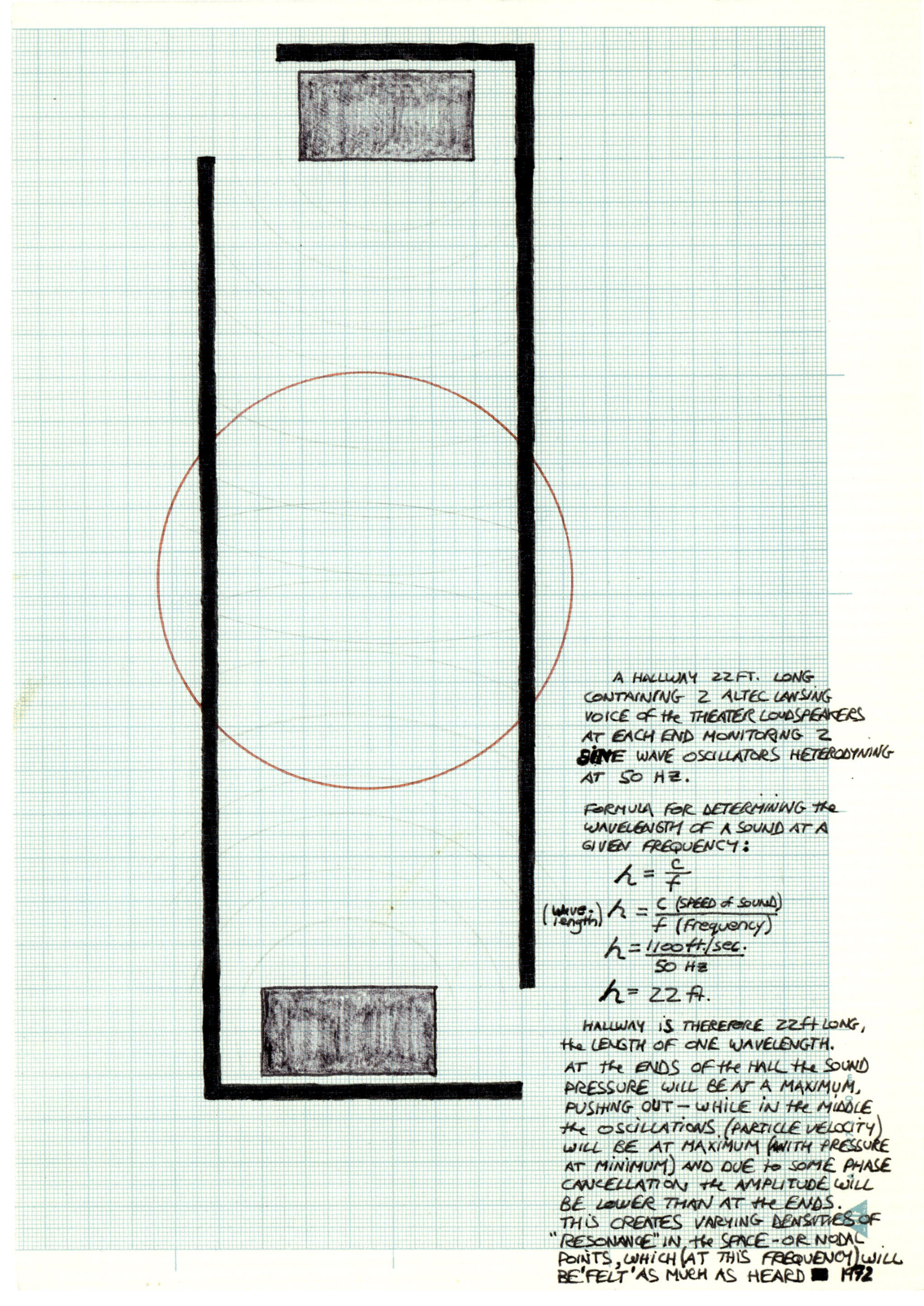

Drawing for sound installation *Hallway Nodes* (1973), 1972

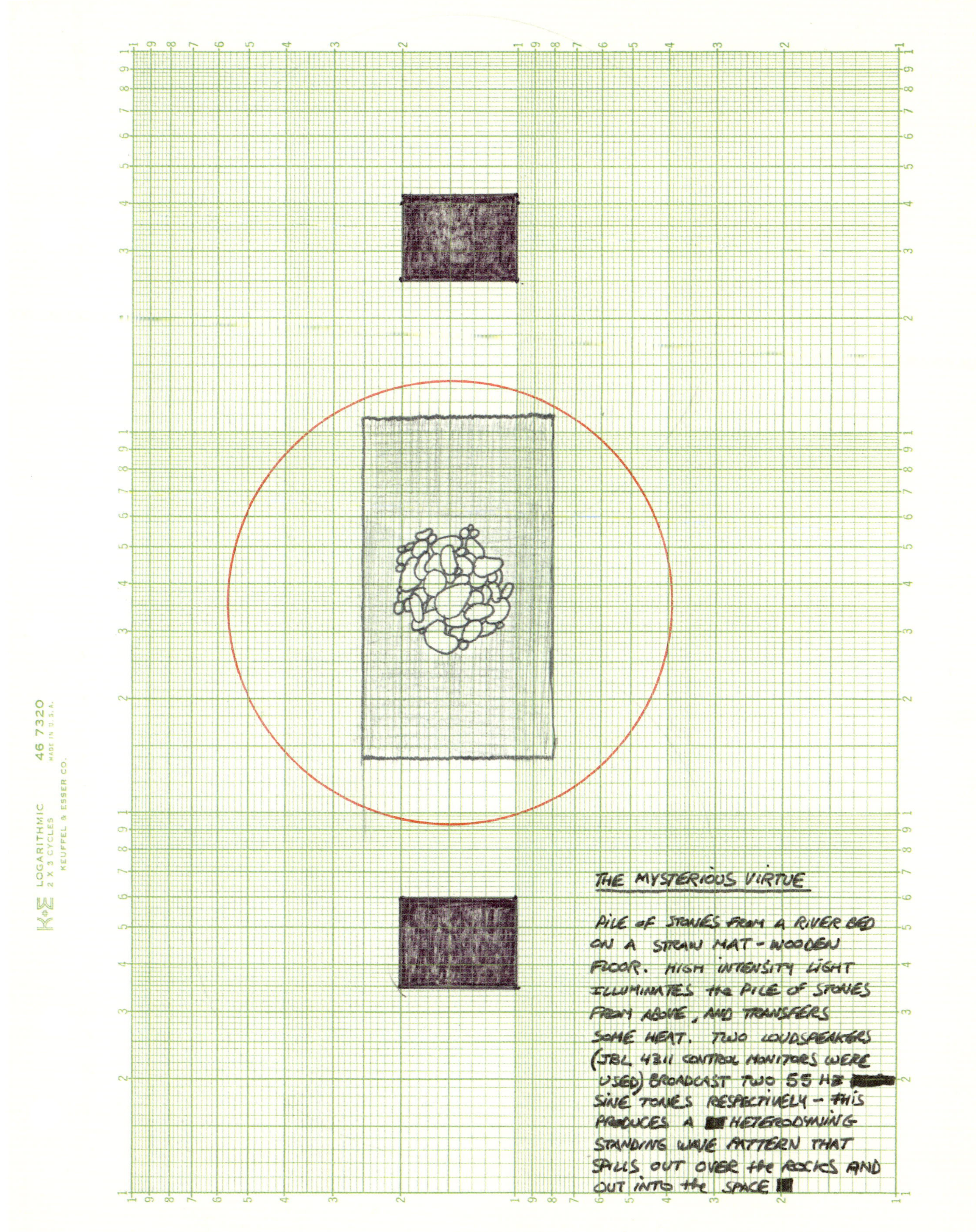

Drawing for sound installation *The Mysterious Virtue* (1974), 1973

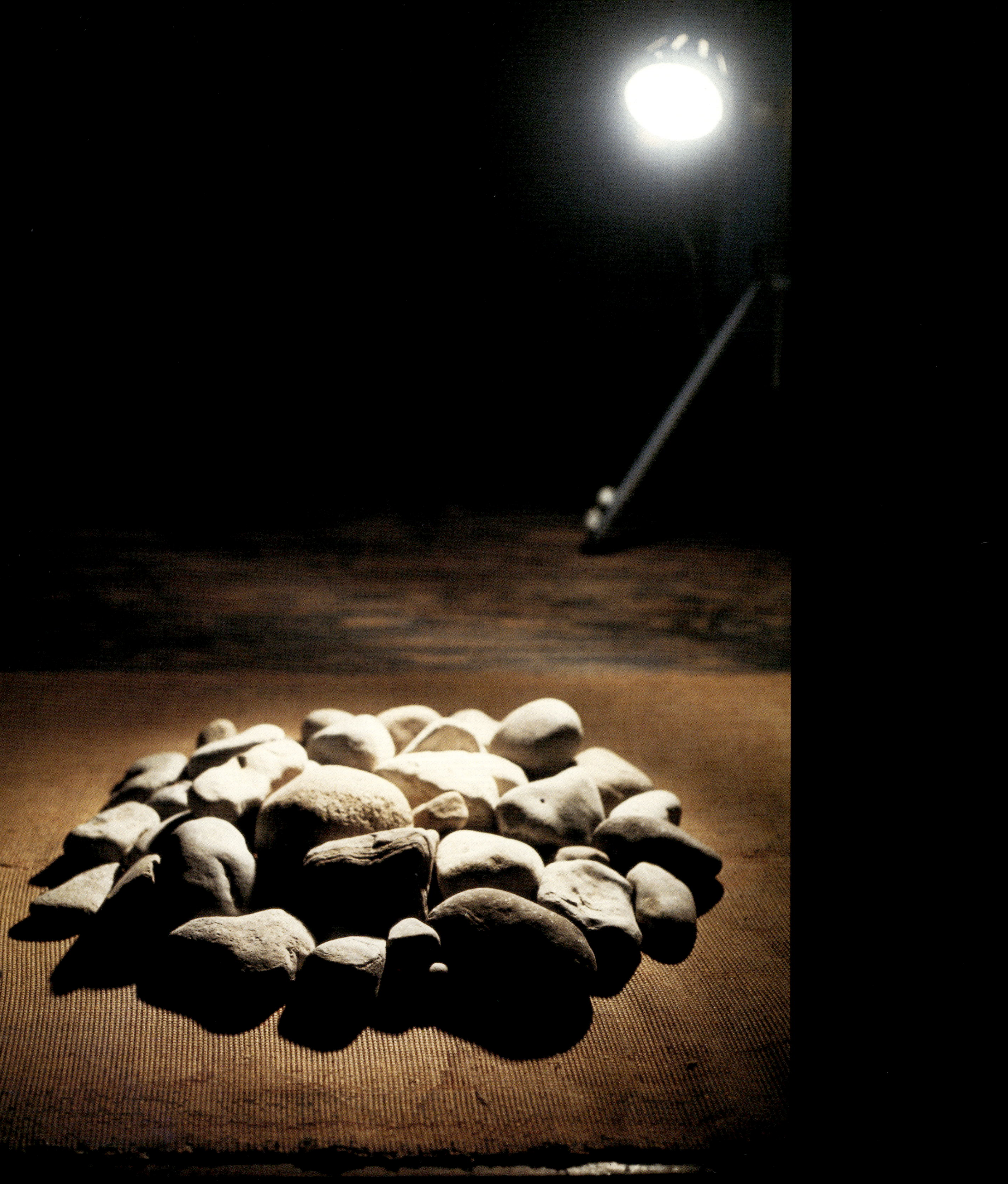

captured in Viola's careful and precise script. Drawings and plans show how ideas and references take shape and inform the visual form and content of specific artworks. In the 1970s especially, he focused on creating beautiful drawings of sound sculptures, some of which, such as *Hallway Nodes* (1973) and *The Mysterious Virtue* (1974), were later produced and performed.

Through the pages of the Notebooks, one can follow Viola's interest in tradition and the continuities of life articulated through family and childhood memories. Viola often tells the story of the Ise Grand Shrine in Japan, which is reconstructed to exact and ancient specifications every twenty years on an adjacent site as part of a continuing process of meditation, renewal, and preservation. The living shrine in Ise captures an idea of tradition as the means to both preserve and embody an art form and sacred memory. The shrine's immortality lies in its continual rebuilding, just as the river lives on in its ongoing flowing power. For Viola, change itself is what gives time its continuity.

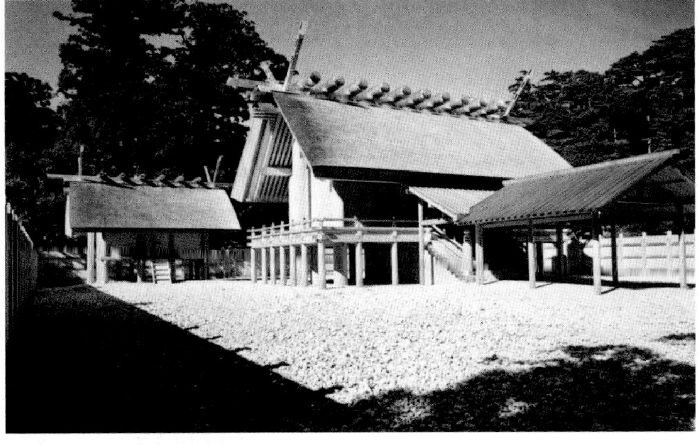

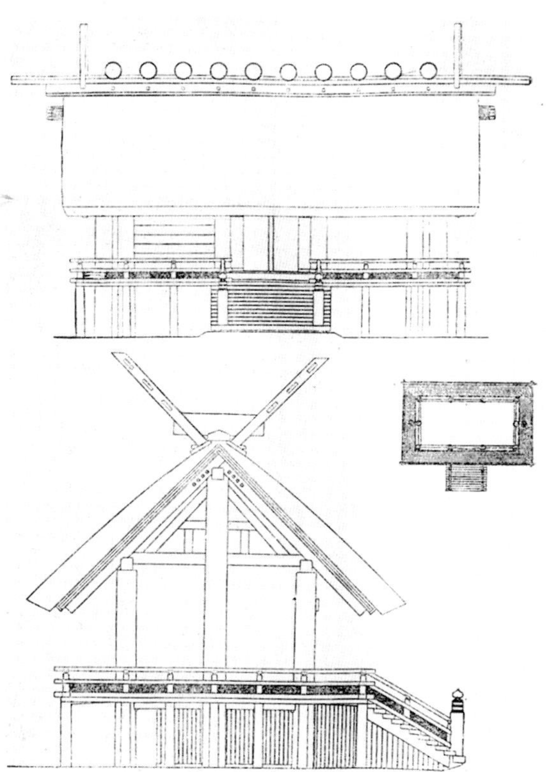

Viola's interest in conveying bodily experience and expressing inner feelings in his art followed from his investigations into world religions and their spiritual texts. At the same time Viola was fascinated by the many traditions in world art created to convey and express visually those inner spiritual feelings and theological narratives. The materialization of time and the treatment of art-historical images come to the fore for the first time in such installations as *The Greeting*. In this piece, Viola stages an action that takes 45 seconds in real time but makes it unfold over 10 minutes. *The Greeting* was inspired by Pontormo's Mannerist painting *Visitation* (1528–9), which Viola had seen in reproduction in an art book and could not get out of his mind. He created *The Greeting* in 1995, one of five new installations for the U.S. Pavilion at the 46th Venice Biennale. As the performers move to embrace, their emotions are expanded in time in the same way their gestures and movements gradually unfold. At once painterly in composition, sculptural in its treatment of the figures, and cinematic in its presence, *The Greeting* is an early example of Viola's reflections on historical aesthetic achievements and world culture and ideas.

It is interesting to follow the way Viola creates work in response to a space or situates installations in different environments. In both cases, the artist's approach brings out the complexity and yet openness of the work's intense visual experience. Viola achieves a balance between the aesthetics of the work and the formal demands of the exhibition space; the installation takes on a new resonance within the space and the space is transformed by the work. The first instance occurred in 1986 when *Room for St. John of the Cross* (1983) and *Reasons for Knocking at an Empty House* (1982) were shown in France at La Chartreuse, Villeneuve-lez-Avignon. Other examples include *The Crossing*, created for the Chapelle Saint-Louis de la Salpêtrière in Paris in 1996; the installation of *The Messenger* in

Opposite *The Mysterious Virtue* (1974), sound installation

Top Main Sanctuary and West Treasure House, Inner Shrine (Naiku), Ise Shrine, Japan, in 1953

Above Front and side view drawings of the Honden, Ise Shrine

Durham Cathedral in England in the same year; an enlarged version of *Five Angels for the Millennium* for the Gasometer Oberhausen, Germany, in 2003; and *Martyrs* in St. Paul's Cathedral in 2014. In her invaluable role as curator, Perov has been particularly instrumental in sensitively matching the works to the sites. Each site tells a different story and marks a different moment in the trajectory of Viola's career.

The humanist ideals of art take on a new dimension in Viola's video art: he recognizes the traditions of visual art and music that are closely connected to the world's great religions and the profound humanism that is expressed in traditional art forms and cultural practices. Viola's art conveys hope for mankind and a belief in the innate goodness of people, and he sees this belief expressed in the historical arc of the human imagination, from the caves of Lascaux France to the cathedrals of the Italian Renaissance.

How Viola came to this investigation of time and a spiritually informed aesthetic is one of the great stories of late twentieth-century art. It begins with his interest in video and the grounding of an art practice in a phenomenology of the body, a phenomenology that moves from the act of perception and representation to an evocation of the temporal as the means to embody the "body." Viola's moving imagery is grounded in mysticism, a strategy that recalls the French philosopher Pierre Hadot's "spiritual exercises." Hadot writes that "attention to the present moment allows us to accede to cosmic consciousness, by making us attentive to the infinite value of each instant, and causing us to accept each moment of existence from the viewpoint of the universal law of the *cosmos*."[5] In focusing on each instant, Viola articulates an aesthetic whose goal is raising "the individual from an inauthentic condition of life, darkened by unconsciousness and harassed by worry, to an authentic state of life, in which he attains self-consciousness, an exact vision of the world, inner peace, and freedom."[6]

Through the spiritual exercises of his art, Viola has spent time with Buddhist monks, traveled the world, and, most significantly, developed a deep interest in the poet Rumi and the scholar Seyyed Hossein Nasr's extensive writings on Islamic mysticism. A quotation from Nasr in Viola's Project Book of 2002 states: "The identification of material objects with the concrete, and mental concepts with the abstract has had the effect of not only destroying the significance of form vis-à-vis matter on the physical plane itself, but also obliterating the significance of the bodily and the corporeal as a source of knowledge."[7] This statement expresses Viola's attention to the classical traditions and discourses of representation, rather than thinking about art in terms of modernity's investment in psychoanalysis and postmodernism's emphasis on self-referential strategies. It is within Nasr's classical traditions that Viola discovers the mysteries still relevant to our times that he wishes to reveal in all of their urgency and ambiguity.

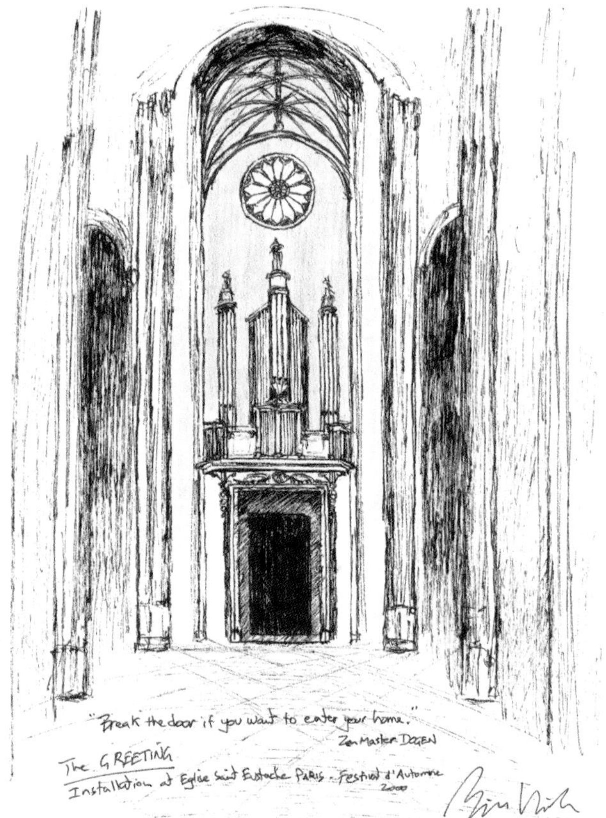

Above Proposal for *The Greeting* (1995) in L'église Saint-Eustache for Festival d'Automne à Paris, September 21, 2000

Opposite *Reasons for Knocking at an Empty House* (1982), La Chartreuse, Villeneuve-lez-Avignon, France, July 1986

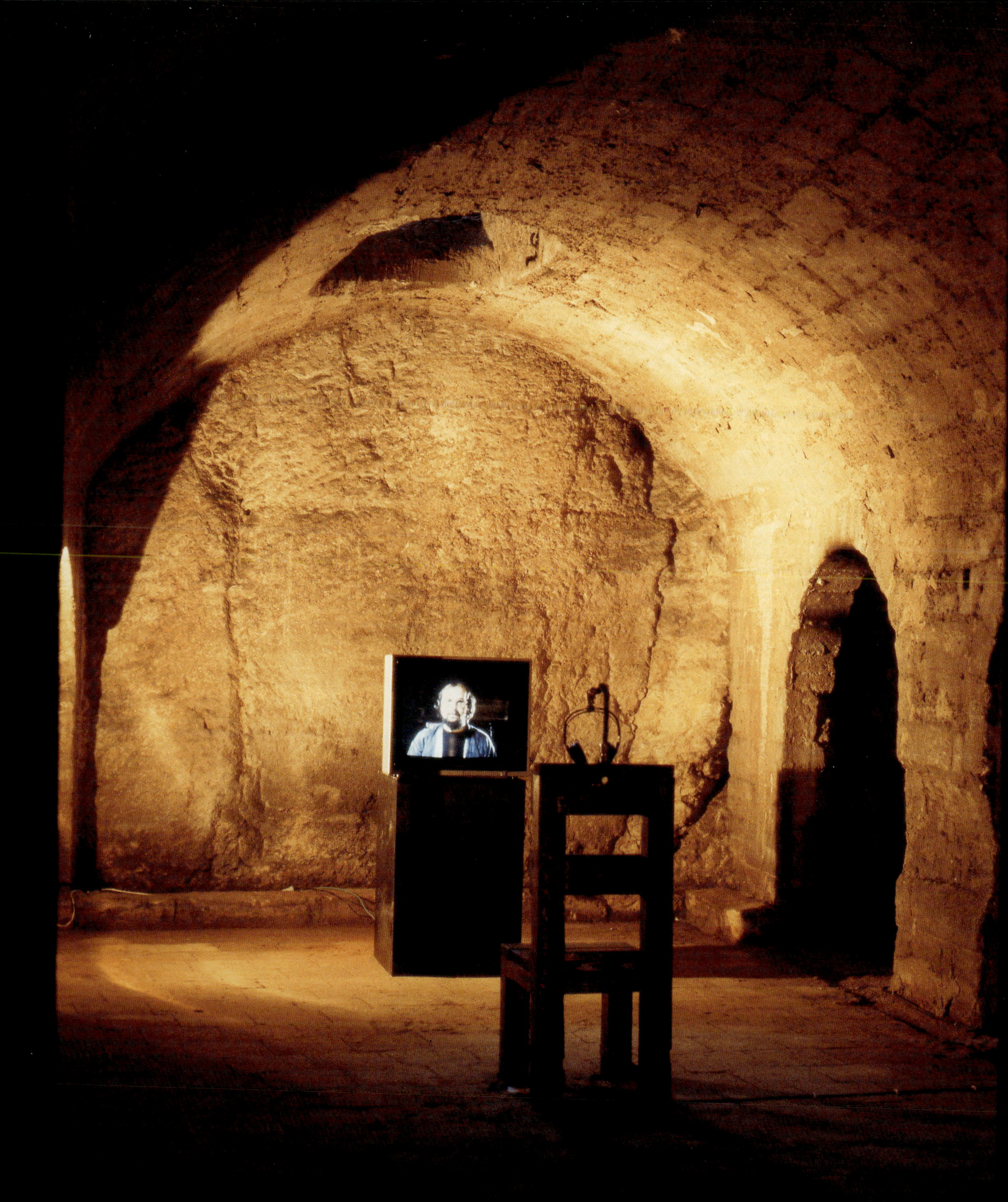

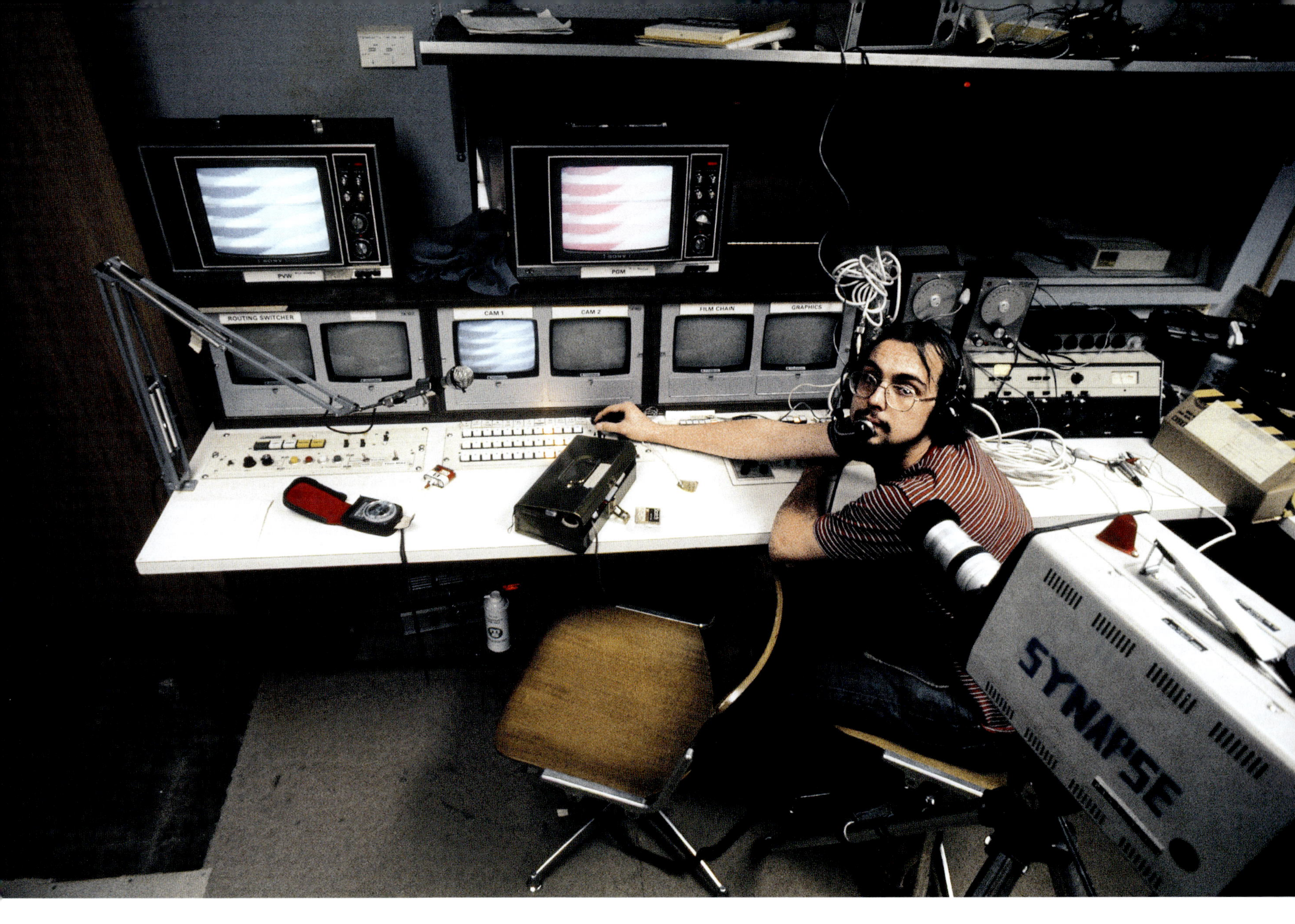

Bill Viola creating *Information*, Synapse, Syracuse University, NY, 1973

CHAPTER ONE

THE DISCOVERY OF VIDEO

I see that media technology is not at odds with our inner selves, but in fact a reflection of it.

—Bill Viola, "Presence and Absence: Vision and the Invisible in the Media Age," 2007

The way the Self arrays itself is the form of the entire world.

—Zen Master Dogen, quoted in Bill Viola's "Peter Campus: Image and Self," 2010

In his imagery, Viola draws on the emotions, on a catalytic, reflective place within himself. His work stands apart from much of contemporary art, engaging with the ideals of beauty as it moves away from the strategies of the post-Duchampian conceptual art practices that have dominated not only contemporary art-making but also academic art history, critical writing, and curatorial practice.

In tracing the trajectory of Viola's art and its influences, I will begin with a film by Stan Brakhage created between 1961 and 1964 entitled *Dog Star Man*. As a film curator and scholar, I am fascinated by the connections and differences between film and video art. There are few artists whose work matches Viola's in ambition and scale of imagination. Stan Brakhage, the most important filmmaker of his time, was one of those artists. *Dog Star Man* has been described by the film historian P. Adams Sitney as a mythopoeic work, which he sees as descending from the Romantic poets and the transcendental return to nature in American literature. Brakhage makes reference, in his writings, to the modernist poetics of Charles Olson and his radical break with the figurative use of language. *Dog Star Man* is open to interpretation, but as the film scholar Fred Camper has written about the *Prelude* to *Dog Star Man*, "It is the beginning of the film, the beginning of the dreamer's ... dream and perception: it is the beginning of the universe."[1] Seen in its entirety, Brakhage's *Dog Star Man* speaks to

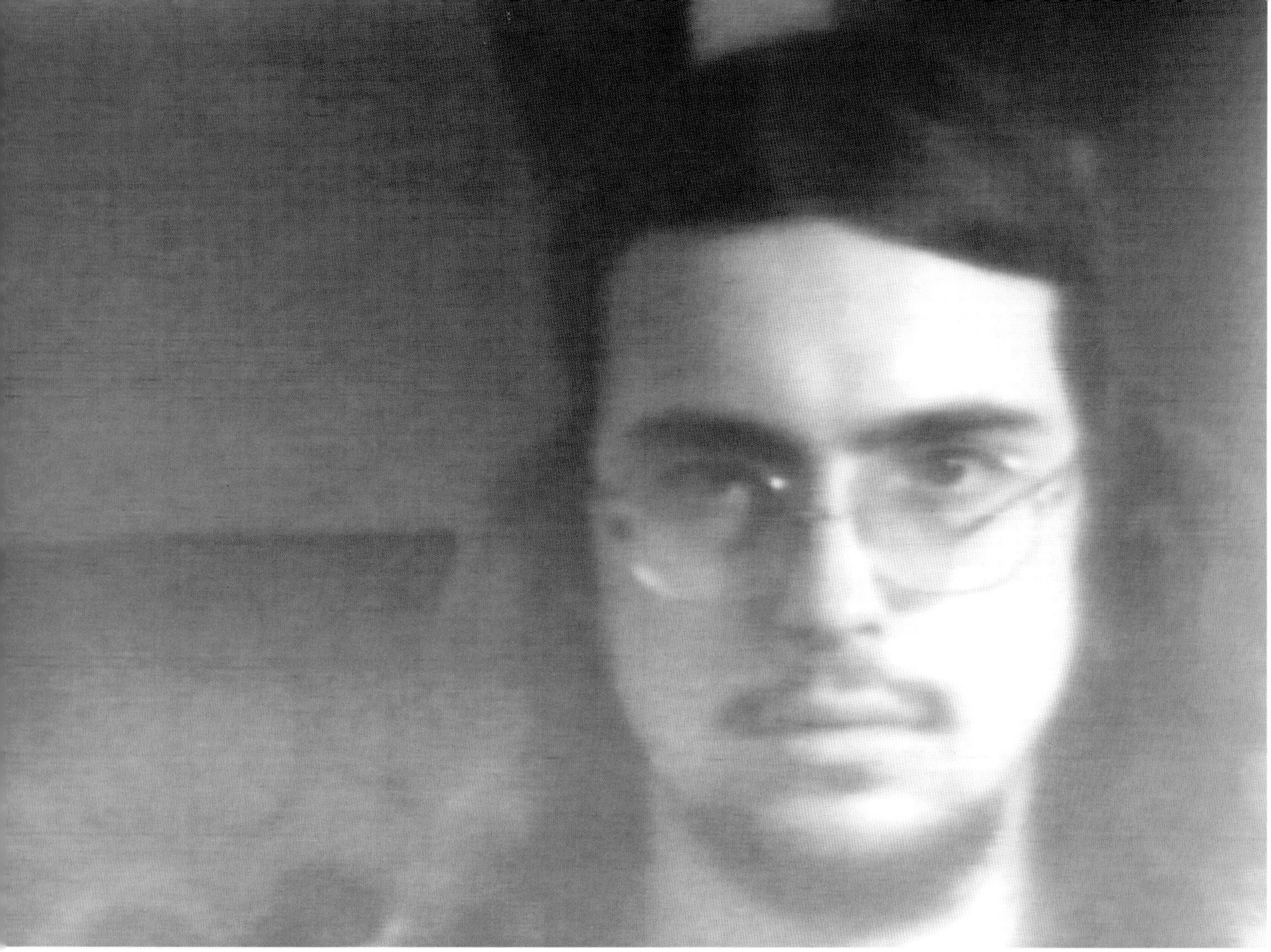

Viola's cosmic view. Brakhage's abstractions, scratched directly onto the celluloid, and his use of the anamorphic lens as well as tracking, and a slow and rapidly moving handheld camera, liberated film from the codes of classical cinema. This is mirrored in Viola's early treatment of the properties of video, with Viola further pushing the medium when he turned the video apparatus onto itself, as in *Tape I* (1972), one of his first video works. Viola describes this process in *Tape I* as

an attempt to stare down the self. A camera, with its live image displayed on a monitor next to it, is seen viewing its own reflection in a mirror when a man enters the room. He sits in front of the mirror, breaking the line of sight and thus becoming both the subject and the object of a self-portrait. He stares into the lens, maintaining eye contact and focused concentration with the unseen viewer. A low howling sound is heard, the noise of the camera's microphone in low-level feedback with its own speaker. The man stares at us for a long time. Suddenly, without a warning, he bursts out with a loud violent scream. He then gets up and physically stops the videotape in the recorder with his hand, creating a violent disruption of picture and sound that plunges the screen into snow.[2]

Tape I (1972)

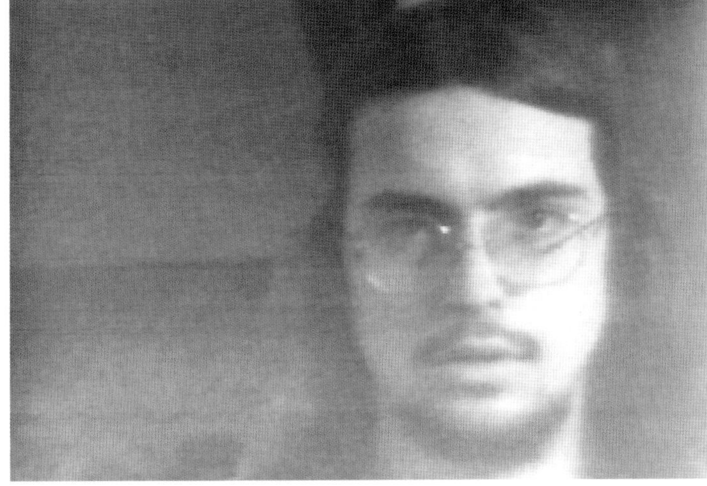

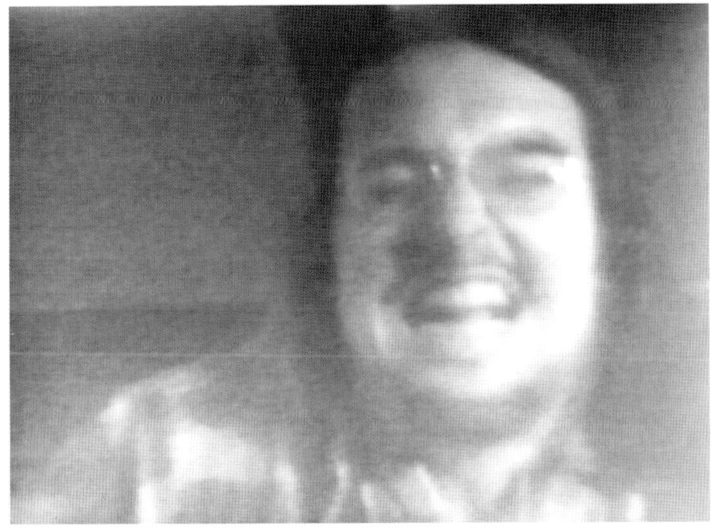

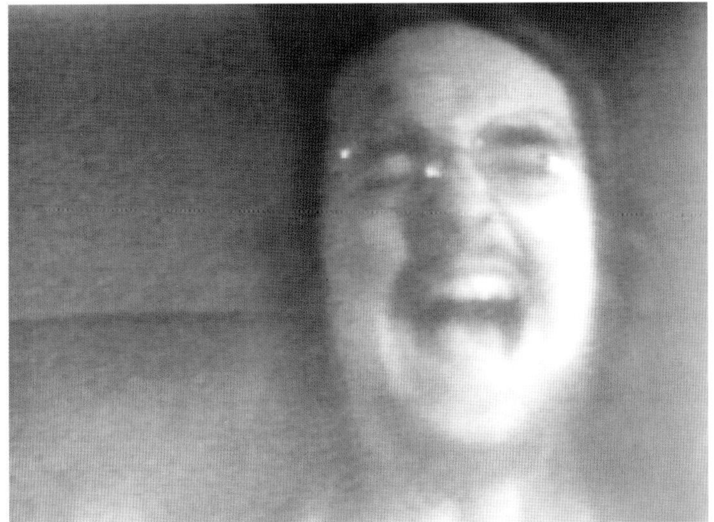

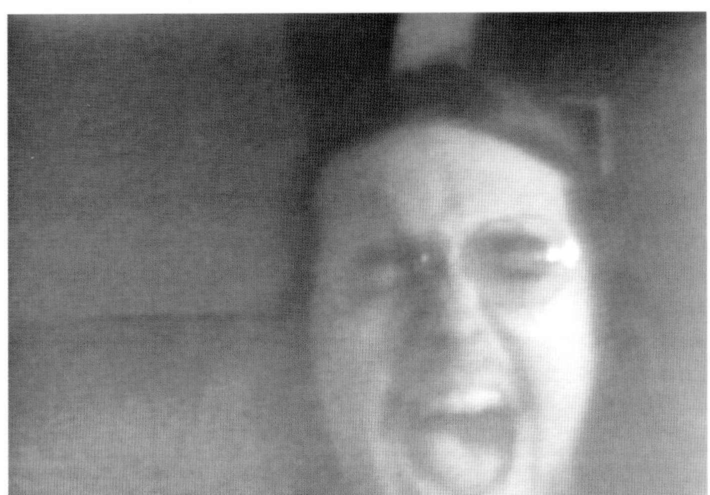

In *Migration* (1976), an elegant and evocative work, Viola plays with the optical properties of the medium as we observe moving shapes of color unfold to reveal a scene in which the artist walks into the image and sits at a table. On the table is a still-life arrangement of a cereal box, some fruit, and a bowl filled with water. The regular beat of a gong marks the passage of time. The camera brings into focus a spigot from which water is dripping into the bowl. The gradually emerging drops of water fill the screen and reveal in close-up the reflection of the artist. The final image of his face shaped by the drop of water brings the work full circle as the natural reflection in the water processes the image much as the electronic system of video transforms what it records. Writing about *Migration*, Viola notes that the piece "evolves into an exploration of the optical properties of a drop of water, revealing in it an image of the individual and a suggestion of the transient nature of the world he or she possesses within."[3] It is this creative dialogue between technology and nature, process and time that becomes a key element of Viola's videotapes and installations. Viola's exploration of the moving image in *Tape I*, *Migration* and the installation *He Weeps for You* (1976) conveys a transcendence of place and experience through a self-reflective exploration of the camera and human eye as conveyers of experience and windows onto our selves and the world around us. This sequence of artworks also reveals how the artist follows a creative path through his single-channel videotapes to the closed-circuit installation of *He Weeps for You*, in which the particle of matter, the drop of water, seen on the videotape *Migration* is made visible as a real-time event in the space and on the screen.

Three years later, Viola produced *Chott el-Djerid (A Portrait in Light and Heat)* (1979), a profound reflection on nature and his most Brakhage-like contemplation of the natural world and its expressive power. He writes that, standing in the Sahara, all you can do is "peer out into the void, watching. Standing there, you strain to look further, to see beyond, strain to make out familiar shapes and forms. You finally realize that the void is yourself. It is like a huge mirror for your mind."[4] Kira Perov, writing in the catalogue for the exhibition "Bill Viola: Visioni interiori," which she curated for the Palazzo delle Esposizioni in Rome in 2008–9, offers a perceptive understanding of Viola's vision:

So how does Bill reveal his inner visions, visions that evoke in us such complex responses? How does he create these environments that we can inhabit so easily? These were not the first questions that came to my mind when experiencing the work for the first time but once Bill and I decided to journey together, over the past three decades I have been privileged to be part of the answer.

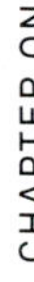

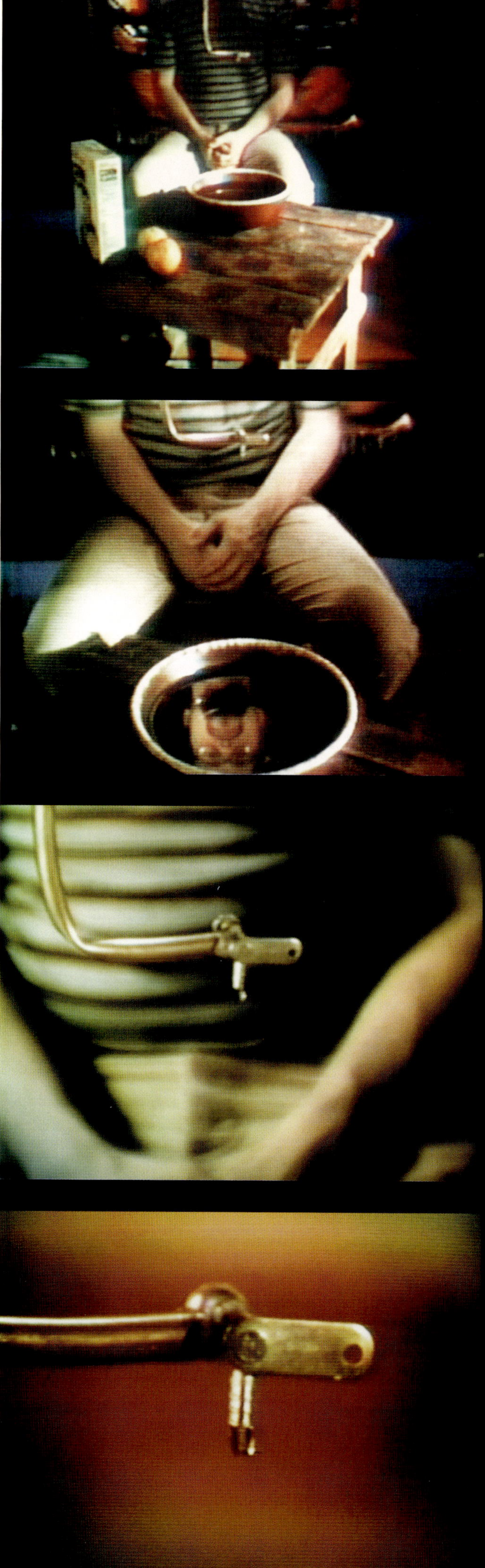

Migration (1976)

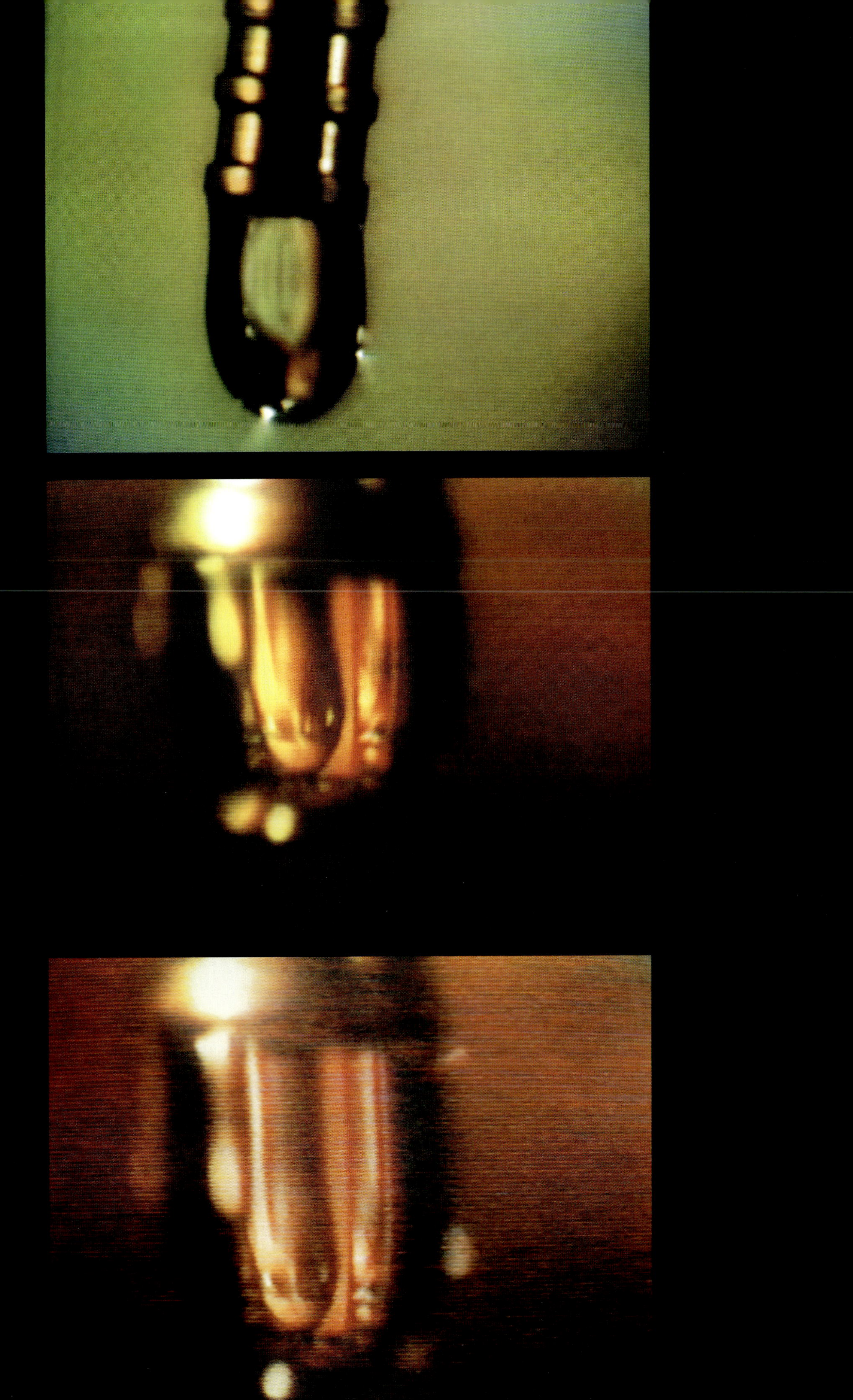

I learned that there are no tricks, no sleights of hand—all the images are derived from reality: real fire, real water, real storms, real deluges. Bill had realized some time before that the most interesting questions are usually right in front of you, present both in the human and non-human worlds, and that all you need to do is to look. And that is what we did.[5]

Perov speaks to a distinctive feature of what one experiences in Viola's work: the sense of the "poetic real," the uncanny quality of seeing something happen that is "derived from reality" and yet is more than reality.

In his exploration of the limits of the moving image, Viola creates a virtual catalogue of shots and metaphors that expand and comment on sensory perception. *The Passing* (1991), with its evocative visualization of birth and life and dream states across a richly imagined landscape, is closely related to the epic *I Do Not Know What It Is I Am Like* (1986). This 89-minute videotape is Viola's meditation on being a video artist. Viola creates a powerful video essay on the sensory reception of nature and the cycles of life and death. It becomes an ecstatic catalogue of moving-image reveries on time, landscape, and all living creatures. Viola views his art, and the place of landscape and culture in *I Do Not Know What It Is I Am Like*, as a global spiritual quest of limitless study and meditation. It is an embrace of the life of "animal consciousness," which was the original working title of the piece. Viola's *Inner Passage* (2013), a recent work, moves the human trek across the landscape into the brain and the memories and experiences it contains, capturing the unfolding presence of human perception.

Viola's later artworks explore the human expression of feeling, although the cause of that feeling is not visible. He does not edit his works to create a narrative logic of cause and effect or to manipulate the viewer into a state of mind. Rather, his videotapes are composed of recorded movements, like a musical composition, that are linked to create an entire work. The power comes from the individual shot, the intensity of the composition, the treatment of movement, the creation of an unfolding scene, and the unanticipated opening into another imaginary space, without narration.

The seedbed for Viola's early and formative development as an artist occurred after he entered Syracuse University as a freshman in 1969. He expected to study advertising, which his father thought would make a good career. He found it boring, however, and discovered the university's newly developing art program, "Experimental Studios." The openness of the academy in the United States in this period was reflected in the program, which Viola found challenging, flexible, unconventional, and non-dogmatic. Professor Jack Nelson, who was brought in to manage the program, was, Viola noted, a "renegade" and the "most interesting person I had met."[6] After creating his own studio, Nelson asked the university for video cameras and

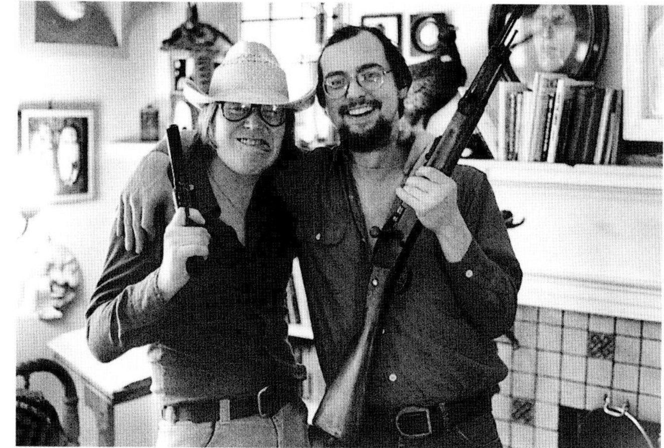

Jack Nelson and Bill Viola, Syracuse, NY, *c.* 1974

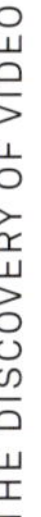

Carol Huggler and Bill Viola recording Carl Geiger's
Multi-origination Dance Piece, Syracuse University, NY, *c.* 1972

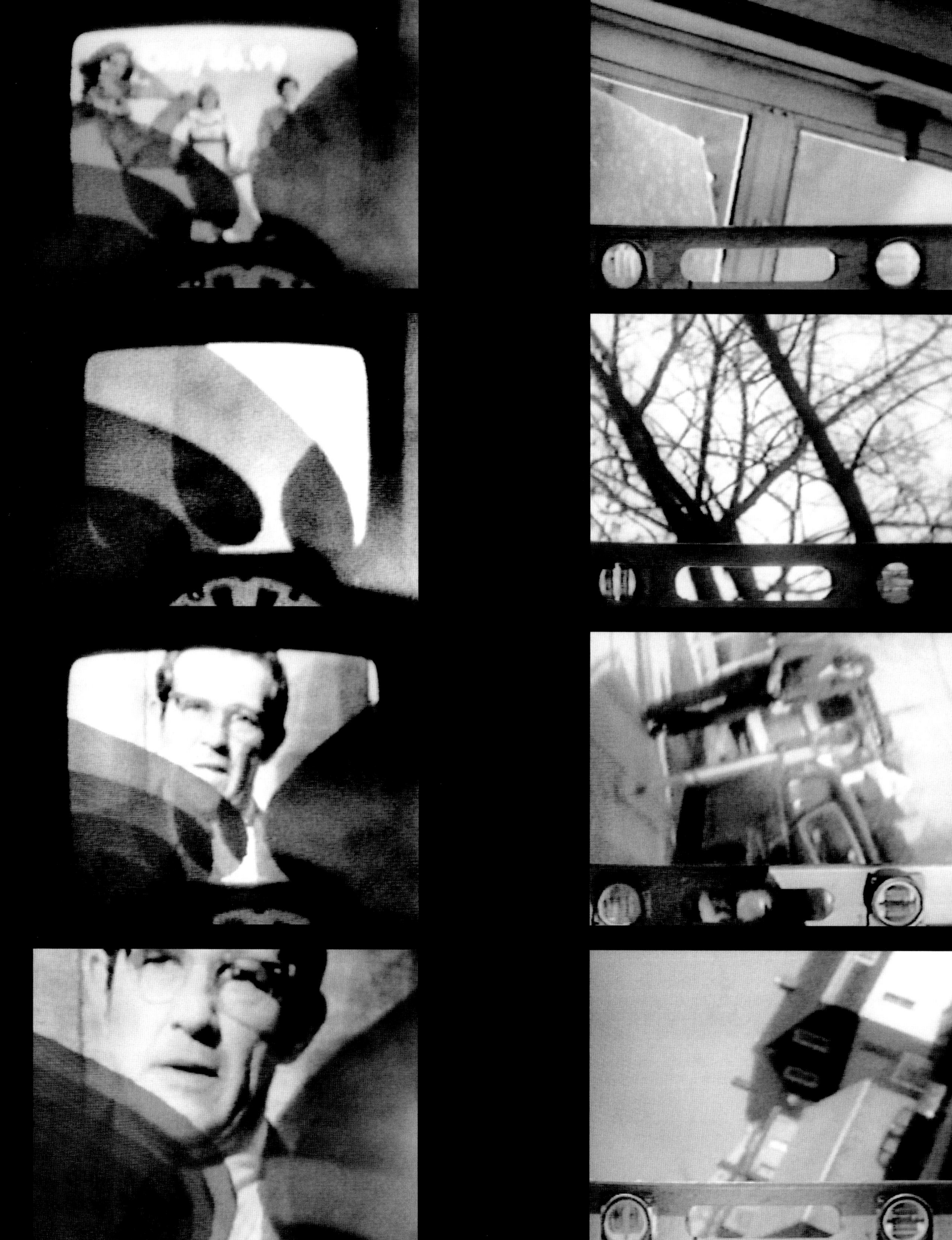

equipment, establishing what eventually became the Synapse Video Center, an important early media resource built and managed by students. Synapse ignited a process of discovery for Viola, providing him with a place to gain access to video equipment. There, he created such early works as *Cycles* and *Level* (both 1973). At Synapse he also established friendships with fellow art students, many of whom would play a key role in the emerging field of media art. One such student was David Ross, who became the country's first video-art curator at the Everson Museum of Art in Syracuse. Under the direction of James Harithas, the legendary museum innovator, the Everson Museum provided Ross with an opportunity to expose to the wider world such artists as Nam June Paik, Juan Downey, and Peter Campus. Viola had his first one-artist exhibition at the Everson Museum, in 1973. That was followed by an exhibition of his videotapes and installations at The Kitchen, New York, in 1974. Later, in 1997, as director of the Whitney Museum, New York, Ross organized a twenty-five-year survey of Viola's work that traveled to five international venues.

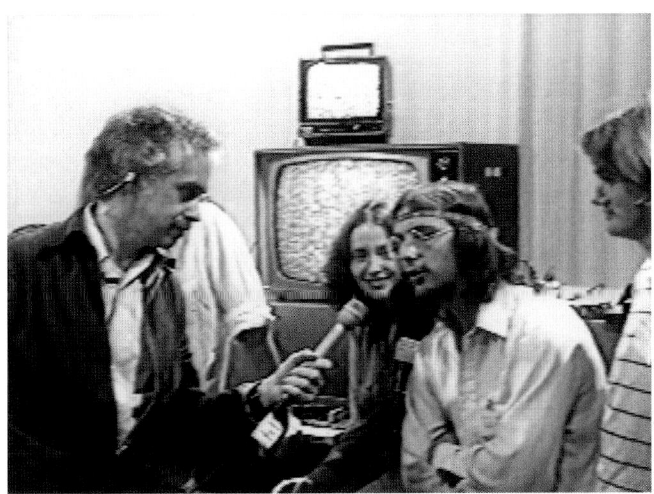

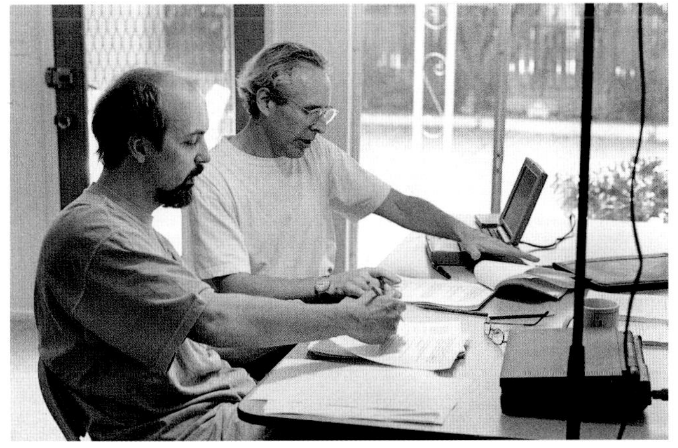

Through Ross, Viola met Gene Youngblood and was introduced to his book *Expanded Cinema* (1970). "All of a sudden," Viola recalls, "we had a purpose. We were at the beginning when things opened up."[7] Youngblood's *Expanded Cinema* described film and video as an open discourse, a laboratory of creative exploration. The book remains a seminal text in the transformation of the moving image in late twentieth-century art, and it laid the groundwork for the next generation of art-makers. Youngblood's book identified the importance of Nam June Paik as a pioneering artist who was creating a new art form. In 1974 Paik had a one-artist exhibition at the Everson Museum, and Viola worked on the show and assisted in the installation of Paik's landmark work featuring plants and television monitors, *TV Garden* (1974). Viola's friendship with Paik continued over the years and shaped Viola's understanding of the potential of video. The formative experiences of working on Paik's *TV Garden*, as well as David Tudor's *Rainforest IV*, set the stage for his own inquiry. But it was the video work of Peter Campus that most significantly shaped Viola's treatment of video. Viola met Campus when he helped the artist install his exhibition at the Everson Museum ("Peter Campus," 1974). He was impressed with Campus's achievements and referred to him as "my hero."[8] Campus's treatment of space and his interest in consciousness and cognitive science were deployed in a remarkable series of installations and videotapes. Viola's *Tape I*, shot in black and white, reflects on his own presence within the virtual space he occupies between two monitors. Seeing this alongside Campus's *Double Vision* (1971), a key work that explores two camera set-ups and the dislocation of space, is to recognize Campus's formative influence on Viola.

It is important to see these changes in art practice in the context of the profound institutional transformations taking place during the 1960s

Opposite, left *Cycles* (1973)

Opposite, right *Level* (1973)

Top Russell Connor interviewing Bill Viola, Marge Monroe, and the Rainbow Video group, *First Half-Inch Video Festival Ever*, WGBH TV, Boston, MA, 1972

Above Bill Viola and David Ross, working on the 1997 Whitney exhibition, Long Beach, CA, March 1997

and 1970s. It was a time of political and social upheaval leading to an expanding culture of public funding and a generational change in the academy. The transformation of broadcast television through public television and the development of cable and public-access television was important to the growing presence of independent video. The new opportunities for access to television heralded its development into a true means for communication, not a one-way channel for commercial broadcast limited to network television. Forms of media collectivism as a means to share resources and open a public dialogue on political issues emerged within independent video. Published by the pioneering production group Videofreex as a resource guide, *The Spaghetti City Video Manual* (1973) featured a section devoted to videotapes in distribution, an eclectic mix of innovative documentary videos on subjects ranging from anti-war commentary, gay and lesbian rights, and black liberation, together with image-processing and conceptual and performance-based work. Genres were not isolated from one another but seen as a community of possibilities and interests.

Looking back at this formative era, it cannot be stressed enough how the very notion of collaboration, the *communitas* of Paul Goodman, the liberation politics of Herbert Marcuse, and the psychoanalytic writings of Norman O. Brown were shifting the ground of art practice at a time when real change seemed possible. The field was fueled in large part by public funding coming from, at the federal level, the National Endowment for the Arts and, on a state level, the New York State Council on the Arts, the strongest and richest state arts agency in the country; it was also being supported by such private institutions as the Rockefeller Foundation, the leader in video art funding, and the MacArthur Foundation, which issued grants to fund equipment for media arts centers nationally. Local artist-run alternative spaces were established, such as The Kitchen, founded by video artists Steina and Woody Vasulka, and were soon creating innovative new platforms that combined production and exhibition. In the arena of television, public access provided communities with the means to create their own programs, and the "TV labs" at the television stations WNET in New York—where Viola was an artist-in-residence from 1976 to 1981—and WGBH in Boston made the resources of television studios available to video artists.

It is important not to confine Viola's achievement to one part of the art world, but to see his inquiry into ideas and art-making as drawing on an archive of global culture. His work is inspired by a desire to break free from a conceptual formula and to imagine art as opening up a humanistic dialogue with the viewer. We see in Viola's art a world reframed by the camera and transformed by the narrative the artist creates. Viola is aware of film's grand narrative ambition in his videos, but he also absorbs and

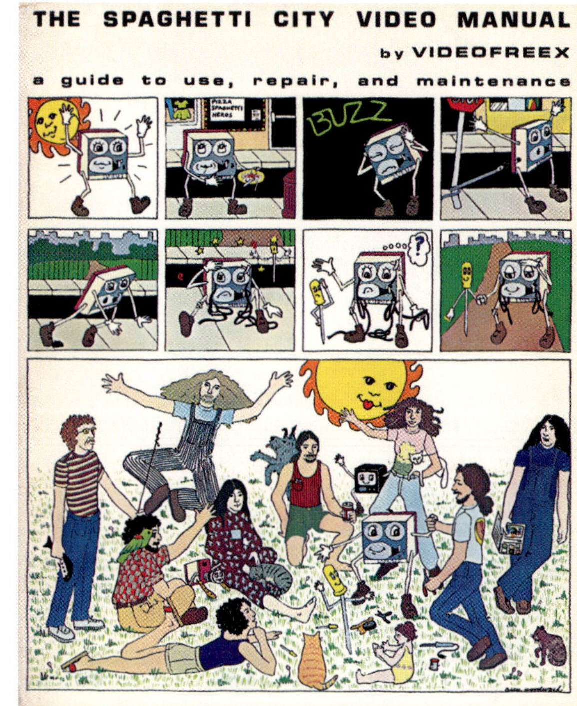

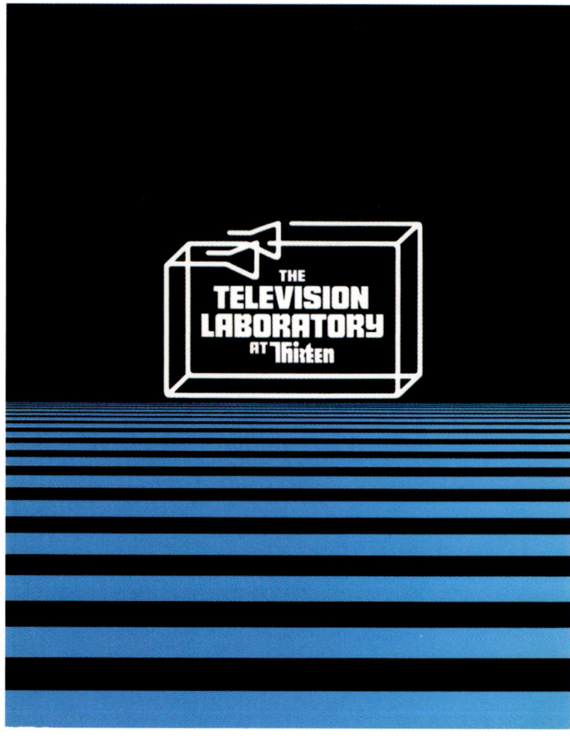

Top Videofreex, *The Spaghetti City Video Manual* (1973)

Above *A Report on the Television Laboratory at WNET/Thirteen 1972–1978*

Opposite Peter Campus, *Shadow Projection* (1974), installation (left), and *Double Vision: Convergence* (1971), videotape (right)

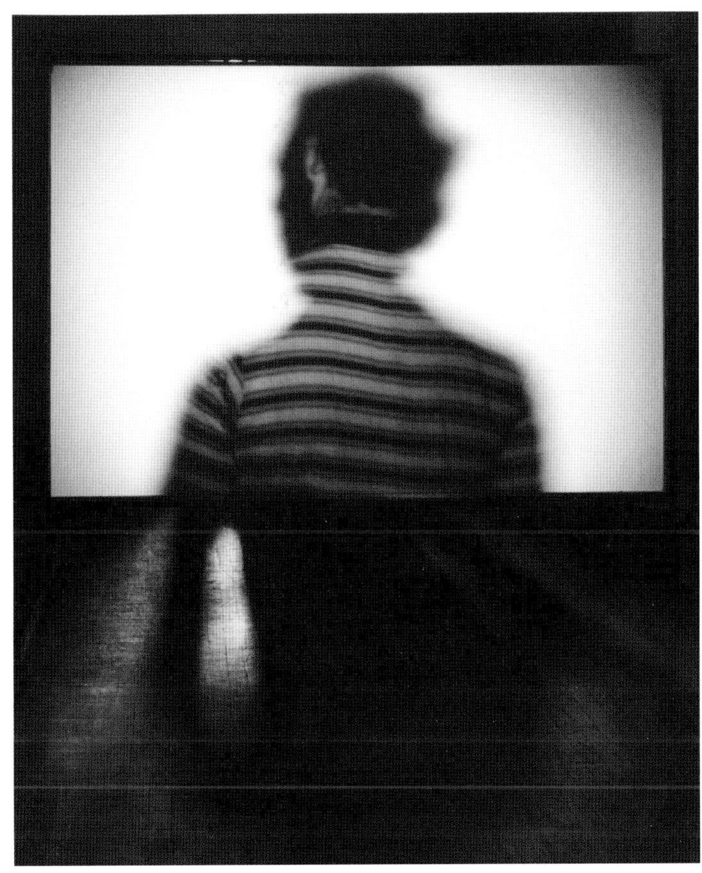

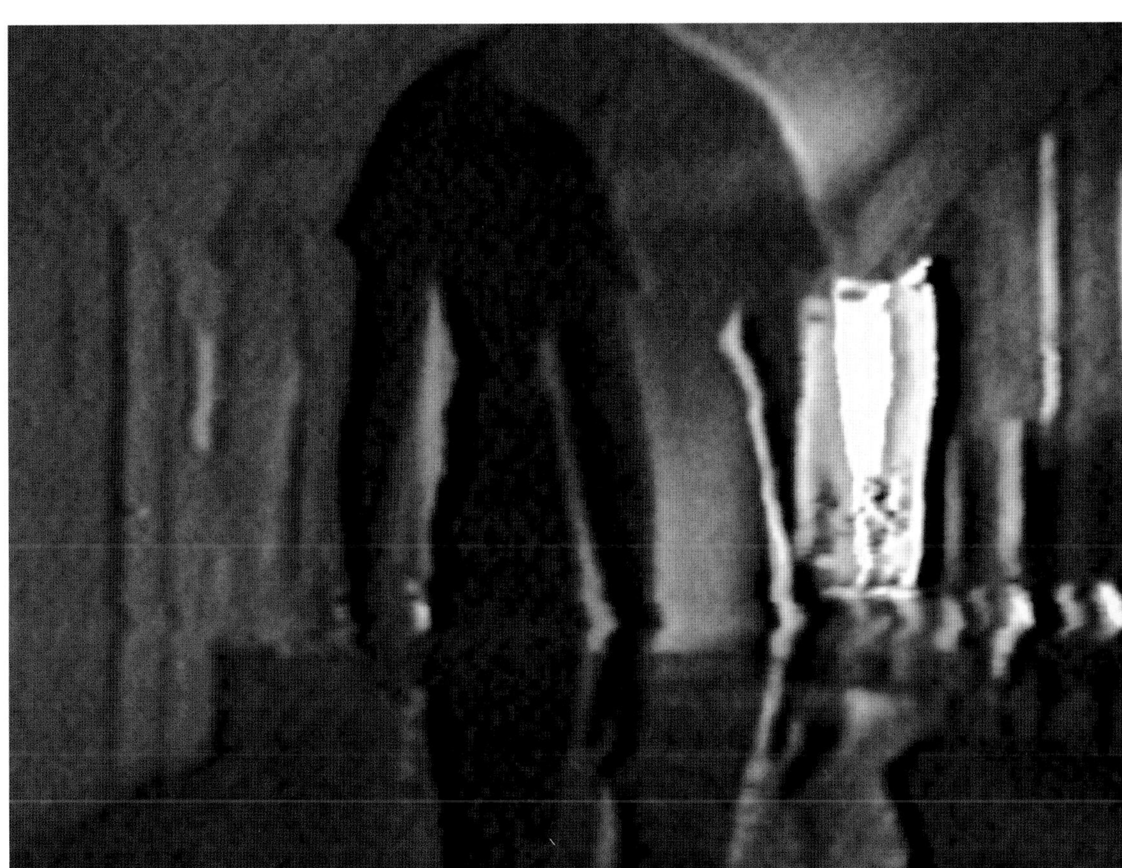

transcends that past in his discovery of video's immediacy and its potential as a recording and image-transforming medium.

I was impressed with Viola's recollection of the formative influence of the world he discovered in the late 1960s, as he was moving away from his past and his parents toward the emerging video culture. David Tudor, Nam June Paik, and Peter Campus, notes Viola, were the "three people who influenced me the most."[9] These three artists embody key aspects of his lifetime art project: transforming technology, empowering a new way of making moving images, and fashioning new ways to see the world around us. Viola recognized video as the path to follow.

As a new and newly accessible medium that captured Viola's attention, video must be seen against the cultural background of the avant-garde cinema and new music, and the political and cultural change percolating when he entered Syracuse University in 1969. Viola was attracted to the flexibility of video and the live, immediate presence of the moving image. For him, this real-time process was the key to unlocking the possibilities of the medium. It was not about establishing a means to create a finished work, but about the infinite possibilities of building out in a variety of directions at the same time that appealed to Viola. His experiments with closed-circuit television allowed him to understand how he could manipulate space, such as in works like *Localization* (1973), which was "concerned with the idea of

LOCALIZATION : A VIDEO STRUCTURE FOR TWO-WAY CABLE SYSTEM.

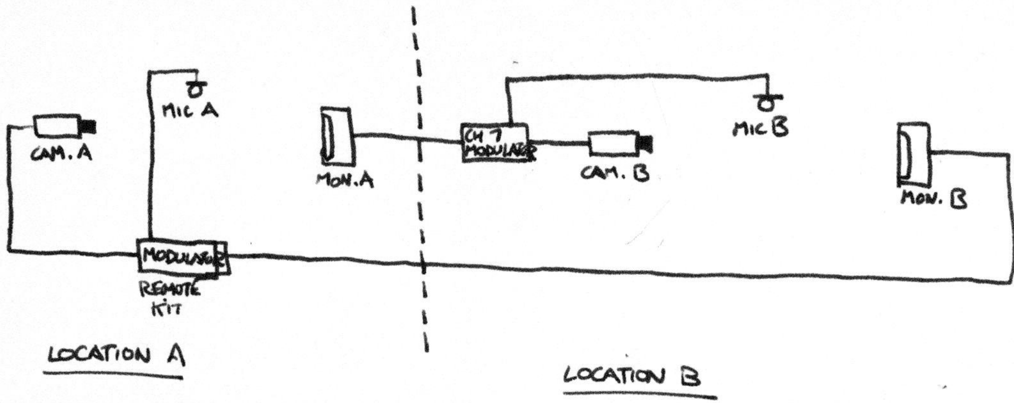

CAMERAS SHOULD BE TAPED UP (CONTROLS etc.) TO PREVENT PEOPLE FROM FOOLING AROUND. FEEDBACK FROM the AUDIO CAN SOMETIMES BE A PROBLEM.

THE CAMERAS ARE ABOUT 20-30 FEET FROM the MONITORS, AND THEY FRAME the MONITORS SO THAT PLENTY of OUTSIDE SPACE IS APPARANT.

NEED
- 2 CAMERAS (PANASONIC) – ONCE SET UP - TAPED OVER.
- 2 TRIPODS
- 2 MONITORS (RCA – minimum RCA types)
- 2 MICS – Hanging from ceiling overhead
- 2 MODULATORS (audio/video)

APPROXIMATE FRAMING of MONITOR

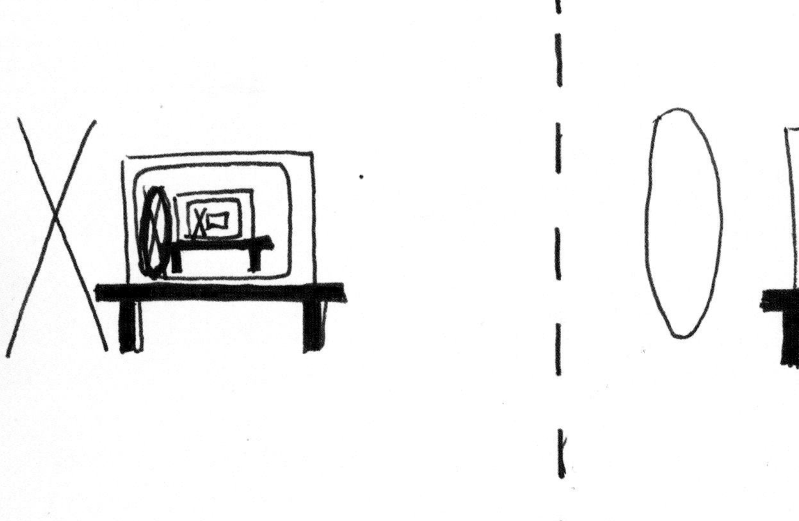

Localization (1973), diagram (above); installation views, Syracuse University, NY (opposite)

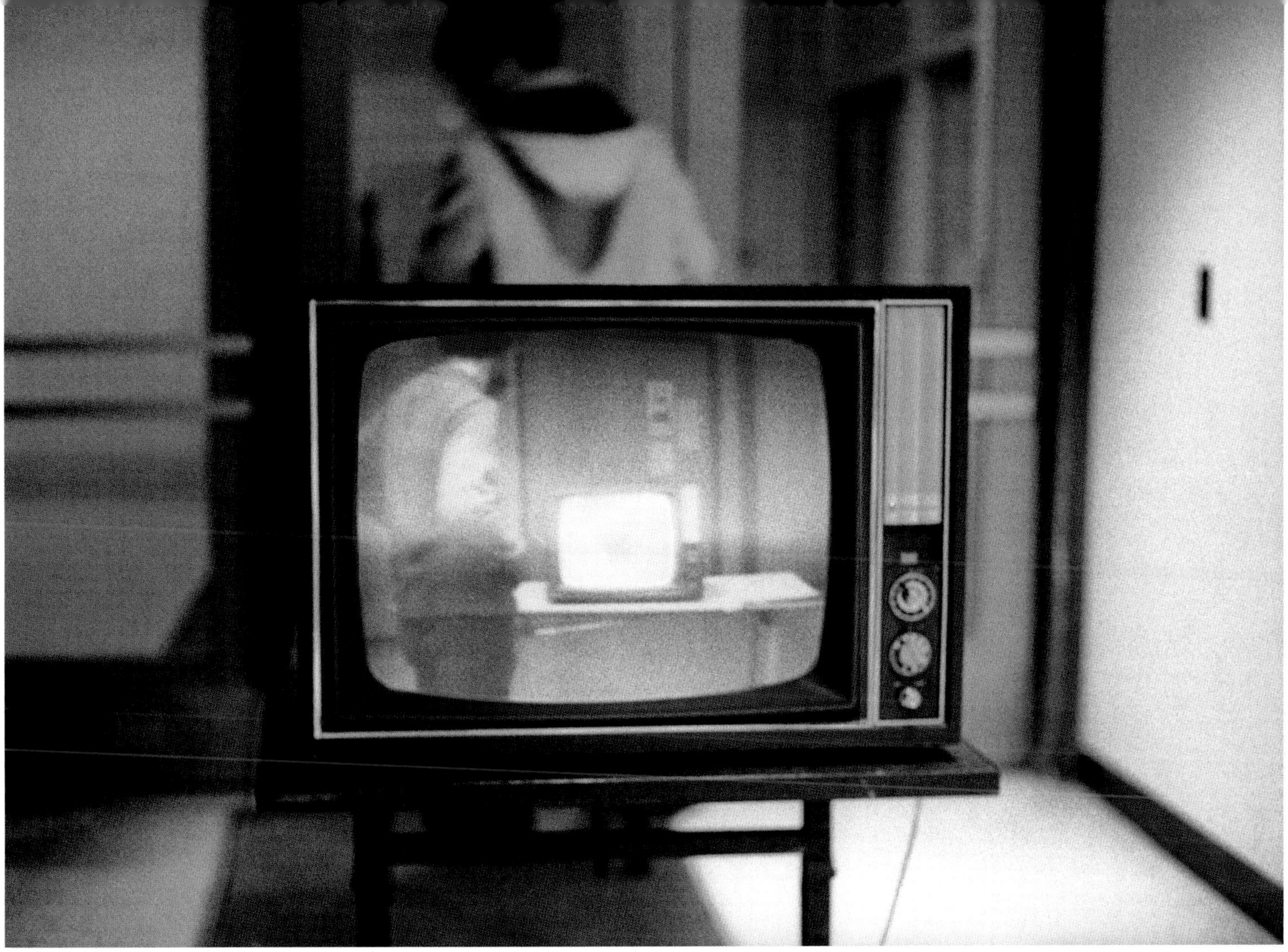

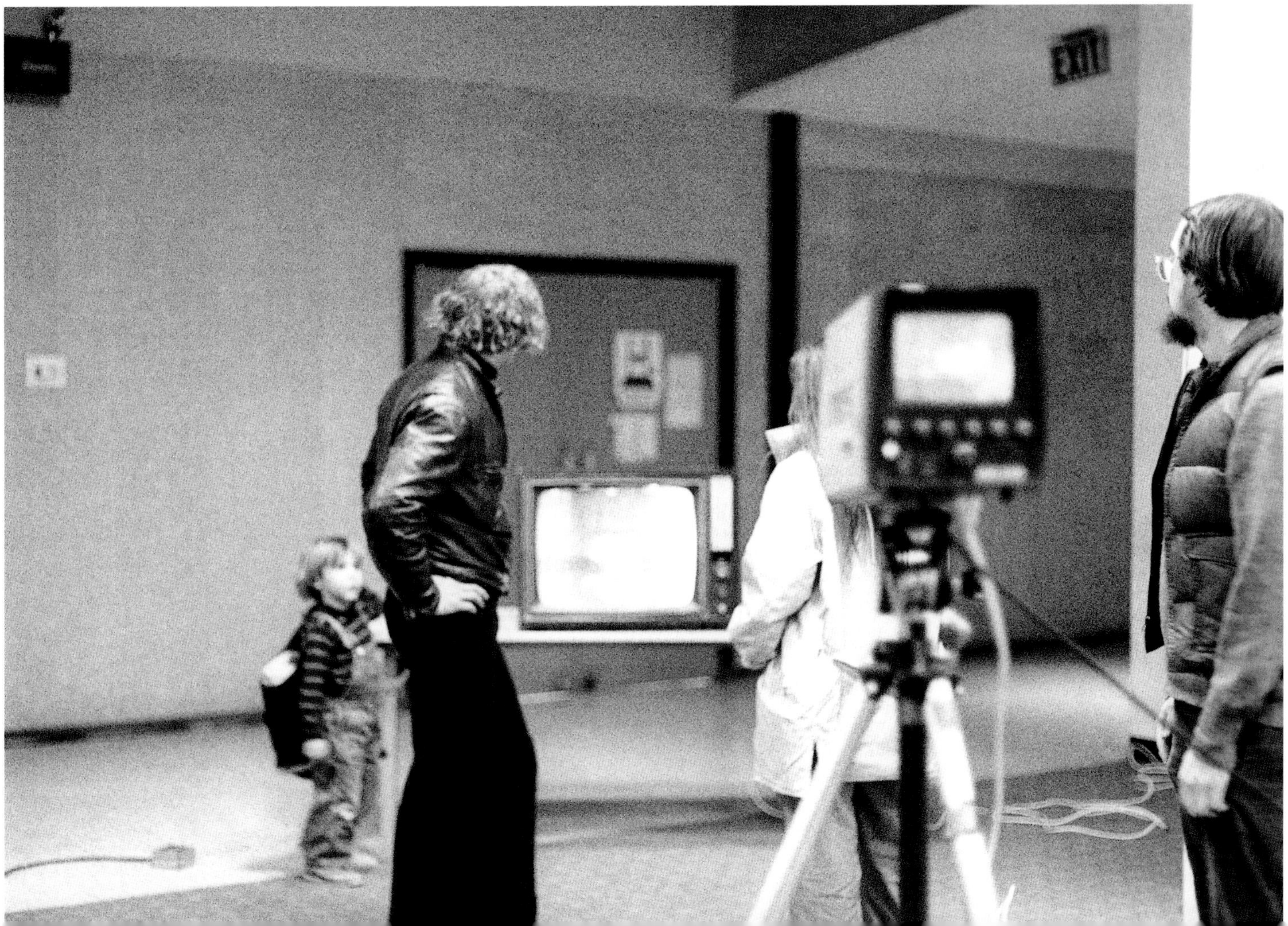

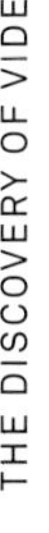

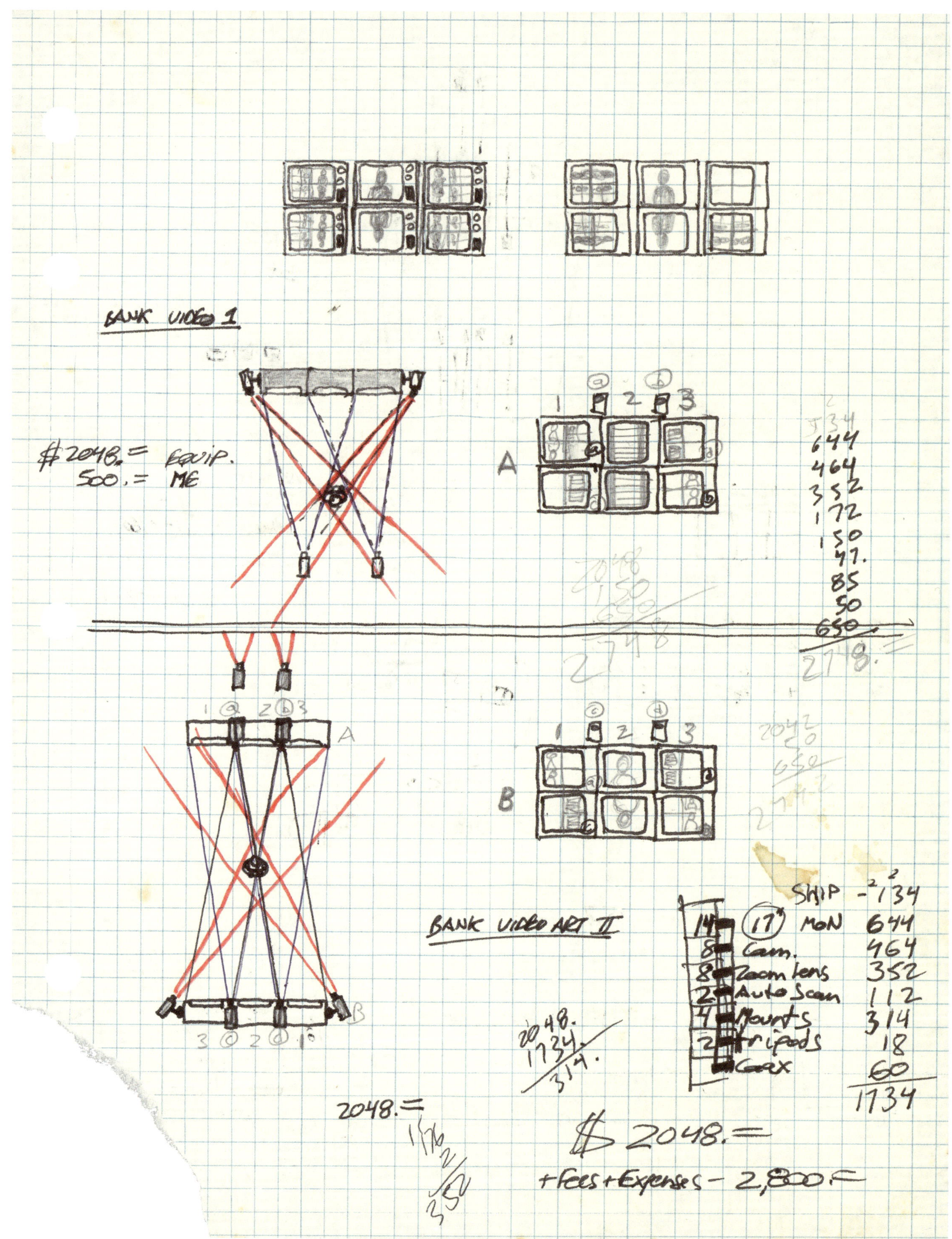

Bank Image Bank (1974), drawing, 1973 (above); Bill Viola and installation view, Lincoln First Bank, Rochester, NY, January 1974 (opposite)

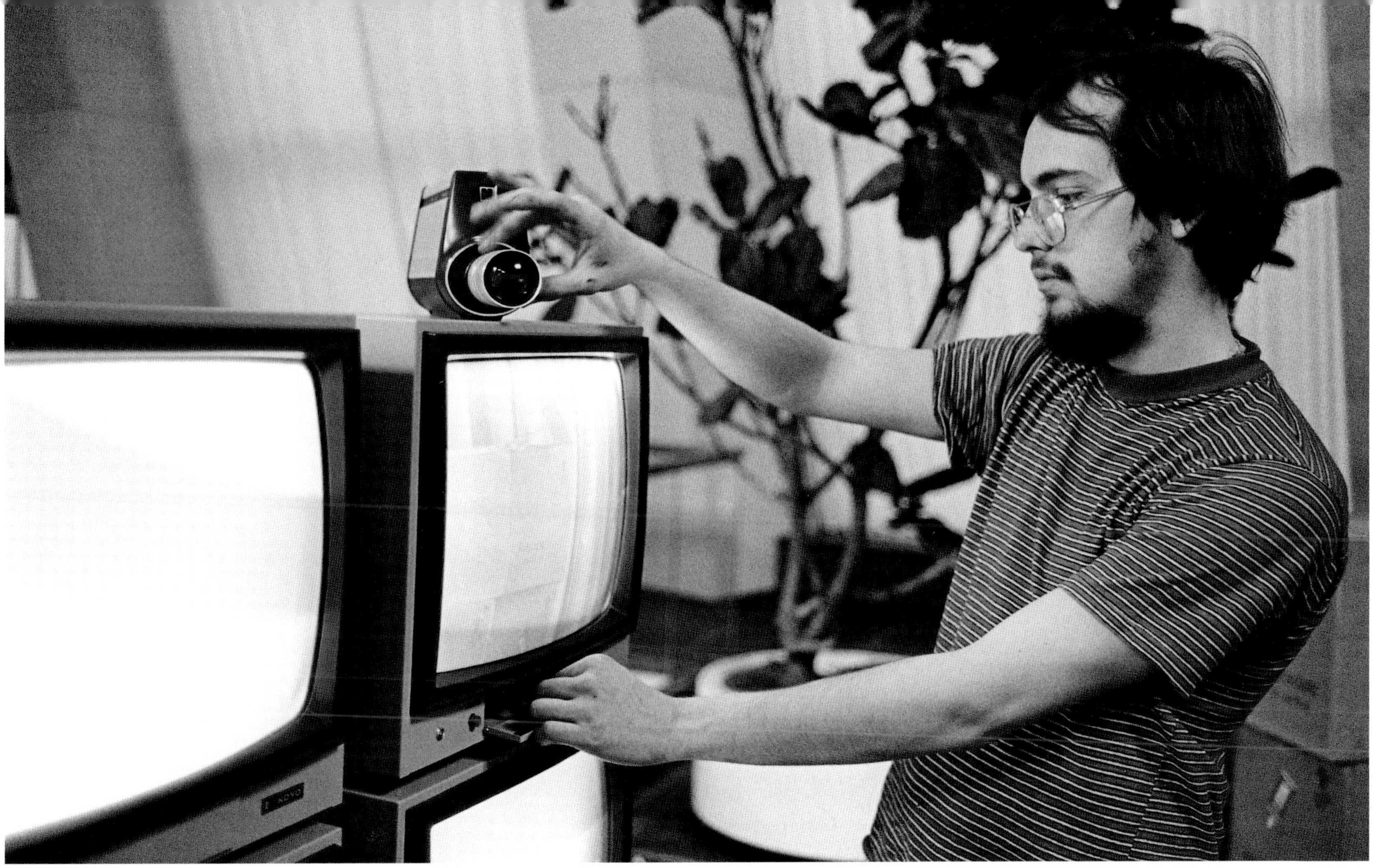

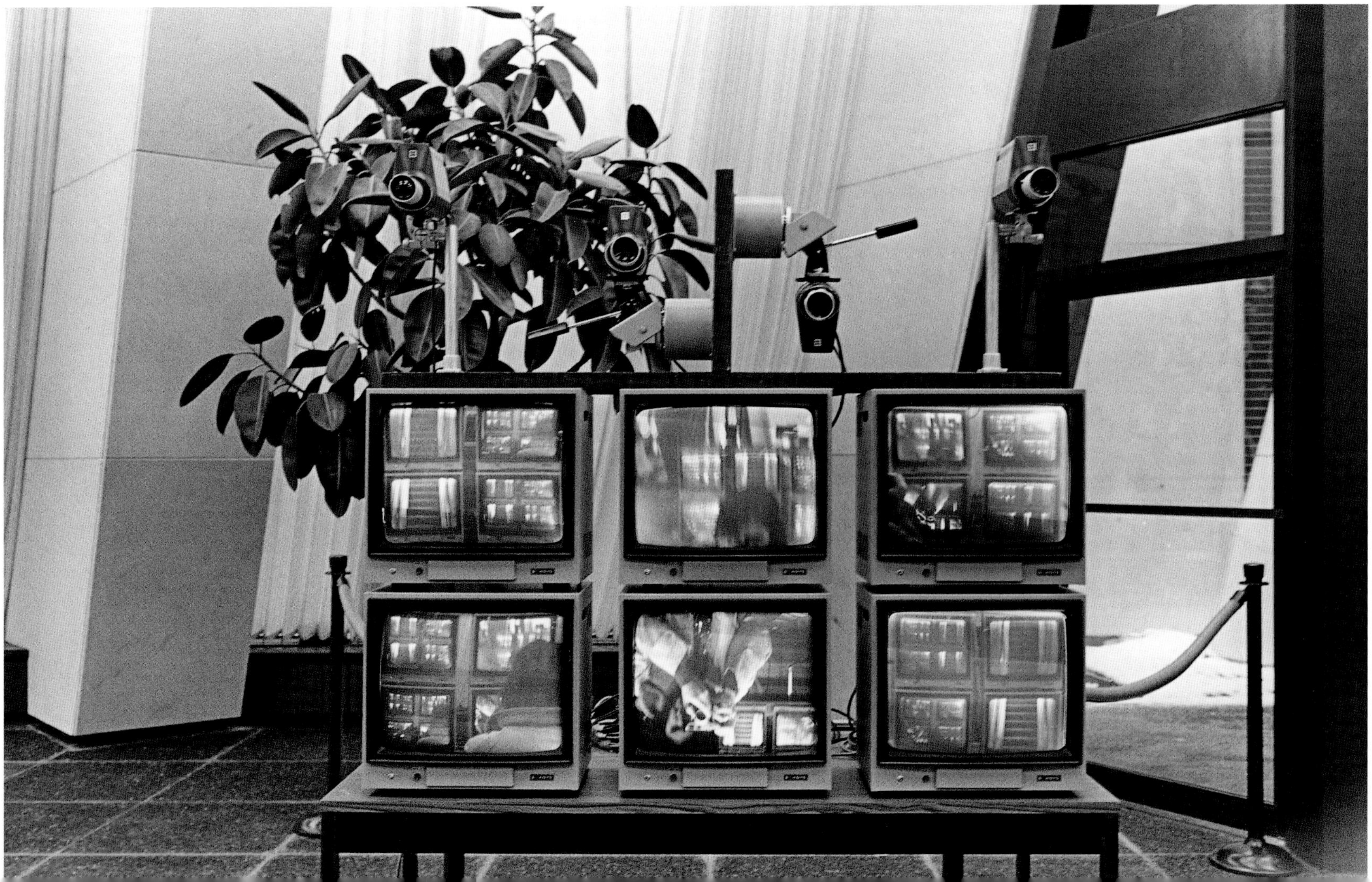

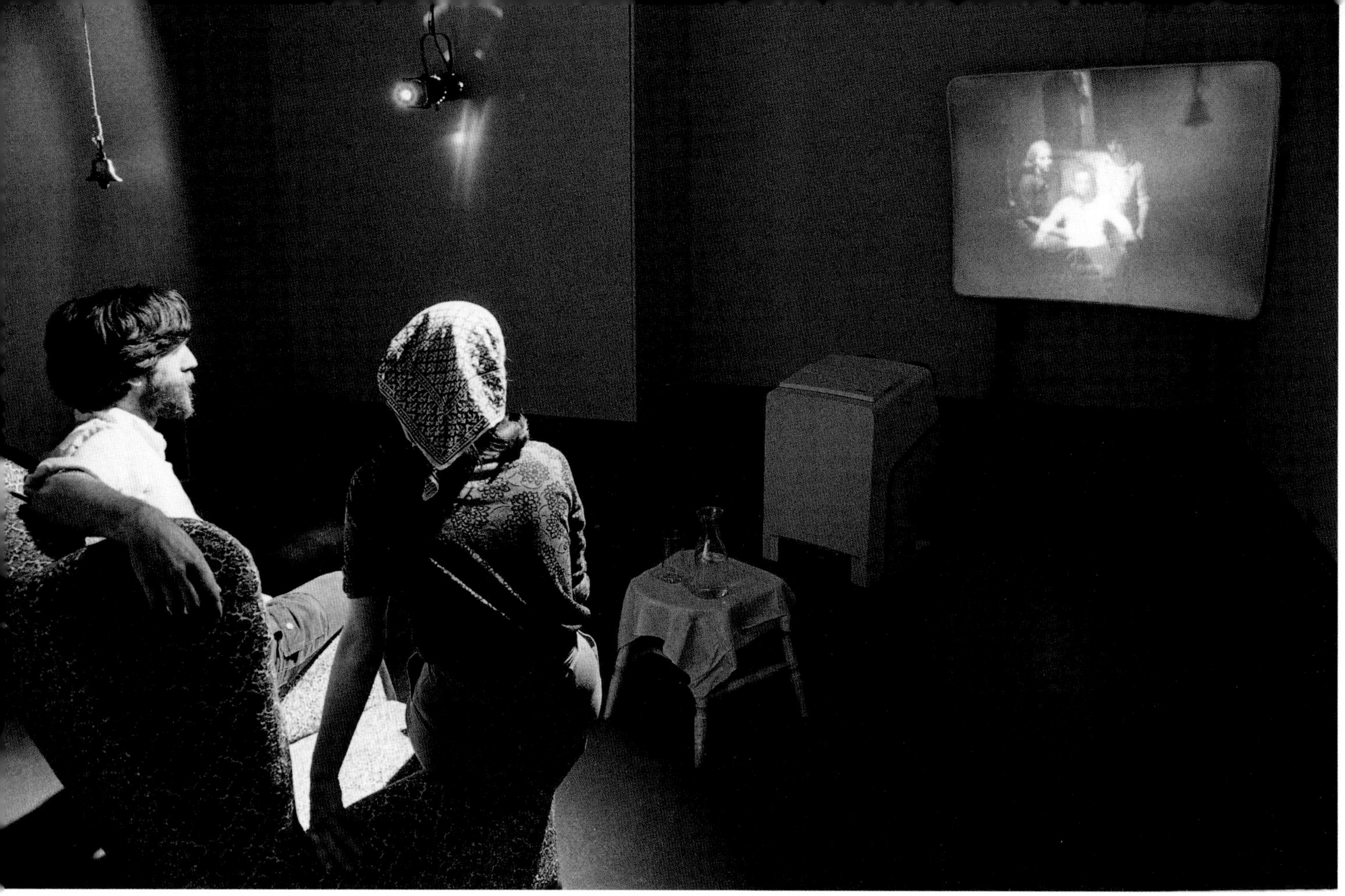

inserting one space into another,"[10] or *Bank Image Bank* (1974), where eight live video cameras were used to alter the geometry of the space in which the viewer found themselves. With the installation *Olfaction* (1976), he attempted to change the notion of linear time by using prerecorded video combined with live camera to create a "mix" of the past and the present, a concept that he had previously explored in the exhibition "Rain–Three Interlocking Systems" at the Everson Museum in 1975. David Tudor and Nam June Paik are foundational to understanding Viola's aesthetic, and the friendship and opportunities offered by his friend and fellow student David Ross were key to his ability to imagine the possibilities of the medium as an art form.

It is important to recall that Paik entered video through performance and music. In his first one-artist exhibition, "Exposition of Music—Electronic Television," held at Galerie Parnass in Wuppertal, Germany, in 1963, he transformed the television set into an interactive medium and a sculptural object. Paik ripped television from the context of the commercial entertainment channels, and his conceptual transformation of the medium reworked it into an art form. Just as Tudor created a new form of aural expression, Paik saw video as an open medium that relied on chance and change, rather than a prescriptive, closed system of production.

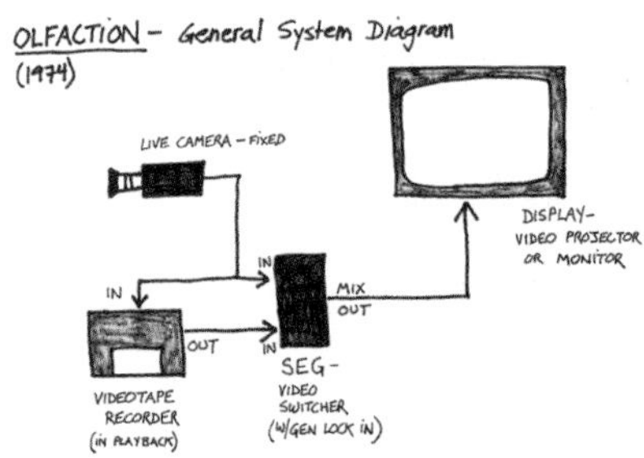

Above *Olfaction*, installation, The Art Galleries, California State University, Long Beach, CA, September 1976 (top); *Olfaction* system diagram, 1974 (bottom)

Opposite "Rain—Three Interlocking Systems," Everson Museum of Art, Syracuse, NY, December 1975

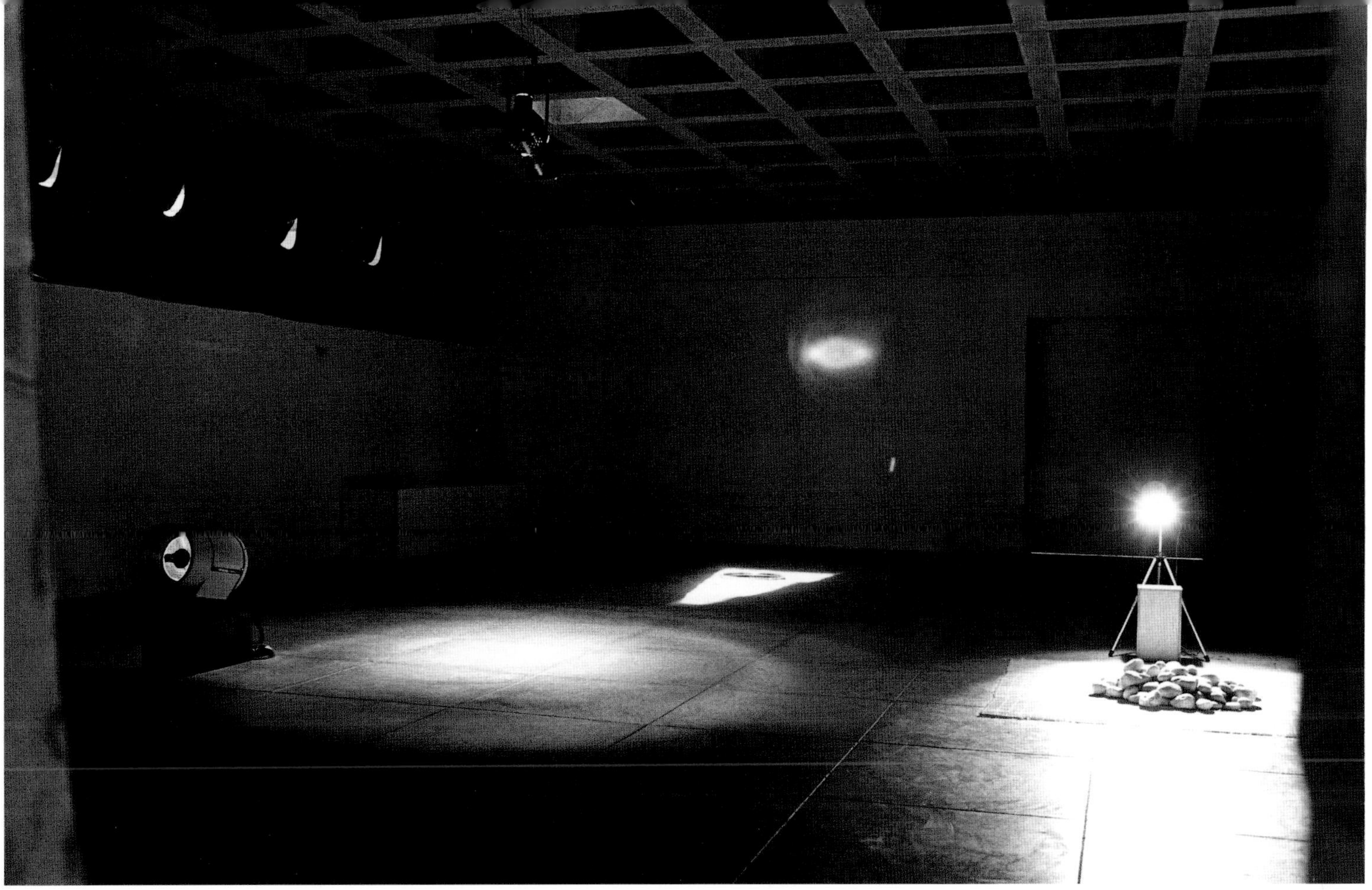

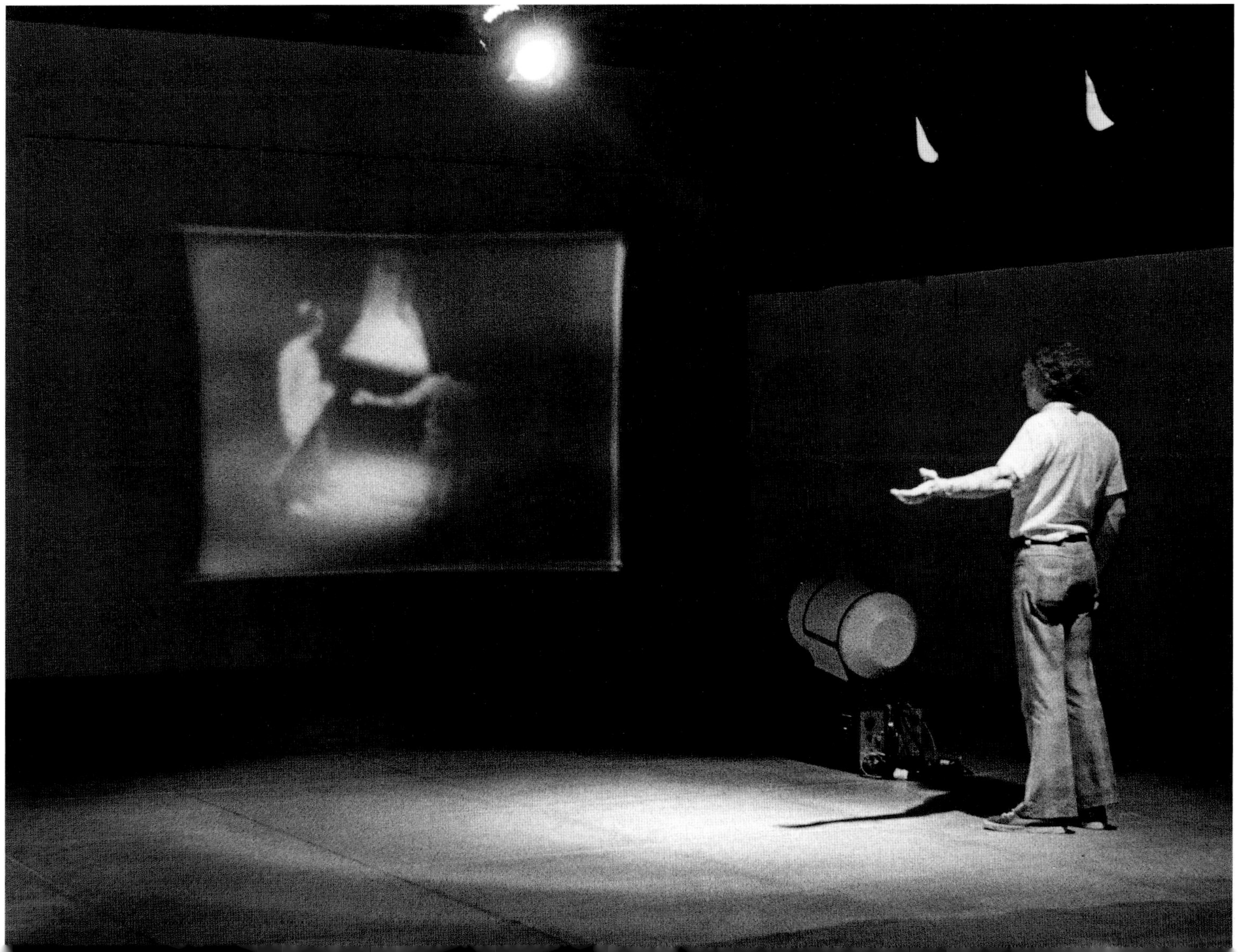

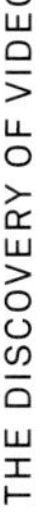

Largely produced at Synapse, Viola's early videotapes were shot in black and white and are best described as experimental forays into self-discovery. His approach to the medium was "about the moment," and his methods varied.[11] He was inspired, he says, by how Paik saw this "vision machine, knows that it's coming to the West," and was "ahead of the curve."[12] Paik had a holistic view that was not about a single medium. While Viola was Paik's assistant for his exhibition at the Everson Museum, and later at Paik's Westbeth studio in New York City, he felt a "huge, important connection" to the artist and to Paik's exploration of the medium of video.[13] "You felt in your gut," he recalled, "that it is the crystal of something that will expand."[14] Later, Viola traveled to the Solomon Islands to shoot video for Paik's seminal videotape *Guadalcanal Requiem* (1977). That experience inspired Viola's own representation on video of the Solomon Islands's Moro Movement. In two videotapes, *Memories of Ancestral Power (The Moro Movement in the Solomon Islands)* and *Palm Trees on the Moon* (both 1977–8), Viola chose not to employ the traditional codes of the documentary genre, such as voiceover to direct and explain the action. Rather, his videotapes used an observational technique that respected the subject and gave voice to the Moro people and their traditions. Viola recognized that video was the first global medium, embracing Europe, Asia, and Latin America: "because you were seeing the same thing at the same time," he explained, "it was the first medium to go global at its start."[15] His travels also took him to Java, to record traditional music and dance, and to Japan, where he was able to show his work and have exchanges with local artists.

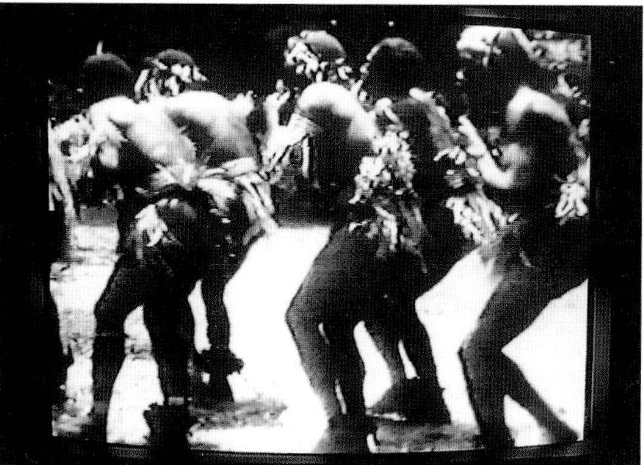

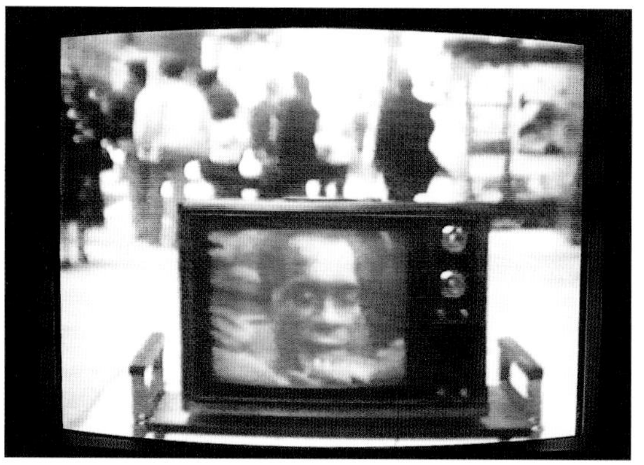

Viola quickly began learning about the technology behind the medium. With the technical skills he acquired, for example, he helped to install the cable television system in the cafeteria that was being transformed into Synapse. He also found work as the assistant to the pioneering television producer Russell Connor at the Cable Arts Foundation (an organization set up in 1973 to get work about art on cable television in New York), and was the cameraperson on Connor's video documentary *To Sienna with Love* (1978). But it was Viola's desire to push the medium that led him to test its limits and find where it would break down. Viola was exploring the break from the normative, the disruption of the professional veneer and surface.

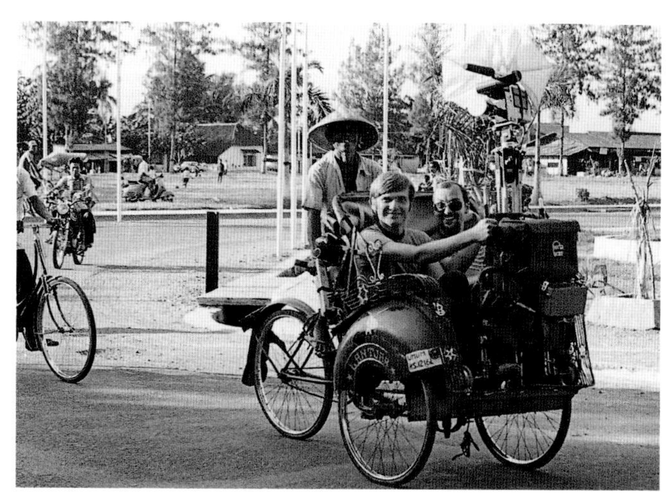

Initially, Viola's interest was in form, in how the medium could be shaped to create and negotiate different places—both literally and metaphorically—and in how it related to his own being. In *Tree Noise* (1973), Viola spent time at the top of a tree, among its canopy of branches and leaves, and attuned his senses to the ecology of this above-ground environment, exploring how he placed himself within it. He then installed pieces of text and Polaroid photographs of the treetop in the student exhibition space at Syracuse University. The Polaroids gave immediacy to the images as he spent time reflecting on his experience. The fragmented

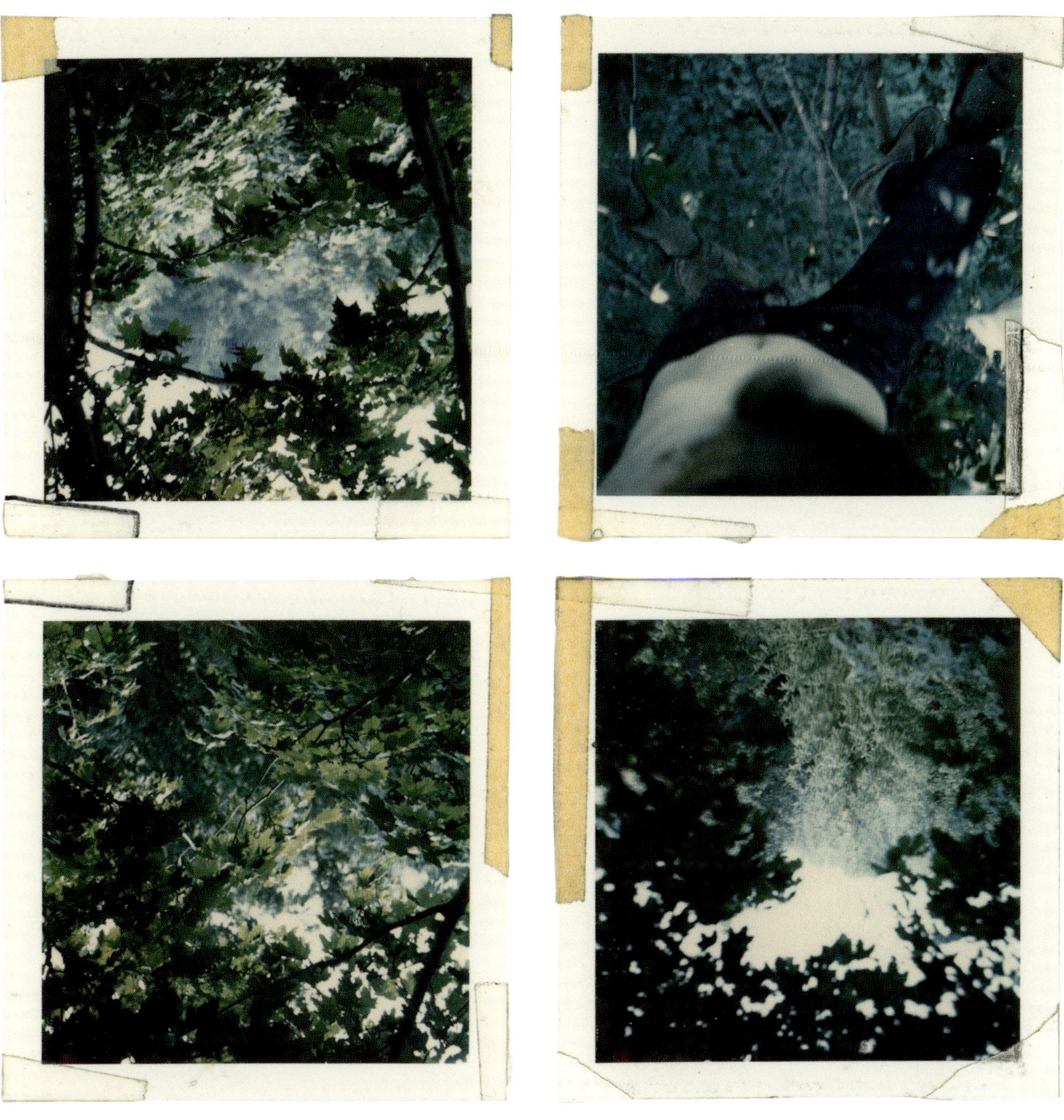

Opposite, top *Palm Trees on the Moon* (1977–8)

Opposite, center *Memories of Anscestral Power (The Moro Movement in the Solomon Islands)* (1977–8)

Opposite, bottom Bob Bielecki and Bill Viola in Java, Indonesia, December 1977

Above Polaroid documentation by Bill Viola of his performance *Tree Noise*, Syracuse, NY, 1973

immediacy of the images played with the idea of photographic evidence and how one perceives the environment in real (past) time. As we shall see in a number of his videotapes (*A Million Other Things (2)*, 1975, *Return*, 1975, *The Semi-Circular Canals*, 1975, *The Morning After the Night of Power*, 1977, *The Reflecting Pool*, 1977–9, *Moonblood*, 1979–80), Viola often goes out into the environment to establish a point of view. He became interested in different environments and in visualizing spaces, and found that the instantaneousness of the Polaroid was offered on another level by video's electronic moving image, which could also see and record the present, in "real" time. In such early works as *Tape I*, he felt that "the image you are receiving is just the first layer. Manipulating the image, it would break up a palette. That was the key. I was starting to read Rumi."[16] The spiritual openness to consciousness inherent in the visionary poetics of the Sufi master added another dimension to the capacity of this artist's new medium. For Viola, the linking of art and ideas, aesthetics and experience, established the media arts as the art of our time.

Instant Replay (1972), *The Breathing Space* (1973, a sound sculpture), *Hallway Nodes* (1973, a sound piece), *Bank Image Bank*, *Return*, *Il Vapore* (1975), *Four Songs* (1976, including *Junkyard Levitation* and *The Space Between the Teeth*), *He Weeps for You*, *The Morning after the Night of Power*, *The Tree of Life* (1977), *Chott el-Djerid*, *The Reflecting Pool*, and *Hatsu-Yume (First Dream)* (1981) laid the foundation for the videotapes and installations that followed. A metamorphosis of Viola's intentions and ideas informed this sequence of artworks as he emerged out of his undergraduate years and joined the video art world of the 1970s and, subsequently, the global, time-based art world of the 1980s. Viola did much to shape the scale and ambition of these art worlds. He left aside postmodern popular culture and replaced it with an inquiry into our global cultural heritage, the classical past, and ways of transcribing and imagining the invisible forces of nature and a spiritual vision. However, it was Viola's interest in "how to use a visual medium to represent invisible things" that attracted him to video and to his pursuit of the unseen.[17] "Video was always showing me invisible things all the time, either technically, in terms of infrared cameras, or circumstantially, in terms of a recorded moment that no longer exists."[18]

As we saw in his earliest videotapes such as *The Space Between the Teeth*, Viola cleared space for the landscape and body as twin embodiments of the living organism of nature. In his Notebooks, drawings of natural forms and the human body offer signs of the world that he is composing in the context of his writings, which locate the spiritual in our being and richly imagined natural environment. It is important to recognize Viola's theoretical intention: a pursuit of meaning through the electronic moving image. Viola's genius was to observe and learn from what was taking place around him and build on an intuitive understanding of the medium's self-reflective capacity to represent action. Not unlike the work of other artists using video at this time, such as Bruce Nauman and Richard Serra, Viola's videotapes became the basis for his future work. However, in Viola's case, his work moved away from conceptual and purely formal intention to an exploration of subjectivity and the creation of a transcendent experience through a renewed aesthetic of beauty.

Viola does not copy or reinterpret the arts of the past; rather, as we read in his Notebooks, they are inspirations that set Viola's mind in new directions and inspire connections between the past and present through the issues he is exploring. We see the full articulation of an epistemological representation of the body occupying a world of narrative possibilities in works ranging from *The Space Between the Teeth* to *I Do Not Know What It Is I Am Like*.

In such early pieces as *The Morning after the Night of Power*, we see how Viola pursues his interest in the properties of video through a richly imagined conceptual narrative space. The piece was distinguished by his active inquiry into the nature of video combined with the spiritual texts he was reading at the time. "The 'night of power,'" he wrote, "is described in the Koran as a moment when angels descend from the heavens to impart the divine inspiration."[19] In this work, Viola continued his exploration of time-lapse and prolonged observation that he had begun in 1975 with *A Million Other Things (2)*, recording changes in sound and light on objects in a room over the course of several days.

For Viola, video and audio became the means to consider what art might become. Because he was not caught up in the avant-garde movements of Fluxus, Conceptual, Process, or Performance art, he could determine his own path, which was a self-reflective one both in terms of his presence in the work and what he was learning about world culture and mysticism. Coming from the margins of the art world—the suburbs of New York City, Syracuse University—allowed him to explore new possibilities. Viola's worldview was a generous and open one. He was looking and exploring and sensing the possibilities. He did not become a member of a video collective, but he did visit some and saw films and videos by Nam June Paik and Peter Campus, Juan Downey and Frank Gillette, at the same time as he participated in experimental audio performances. Viola's father worked for Pan American World Airways, which gave Viola the means to travel to Europe to attend such festivals as EXPRMNTL, the Knokke Experimental Film Festival in Belgium. A year after he graduated, from 1974–6, he became technical director of production at art/tapes/22 in Florence, a video initiative that brought him into contact with a diverse community of international artists, including Giulio Paolini, Jannis Kounellis, Mario Merz, Vito Acconci, Joan Jonas, and Terry Fox. At the same time he had access to some of the finest art in the Western world, which would later greatly influence his work. But Viola's independence from any school of art or art-historical movement made him uniquely positioned to fashion his own path. His body of work is defined by his interest in spiritual and aesthetic issues, from a global yet idiosyncratic position. His work took shape around these twin poles over a twenty-year period from the 1970s to the 1980s, and it continues to develop and change to the present day.

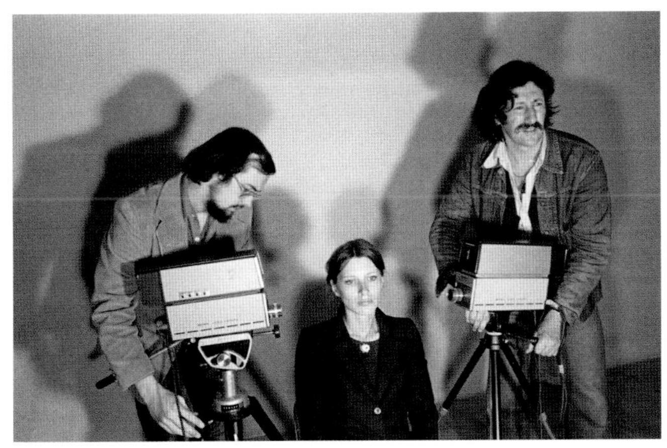

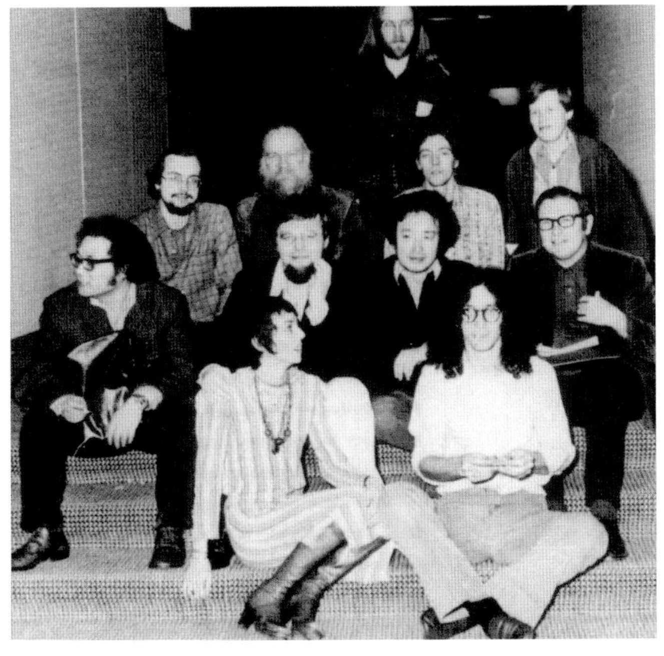

Top Bill Viola, Muriel Olesen, and Gerald Minkoff, art/tapes/22, Florence, Italy, April 1975

Above Video artists and curators, EXPRMNTL, the Knokke Experimental Film Festival, Belgium, December 26, 1974 (left to right, front row: Wendy Clarke, Jean-Pierre Boyer; second row: Taka Imura, Woody Vasulka, Nam June Paik, Gerald O'Grady; third row: Bill Viola, Ed Emshwiller, Kit Galloway, Steina; back row: Walter Wright)

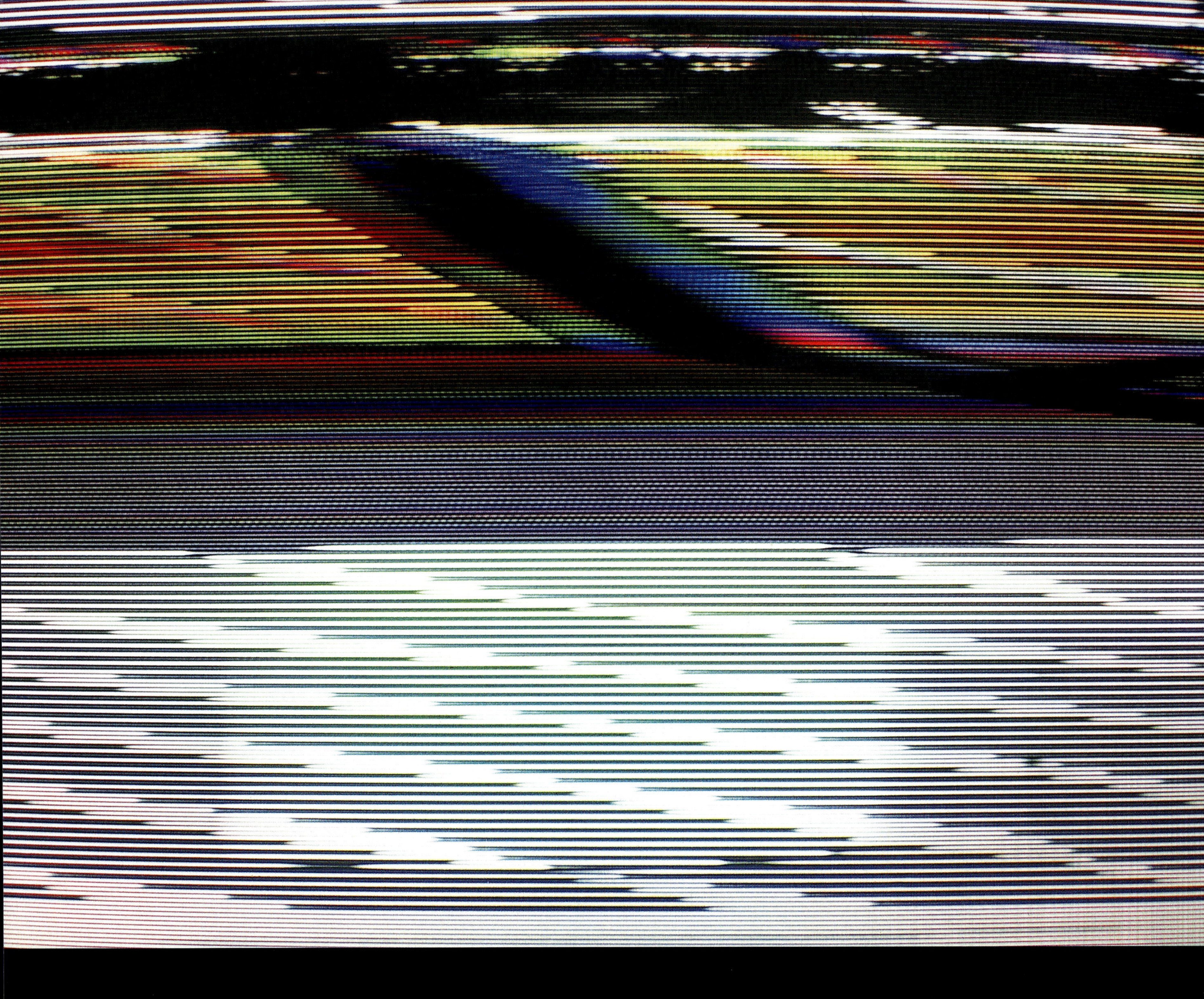

CHAPTER TWO

1970s: REFLECTIONS ON NATURE AND TIME

No beginning/No end/No direction/No duration
Video as mind

—Bill Viola, Note, 1980

The first twenty years of Viola's artistic practice moved toward a vision of reality in which the form his art takes creates a ground for capturing the forces of nature. How, through the optics of a moving-image recording technology, could he create a "vision of reality" absent of form? Here, I want to consider one of Viola's earliest works, *Information* (1973), beginning with his description of the chance encounter with a recording system that resulted in its creation:

Information **is the manifestation of an aberrant electronic non-signal passing through the video switcher in a normal color TV studio, and being retrieved at various points along its path. It is the result of a technical mistake made while working in the studio late one night, when the output of the videotape recorder was accidentally routed through the studio switcher and back into its own input. When the record button was pressed, the machine tried to record itself. The resulting electronic perturbations affected everything else in the studio: color appeared where there was no color signal, there was sound where there was no audio connected, and every button punched on the video switcher created a different effect. After this error was discovered and traced back, it became possible to sit at the switcher as if it were a musical instrument and learn to "play" this non-signal. Once the basic parameters were understood, a second videotape recorder was used to record the result.** ***Information*** **is that tape.**[1]

This videotape is, in many ways, Viola's urtext. It displays the qualities that mark his work throughout his career. Viola is so attuned to the medium that

Information (1973)

he is open to the possibility of "accidents" to show something we haven't seen. Viola explores a deep interest in the musicality of the medium, the way rhythms compose themselves in terms of what unfolds on the screen, as well as how sound adds another dimension to our perception of the work.

Information is, in a sense, a combination of David Tudor's treatment of sounds and instruments in *Rainforest IV* and Nam June Paik's openness to chance. Paik's treatment of video in the 1960s and 1970s, through the development of the video synthesizer and the direct treatment of the cathode-ray tube with magnets, is exemplified by *Demagnetizer (Life Ring)* and *Magnet TV* (both 1965). The properties of the cathode-ray tube, virtual electronic spaces, and a distortion of the received broadcast signal create the imagery we see in Paik and Jud Yalkut's *Video Tape Study No. 3* (1967–9), in which a recorded television image emerges out of the electronic "snow." *Information* also recalls Paik's early use of the Paik-Abe Video Synthesizer in *Experiments with David Atwood* (1969) and the 4-hour live interactive telecast from the WGBH studio entitled *Video Commune* (1970). In *Information*, the figure of the American visionary architect and inventor Buckminster Fuller is seen and heard and then disappears into the electronic noise and abstract "chatter" between sound and image as they feed off each other in a disruptive loop of self-cannibalization. *Information* speaks to Viola's attention to the possibilities of the moment. Key to his work is the video's locus in the real-time formation of the moving image. Video, in its closed-circuit modality, creates the possibility of an active, first-hand treatment of the image, since it is being recorded and manipulated in real time, as opposed to film, which is developed and edited later.

All of Viola's work from this period treats the temporal and the aural dimensions of video as a coherent audio-visual composition. Time becomes a powerful component in his work: as we see the image unfold, we become more aware of its making. There is a self-consciousness to the early work that is enhanced by the presence of the artist in its fashioning. This meta-strategy reframes the image in a constant process of construction and destruction. Fuller's fragmentary language and presence in *Information*—for example, when he says, "I don't think nature is using..."—is filled in by building and crashing feedback caused by the chance operation of a self-deflecting system. The soundtrack plays off the striated lines and reframing video image on the monitor's screen. The soundtrack of *Information* sounds uncannily like sprocket holes running through a projector, giving the videotape the characteristics of film. This is reinforced in Viola's instructions for the work to be exhibited in a darkened theatrical situation, not in the form of a monitor on a pedestal in an open gallery space. Just as Viola became more aware of the unique character of the electronic image in his first videotapes and installations, he also saw how his process created its own chance operations, exposing the instrumental possibilities of a medium that was feeling the push and pull of its great predecessor, the cinema.

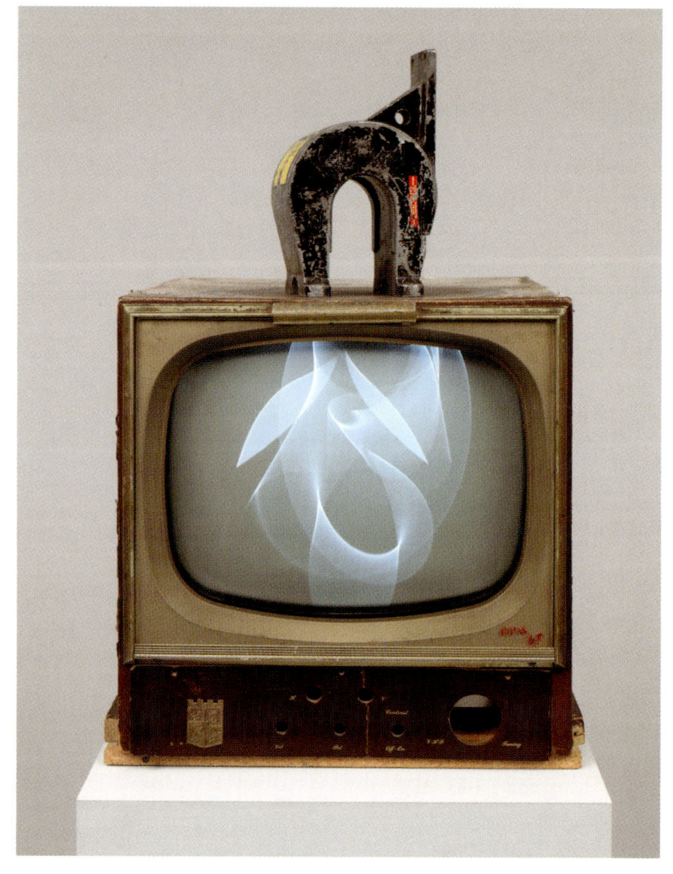

Above Nam June Paik, *Magnet TV* (1965)

Opposite and following two pages *Information* (1973)

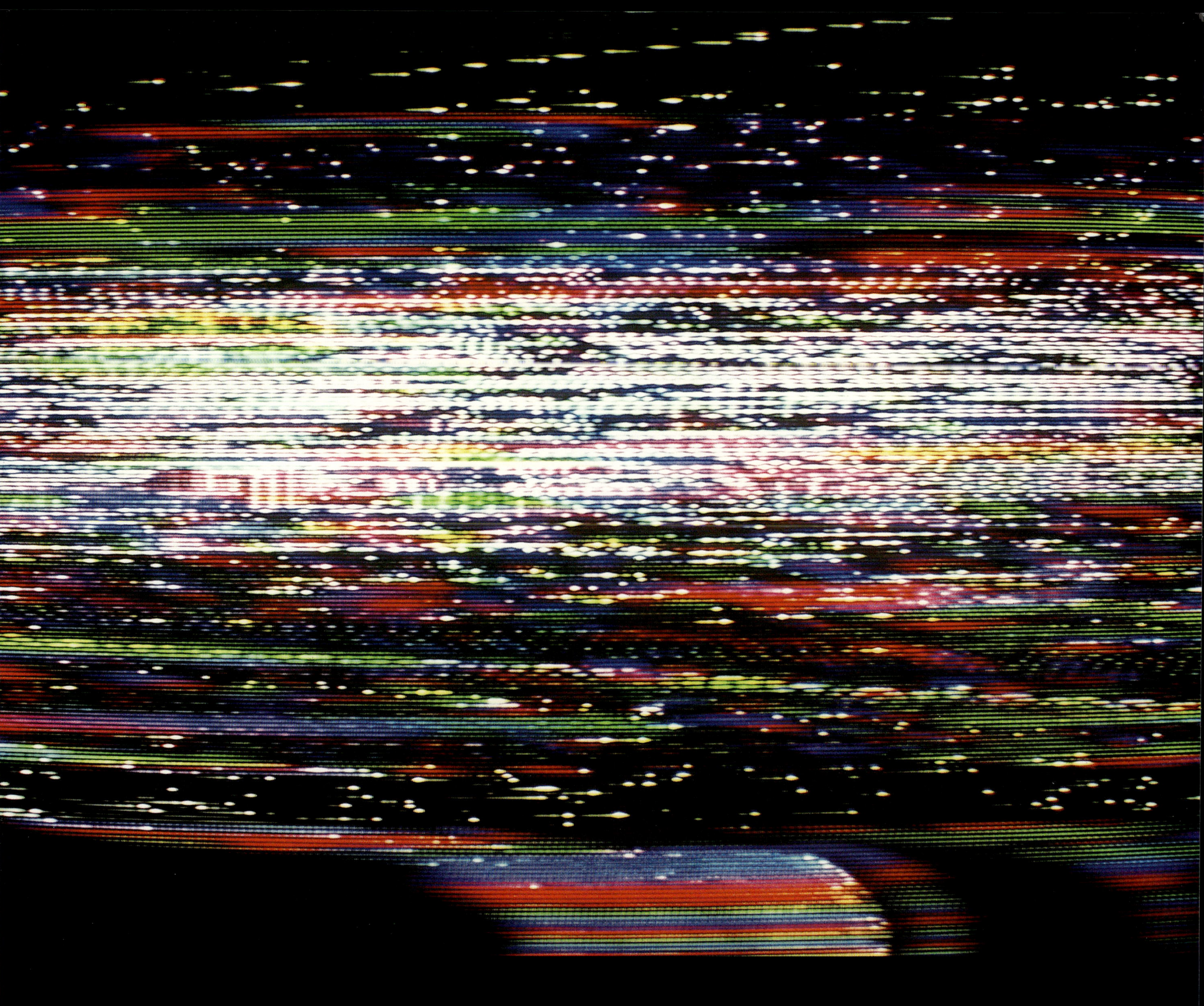

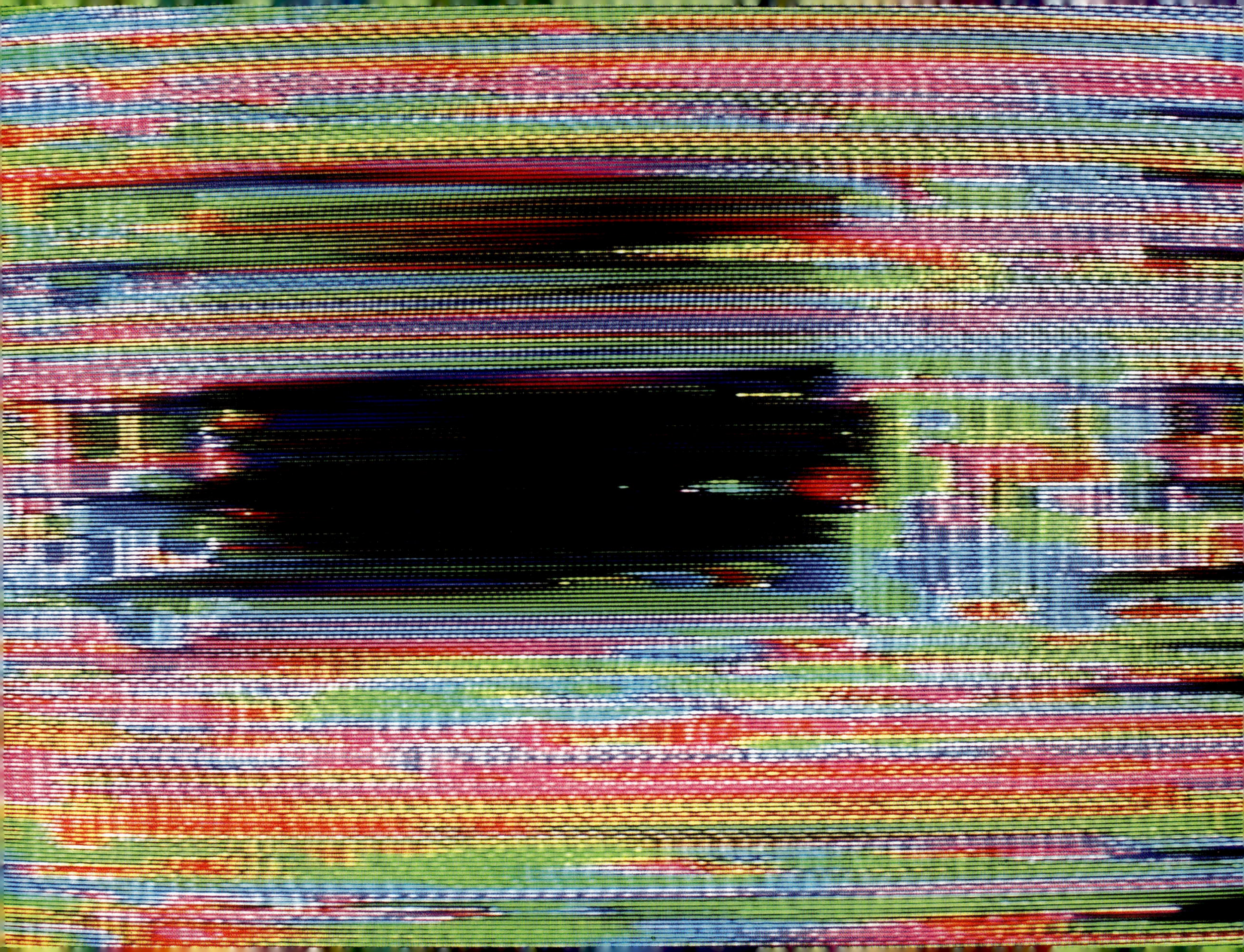

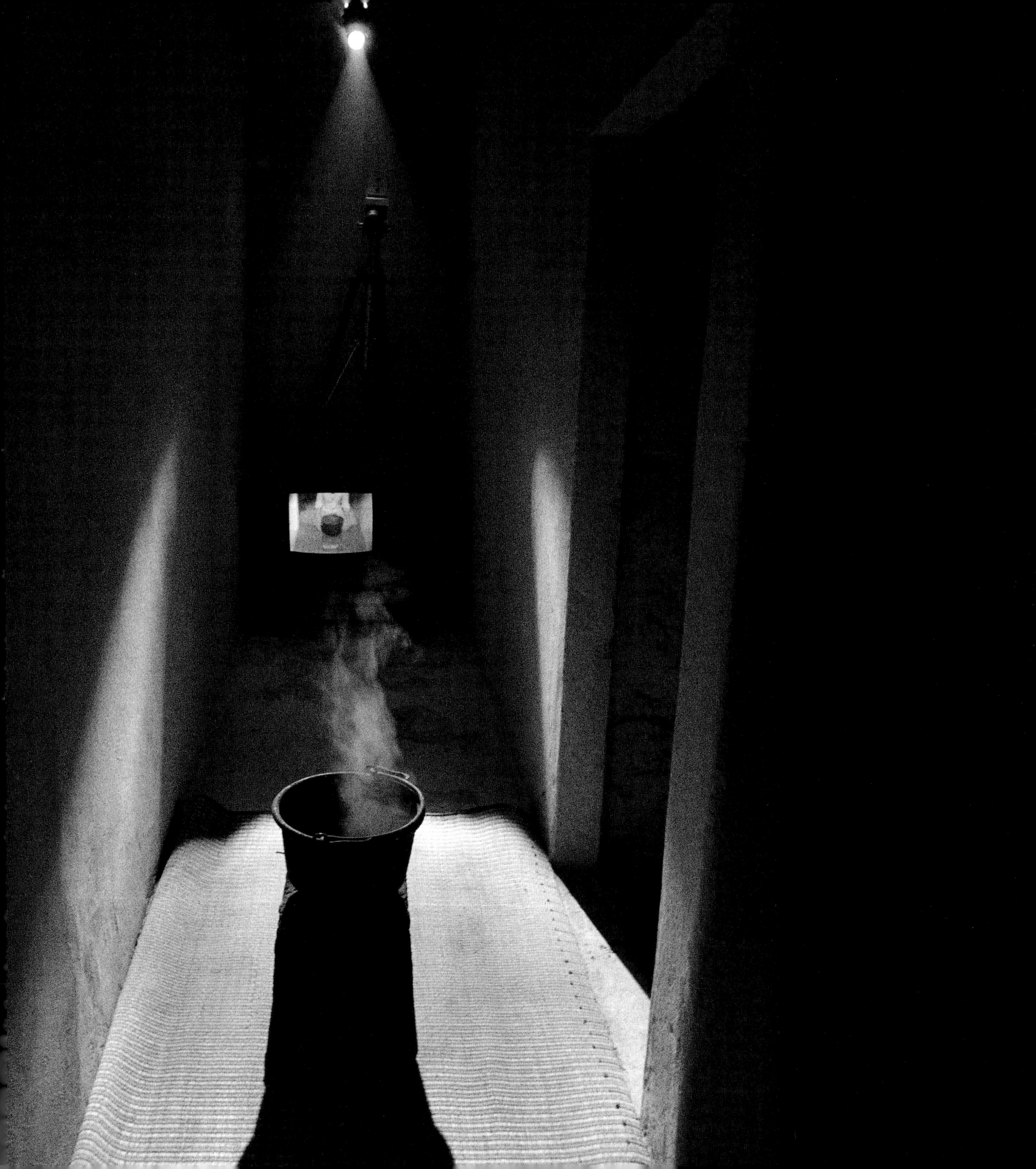

Bill Viola
Walking into the Wall 1973

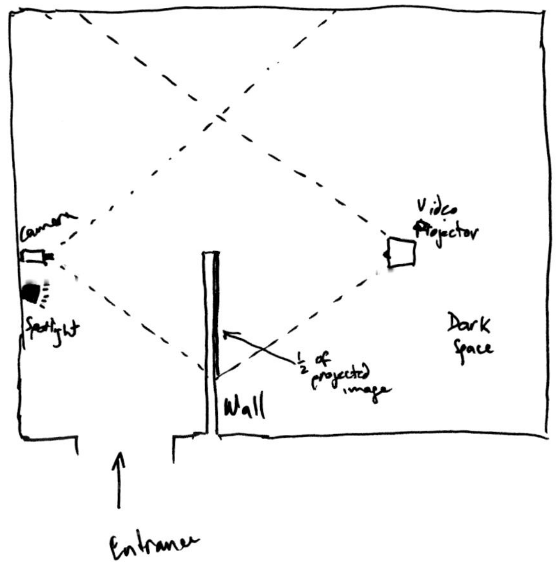

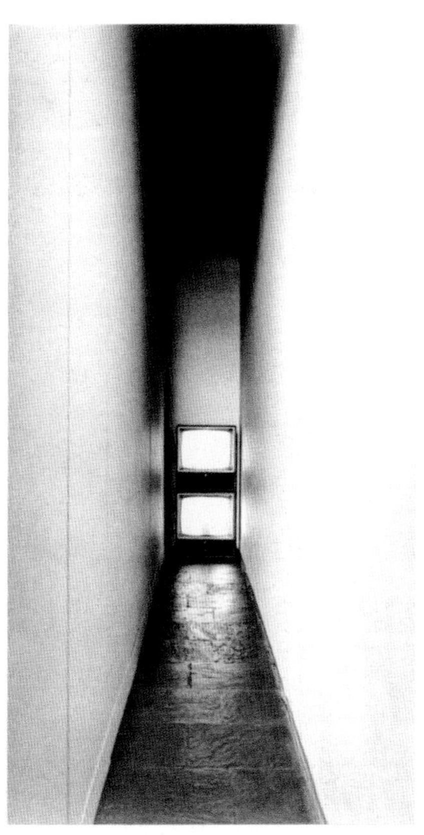

Opposite *Il Vapore*, Zona, Florence, June 1975

Top *Walking into the Wall* (1973), diagram

Above Bruce Nauman, *Live-Taped Video Corridor* (1970)

The basic qualities of process and chance that inform *Information*, and the interplay of the recording and playback system that shapes the experience of the piece, laid the groundwork for what would be a poetic and expanded form of experimentation in the single-channel videotapes and installations of the 1970s. One of the first was *Il Vapore* (1975), which Viola created while in Florence. Here, he describes the two stages of the installation:

First, after the space is set up and the iron pot, mat camera, and lights, etc., are all set in their fixed positions, a videotape was made of myself kneeling before the pot, pouring water from a separate bucket into it with my mouth. A microphone was placed close to pick up water sounds. This process was slow and deliberate, lasting one hour, and occurred as a solitary performance, the space locked and closed to the public. Next, eucalyptus leaves were put into the pot and the water brought to a boil from a small camping stove previously placed underneath. The one-hour tape was rewound, and played back, the audio being monitored directly on a small speaker under the video monitor. The video was sent into a SEG (special effects generator) and mixed (50% dissolve) with the signal from the light camera. Since the camera and objects were never moved, the taped space and the live space line up exactly in the mixed image on the monitor. The only thing to have changed, myself pouring water in the pot, could be seen and heard in the monitor's space, but in the actual room, no person was there sitting in front of the steaming pot. Stage two—the audience is let in. The installation begins. Eucalyptus vapors have filled the space with a strong menthol smell. Persons can see themselves on the monitor live, in the background behind the pot, and simultaneously, the figure of a person filling the pot with water is also visible and audible, co-existing with them in the same space. Past and present tense co-exist equally.[2]

The exhibition of *Il Vapore* in Zona, a non-profit art space in Florence, was one of Viola's first shows in Europe.

Il Vapore layers time and experience to create an audio, visual, sensory installation. Other works show Viola's interest in space and the perception of movement. *Walking into the Wall* (1973), for example, employs a closed-circuit camera to show, through the projected image, viewers entering a space and appearing to walk into a wall, so that participants and observers become disoriented by the camera's point of view in relation to the projected image, which seems to show the viewer in a different place. In displacing the viewer and the space, *Walking into the Wall* is an interesting analogue to videotapes that deal with point of view and the reorientation of space and action, such as Bruce Nauman's *Live-Taped Video Corridor* (1970). In this work, a narrow, confined space is seen on a monitor from the camera's point of view, as well as on prerecorded videotape, thus mixing present and past.

Il Vapore uses technological innovation to bring the meditative process of preparing tea into the present tense on video.

The ability to make the present tense tangible is intimately linked to the closed-circuit capacity that characterizes video. The video camera's capability to record something while displaying it in real time on a monitor redefined the construction of the moving image. Previously, artists needed to process film before being able to see what they had shot with their camera, creating a delicate balance of intention between what the artist imagined was being recorded and what the final film looked like when projected. This ontological difference becomes a subtext to the creative process. Viola immediately understood that, as a creative medium, the electronic moving image was profoundly enabling in its infinite possibilities. In the videotape *Olfaction* (1974), for example, recordings of past and present actions are shown at the same time. His work is not about the product of image processing, but about the real-time discovery of what can happen through chance with the closed-circuit video system. Viola's openness to the unexpected runs throughout his creative life. After looking at his later work, and as a result of conversations with Kira Perov, it became clear to me that chance—the unexpected opportunity that arises during a shoot in the desert, say, or in another culture—could produce something that would later become the focus of a new work. Video is not a piece of Viola's art practice, but rather the centerpiece of his creative life.

The way in which the closed-circuit system opens our understanding of moving-image making takes on a vivid and immediate form in Viola's *He Weeps for You* (1976), dedicated to his Syracuse University teacher and mentor Jack Nelson. This was Viola's first internationally recognized installation, which he describes as an "ensemble of elements [that] evokes a 'tuned space,' where not only is everything locked into a single rhythmical cadence, but a dynamic interactive system is created where all elements (the water drop, the video image, the sound, the viewer, and the room) function together in a reflexive and unified way as a large instrument."[3] Viola's drawings and conceptualizations of the installation in his Notebooks show how he first imagined the piece.

The real-time video image is central to *He Weeps for You* and, by extension, to everything Viola has created. By locking in all the elements to create an interactive, reflexive, and unified instrument, he defines the power of the image on the screen, which shows on a large scale a tiny drop of water emerging from the copper pipe suspended in the room. As the drop grows, it becomes at once more prominent and more fragile. Standing in a beam of light, the viewer is captured in the drop and becomes visible on the screen as the drop is magnified. When the drop of water falls to the ground, it hits a drumhead with a microphone underneath, and in this way the sound is amplified on speakers in the room, enlarging the scale and significance of

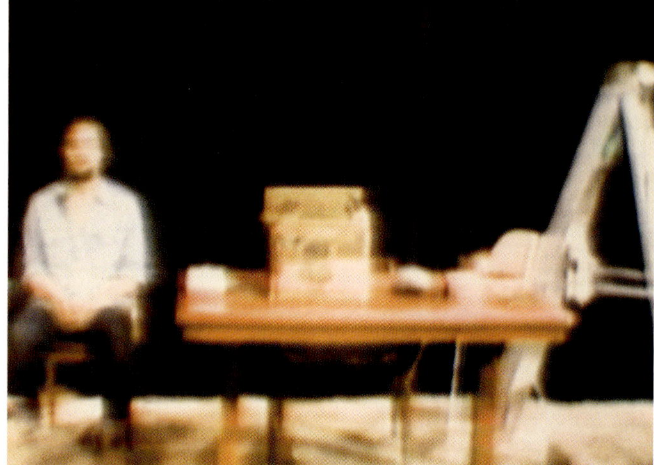

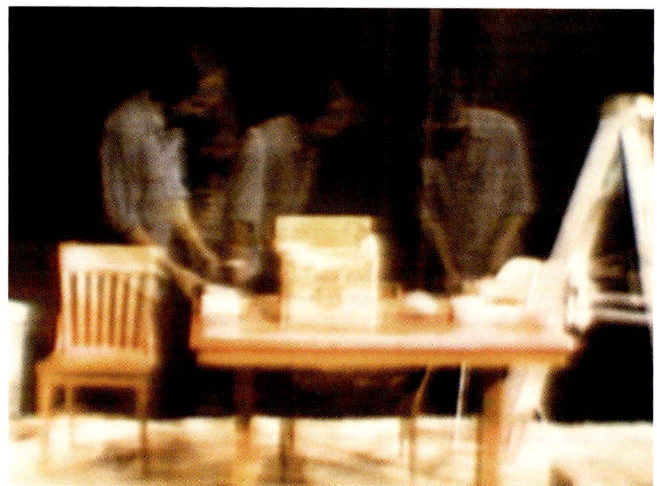

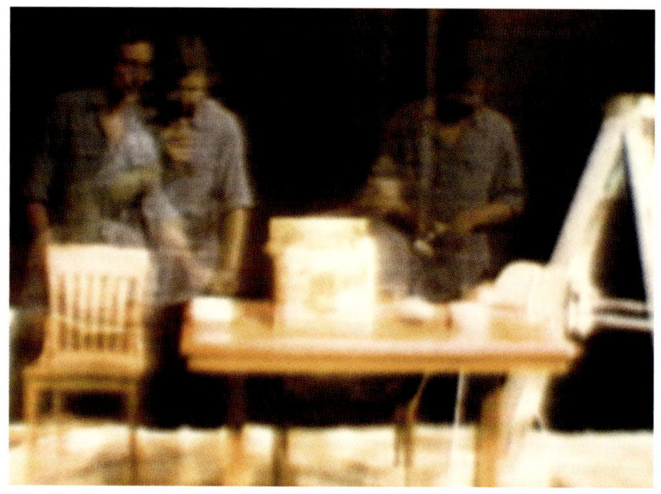

Above *Olfaction* (1974), videotape

Opposite *He Weeps for You* (1976), first description, Notebook, October 7, 1975

Next page *He Weeps for You*, drawing, January 1976

Following page *He Weeps for You*, first version, Watson Hall, Syracuse University, NY, May 1976 (top); *He Weeps for You* (1976), Museum of Modern Art, New York, NY, 1979 (bottom)

10-7-75

DO TINY DROPLETS OF MOISTURE REFLECT ENTIRE ROOM SPACES.

DRIPPING FAUCET PIÈCE.

A CLOSE-UP VIDEO CAMERA ON THE MOUTH OF A DRIPPING FAUCET. A SECTION OF THE SPACE VERY WELL-LIT. AS EACH DROP SLOWLY FORMS, OUTWEIGHS AND DROPS A WORLD IS BORN AND DIES.

THE VIDEO CAMERA PICKS UP THE REFLECTION OF THE ROOM IN THE DROP—AND VIDEO PROJECTS THAT UP ON THE WALL. THE IMAGE SLOWLY FORMS, ENLARGES, DISTORTS AND DISAPPEARS AS THE DROP FALLS AND LANDS ON A GREATLY AMPLIFIED SURFACE. THE ROOM IS LIT FROM THE TELECAMERA DRIP AREA OFF DIAGONALLY TO A FAR CORNER. $\frac{2}{3}$ OF THE WAY OUT A CHAIR IS PLACED IN THE LIGHT. SO IT IS PICKED UP DIRECTLY IN THE DRIP REFLECTION. A STRAP IS ON THE CHAIR. INVITATION TO A WATER TORTURE.

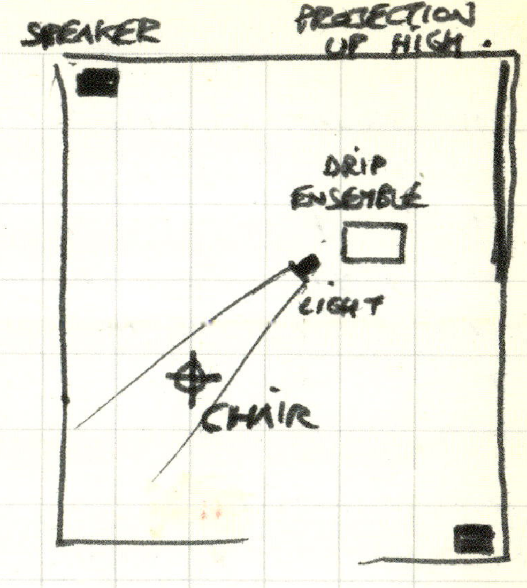

RE-DO PLANT TORTURE WITH TRANSDUCER ON THE BOARD TO SHAKE THE LEAVES.

I AM LOOKING —

A PERFORMANCE - ME IN A ROOM ON A CHAIR - A BRIGHT SPOTLIGHT SHINES OUT INTO THE ROOM FROM MY ZONE. EYES WIDE OPEN I WATCH THE SPACE.

A CLOSE UP VIDEO CAMERA PICKS UP THE REFLECTIONS OF THE SPACE OFF THE SURFACE OF MY EYE.

POSSIBLY TWO MONITORS UP HIGH OVER EACH SHOULDER AS THE EYES THEY BLINK TOGETHER

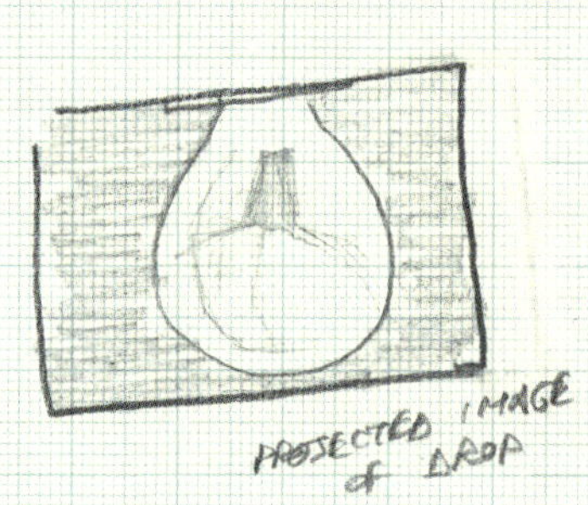

HE WEEPS FOR YOU

VIDEO-SOUND INSTALLATION

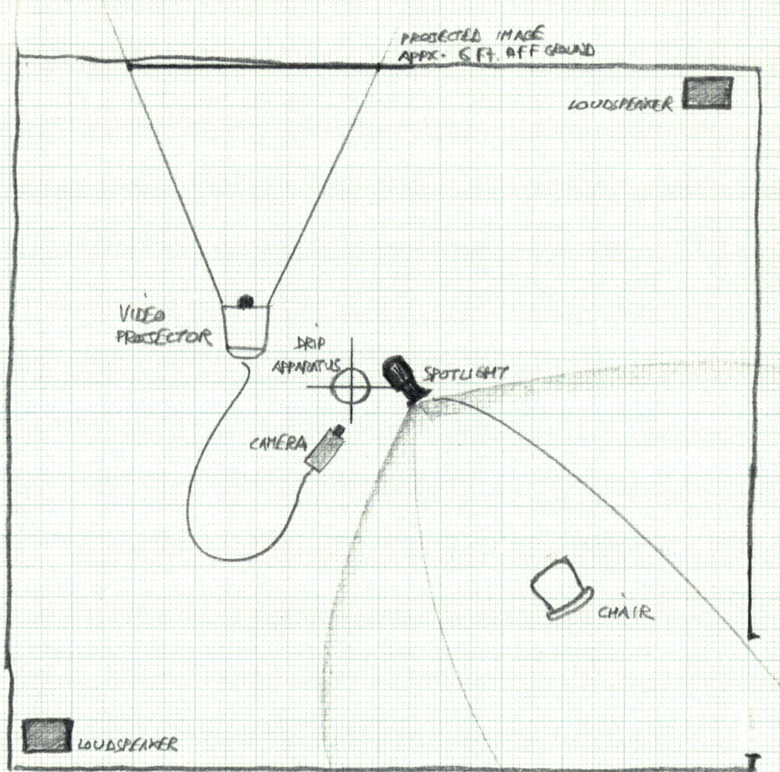

THE SITUATION CENTER CENTERS ON DRIPPING WATER EMERGING AT A VERY SLOW RATE FROM A SMALL TUBE ABOUT HEAD HEIGHT. IT LANDS ONTO AN AMPLIFIED PIECE OF SHEET METAL, THE CONTACT MICROPHONE IS CONNECTED TO THE LOUDSPEAKERS IN THE CORNERS. A HIGH INTENSITY SPOTLIGHT IS PLACED NEXT TO THE DRIP APPARATUS ABOUT 1 FOOT AND ½ LOWER THAN THE EMERGING DROP. IT DOES NOT ILLUMINATE THE DRIPPING WATER, BUT SHINES OUT INTO THE SPACE, CENTERED ON A WOODEN CHAIR. THE VIDEO CAMERA WITH A CLOSE-UP MACRO LENS FOCUSES IN ON THE DROP, FACING, AT ANGLE, AWAY FROM THE CHAIR. THIS IS ATTACHED TO THE VIDEO PROJECTOR, WHICH IS ELEVATED TO PROJECT THE IMAGE ABOUT 6 FEET OFF THE GROUND. A PERSON ENTERING THE SPACE WILL BE MET BY A DIRECT SPOTLIGHT. THEY WILL BE ABLE TO SEE THE CHAIR DIRECTLY AHEAD, AND, UP ABOVE THE GLARE IN THE BACK, THE PROJECTED IMAGE OF A HUGE DROP, SWELLING UP, FILLING THE PICTURE, THEN FALLING OUT OF THE IMAGE FOLLOWED BY A LOUD SOUND FROM THE AMPLIFIED SHEET METAL. AS THEY ENTER THE SPACE, AND THUS PASS THROUGH THE LIGHT, THEY MIGHT NOTICE THAT EACH TIME THE DRIP SWELLS, THE VIDEO CAMERA IS PICKING UP THEIR IMAGE AND THE CHAIR, AS REFLECTIONS OFF THE SURFACE OF THE DROP. EACH TIME THEY ARE REVEALED WITHIN THE DROP, IT FALLS, DESTROYING THE TINY WORLD WITHIN AND THEMSELVES ALONG WITH IT.

JANUARY 1976

LES PAPIERS CANSON _ FRANCE

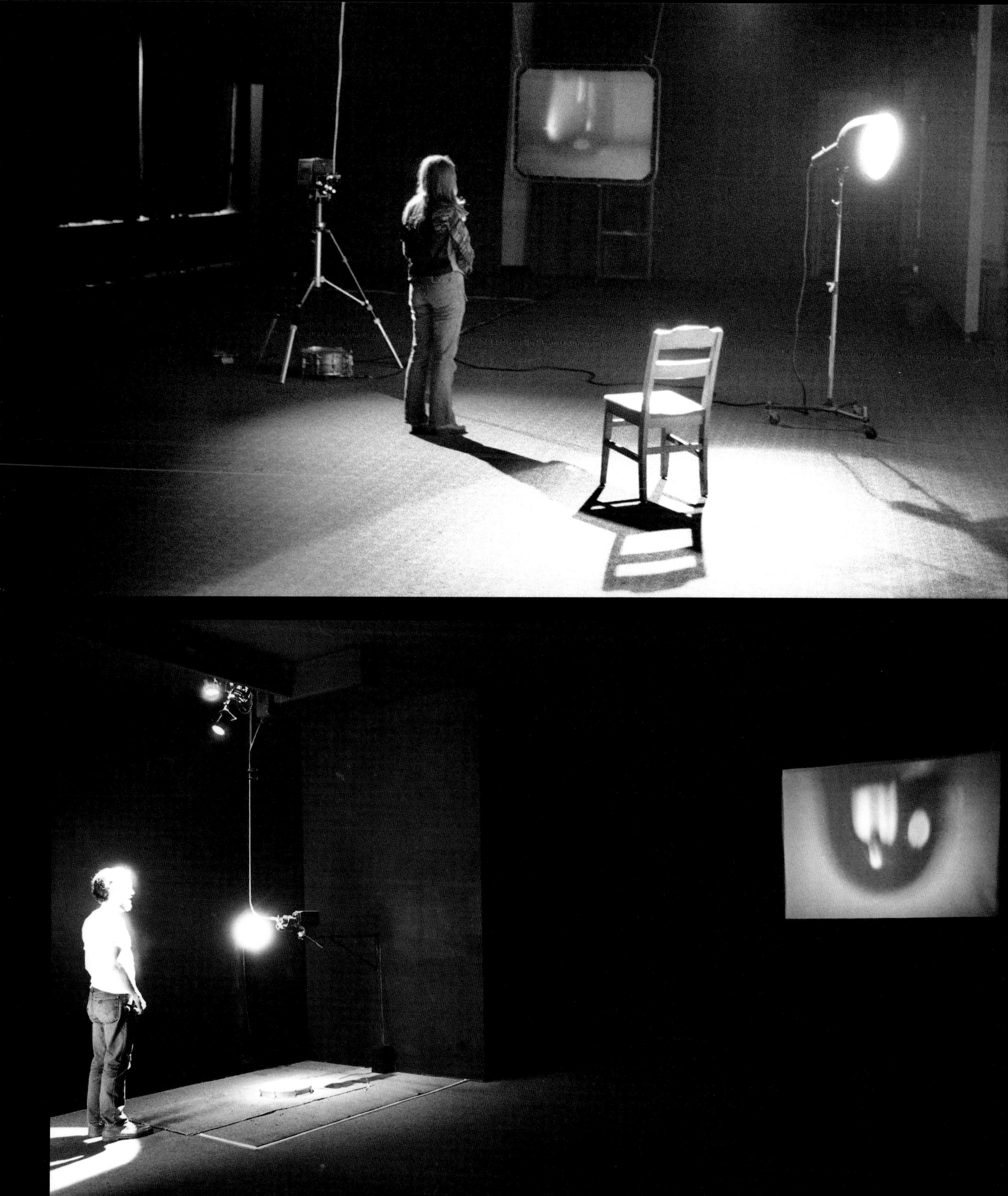

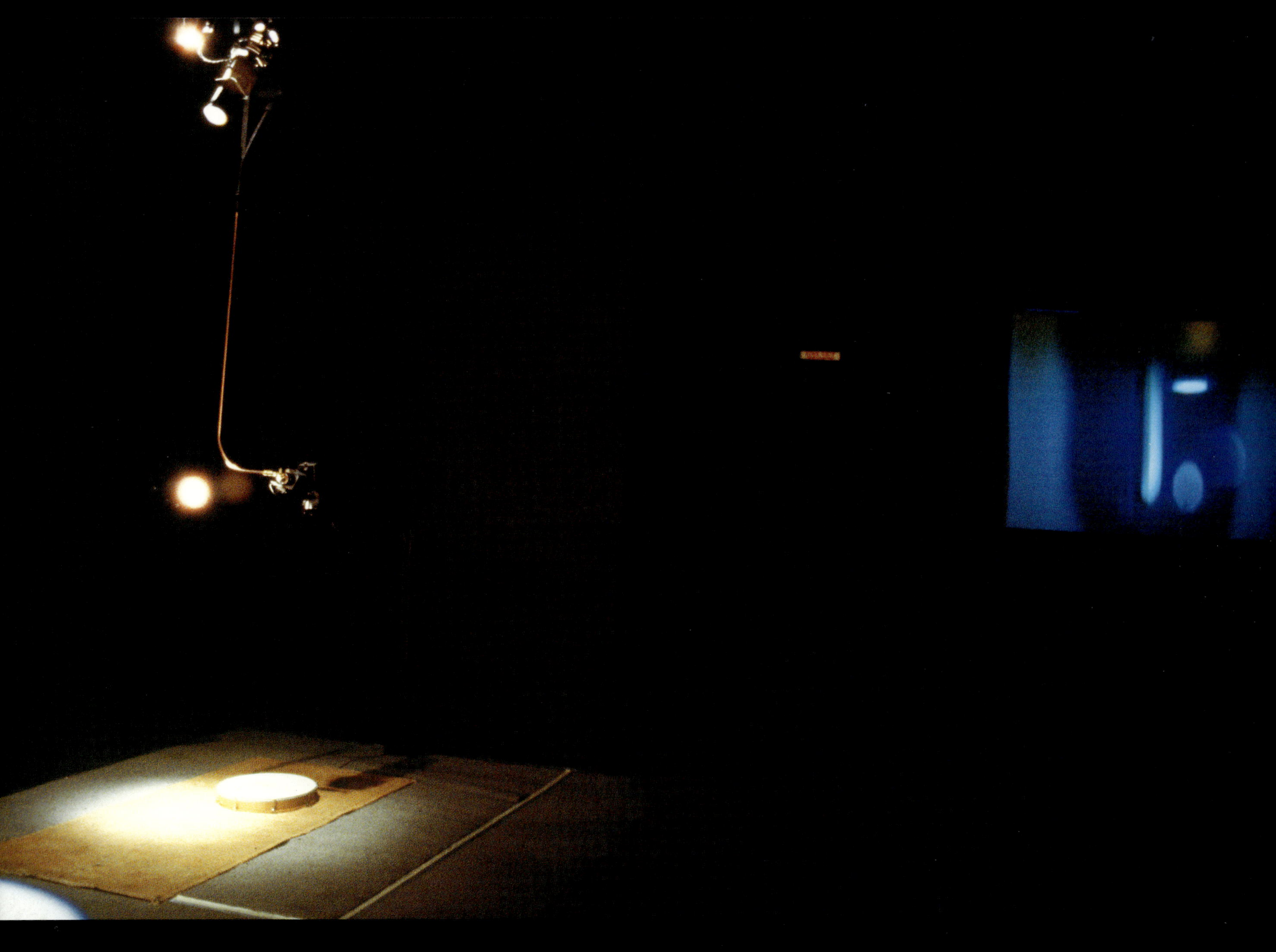

He Weeps for You (1976)

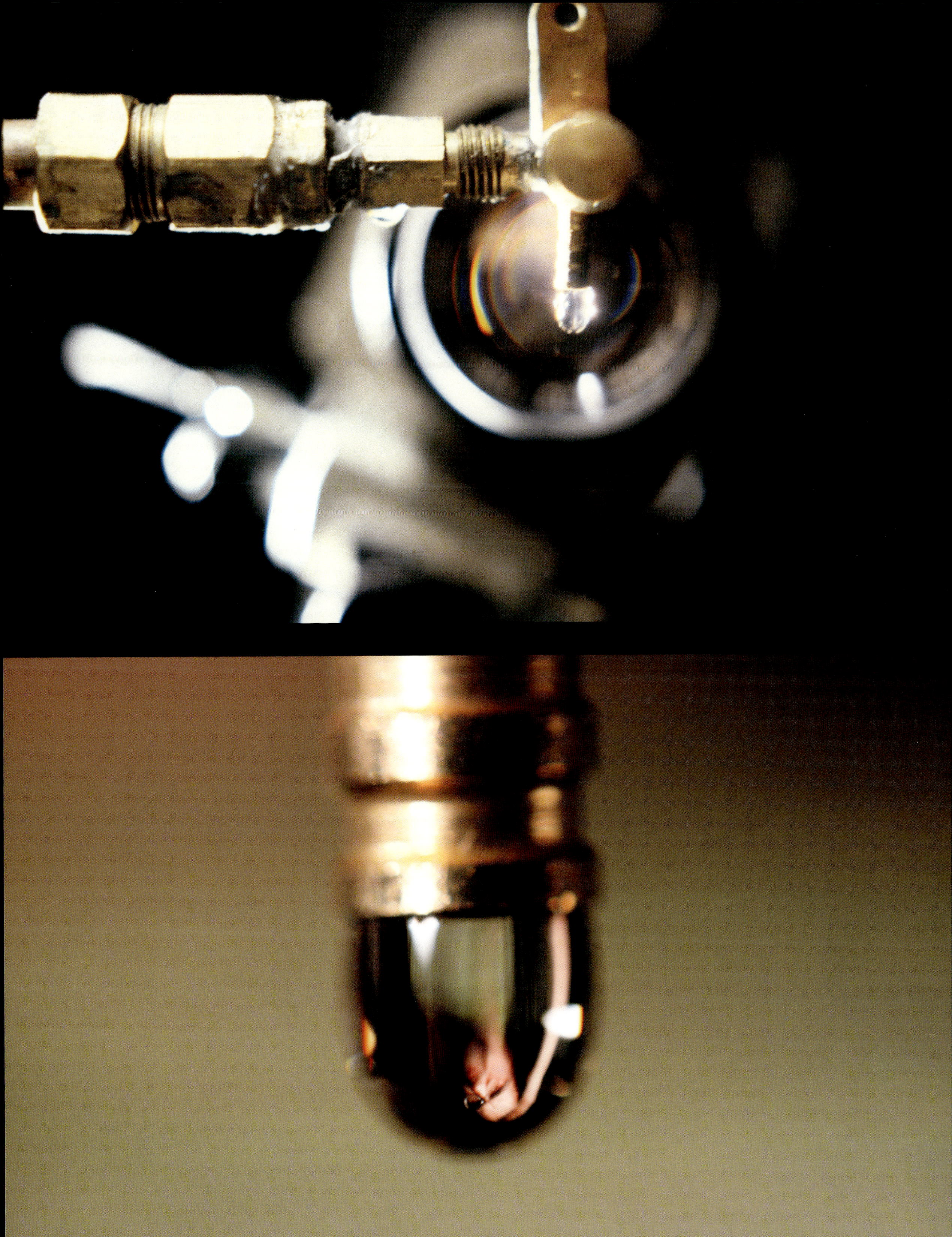

the drop. The temporal dimension is a key factor, as the slow formation of the drop of water establishes a narrative of discovery, expectation, and surprise on behalf of the viewer, who follows what is happening to the falling drop, concluding in the shock of the sound it makes as it hits the drumhead in this otherwise silent process.

The exposure of the copper pipe and the presence of the video camera acknowledge the instrumentality of the piece. In this way the process of interactivity between camera and water feels less deterministic; the action unfolds naturally. Unlike interactive artworks that operate using a stimulus/response—an action followed by a reaction—Viola's piece works itself out through the logic of the drop of water emerging and falling to the ground. The drop acts as a screen, reflecting the viewer, whose own real-time presence plays off that of the video projection of the water. As Viola notes, "With every moment a world is born and dies, And know that for you, with every moment come death and renewal."[4] This installation was exhibited at the international art exhibition Documenta 6, held in Kassel, West Germany, in 1977. The video section was curated by Wulf Herzogenrath, an early supporter of video art who would become a good friend of Viola.

He Weeps for You anticipates issues that Viola revisits in such later works as *The Tree of Knowledge* (1997), his first interactive computer-graphics installation. Produced at the Zentrum für Kunst und Medientechnologie (ZKM) in Karlsruhe, Germany, in collaboration with the artist and programmer Bernd Lintermann, *The Tree of Knowledge* is a time-based projection of a computer-generated tree that grows and passes through its seasonal cycles as you walk through a narrow corridor toward it; as you come closer to the screen it loses its leaves, ages, and dies. When you return down the corridor, the tree reverses in time and becomes a sapling again. At any point the viewer can freeze-frame a moment in the tree's development by standing still. According to ZKM's website, "The tree, with a design that incorporates all seasonal markers, symbolizes the various stages of life. The corridor functions as a metaphor for the constraints and obligations for the human path through life."[5]

The Tree of Knowledge represents a life cycle transcribed in a composed performative action that sheds light on how Viola represents time. It is also a real-time interaction with aging and the passage of time, with the piece unfolding through the movement of the viewer. In *The Tree of Life* (1977), to quote Viola's own description of the work, "a large oak tree standing alone in an open field was spotlit by a high-powered searchlight beam positioned a quarter of a mile away. The searchlight was turned on in the late afternoon. As the daylight faded, the beam gradually became visible and the tree glowed with luminous intensity into the night. A negative shadow of its dark form was cast out across the valley, visible for several miles. The moon was also seen at times coming through the clouds behind

Eternal Life, drawing, May 10, 2009

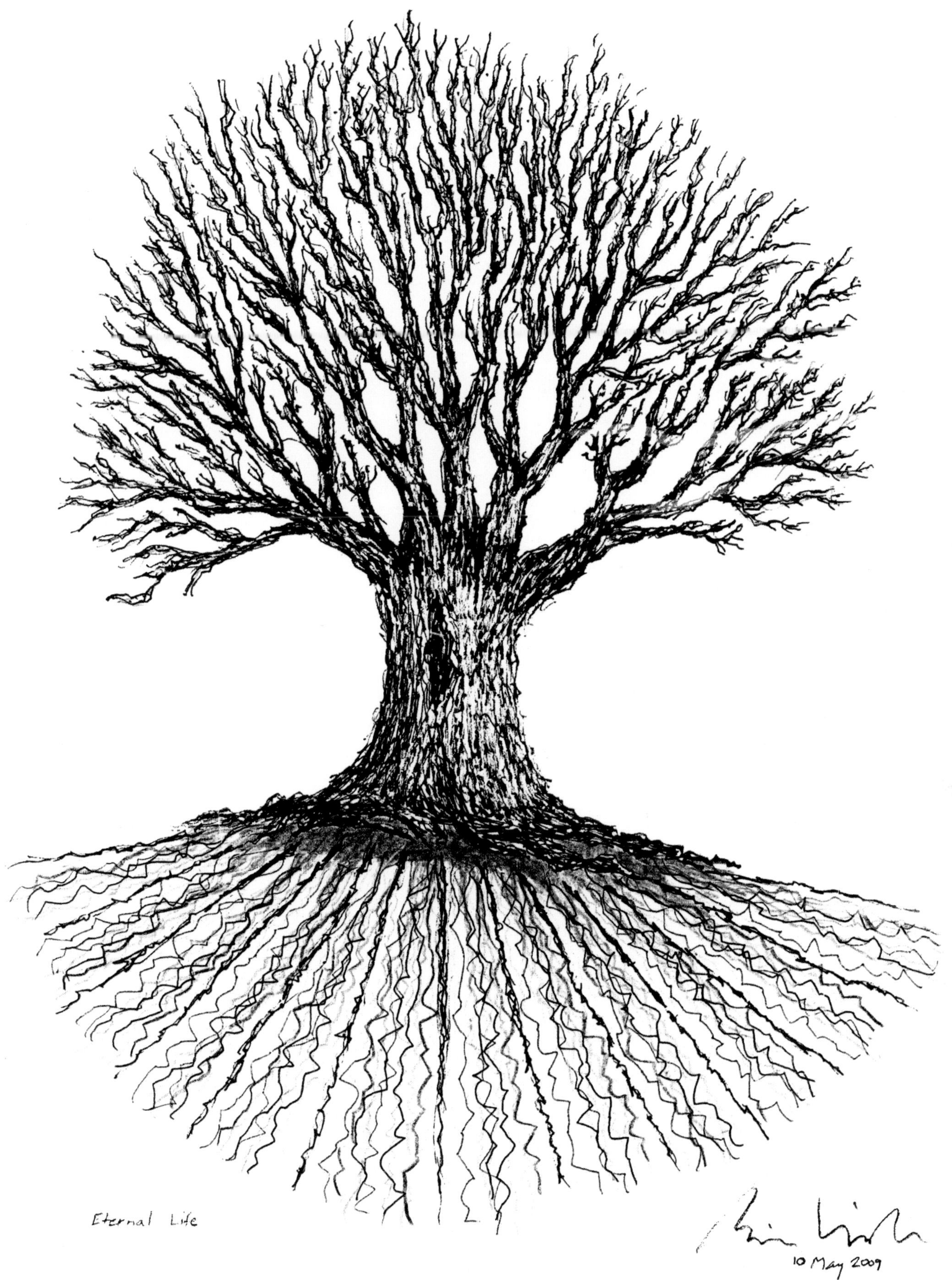
Eternal Life
10 May 2009

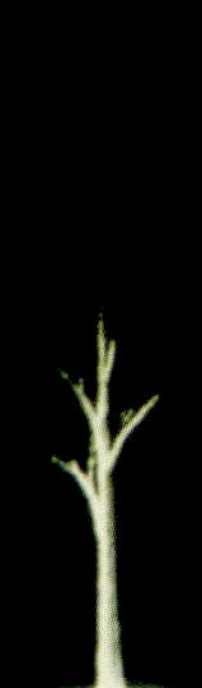
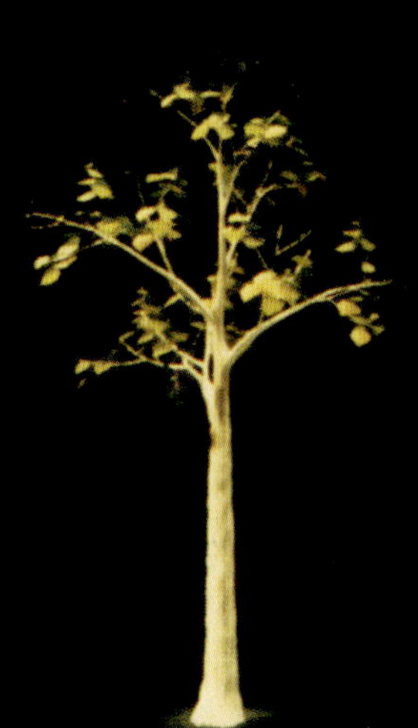
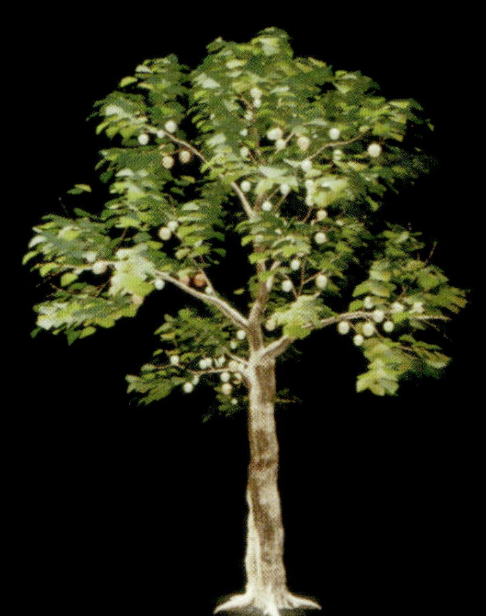

The Tree of Knowledge (1997), interactive computer/video installation

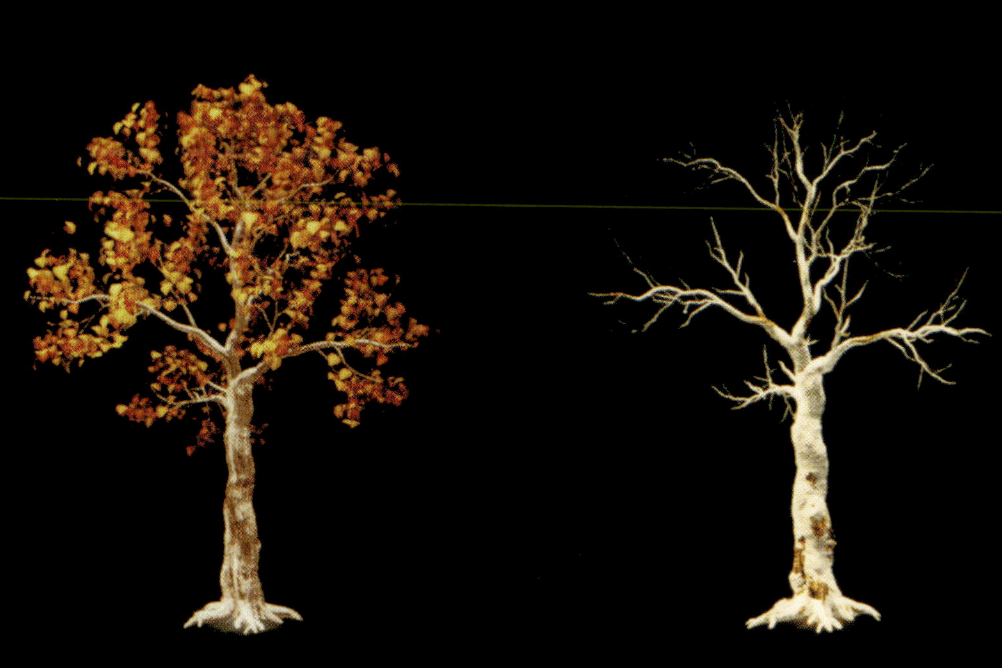

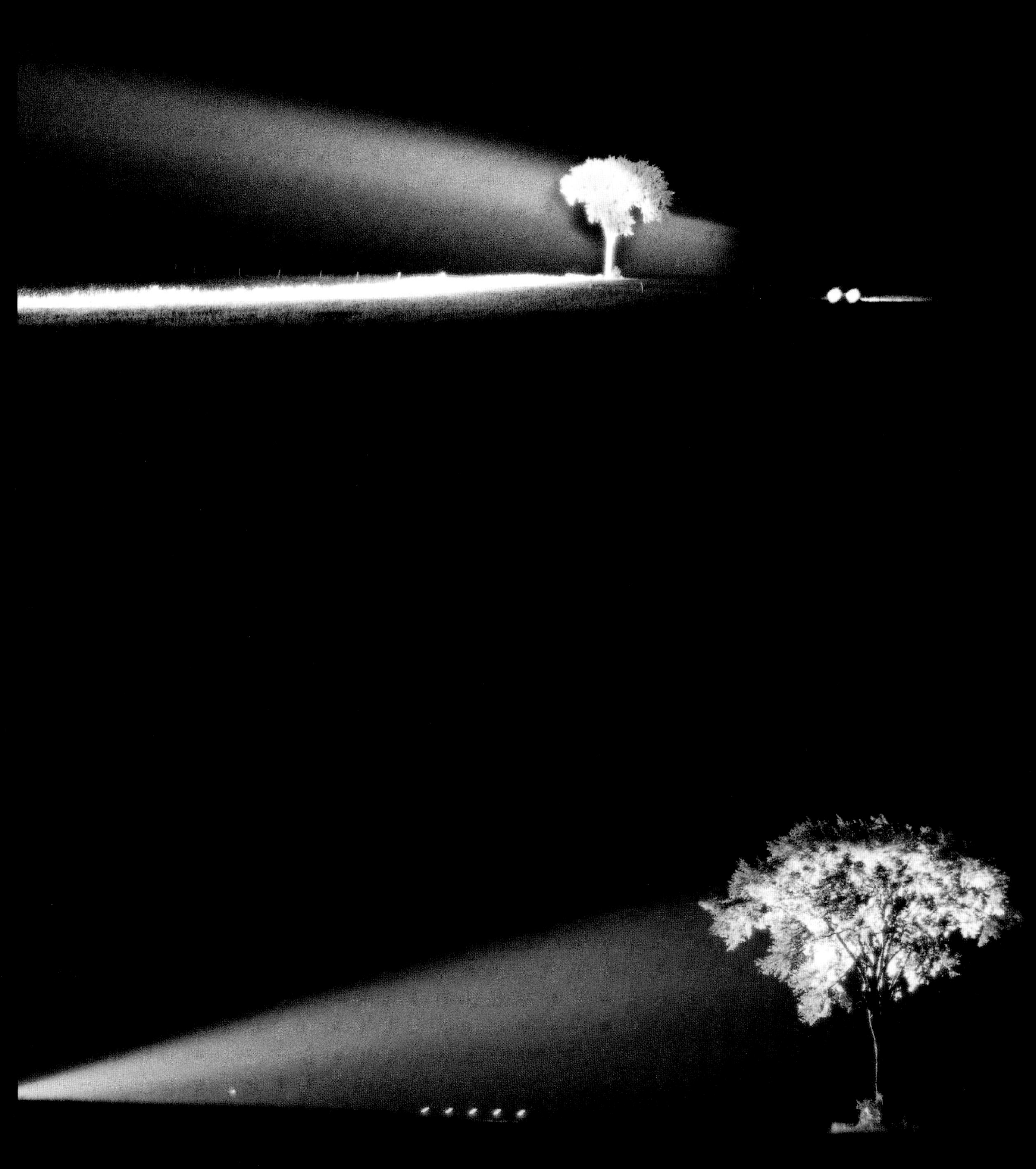

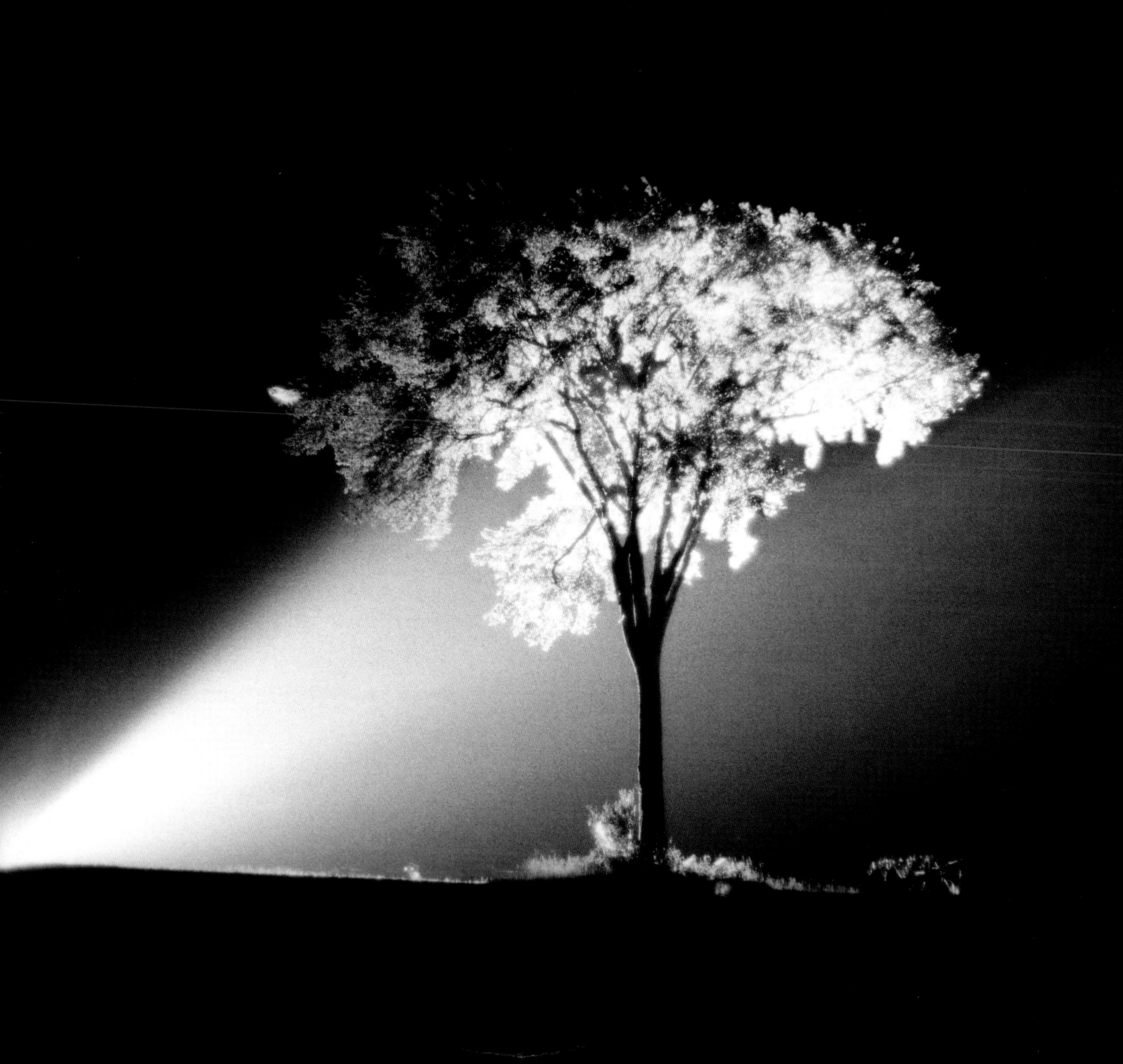

The Tree of Life (1977), 5-hour, one-night event, Fort Edward, NY

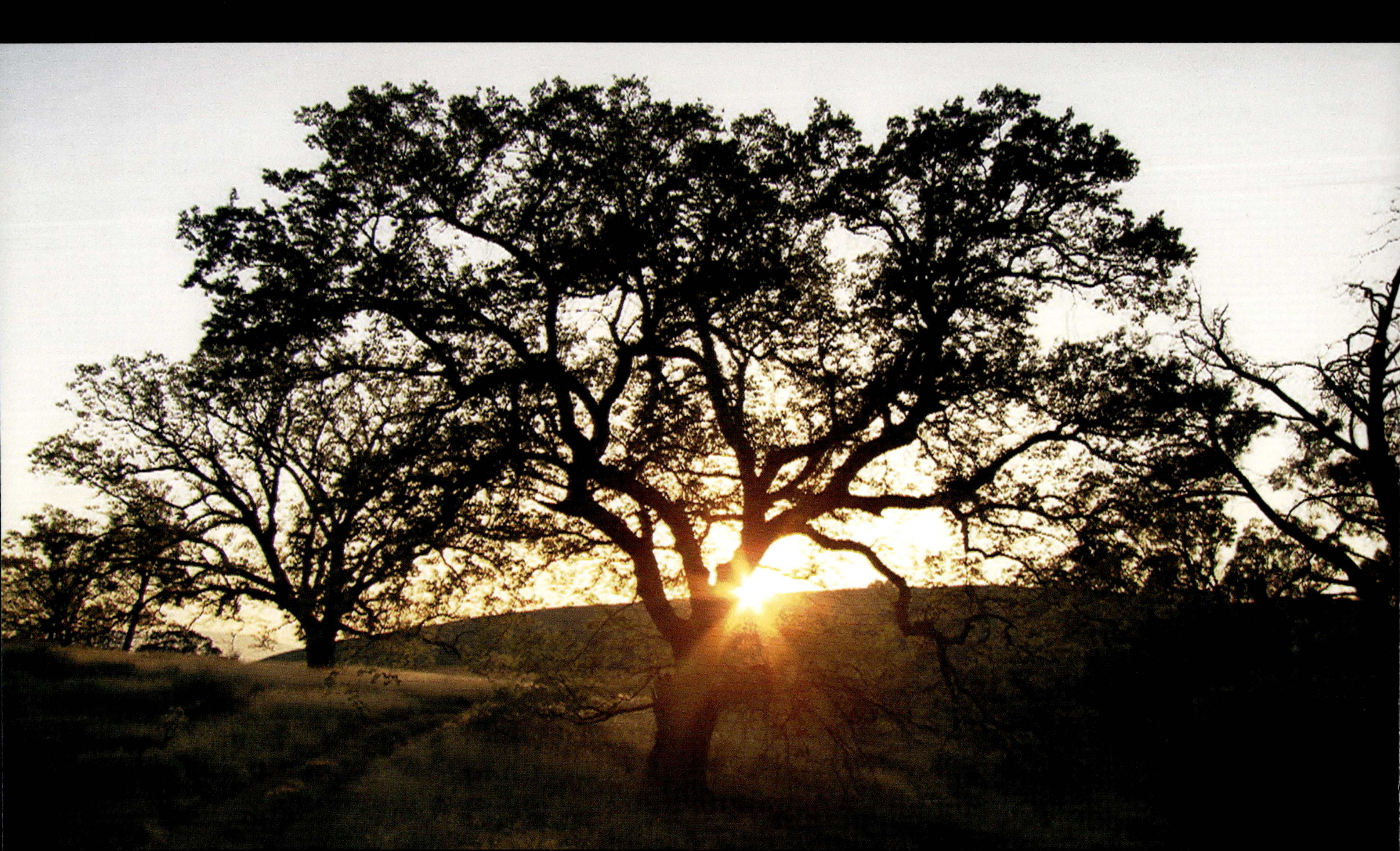

the tree. The beam was turned out several hours after the sun had set."[6] We can see how Viola is exploring the tree by isolating the object *in situ*. It becomes a real-time event in which the light from the searchlight and the fading of the day as the sun sets move the tree from the natural light of the environment to the focused, artificial light of the beam.

The Darker Side of Dawn (2005) is a large image of a tree projected on a wall, described by Viola as a

study of an old California oak tree on a hillside in the mountains north of Los Angeles from the first light of dawn to full sunlight and beyond. A fixed camera registered the subtle shifts of color and luminosity of the changing natural light from daylight to complete darkness over several days. The recordings were edited to create a condense time-lapse document of the continuous passage of time at dawn, moving slowly into night, with the goal that there was no apparent movement of light or shadow visible. The changing illumination and subtle shifts of color in the image are felt rather than seen, and it is only the occasional gust of wind through the branches that visibly animates the tree. The work continuously cycles from night to dawn to night, and in between each cycle the extremes of light and dark are attained.[7]

This complex, 60-minute projection is displayed on a wall in a darkened gallery. Time is presented as a composition of stillness and movement, marked by the glow of light and the passing of the day. Viola's seamless editing results in a work of magisterial beauty with an intimate transaction between the viewer and the work.

Both *The Tree of Life* and *The Darker Side of Dawn* describe a complex intermixing of observation and meditation on the natural, the unfolding of time, and the presentation of the cycles of nature through the artificial searchlight and the natural sunlight. Both pieces demonstrate the trust that Viola has in his vision and his capacity to illuminate—literally and metaphorically—the natural world. Viola's work does not read as a conceptual strategy for exploring a secular phenomenon, but rather as a process that unfolds with a lyrical intensity. His aesthetic approach, in its celebration of wonder, enchantment, and beauty, marks his difference from other artists of his generation. He is not working to create an artificial representation of what we presume to be real. He wants it to be seen as real, with no ironic interplay between the real and the "real." The honesty of Viola's images lies in his effort to capture life as a breathing thing, not an artificial sign.

Viola's transformation of the moving image into a means of cataloging and transcribing changes in sound and image took shape in his single-channel videotapes created in the late 1970s, culminating in his

The Darker Side of Dawn (2005)

masterpieces *Chott el-Djerid (A Portrait in Light and Heat)* (1979) and *Hatsu-Yume (First Dream)* (1981). Just as Viola is deconstructing video to its basic principles, he recognizes the power that the cinematic, theatrical tradition gives to his tapes. The videotapes that led up to those seminal pieces are a series of collected works: *August '74* (1974), *Red Tape (Collected Works)* (1975), *Four Songs* (1976), *Memory Surfaces and Mental Prayers* (1977), and *The Reflecting Pool—Collected Work 1977–80*. Viola likens these works to "albums": collections of individual titles that, when played together, compose a whole. These works are Viola's testing ground, the place where his ideas are developed; they become catalogues of image references that will be picked up in later installations. It is a practice that one can follow through all of his single-channel videotapes, and understanding these tapes and their relationship to the installations is the key to unlocking Viola's work and appreciating its subtle range and the great care that he invests in all of his pieces. Rather than providing a descriptive catalogue of these tapes, I shall pick out specific titles and issues that can be traced throughout his working life. What follows is a weave that loops backward and forward in time in order to explore Viola's career as a deliberate effort to return to what he felt early on was the power of art and imagination. His goal has been to evoke experiences and create images that both astonish and convey the poetic possibilities of a medium seen as a new form of temporal expression.

The position that the camera takes in video echoes that of the viewer, with the added immediacy that characterizes the electronic moving image. As discussed earlier, the importance of closed circuit video is in the sense of the present tense that it conveys, a reflection of the feeling that television is live. This sense is expressed in early videotapes by Bruce Nauman and others that run the length of the tape and are unedited. They simply unfold from the camera's point of view, whether it is handheld, as in Charlemagne Palestine's *Running Outburst* (1975), or shot from a tripod, as in William Wegman's *Selected Works: Reel 1* (1970–2). In *A Non-Dairy Creamer* (1975), part of *Red Tape (Collected Works)*, Viola shows his reflection in the coffee that fills a cup; the reflection disappears as the coffee is consumed. Viola has described this tape as the "eradication of the individual by self consumption," a tactic that directly acknowledges the artist and point of view are the same.[8] Viola's recorded image becomes a real-time reflection of the artist consumed both by the artist and by the camera.

Another example from the same collection is *The Semi-Circular Canals* (1975), a work whose title refers to the part of the human ear that gives us balance. In this piece, we see the artist seated in the center of the shot. The camera facing him is placed on the same platform on which he is seated. The platform spins, giving the background, which becomes a blur, the sense of rapid movement. The seated artist, occasionally drinking water from a glass, remains still, placing his physical presence as a marker in a

A Non-Dairy Creamer (1975)

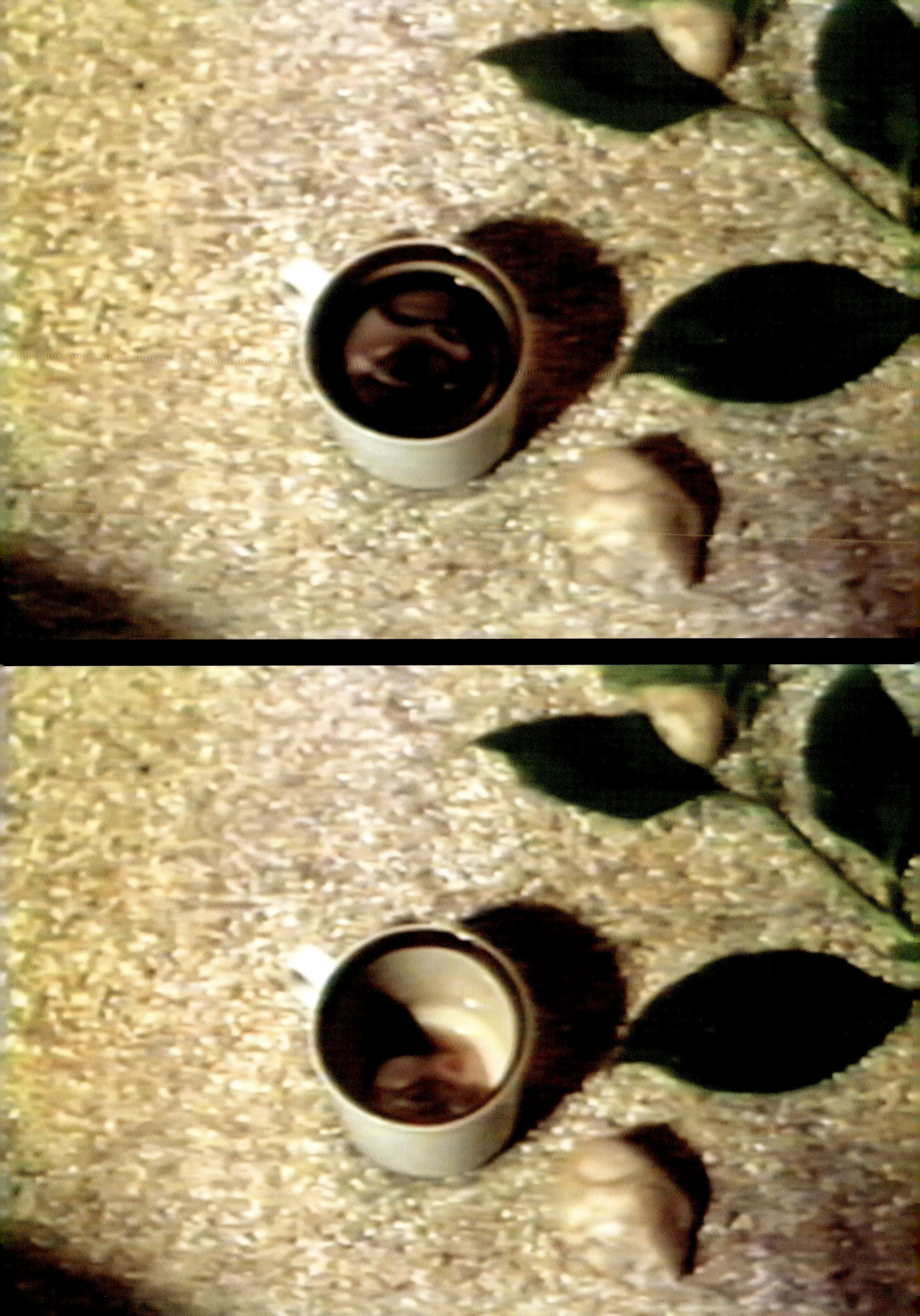

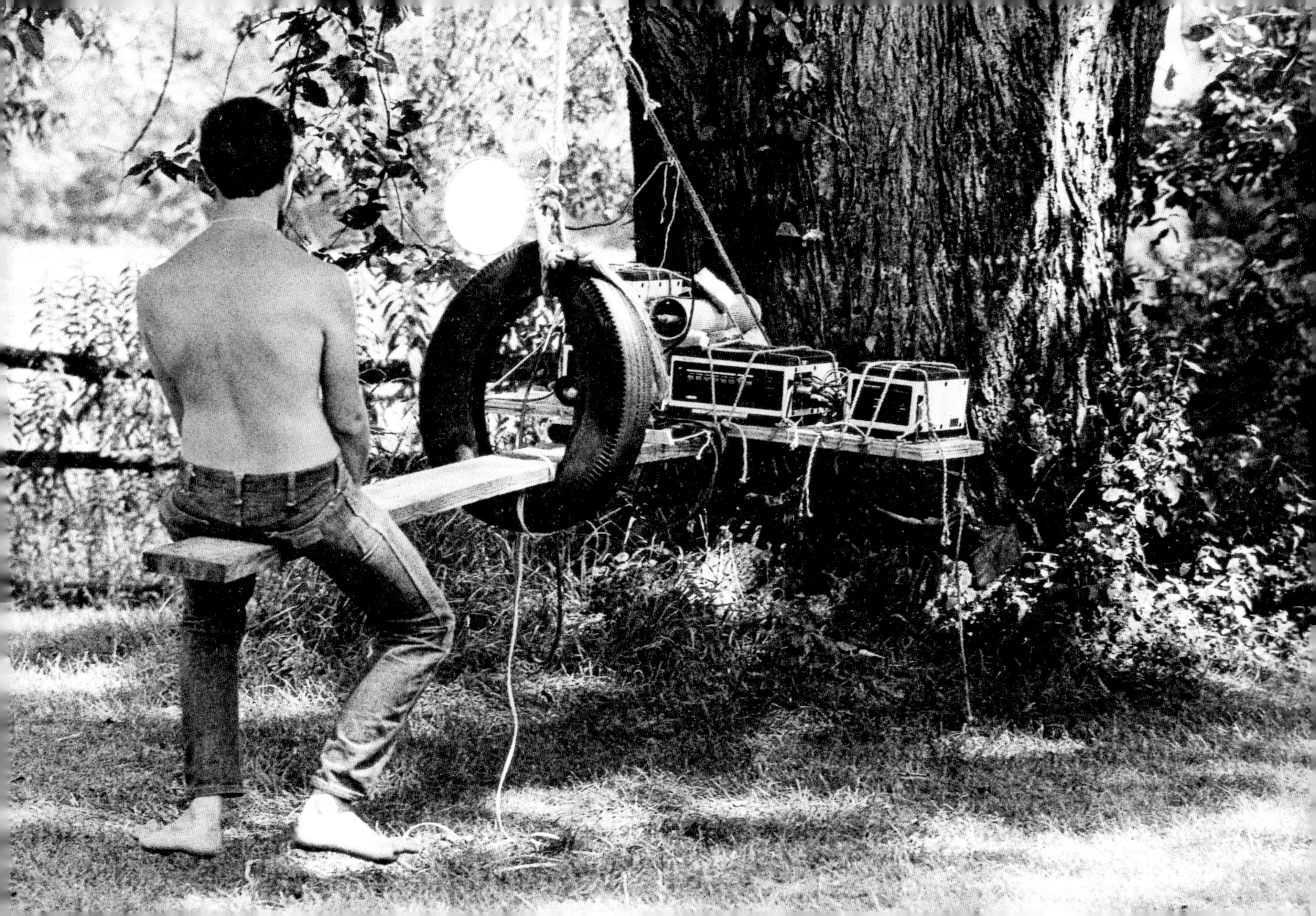

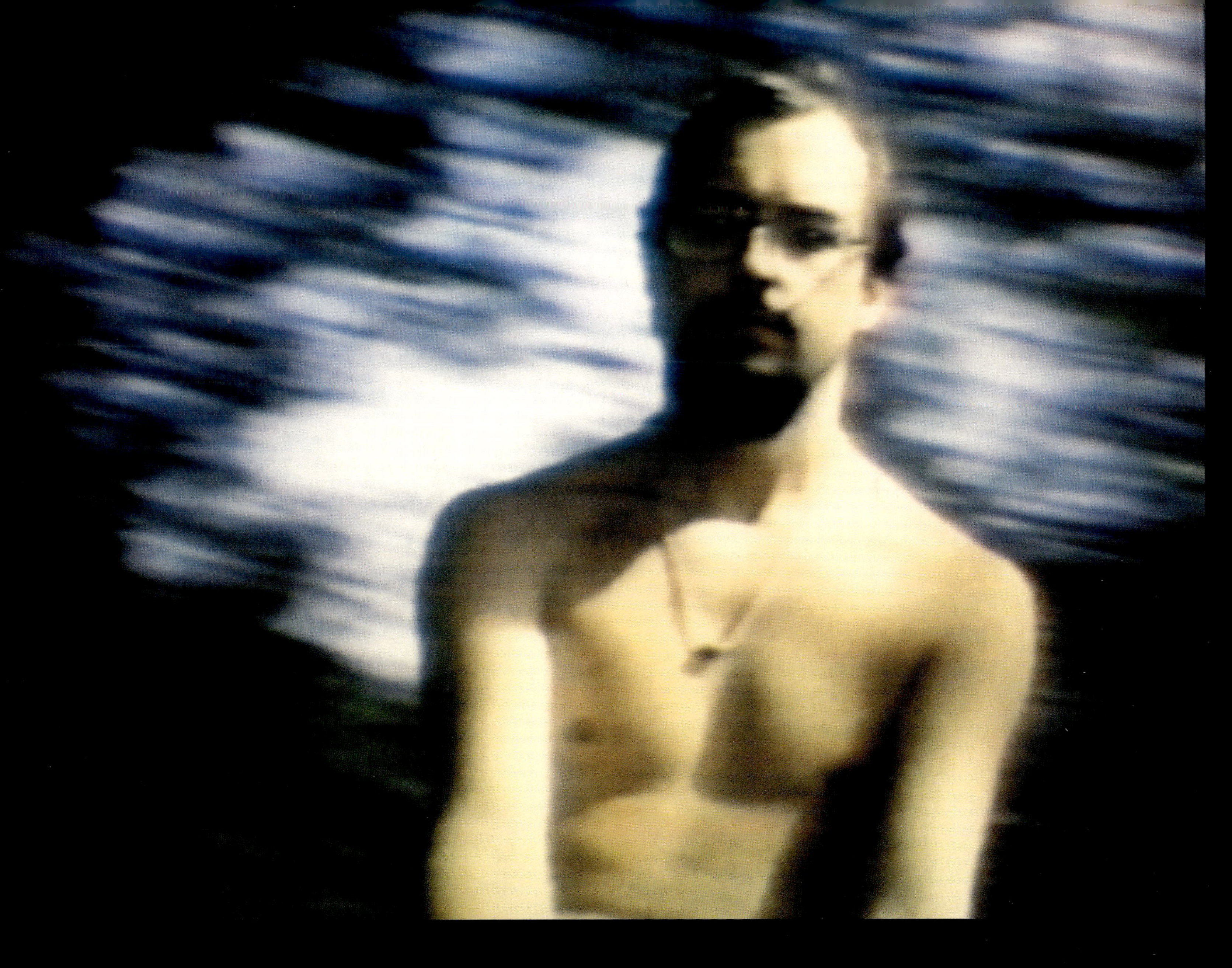

shifting and changing visual and aural environment. Once again there is a fixed perspective and point of view: the camera controls what we see and transforms it, since our peripheral vision cannot complete and correct our view. The monitor screen serves as a small window onto the world and cannot account for the larger perception of the space. The camera becomes like the artist—an eye staring straight ahead, immovable and static. The video is interrupted by an occasional black screen or color bars, and the screen turns yellow toward the end. These breaks acknowledge the material basis and fragility of the process and return the image to its origin in the electronic.

The landscape that turns into an abstract surface in *The Semi-Circular Canals* is replaced in *A Million Other Things (2)* (1975) with a scene at the edge of a large pond, which passes through day and night and back again, concluding at night with a person illuminated by an electric lamp. The work, which also forms part of the *Red Tape* collection, was produced at ZBS Media, Fort Edward, New York, with the assistance of Bob Bielecki, a sound engineer who would help Viola with several of his early sound pieces and videos. In the context of Viola's body of work, this is a significant videotape, in which he captures the individual in nature, recorded in time and occupying a space determined by the camera's point of view. It is a chronicle of time imagined across a body of water, with the artist making slight time shifts through the editing process that capture changes in light and movement, thereby creating a temporal composition out of the passage of time. The figure continues to be illuminated by the artificial light as dusk approaches. This moment is marked by the figure walking to a small dock and throwing a rock into the pond. The tape concludes with a sense of returning to the beginning. The endless cycles of nature mark time and space as coordinates to capture the body in place and in movement. The importance of this tape lies in its simplicity; it is an example of Viola's romantic landscape, a concept that haunts all of his later work. The romance that Viola has with the natural landscape is framed by his idealization of time. For Viola, landscapes and time are not tied to a rigid semiotic system of expression; rather, they link his art to states of being and the rhythms of life. Recorded over eight hours, this work represents Viola's first use of time-lapse, a technique that he would employ often in his art practice over the coming years.

Time, which is integral to the moving image and its reception, is the key to unlocking Viola's art. In his early videotapes, time emerges as central to the question of what it means to be, to exist. His notion of time and its influence on his video pieces are shaped by a mix of theology, classical painting, naturalism, and language, and each informs the artist's experience and his art-making. Although Viola's interest in art is founded in modernism and the avant-garde movements of the late twentieth century, especially in

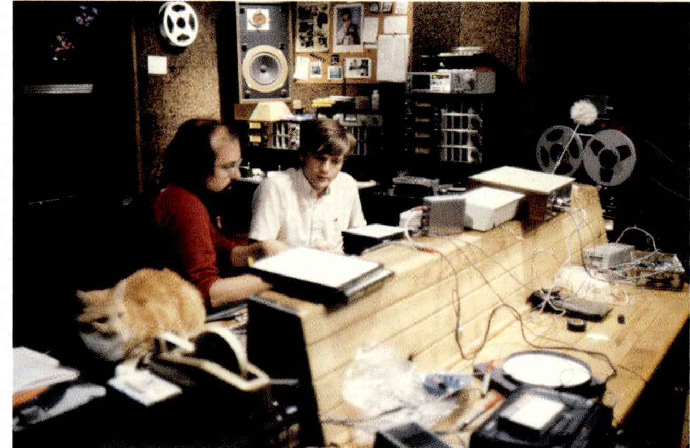

Above Bill Viola and Bob Bielecki, sound studio, ZBS Media, Fort Edward, NY, July 1982

Opposite *A Million Other Things (2)* (1975)

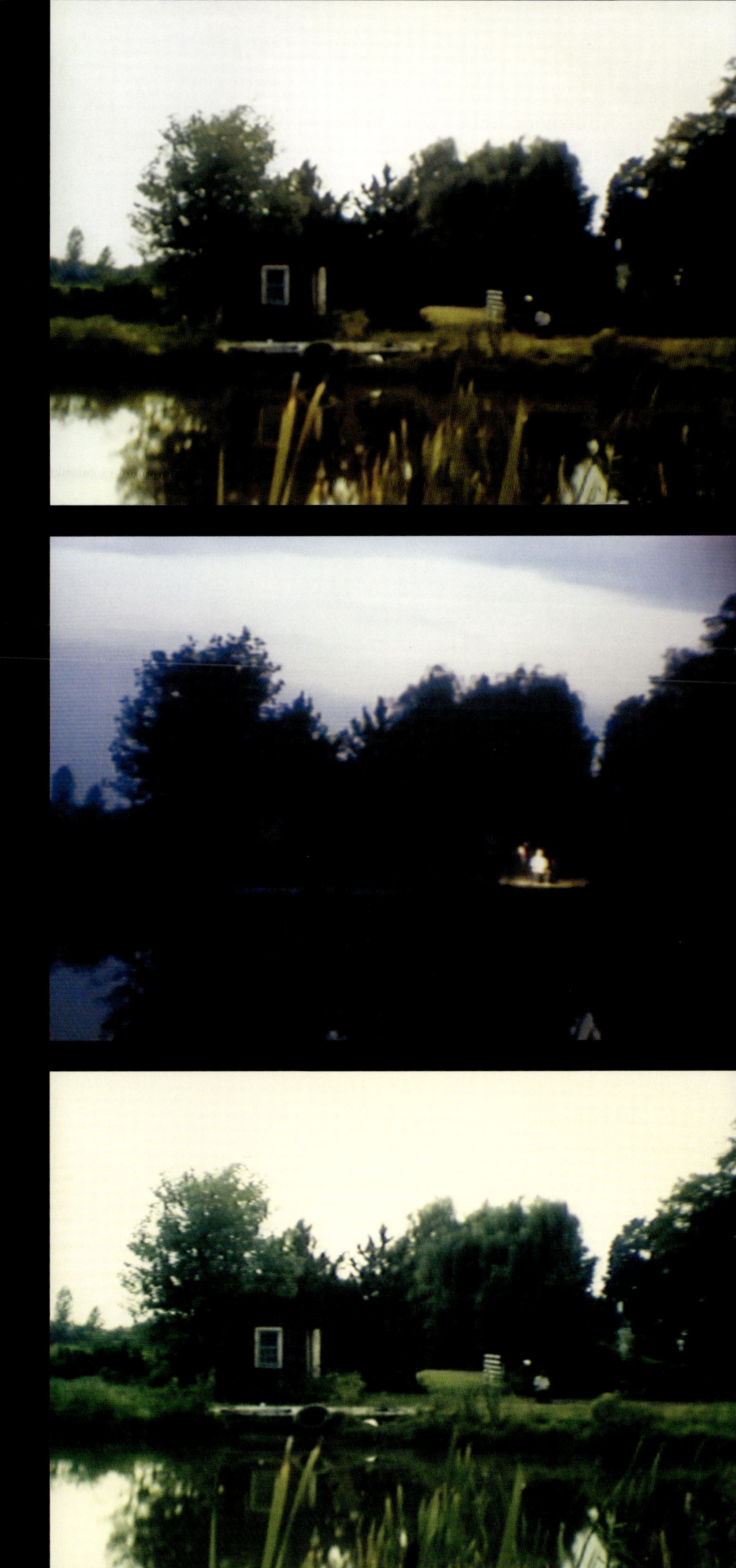

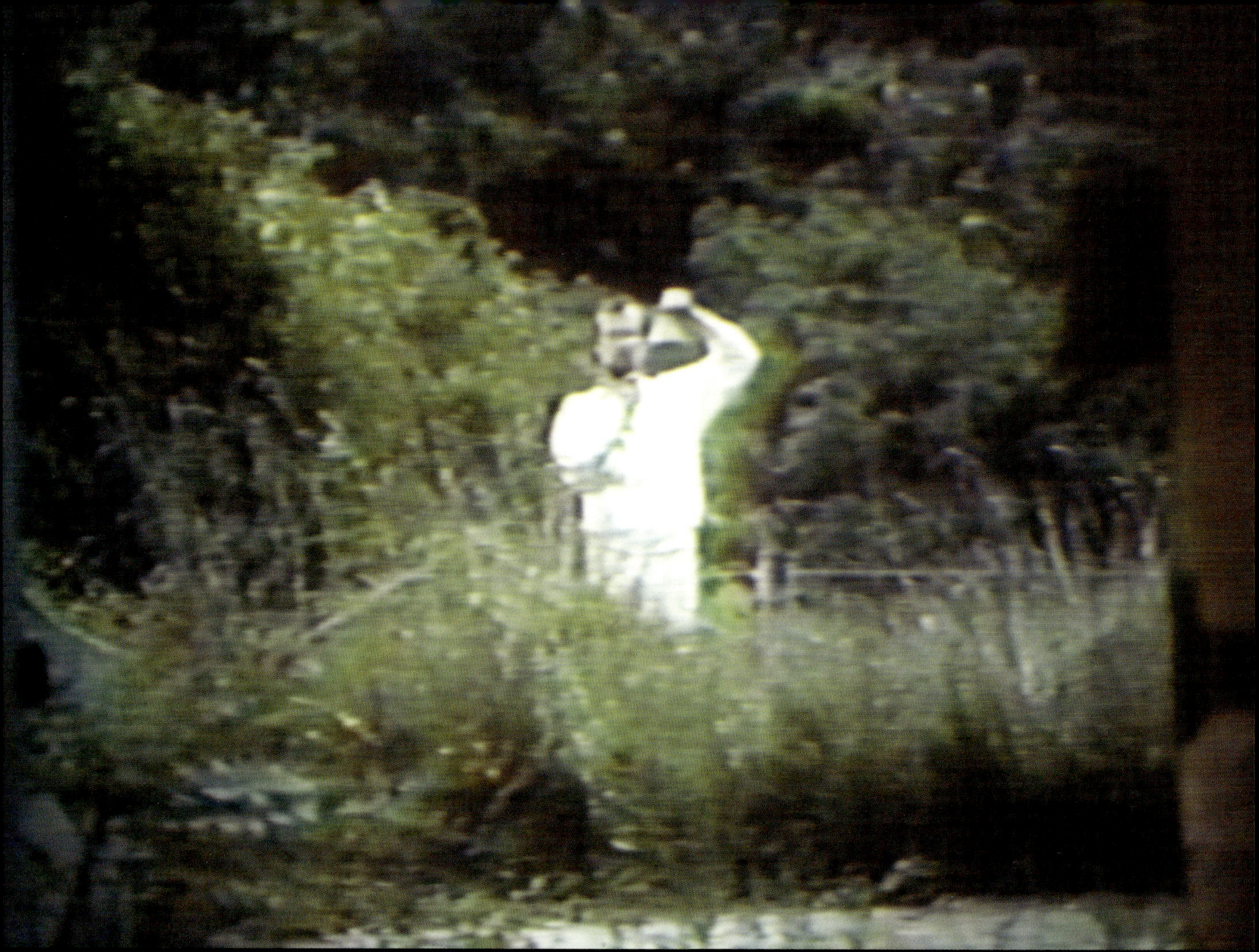

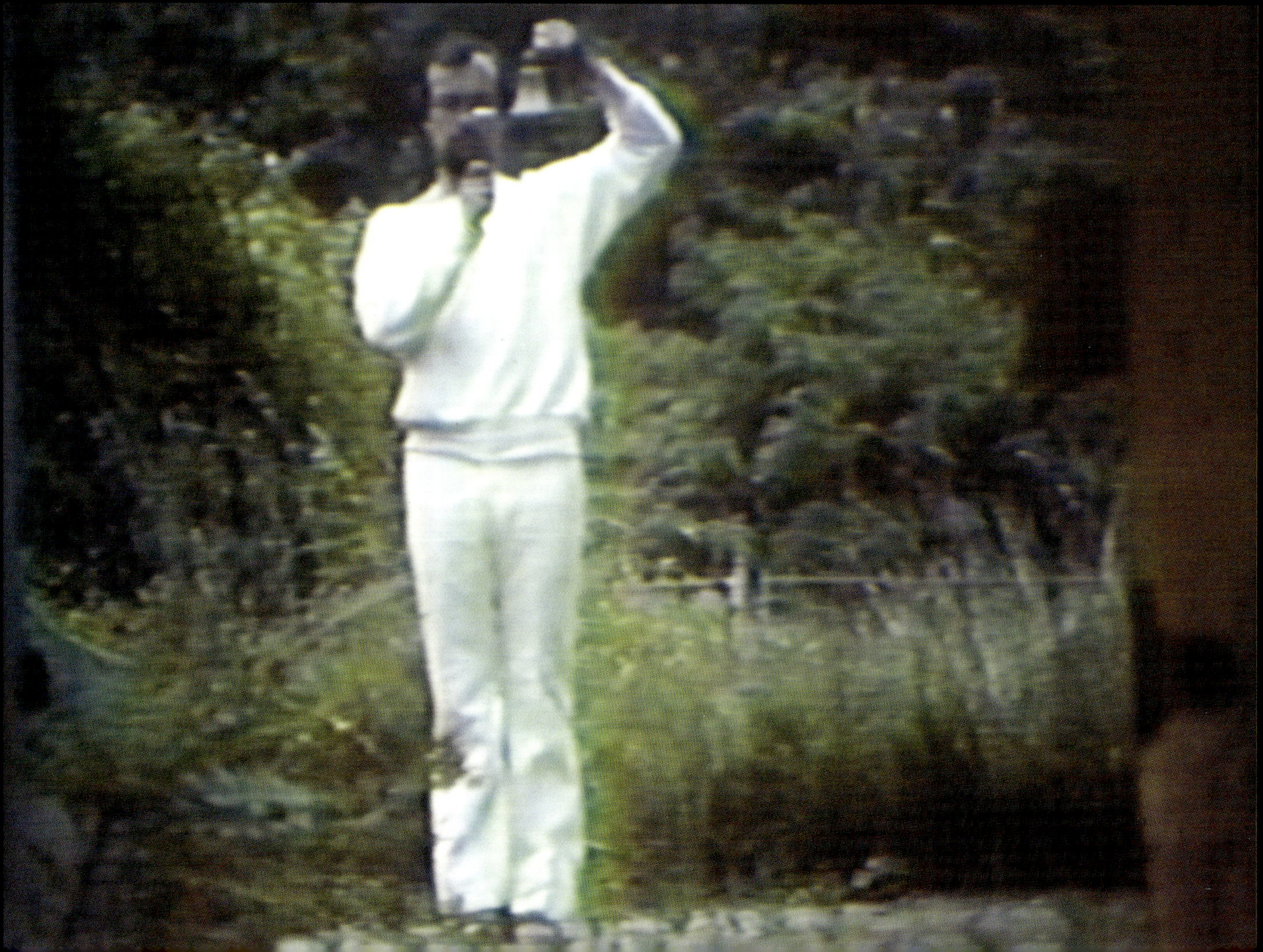

music and video, his return to the body is reflected in the spiritual languages of early Christian thought and mysticism. This complex interweaving of sources is clarified further in his work of the 1980s and 1990s, and reaches an apotheosis in the first decades of the new millennium. This became apparent as I began to spend time with the artist in his study, where he keeps his library and writes his Notebooks. This space is a living archive, which the artist draws on by writing quotations in his Notebooks to help illustrate, or better embody, the ideas he is looking to visualize.

There is, in Viola's art at this time, a growing desire to create an ontology and theology of reflection on the world. In part, he achieves this by retrieving the ecstatic in art from the sensory. This is laid out in *Red Tape*, *Four Songs*, and *The Reflecting Pool*. Each of these collections either directly or indirectly seeks to reclaim a connection to the world. *Return* (1975), part of the *Red Tape* collection, has a simple and straightforward structure. Viola, dressed in white and viewed through an open doorway, can be seen standing in a garden holding a bell. He moves deliberately for a few steps and then rings the bell. Viola writes, "As the tape progresses, each time the bell is struck, a rapid edit sequence carries the figure back through each previous position where the bell was rung... Finally reaching his destination, he arrives at the camera, where his body momentarily blocks the view."[9] The piece elaborates a set of sequences where a place is marked by the ringing of the bell, which is then followed by edits that move Viola forward. He positions himself in the shot to move from deep space across a temporal path to the camera. This editing-together of his positions is both a technique and a strategy to compose the space. From the individual works that constitute Viola's other early collections, *The Reflecting Pool* and *Four Songs*, we can trace a further elaboration of the body within specific spaces.

The Reflecting Pool (1977–9) is a meditation on the quietness of movement. Here, video provides a firsthand look at the position the body takes in the blur of flight. From the camera's point of view, we look across a pool, where the artist emerges from the greenery to stand at the edge of the water. Suddenly, Viola leaps and, with a shout, hugs his legs to his chest in a fetal position. In this moment, the marked difference between video and photography or the motion picture is both highlighted and exploited by Viola. The English photographer Eadweard Muybridge's early photo sequences, which break down the locomotion of animals and human beings, are set against a measured-grid background and provide an empirical and precise sequence of frozen points in time. These sequences are like flip books, in which each "moment" is a still photo that is animated into movement as the pages flash by. It suggests an early form of the cinema, in which individual "still" frames move through the apparatus of the projector so that we perceive the sequence as continuous movement. The electronic blur that freezes Viola's jump over the pool, on the other hand, is a wash of color and

Return (1975)

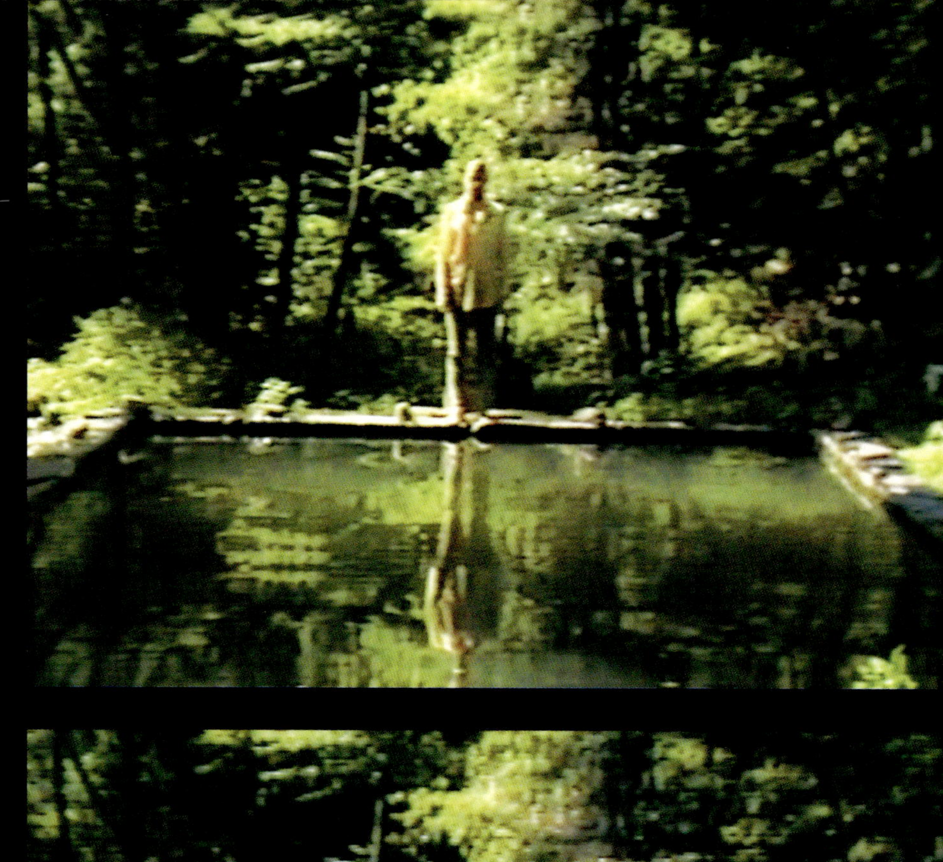

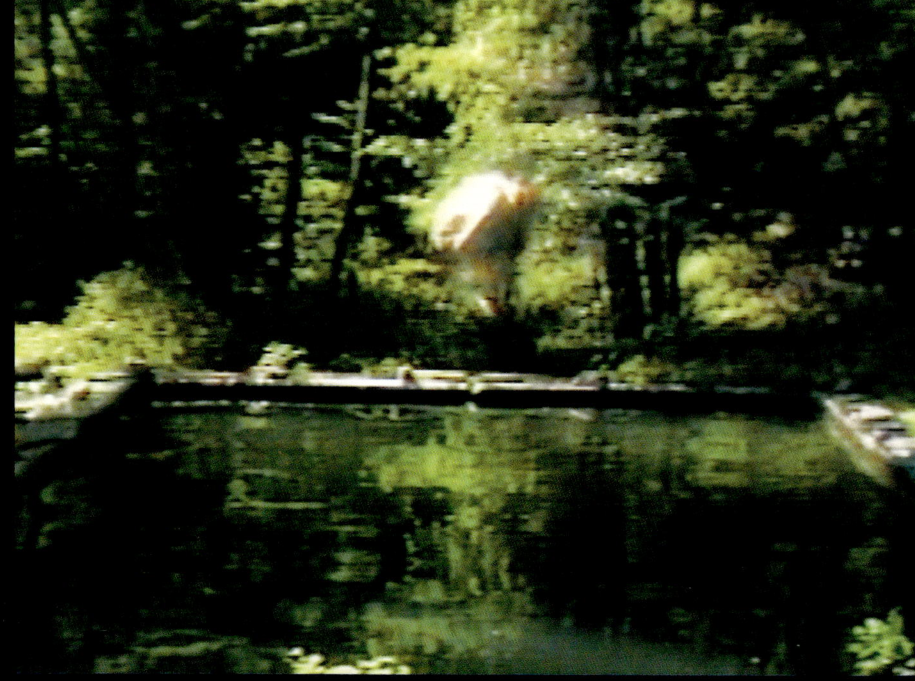

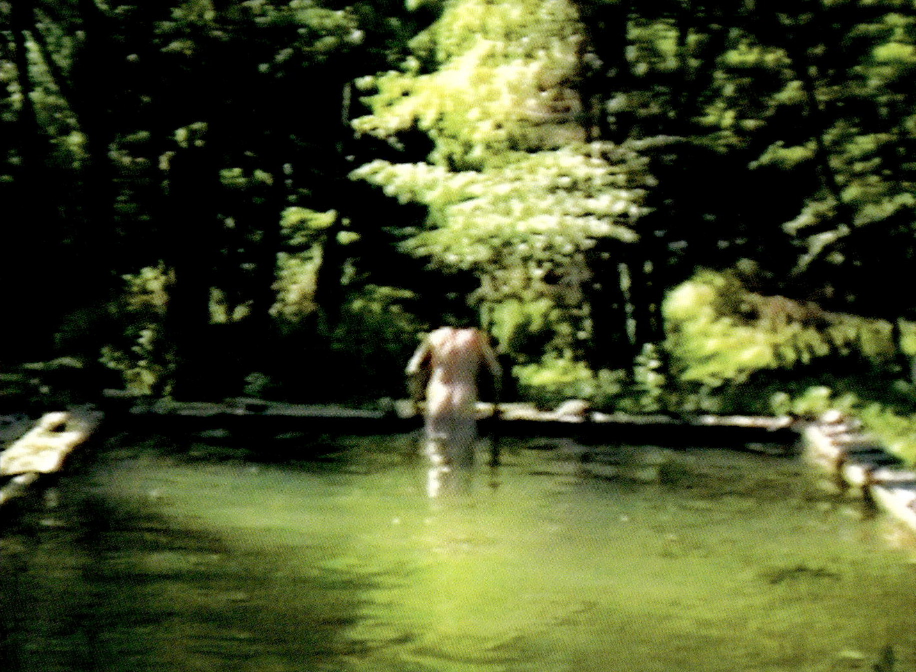

The Reflecting Pool (1977–9)

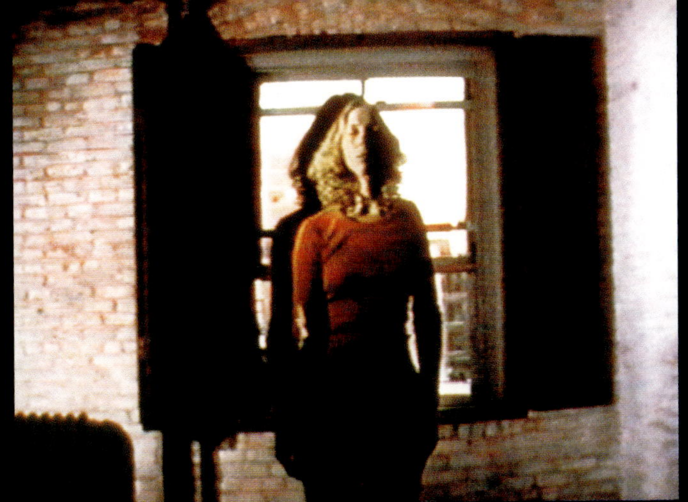

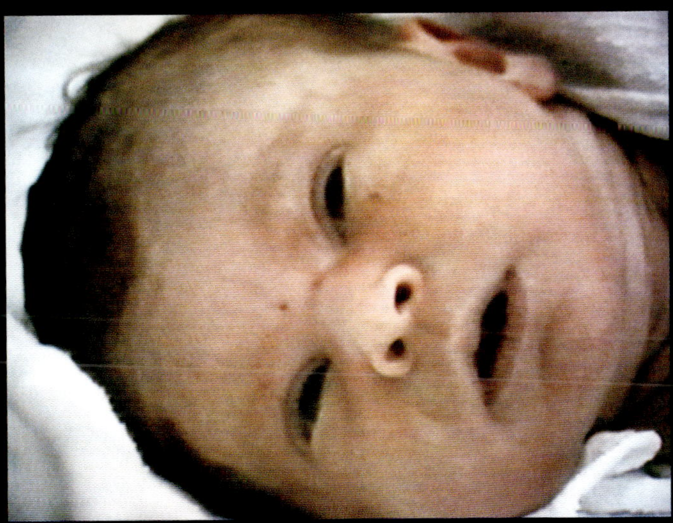

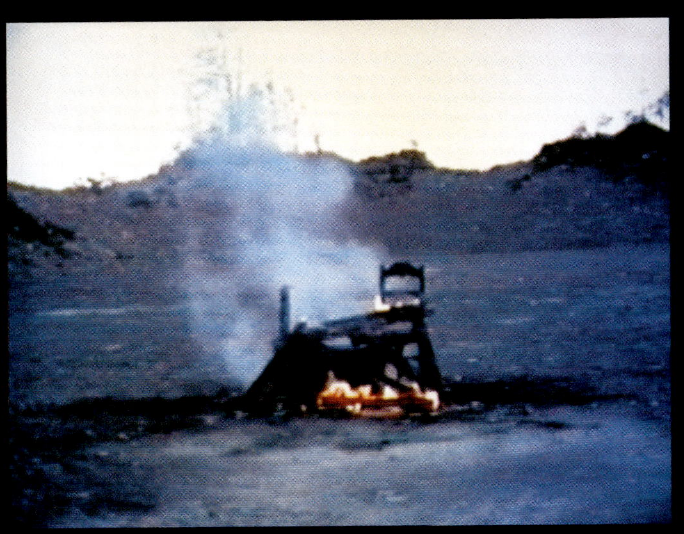

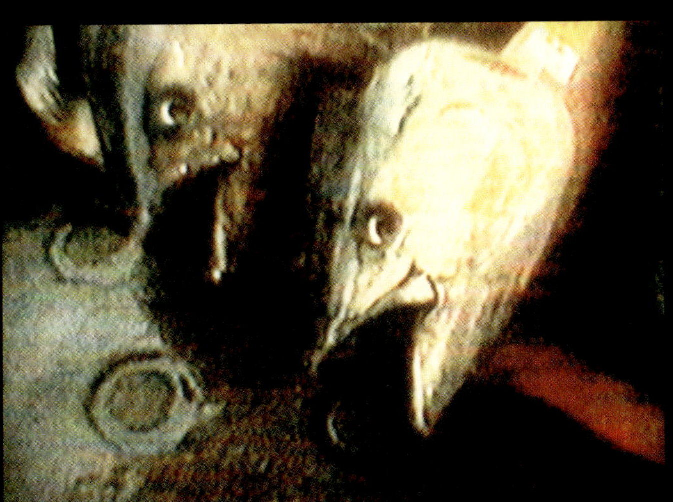

Top to bottom *Moonblood* (1979–80), *Silent Life* (1979), *Ancient of Days* (1979–81), *Vegetable Memory* (1978–80); all on this spread from *The Reflecting Pool—Collected Work 1977–80*

shape. Like a paintbrush that conveys the sense of a captured moment, the video system softens the outlines of precise measurement into a suggestion of movement held in place. Below his suspended body, the water moves as if opened by his plunge, then seems to close again. The pool takes on a life of its own, acting like a screen reflecting and capturing movement as past and future time. Reborn, Viola emerges naked from the pool and follows the path he arrived on as he disappears into the surrounding foliage. Water is a key motif in Viola's work. For him, the movement of the body through space, as well as above and through water, becomes the means to represent and to further articulate the poetics of the body in movement. As we shall see, these ideas recur in such video installations as *The Messenger* (1996) and *The Crossing* (1996), as well as in his most recent work.

An ongoing exploration of the tension between stasis and motion can be seen in such early seminal works as *The Space Between the Teeth* (1976), part of *Four Songs*, in which we see Viola at the end of a corridor having a drink of water and then seating himself in a chair and staring at the camera. He screams suddenly, and the camera dollies back to the other end of the corridor. With each subsequent scream, the camera moves toward him until it ends at his teeth. As it gets closer, the tape cuts alternately to a kitchen scene until the hallway shot has disappeared and the camera dollies toward a sink filled with water. Viola walks into the kitchen and washes some dishes in the sink. Leaving the faucet running, he exits the scene. The camera continues to dolly and for a minute we watch as the water continues to run. Suddenly we hear the scream once more as an image of the hallway returns. This turns out to be a black-and-white photograph that is tossed from a bridge where it is swept under the water by a passing boat. This sequence recalls the artist's leaping above the water and then vanishing in *The Reflecting Pool*. Here, the still photographic image is tossed into the air, only to land on the surface of the water and be swept under. The artist is exploring a crucial move toward transcendence by showing that the still image, which captures the moment, is ultimately fragile and impermanent. In this way the work indirectly anticipates *The Messenger* and *The Crossing*, in which spectacle gives presence to astonishment and wonder. In *The Messenger* this happens through the submerged and revealed body, and in *The Crossing* through the primary elements of fire and water. *The Space Between the Teeth* could not have been made without the computer-editing techniques that had only recently been developed.

Viola's domestic scenes in kitchens, dining rooms, garages, gardens, lawns, and fields are not ironic but portray working and living spaces. Two videotapes, *The Morning After the Night of Power* and *Sweet Light* (both 1977), part of the collection entitled *Memory Surfaces and Mental Prayers* (1977), tap into another feature of the spaces he creates for the camera, namely the workplace or desk. Viola foregrounds the spiritual and stresses

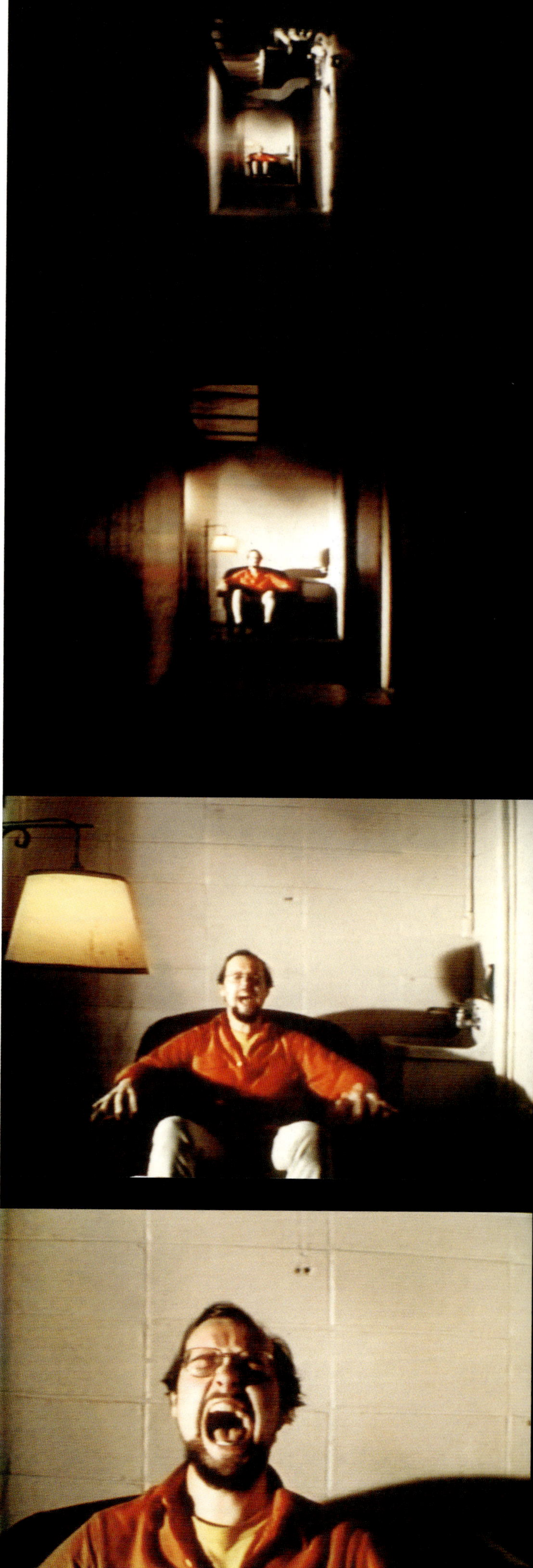

The Space Between the Teeth (1976)

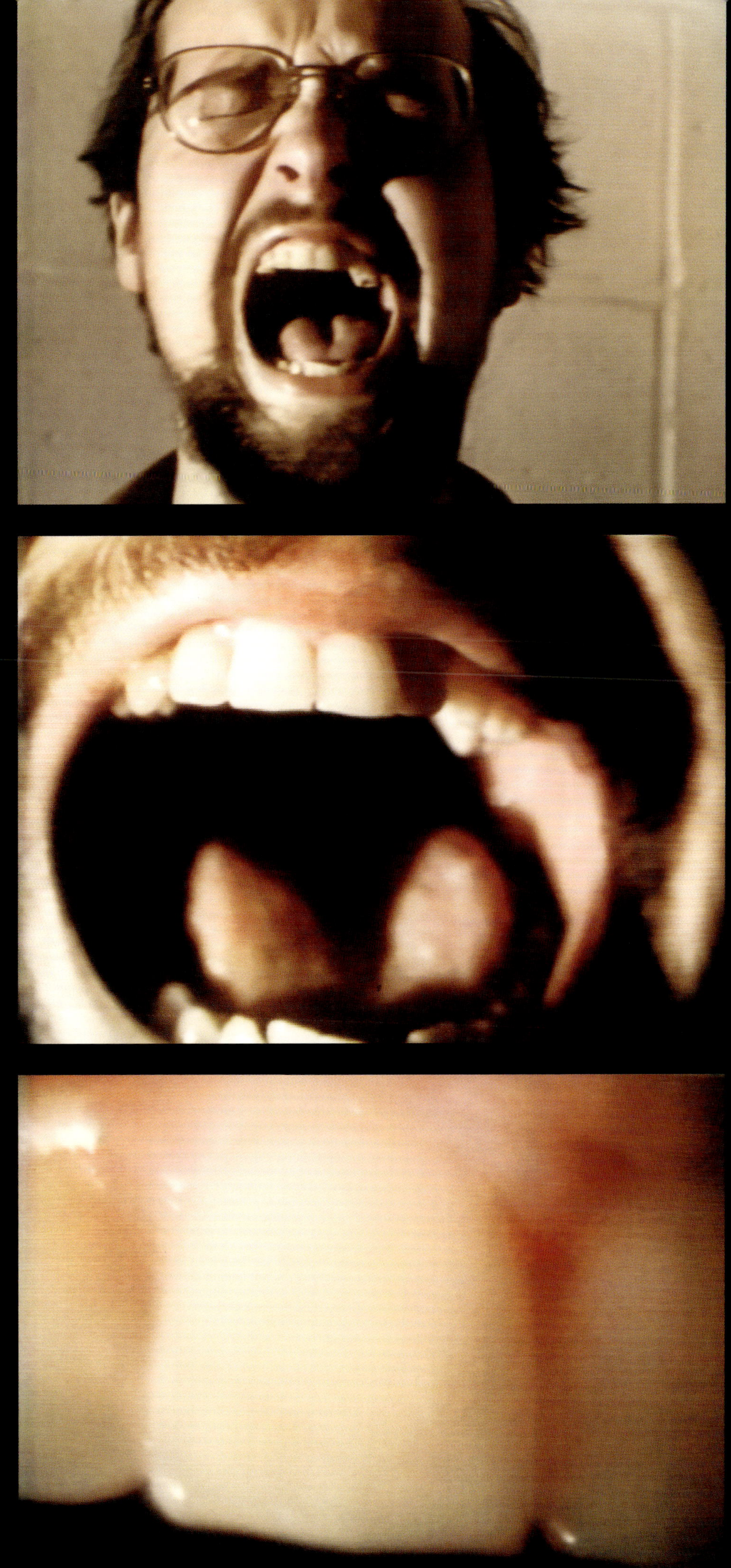

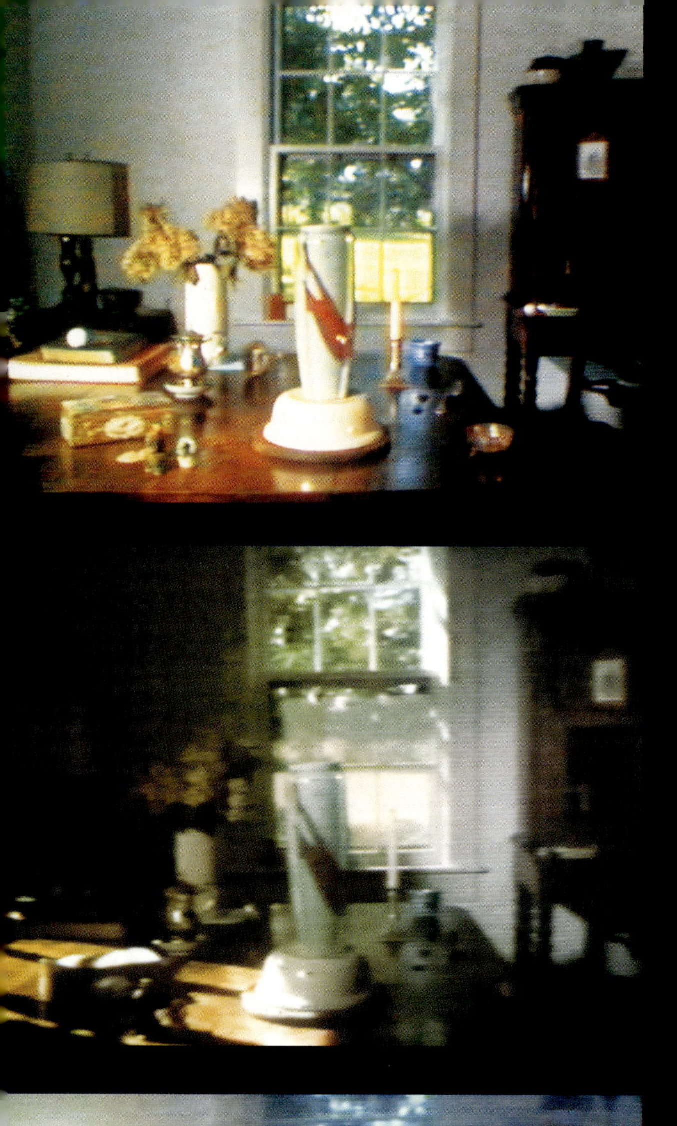
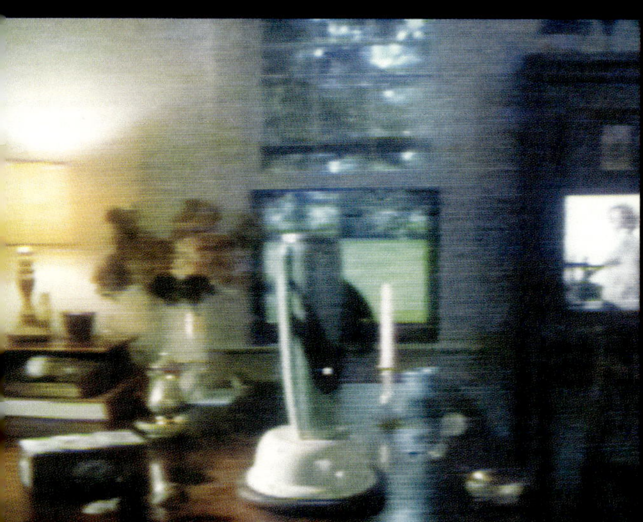
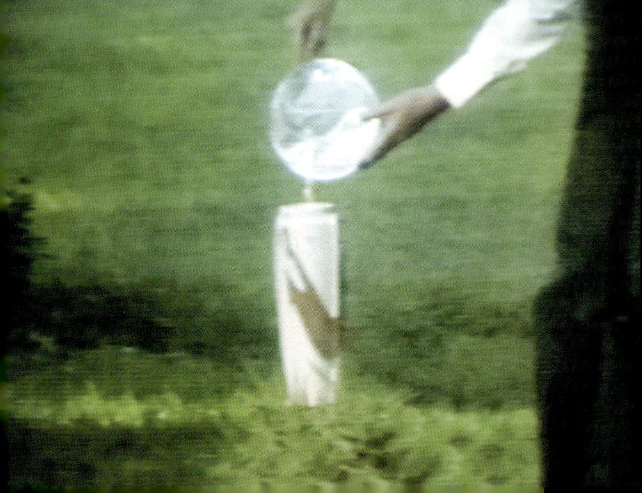

the importance of Rumi to his aesthetic, which is evidenced in his early Notebooks. His interest in the spiritual inspires him to infuse the everyday moment and the handmade object with the power of the human imagination. Rather than reducing the craft of production to an industrial process, he is looking to recover the spirit of the human in our creations. Viola observes that the blue vase in *The Morning After the Night of Power* reflects light, shadow, and movement: "As the condensed stillness of pure duration becomes activity, events hover at the edge of awareness until a final culminating action of transcendent liberation."[10] To understand Viola's engagement with Rumi and other mystics, it is instructive to recall the words of the German theologian Karl Rahner. In one of his prayers, he writes, "Theologians call Your silence in such a decisive hour the 'dark night of the soul,' and those who have experienced it are 'mystics.' These are the great souls who have not merely 'lived through' this hour of decision, as all men must, but have been able *to watch themselves in the process, to be somehow witnesses of their own reactions*."[11] The final few words, emphasized here by me, capture Viola's reflective turn of the camera on himself and what he discovers around him. The vase is not what it appears. *The Morning After the Night of Power* also recalls the scene in *I Do Not Know What It Is I Am Like* (1986) in which the desk and video monitor are the workplace of the imagination, as Viola looks at videotapes and reads texts. The tabletop in *The Morning After the Night of Power* is lit to capture specific objects, with the vase holding the central position.

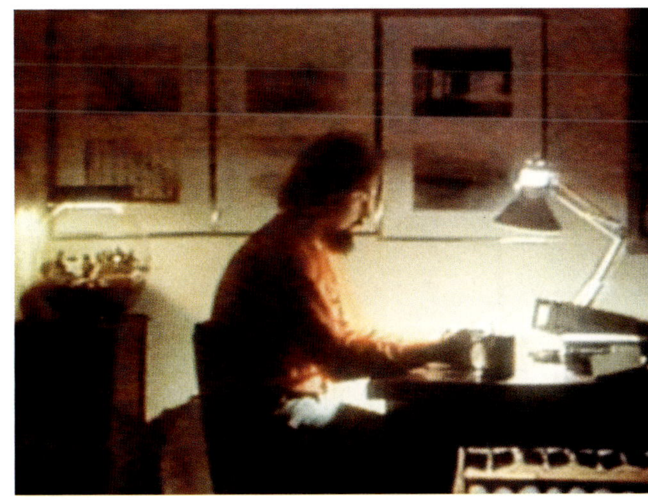

In *Sweet Light*, language is left as a scrap of paper on the floor. The words take flight in the nighttime light as pathways to experience, not uttered or written but seen. The work begins with Viola at a desk; he gets up and tosses a crumpled piece of paper on the floor, and an insect lands on the paper. Here, the visible and invisible intermingle. As Viola writes, "A moth emerges from a discarded letter as the spirit of a dead thought and—after an attempted flight to freedom—an individual appears, is inexorably drawn into the source of light, and consumed."[12] The tracings of the moth in flight in the darkened space fill out the void as light, illumination, and life. The moving air captured in the moth's flight, the words written on a piece of paper, all become the shapes and ideas of Viola's art. There is a balance in his aesthetic: his art speaks to the ability to look inward and recognize the wholeness of being. From this perspective the human body becomes an emblem of wholeness. As the early Christian theologian Saint Augustine wrote, "I looked carefully and saw that, in corporal beings, one thing is the whole and thus the beautiful, while another is that which is harmonious because well adapted to something other than itself, like a part of the body to the whole or a shoe to the foot."[13]

Opposite *The Morning After the Night of Power* (1977)

Above *I Do Not Know What It Is I Am Like* (1986)

Sweet Light reveals in Viola an intimacy with video and a pleasure in discovering its capabilities—how it can be controlled and can elicit surprise from the viewer. One is reminded of how video enabled Viola's worldview and his eventual rejection of an impersonal modernity in favor of a holistic view of humankind, nature, and belief. Viola struggles to push himself into the present by creating a caesura, a break, in the camera's omnipotent stare. He does this by relinquishing his body to the apparatus of the cinema, and in so doing he reminds us of the fragility of the self on the surface of the image. Viola's art breaks the pictorial plane by embracing the possibility of a humanist reconstruction of birth and death as the central node for understanding being. First, however, Viola needs to position his own body at the center of his work, a space that will be filled by others in future works.

Viola's early videotapes and installations, although focusing on the body, possess an impersonal quality and do not convey the emotion and feeling of the later work. The body in *The Messenger* emerging from the depths, and the transformation of the body in *The Crossing*, represent a suggestive break into an exploration of emotions. A similar transition happens in the videotapes from the mid-to-late 1970s, which explore the perceptual capacity of the medium to represent time and physical being through the body and the voice of the artist himself, who plays a role in each of these tapes. Viola is present less to expose himself, as actors will in later tapes and installations, than to test himself and his medium. An incisive and all-encompassing openness to technological developments in the medium marks the difference between Viola's approach to his work and the reductive conceptual and performative strategies of the art of this period. In these early tapes, Viola learns about staging the performance and bringing time into a narrative formation of experience. The notion of transcendence is beginning to emerge, as well as the ecstatic. In *The Space Between the Teeth*, the shout becomes an organic manifestation of the person calling out to the world in an effort to break through the architecture of the hallway and into the natural world, in the form of the body of water into which the still image of Viola in the hallway is ultimately thrown. As the French philosopher Jean-Luc Marion wrote on the paradox of the visible in art, it ultimately "make[s] visible that which one should not be able to see and which one is not able to see without astonishment."[14]

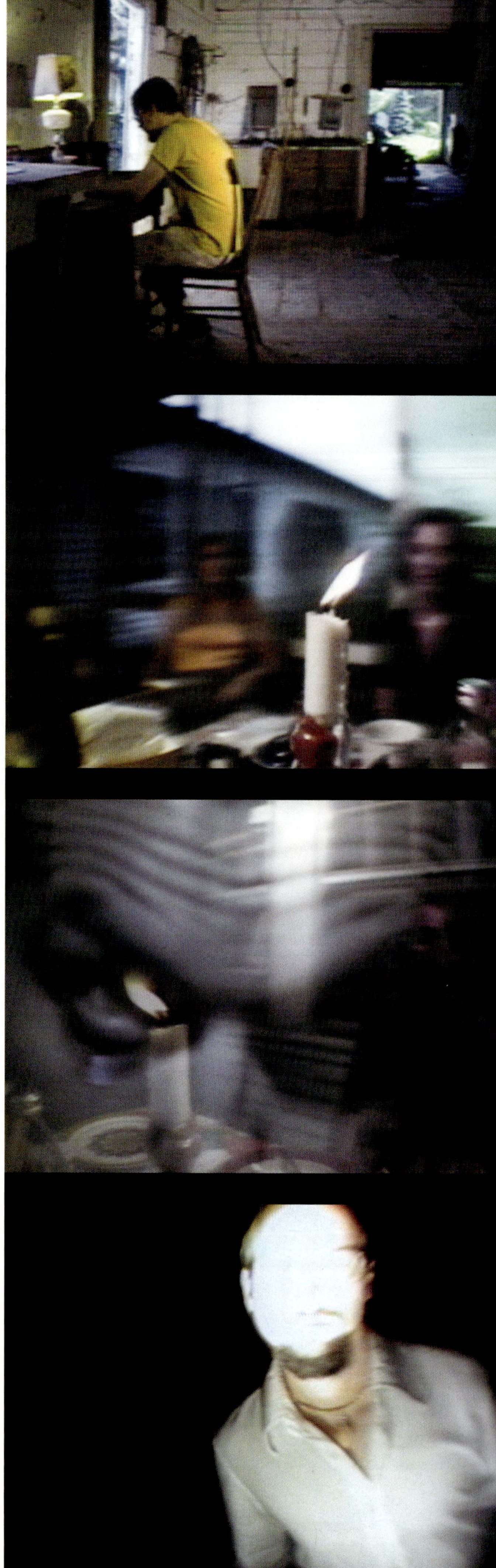

Sweet Light (1977)

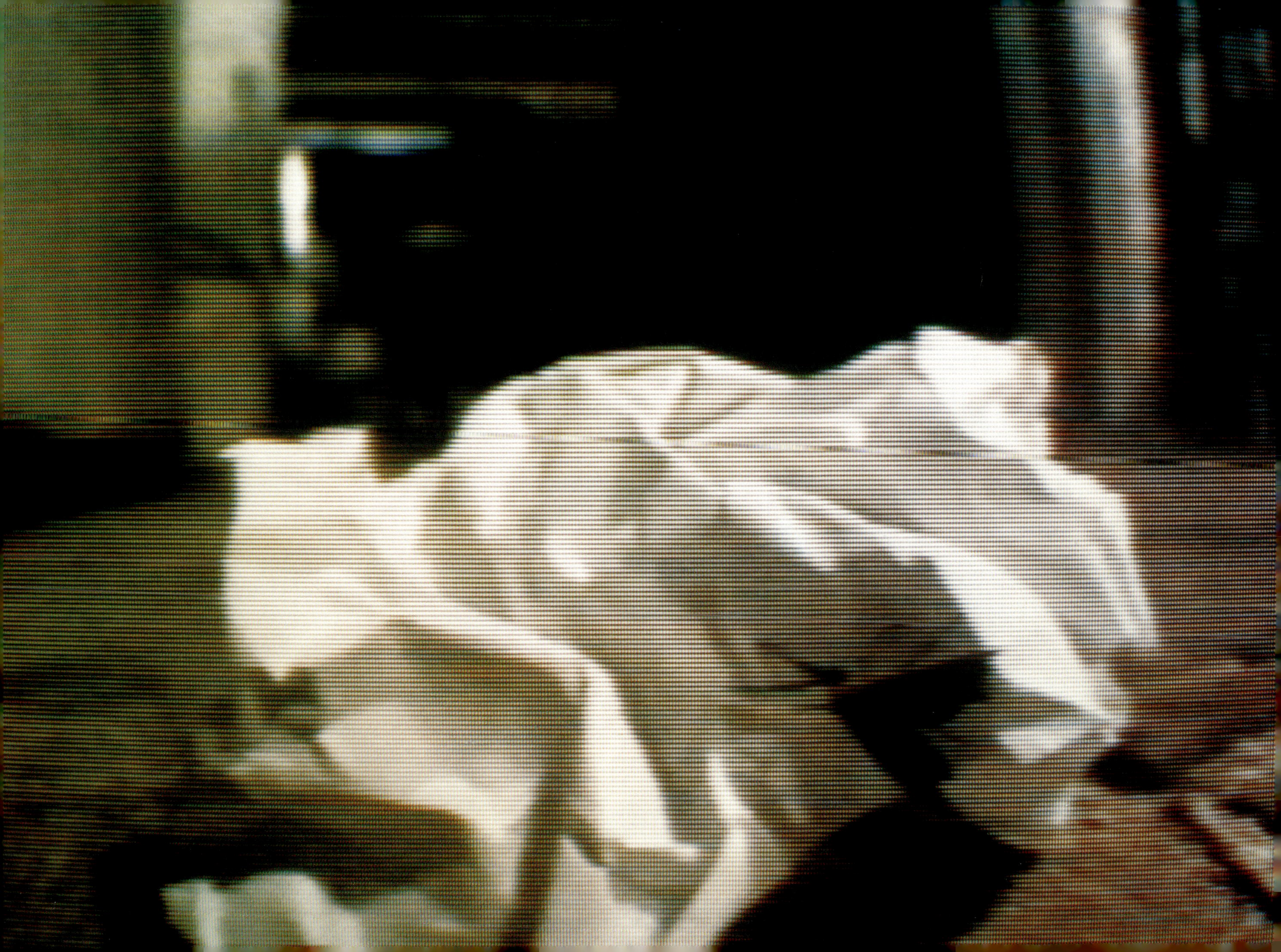

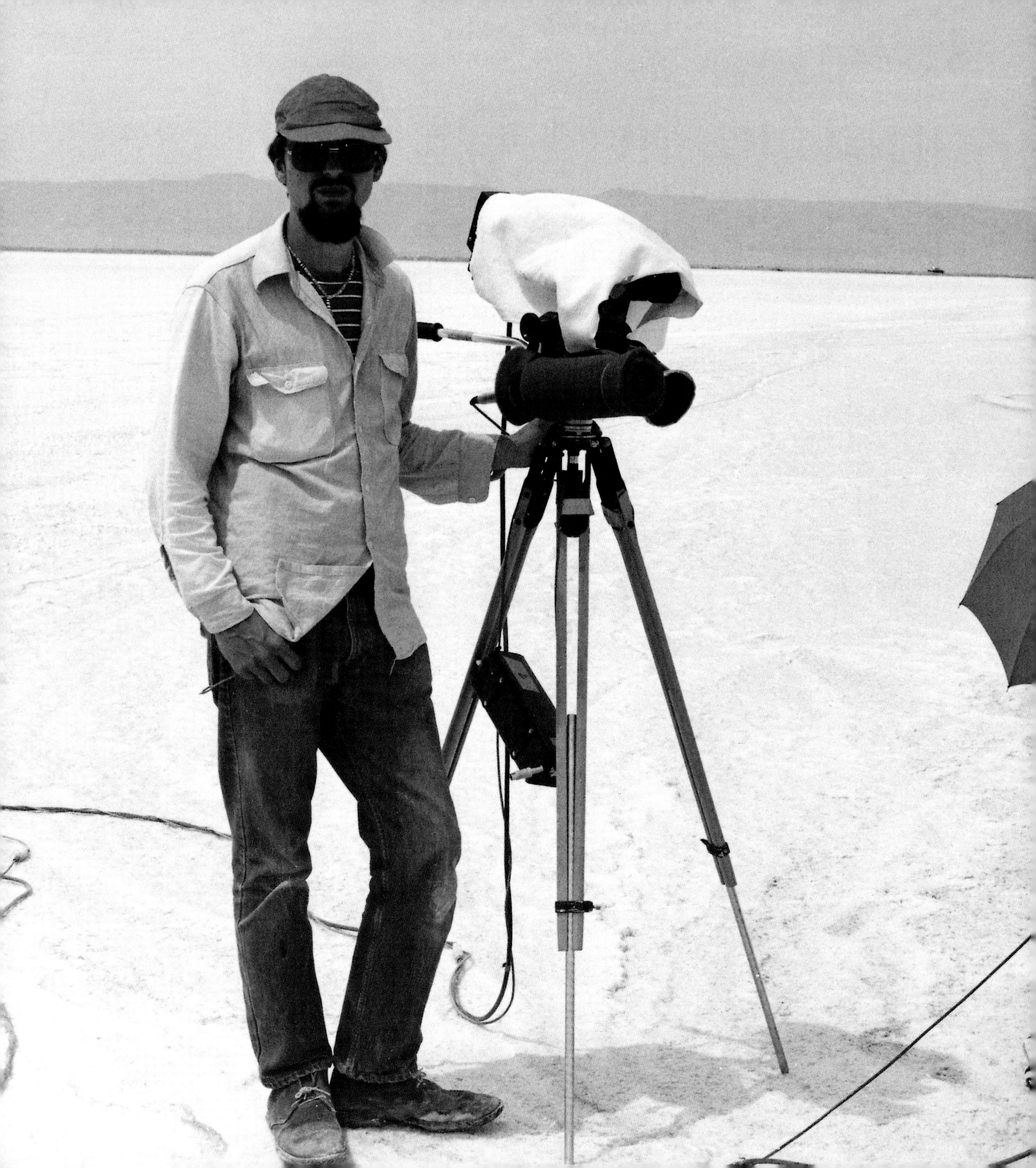

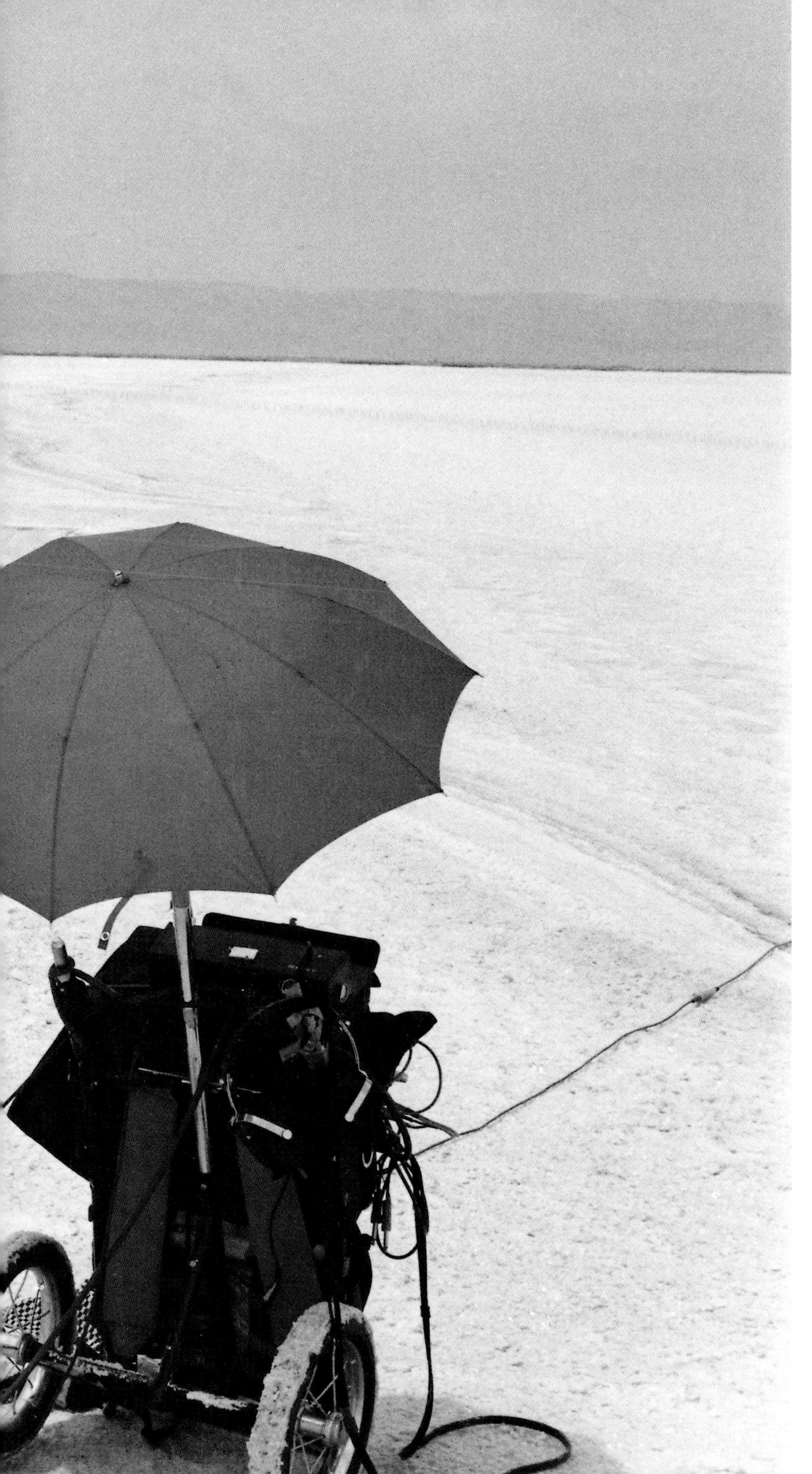

Bill Viola on location for *Chott el-Djerid (A Portrait in Light and Heat)*, Chott el-Djerid salt lake, Tunisia, May 1979

CHAPTER THREE

1980s: EXPANDED VISIONS OF LIFE AND MEMORY

We are all moving images!

—Bill Viola, Notebook, August 12, 2013

Viola realized early in his career that his art was a personal reflection of his being in the world. He had discovered in video the perfect medium to explore what he saw and to learn from what he could not see. The camera gave him the means to experience the world alone with the knowledge that he could share what he learned through the camera. Viola felt increasingly attuned to nature and the mysteries of the natural world through his art. He has a kinship with the poet William Wordsworth, who saw in nature the means to reflect on his life through poetry.[1] In *Return* (1975), when Viola looks out of a window and sees himself in nature, or in *Ancient of Days* (1979–81), when the snow-capped mountain appears, disappears, and reappears with a child in the foreground, it is clearly the artist going back to nature, which was visible and then rendered invisible by clouds. Viola returns to these themes in the single-channel videotapes and installations of the 1980s.

I would describe such collections as *August '74* (1974) and such individual works as *Sweet Light* (1977) and *Silent Life* (1979) as experiments or tests, probing various ways of working with video. This does not, however, lessen their importance. In *Silent Life*, we observe newborn babies in incubators. Viola directs his camera at their faces and hands, and into their eyes. It feels like a search for something, that ineffable quality of the newborn. In *Sweet Light*, which is a more developed piece, the various parts have a feeling of discovery, similar to looking through the pages of a sketchbook. A fascinating early example of Viola's pursuit of a "looking and trying to see more" strategy is *Instant Breakfast* (1974, from the collection *August '74*). Viola uses a strobe light to illuminate a scene so it explodes into view and then disappears just as quickly, a technique that the artist would

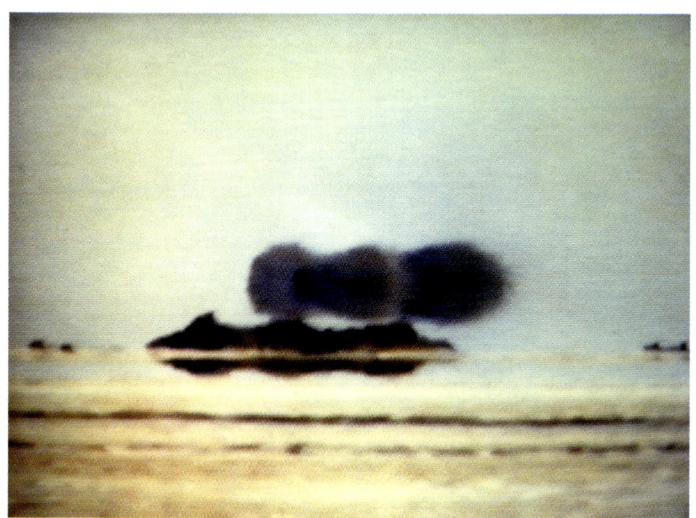

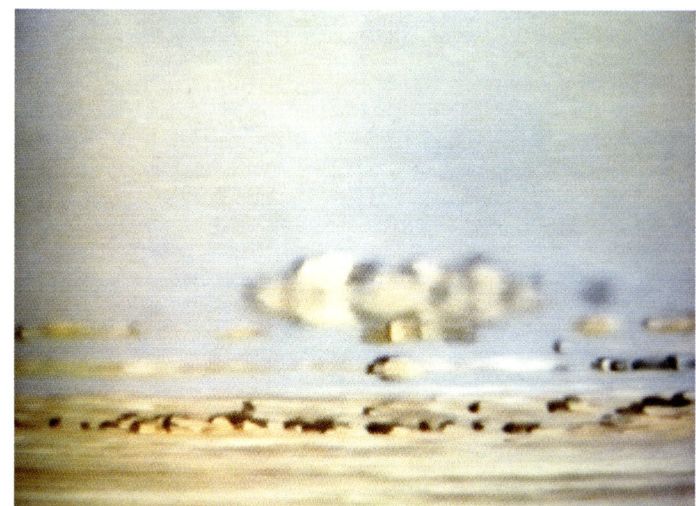

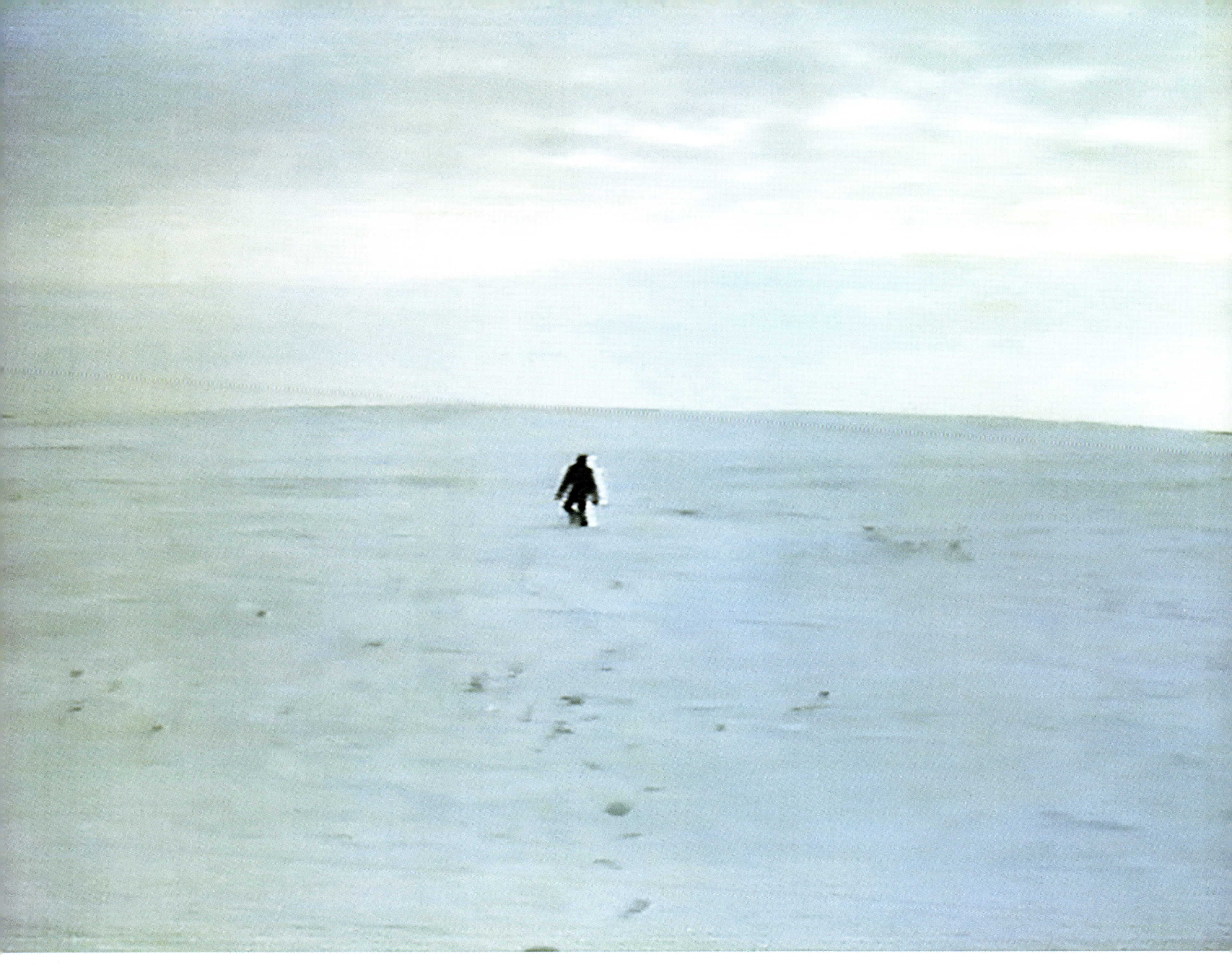

Chott el-Djerid (A Portrait in Light and Heat) (1979)

later employ in his installation *The Sleep of Reason* (1988), in which the space suddenly darkens and the walls reveal dreams of violence and explosive terror. In *Instant Breakfast*, however, the sequence is more about looking and revealing. The soundtrack suggests something being built and broken, with an occasional voice heard. It is about process, and the glimpses provided by the light reveal little, suggesting that we are in a closed and secretive place that the camera can record in the dark but not reveal through the light. What is this place that we "see" in *Instant Breakfast*?

The centrality of vision in the early videotapes takes on another dimension in a sequence of single-channel videotapes and installations that together describe one of Viola's most sustained and accomplished bodies of work. Viola's reputation as an artist would be secured on the basis of *Chott el-Djerid (A Portrait in Light and Heat)* (1979), *Hatsu-Yume (First Dream)* (1981), *Room for St. John of the Cross* (1983), *The Theater of Memory* (1985), *I Do Not Know What It Is I Am Like* (1986), *Passage* (1987), and *The Sleep of Reason* (1988). While these pieces follow from his earlier work, they also set the stage for what he would create throughout the 1990s and at the beginning of the new millennium. Essentially, each of these works represents a single chapter in a philosophic-poetic text that unfolds over seven parts. The scope and range of Viola's achievement are virtually unmatched by any other artist of his generation.

I am reminded of the words of the French poet André du Bouchet: "Nothing is lost of what escapes me."[2] In all of these pieces we feel that Viola is revealing something that he has discovered and that we have never seen. Through the eyepiece of the camera or the elements brought together in the installation, the artist, and of course the viewer, finds the unexpected. But there is something else going on here as well that has to do with memory and the act of forgetting—the memory of birth, the markers of life, aging, and death. Across the arc of life, we cherish memory and feel the loss of forgetting. Video is a virtual memory bank that represents not only what we see and remember but also what we forget. Or should we say that forgetting is another memory? Do we ever truly forget? I think not. This ambivalent tension between memory and forgetting is part of the uncanny insight that Viola brings to his artworks and the power that resides in our experience of them.

The representation of the landscape, which is one of the central motifs of art, sets the stage for *Chott el-Djerid*. Its subtitle, *A Portrait in Light and Heat*, captures the phenomenological act of looking and seeing a double virtual reflection. The camera records a series of mirages on the surface of the chott, a dry salt lake in the Sahara, including distant images of people walking and moving in vehicles across the horizon. Viola writes: "Through special telephoto lenses adapted for video, the camera confronts the final barrier of the limits of the image, the point where the breakdown of normal conditions, or lack of visual information, causes us to reevaluate our

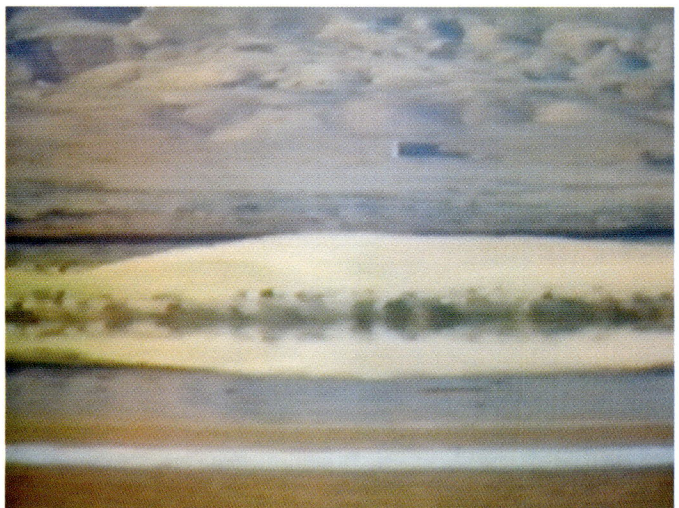

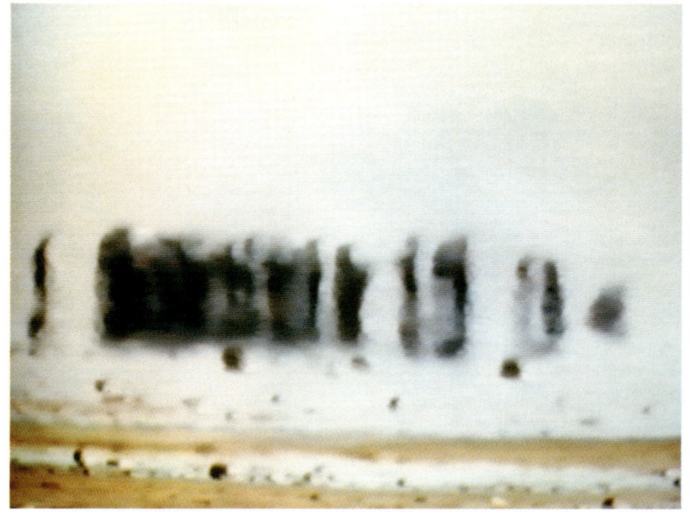

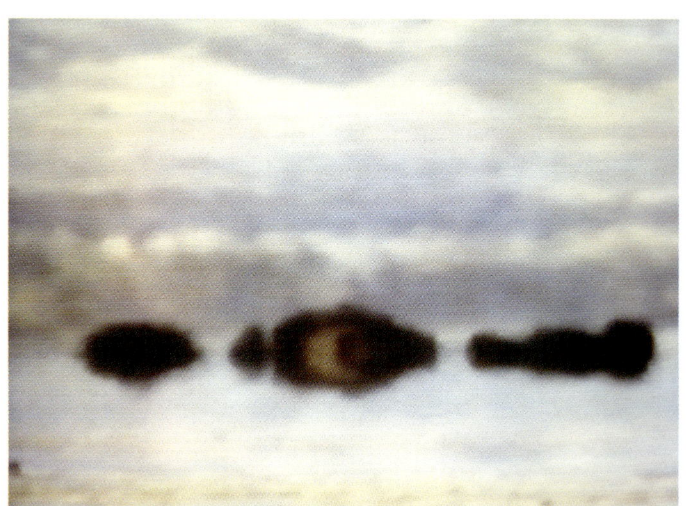

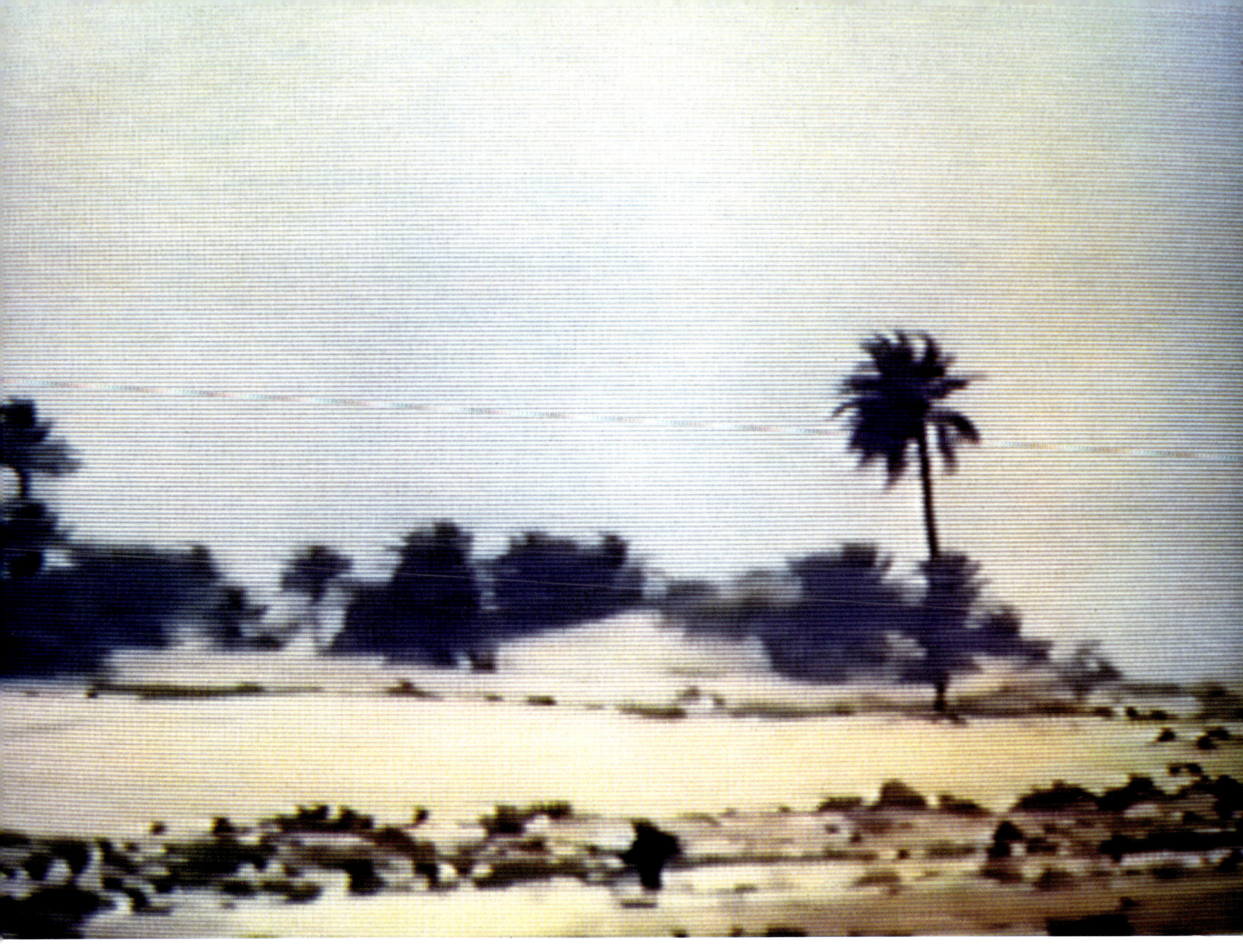

Chott el-Djerid (A Portrait in Light and Heat) (1979)

perceptions of reality and realize that we are looking at something out of the ordinary—a transformation of the physical into the psychological. If one believes that hallucinations are the manifestation of some chemical or biological imbalance in the brain, then mirages and desert heat distortions can be considered hallucinations of the landscape. *It was like physically being inside someone else's dream*."[3]

Viola's treatment of the landscape as giving off its own hallucinations, which we then enter, is a key trope of his work, to be found as well in *Inner Passage* (2013). I will return later to this piece because of its seminal role in recalling a key focus of the artist: the representation of consciousness. In *Chott el-Djerid*, we enter into nature and see recorded through the optics of video what we can only imagine. As Perov recalls: "In recording the snow footage in Saskatchewan [with which the piece opens], Bill used a portable stove placed under the lens to create heat-wave distortion of the snowy fields and distant objects to simulate the heat waves of the desert. The method of recording was to drive through the landscape to collect images, very different to studio work that was prevalent in the earlier pieces. But the human figure within the vastness of their environment was always an important part of the reason for the journey."[4] Perov and Viola both appear in the piece, along with a group of tourists captured by Viola's telephoto lens as dancing heat waves. The physical exertion of creating *Chott el-Djerid*, the movement of equipment across the desert and snow-covered landscapes, and the chance opportunities offered in each site, are a growing part of Viola's art project. Viola and Perov recorded the desert footage in Tunisia, enduring summer heat and a lack of clean water and fresh food. Perov's photographic documentation of their work and experiences together remains central to appreciating the detail and ambition of each project, and results in images that are influential in shaping the reception of Viola's work.

In *Hatsu-Yume (First Dream)*, Viola continues to explore perception and the phenomenological, as well as the tension between tradition and the new, the urban and nature. The work covers a day in Japan, from the rural, myth-filled north to the artificially lit metropolis of nighttime Tokyo. The opposites that subtend this piece are marked by key words: "structured on the *cycle* of one day, the dividing line of *light* and *darkness*, the *ancient* and the *new*, *nature* and *city*, *object* and *subject*, *rational thought* and *unconscious insight* [emphasis added]."[5] This encyclopedia of terms informs this piece and virtually all of Viola's later work. These final oppositions are as revealing as the "hallucinations" of the landscape in *Chott el-Djerid*. In juxtaposing the terms "object" and "subject," "thought" and "insight," Viola raises the possibility that an "object" could be a "subject" or a "thought" defined as an "insight." It is the fluid movement of these terms that expresses Viola's desire to turn this meditation on a place and culture into a celebration of

Hatsu-Yume (First Dream) (1981)

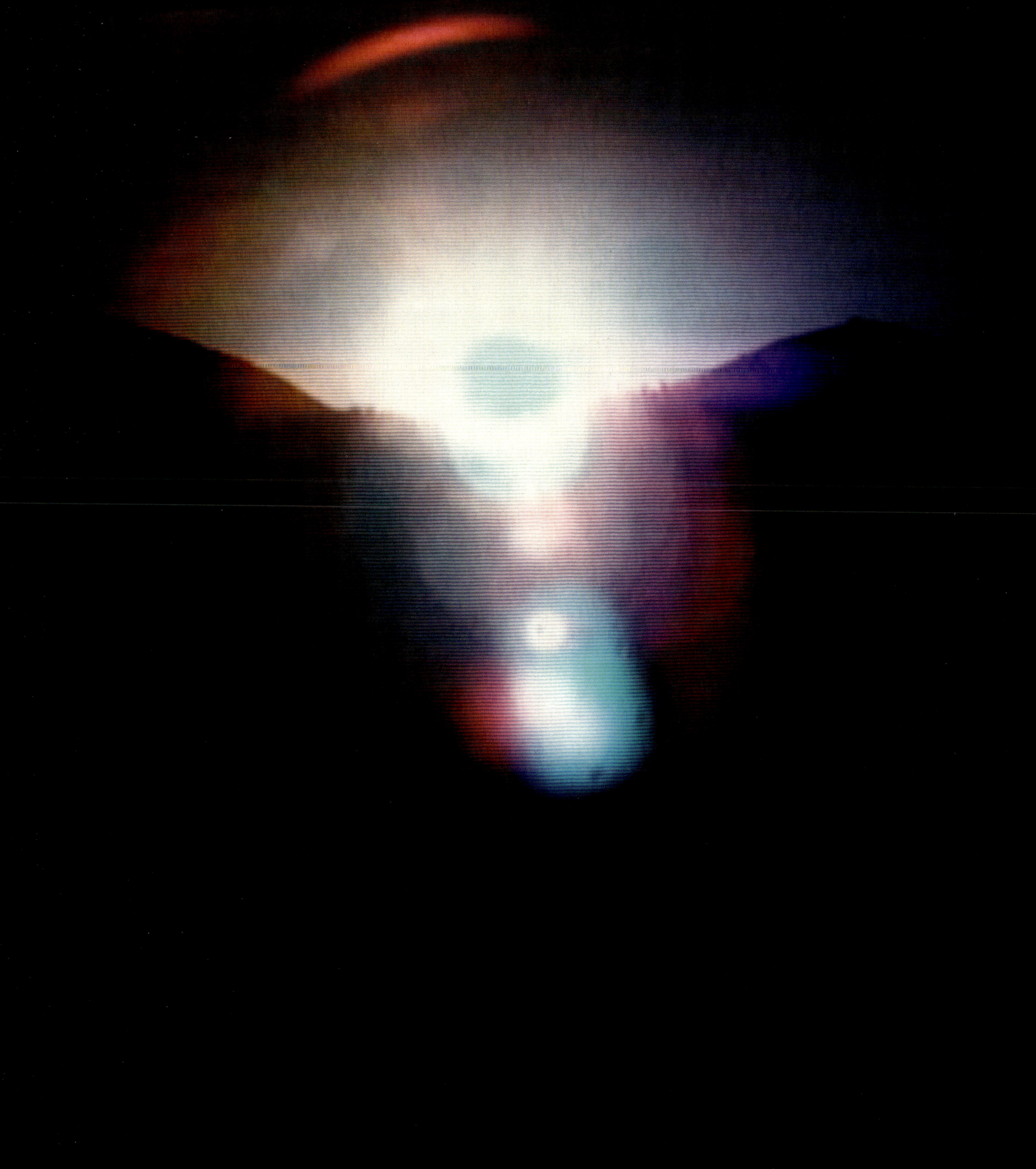

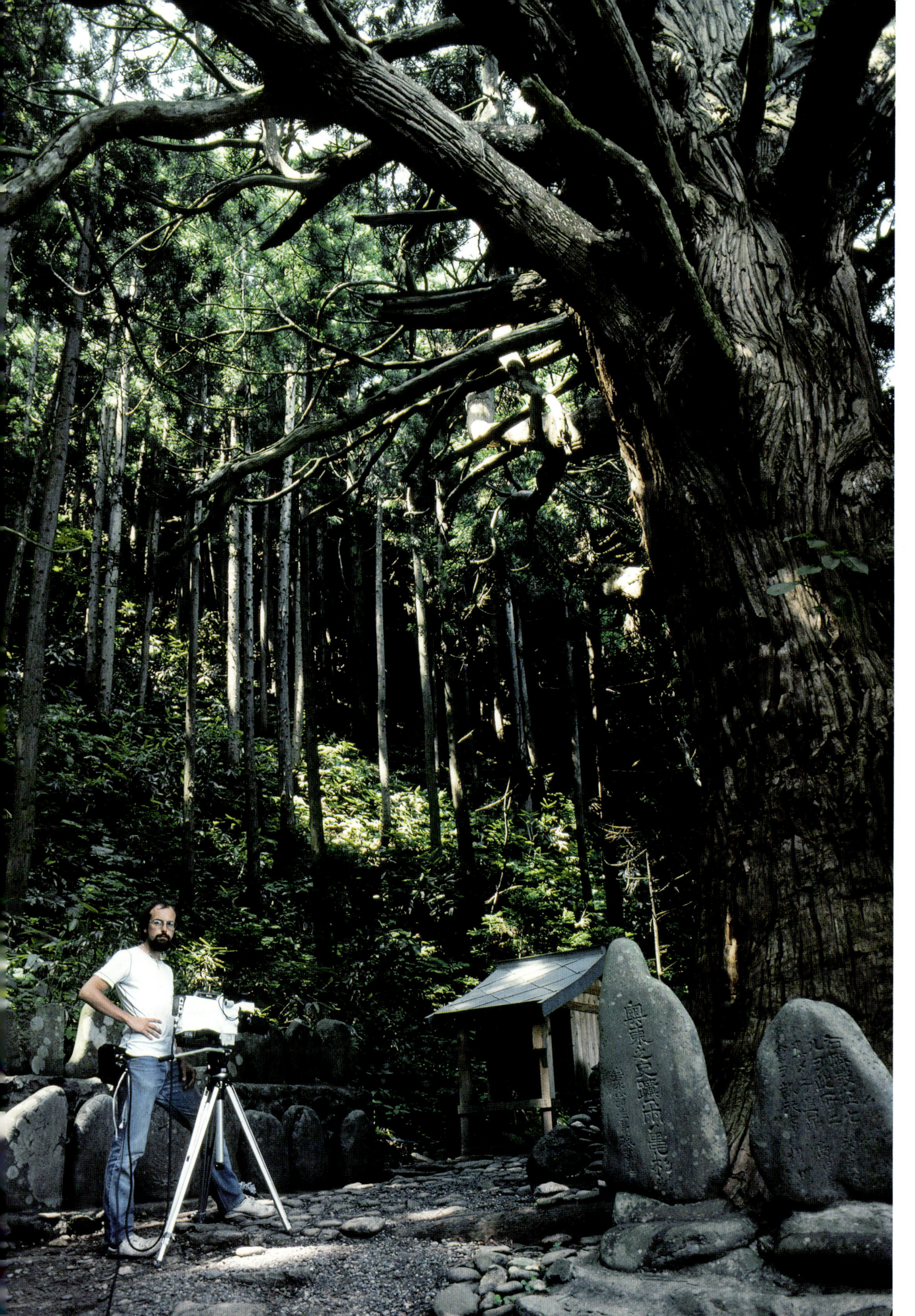

Left Bill Viola and sacred tree, on location for *Hatsu-Yume (First Dream)*, Tohoku, Japan, April 1981

Opposite *Hatsu-Yume (First Dream)* (1981)

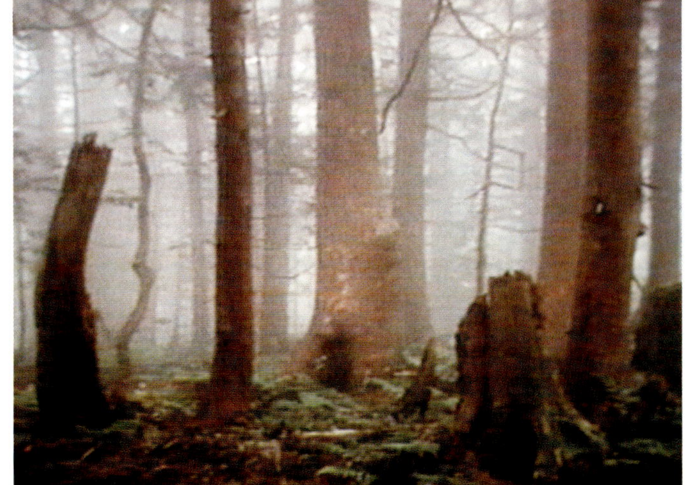

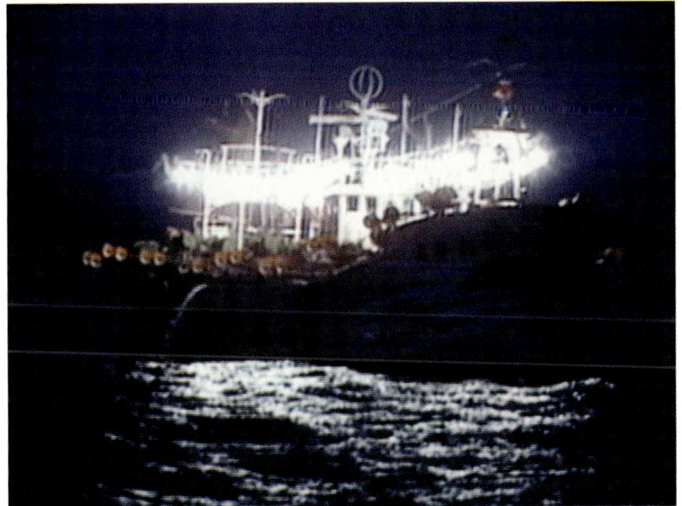

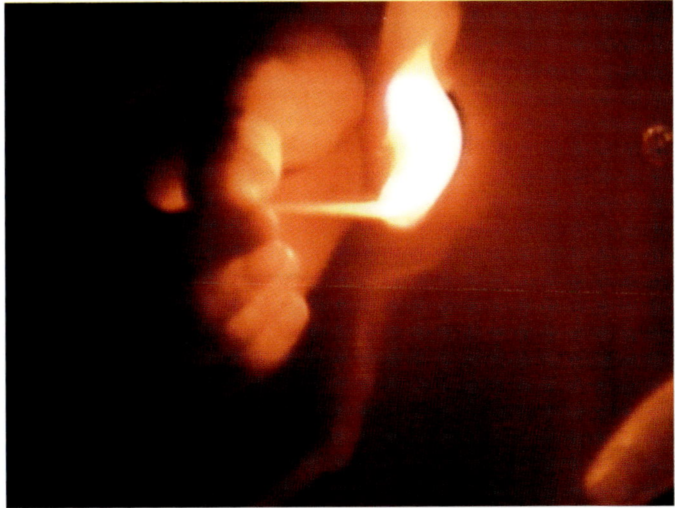

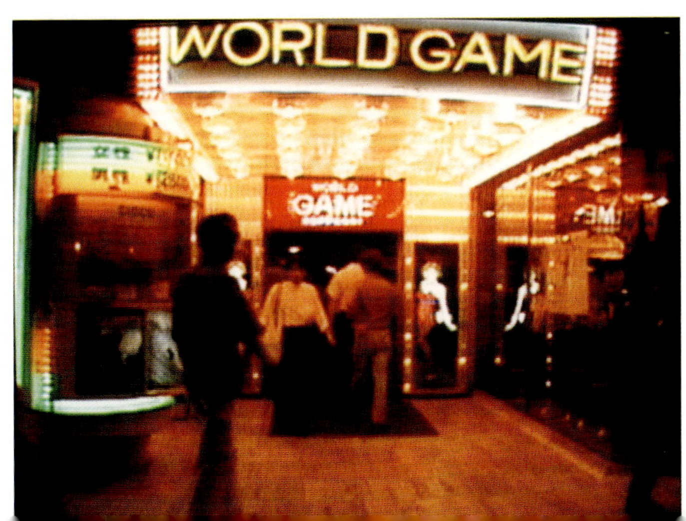

the thinking eye. The work is, in fact, more complicated than the artist's binary catalogue given above might suggest. As Viola writes,

Toward the end of the tape, after a purgation through light and color during a deluge from a violent rainstorm on a car windshield, fish appear as rippling gold and orange hues under the surface of the water. The *disembodied consciousness of the roving camera* finally takes root on the night streets of Tokyo when an individual emerges from the urban landscape to strike a match flame. Sweeping the glare of a bright light directly into the lens, he finally disappears into the night shadows of a bamboo forest, trailing the silver-purple thread of a fading afterimage on the camera tube, recalling the first rays of sunrise that pierced the darkness at the beginning of the work. The piece unfolds in extended time as a visual trance about light and its relation to water and to life, and also its opposite—darkness or the night and death. Here, video treats light like water—it becomes a fluid on the video tube. Water supports the fish like light supports the man. Land is the death of the fish. Darkness is the death of man [emphasis added].[6]

The language Viola uses to describe *Hatsu-Yume* embraces states of mind linked to such concepts as "visual trance," in which the camera takes on a "consciousness." Light becomes a "fluid on the video tube," extending the metaphor to water supporting fish like light supports and reveals humankind. This use of metaphor to describe what we see on the screen and to convey the ecology of life for humans and animals is a strategy that the artist employs in such later pieces as *I Do Not Know What It Is I Am Like.* The "disembodied consciousness of the camera" characterizes Viola's view of video as an extension of the body. Here, the camera is not a mirror of consciousness but a mind functioning in a way that conveys a different representation of the world, one that is a process of discovery, making visible the invisible. This idea comes to the fore in *Hatsu-Yume* in the rain sequence, in which the front windshield of a taxi is recorded from inside the car, the blades sweeping across the glass conveying washes of color from the lights of the city through which the taxi is moving. The materialization of light, with colors becoming streams of liquid as the action is slowed down, is echoed in the soundtrack, which slows down the ambient sounds of the city. To the naked eye in real time, such a view of water would be a complex set of agitated movements and sounds. Through the "disembodied consciousness of the camera," it becomes something else. The water brings to life the human-made environment as if we were below the sea. Viola emphasizes this movement when the camera's focus on the windshield gradually fades into goldfish swimming in a stream. *Hatsu-Yume*, like all of Viola's videotapes, deserves a close-shot analysis, so as to reveal the complex connections that he makes in his single-channel pieces. Unlike film, in which

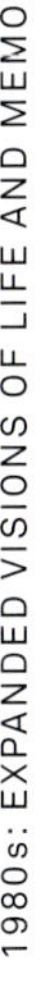

the editing of frames of celluloid composes the action in time, the electronic flow of video softens the "cut," conveying on another level the seamless apprehension of the world through our optical and cognitive systems.

Viola's opportunity to work in Japan came about through the Japan–U.S. Friendship Commission Creative Artist Fellowship he was awarded in 1980. That year Perov and Viola married, and together they settled in Tokyo and traveled throughout Japan. They also began to study with the Zen master Daien Tanaka. "Since the grant enabled us to travel for research and to study the Japanese culture," recalls Perov, "the eighteen months we spent in Japan had an enormous influence on Bill's work. All forms of the Japanese culture were explored and experienced: painting, especially Zen painting, and calligraphy, sacred art, the architecture and gardens of temples and shrines, crafts (paper making, basket weaving, pottery), and the performing arts such as Kabuki, Bunraku, and in particular the slowly moving ancient theater of the Noh. We witnessed Shinto fire walking ceremonies, traditional Sumo wrestling in small villages, and all manner of sacred festivals in small temples and shrines."[7] The following year Viola became an artist-in-residence at Sony Corporation's Atsugi research laboratories, and with additional funding from WNET in New York, Viola and Perov were able to shoot and edit *Hatsu-Yume*. Viola also gained access to the latest technological developments and was given the opportunity to work with the Sony engineer Yasuo Shinohara, who created a device that enabled the precise control of temporal sequencing and editing techniques that we see in *Ancient of Days*.

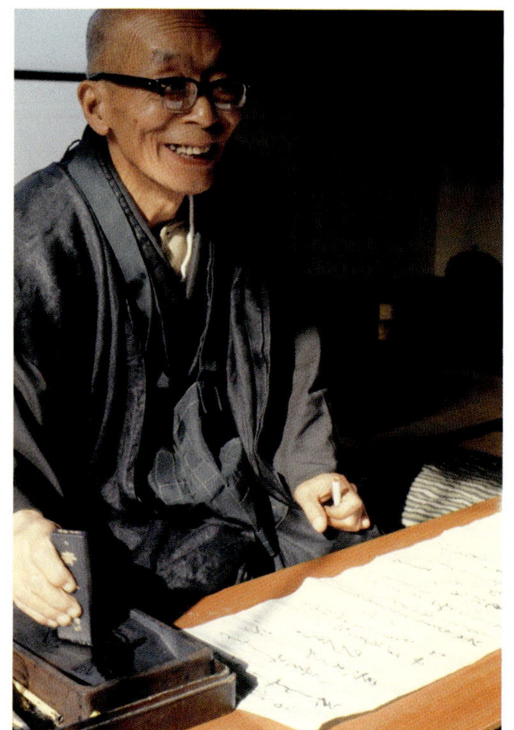

The astonishing ambition of *Hatsu-Yume* and the subtle range of textures and experiences that it conveys were unmatched by anything else being made at the time. Significantly, Viola's access to technology did not result in slick and commercially accepted techniques. Rather, he worked against the grain, challenging himself and the engineers at Sony through the new forms he was creating. Viola was taking the first bold step along a path toward exploring a radical aesthetic that would bring single-channel video to a new place, one structured not by a playful inversion of genre and narrative but by a visualization of the unseen. His sixteen months spent with a Zen master intensified his strong belief in forging a multicultural and deeper spiritual sensibility. His interest in art history was also connected to an ongoing study of Japanese poetic and spiritual texts. He was not researching contemporary art practices but believed instead that video offered the means of establishing a new phenomenological ground for a visual, aesthetic experience.

After returning to the United States, Viola and Perov settled in Long Beach, California, where they have remained and raised two sons. Perov recalls the return to America:

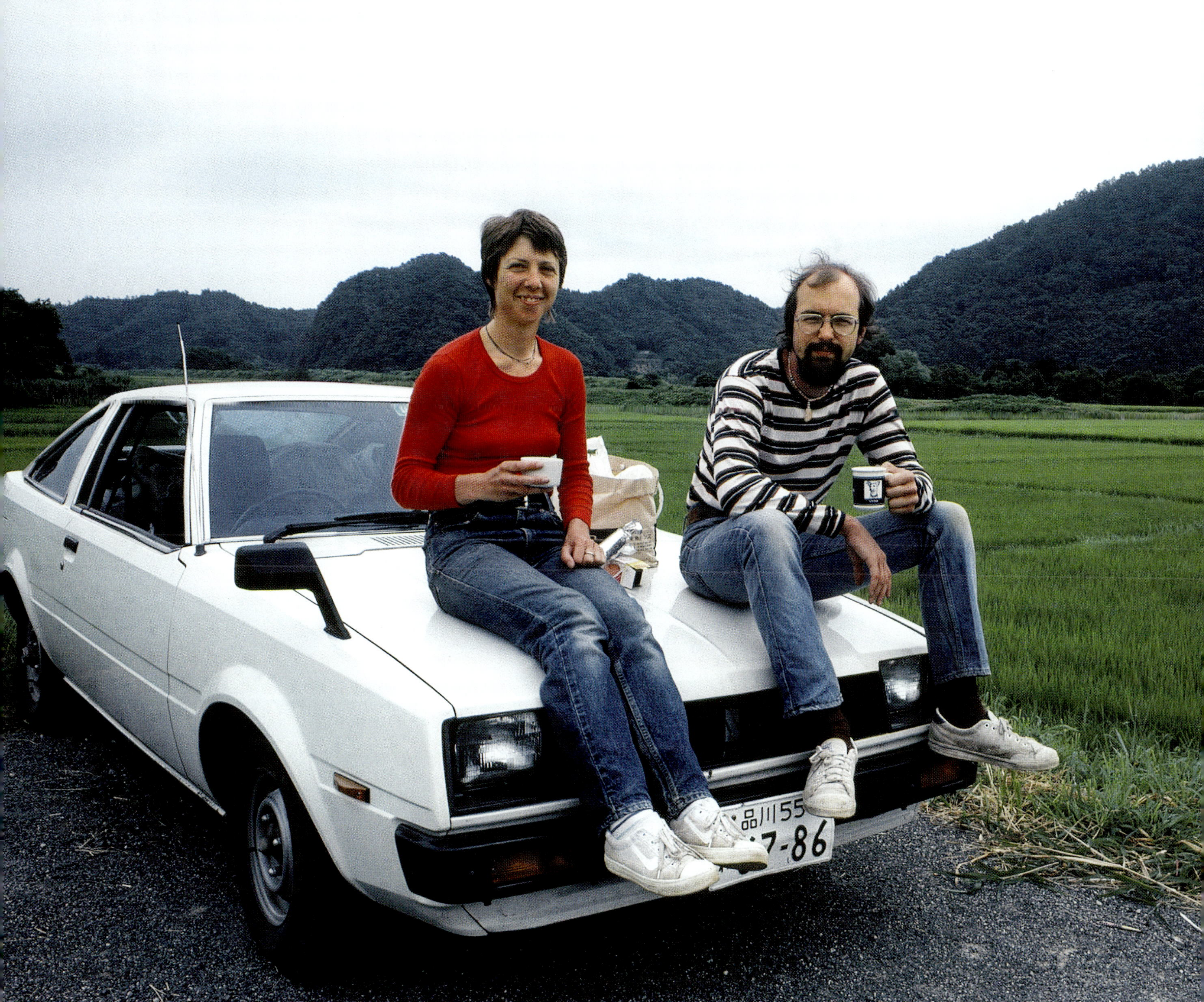

Opposite Daien Tanaka at Abe family temple,
Isu Peninsula, Japan, November 1980

Above Kira Perov and Bill Viola on location for *Hatsu-Yume (First Dream)*,
Tohoku, Japan, April 1981

California offered many different possibilities for the creation of new work. On the other side of the Pacific from Japan, the landscape was similarly rich with mountains, ocean coastline, forests, but in addition there were the vast deserts. In Japan, it seemed that everywhere you traveled you could find cultural objects, a grouping of stones or a makeshift shrine, but in California nature was vast, overwhelming, and often devoid of human presence. Bill began to produce large room-size installations and bring nature and objects once more into the gallery. From 1982 to 1989 he created eleven major installations and five videotapes, including the 89-minute single-channel encyclopedic work *I Do Not Know What It Is I Am Like,* which took us three years to complete.[8]

The spiritual dimension of Viola's aesthetic and his ongoing interest in memory inform two large installations from this period, *Room for St. John of the Cross* and *The Theater of Memory*. Both works combine video with other materials and, in doing so, foreground the centrality of the moving image to the construction of his artwork. *Room for St. John of the Cross* continues Viola's interest in the space of the installation as a means of combining various elements linked by the video image and as a stage on which to explore how the senses receive the world and how video can mediate it. Objects from nature become part of the work: a large dead tree in *The Theater of Memory*, and peat moss in *Room for St. John of the Cross*. Viola succinctly describes the piece:

A small black cubicle (6 × 5 × 5½ feet) stands in the center of a large dark room. There is a small window in the front of the cubicle where a soft glow of incandescent light emerges. On the back wall of the space, a large screen shows a projected black-and-white video image of snow-covered mountains. Shot with an unstable hand-held camera, the mountains move in wild, jittery patterns. A loud roaring sound of wind and white noise saturates the room from two loud speakers.

The interior of the cubicle is inaccessible and can be viewed only through the window. The inner walls are white. The floor is covered with brown dirt. There is a small wooden table in the corner with a metal water pitcher, a glass of water, and a 4-inch color monitor. On the monitor is a color image of a snow-covered mountain. Shot with a fixed camera, it is presented in real time with no editing. The only visible movement is caused by an occasional wind blowing through the trees and bushes. From within the cubicle, the sound of a voice softly reciting St. John's poems in Spanish is barely audible above the loud roaring of the wind in the room. The Spanish poet and mystic St. John of the Cross (1542–91) was kept prisoner by the religious establishment for nine months in 1577. His cell had no

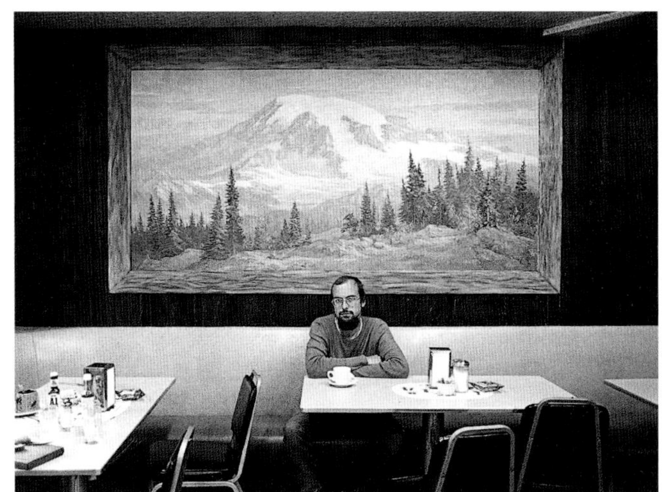

Above Bill Viola, Mt Rainier coffee shop, WA, August 1979

Opposite *Room for St. John of the Cross*, proposal for exhibition "Video as Attitude," May 1983

BILL VIOLA

ROOM for ST. JOHN of the CROSS

Video/Sound Installation

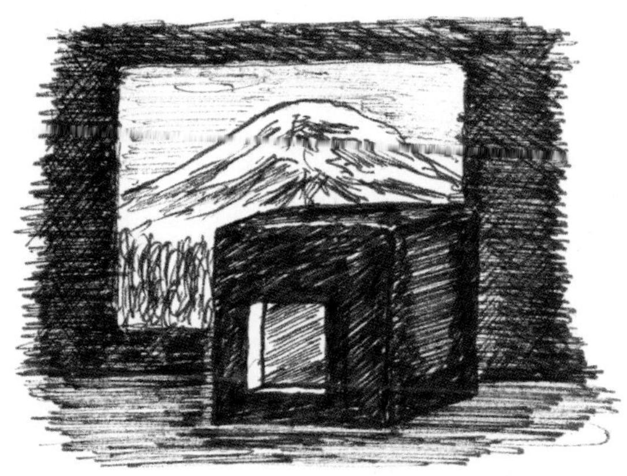

EMPTY BLACK CUBICLE
(ROOM of the SELF)
IN A DARK SPACE.
INSIDE, A CANDLE AND
A STILL MOUNTAIN.
OUTSIDE, A MOVING
MOUNTAIN AND the
SOUND of the WIND.

1. 4 x 5 x 6ft. THICK-WALLED CUBICLE (BLACK)
2. VIDEO PROJECTOR (BLACK + WHITE)
3. 3/4" VTR PLAYBACK (2)
4. " TABLE TOP TV (SONY TRINITRON) SONY KV-4000
5. PROPS - SMALL WOOD NIGHT TABLE, CANDLE
6. STEREO SOUND SYSTEM (2) 1. 60 WATTS/CH. (ROOM)
   2. 30 WATTS/CH. (CUBICLE)

TOP VIEW

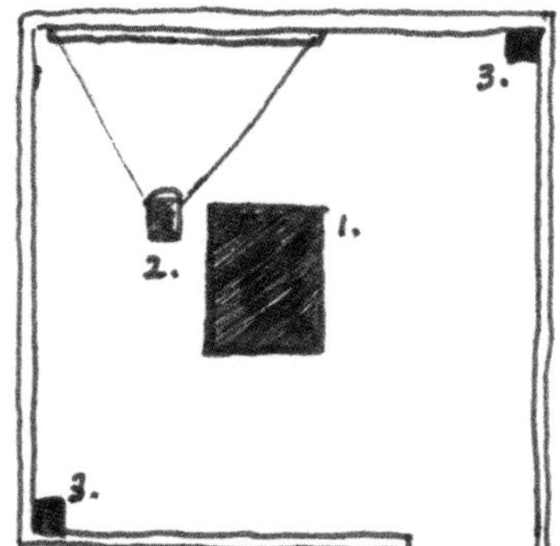

- ROOM - APPX. 20 x 30ft.
DARK, NO WINDOWS

1. CUBICLE
2. VIDEO PROJECTOR
(OVERHEAD MOUNT)
3. LOUDSPEAKERS

LOCATION of EXITS VARIABLE,
BUT VIEWERS SHOULD APPROACH
the PIECE from the REAR of
the ROOM.

FLOW CHART

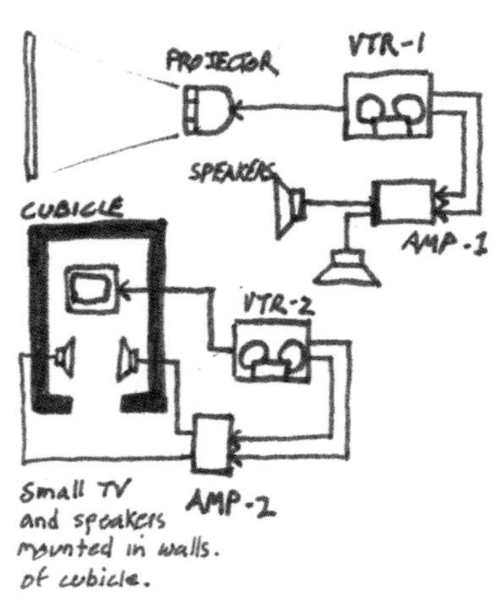

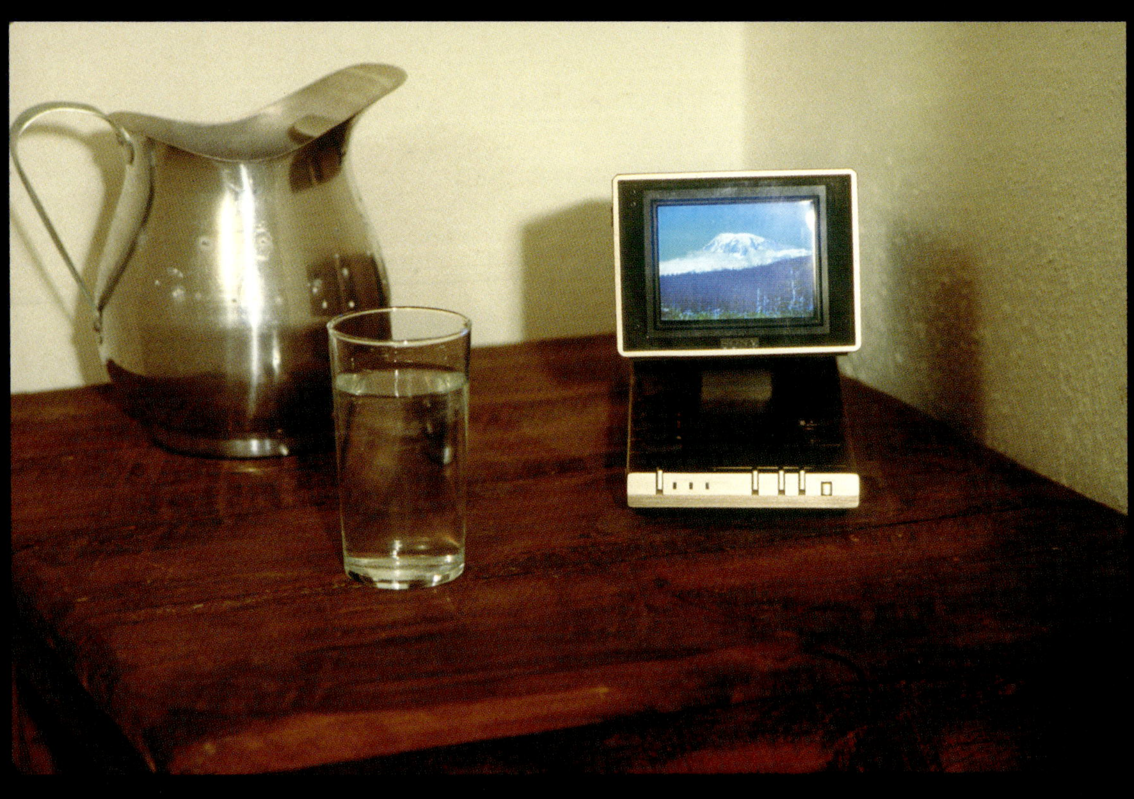

Room for St. John of the Cross (1983)

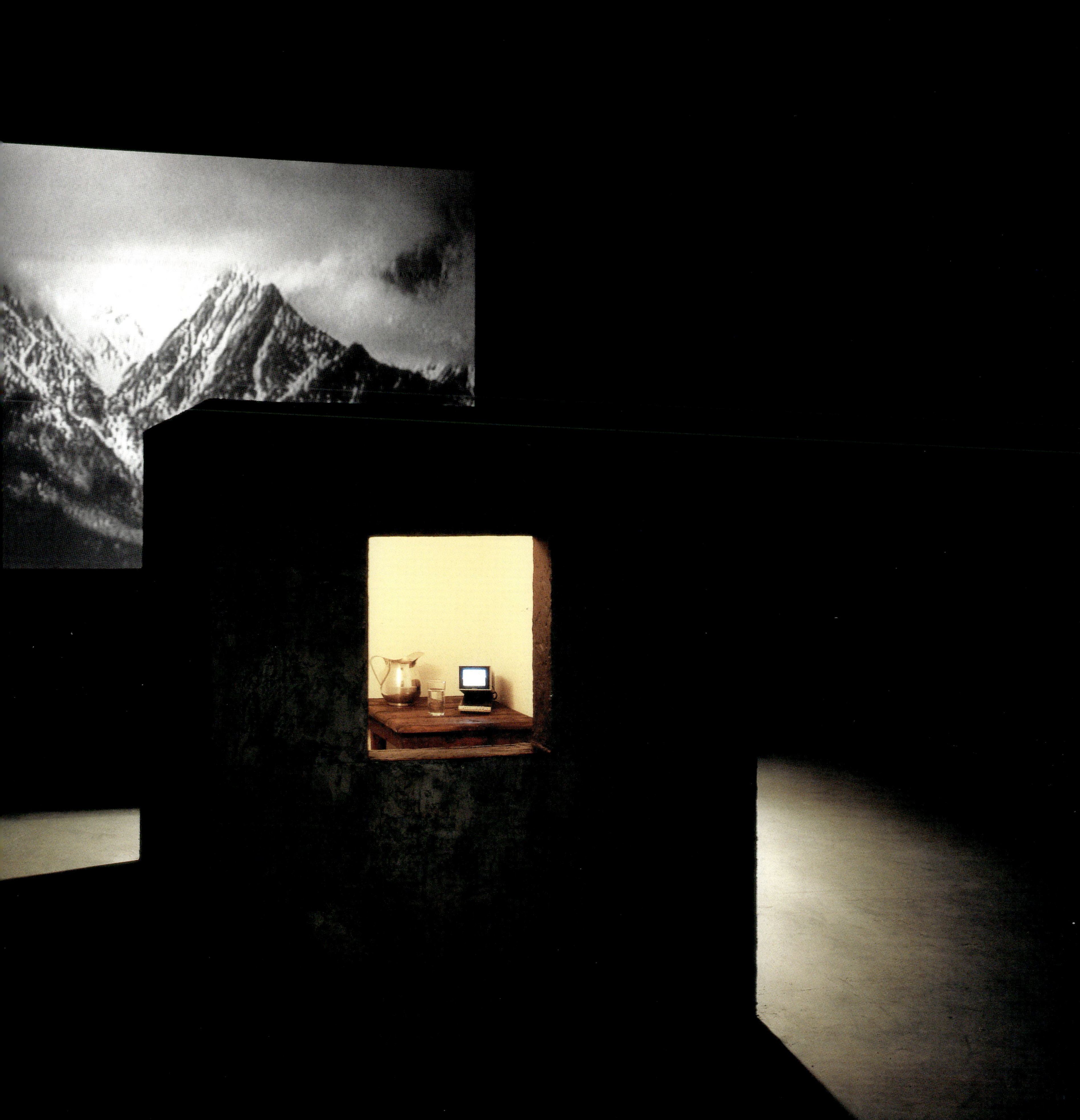

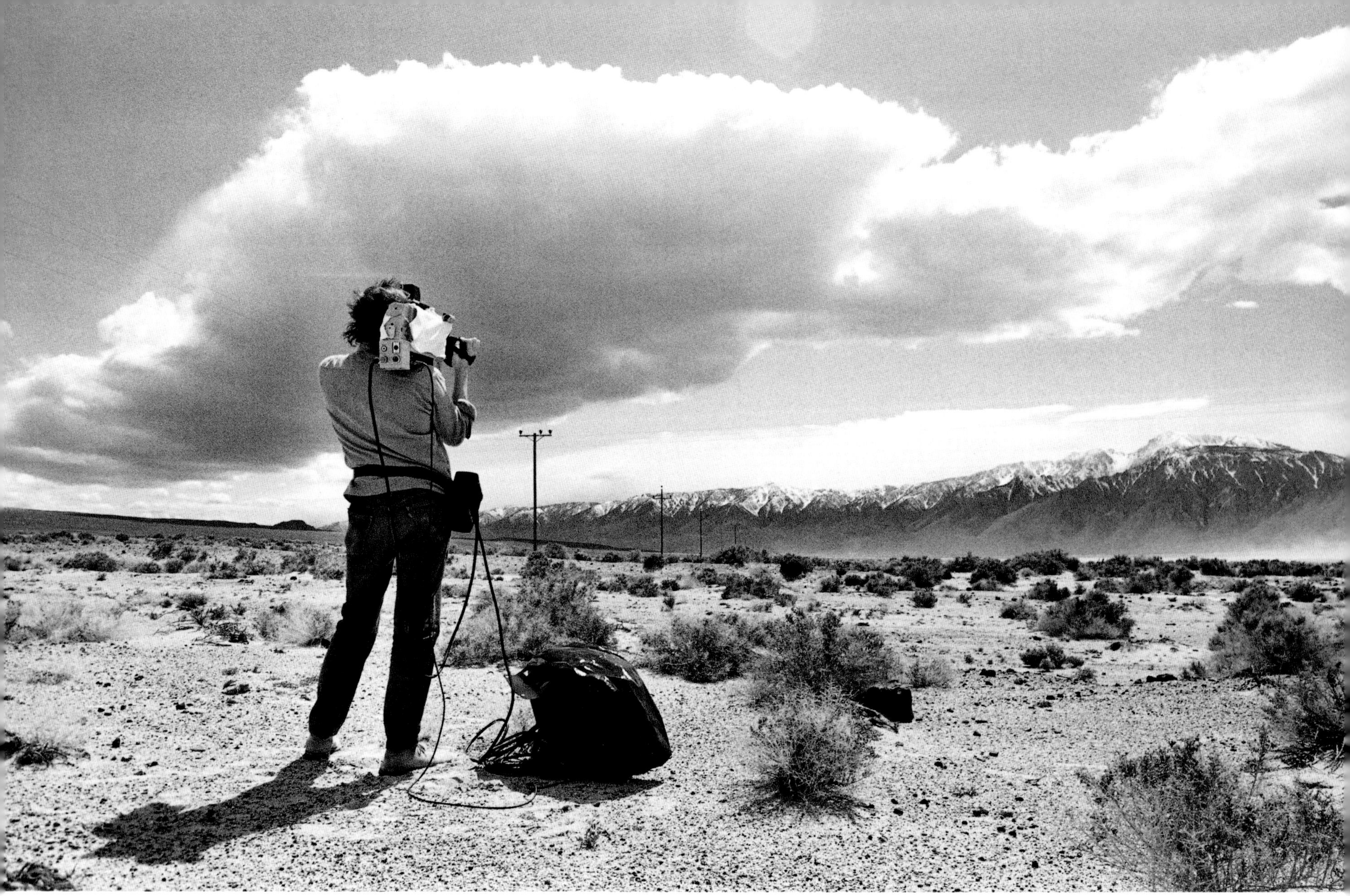

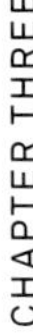

On location for *Room for St. John of the Cross*, recording Sierra Nevada mountains near Lone Pine, Owens Valley, CA, April 1983 (above); details of large screen projection (opposite)

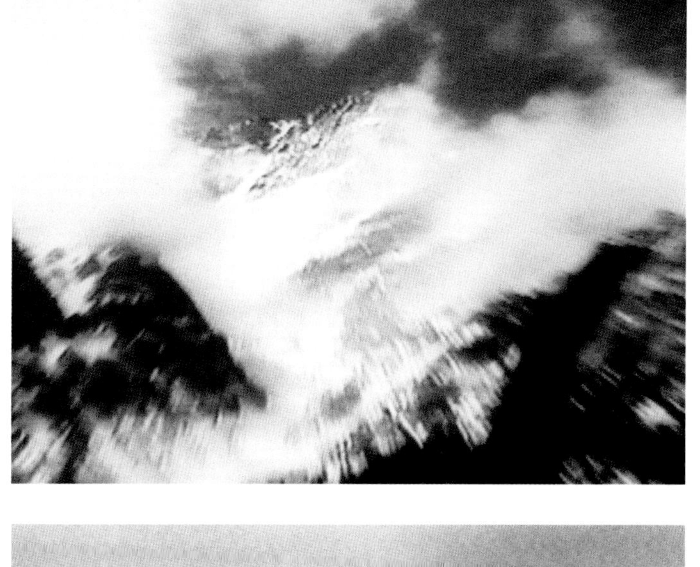

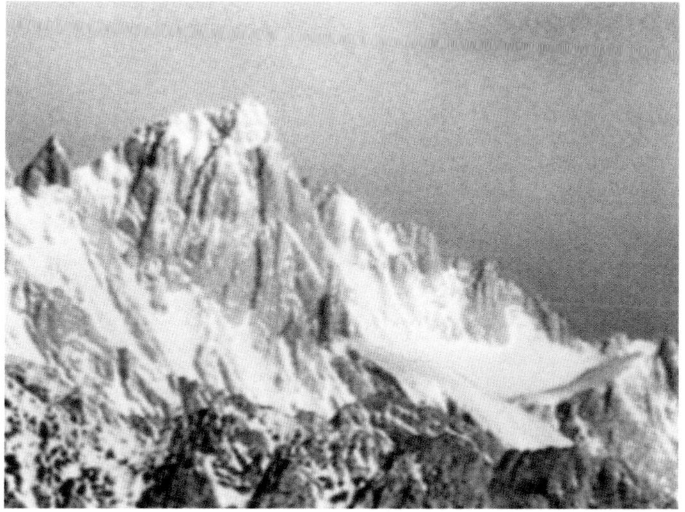

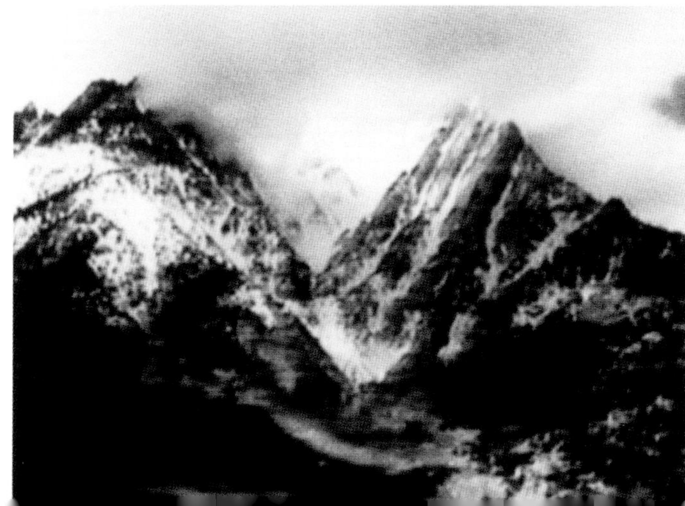

windows and he was unable to stand upright. He was frequently tortured. During this period, St. John wrote most of the poems for which he is known. They often speak of love, ecstasy, passage through the dark night, and flying over city walls and mountains.[9]

Viola's description reads like one of his videotapes, in which image and sound create a landscape of the imagination guided by the "disembodied consciousness of the camera." Here, it is the embodied consciousness of St. John, conveyed through his words, that speaks to the "passage through the dark night…and flying over city walls and mountains." Viola quotes from one of St. John's texts: "To come to the knowledge of all, desire the knowledge of nothing," an extract that speaks to an openness to experience, to drawing in the unknown, to capturing the sense of chance caught by the camera.[10]

Room for St. John of the Cross is laid out as a set of experiences that one can either discover or ignore. Moving through the space, the visitor is plunged into the tumult and noise of St. John of the Cross's world: "Why does the soul call the divine light that enlightens the soul and purges it of its ignorances a dark night? The answer to this is that for two reasons this divine wisdom is not only night and darkness, but also pain and torment. The first is because the divine wisdom is so high that it transcends the capacity of the soul, and therefore in that respect is darkness. The second reason is based on the meanness and impurity of the soul, and in that respect the divine wisdom is painful to it, afflictive, and also dark."[11] In the late 1560s St. John of the Cross met the Spanish mystic Teresa of Ávila and joined her reform movement. Teresa authored works that are central to Christian mysticism and wrote of the piercing, or "transverberation," of her heart, an experience that resonates with St. John of the Cross's words: "The pain and this bliss carried me out of myself, and I could never understand how it was. Oh, what a sight a wounded soul is—a soul, I mean, so conscious of it as to be able to say of itself that it is wounded for so good a cause!"[12] The mystics suggest that to experience the ecstatic opening of the soul to the purity of God and the transcendent pain is to experience the fullness of being in the light of God. These beliefs and texts strengthen Viola's sense that video offers us the means to open ourselves to the unimaginable. The mystics address, in abstract and incorporeal ways, the experience of divine pain felt not through torture but in contemplation of one's own flaws.

Viola's *Room for St. John of the Cross* offers a path by which to search for the ineffable through projections suggesting a churning consciousness and through words spoken in the restricted space of the cell. In the room we overhear the saint's words spoken in Spanish, barely audible and yet coming to terms with the violent eye of God looking for the soul to be cleansed of impurities. Viola brilliantly resists a reductive view of the mystics, instead

Bill Viola - Video/Sound Installation

WHITNEY BIENNIAL 1985

The Theater of Memory (1985)

A large tree with roots exposed and bare branches leans diagonally across the room from the near floor at the entrance to the far corner at the ceiling. One hundred small lanterns are hung on its branches, with a few strewn on the floor. Up on the rear wall is a large video projected image. The image is predominantly electronic noise and static patterns. Occassionally, recognizable images are seen trying to break through, but they never come in clearly. Bursts of static and noise come through the speakers, as if a loud clear sound was about to come on, but never does. There are long silences between the bursts of noise. The lanterns on the tree flicker as if short circuiting. The only light in the room comes from the lanterns and the glow of the video image. The only continuous sound in the room is that of a delicate wind chime on the tree being blown by a small fan out of the audience's view.

- (1) Color Video Projector
- (1) 3/4" Video Cassette Player
- (1) Stereo Sound System
- (1) Projection Screen
- (1) Small Electric Fan
- (100) Electric Lanterns
- (1) Wind Chime
- (1) 40 ft. dead tree

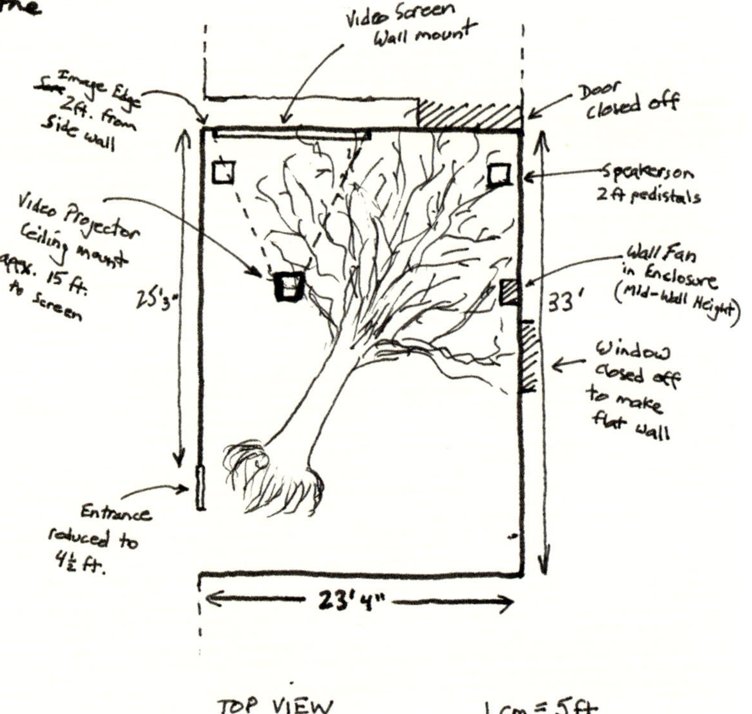

15' appx
1 ft
Image
Ceilings 14'4½" (?)
Speaker
33'

SIDE VIEW

Room will be painted flat black.

TOP VIEW

1 cm = 5 ft.

The Theater of Memory, proposal to the Whitney Museum of American Art, New York, NY, 1985

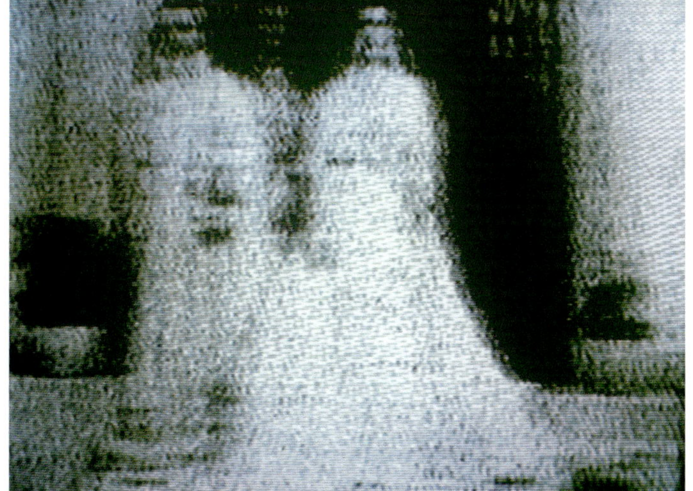

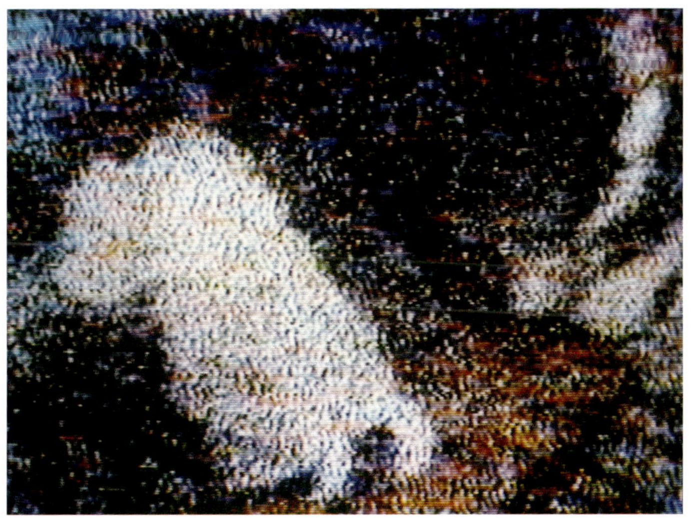

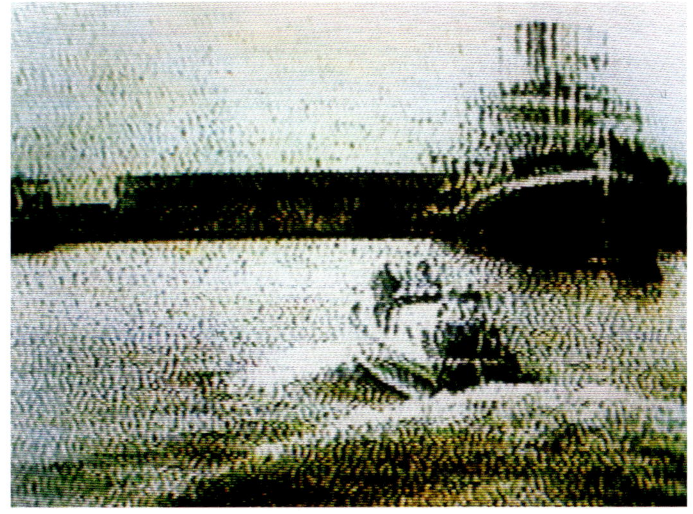

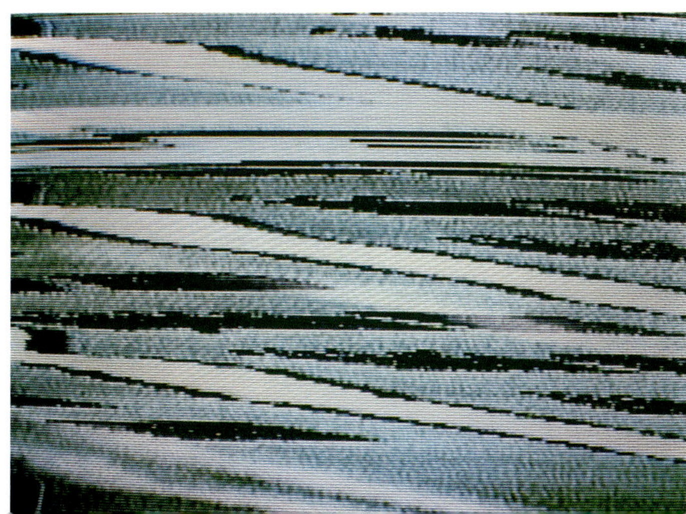

contextualizing their words within the world they occupy. He makes that world at once distant and present. Viola's interest in the mystics, Christian and Islamic, is evident throughout his work. As a MacArthur Fellow (1989–94) and a recipient of a Getty Research Institute Fellowship (1998), Viola met leading intellectuals and scholars who further inspired his creative exploration of diverse bodies of knowledge. Here, he pursues his intuitive and subtle reading of spiritual texts and images that he had begun in college. The visualization of historic ideas, from prehistoric cave paintings to medieval and Renaissance imagery and thought, speaks to the artist's desire to absorb and anchor the powerful intuition he feels and wishes to express through his art.

Room for St. John of the Cross becomes a means for Viola to explore, in a variety of new ways, the states of consciousness he is representing in his videotapes. *The Theater of Memory* is linked to both *Room for St. John of the Cross* and Viola's earlier and later work. With *The Theater of Memory*, Viola demonstrates a complex negotiation of a variety of issues surrounding video as an artist's medium, and displays his command of the installation, in his use of different materials to compose a whole experience. Once again, Viola creates something distinctly his own; he refuses to let the objects and images he brings together fall into an easy and reductive interpretation. I shall begin with the artist's own description of the installation, as it effectively lays out the key elements of the work and the issues it addresses:

A large tree leans diagonally across the room, its exposed roots at the floor near the entrance, and its bare branches stretching to the ceiling at the corner of the space. Fifty small electric lanterns are hung on its branches. Up on the rear wall is a large video-projected image. The picture is dominated by electronic noise and static patterns. Recognizable images are seen trying to break through, but they never come in clearly. Bursts of loud static noise come through the speakers, as if a loud clear sound were about to come on, but never does. There are long silences between the bursts of noise. The only light in the room comes from the flickering lanterns and violent flashing of the video image. The only continuous sound in the room is the delicate tone of a small wind chime hanging from a tree branch. There has been much speculation, scientific and philosophical, on the causes and processes of the triggering nerve firings in the brain that recreate patterns of past sensations, finally evoking a memory. Central to the brain's operation is the fact that all its neurons are physically disconnected from each other and begin and end in a tiny gap of empty space. The flickering pattern evoked by the tiny sparks of thought bridging these gaps becomes the actual form and substance of our ideas. All of our thoughts have at their center this small point of nothingness.[13]

The Theater of Memory (1985), details of large screen projection

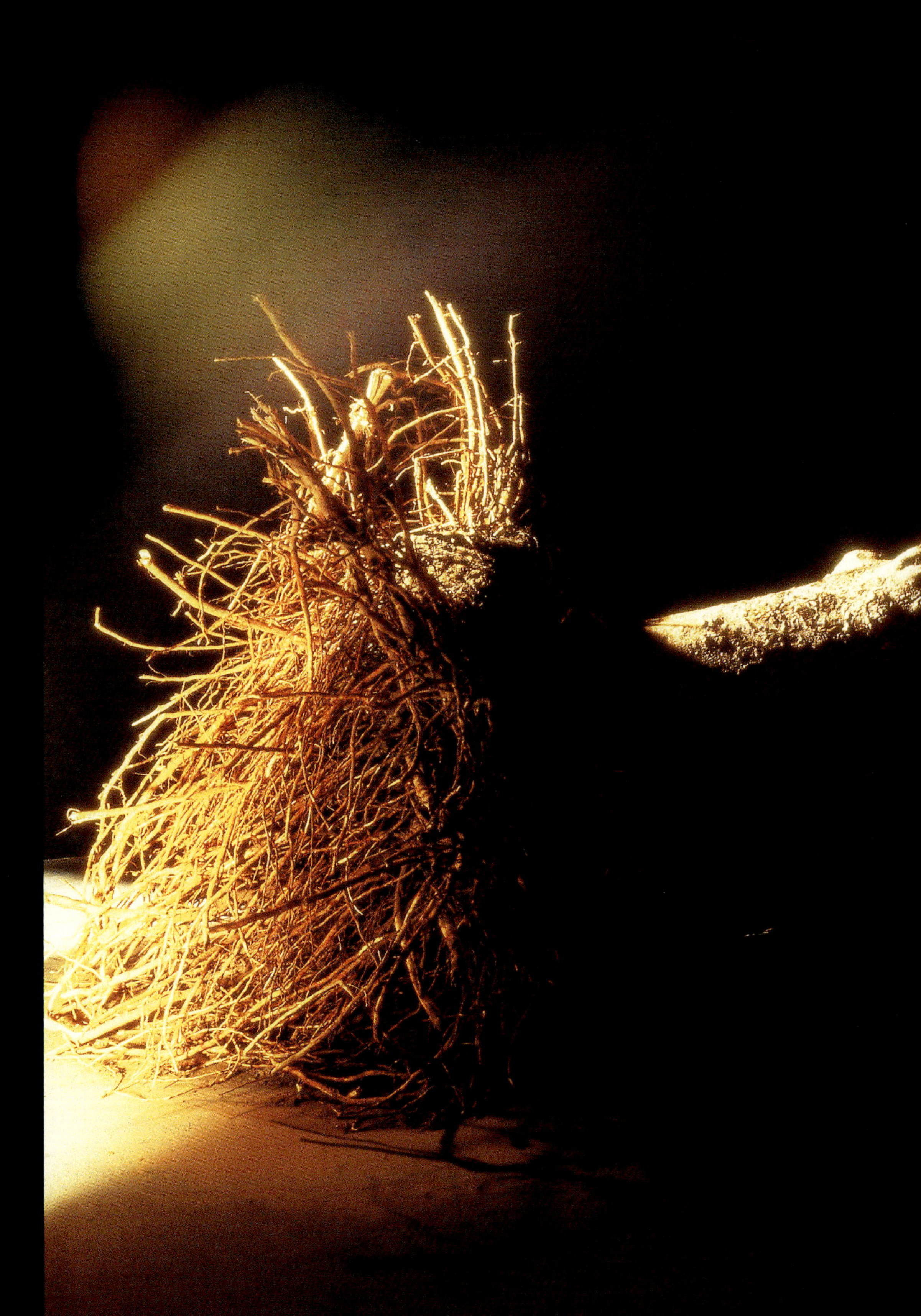

The Theater of Memory (1985)

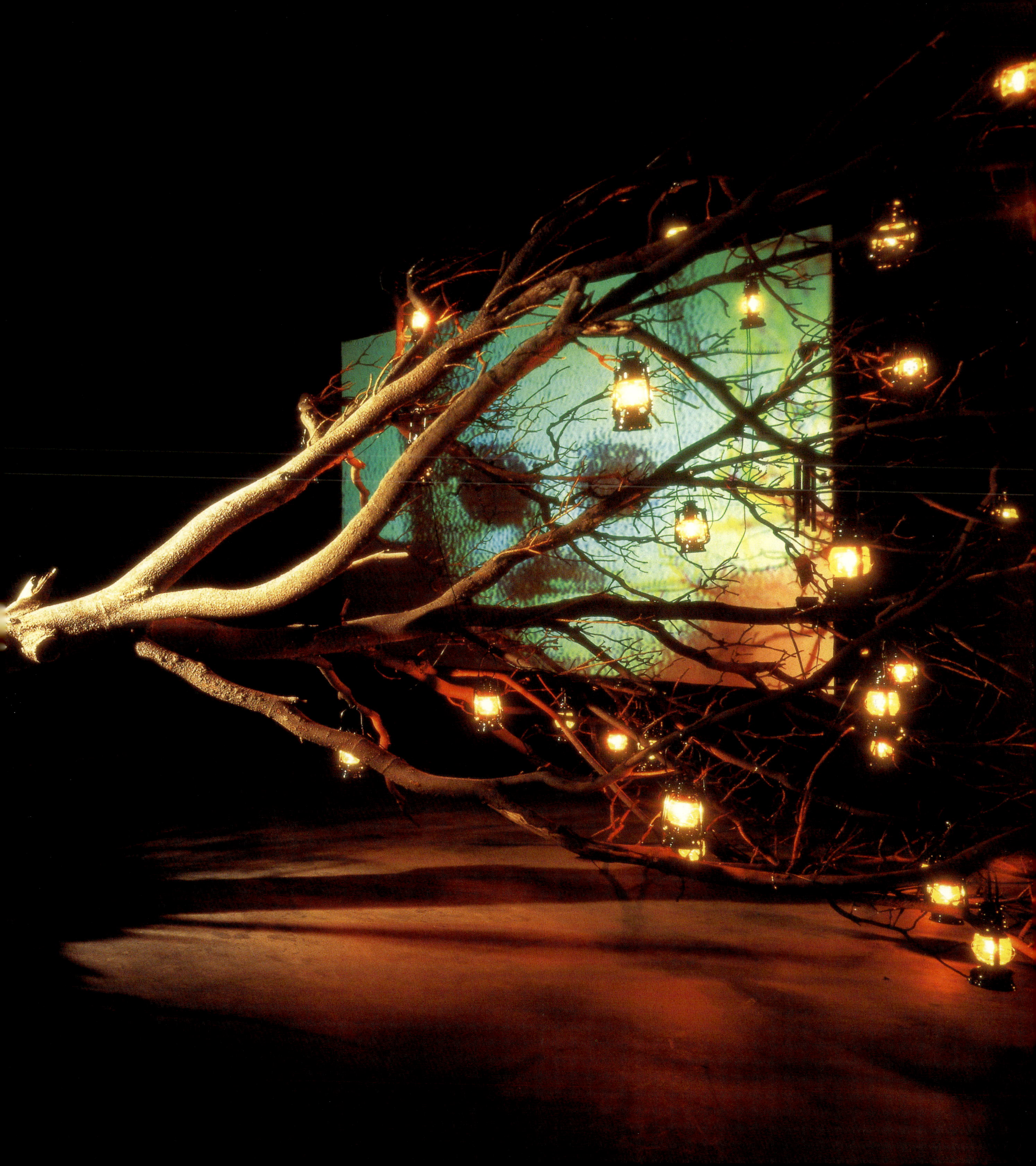

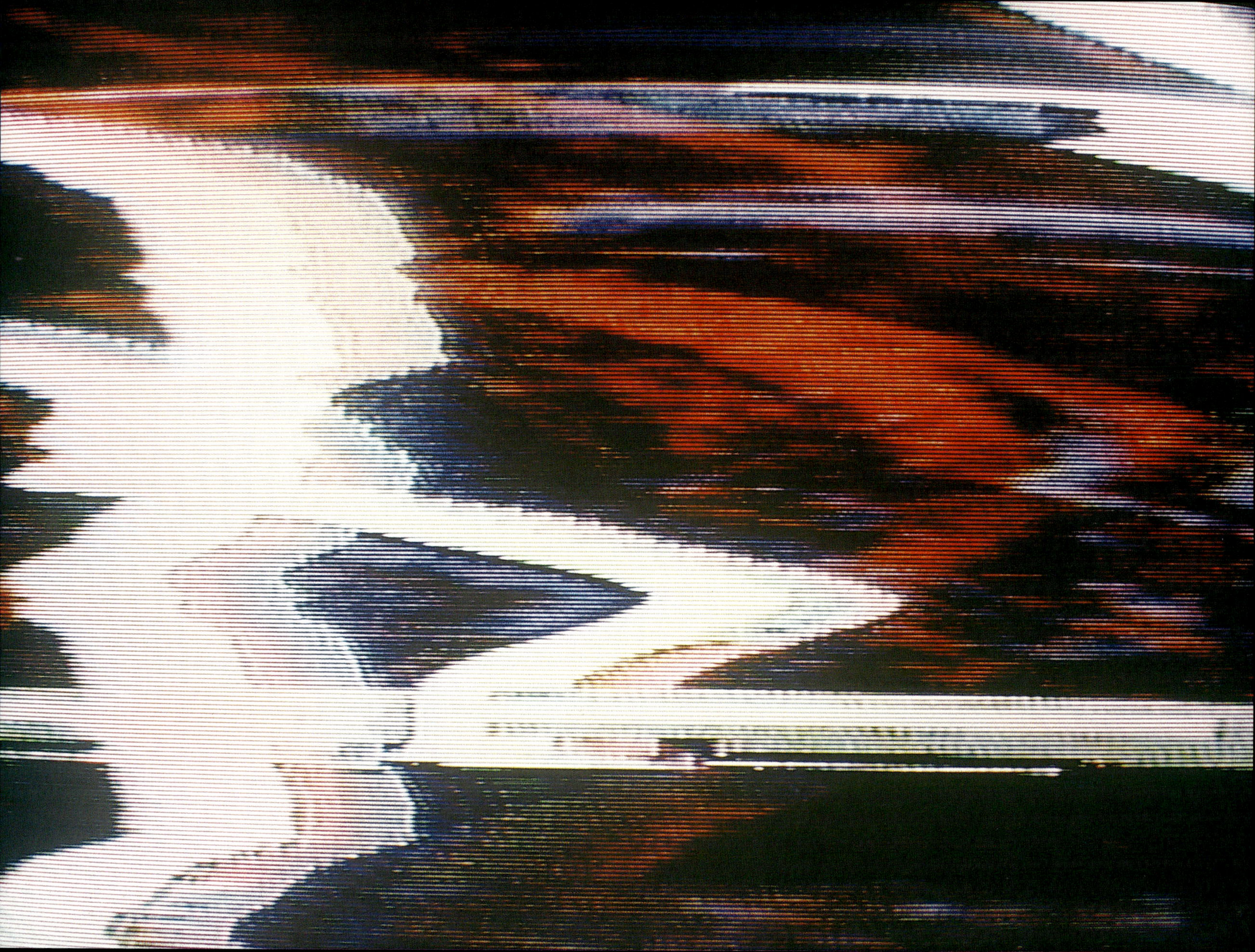

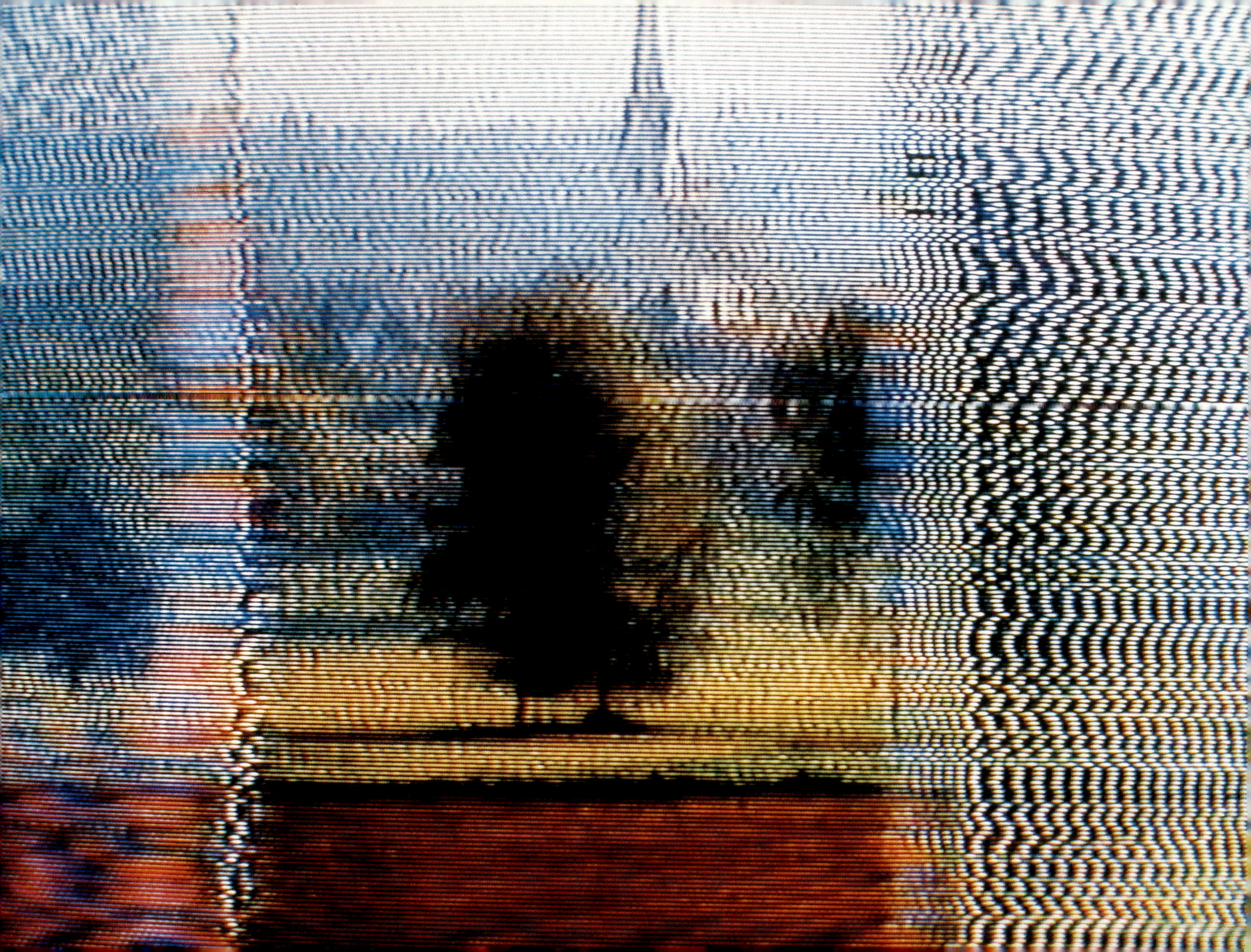

In advancing Viola's thinking about thought and memory, this fascinating text returns us to some of the cognitive issues discussed earlier. *The Theater of Memory* furthers Viola's desire to make ideas the basis of his aesthetic. Here, he is not drawing directly, or exclusively, on the visionary experiences of the mystics, as we saw in *Room for St. John of the Cross*. Rather, he is bringing nature to the fore with the uprooted tree, its roots and branches being a model for the brain, while the flickering lamps and the projection stand in for the synapses and the formation of images and thoughts through the workings of our cognitive instruments. The lamps also link the work to *Hatsu-Yume*, in particular the lights on the boats that trace their presence on the surface of the water.

I have special memories of *The Theater of Memory*, since I commissioned it as a curator for the Whitney Museum of American Art Biennial in 1985. Locating a suitable tree in New York City and getting it into the museum was something of a challenge; when the tree was brought into the building, it shattered the glass front doors. The presence of the tree in the gallery was vivid, and the projection was disturbing, as it broke the expected tranquility of the tree and returned viewers to the surprising nexus of the brain and a flickering perception. The video element of the work clearly recalls *Information* (1973) in the way it processes violent feedback and breaks down to build up an image. It also recalls *Instant Breakfast*, *Sweet Light*, and the "disembodied" camera of *Hatsu-Yume*, in which movement, sounds, and high- and low-end technology describe the uprooted self as it moves through the chaos of our modern world. The tension between the uprooted tree, the technology that flickers into presence and then disappears amid electronic noise, and the chimes all recall the stability of nature. It offers a meditation on the vulnerability of the environment in the unstable technological worlds we inhabit.

The imagery that Viola creates in his single-channel videotapes and installations is not an ironic construct. Rather, it is grounded in the belief that what we experience through the artwork gives us an insight into ourselves. The references to iconic artworks from history in such pieces as the works in the "Quintet" series (2000–2), as well as in such installations as *Going Forth By Day* (2002), are in service to Viola's belief in drawing on earlier notions of perspective and the representation of narrative and time. They allow the artist to open up a dialogue on experience in the present through the capacities of new media. This will become clearer in later works that feature staged narratives, such as *The Greeting* (1995) and *Going Forth By Day*. But there is no question that an important set of issues is beginning to coalesce with the creation of *The Theater of Memory* and *Room for St. John of the Cross*, preparing the way for Viola's break from the display of mystery, as seen in his earlier work, and his move toward the expression of emotion and a cognitive centering of human experience.

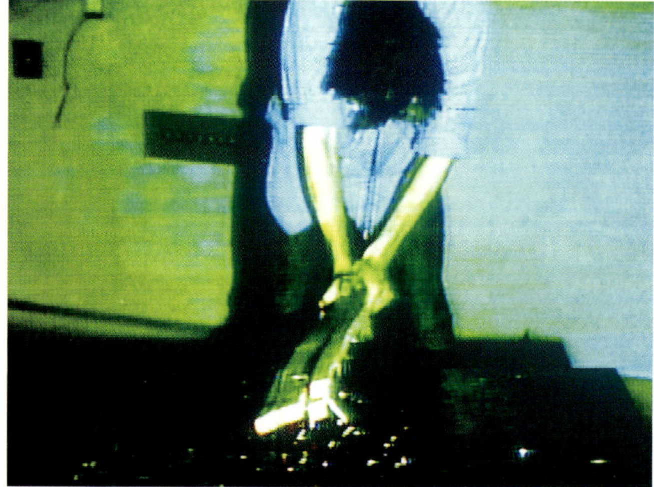

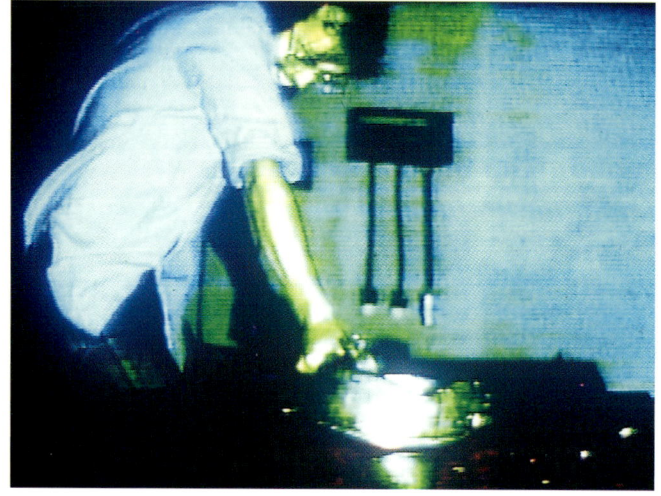

Above *Instant Breakfast* (1974)

Opposite *I Do Not Know What It Is I Am Like* (1986)

This break is signaled by *I Do Not Know What It Is I Am Like*, his epic videotape from 1986.

I Do Not Know forms a bridge between Viola's earlier pieces and the work that follows. Ambitious in scale and imagination, it stands as one of the most commanding artworks of the late twentieth century. In common with works from this period by other artists, such as Francesc Torres's *The Head of the Dragon* (1981), which links human aggression to deep-seated cognitive structures within the "reptilian" brain, Viola's piece, to use the artist's own words, is an "investigation of the inner states and connections to human consciousness we all carry within."[14] Viola acts as a witness to the world by creating a kind of grand encyclopedia of life and transcendence. He is a postmodern adventurer, tracing out the lineages of animal and human consciousness through direct observation.

Below is an extract from an extended piece of writing by Viola on *I Do Not Know What It Is I Am Like*:

In our horizontal models of time and movement, our image of the sediments of time, our expressions of "down" through history and "up" through evolution, the vertical pole becomes the continuous present, the connecting thread, the simultaneous, perpetual "now" that we are living at this instant and have always lived. It is the single point that, when displaced becomes the line, becomes the surface, becomes the solid forms of our world and minds, and that, without the imparted energy of movement (time) or the direction of movement (space), becomes the point once more, a process incremented by our breath as we each recapitulate its great form in the course of our individual journey.

As the gateway to the soul, the pupil of the eye has long been a powerful symbolic image and evocative physical object in the search for knowledge of the self. The color of the pupil is black. It is on this black that you see your self-image when you try to look closely into your own eye, or into the eye of another . . . the largeness of your own image preventing you an unobstructed view within. It is the source of the laughter that culminates the staring game that young children play, and the source of the pressure that a stranger feels on their back in public as they turn to meet the eyes they know are there. It is through this black that we confront the gaze of the animal, partly with fear, with curiosity, with familiarity, with mystery. We see ourselves in its eyes while sensing the irreconcilable otherness of an intelligence ordered around a world we can share in body but not in mind.[15]

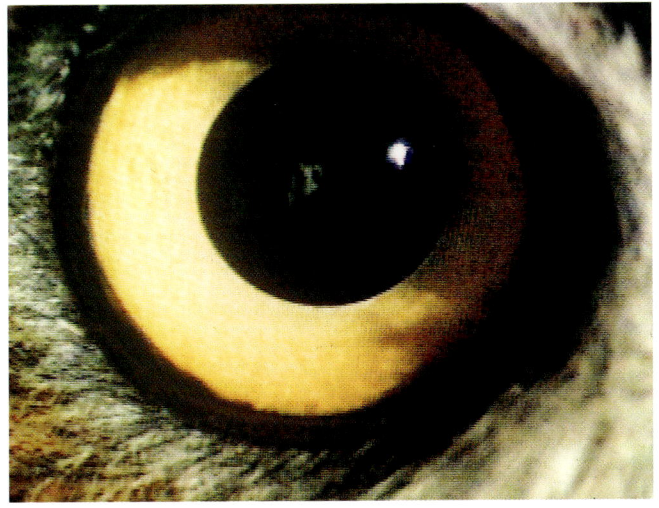

"Movement" and the "eye" are two key terms in Viola's text. They are central to the focus of the work itself: the phenomenological investigation of the axis of time and perception. They also shape what is a pivotal point

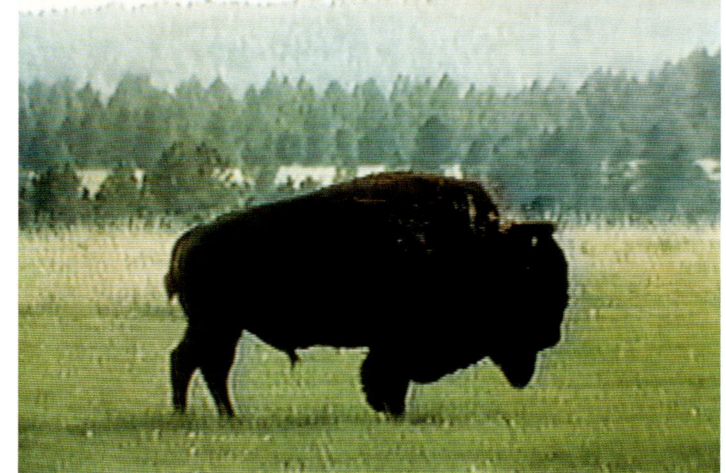

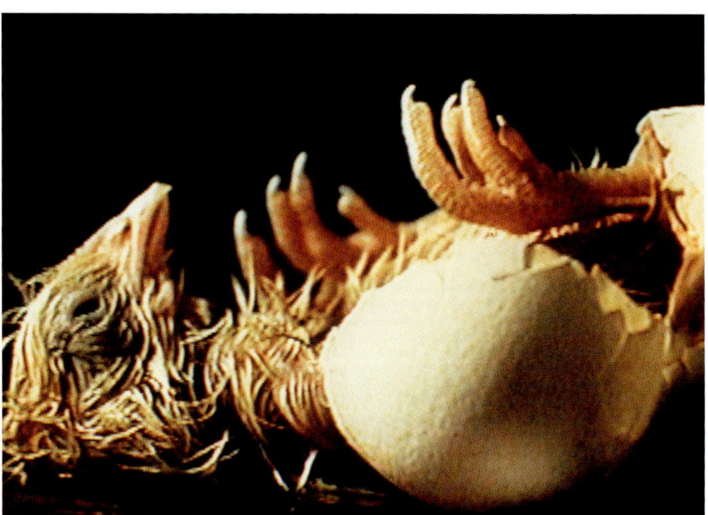

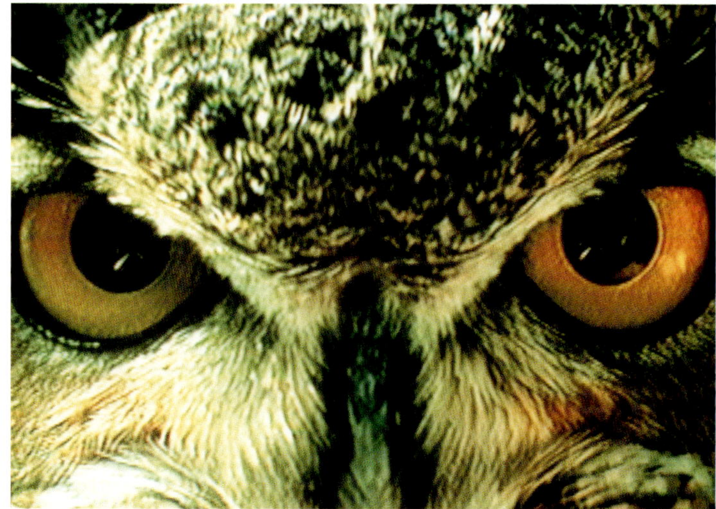

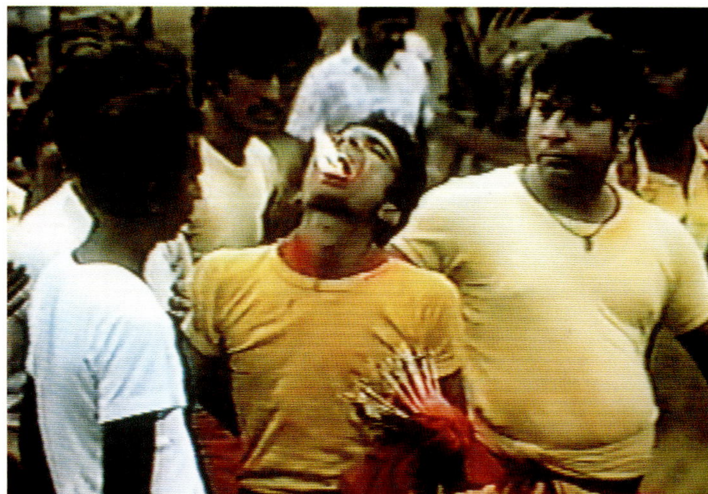

Grazing as Pure Meditation

Remember – my plan for living with grazing animals came from shooting the storms out on the Saskatchewan prairies.

Those cows and I sat there for 8 hours. They were much more at home than me. They just 'sat'. Pure meditation, prairie mind. at one with the landscape.

I desired to record this state of mind as the first idea to do the animal piece.

Above Note, Animals Sketchbook, 1986

Right and opposite *I Do Not Know What It Is I Am Like* (1986)

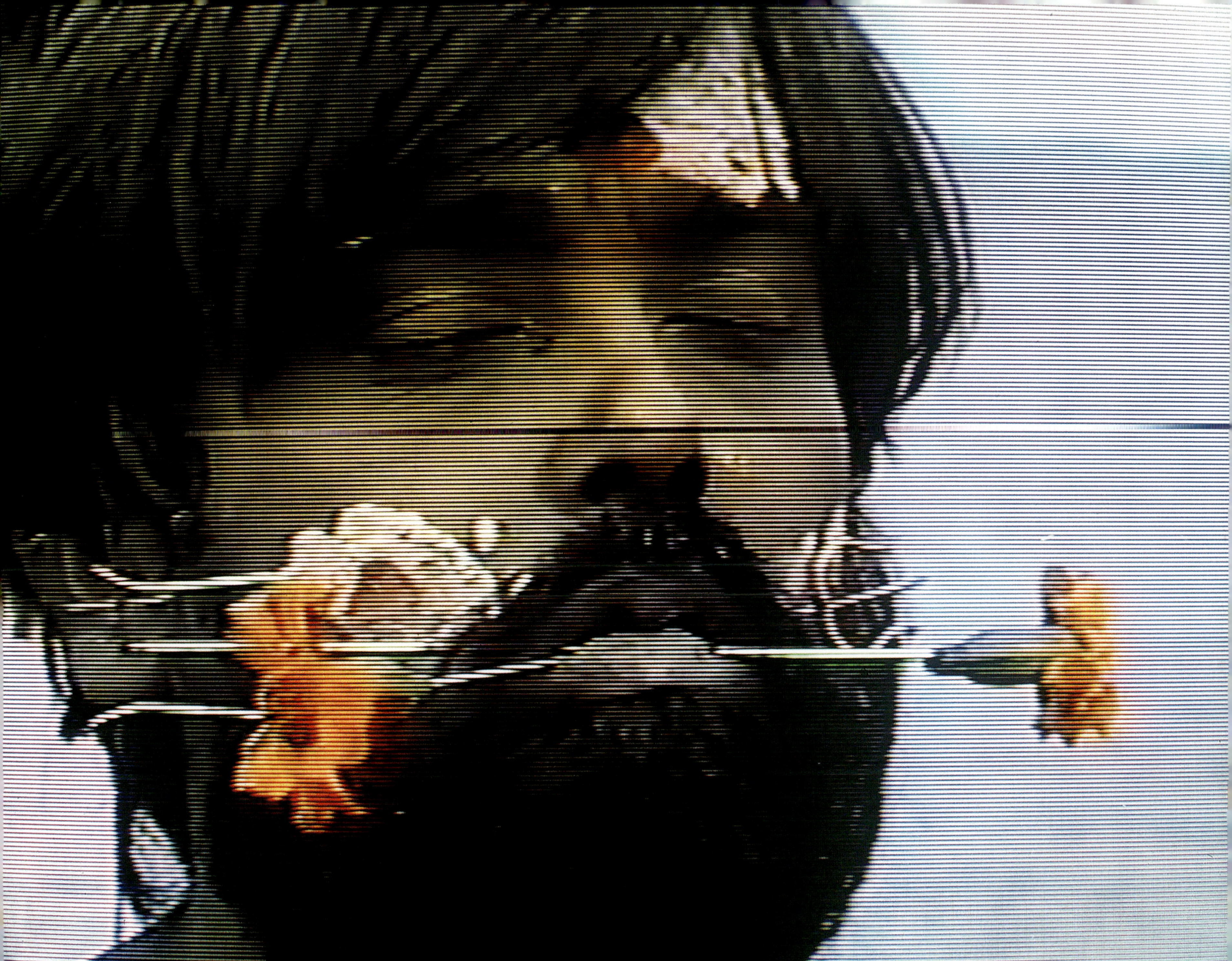

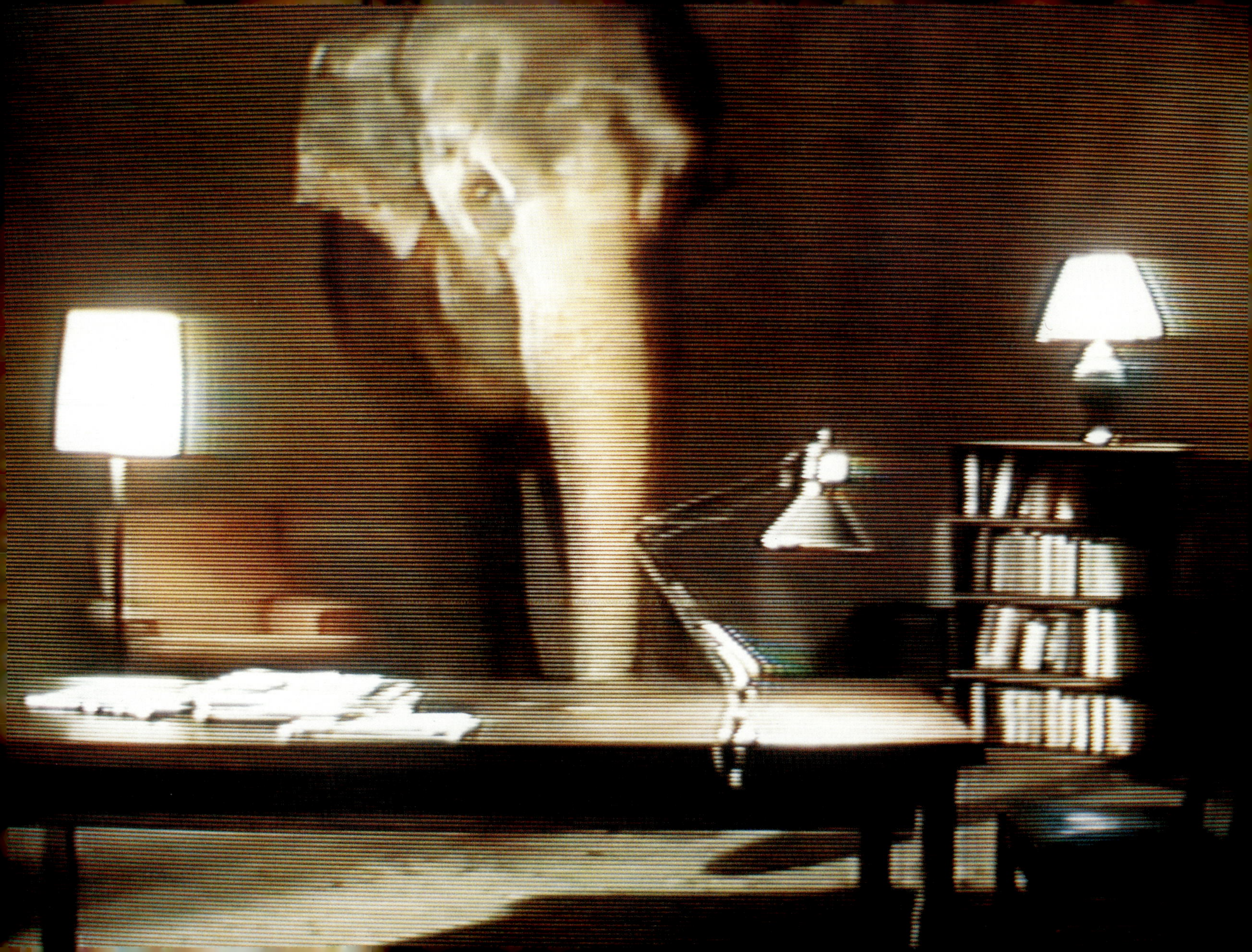

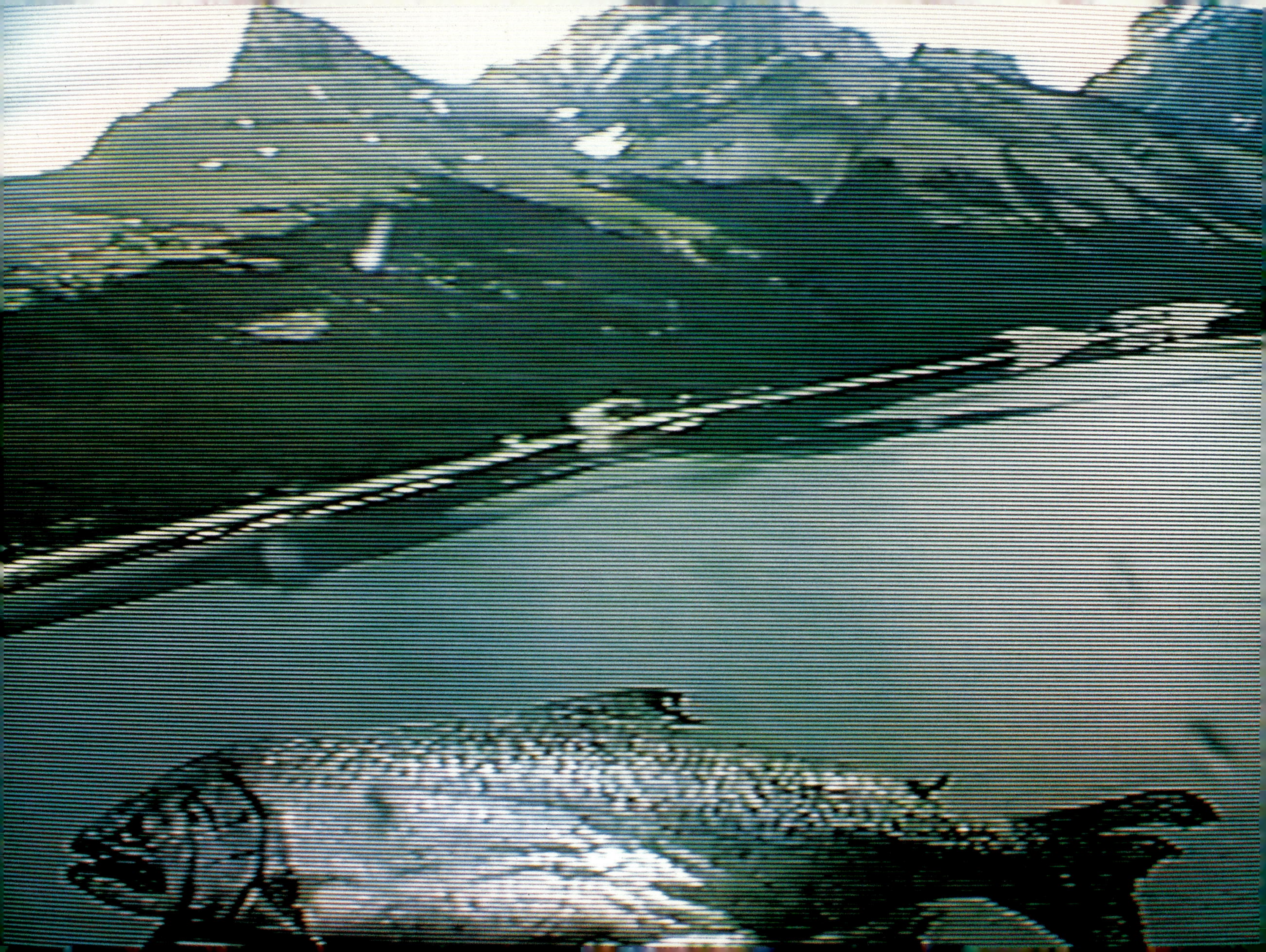

in the tape—namely, Viola's discovery through the telephoto lens attached to his video camera that he can see himself and his camera captured in the eye of an owl. This sequence was shot while Viola was an artist-in-residence at San Diego Zoo, and I remember him calling to tell me of his discovery. The apparatus of the camera and the animal's eye become one with the artist's eye. The movement of the zoom reveals the struggle and excitement of discovery, and can be found elsewhere in Viola's art. The equation of the eye with movement finds an epistemological balance as we watch the artist in real time explore through his camera and discover his reflection in the bird's eye. Created over a three-year period, *I Do Not Know What It Is I Am Like* even contains scenes that were recorded when Viola and Perov were living in Japan. Perov recalls the making of the work: "Our search for animal and human consciousness took us to, among other locations, South Dakota to observe bison, to Fiji to record the Hindu fire-walking ceremonies of the Tamil Indians, to various zoos and aquariums, and to Banff, Canada, to fly a large fish by helicopter over a glacial lake surrounded by snowy mountains, where we stayed a week to watch it decompose in the forest. The piece was originally called *Animal Consciousness*; Bill was of course including the human being in this working title."[16]

After the grand quest for knowledge and experience in *I Do Not Know What It Is I Am Like*, the presence of time and the everyday world are foregrounded in *Passage*, one of Viola's major installations. The temporal aspect of Viola's work has, as I have argued elsewhere, always been central to his aesthetic. In *Passage*, the way space is broken up is mirrored in the soundtrack, and the freezing of time as a phenomenal experience becomes key to what is a profound meditation on the medium of video. The work was commissioned by the Museum of Modern Art, New York, for Viola's one-artist exhibition there in 1987, organized by then associate curator Barbara London, a longtime supporter of the artist. Viola's description of the work begins with the technical details:

A narrow corridor 20 feet long leads to a small inner room. One large wall of this room is actually a rear-projection screen displaying a moving image, floor to ceiling, wall to wall, 18 feet wide by 12 feet high. A videotape of a four-year-old's birthday party is playing back at 1⁄16 normal speed. Sounds and images fill the room as the original 26-minute videotape now takes approximately seven hours to unfold, playing through once a day. The room's architecture places the viewer uncomfortably close to this large image, overwhelming in its scale. The original event becomes monumental, in time as well as space.[17]

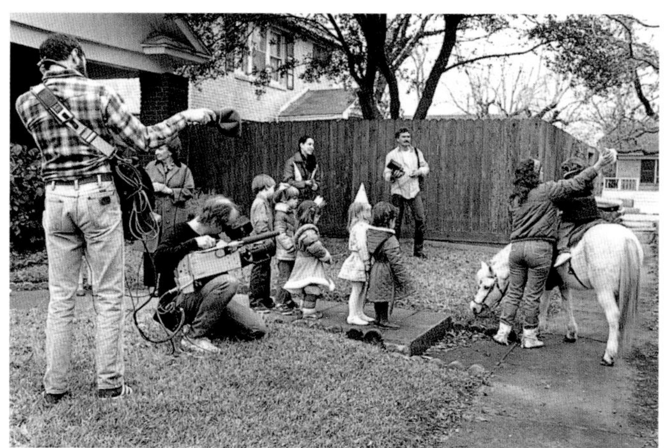

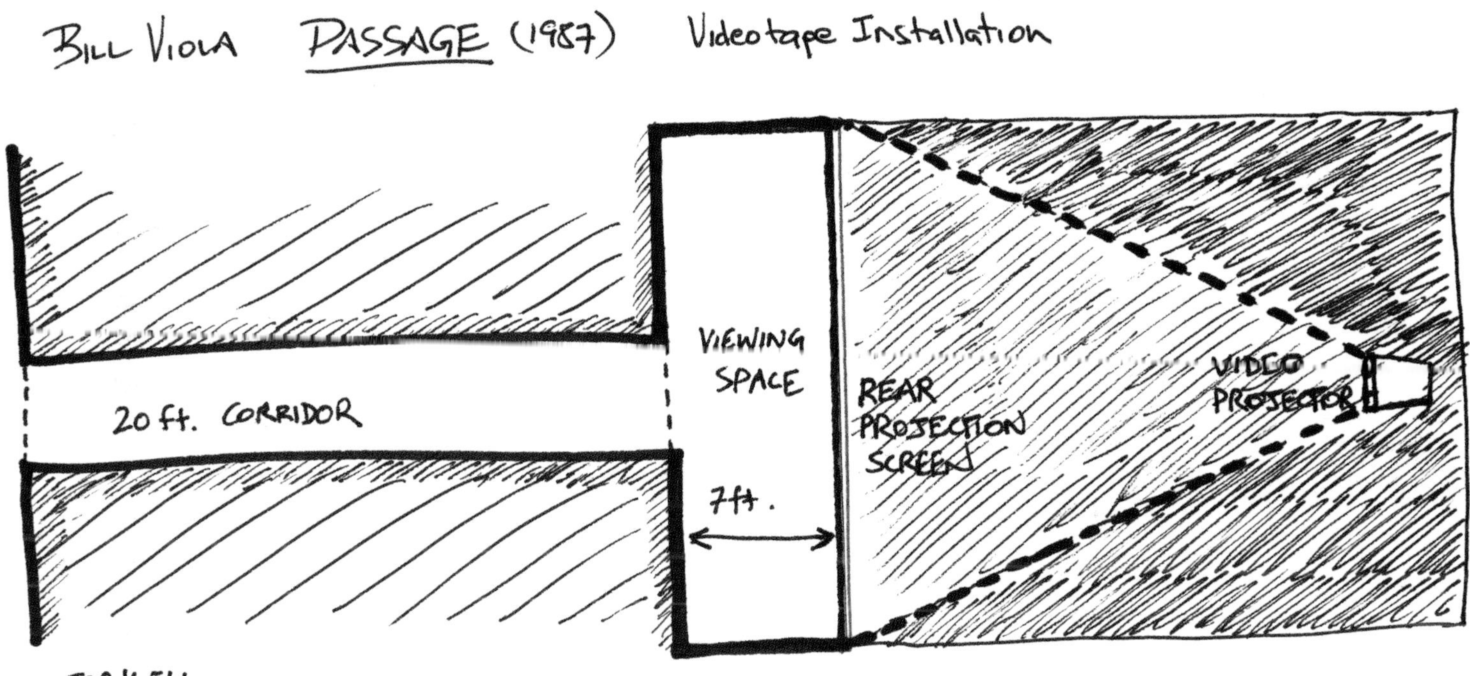

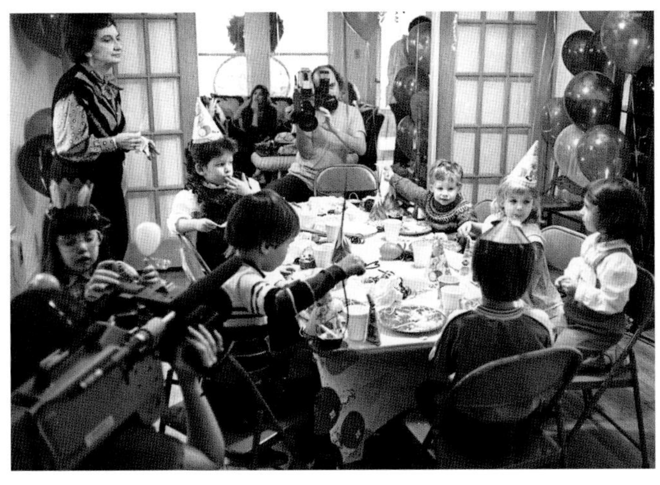

Opposite and above On location for *Passage*, private home, Houston, TX, February 21, 1987

Top Floor plan for *Passage*, 1987

Here, Viola focuses on the physical dimension of the installation, including the scale of the moving image, the distension of time, and the viewer's close proximity to the moving image. Viola's observation that the "original event becomes monumental, in time as well as space," is key to considering the impact of the piece. I remember visiting the work at its premiere, and the physical nature of the images was made more immersive with the slow unfolding of time and the almost claustrophobic intimacy engendered by the narrow passageway leading to the viewing area and the short distance inside the room from the huge screen. Viola reflects on the physical aspect of the installation as he describes the work as being

an architectural structure enclosing time. *Passage* is a hybrid between the forms of installation and single-channel videotape. The installation is constructed in the physical form of the archetypal emblem of transition and transformation, the tunnel or long narrow passageway, which ultimately refers to the original passage through the birth canal. The structure frames an image that transcends human scale in both time and space, placing it in the internal or subjective domain of memory and emotive association. The child's birthday party, a familiar rite of passage and a contemporary vestige of an ancient perennial ritual, retains some of its ritualistic and mythic stature through the manipulation of space and the extreme extension of time.[18]

Time becomes embodied in memory and ritual and what Viola calls "emotive association," the recall of our own everyday rituals through the performance of the child's birthday.

From my initial experience of viewing *Passage*, I also recall how immediate and present the video images were. Perov remembers the first time they turned on the installation:

The images were gorgeous, they were slowed down to single frames and we could see every one of them in the 7½ hour period as they stepped one after another. They each resembled giant paintings evolving from one frame to the next, and since the camera movements of the shoot are quite wild and fast with many zooms, the paintings smeared in slow motion and then came into focus as the camera stops briefly on a cake, a child, or the close-up of a face. Emotions are extended until we can't stand to look at them any longer: the delight of the candles, a happy pony ride, the blowing of the party horns. The sound is also stretched like the images, and bellows deeply in long slow tones, creating a score for this dreamlike otherworldly experience. The piece was like a series of frescoes. I was pregnant with our first child and I felt his first movements in response to the deep sound.[19]

Throughout his career, Viola has deftly ignored the postmodern tactic of appropriation while grounding his self-reflective strategies in nature, looking outward toward the past and following the silent passage of time, as we have seen in *I Do Not Know What It Is I Am Like*.

From the archetypal interior space of *Passage*, we move to an installation that explores the unconscious of dreams. *The Sleep of Reason* is one of Viola's most dramatic pieces. It employs a computer-controlled self-generating system that determines the timing of the projection of the moving images. The explosive narrative engulfs the viewer and brings to the fore the nightmare worlds we sometimes pass through during sleep. The work was inspired by Goya's etching *The Sleep of Reason Produces Monsters*

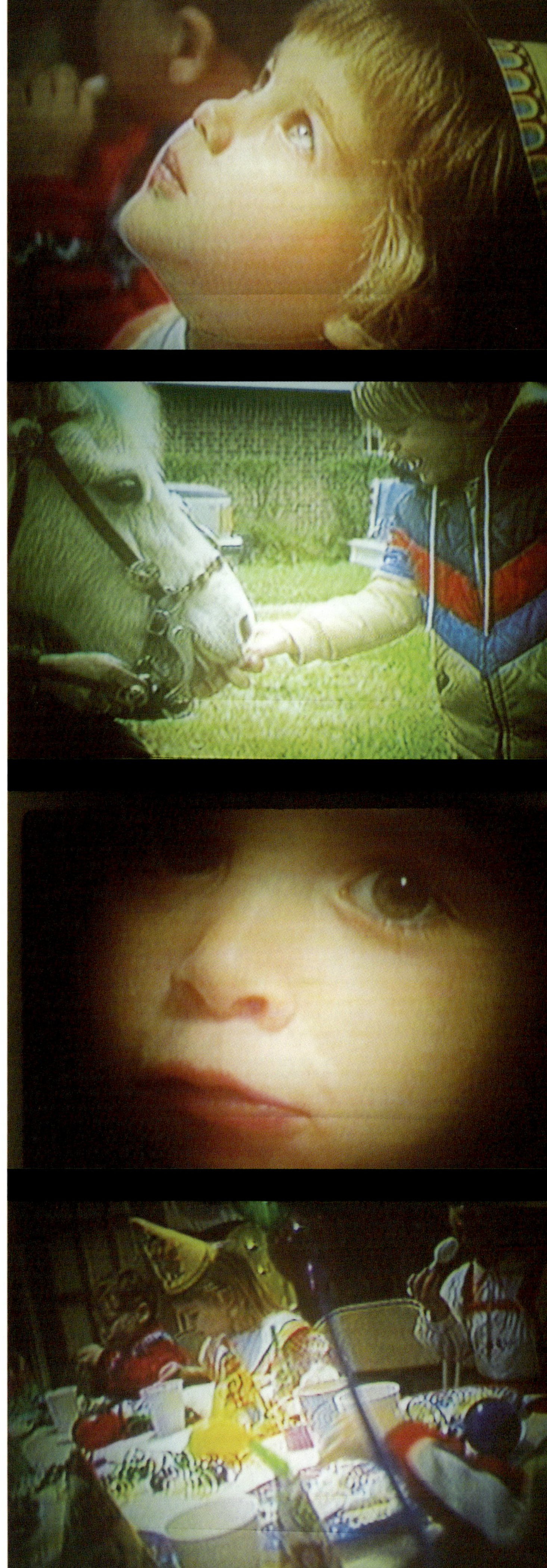

Right, opposite, and following two pages *Passage* (1987)

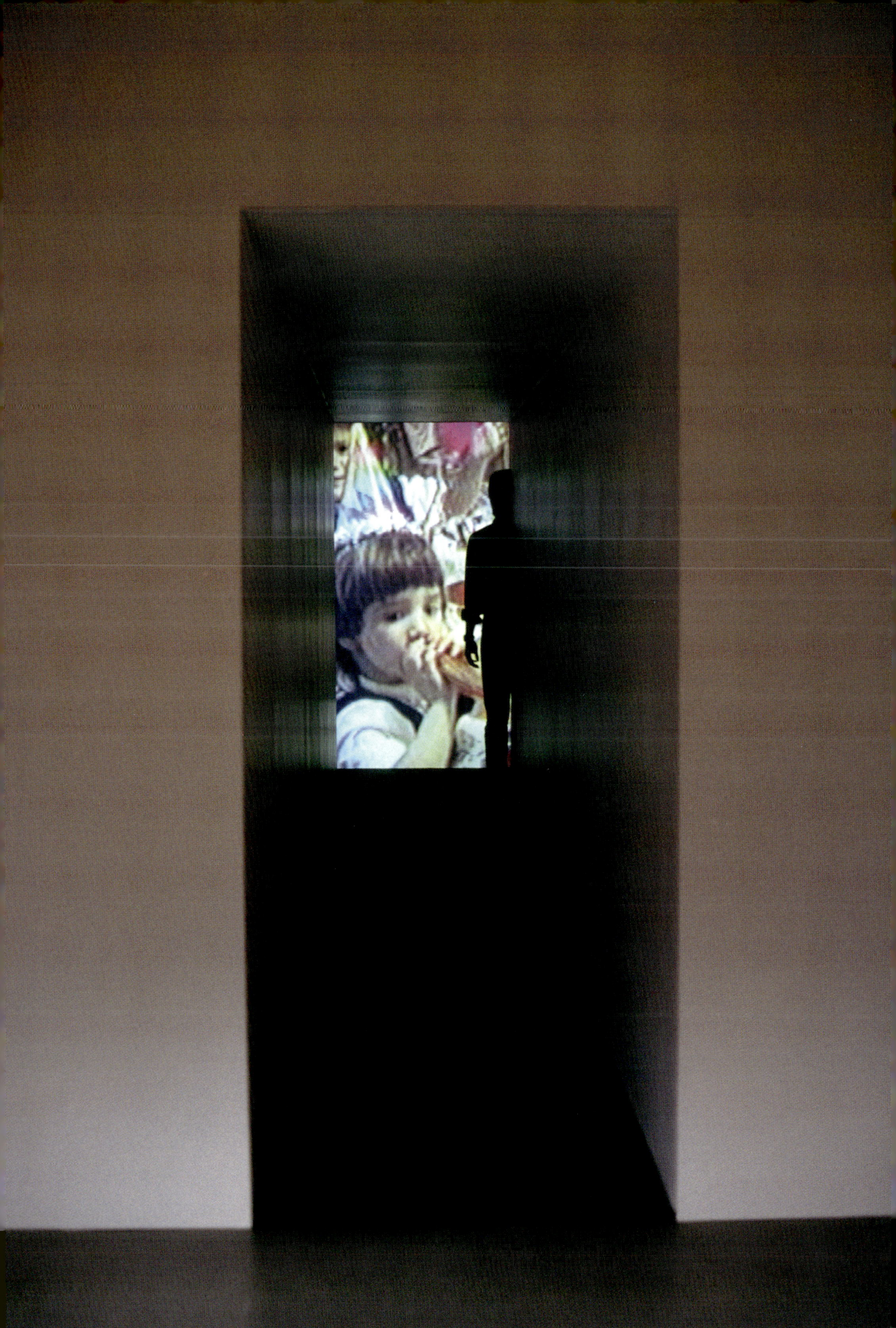

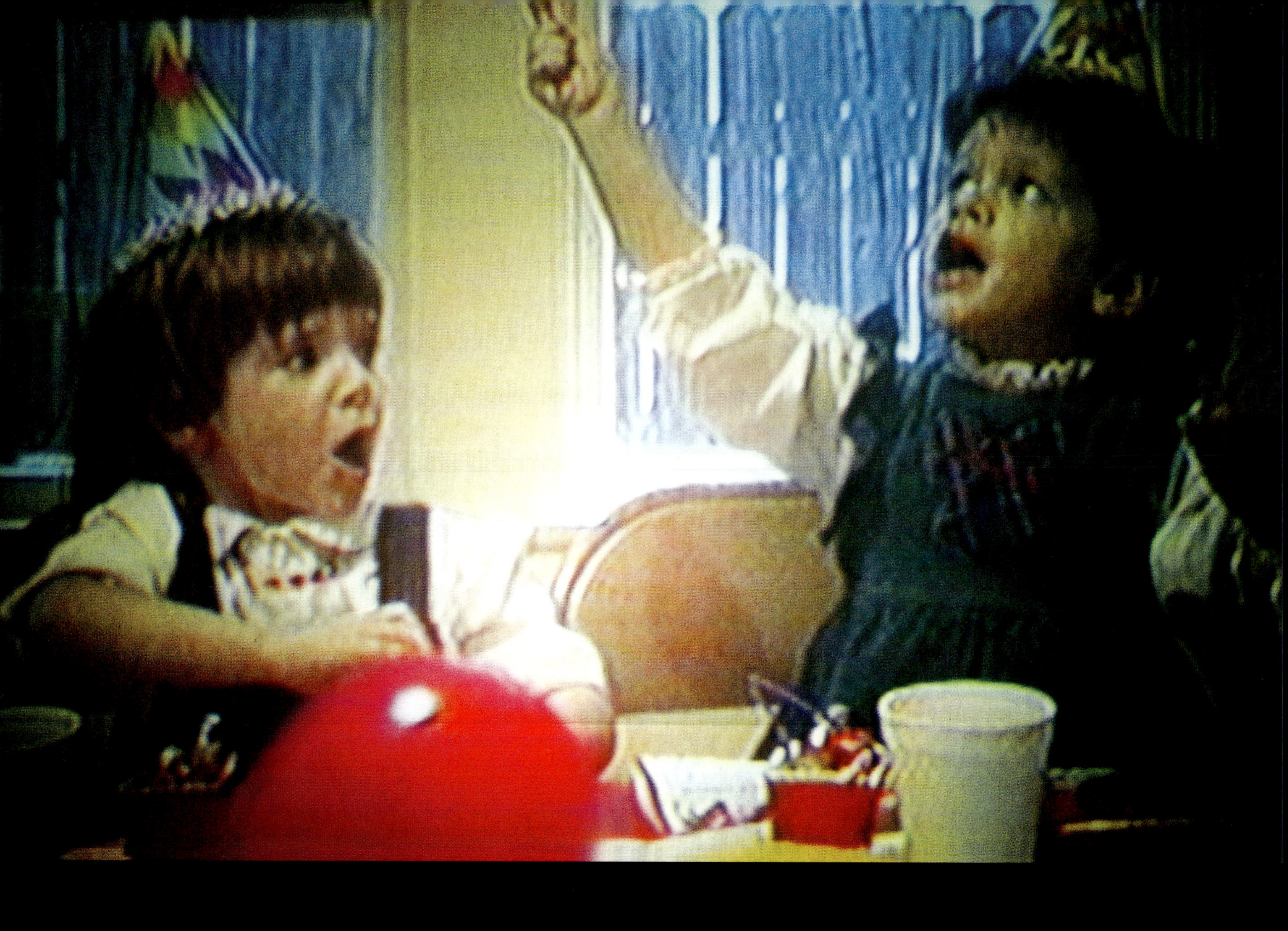

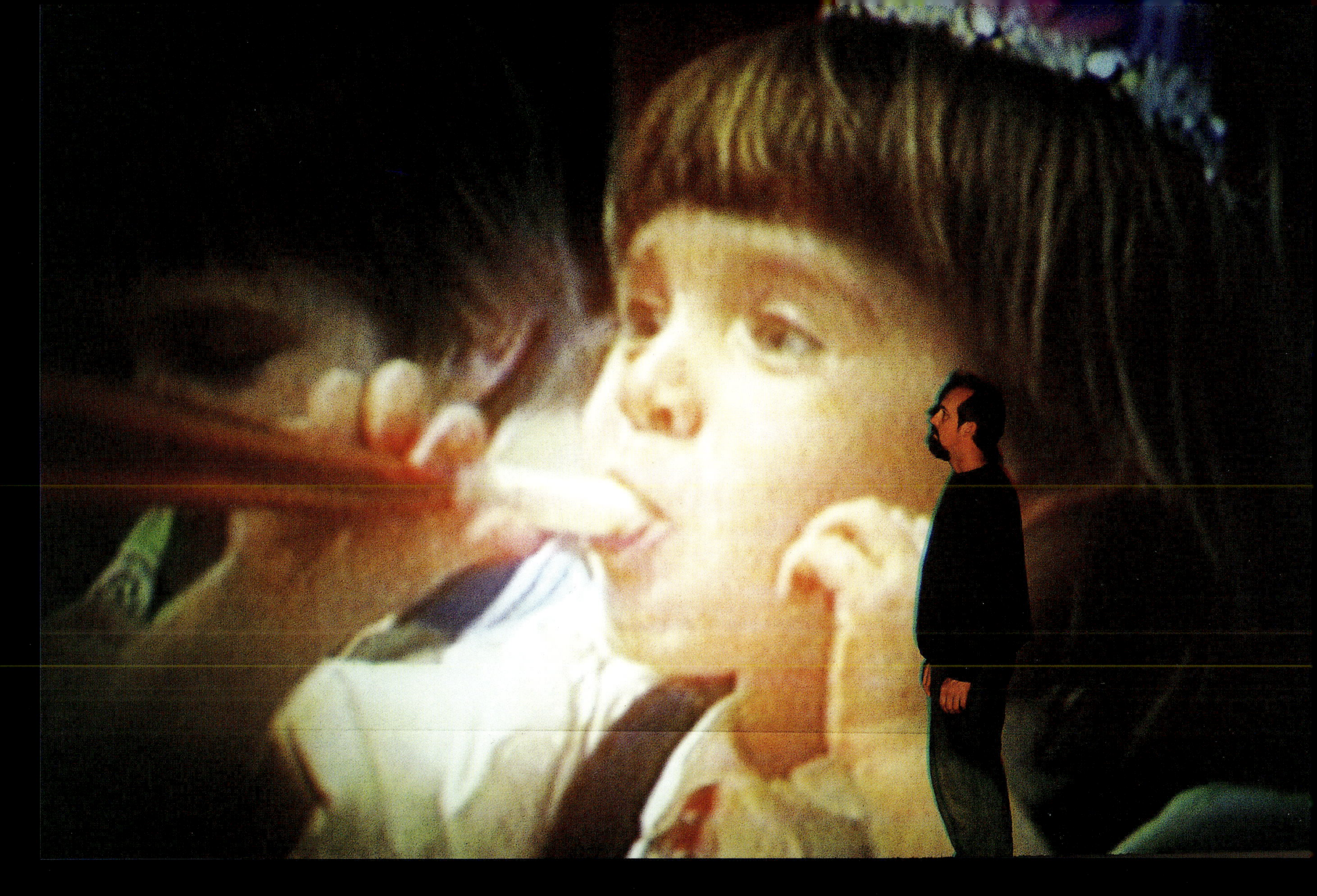

(1799), one of the artist's most biting criticisms of what he perceived as the corrupt and demented Spanish society of the time. The etching portrays bats and owls threatening a person while he sleeps. Viola's *The Sleep of Reason*, to quote his own description of the work, consists of

a wooden chest in an empty room, [on which] a black-and-white monitor shows a close-up of a person sleeping. The sleeper's night sounds are heard softly. A vase with white roses, a small lamp, and a digital clock are also on the chest top. The floor of the room is carpeted and the space illuminated. Suddenly, the lights cut out and the room is plunged into total darkness. Large color moving images are seen covering three of the walls, and a loud disturbing sound of moaning and roaring fills the space. Just as suddenly, the images vanish, the lights come back on, and the room returns to normal. It is as if a momentary glimpse of another, parallel world has appeared, the dark underside of a familiar well-lit environment. The blackouts occur at random periods, behaving like unpredictable "image seizures" from some incurable schizophrenic affliction of the room. Present for only a few seconds, they can reoccur anywhere from less than one second to several minutes later, impossible to anticipate. The three projections of imagery on the wall are from a single videotape. Images include fire burning out of control through city buildings, fierce attack dogs lunging at the camera, wild movement through a forest at night, moving X-rays of human beings and animals, and a provoked owl flying into the night.[20]

For me, the projections in *The Sleep of Reason*, as described here by Viola, are representations of the dream state. As Freud notes in *On Dreams* (1901), "The manifest content of dreams consists for the most part in pictorial situations"[21]—in other words, a visualization of the nightmares that inhabit our sleep. The neurological processes bring to the surface both real and imagined combinations of scenes drawn from deep in our past or our anxiety about the future. Some of the sequences in the installation are taken from *I Do Not Know What It Is I Am Like*, Viola's epic catalogue of perceptual experiences and representations of states of mind. *The Sleep of Reason* functions as a set describing the elements of a domestic scene. We step into the sleeping person's mind and are bombarded by his thoughts. Viola's diagnosis of the installation as representing "image seizures" from an "affliction of the room" traps both the sleeper and the viewer in a space that is "schizophrenic," breaking down into random images of aggression and violence. Viola's analysis suggests that the built space, the corridors and passageways we move through, are alive and potentially disturbing. It speaks to an anxiety about where to mark the point of separation between our own emotions and those of others. *The Sleep of Reason* is in keeping

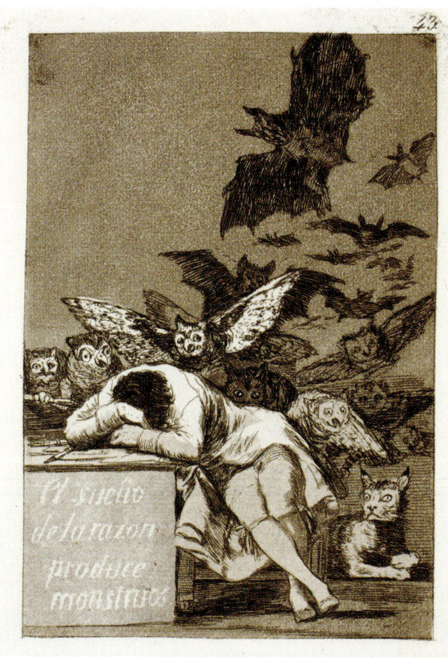

Above Francisco de Goya y Lucientes, *The Sleep of Reason Produces Monsters* (1799)

Opposite *The Sleep of Reason* (1988)

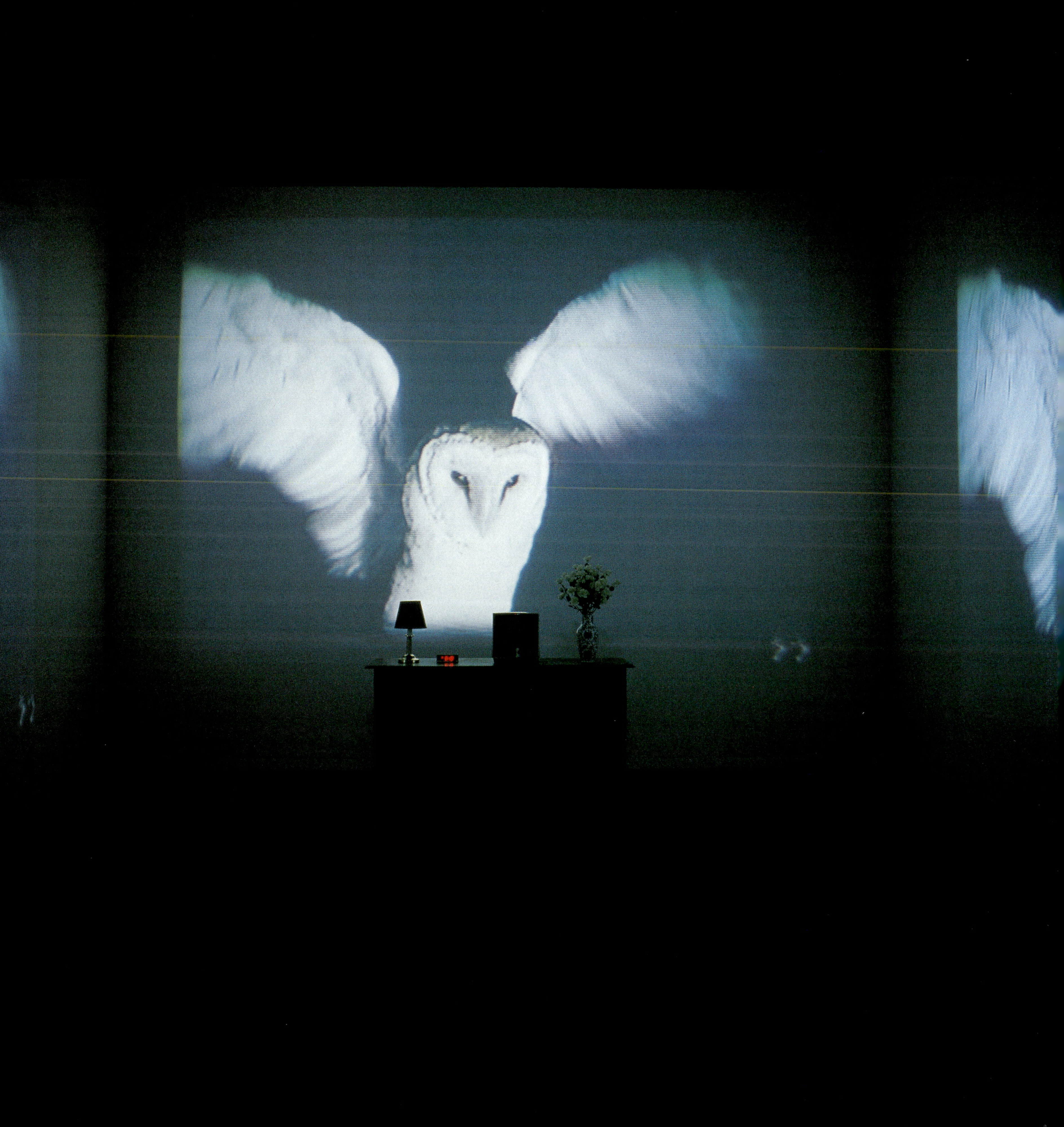

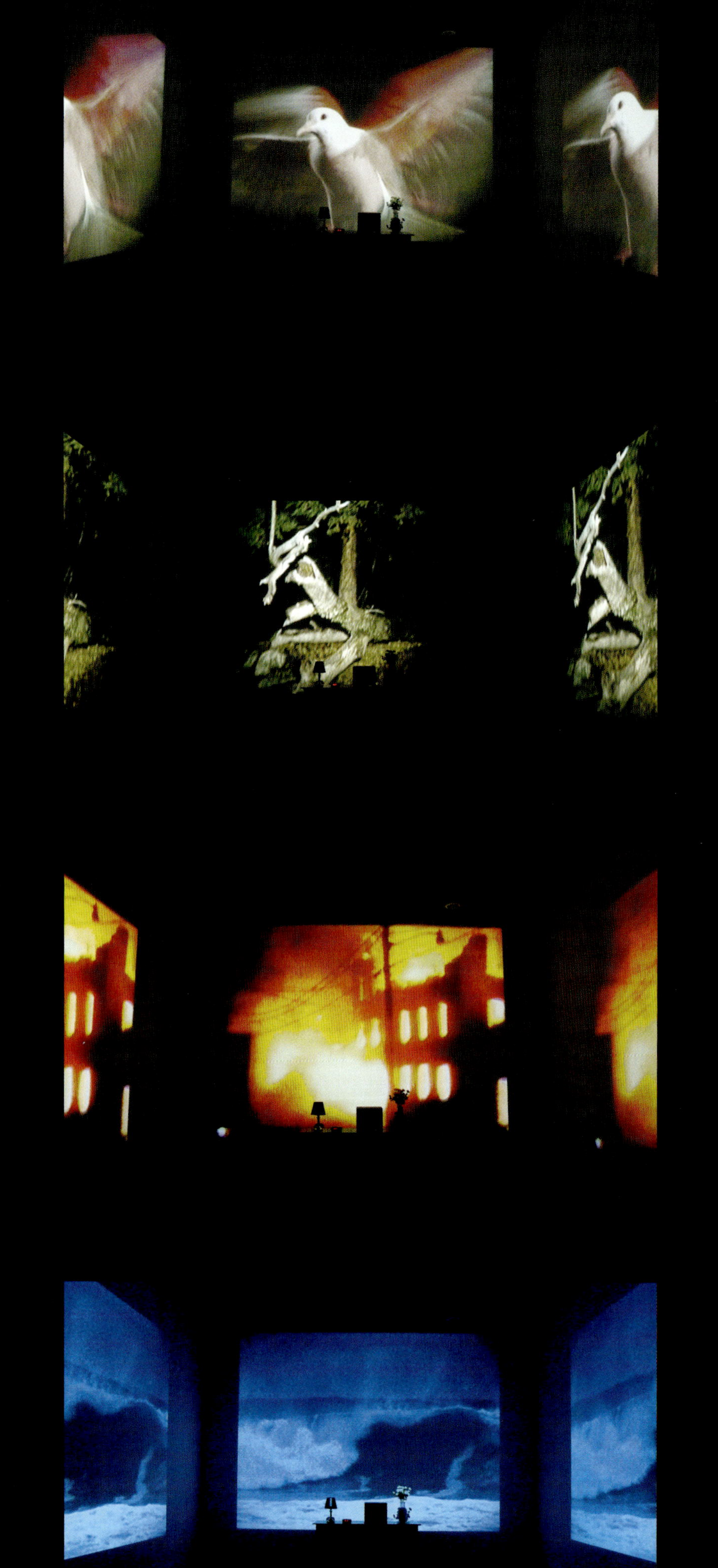

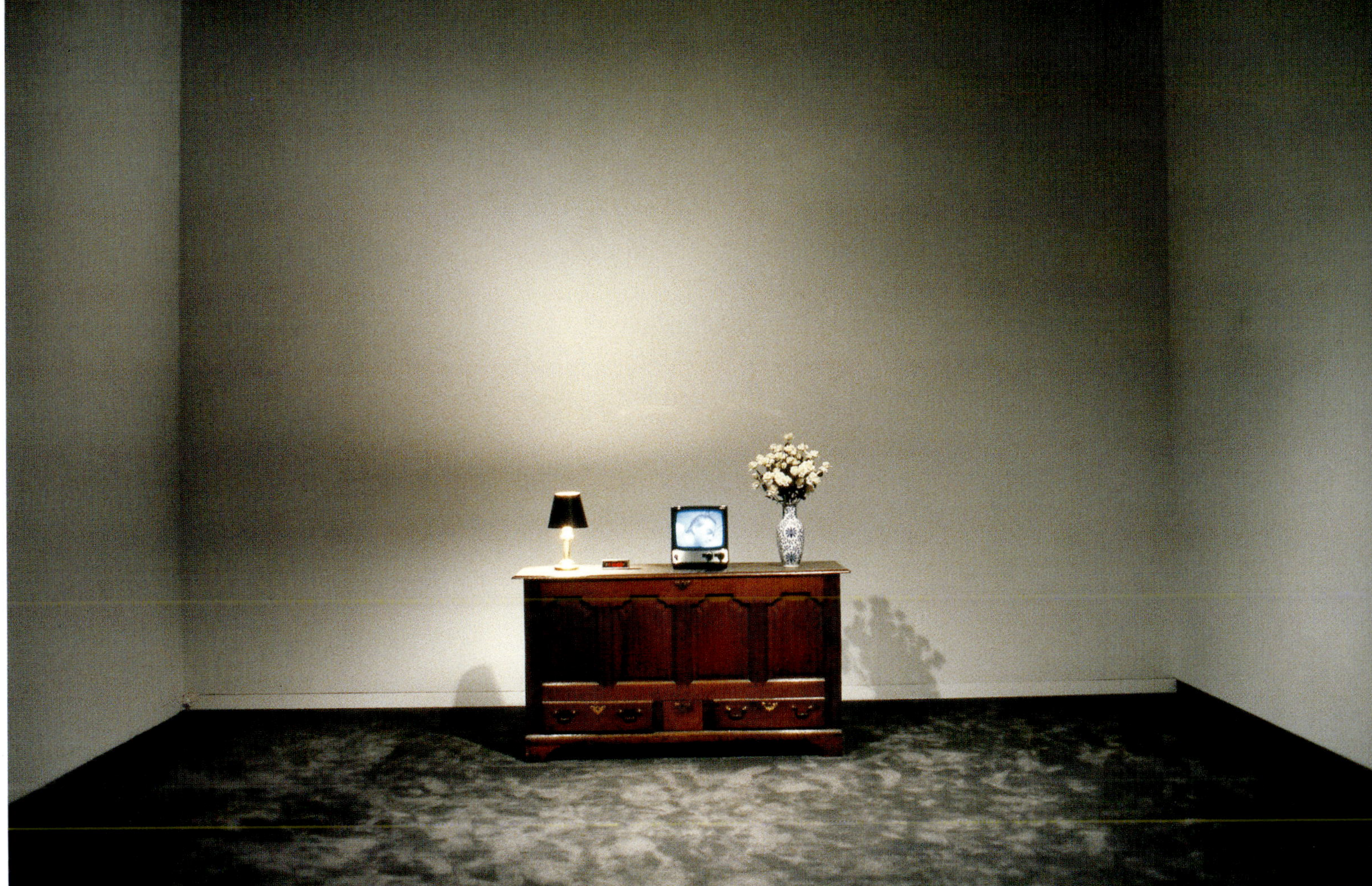

with Viola's other work in using the event, the single-channel videotape or the installation, to capture and foreground our world. The entire space becomes the interior of Viola's imagery, and we cannot escape what he sees and records.

An ethical dimension to Viola's art follows upon his earlier treatments of sensory phenomenon and human consciousness. The virtues of spiritual and moral balance come to dominate his later work. But his work from the first half of the 1990s explores the body and opens up the installations as a means to expand our perception and our understanding of the medium.

The Sleep of Reason (1988)

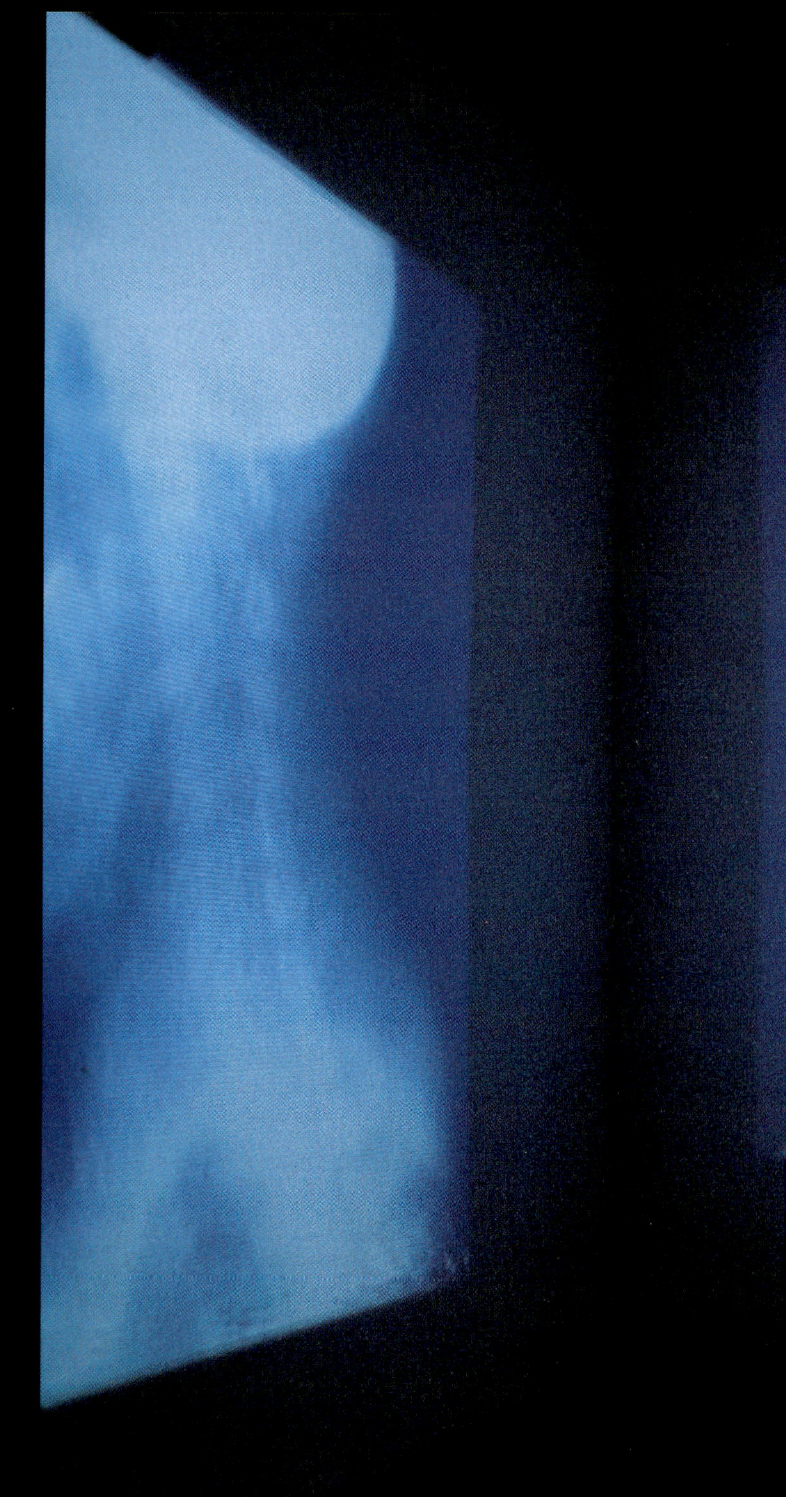

The Sleep of Reason (1988)

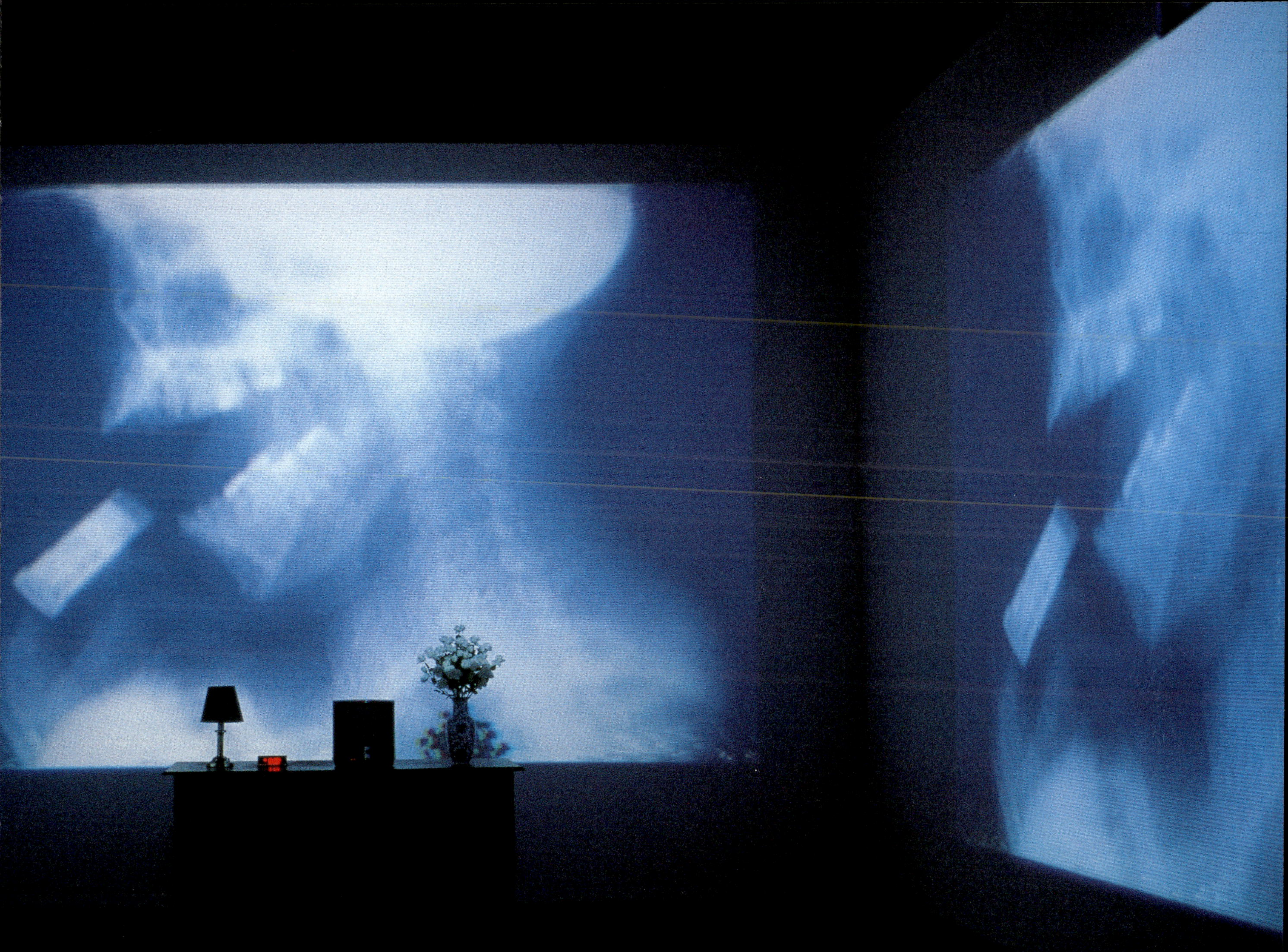

Bill Viola

PROPOSAL for INSTALLATION - FRANKFURT 1990

ARCHITECTURAL PLANS: TOP VIEW

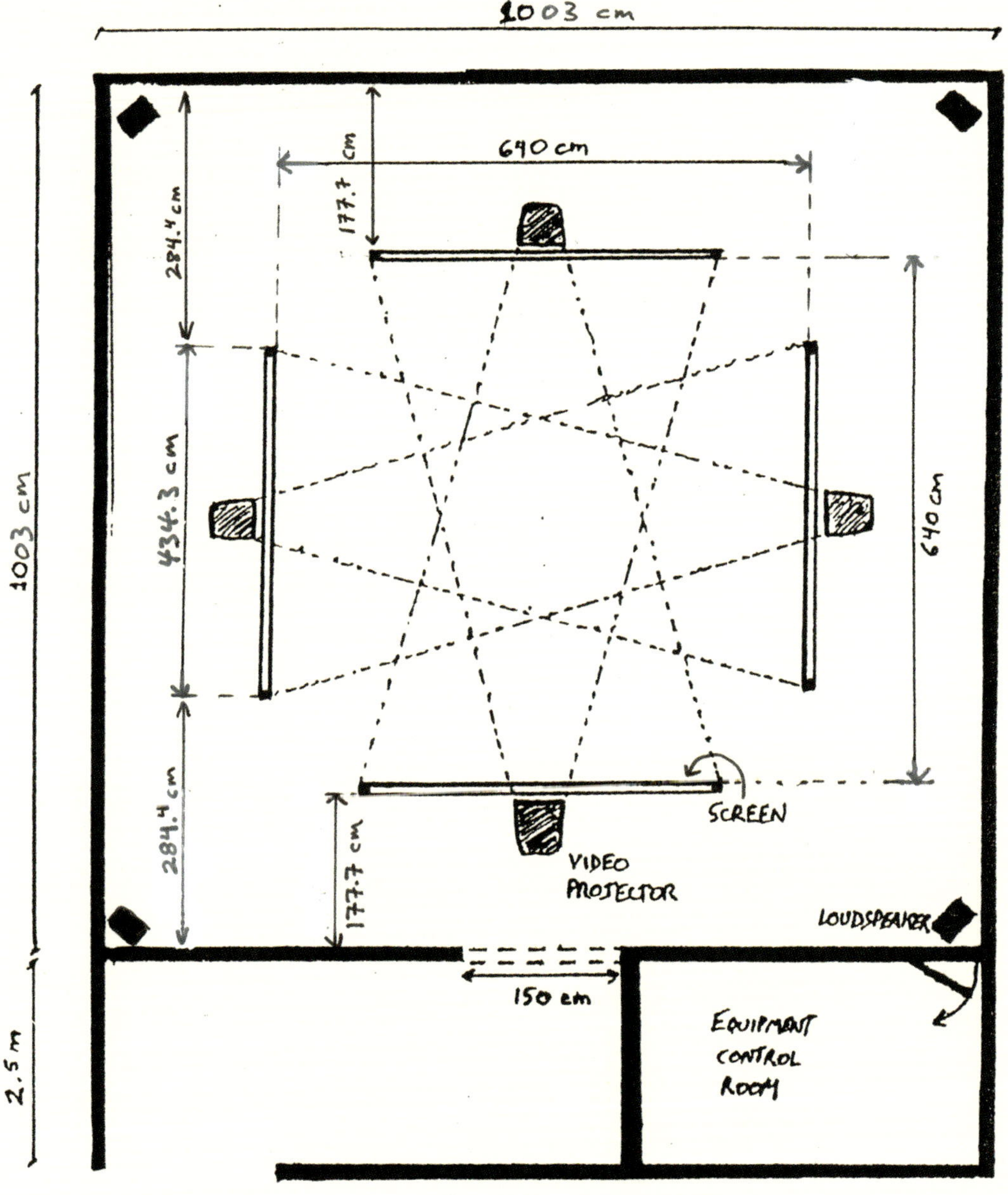

ALL WALLS AND CEILING PAINTED FLAT BLACK.

PROJECTORS: CEILING MOUNT. (Possibly sound proofed)

SCREEN DIMENSIONS: 434.3 X 327.6 cm (171" X 129")

ALUMINUM FRAME, 2 SIDED MATERIAL

SUSPENDED from CEILING, (Bottom edge appx. 61 cm from Floor)

Ceiling - 4.65 m (15 ft. 3 in.)

CHAPTER FOUR

1990s: THE JOINING OF THE SPIRITUAL TO THE AESTHETIC

It only takes an instant for an impression to become a vision.

—Bill Viola, Note, January 21, 1985

Every part of a space contains knowledge of every other.

—Bill Viola, Note, July 6, 1975

Viola's art in the early 1990s explores dimensions of time and perception on a larger scale than before in an effort to represent how our view of the world is compounded by innocence and an anxiety that comes from the fragility of the worlds we experience. Our innocence derives from our earliest life experiences and the freshness of a child's vision. To borrow the words of the American cultural critic Kathleen Stewart, Viola's art is dedicated to finding the "physical trace" coming from the "immanent fragments of sensory experience and dreams of presence."[1] The traces on his monitor screens and the moving images projected into the spaces created by his installations house Viola's deepening "investment in the unfolding of things."[2]

This is a rich period in Viola's art-making, and the selection of artworks that follows is intended to highlight certain key features of his work during these years, features that describe a growing interest in the perceptual and personal informed by a spiritual and aesthetic turn in his art. *The Stopping Mind* (1991), a video installation made up of projected images and sound, is based, as Viola notes, "on the age-old desire to stop time."[3] As early as 1974, in *Instant Breakfast*, Viola used the strobe light and its effect on our visual perception to capture a flash of time, which appears and disappears in an instant. Seventeen years later, we are immersed in a field of moving images that "deals with the paradox of thought (memory) and experience—the underlying propensity of the mind to retain or arrest experience in the face

The Stopping Mind (1991), proposal for Museum für Moderne Kunst, Frankfurt, 1990

of the dynamic nature of both the experience and the perpetual movement of consciousness itself."[4] *The Stopping Mind* takes its inspiration from *The Unfettered Mind: Writings of the Zen Master to the Sword Master* by the Japanese Zen master Takuan Sōhō (1573–1645). This text had a profound influence on Viola, and he used it as a guide in his exploration of time in such installations as *The Stopping Mind*.

Abiding place **means the place where the mind stops.**

In the practice of Buddhism, there are said to be fifty-two stages, and within these fifty-two, the place where the mind stops at one thing is called the *abiding place*. Abiding signifies stopping, and *stopping* means the mind is being detained by some matter, which may be any matter at all.

To speak in terms of your own martial art, when you first notice the sword that is moving to strike you, if you think of meeting that sword just as it is, your mind will stop at the sword in just that position, your own movements will be undone, and you will be cut down by your opponent. This is what *stopping* means.[5]

The Stopping Mind is a complex temporal and aural experience. Central to the work, as Viola describes it, are

four large screens suspended from the ceiling, parallel to the four walls of the room, positioned to describe the sides of a cube open at the corners. Four separate but related images are displayed on the screens. The images are static and the room is silent, except for the sound of a voice quietly whispering in a rapid, unceasing chant that describes the passive loss of bodlly sensation in an unknown black space. Suddenly, without warning, the images simultaneously lunge into movement, momentarily coming to life in a wild burst of frantic motion and loud cascading sound. After only a few seconds, and equally without warning, they freeze again and become silent and still as fixed frames. The image sequences are all shot with a constantly moving camera. They are characterized by incessant activity and violent motion, and center on the theme of physical struggle with the material world. They often contain oblique images of an individual engaged in such a struggle.[6]

In the middle of the room a loudspeaker sits inside a parabolic reflector, and the recording of the artist's monologue can only be heard if the viewer stands in the center of the space. This fascinating text is emblematic of the perceptual and experiential struggle at the heart of Viola's project. I intend to focus on the "self" that is composed and speaking within the installation.

Text for *The Stopping Mind*, transcribed from 1991 audio recording

There is nothing but black. There is nothing but silence. I am lying in a dark space. I can feel my body. I can feel my body lying here. I am awake. I feel my breathing, in and out, quiet and regular. I can feel my breathing. I move my body. I slowly roll over and look up. I see nothing. There is nothing. There is no light. There is no darkness. There is no volume. There is no distance. There is no sound. There is no silence. There is the sensation of space, but without an image. There is no image. There is the sensation of my body with its extension and the weight pressing down. I can feel my body and this is the silent voice ringing in the darkness. A voice ringing in the blackness. I bring my hand up to my face. I move my hand but there is nothing. I move my hand back and forth and I feel the slight movement of air across my cheek. The air moving across my cheek but I see nothing. Nothing in the blackness. My body does not move. I lie completely still. My body is still. The silence becomes heavy. The silence is heavy around my body. There is a slight ringing sensation in my ears. The silence is ringing in my ears. My mouth feels dry and my body lies still. Completely still. I don't move. I don't move my body, not even to swallow. Slowly I become aware of the loss of sensation in my limbs. The loss of sensation in the darkness. The loss of sensation of my body. I don't know how long I have been lying like this. I don't know how long I've been lying here. Lying in the silence. My body lying in the darkness. I imagine the black space. I imagine the silence. The darkness of no image. The silence of no sound. I imagine my body. I imagine my body in this dark space. The space is like a large black cloud of soft cotton, silent and weightless. A soft black mass slowly pressing in around my body. I can feel it slowly pressing in around my body. Pressing in around me. Everything is closing down. Closing down around my body. It's closing down around me until only a small opening remains. A small opening around my face. Only a small opening around my face remains. Outside of this—the oblivion of nothing. The oblivion of nothing. Outside of this there is only darkness. Only the blackness. There is nothing. I am like a body under water breathing through the small opening of a straw. A body under water breathing. Breathing through a small opening. Finally, I let that go. I let it go. I feel myself submerge. Submerging into the blackness. Letting go. Sinking down into the black mass. Submerging into the void. The senseless and weightless void. The great comfort of the senseless and weightless void, where there is nothing but darkness. [Repeat from beginning]

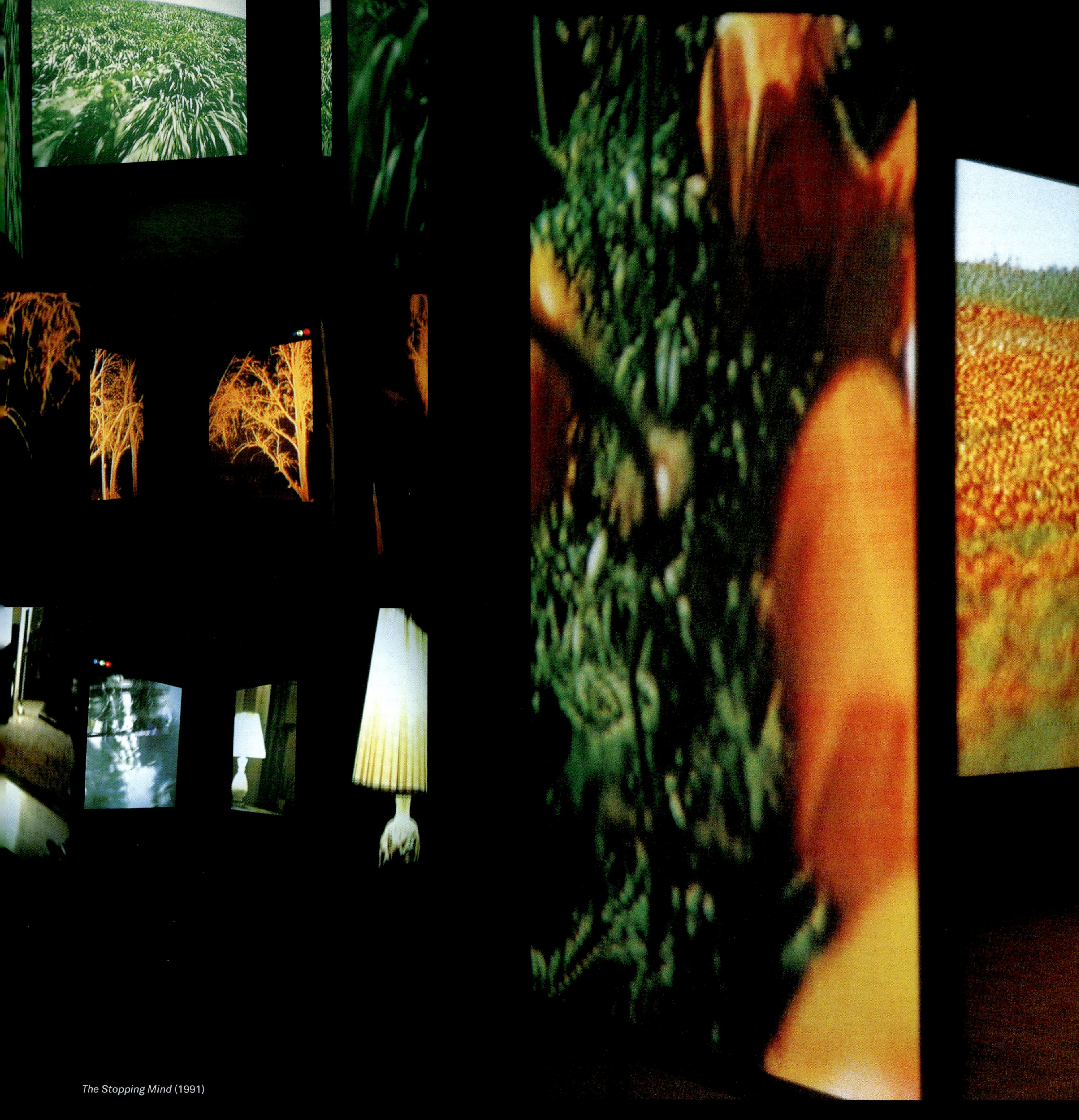

The Stopping Mind (1991)

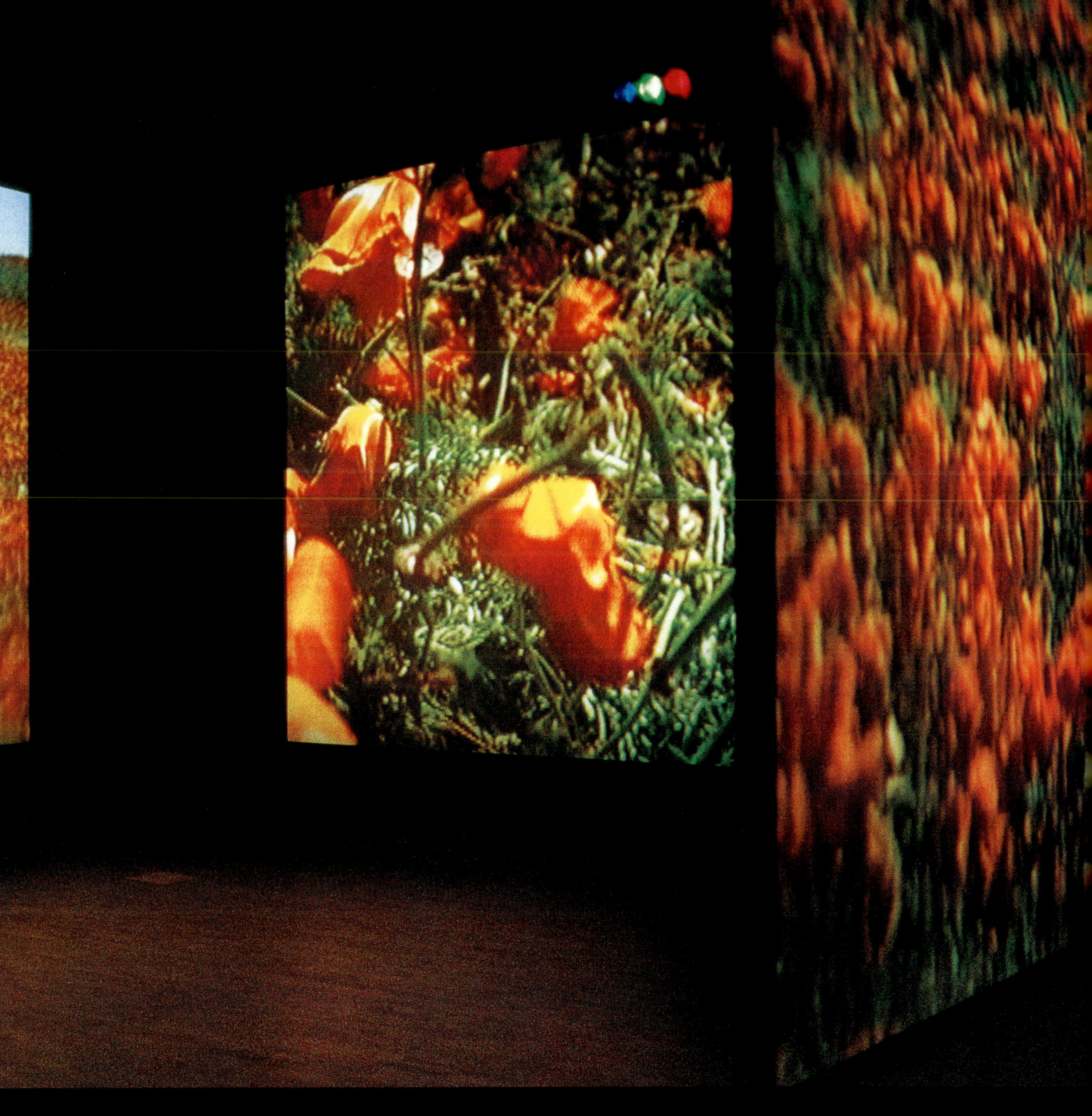

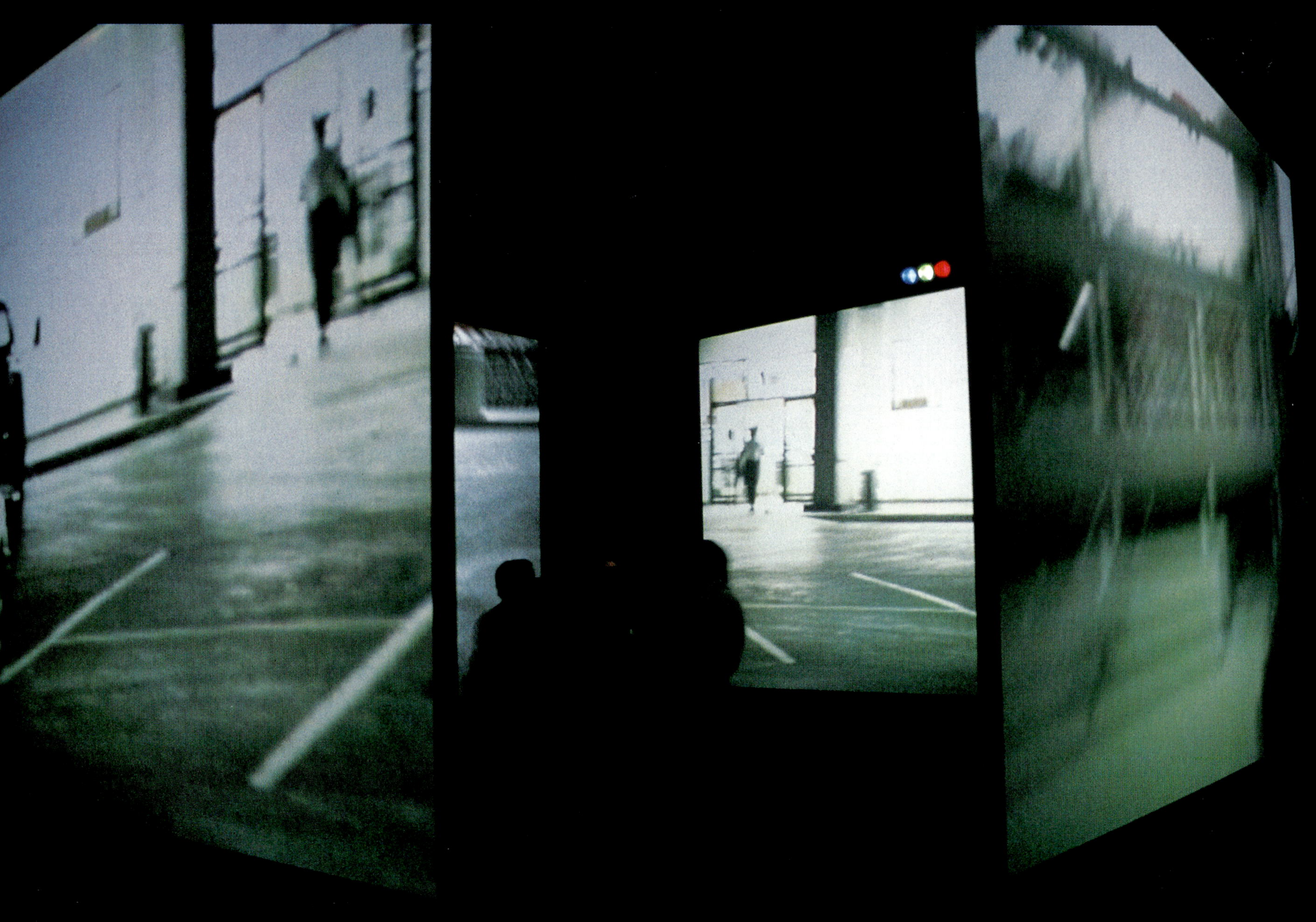

It is the voice of the artist, and it speaks to a sense of fragility at the center of a disturbing cacophony of moving images. It is the voice of a man dying.

Viola's description of the installation continues: "The imprisoned time of the still images can unleash itself at any moment and, once witnessed, the potential for the resumption of their violent activity is imminent and constantly present in the space. The intervals between each onslaught of motion are random and unpredictable, occurring anywhere from several seconds to over a minute apart. If allowed to play continuously, the material would be overwhelming and unbearable. The constant soft monotone of the chanting voice is focused acoustically in the center of the room and provides the only stable reference point in the space."[7] The artist is setting in motion an experience that will confront the viewer. The self of the artist's voice is not, however, the "ego" that is constructed in the work of Vito Acconci in such videotapes as *Undertone* (1973), in which he is the subject directly confronting the viewer, or *The Red Tapes* (1976), in which he composes and responds to the psychic and architectural/ideological space of "America." In those works the position of the artist vis-à-vis the camera and viewer is staged as a narrative foregrounding of the power of language in articulating what is visible and imagined through the dialectical opposition of the artist as speaker and the viewer as mute witness mediated through the camera. Viola's text from *The Stopping Mind* is more closely aligned with John Cage's account of being in the anechoic chamber at Harvard University, where "there was no sound."[8] As recounted by Cage in Nam June Paik's videotape *Global Groove* (1973), when he asked the attendants what it was he was hearing, they replied that it was the sound of his blood moving through his body. The sounds of the body made audible in absolute silence relate to the cacophony of images and words, the unconscious free association of word and image that assaults the viewer in *The Stopping Mind.* The viewer *becomes* the artist.

As interesting as it is to consider Viola's text in the context of *The Stopping Mind*, it is a powerful description of a state of being that brings into focus his entire body of work. The struggle to come to terms with the world and the passage of time bracketed by birth and death are subjects he addresses throughout his work. If we cannot imagine life before we were born, will our death be like our world was before we were born? Ultimately, this is a metaphysical/theological question that we seek to understand as we experience our everyday lives, observing the world and all it offers in life. Should we understand the world of nature as the Romantic poets did or create a new society as various utopian movements sought? Viola suggests that within the "paradox of thought (memory) and experience," we can find a space where we can be shielded from the "still images [that] can unleash" themselves at any time. The violent beauty of *The Stopping Mind* and the explosive presence of the moving images do save one from the "oblivion

The Stopping Mind (1991)

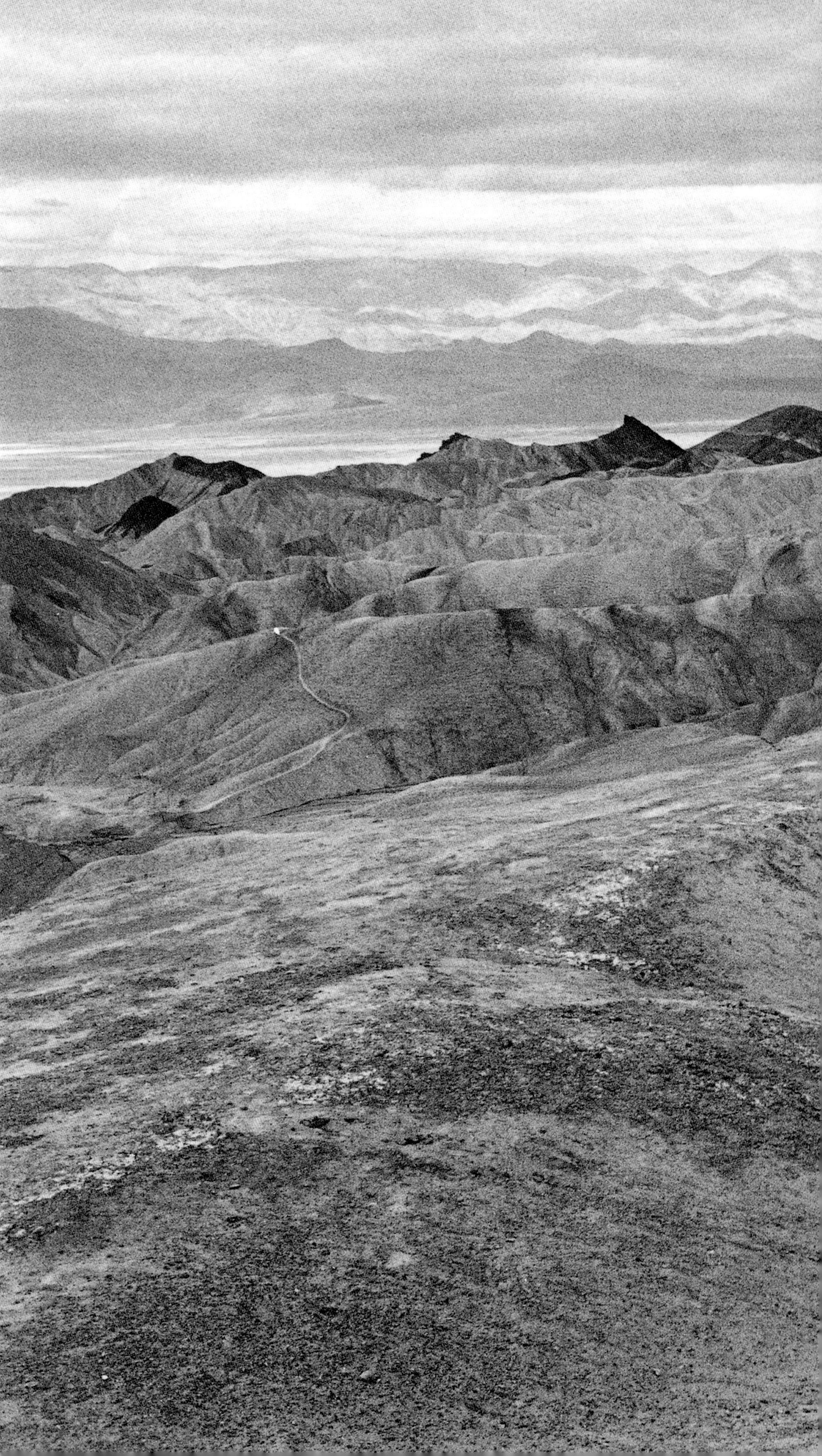

 Bill Viola, Zabriskie Point, Death Valley, CA, May 1982

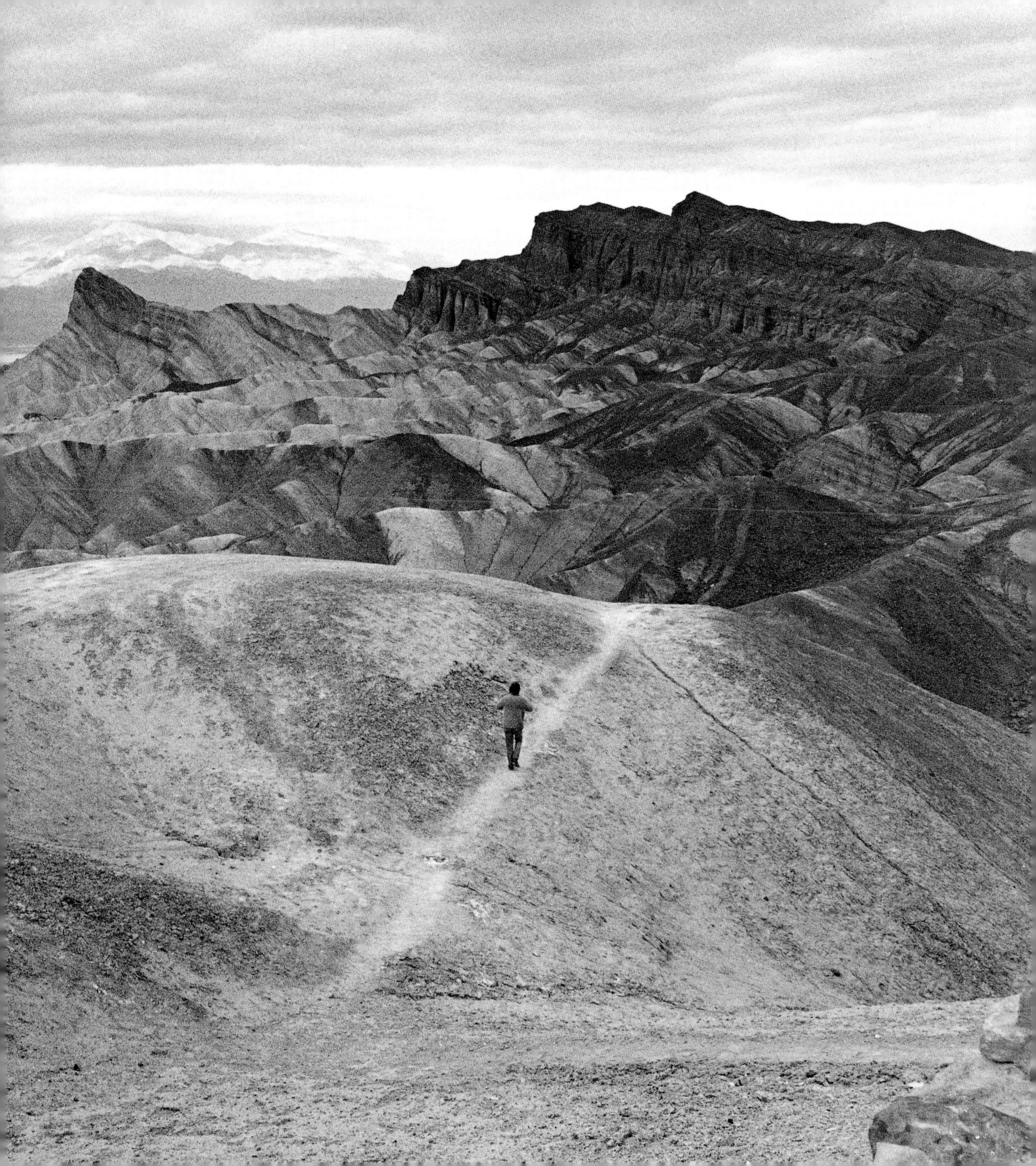

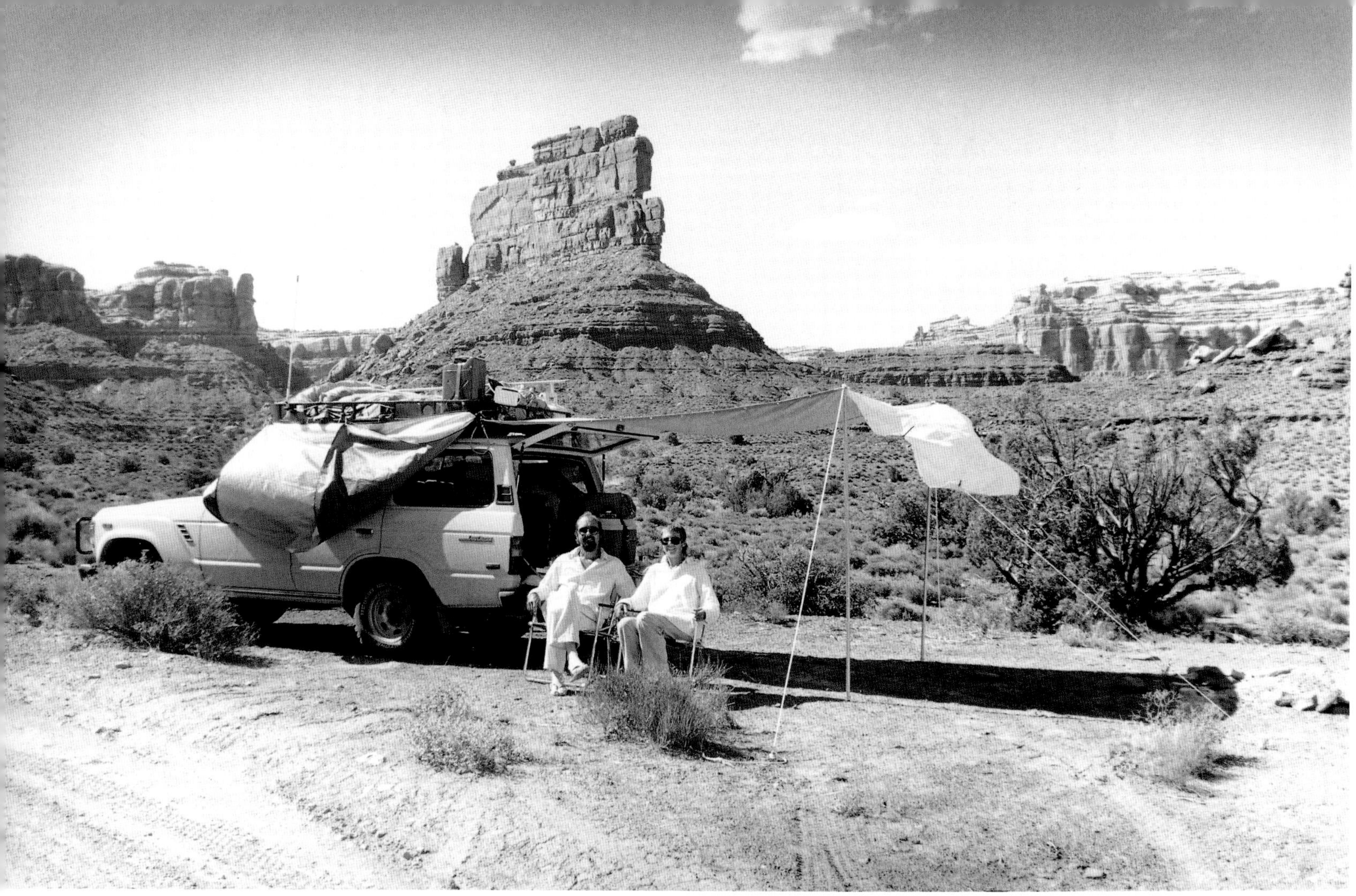

of nothing," the world before we were born, which disappears with death. I would argue that it is our hope in the future of humankind, the "collective history that carries on," that makes our lives bearable.[9] Whether there is an afterlife is less the point than whether there is a future for humankind, an argument eloquently made in Samuel Scheffler's book *Death and the Afterlife* (2013): "the expectation that others will survive me, that humanity will go on, is necessary for me valuing much of what I do, the recognition that I will *not* survive, that my life will *not* go on, is likewise necessary for my valuing much of what I do."[10] As we near death, the cognitive function that persists to the end is hearing. It is Viola's voice that speaks to the rush of images of the world seen, remembered, and heard at the end of *The Stopping Mind*.

Some of the issues raised by Viola in *The Stopping Mind* are pursued by the artist in the single-channel videotape *The Passing*, completed in 1991. Here, Kira Perov recalls the making of the work:

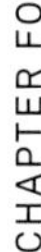

Production for *The Passing* began in 1987, when we traveled for five months throughout the southwestern United States camping in remote areas of Utah, Colorado, Arizona, and New Mexico. We made daytime and nocturnal

Above Bill Viola and Kira Perov on five-month shooting trip for *The Passing* (1991), Valley of the Gods, UT, June 1987

Opposite *The Passing* (1991)

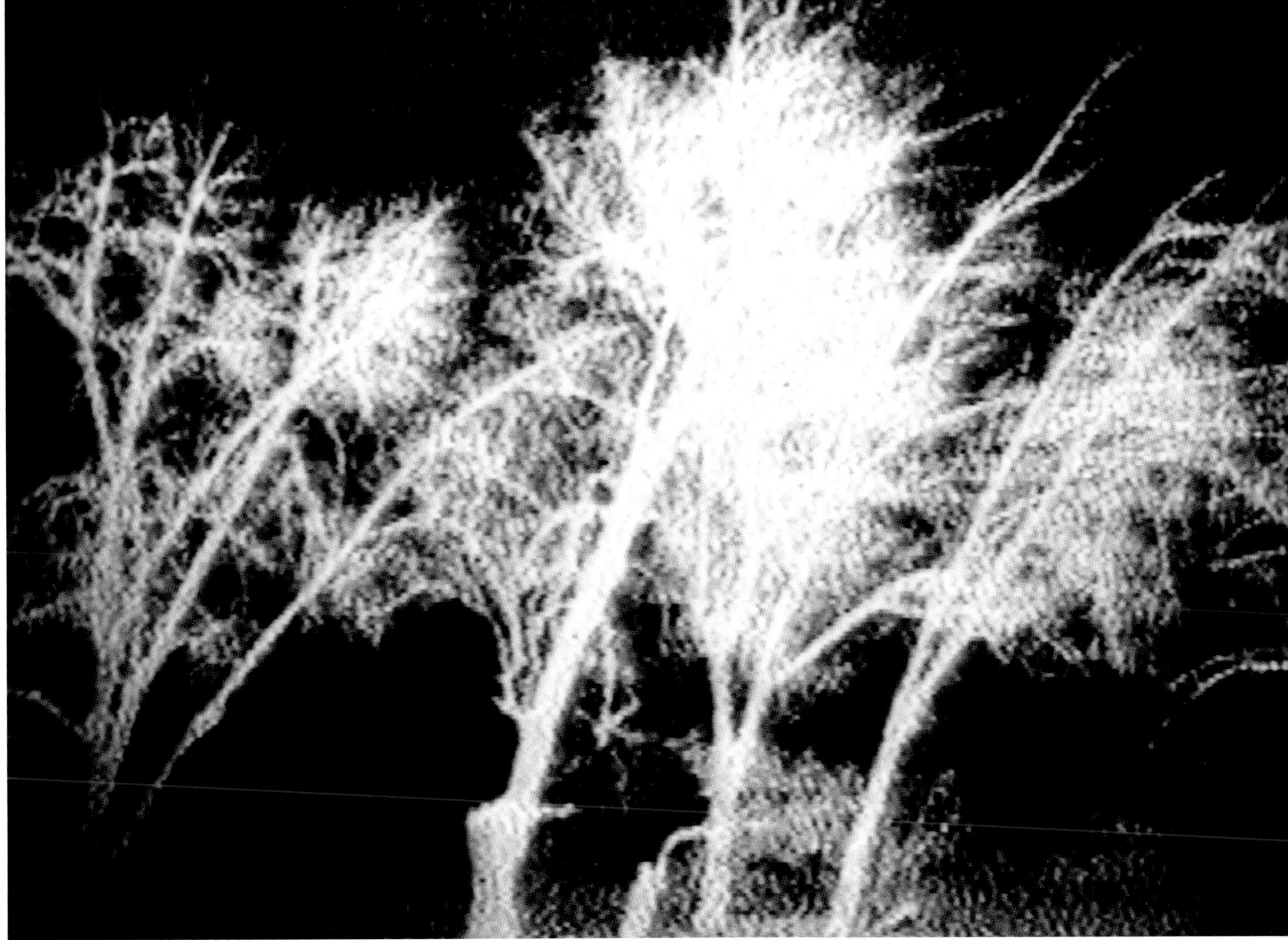

black-and-white recordings of the desert and studied ancient Native American archeological sites, one of my passions. Bill was commissioned by Das kleine Fernsehspiel of ZDF German television to produce a work on desert landscapes, and with the grant we purchased a Land Cruiser, loaded it up with camping supplies, food, and equipment and began an extended emersion into the vast landscapes of the Southwest. Bill did not bring a color video camera, but we had two black-and-white surveillance cameras, one infrared, that created beautiful dreamy images, and a military night surveillance camera, the Lunar Lite, that could record grainy images in moonlight and the side of a whole building at night lit with only a flashlight. I was pregnant with our first son for the last three months of the trip. Bill hit a writer's block on this piece and the work was not completed or resolved for three years, until soon after the death of his mother in 1991 (to whom the work is dedicated), when he realized that his art was actually his life and that he could bring the personal into his studio.[11]

The 54-minute running time of *The Passing* allowed for a virtual catalogue of techniques, which take on different aspects and intensities in later work. Such variety was made possible through the use of modified

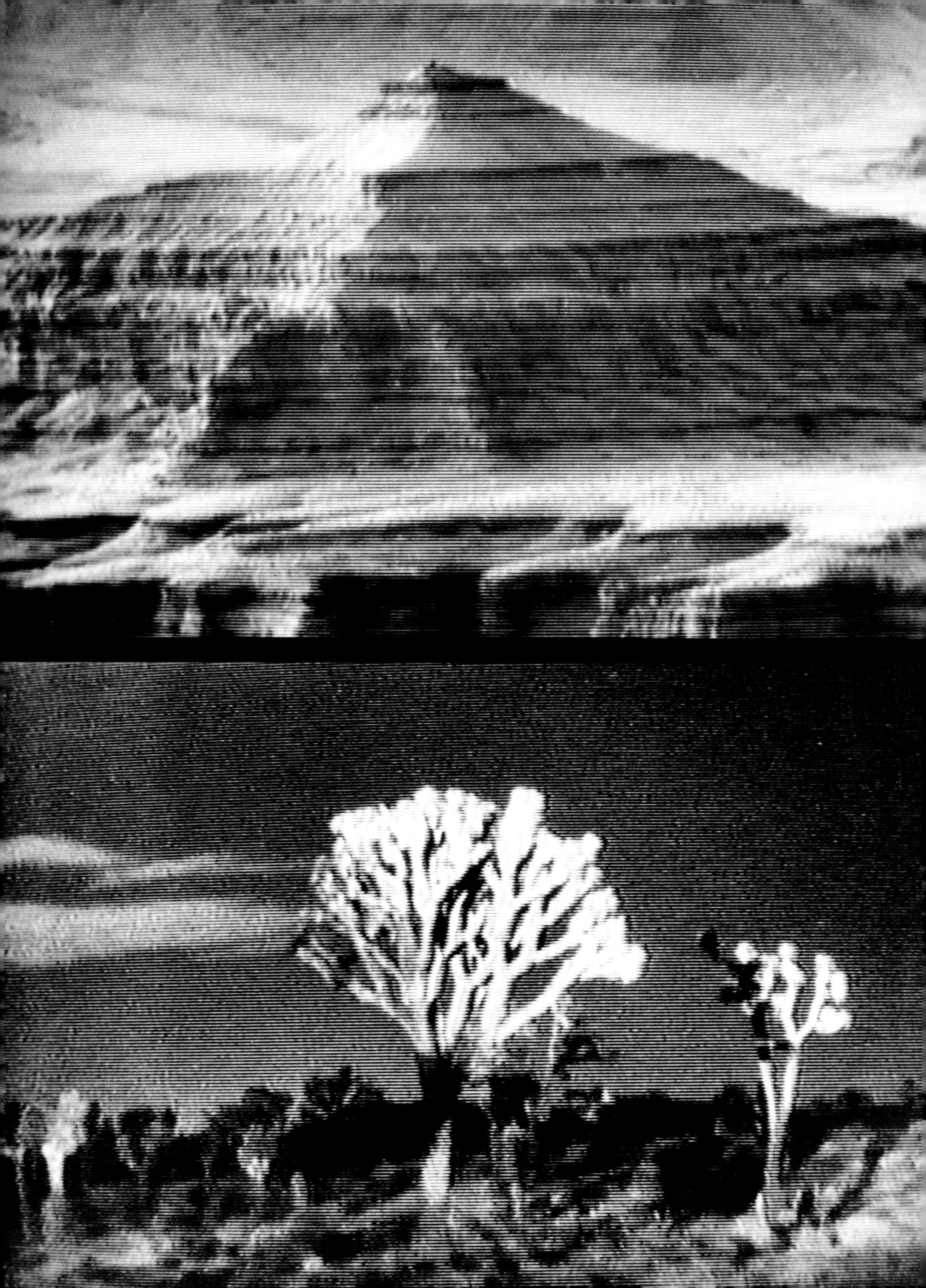

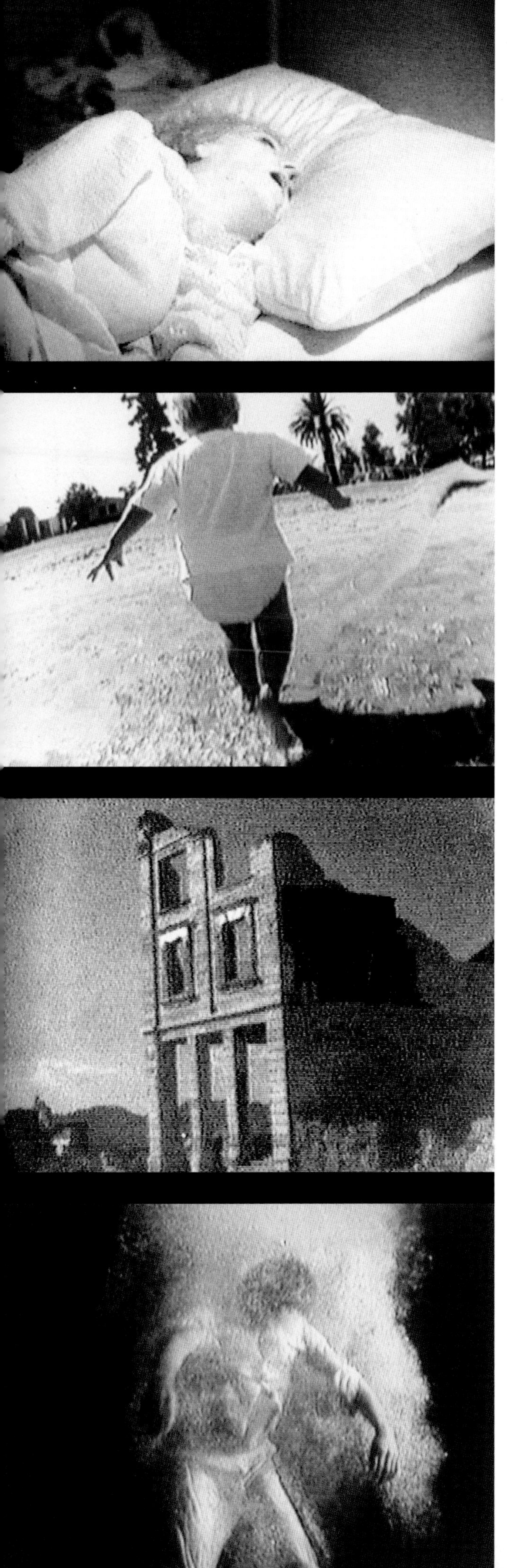

equipment, including image intensifiers and infrared cameras that allowed black-and-white recording of images at the very threshold of visibility. Key visual elements include the metaphor of the eye, the body under water, and the unconscious rendered in dream-like states of perception. Viola succinctly states the distinctive features of the work: "A personal response to the spiritual extremes of birth and death in the family. Black-and-white nocturnal imagery and underwater scenes depict a twilight world hovering on the borders of human perception and consciousness, where the multiple lives of the mind (memory, reality, and vision) merge."[12] The wonderful concept of the "lives of the mind" being "memory, reality, and vision" and the exploration of the edge of consciousness are certainly familiar from Viola's earlier work. But here, Viola moves away from the texts of the mystics and the phenomenon of the video-recording system toward a narrative located in two major life events, namely the birth of his first son in 1988 and the death of his mother in 1991. This move signals a shift in his work from the epistemological catalogue of human experiences in *I Do Not Know What It Is I Am Like* (1986) to the personal. At the same time, Viola creates the first sustained narrative work based on the phenomenology of reception in the history of video art. By "narrative," I am not describing a story with a beginning, a middle, and an end, all focused on a dramatic denouement that results in emotional catharsis and closure. Rather, I am describing the shaping of images in order to come to terms with the experiences of change, the birth into being, and the end of consciousness.

Viola's *The Passing* is a testament to the possibility of art living on and, in the process, embodying the soul. The ethos of narrative and documentary as records of a life, although central to the history of cinema, has long been elusive for artists working in video. In part, this is due to the early history of cinema being divided into the imaginary, as represented by the magical, fantastical films of Georges Méliès, and the record of daily life identified with the work of Auguste and Louis Lumière. This division has haunted cinema and often marginalized the reception of the documentary in the pantheon of the art of film. Artists working in video have made the document a central strategy of their art practice, thereby making "documentary" a fluid and open term. *The Passing* is an outstanding example of the way in which Viola combines documentary and narrative to link life and death in a work of the imagination. His visualization of life and death, expressed through symbols (as the train rushes through the tunnel) and as a record of fact (as Viola's mother hangs on to life in her hospital bed), gives powerful meaning to the work. *The Passing* does not represent a causal chain of events, but rather a movement that gives equal power to night visions of the desert and of children swimming underwater to convey the artist's feelings toward life as it continues and ends. Viola moves these images into freestanding installations that draw their power from the images themselves

The Passing (1991)

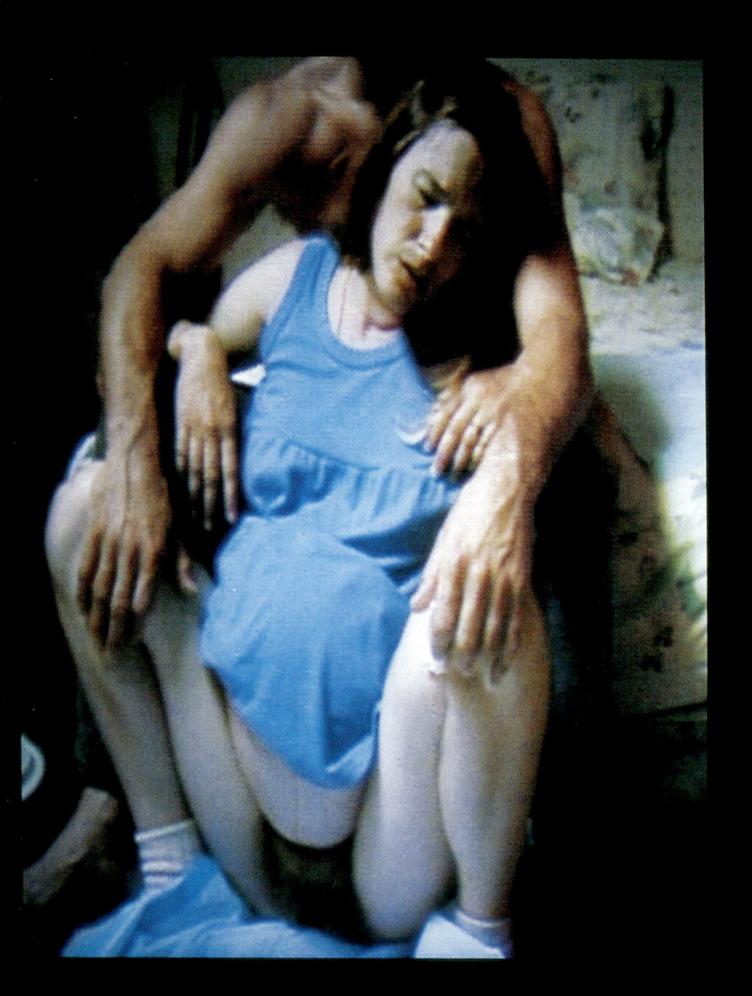

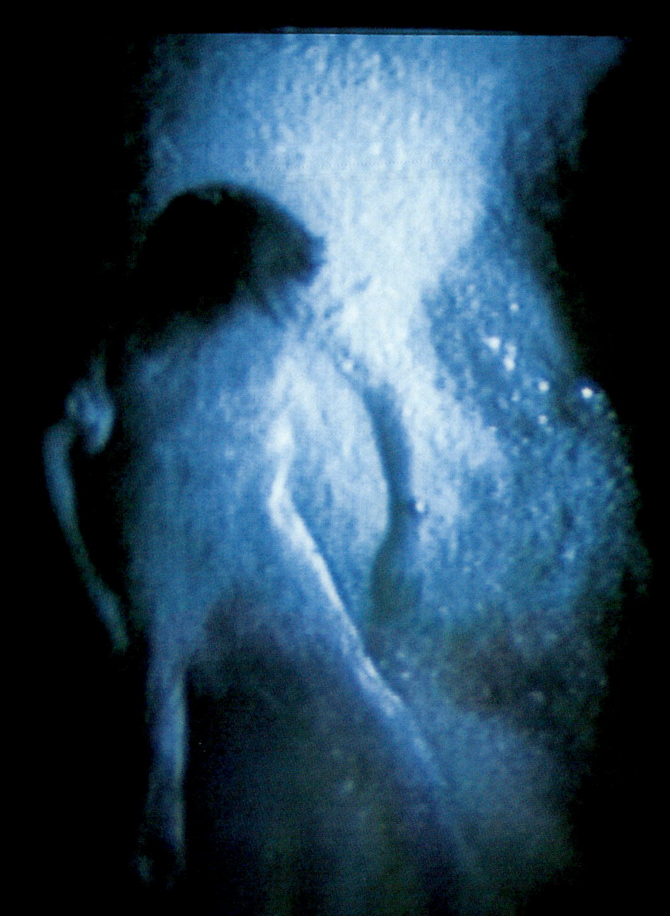

as well as from the artist's association with specific imagery as embodying the personal and the experiential. Viola pushes the visual to embody emotion, giving his images meaning. He wants you to feel something, to bring you, the viewer, into the pain and mystery that he finds in life and his spiritual quest for meaning. He continues to forge his own path through the contemporary art world, avoiding the tropes of irony and distantiation that are hallmarks of modernism and postmodernism.

In the early years of the 1990s, Viola's single-channel and installation pieces oscillate between the phenomenology of sight and the grounding of images in life. It was a time of change, and the year 1992 proved especially busy. "At the end of 1991," recalls Perov, "our second son was born, Bill rented a large studio, and for the first time [1992] we began a relationship with two private galleries, Anthony d'Offay in London, and Donald Young Gallery, Seattle. Bill completed an incredible nine installations that year, continuing to explore the themes of sleep, dreams, birth, and mortality; it was as though everything was expanding and exploding. We also began to work in high-speed 35mm film to achieve extreme slow motion that video was not able to match. It was the beginning of a longtime collaboration with our director of photography, Harry Dawson. Having a large studio with an 18-foot-high ceiling, Bill was able to explore a variety of new materials, physical and electronic, and for the first time he could see how the installations appeared in space before they were shown to the public. He created such video 'sculptures' as *Heaven and Earth*, which incorporated a wooden column with stripped monitors; he made a work using a large LED screen that displayed a live news feed; he used new tiny projectors to make a seven-channel autobiographical work, *What Is Not And That Which Is*; he designed a work for a window that would play for 24 hours; he explored once more the triptych altar model to create *Nantes Triptych*, a bold and simple statement on birth and death for the Chapelle de l'Oratoire, Musée des Beaux-Arts de Nantes, France; and brought in seven 55-gallon oil drums, and filled them with water after installing black-and-white images of people sleeping on monitors on the bottom of the barrels, which became *The Sleepers*, a commission for the Musée d'Art Contemporain de Montréal."[13] By the end of 1992, Perov had organized, together with German curator Marie Louise Syring, a touring exhibition of seven of these important recent installations and a selection of videotapes that were premiered in six European cities, beginning with Düsseldorf. "It was the first time we had traveled such a large installation show," as Perov remembers, "and the work made an impact. People still remember that exhibition."[14]

Commissioned by the Institute of Contemporary Art in Philadelphia, *Slowly Turning Narrative* (1992) is a dramatic example of what Viola calls "sculpting with time."[15] The installation frees the screen from the wall,

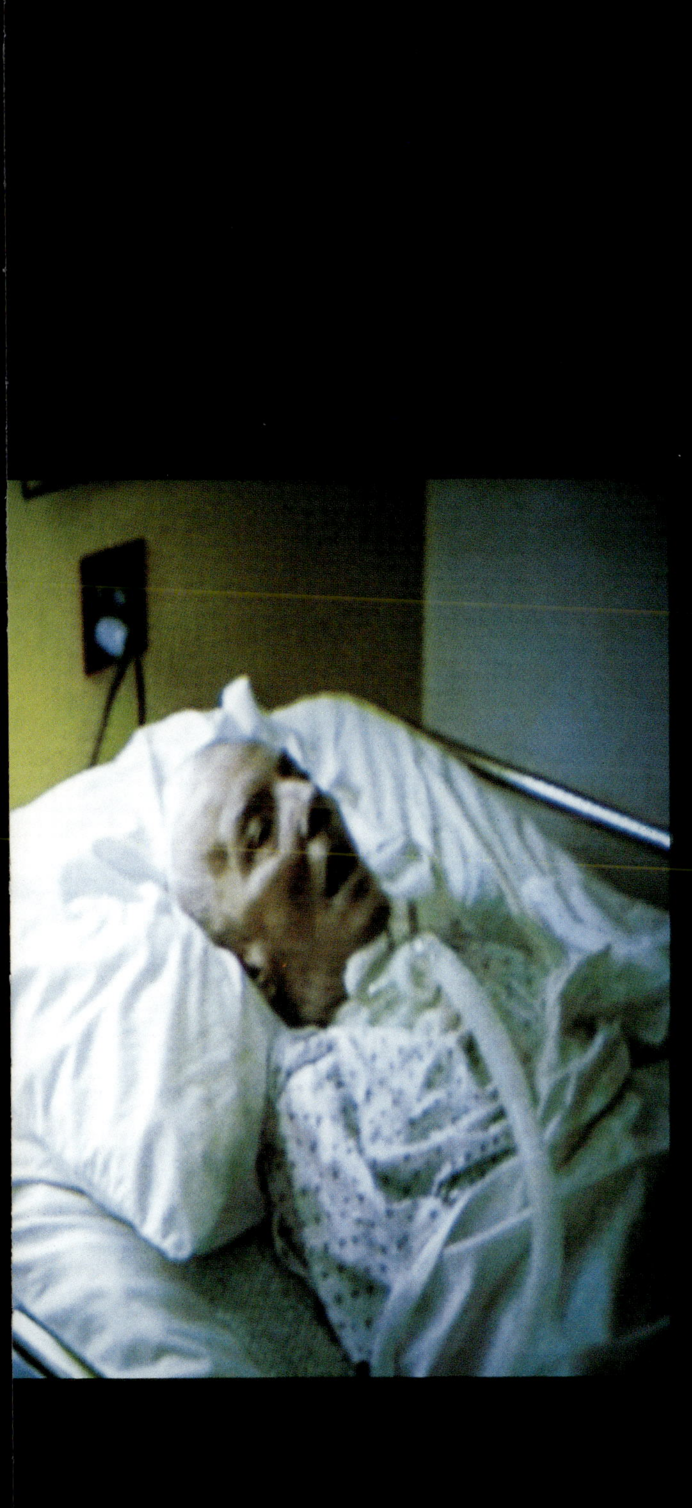

Nantes Triptych (1992)

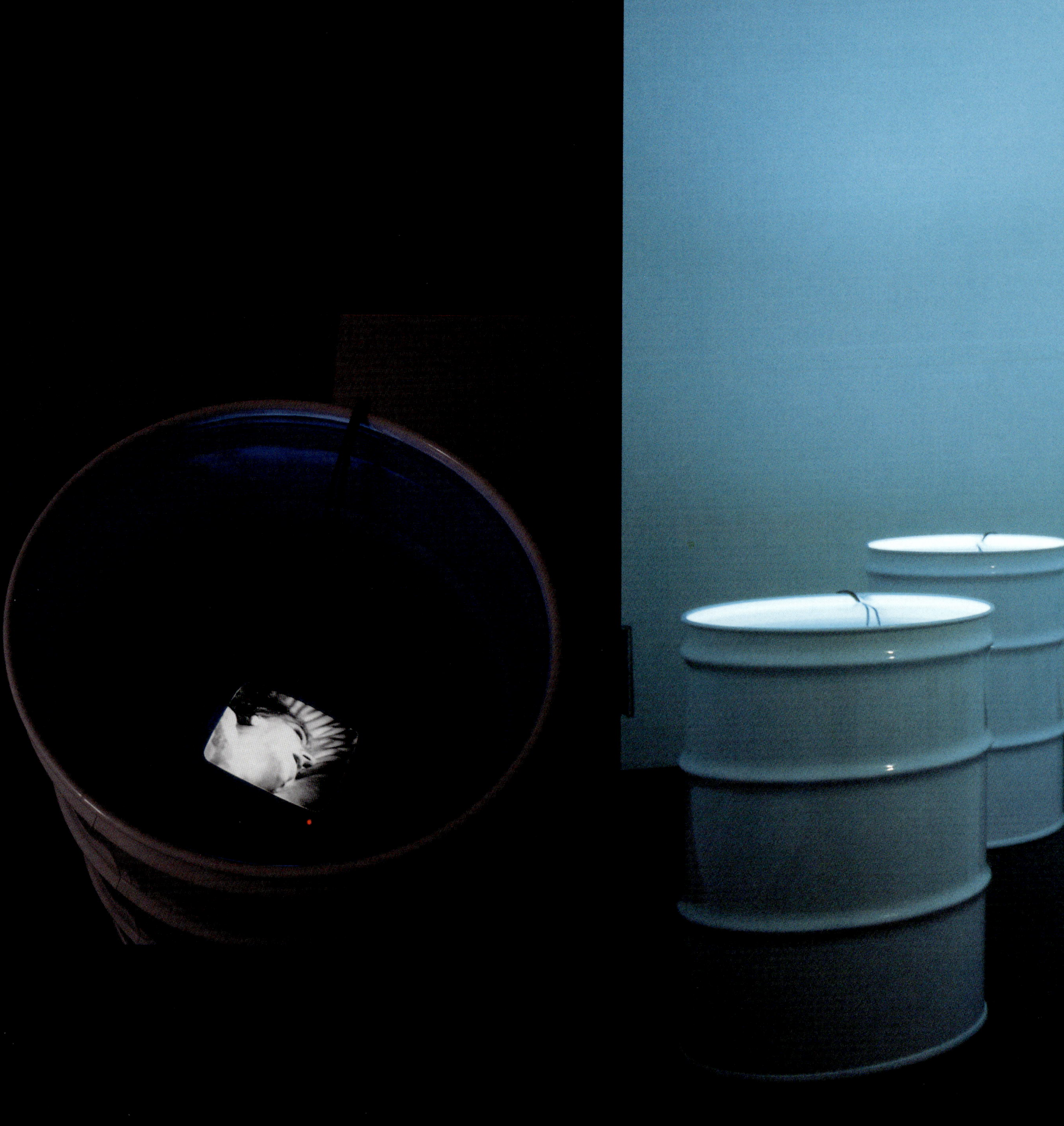

The Sleepers (1992)

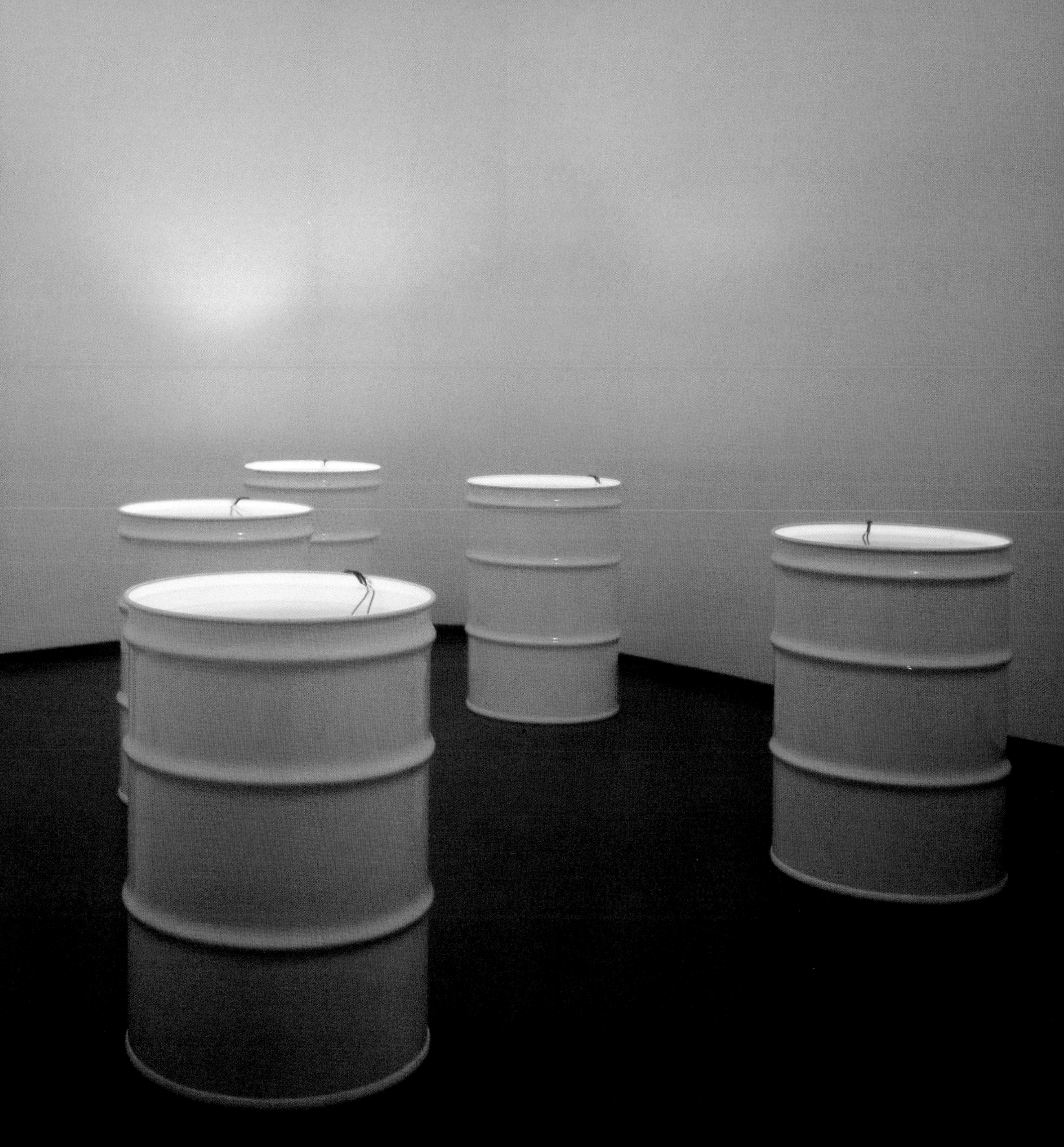

rotating and shifting our reception of the moving image. Here is Viola's technical description of the work:

A large screen (9 × 12 feet) is slowly rotating on a central axis in the center of a large dark room. Two video projectors are facing it from opposite sides of the space. One side of the screen is a mirrored surface, the other side a normal projection screen. One projector shows a constant black-and-white image of a man's face in close-up, in harsh light, appearing distracted and at time straining. The other projector shows a series of changing color images of young children moving by on a carousel, a house on fire, people at a carnival at night, kids playing with fireworks, etc., characterized by continuous motion and swirling light and color. On the black-and-white side, a voice can be heard reciting a rhythmic, repetitive chant of a long list of phrases descriptive of states of being and individual actions. On the color-image side, the ambient sounds associated with each image are heard. The beams from the two projectors distort and spill out images across the shifting screen surface and onto the walls as the angle of the screen alternately widens and narrows during the course of its rotations. The mirrored side sends distorted reflections cascading across the surrounding walls—indistinct gossamer forms that travel around the perimeter of the room. In addition, viewers in the space see themselves and the space around them reflected in the mirror as it slowly moves past.[16]

Separately, Viola has described the experience and meaning of the installation:

The work concerns the enclosing nature of self-image and the external circulation of potentially infinite (and therefore unattainable) states of being all revolving around the still point of the central self. The entire room and all persons within it become a continually shifting projection screen, enclosing the image and the reflections, including a self-reflection of the space and viewer, and all locked into the regular cadences of the chanting voice and the rotating screen. The entire space becomes an interior for the revelations of a constantly turning mind absorbed with itself. The confluences and conflicts of image, intent, content, and emotion perpetually circulate as the screen slowly turns in the space.[17]

These two texts highlight the twofold structure of the piece. There are issues of scale and shifting planes of movement, in terms of the screens themselves as well as what is projected on them. The viewer is physically caught up in the unfolding spectacle of everyday and strange events shifting around the "still point of the central self" and embodying the "potentially infinite states of being." The mind is projected onto the screens like the

5TN Voice Text

"Past the one..." Text

~~(From intro:)~~

the one who goes
the one who does
the one who feels
the one who knows
the one who breathes
the one who moves
the one who stands
the one who sleeps
the one who turns away
the one who looks
the one who comes
the one who calls
the one who returns
the one who remembers
the one who fails
the one who runs
the one who lives
the one who expects
the one who sees
the one who allows
the one who forgives
the one who hates
the one who makes
the one who pleads
the one who cries
the one who falls
the one who creates
the one who forgets
the one who betrays
the one who screams
the one who loves
the one who smells
the one who feels
the one who lies
the one who agrees
the one who follows
the one who leads
the one who deceives

the one who doubts
the one who carries
the one who resolves
the one who discovers
the one who dies
the one who fights
the one who responds
the one who fears
the one who leads
the one who completes
the one who abandons
the one who receives
the one who surrenders
the one who avows
the one who prays
the one who gives
the one who denies
the one who takes
the one who stops
the one who sits
the one who kills
the one who rests
the one who dreams
the one who cuts
the one who pulls
the one who pushes
the one who destroys
the one who fires
the one who blames
the one who writes
the one who retreats
the one who lies
the one who drives
the one who gathers
the one who helps
the one who hurts
the one who eats
the one who robs
the one who keeps
the one who shares
the one who accuses
the one who cheats
the one who supplies

the one who demands
the one who buys
the one who swallows
the one who shits
the one who fucks
the one who increases
the one who threatens
the one who spits
the one who pisses
the one who blinks
the one who hears
the one who touches
the one who changes
the one who grows
the one who shrinks
the one who roots
the one who stabs
the one who brags
the one who whispers
the one who announces
the one who refines
the one who conceals
the one who chokes
the one who relies
the one who finds
the one who meets
the one who waits
the one who dives
the one who scrapes
the one who starves
the one who fills
the one who learns
the one who cleans
the one who uncovers
the one who disappears
the one who consumes
the one who solves
the one who flies
the one who crushes
the one who punctures
the one who upsets
the one who disturbs
the one who centers

the one who tells
the one who turns
the one who escapes
the one who lunges
the one who avoids
the one who sucks
the one who cares
the one who endures
the one who drops
the one who cracks
the one who interrupts
the one who annoys
the one who defines
the one who knocks
the one who reveals
the one who disturbs
the one who arrives
the one who embraces
the one who silences
the one who strikes
the one who nurtures
the one who catches
the one who drops
the one who adds
the one who removes
the one who distills
the one who reflects
the one who explains
the one who ignores
the one who hits
the one who delays
the one who keeps
the one who shoots
the one who hides
the one who accomodates
the one who heals
the one who describes
the one who defies
the one who closes
the one who informs
the one who travels
the one who speaks
the one who transforms

the one who overrides
the one who commands
the one who rules
the one who stifles
the one who judges
the one who fakes
the one who misleads
the one who releases
the one who contains
the one who gags
the one who farts
the one who squeezes
the one who shifts
the one who shuts
the one who stabilizes
the one who disables
the one who empties
the one who cripples
the one who bleeds
the one who thirsts
the one who desires
the one who obeys
the one who bathes
the one who hungers
the one who enlightens
the one who boasts
the one who prevents
the one who intervenes
the one who constrains
the one who mediates
the one who suppresses
the one who convinces
the one who disciplines
the one who complies
the one who retains
the one who comforts
the one who calculates
the one who climbs
the one who constrains
the one who crawls
the one who believes
the one who rejects
the one who covers

the one who copies
the one who wills
the one who donates
the one who recedes
the one who charges
the one who convinces
the one who qualifies
the one who achieves
the one who wins
the one who loses
the one who darkens
the one who opens
the one who finishes
the one who conceives
the one who purifies
the one who perpetuates
the one who reforms
the one who restores
the one who remains
the one who drowns
the one who refuses
the one who maintains
the one who prevails
the one who undresses
the one who washes
the one who kisses
the one who divides
the one who resists
the one who aligns
the one who measures
the one who delivers
the one who sends
the one who troubles
the one who signals
the one who confirms
the one who holds
the one who decreases
the one who removes
the one who cleanses
the one who negates
the one who signs
the one who extends
the one who profits

Dot matrix printout of thirteen-page text for *Slowly Turning Narrative* (1992)

the one who fulfills
the one who speculates
the one who matches
the one who empowers
the one who simplifies
the one who multiplies
the one who disfigures
the one who clutters
the one who amuses
the one who connects
the one who sustains
the one who deserves
the one who practices
the one who asks
the one who bestows
the one who hides
the one who curses
the one who frees
the one who sets
the one who faces
the one who fixes
the one who deludes
the one who isolates
the one who recalls
the one who submerges
the one who engages
the one who bears
the one who pronounces
the one who pays
the one who responds
the one who sings
the one who lowers
the one who lessens
the one who earns
the one who crushes
the one who splits
the one who sows
the one who suppresses
the one who binds
the one who tightens
the one who operates
the one who stings
the one who plays

the one who nullifies
the one who grieves
the one who ends
the one who laughs
the one who encloses
the one who refers
the one who evolves
the one who declines
the one who searches
the one who discerns
the one who softens
the one who erodes
the one who mourns
the one who passes
the one who establishes
the one who detracts
the one who reproduces
the one who organizes
the one who respects
the one who finances
the one who abstains
the one who summarizes
the one who shortens
the one who deals
the one who lifts
the one who leaps
the one who contracts
the one who damages
the one who cancells
the one who pressures
the one who restores
the one who aches
the one who itches
the one who worries
the one who infects
the one who invests
the one who wets
the one who stains
the one who fills
the one who stays
the one who advises
the one who plans
the one who battles

the one who relates
the one who dismantles
the one who understands
the one who contacts
the one who controls
the one who presses
the one who undermines
the one who spends
the one who speeds
the one who occurs
the one who rocks
the one who lights
the one who blinds
the one who gains
the one who covets
the one who indulges
the one who abuses
the one who instigates
the one who initiates
the one who renders
the one who effects
the one who sounds
the one who lengthens
the one who proceeds
the one who patches
the one who panders
the one who handles
the one who depends
the one who concedes
the one who envisions
the one who enters
the one who applaudes
the one who regulates
the one who enforces
the one who suspends
the one who enrages
the one who rescues
the one who survives
the one who conforms
the one who rents
the one who employs
the one who behaves
the one who overstates

the one who concludes
the one who projects
the one who demeans
the one who subverts
the one who nourishes
the one who howls
the one who blows
the one who copulates
the one who supports
the one who eradicates
the one who confides
the one who serves
the one who permits
the one who reduces
the one who forgoes
the one who honors
the one who slows
the one who bans
the one who sanctifies
the one who secures
the one who locks
the one who attracts
the one who scratches
the one who erases
the one who appreciates
the one who confuses
the one who regresses
the one who degrades
the one who joins
the one who embodies
the one who creases
the one who stimulates
the one who obliterates
the one who anticipates
the one who supervises
the one who slumps
the one who slouches
the one who straightens
the one who migrates
the one who educates
the one who packages
the one who ties
the one who counts

the one who dignifies
the one who wastes
the one who designs
the one who investigates
the one who punishes
the one who categorizes
the one who strains
the one who masters
the one who converges
the one who converses
the one who repeats
the one who relinquishes
the one who authorizes
the one who defaults
the one who promotes
the one who produces
the one who ages
the one who clings
the one who decays
the one who subsidizes
the one who replenishes
the one who collapses
the one who descends
the one who distinguishes
the one who repairs
the one who exhausts
the one who ascends
the one who says
the one who seizes
the one who peeks
the one who works
the one who borrows
the one who belittles
the one who resumes
the one who misunderstands
the one who folds
the one who trembles
the one who hesitates
the one who leans
the one who burns
the one who renounces
the one who concentrates
the one who schemes

the one who sells
the one who stands by
the one who observes
the one who revokes
the one who strengthens
the one who shudders
the one who defends
the one who rages
the one who rapes
the one who masterbates
the one who hunts
the one who weakens
the one who wishes
the one who rises
the one who integrates
the one who trusts
the one who witholds
the one who performs
the one who intimidates
the one who inspires
the one who accumulates
the one who depletes
the one who chooses
the one who exceeds
the one who excells
the one who repels
the one who selects
the one who frightens
the one who denigrates
the one who feeds
the one who scatters
the one who shelters
the one who marks
the one who inflicts
the one who despises
the one who corrects
the one who deforms
the one who moderates
the one who wounds
the one who prides
the one who expires
the one who confounds
the one who penetrates

the one who eludes
the one who satisfies
the one who outlives
the one who uses
the one who breaks down
the one who weeps
the one who murmurs
the one who manipulates
the one who rectifies
the one who complains
the one who applies
the one who appoints
the one who reserves
the one who notifies
the one who clothes
the one who rebuilds
the one who realizes
the one who constructs
the one who wonders
the one who contemplates
the one who disposes
the one who preserves
the one who mobilizes
the one who disintegrates
the one who stores
the one who begins
the one who mistrusts
the one who worships
the one who carries
the one who repents
the one who defeats
the one who recommends
the one who drags
the one who bites
the one who beholds
the one who possesses

the one who is.

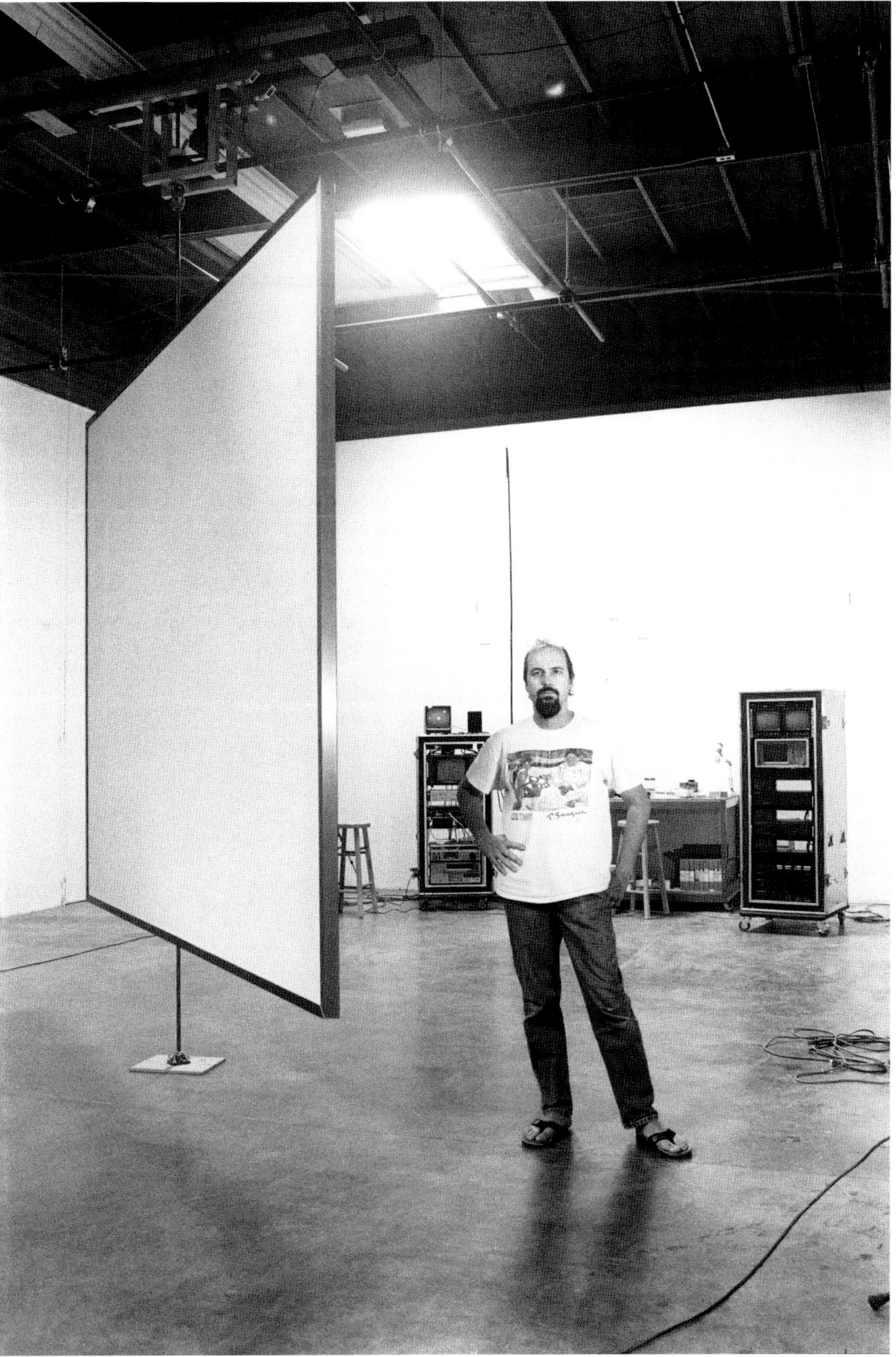

Bill Viola with rotating screen, Bill Viola Studio, Signal Hill, CA, August 1992

The Rotating Screen: Image, Shadow, Mask

Variations:

- Single projector
- Two projectors
- Three projectors

- Double Sided Screen
- Single Sided Screen/Black
- Single Sided Screen/Mirror
- Translucent scrim/screen

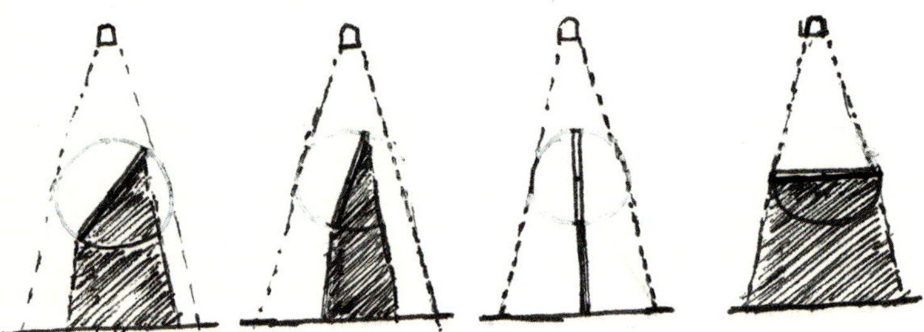

variations with single projector. Umbra/penumbra

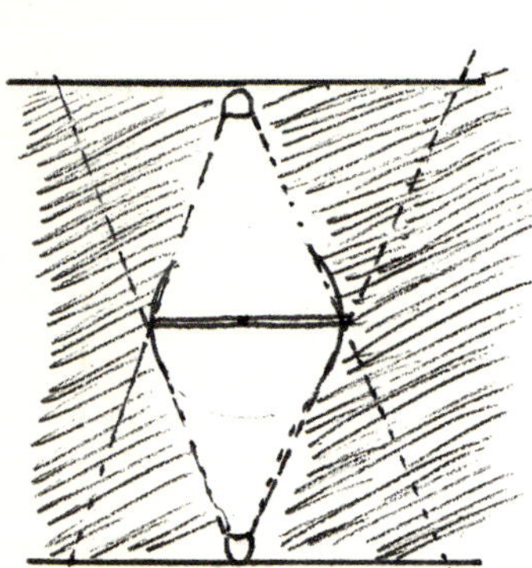

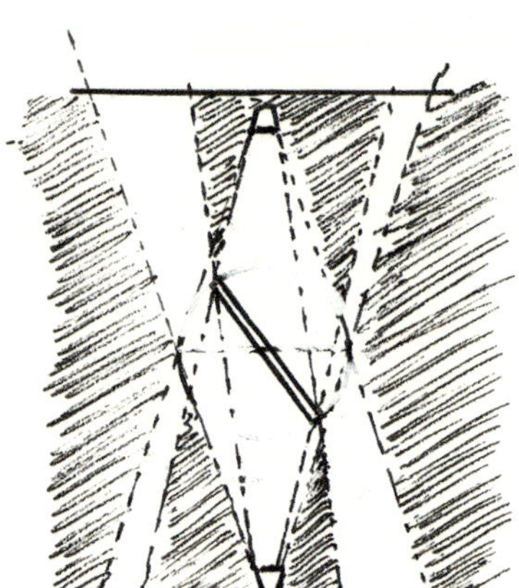

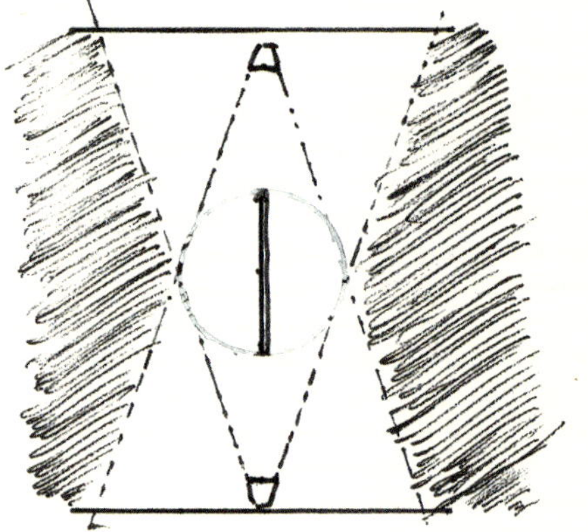

Variations: Two Projectors

Pieces for the Rotating Screen -

- Slowly Turning Narrative: single projector, single sided screen + mirror
- Triptych: three projectors, double sided screen, image ~~collisions~~ overlap
- Collision of Opposites: two projectors, double sided screen, images mask each other
- Collusion of Opposites: two projectors, translucent screen

Above *The Rotating Screen: Image, Shadow, Mask*, drawing, Brockton Triptych Project Book, *c.* July 1988

Opposite and following two pages *Slowly Turning Narrative* (1992)

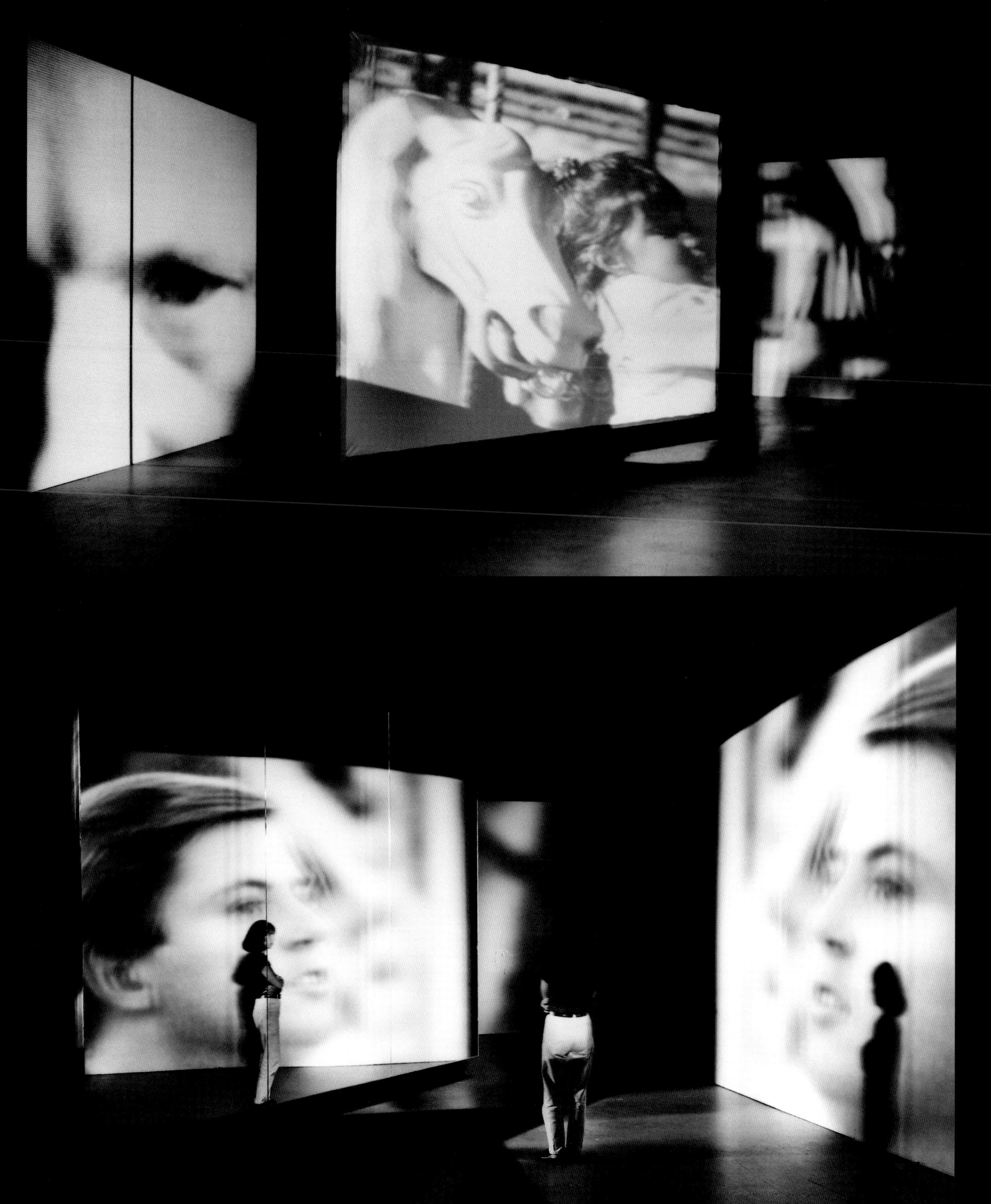

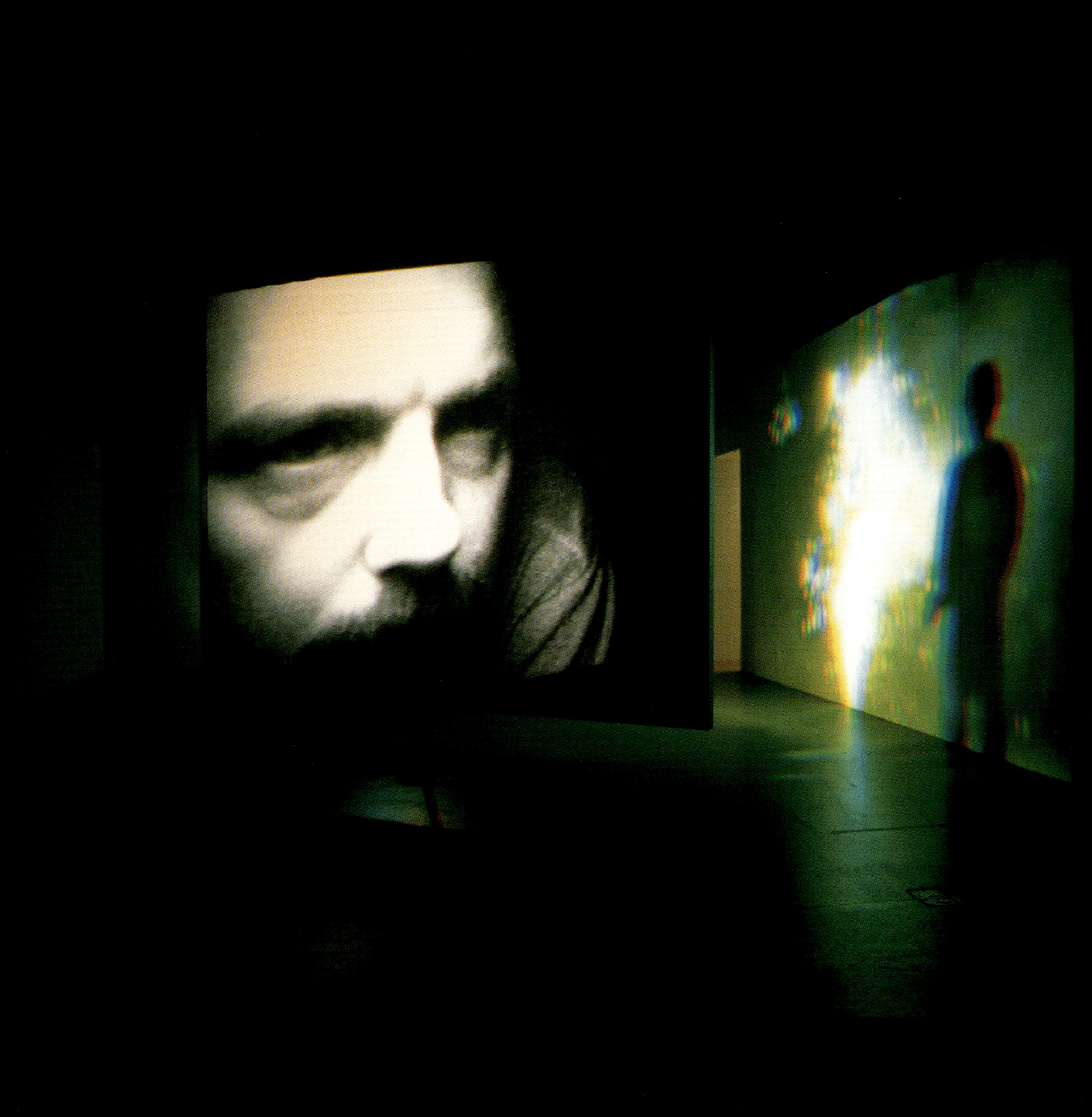

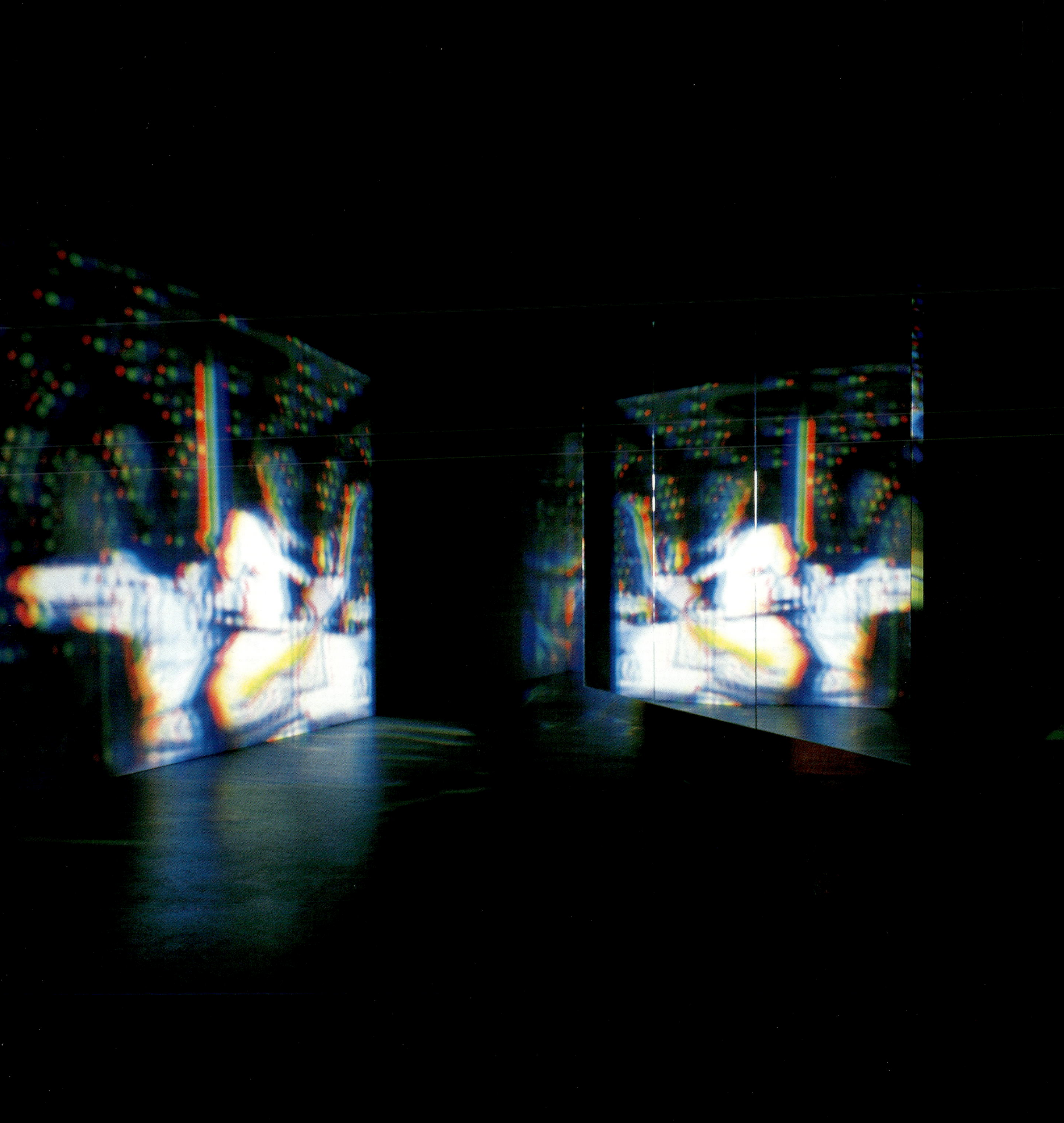

dreams that erupted into view in *The Sleep of Reason*. However, instead of being shocked into consciousness, we are embraced in a moving diorama of dream states that are stitched together with the remarkable text that is continuously chanted by the artist like a dirge. It is the most graphic, compelling, and poetic text that the artist has written in order to capture the hypnotic states of being, the ultimate fragility of the word alongside the image. Neither image nor text anchors or authors the other; rather, they engage in a codependent dance of the one who is the many within the screens of Viola's constantly shifting *tabula rasa* of memories and projected present-tense encounters with the installation.

Slowly Turning Narrative is open to interpretation, and the self-awareness it evokes is specific to every viewer. It causes us to think differently as regards our assumptions about ourselves and others; as Michel Foucault wrote, "There are times in life when the question of knowing if one can think differently than one thinks, and perceive differently than one sees, is absolutely necessary if one is to go on looking and reflecting at all."[18] At this juncture in his life's work, Viola is moving with total assurance toward an understanding of the medium of video as coming into a place of its own. In other words, the moving image of video that caught Viola's attention early on is not "standing in the 'service' of something else," to use Heidegger's conservative argument about technology's "domination" and "conquest" of life.[19] Rather, it is expanding the means for self-reflection and the composition of a poetics that defines itself not in terms of traditional media but through its own properties, which are controlled, or set in motion, by the artist. The videotapes and installations beginning in the early 1990s move Viola's work into a new dimension of representing experience and creating a body of work that speaks to the artist's sense of self and a changing world. The theories of identity, globalism, and theology that emerged at the close of the last millennium have found their champion in an artist not commonly identified with these issues. But a close look at Viola's art will show how his commitment to a changing world arises from a new aesthetics and epistemology of virtue, which we shall consider later in the book. For now, we can continue to trace, through a series of projects, Viola's efforts to place the moving image into a new set of spaces and onto a variety of surfaces, as he signaled in *Slowly Turning Narrative*.

An installation that holds a significant place in Viola's treatment of the image and our perception of the human body in space is *Stations* (1994). In the source of its imagery and the surface onto which it is projected, it contains all the elements of a new representation of the body. The following is Viola's own description of the work:

Stations is an installation for five channels of video projection and sound, focusing on images of the human body submerged underwater. Five cloth

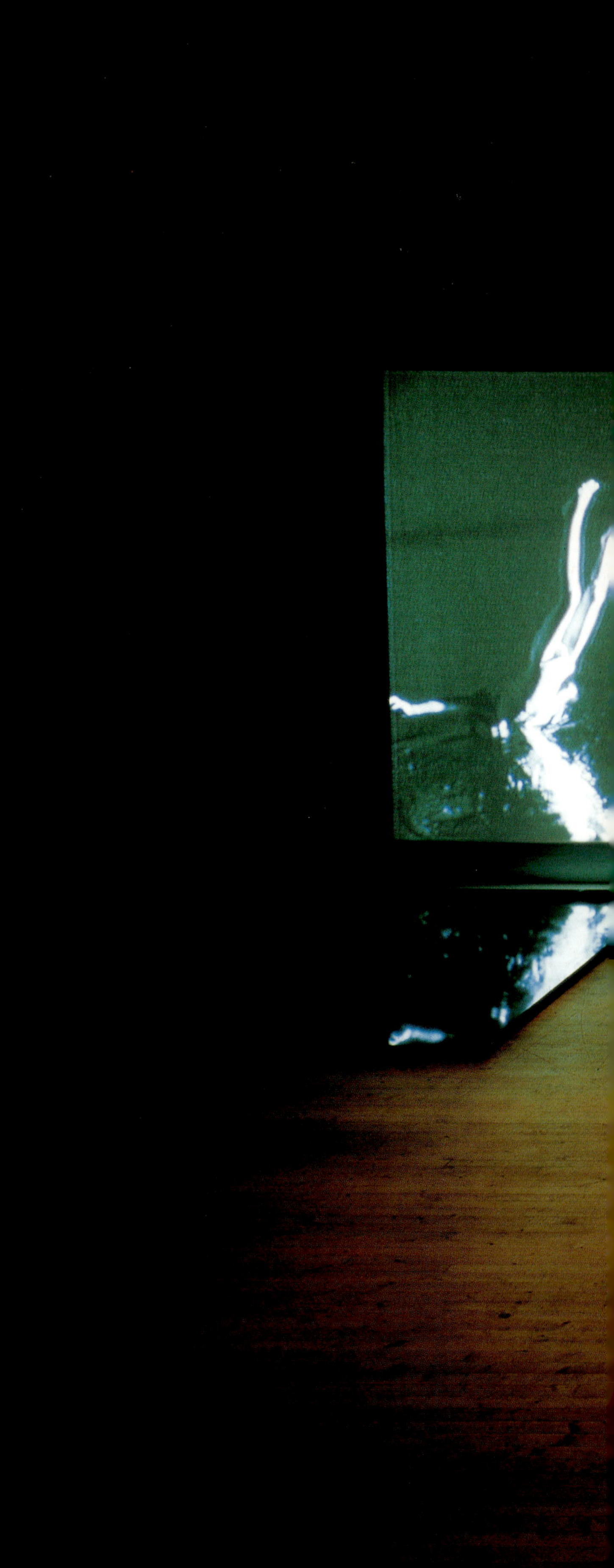

Stations (1994), detail

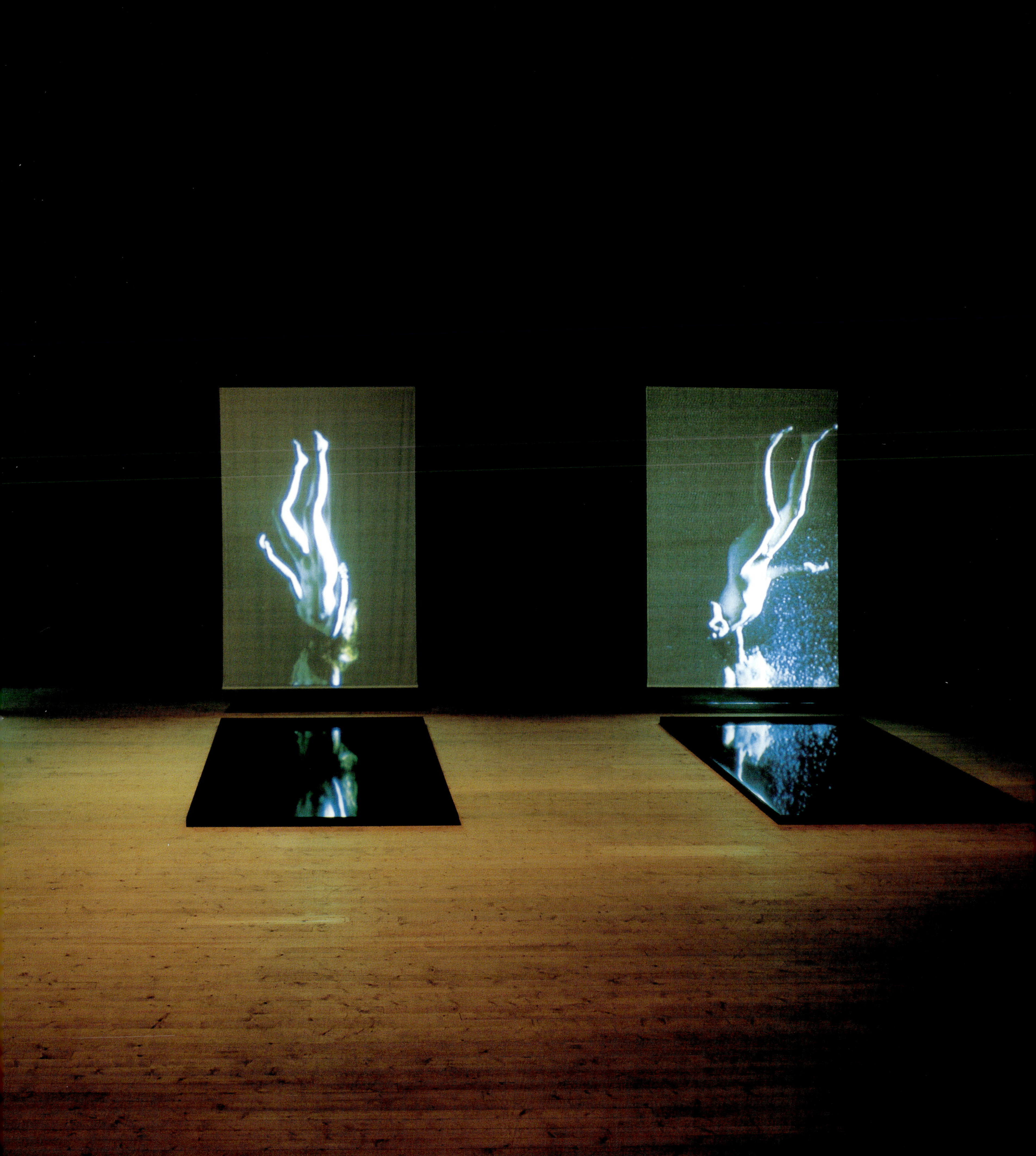

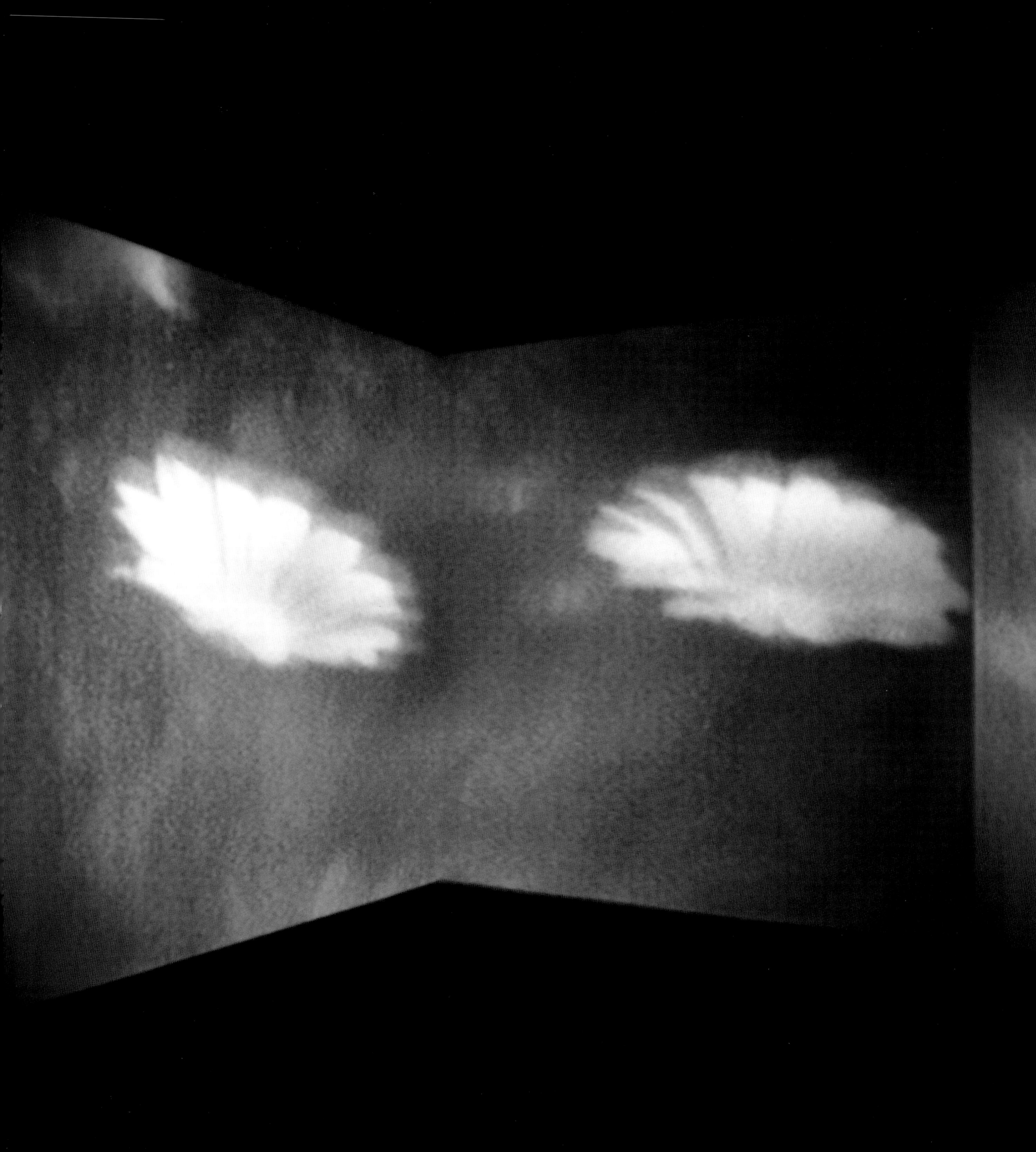

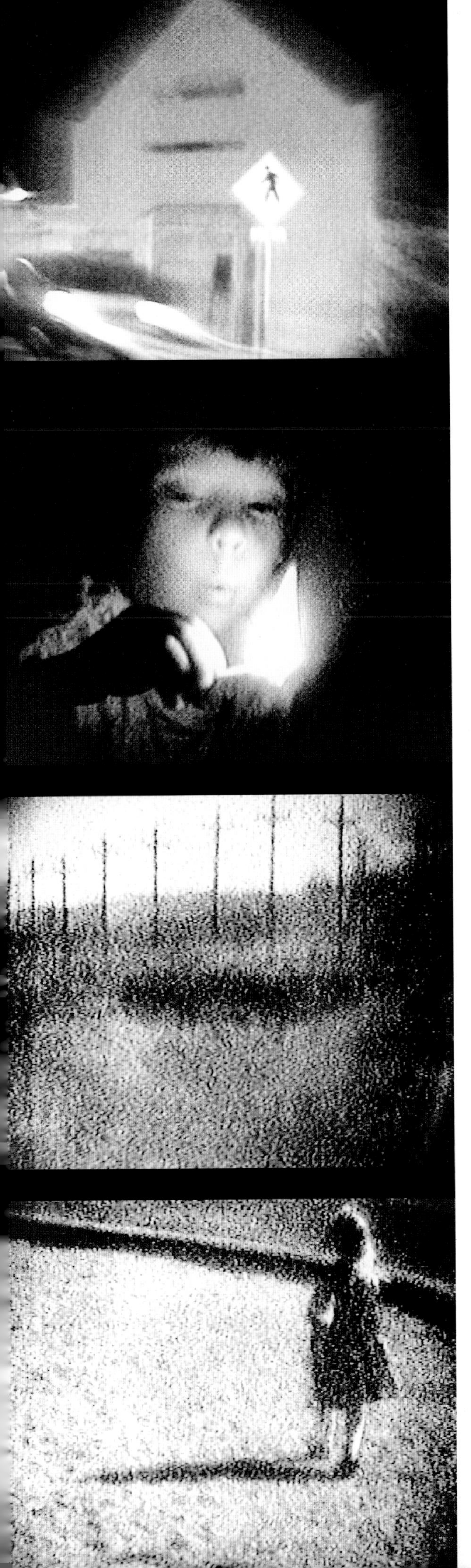

screens are suspended from the ceiling of a large, dark, open space. Under each, a slab of polished black granite lies flat on the floor. The granite slabs are the same dimensions as the screens, on which five different images of the human figure underwater can be seen. The figures are lit with a strong cross light and stand out against the dark void of the background. The submerged bodies hang limp, suspended in space in the subjective tense of slow motion. They are projected upside down and their righted reflections can simultaneously be seen on the polished stone surface below. Underwater sounds are heard locally near each screen. The images play continuously, and at varying intervals the bodies are seen to slowly drift out of the frame, eventually leaving the room dark and silent. Suddenly, the figures plunge into the water in an explosion of light and turbulence. Gradually, the turbulence subsides as they are again slowly at drift until the cycle repeats itself. There is no single viewing angle for the piece, the viewers are free to enter and move about the space at will. An initial surface appearance of eerie, serene beauty resides over a deeper disturbing aspect of muted violence and disorder, with the unrooted, isolated, free floating bodies evoking an eternal state between dream and death.[20]

Anticipating *Five Angels for the Millennium* (2001) and *The Dreamers* (2013), and recalling sequences from *The Reflecting Pool* (1977–9) and *The Passing*, *Stations* occupies a pivotal place in Viola's oeuvre. Its refined use of materials and the drama of its presence develop from the signature "tense of slow motion" and underwater sequences, as well as the use of the fragile scrims and hard stone to anchor our reception of the moving images. In Viola's statement quoted above he describes the "eternal state between dream and death," as the bodies float in a magical liquid space that belies the sense of "muted violence and disorder" that hovers over the exhibition space. A poetic and compelling installation, *Stations* sets the stage for the "Passions" series and the focus on emotions, as well as the environmental treatments of the projected image, in the work that follows.

In *Pneuma* (1994/2009) and *The Veiling* (1995), Viola has created two of his most ethereal and beautiful artworks. They call to mind the German philosopher Martin Seel's term "atmospheric appearing."[21] Seel astutely considers the impression that an object makes, such as how a piece of music can "change the atmosphere in a room."[22] Both *Pneuma* and *The Veiling* place the viewer in the image and create an "atmospheric appearing" out of the changing surface of the moving image, either through the material onto which it is projected (*The Veiling*) or through the construction of the projections that reshape the room that contains them (*Pneuma*).

The brilliance of *Pneuma* lies in its haunting beauty, a flickering consciousness of a moment that composes the space and leaves the viewer with the sense of floating images. Past and present collapse as the viewer

Opposite, left, and following two pages *Pneuma* (1994/2009)

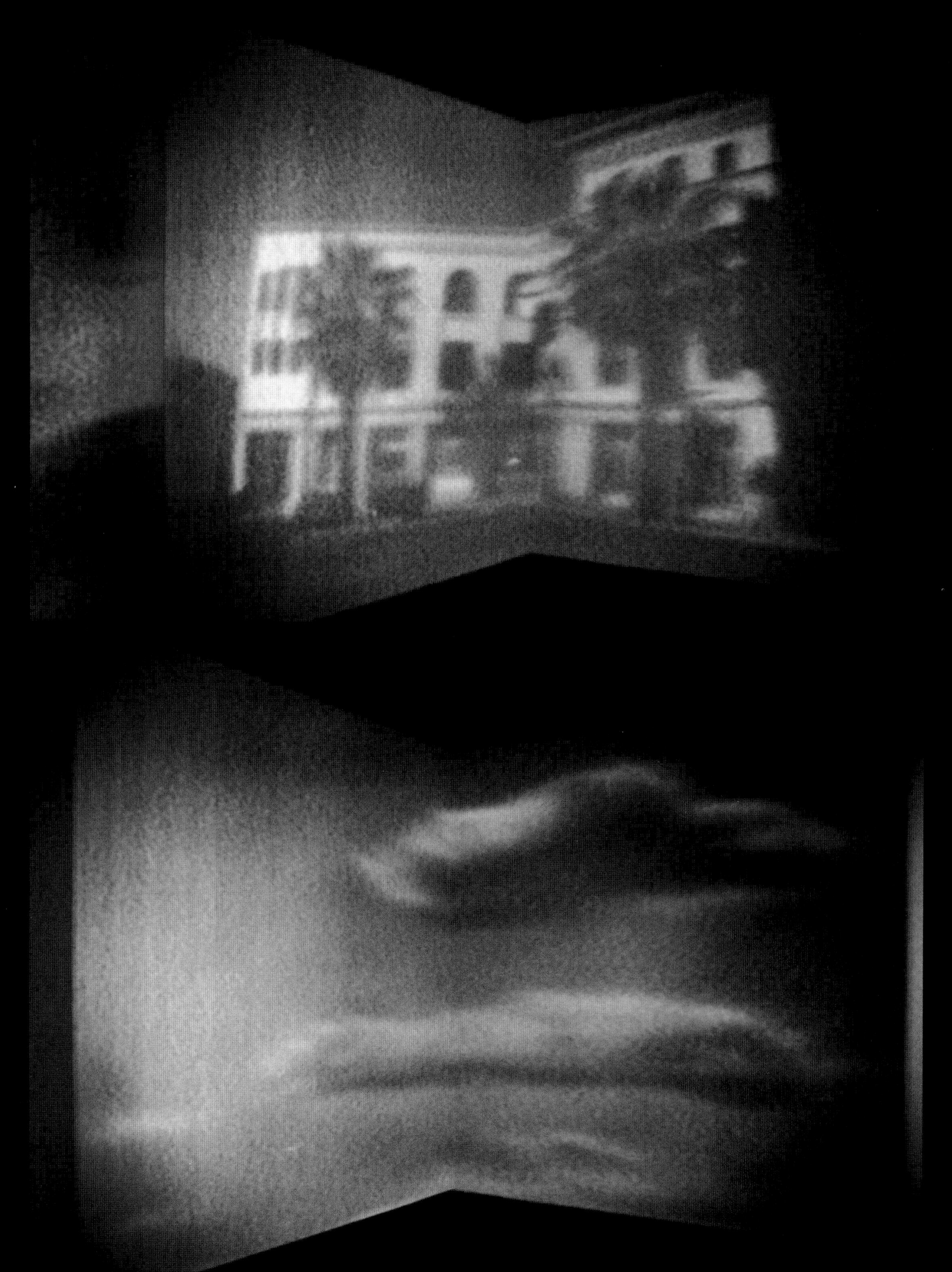

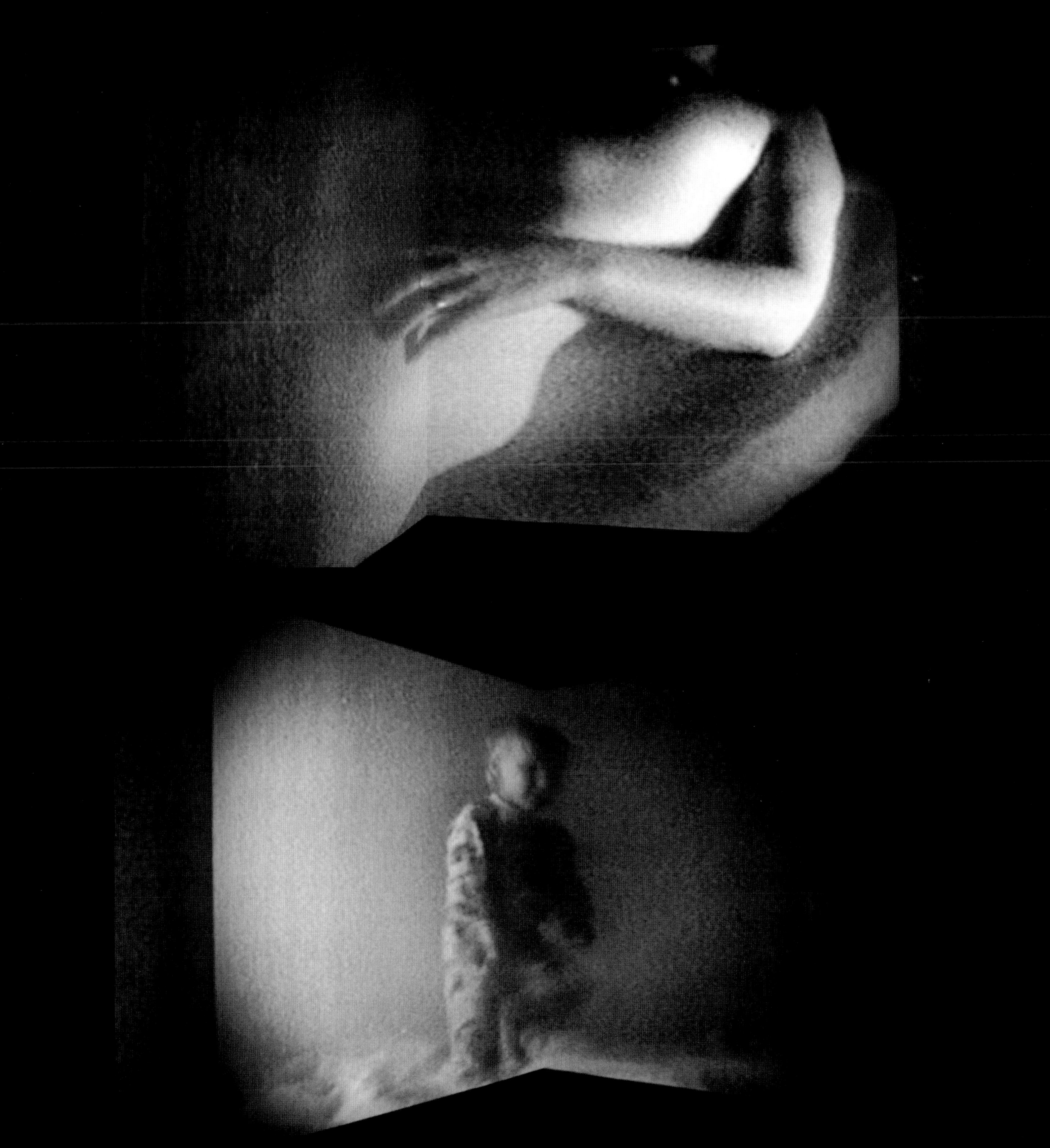

is surrounded by images that appear to be emerging from a timeless night. As Viola describes it, the "moving images are projected in monochrome into the three corners of a dark room. Viewers enter through a door at the fourth corner. The projections fill the walls and overlap with each other, creating a continuous image field that wraps around the room, ending at the entrance area. The sound of white noise permeates the space, and the images appear to coalesce out of the vibrating cloud of abstract grain. Images such as children playing, distant buildings, reflections in a water fountain, and a field of flowers remain fleeting and ambiguous, like a dim memory of a forgotten dream."[23] The themes of flowers, children, and water recur throughout Viola's work, reflecting not only how he continues to discover new things in footage that he has shot over the years, but also how images can take on different meanings in different contexts and projects. The return to certain themes also characterizes Viola's ongoing self-reflective movement through his catalogue of images and the discoveries he makes through the process of shooting.

Regarding the title of *Pneuma*, Viola has said:

"Pneuma" is an ancient Greek word that has no equivalent in contemporary terms. Commonly translated as soul or spirit, it refers as well to breath, and was conceived as an underlying essence or life force, which runs through all things of nature, animating or illuminating the Mind. In the installation, images alternately emerge and submerge into a field of shimmering visual noise, the ground of all images, and hover at the threshold of recognition and ambiguity. Indistinct, shifting, and shadowy, the projections become more like memories or internal sensations rather than recorded images of actual places and events, surrounding and submerging the viewer in their essence.[24]

Viola's turn to ancient thought in both the title and his description of *Pneuma* is an important example of how the artist looks to the poetics of philosophy for the language with which to describe his artworks and the processes involved in their making. Viola's choice of language in describing *Pneuma* is particularly interesting, as it recalls both the early Greek and Stoic philosophers as well as Aristotle's *Physics* and its explanation of physical phenomena. *The Veiling* mirrors Aristotle's thinking about time and the body, the void and contiguity of the human form. As Aristotle notes in the section of *Physics* concerning change, "something which is continuously changing and has not ceased to exist or stopped changing must always either be changing or have changed. But since it is impossible for it to be changing in the now, then at each now it must have changed. Therefore, since there are infinitely many nows, every changing object must have completed an infinite number of changes."[25]

Opposite and following two pages *The Veiling* (1995), drawing and two installation views

THE VEILING

Layers of translucent scrim material catch and diffuse the light of the images

Intersecting
Interpenetrating
Images

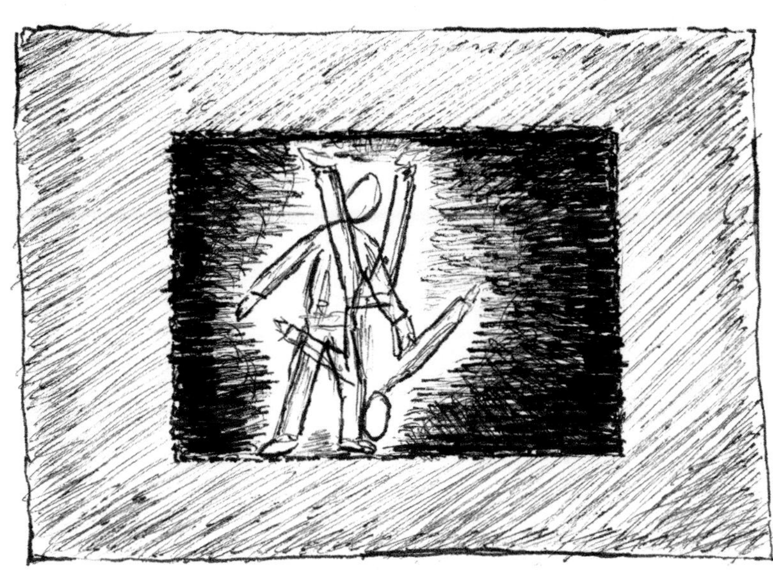

Central Scrim – Images from both projectors meet and align. Figures superimpose

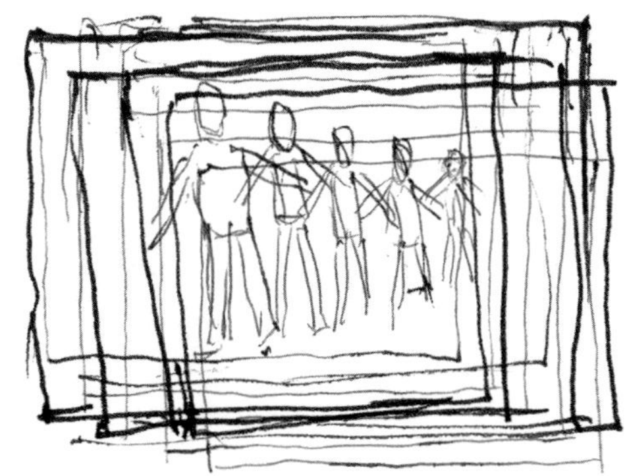

Receding/Advancing figures –
Parallel surfaces of scrims catch light of image and pass through rest to deeper scrim layers.

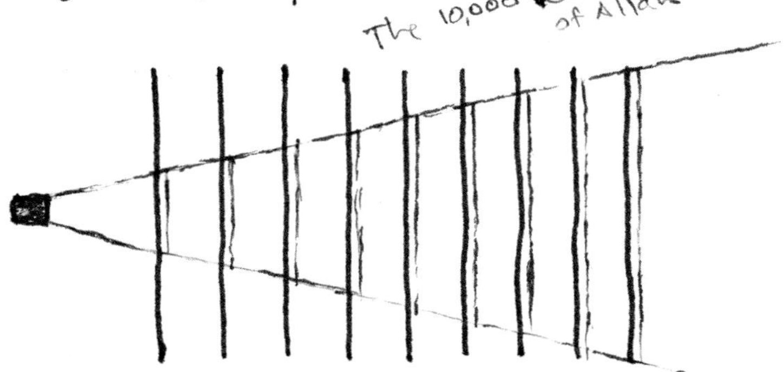

Image light passes through layers of material. It expands in size while getting more dim and diffuse.
Light from one projector crosses with the other

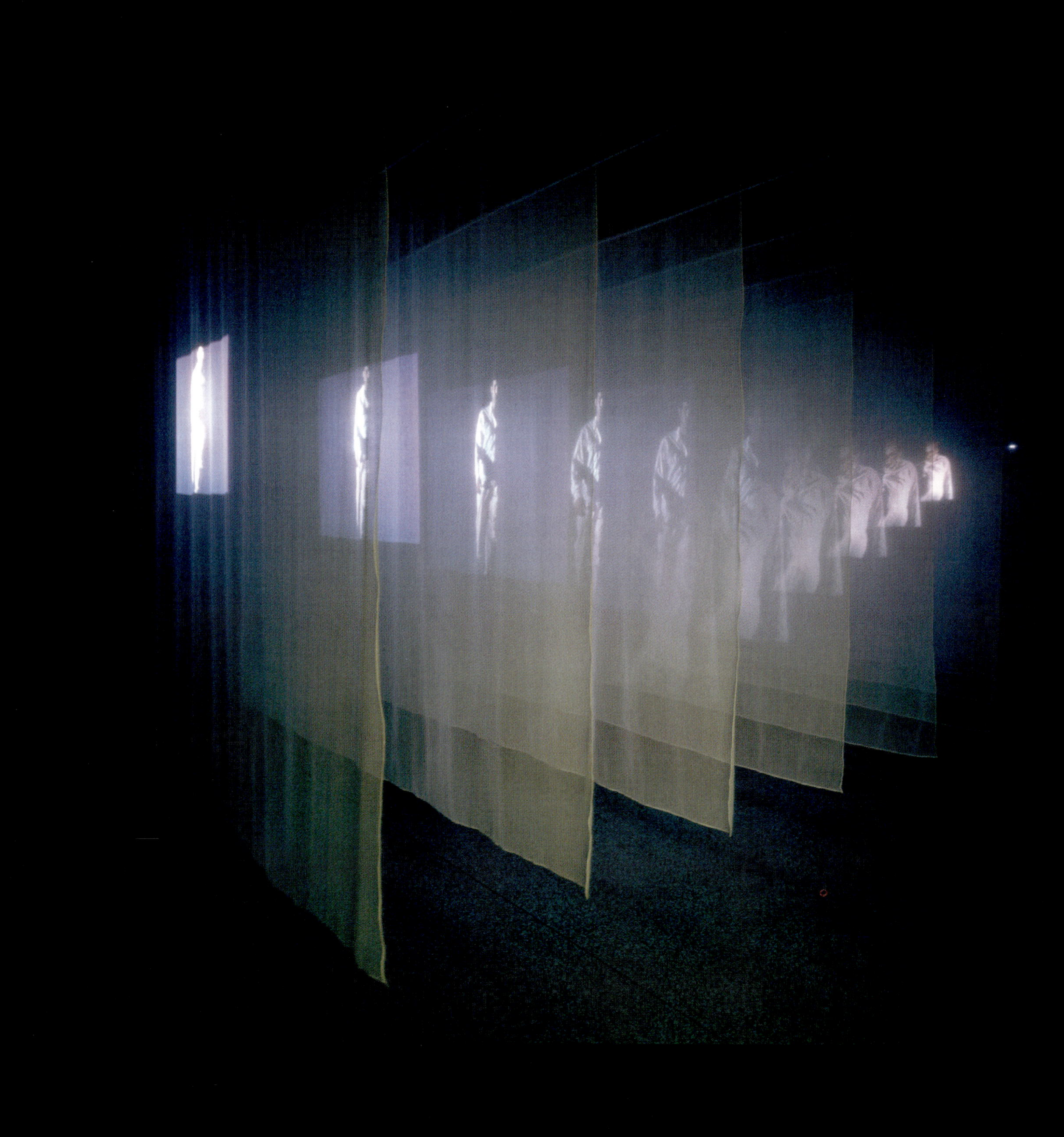

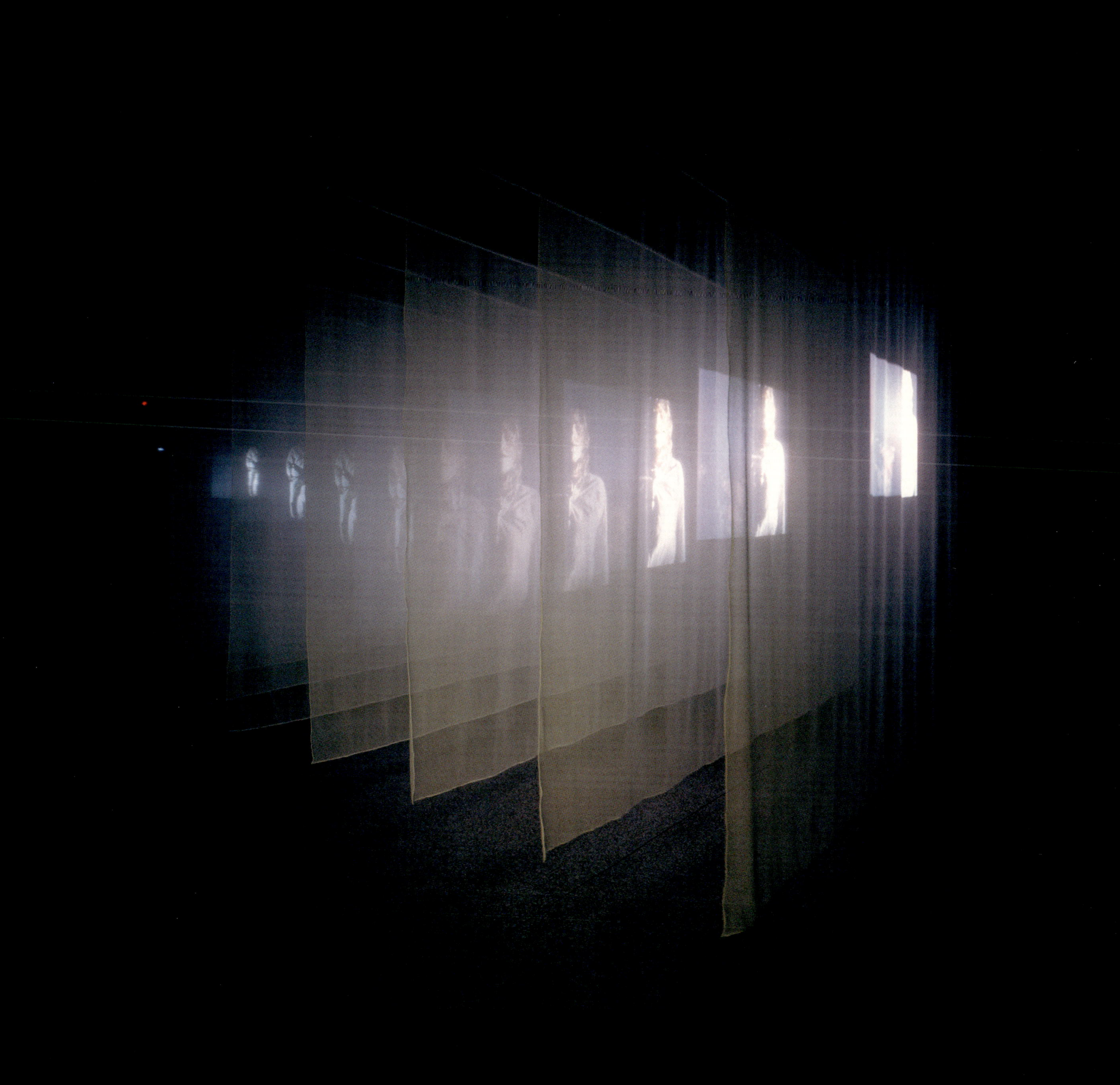

The fragility of the image is embodied in *The Veiling*, one of the five new pieces created by Viola for the U.S. Pavilion at the 46th Venice Biennale. Together with *Pneuma*, *The Veiling* sees the artist move away from his phenomenological representation of perception and his exploration of the nature of the image through its materialization. With both pieces, Viola begins a conversation with the present through the past and establishes the importance of beauty and ethics. The key to *The Veiling* is its structure. Here is Viola's description of the work:

Thin parallel layers of translucent cloth hang loosely across the center of a dark room. Two projectors on opposite ends of the space face each other and project images into the layers of material. The images show a man and a woman as they approach and move away from the camera, viewed in various nocturnal landscapes. They each appear on separate opposing video channels, and are gradually moving from dark areas of shadow into areas of bright light. The cloth material diffuses the light, and the images dissipate in intensity and focus as they penetrate further into the scrim layers, eventually intersecting each other as gossamer presences on the central veil. Recorded independently, the images of the man and the woman never coexist in the same video frame. It is only the light from their images that intermingles in the fabric of the hanging veils. The cone of light emerging from each projector is articulated in space by the layers of material, revealing its presence as a three-dimensionawl form that moves through and fills the empty space of the room with its translucent mass.[26]

With *The Veiling*, Viola brings "breath" into his artwork. According to Stoic physics, "physical objects involve two basic principles, matter and breath. This breath, itself material, pervades all physical objects and the qualities of any particular object are due to the tension of the breath within it."[27] The Stoics further outlined four categories of pneumatic intention, including "rational soul" found in "rational adult humans."[28] Furthermore, "the soul of an individual human being is thus simply the breath present in that individual at a certain level of tension."[29] In *The Veiling*, the moving veils, the material of the fabric, and the human form are fused together as breath, movement, and life, all embodied in both the inanimate object and the human. The essence of video is the moving image, a movement articulated within the shot, composed for projection, as well as shaped through editing. The spirit of Viola's art is about to enter the body as an animating force intended to articulate emotion and reclaim a theological aesthetics in which, echoing the thought of the Swiss theologian Hans Urs von Balthasar, "the beautiful, the true, and the good are found in full and simultaneous companionship."[30]

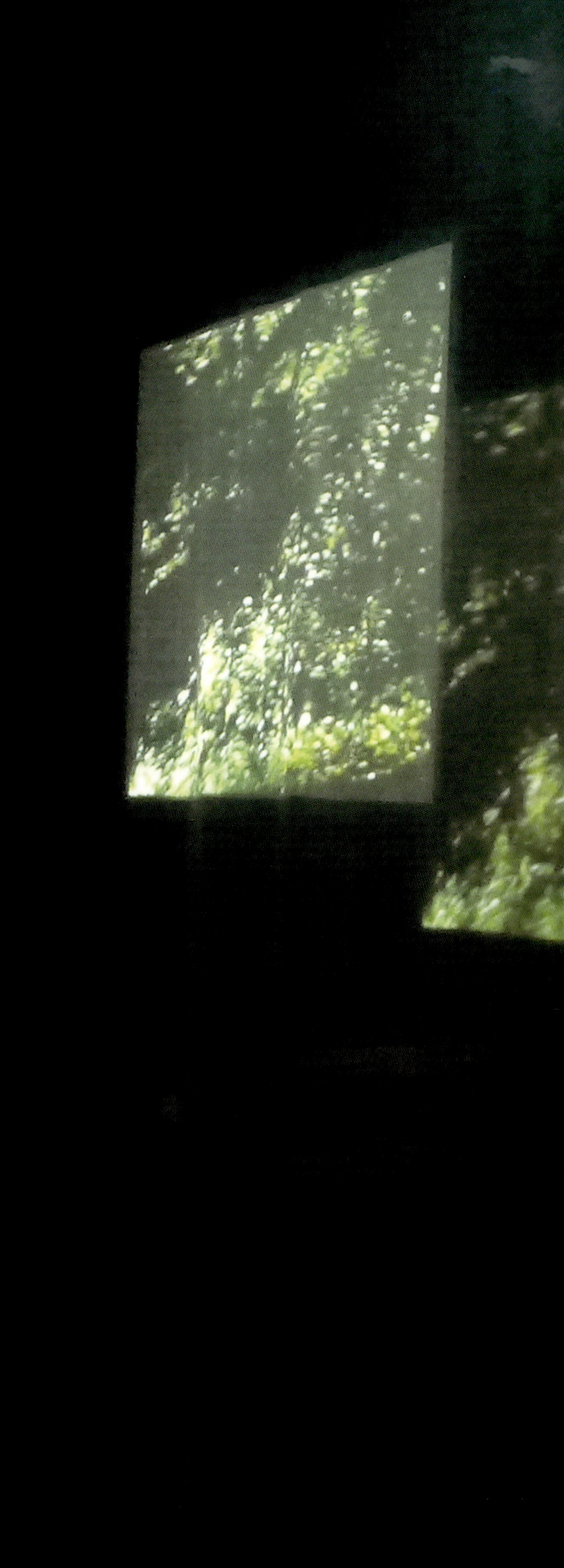

The Veiling (1995)

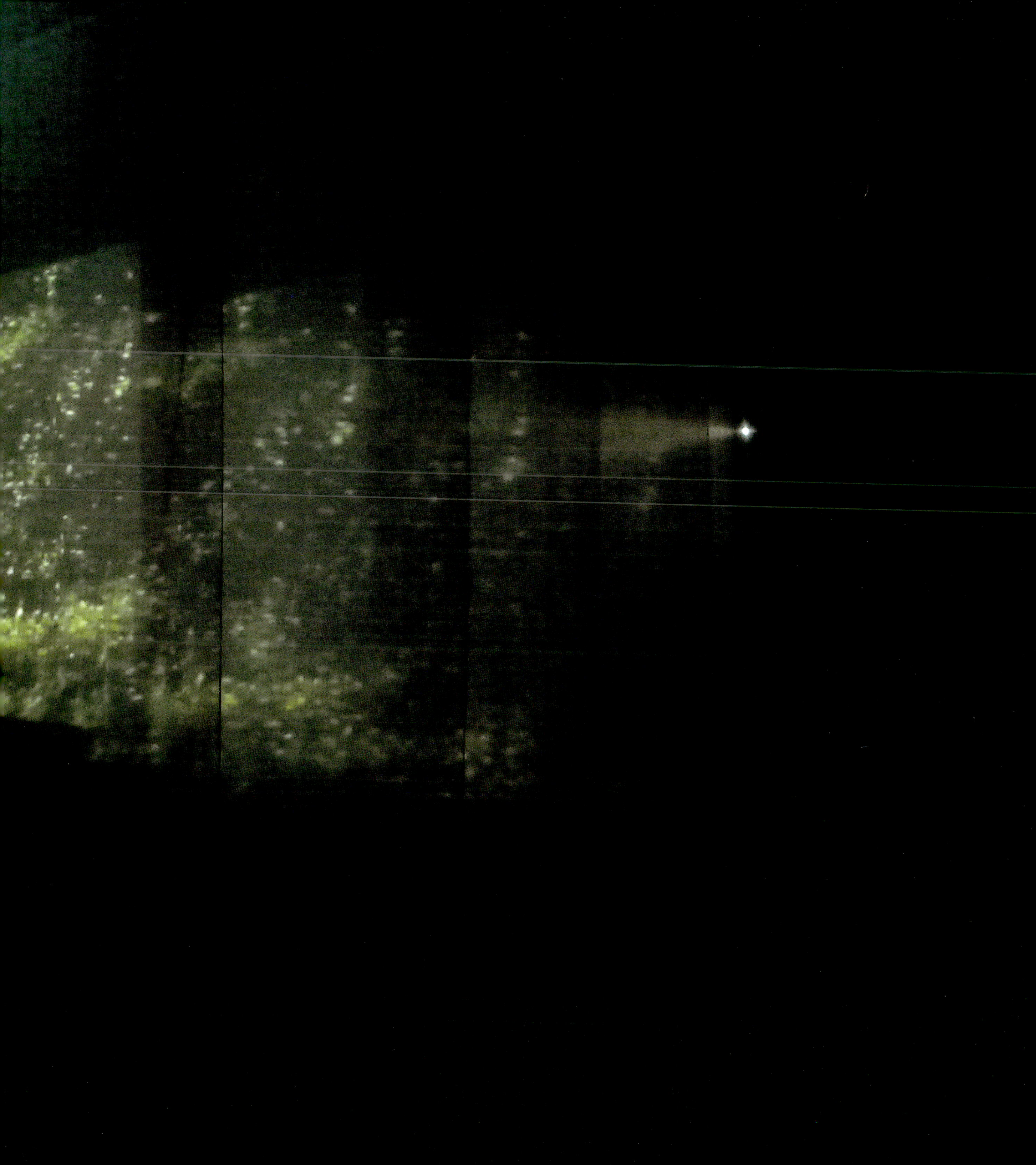

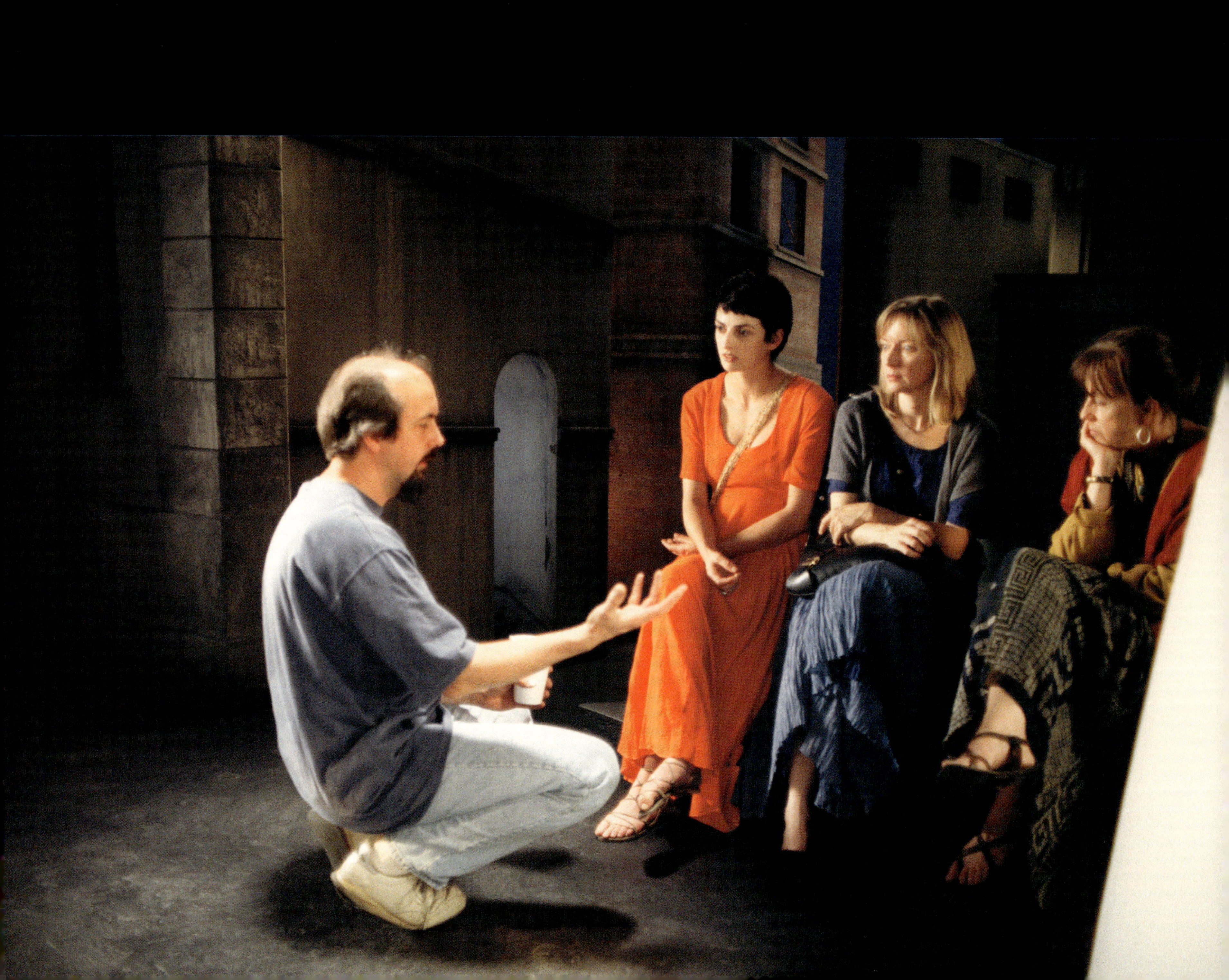

CHAPTER FIVE

1990s: EMBODYING EMOTION ON VIDEO

I have come to realize that the most important place where my work exists is not in the museum gallery, or in the screening room, or on television, and not even on the video screen itself, but in the mind of the viewer who has seen it.

—Bill Viola, 1989

In the 1990s Viola makes a definitive turn to the treatment of the human body through the representation of emotion. It is a step that defines his later work as he elaborates on this theme. The human body and emotions are linked in Viola's work of the 1990s by his treatment of time, which he presents less through the phenomenon of perception, which we saw in the earlier work, and more through a treatment of the deeper meaning of the image. In the works from this period, we can see how Viola's command of the medium allows him to go below the surface of the moving image. His spiritual quest to explore how we understand ourselves and the world around us is inspired by the history of art. In pursuing this goal, Viola furthered his understanding of world religions, as well as the key artworks and genres of painting that expressed spiritual longing and sought to tell the story of religion. However, he was interested not in reproducing paintings on video but in evoking the primary forms of human expression. What comes across clearly in all conversations with Viola is his belief in the flame of human consciousness, which he feels has been lost in today's mechanized and virtual world. He sees it, however, in the imagination of medieval and Renaissance artists creating new ways to represent the spiritual world, be it Islamic, Buddhist, or Christian.

The work that exemplifies Viola's shift of attention to the body in motion within a spiritual space is the video/sound installation *The Greeting*

Bill Viola with performers Angela Black, Suzanne Peters, and Bonnie Snyder on the set of *The Greeting*, Warner Drive Warehouse, Culver City, CA, April 1995

(1995), another of the works he created for the 46th Venice Biennale. "Bill used a high-speed 35mm camera for this work," recalls Perov, "for its ability to shoot 300 frames a second that results in very smooth slow motion, unlike video that had at that time only a fixed 30 frames per second. And for the first time, we were working with actors; the shoot resembled a Hollywood studio. Bill was actually having a set constructed! He was not interested in realism, but in the kind of subtle distortion of the geometry of a scene that you can normally only achieve in a painting."[1] Here is Viola's description of *The Greeting*:

Inspired by Pontormo's Mannerist painting *Visitation* (1528–9), *The Greeting* is a video image sequence projected onto a screen mounted in the wall of a dark room. Two women are seen engaged in conversation. Industrial buildings are visible behind them, aligned in a strange perspective within a barren urban background. As the two women are talking, they are interrupted by a third woman, who enters and approaches them. As they prepare to greet her, it becomes apparent that one of the women knows her quite well, the other less so or perhaps not at all. A slight wind comes up and light subtly shifts as the new woman arrives to great the one she knows, ignoring the other. As the two embrace, she leans and whispers something to her friend, further isolating the other woman. With an underlying awkwardness, introductions are then made and pleasantries exchanged among the three.

Presented as a single take from a fixed camera position and projected in a vertical aspect ratio more common to painting, the actions of the figures are seen in extreme slow motion. An original event of 45 seconds now unfolds as an elaborate choreography over the course of ten minutes. Subtle aspects of the scene become apparent. The unconscious body language and nuances of fleeting glances and gestures become highlighted and remain suspended in the viewer's conscious awareness. Minor shifts in light and wind conditions become central events. At times the background becomes foreground, and other figures are seen in the darker spaces behind the central figures, engaged in unknown activities. The geometry of the walls and buildings appears to violate the laws of optical perspective, and this, together with ambiguities in lighting, all lend a subjective character to the overall scenes. In the end, none of the figures' actions or intentions are explained or become apparent. The precise meaning of the event remains in circulation as an ambiguous, speculative gesture.[2]

Viola's description focuses on the activity of the encounter. In other words, *The Greeting* is not replicating Pontormo's painting; rather, the painting serves as an inspiration for Viola's rendering of this meeting of three women.

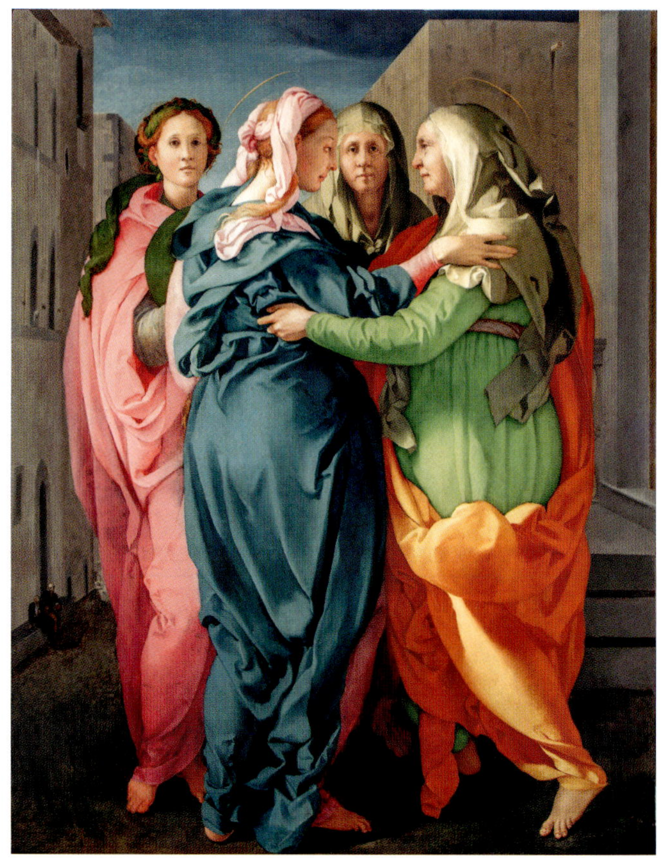

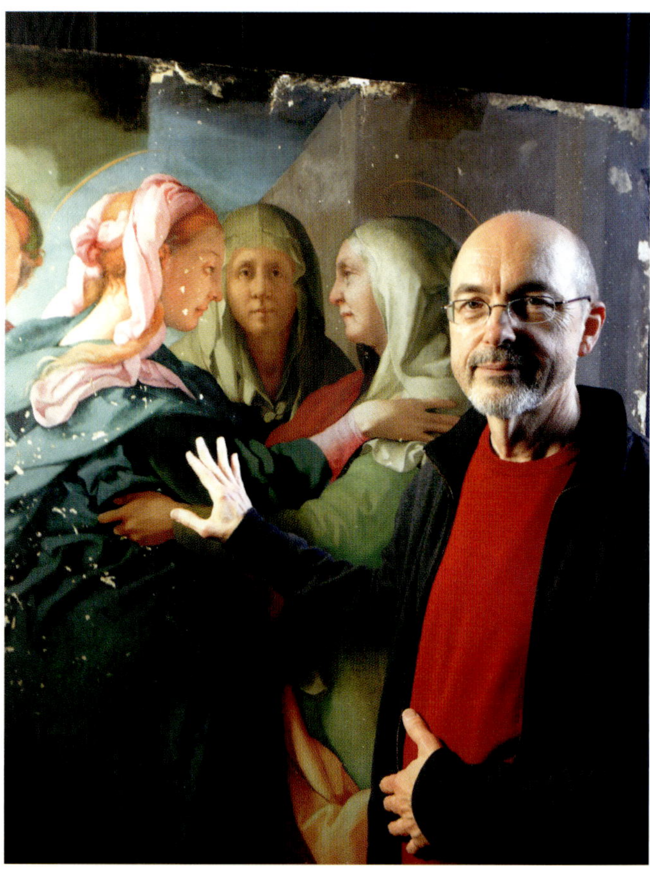

Above Pontormo, *Visitation* (*c.* 1529) (top); Bill Viola with *Visitation* at the restoration studio of Daniele Rossi, Florence, December 15, 2013 (bottom)

Opposite *The Greeting* (1995), stage design

THE GREETING   Architecture of space behind figures.

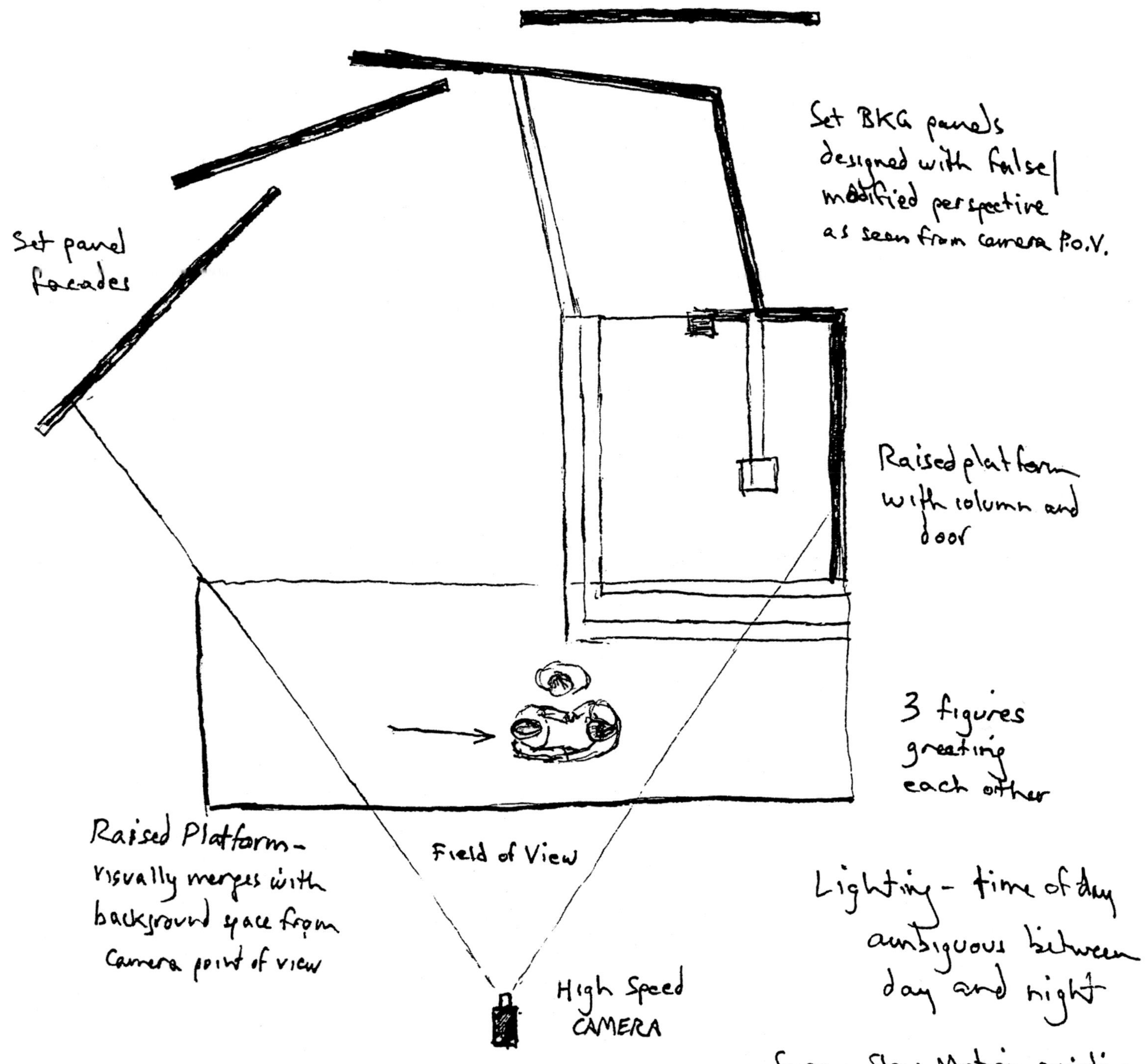

Super Slow Motion recording
300 frames per second
45 seconds of original event becomes appx. 12 minutes of playback time.

Set to be constructed indoors to create view of exterior plaza space with altered geometry.

In the original work there are four figures: the Virgin Mary and Saint Elizabeth meeting, and two women behind them staring straight at the viewer. Viola creates an experience, a narrative, that plays off the Pontormo painting, but which exists in its own space. The woman who is "ignored" in Viola's work lends an ambiguity to the meaning of the encounter, which gains weight through knowledge of the Pontormo. The role of emotion in this scene privileges the viewer and further encloses the action in the extended time of the slow motion. Pontormo's Mannerist folds of cloth are evoked in Viola's expressive use of time to shape the action and lead the viewer to the two women. In a sense, Viola's piece is both more personal and more abstract. It is more personal in its emotional message, and more abstract in not locating the work strictly within the theological narrative of Pontormo's painting.

The Greeting, in which Viola used slow motion most compellingly to make the physical experience tangible for the viewer, was followed by *The Messenger* (1996). Although this work does not reference a specific theological text or painting, it was originally conceived for a cathedral. Thus its emotional power and spiritual significance are enhanced by the cathedral context. Here is Viola's description of the work:

***The Messenger* was originally created for Durham Cathedral, in northern England. A large image was projected onto a screen mounted to the great west door of the church. The image sequence begins with a small, luminous, abstract form shimmering and undulating against a deep blue-black void. Gradually, the luminous shape begins to get larger and less distorted, and it soon becomes apparent that we are seeing a human form, illuminated, rising toward us from under the surface of the body of water. The water becomes calmer and more transparent and the figure clearer on its journey upwards toward us. We identify the figure as a man, pale blue, naked, on his back, rising up slowly.**

After some time, he breaks the surface, an act at once startling, relieving, and desperate. His pale form emerges from the warm hues of a bright light, the water glistening on his body. His eyes immediately open as he releases a long-held breath from the depths, shattering the silence of the image. The forceful primal sound of life resonates momentarily in the space. After a few moments, he inhales deeply, and, with his eyes shut and mouth closed, he sinks into the depths of the blue-black void once more, returning to his origin as a shimmering, moving point of light. The image sequence continually repeats, with the man perpetually rising and sinking, describing the constant circulation of birth and death, and functioning like a great cycle of respiration in the space.[3]

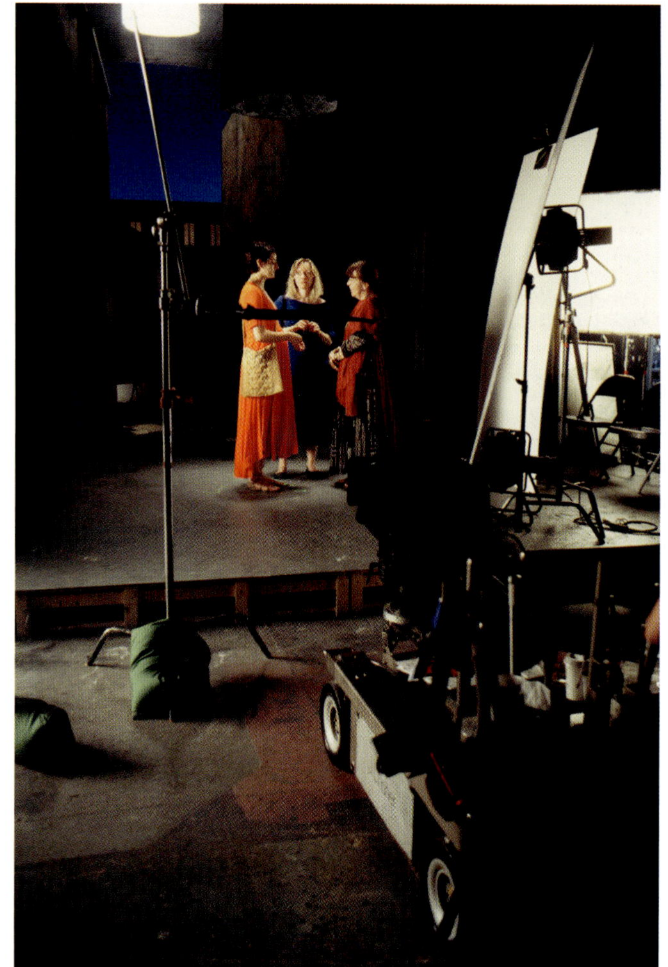

Above and opposite On the set of *The Greeting*, Culver City, April 1995

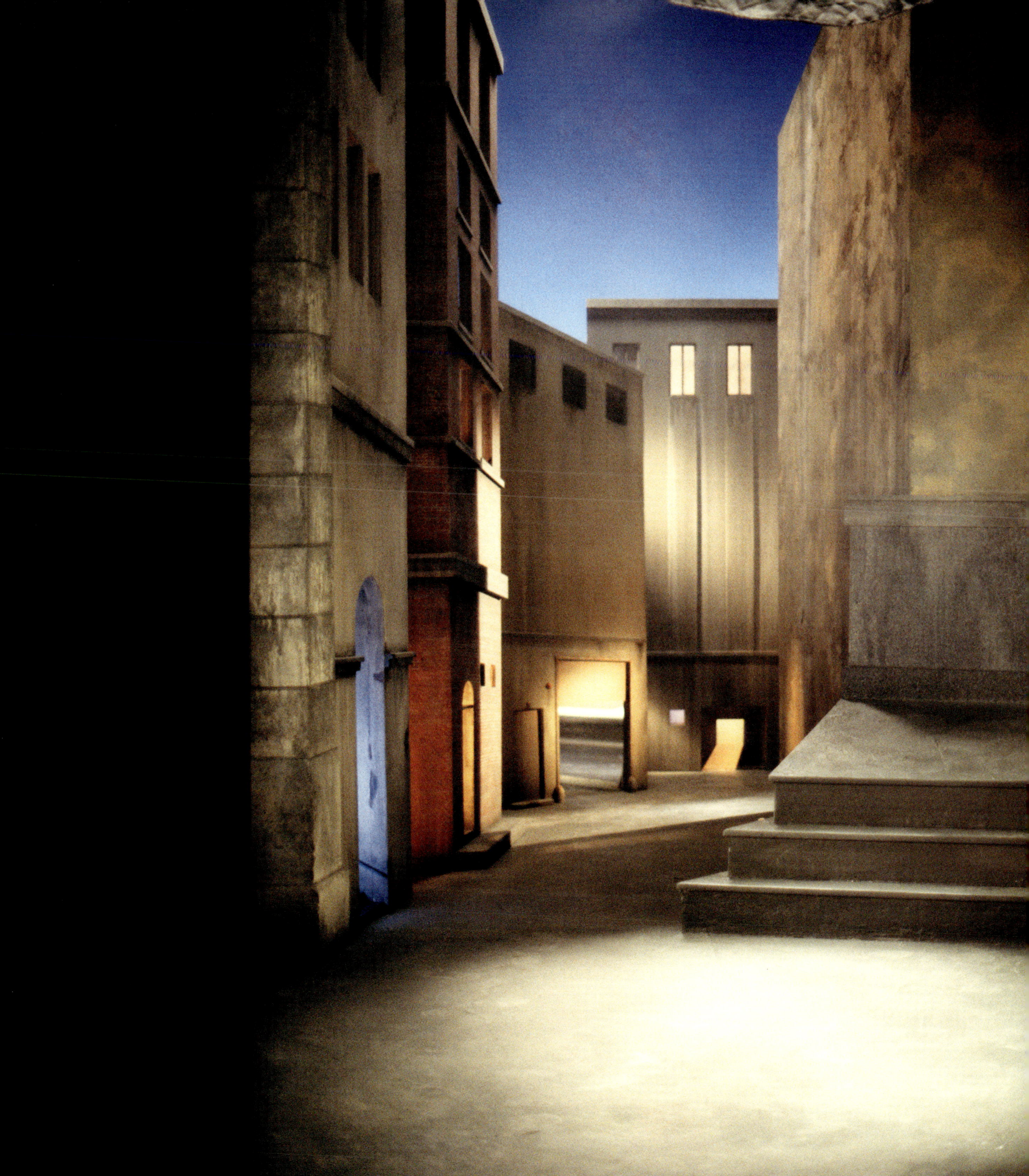

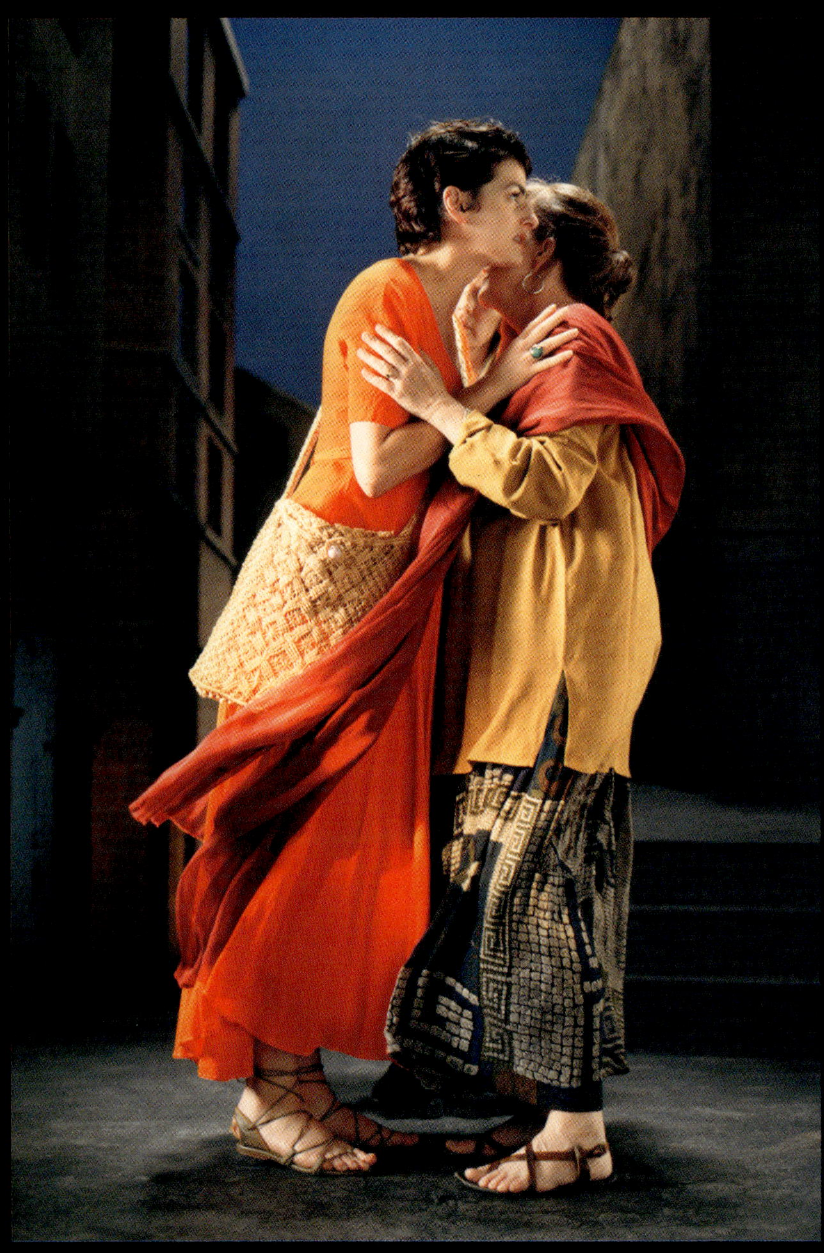

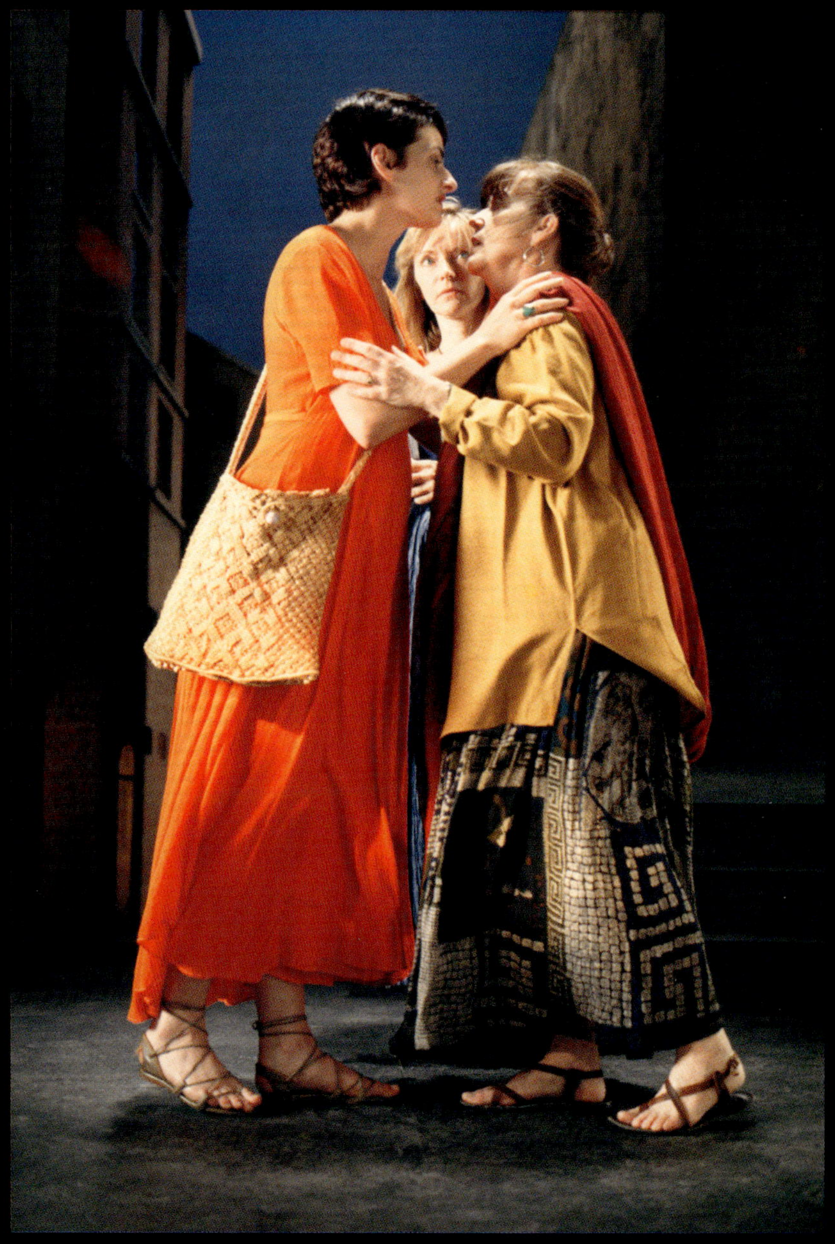

The Greeting (1995)

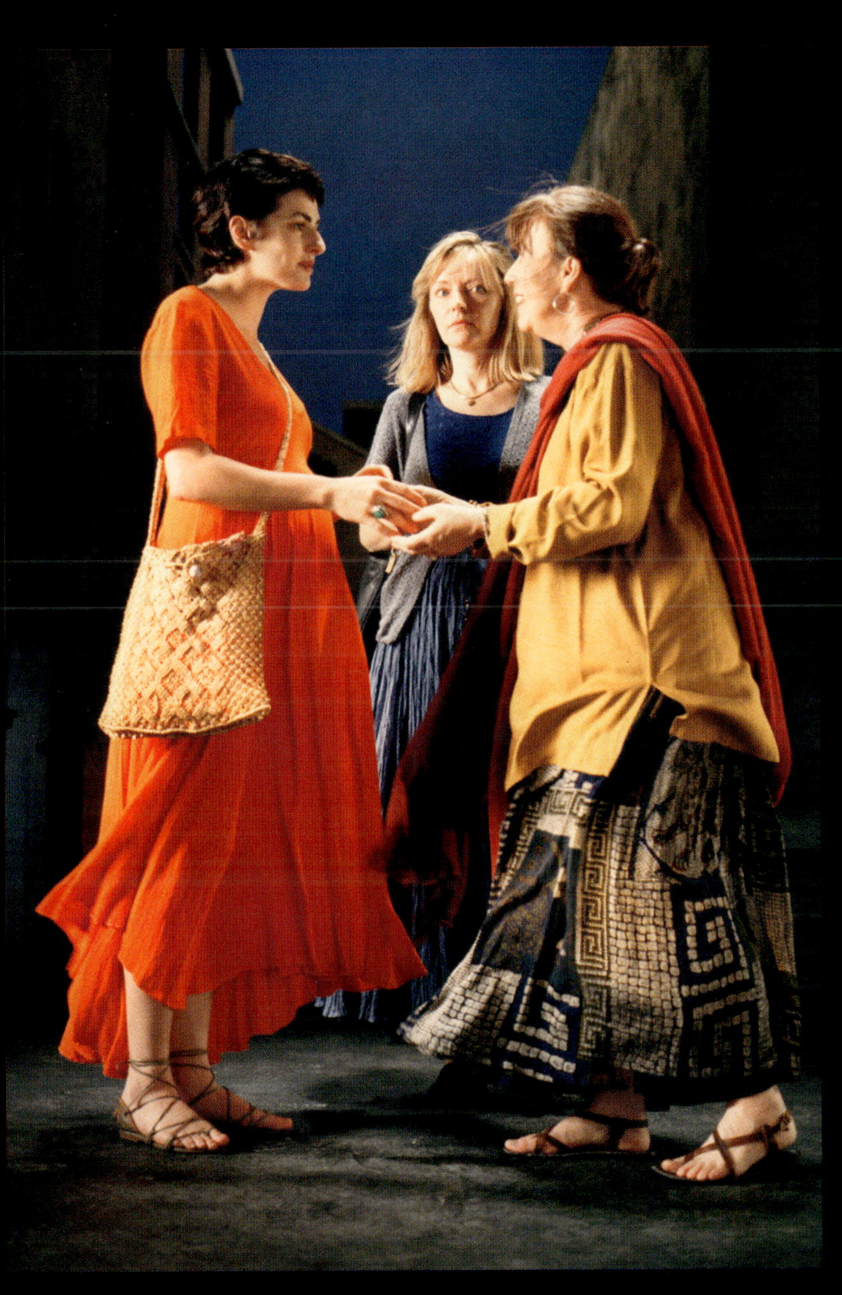

Unlike *The Greeting* that treats the meaning of the event as purely gestural and describes a social dynamic of inclusion/exclusion between the three women, *The Messenger* embodies a more spiritual theme, the "constant circulation of life and death." This is in part a response to the site for which the work was created, a cathedral, where the figure's journey through the void speaks to what we seek from religion and holy places, sanctuaries in which to contemplate life and death. Over a period of 28 minutes, we see five sequences of the man slowly surfacing and then sinking, each representing a cycle of birth and rebirth. The naked figure emerges as a point of light out of the void and continues to the surface as a full-grown human, gasping for the oxygen one needs to sustain life. In the cathedral setting, this figure could be a stand-in for Christ—whose death and resurrection continue as a hymn to life—and the ineffable light that illuminates the trajectory through oppression to freedom, but it could also be interpreted as representing the Buddhist notion of reincarnation. Viola's slow-motion meditation on the body creates its own space within the narrative of the moving image. *The Messenger* can be removed from the context of the cathedral and shown on its own in a museum or gallery, where the mystery of the origins of the image is open to multiple interpretations.

The beauty of following the arc of Viola's art-making is being able to observe how he refines his aesthetic, creating a cumulative impact over time. There is a wholeness to Viola's body of work that is both summarized and expanded by each new piece. Here, Viola describes *The Crossing* (1996), made at the time of *The Messenger*'s creation:

A large double-sided projection screen stands in the middle of a room, its bottom edge resting on the floor. Two video projectors mounted at opposite ends of the room project images onto the front and back sides of the screen simultaneously, showing a single action involving a human figure culminating in a violent annihilation by the opposing natural forces of fire and water.

On one side of the screen, a human form slowly approaches from a great distance through a dark space. The figure gradually becomes more distinct, and we soon recognize a man walking straight toward us, all the time becoming larger. When his body almost fills the frame, he stops moving and stands still, staring directly at the viewer in silence. A small votive flame appears at his feet. Suddenly, brilliant orange flames rise up and quickly spread across the floor and onto his body. A loud roaring sound fills the space as his form rapidly becomes completely engulfed by a violent raging fire. The first soon subsides until only a few small flickering flames remain on a charred floor. The figure of the man is gone. The image returns to black and the cycle repeats anew.

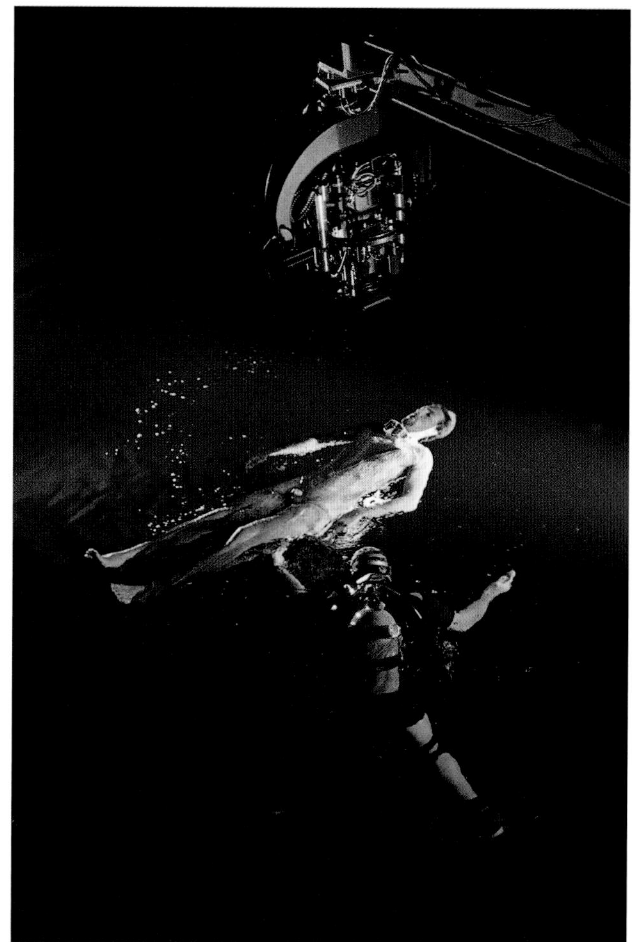

Above On the set of *The Messenger*, performer Chad Walker, Belmont Olympic Pool, Long Beach, CA, August 1996

Opposite *The Messenger* (1996), Durham Cathedral, UK

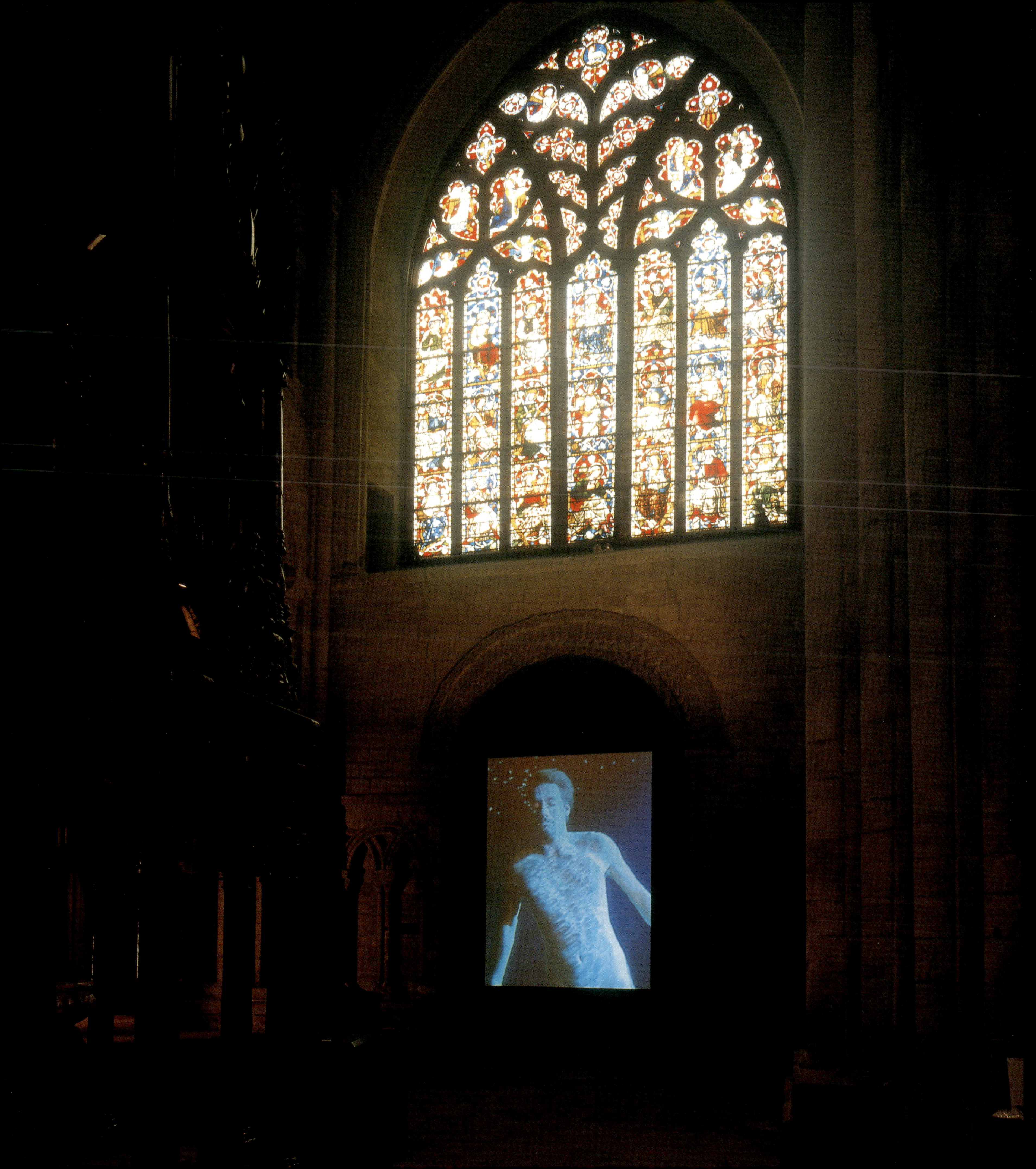

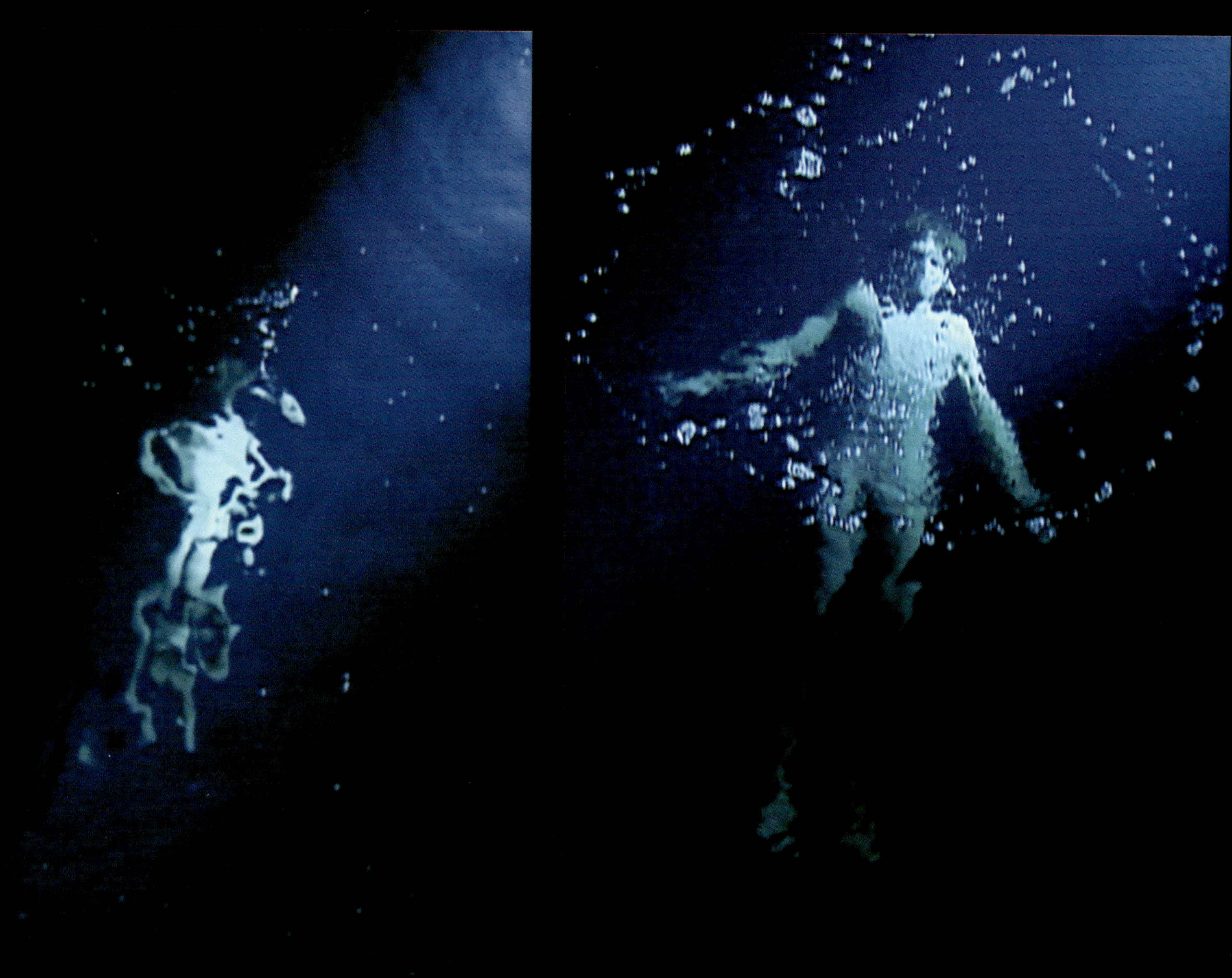

The Messenger (1996)

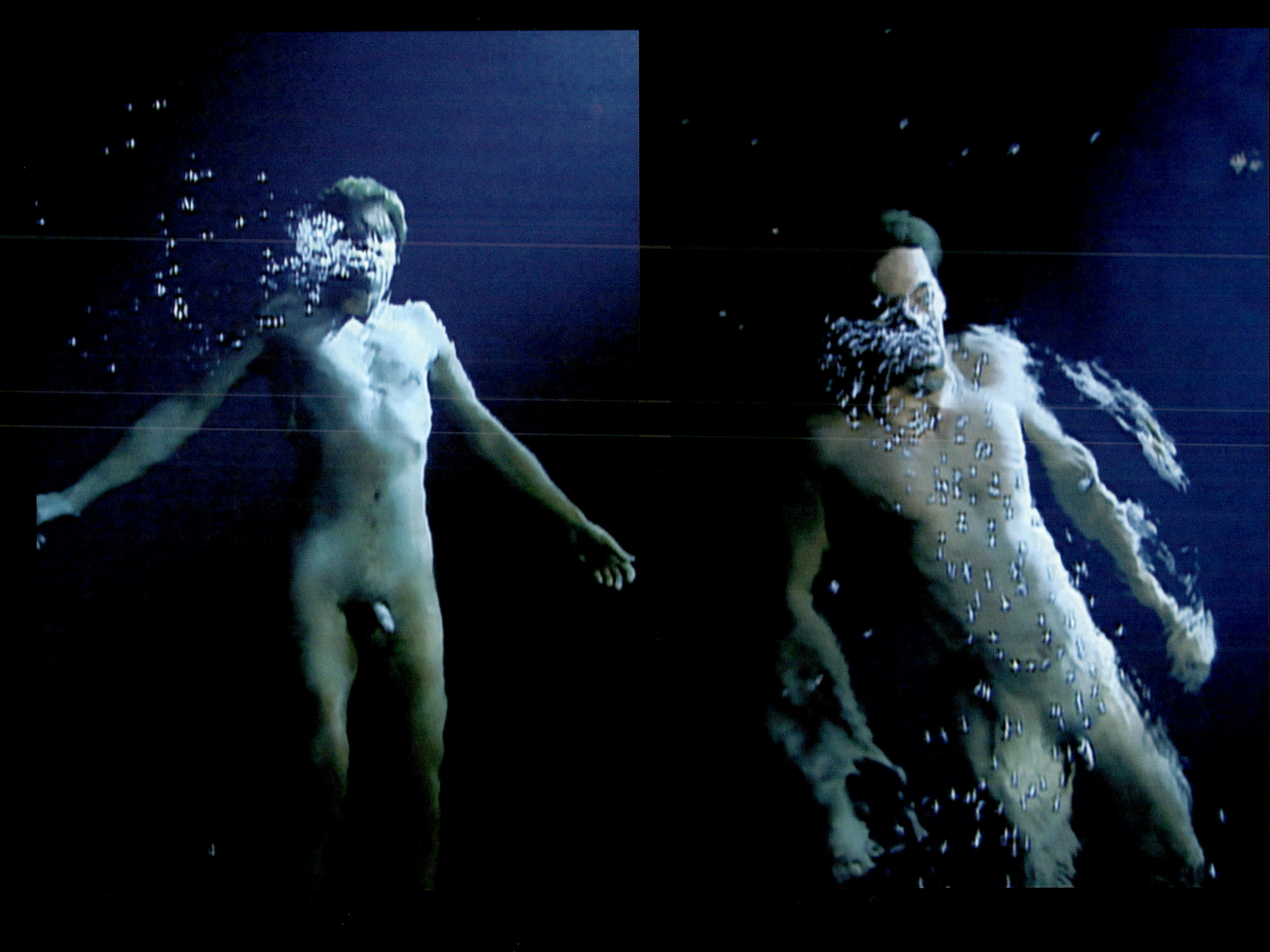

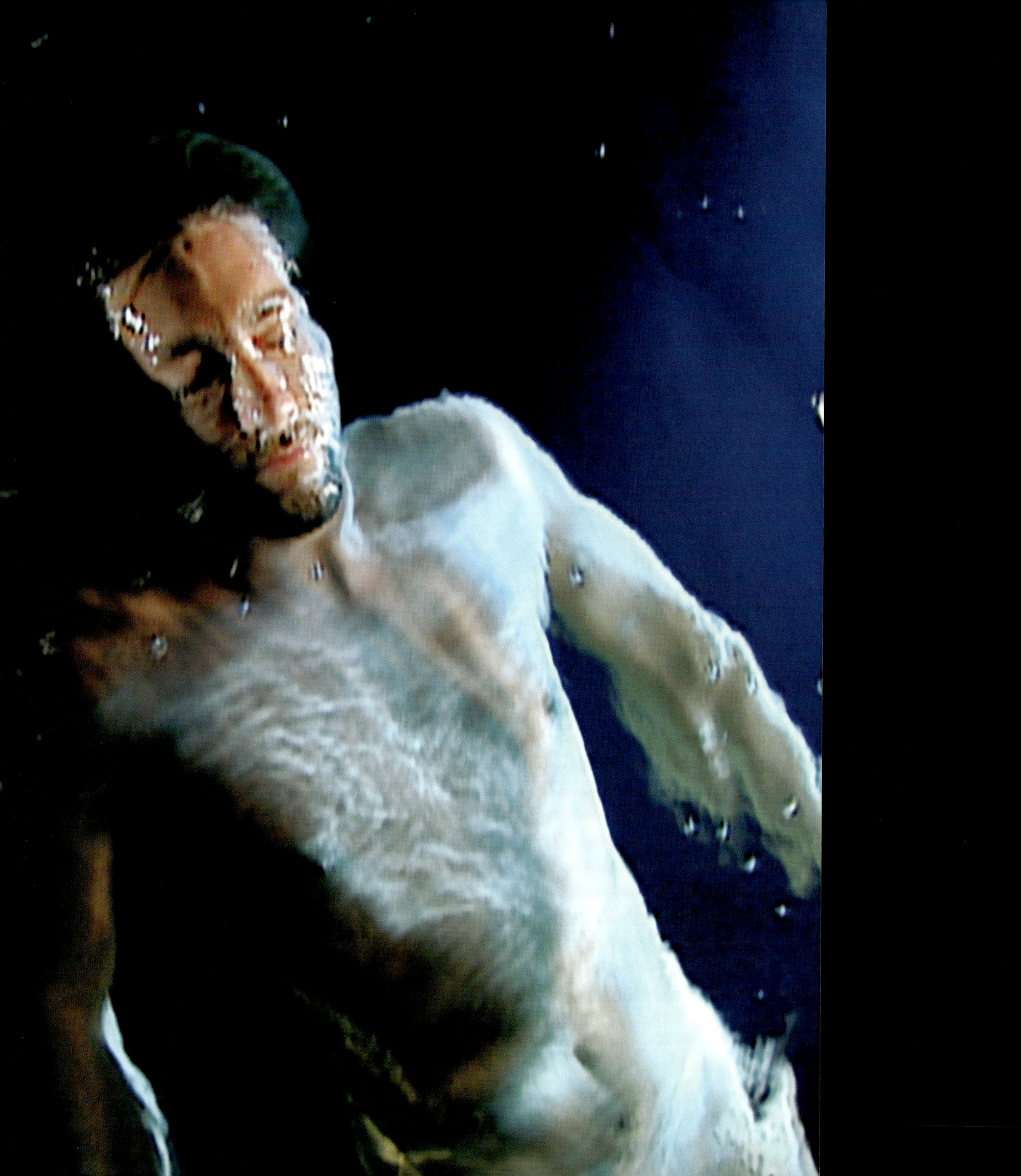

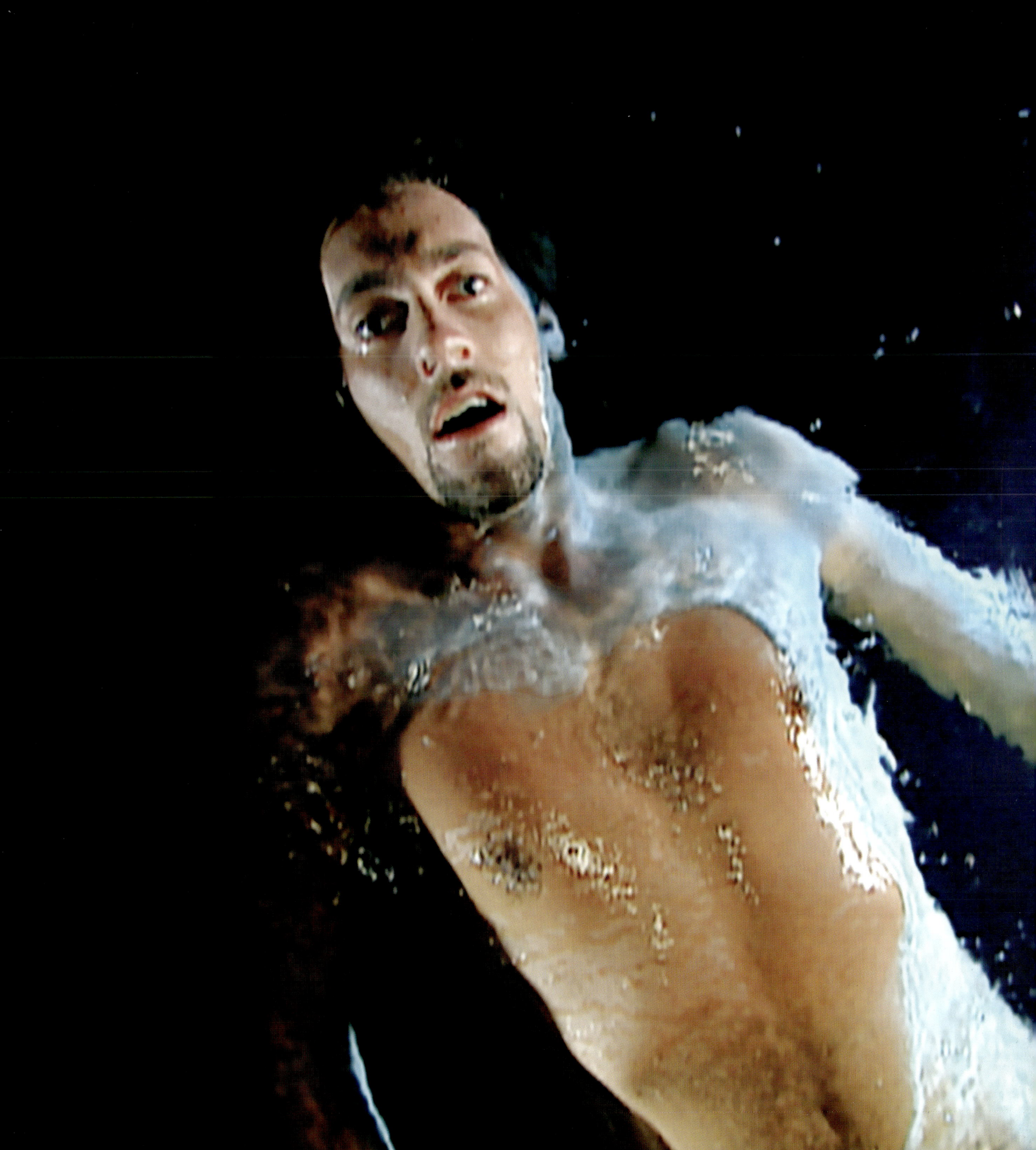

On the other side, we again see a dark human form approaching. He slowly moves towards us out of the shadows, in the same manner as the other figure. Finally, he too stops and stares, motionless and silent. Suddenly, a stream of silver-blue water begins pouring onto his head, sending luminous trails of splashing droplets off in all directions. The stream quickly turns into a raging torrent as a massive amount of water cascades from above, completely inundating the man as a loud roaring sound fills the space. The falling water soon begins to subside and trails off, leaving a few droplets on a wet floor. The figure of the man is gone. The image then returns to black and the cycle repeats anew.

The two complementary actions appear simultaneously on the two sides of the screen, and the viewer must move around the space to see both images. The image sequences are timed to play in perfect synchronization, with the approach and the culminating conflagration and deluge occurring simultaneously, energizing the space with a violent raging crescendo of intense images and roaring sound. *The two traditional natural elements of fire and water appear here not only in their destructive aspects, but manifest their cathartic, purifying, transformative, and regenerative capacities as well. In this way, self-annihilation becomes a necessary means to transcendence and liberation* [emphasis added].[4]

Viola here makes one of his clearest statements about how he sees the forces of creation and destruction as being linked. It is within the loop of the video projection that the transcendence occurs. The endlessly returning figure that is washed away with water and consumed by flames returns to an experience depicted as a serenely purifying, not cataclysmic or destructive, event. It is also an event emptied of emotion, where the power of nature and humanity recedes in a purifying reserve. It is this linking of beauty to emotion and the powers of seeing that, over the following decade, brings Viola's work to the forefront of an ethically grounded aesthetic, an investigation that locates itself in the transactions between people and within the individual.

The compelling emotional power of Viola's work distances his aesthetic from a simple rejection of modern life; he complicates the position of the self in creating its hold on life in the face of the certainty of death. These are issues that continue to inhabit Viola's art as he explores new ways in which to speak to the human condition. Once again, developments in video technology gave the artist a new electronic surface on which to create. As Viola notes,

There is a revolution going on right now in display technology. I'll never forget when, in 1998, an engineer friend [Thomas Piglin, with whom Viola

Opposite Drawing for *The Crossing*, proposal for Festival d'Automne à Paris, January 1996

Following two pages *The Crossing* (1996)

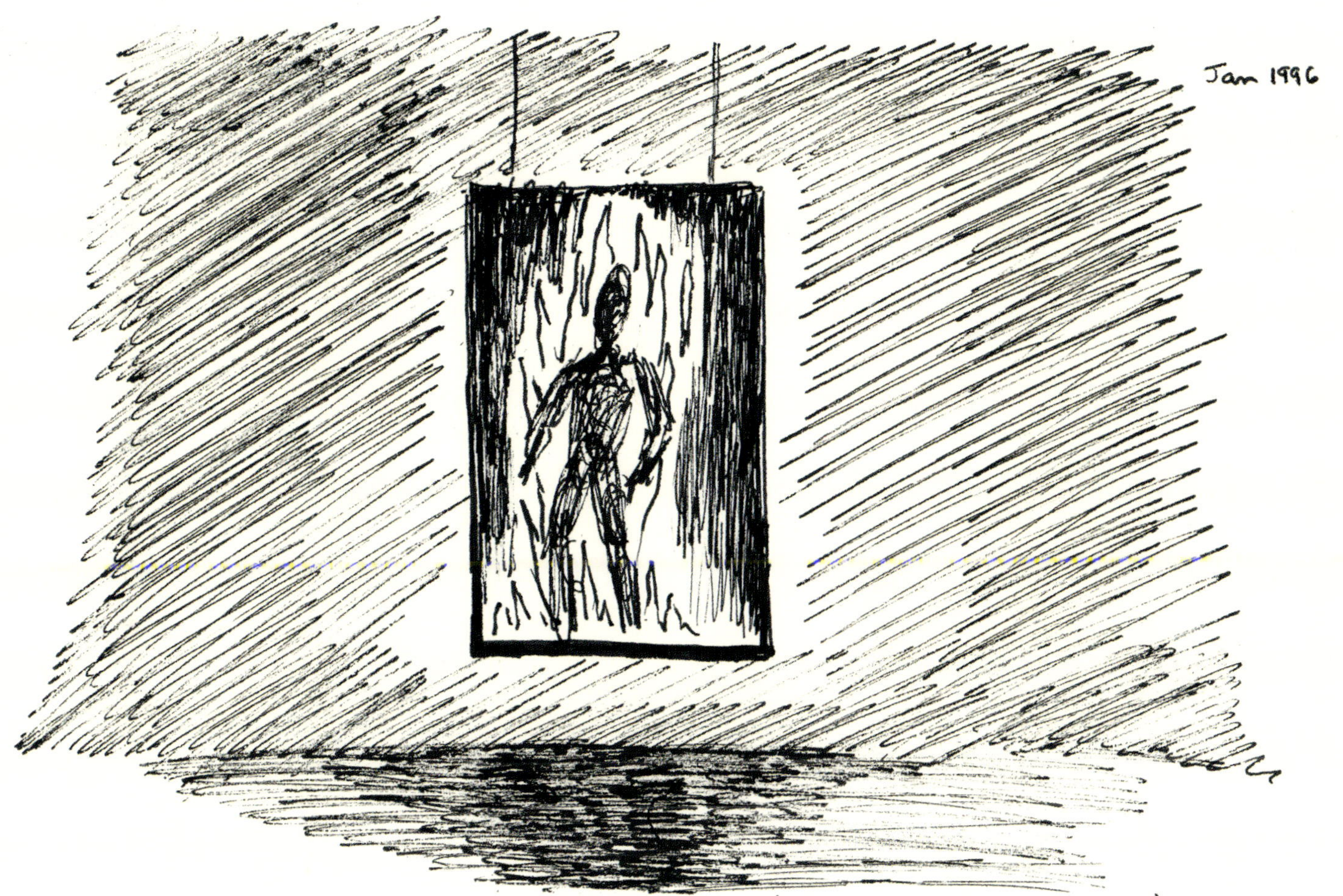

Bill Viola Project for Festival d'Automne
Chapelle St. Louis Salpetriere

MAN ON FIRE (1996)

A large screen (5m high by 3m wide) is freely suspended in the Chapelle space. On it is projected an image of a man moving around slowly in a dark obscure space. The image is indistinct, grainy, black and white. The features and identity of the figure are not clear. After some time, the man is seen to cease his motions, and suddenly, brilliant orange flames appear at his feet and quickly spread to his whole body. His form is rapidly consumed by the fire and disintegrates in the heat and flames, returning the image to darkness. The cycle then begins anew.

Continuous projection on a suspended screen in a dark space. Stereo sound accompanies the image.

Bill Viola

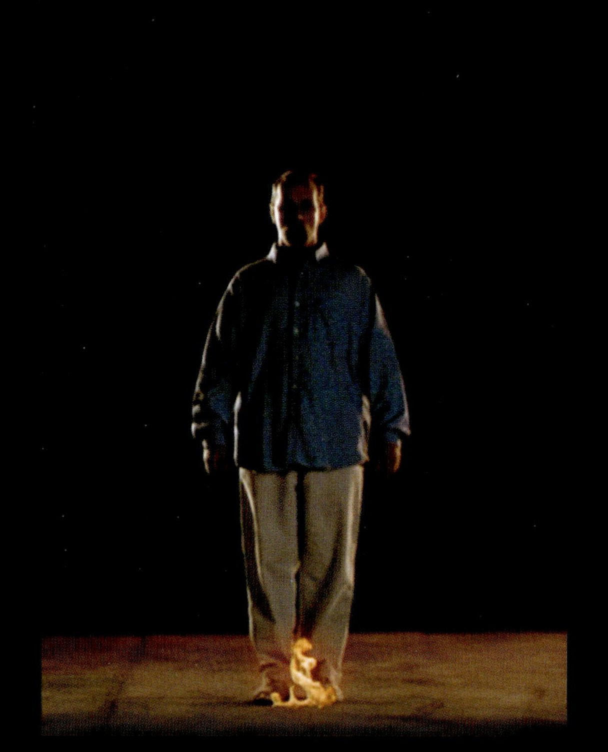
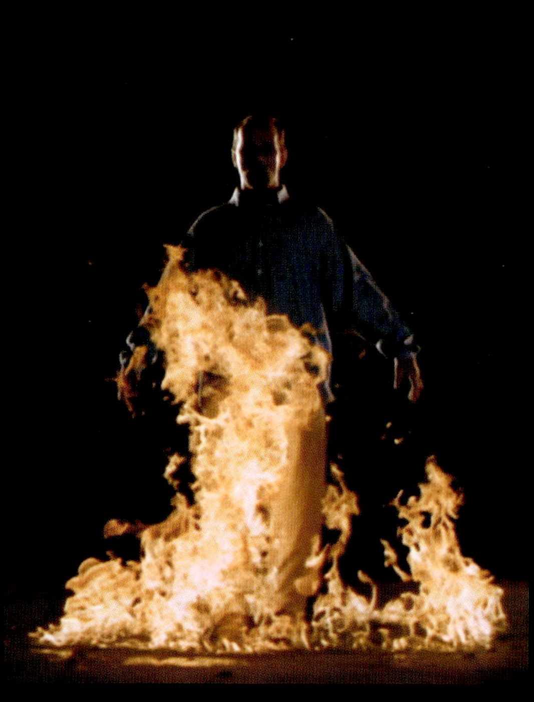
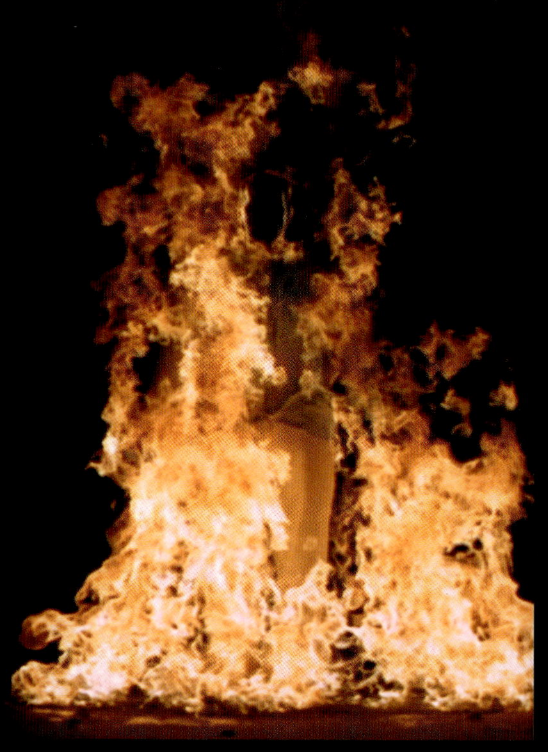
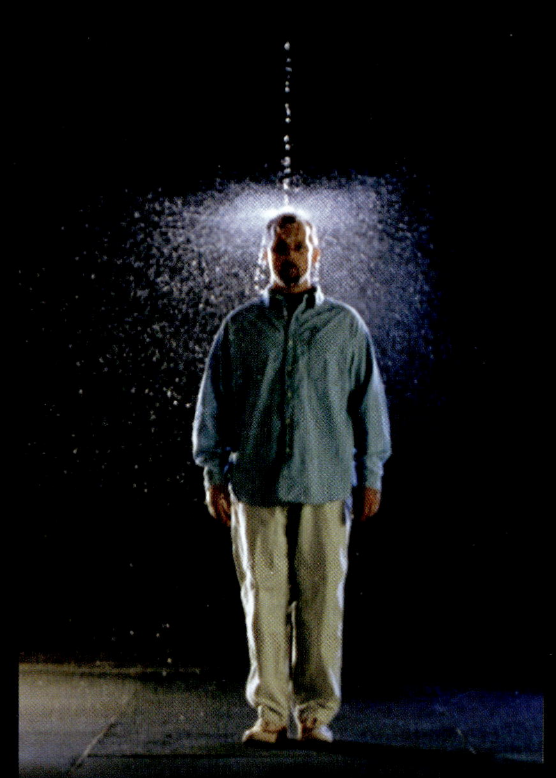
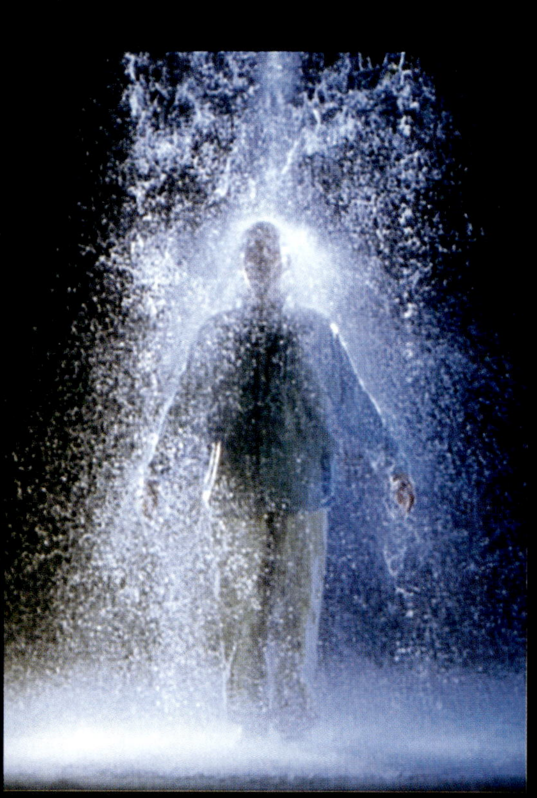
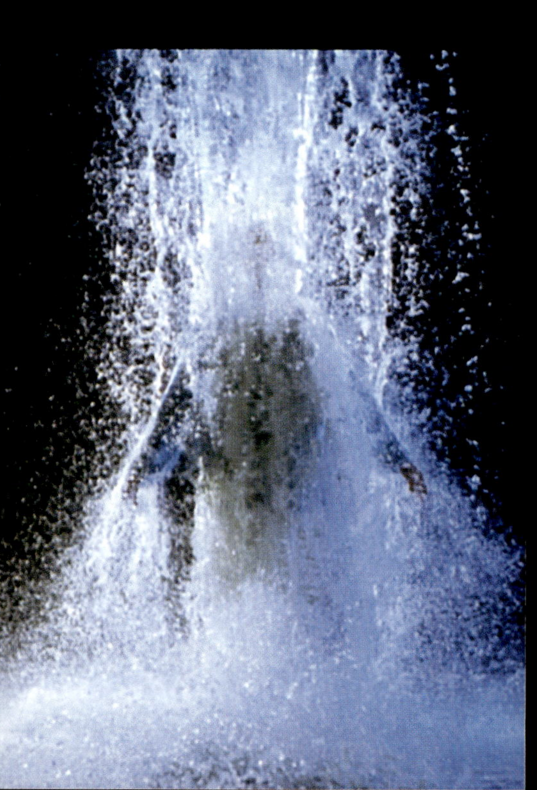

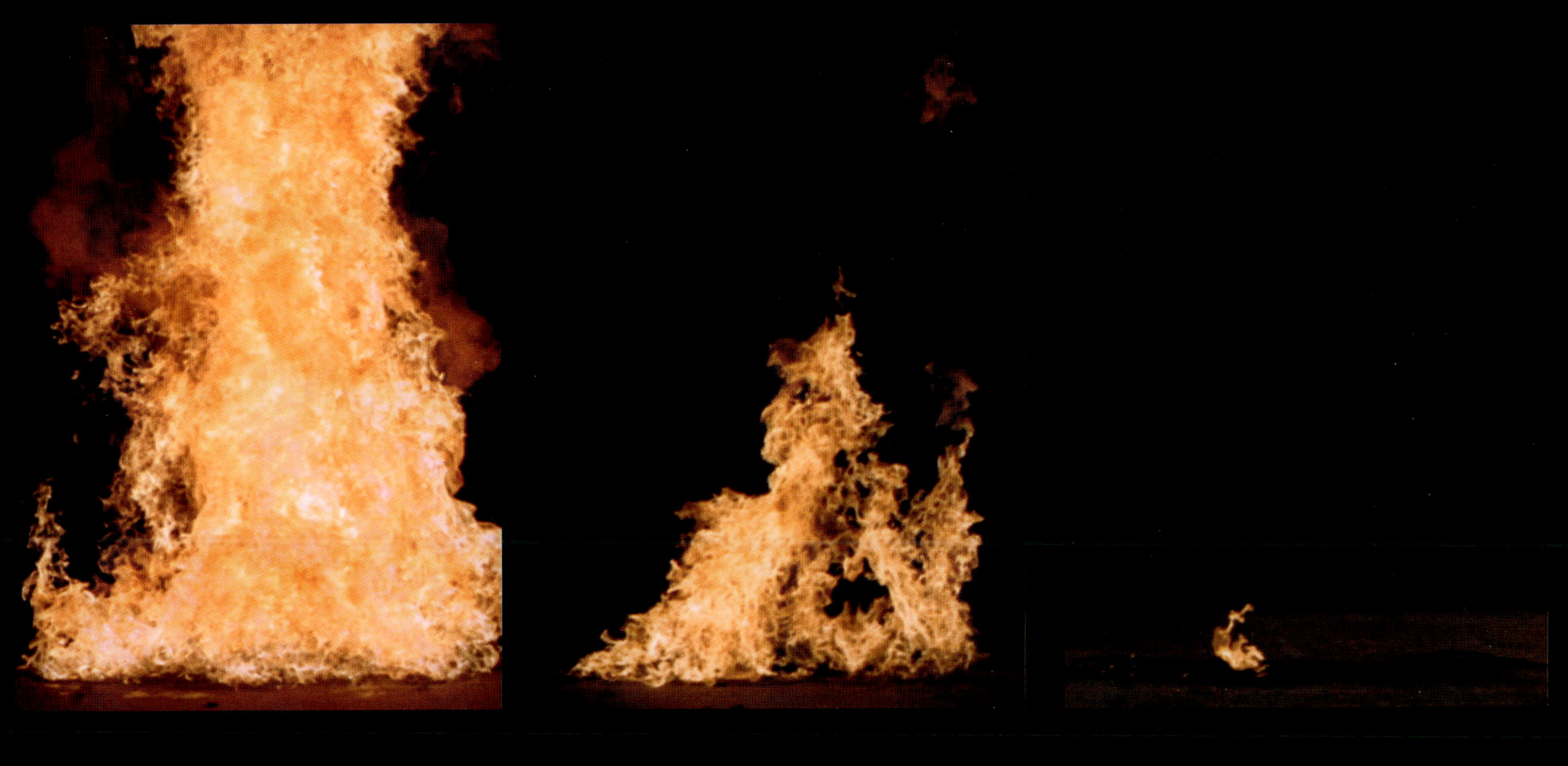

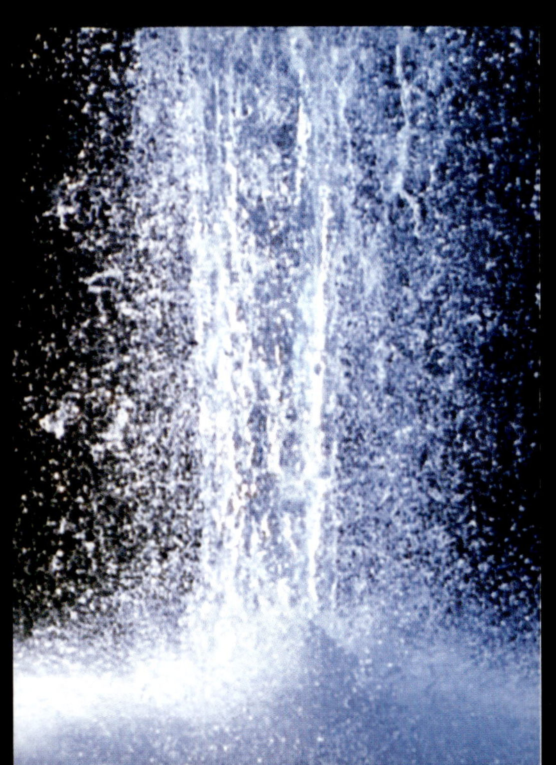

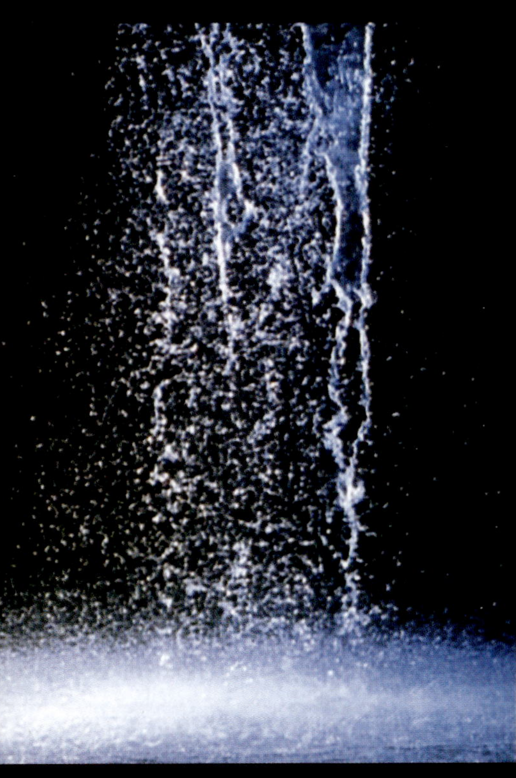

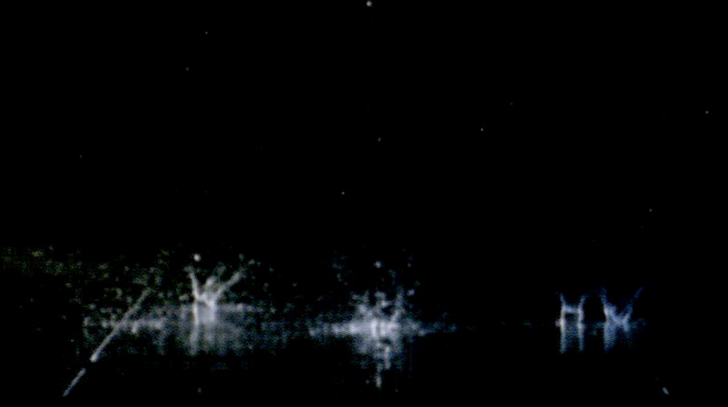

had been working since 1982] brought one of the first of these new generation of LCD flat panels into my studio for us to evaluate. When we turned it on, I couldn't contain myself. This was a new technology adrenaline rush I hadn't felt in years. I knew I was seeing a new step in the evolution of the moving image. It had none of the characteristics of the television monitor, the old cathode-ray tube. There were no scan lines, no electronic colors, or harsh edges. The image had a soft, satin-like quality because there was no glass in front of the picture. It was photographic, but it also had a texture, a really unique physical appearance more like the page of a book than an electronic screen. And the source of the image was digital, which meant high resolution and low noise. But the scale was most startling. I found myself falling into the image, getting lost in its aura, and it was only 16 inches wide.[5]

This discovery of a further transformation of the moving image elevated the artist's work to a new level of detail and compositional power and, in the process, provided the viewer with a novel aesthetic experience. The new small flat screens were also ideal for portraiture. Their small size, combined with high-speed 35mm film or High-Definition video recordings, gave the works a highly photographic look that could compare in detail with large-format photography.

To achieve this high-end, "photographic" look, Viola and Perov again assembled a crew. It is important to mention here Viola's "voice" and the way in which his spoken reflections on his work provide the insight and understanding that the cast and crew of the productions need in order to achieve the artist's vision. The "script" of his comments and observations begins with the words and drawings in the Notebooks. The steps taken from the Notebooks to the realization of an artwork are complex. Perov, as executive producer of the works and executive director of the Bill Viola Studio, oversees every aspect of the production of the videotapes and installations with a team of longtime collaborators, including producers, camera operators, lighting and special effects crew, and actors. Viola conveys to the actors on the set, as well as the technicians, what he wants to capture in the work, but responsibility for the successful completion of the stages leading up to this point rests with Perov. The nature of her collaboration with Viola is a close one.

The catalogue for Viola's exhibition "The Passions," which presented many of the artist's works on the emotions at the J. Paul Getty Museum, Los Angeles, in 2003, features a helpful essay by the exhibition's curator, John Walsh, and a conversation between Viola and the German art historian Hans Belting. The essays in the catalogue describe a conversation between Viola's video pieces and the classical tradition in painting. While these texts are certainly informative in showing how Viola worked with actors, developed

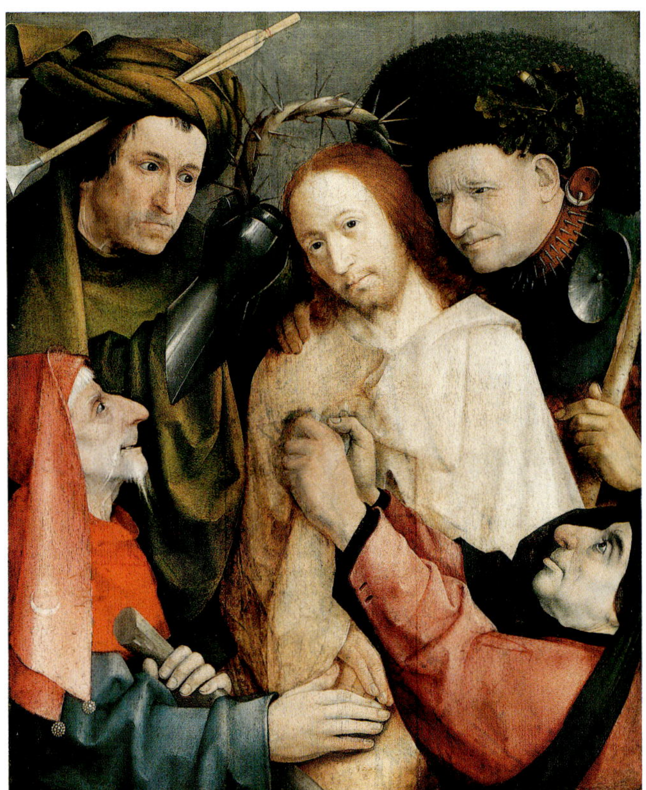

Above Hieronymus Bosch, *Christ Mocked (The Crowning with Thorns)* (c. 1490–1500)

Opposite *The Quintet of the Astonished* (2000)

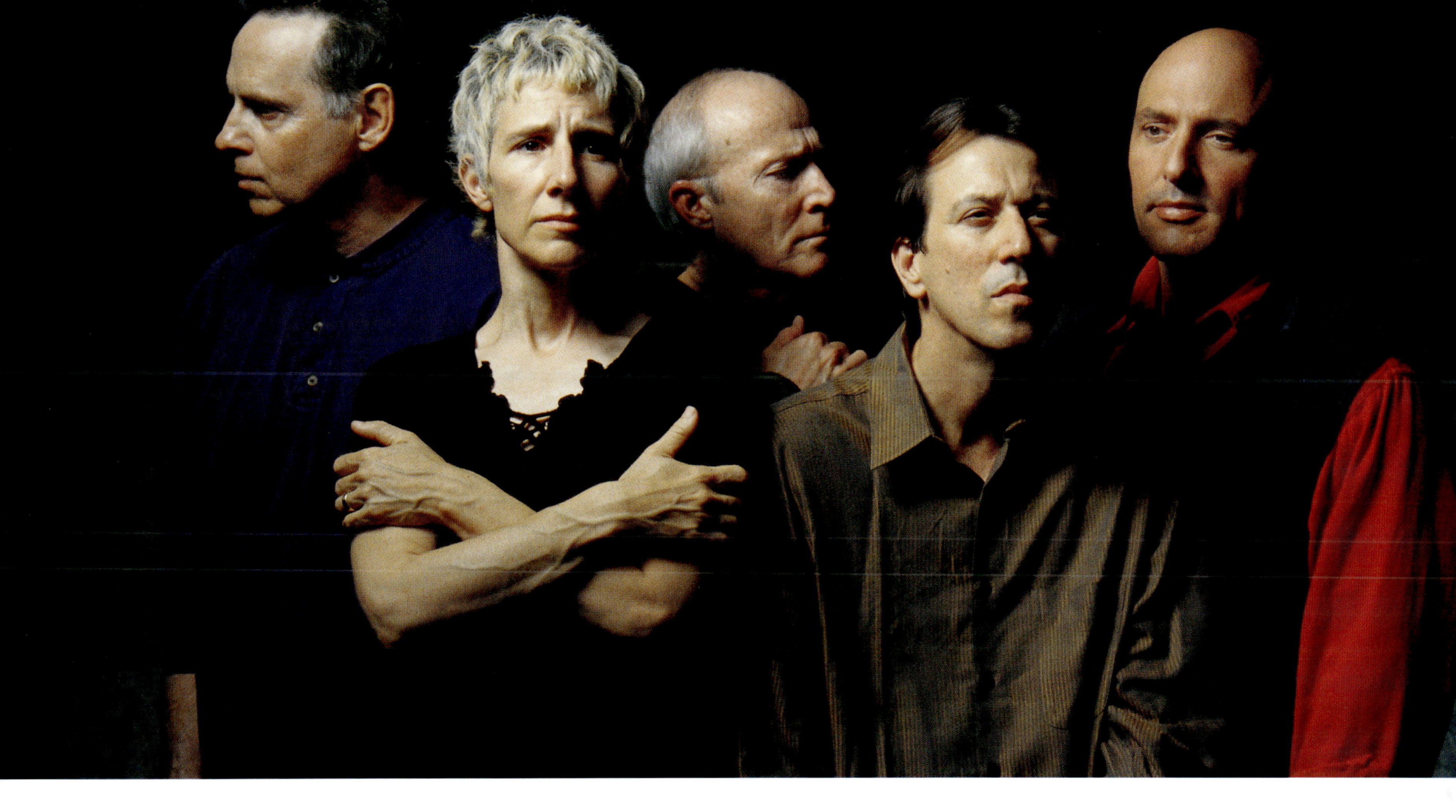

scenes of emotion, and referenced formal issues, I would like to suggest that Viola's self-reflective process results in artwork that speaks to an awareness of our fragility as individuals and within communities, to Heidegger's being-toward-death rendered not as a nihilistic trap but as an opening to self-consciousness and self-awareness. This complex move can be seen in three pieces from the exhibition: *The Quintet of the Astonished* (2000), *Catherine's Room* (2001), and *Five Angels for the Millennium* (2001), a work that was shown in addition to the "Passions" series. Each focuses on the human figure: *The Quintet of the Astonished* echoes in representational detail classical group portraits of figures; *Catherine's Room* directly acknowledges the spiritual abode of the female saint by using a classical predella sequence of LCD flat screens; and *Five Angels of the Millennium* projects on five large screens the breathtaking sight of five figures plunging into water.

In its grouping of individuals whom Viola directs as a composition in time, *The Quintet of the Astonished* takes its inspiration from *Christ Mocked*

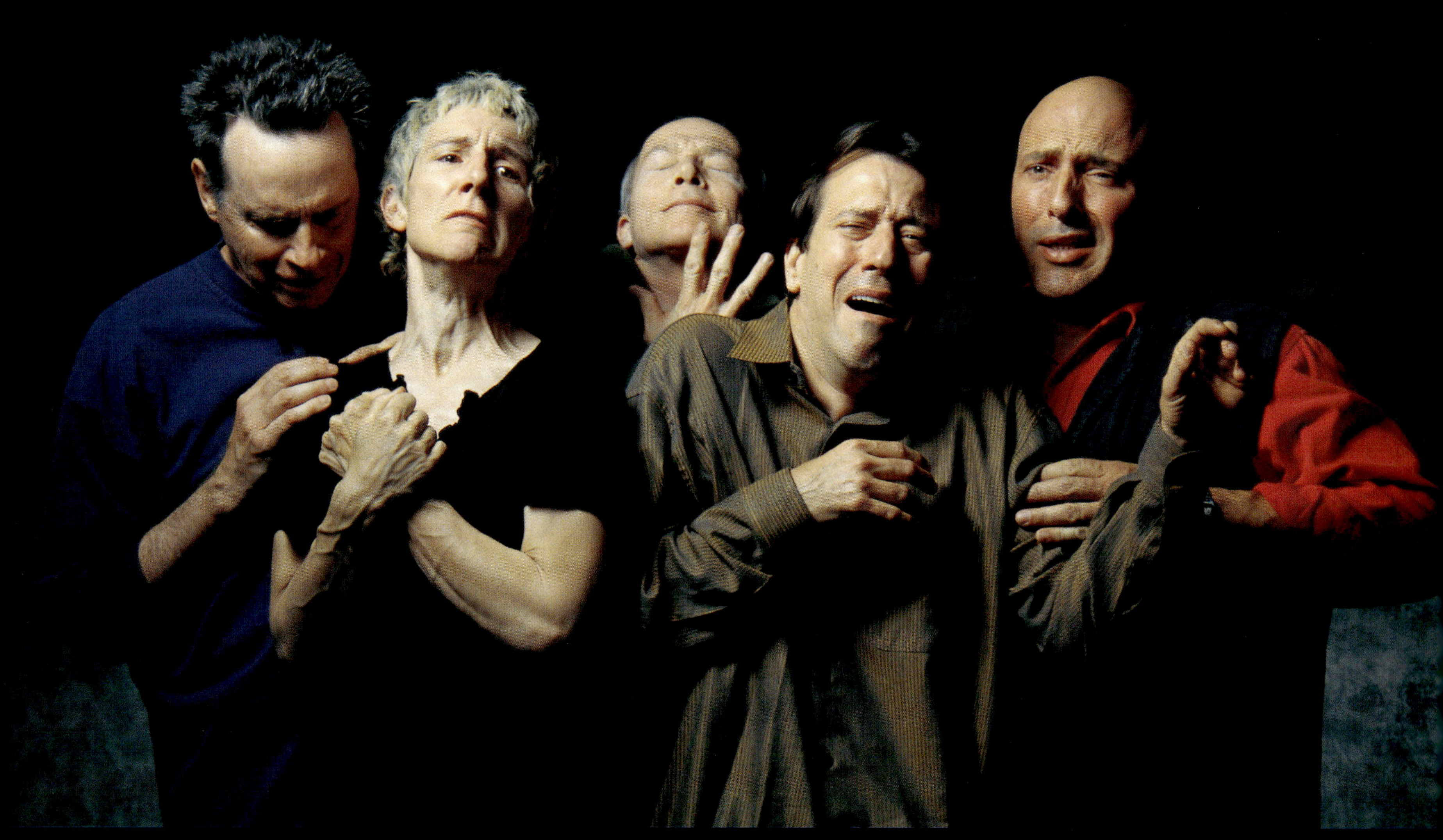

The Quintet of the Astonished (2000)

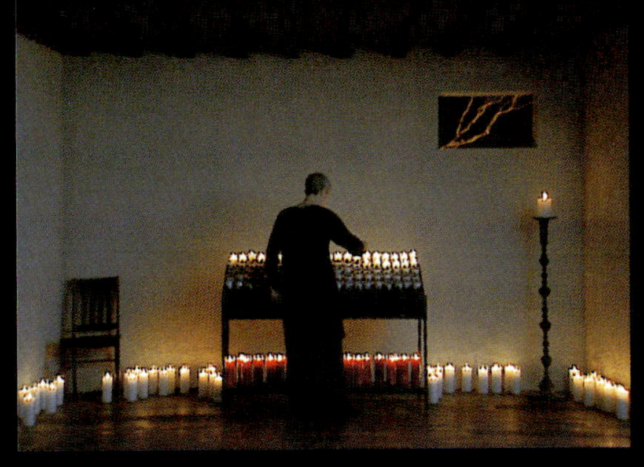
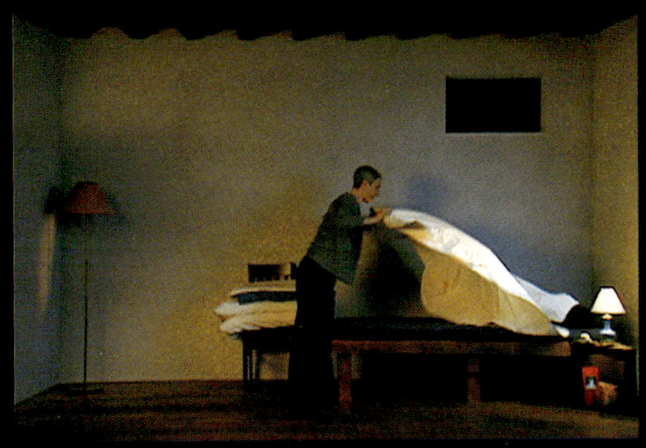
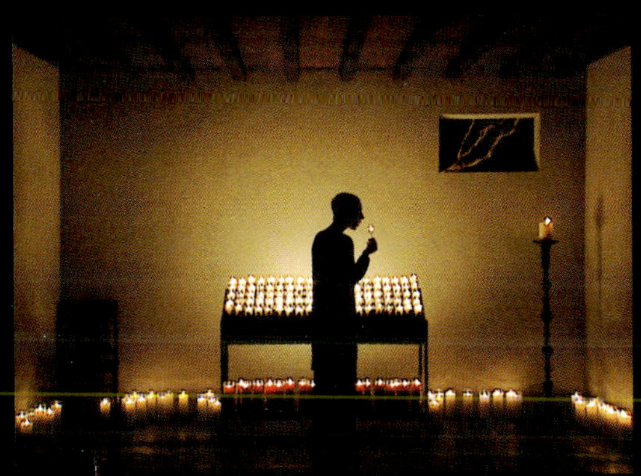
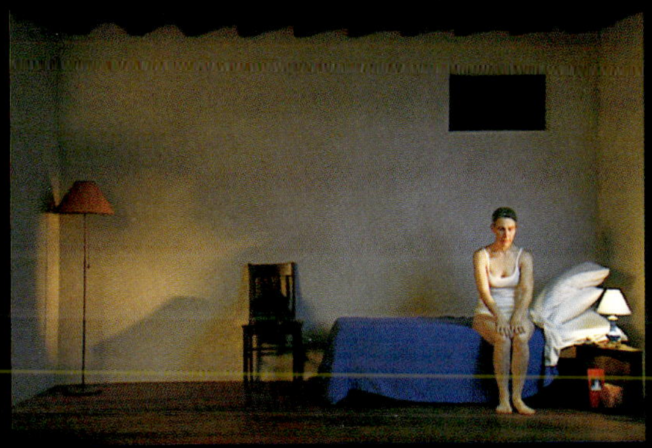
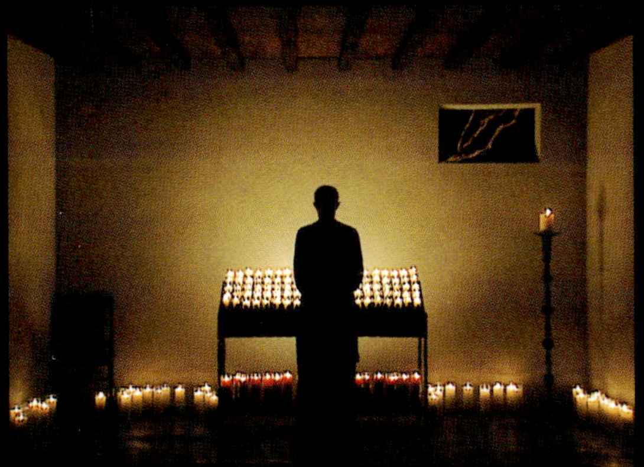
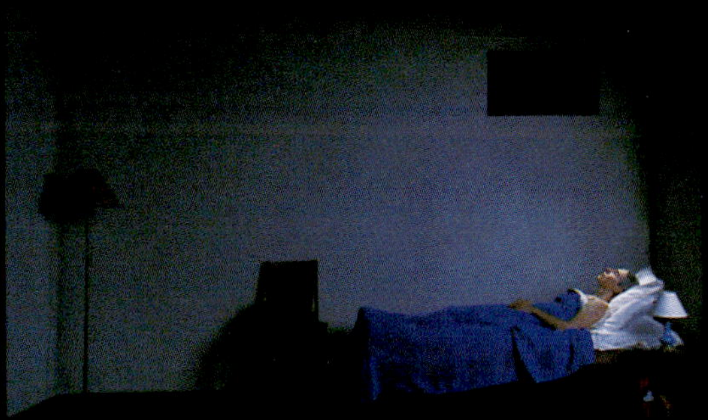

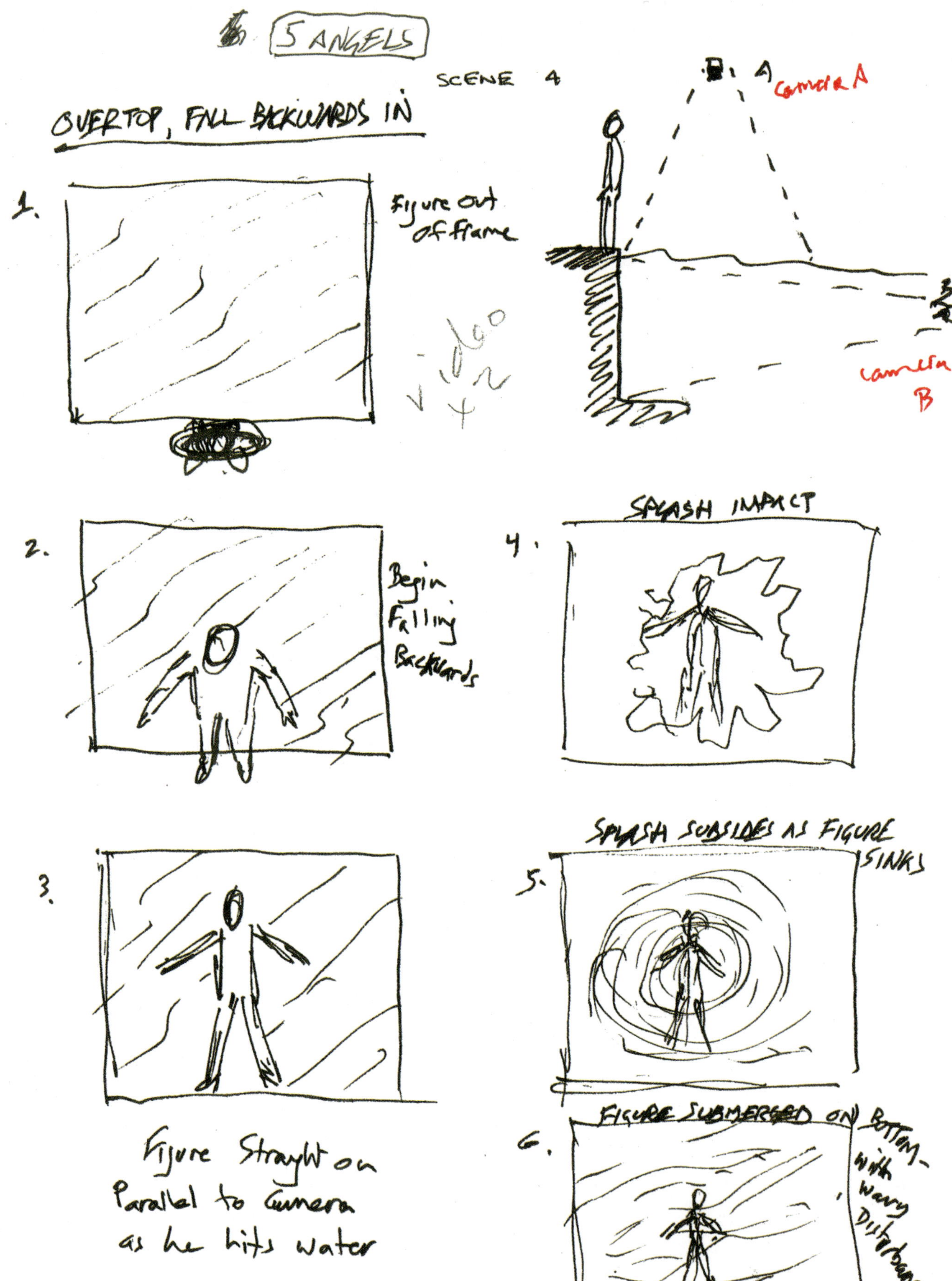
5 ANGELS
SCENE 4
OVERTOP, FALL BACKWARDS IN
A Camera A
1. Figure out of frame
video 4x2
Camera B
2. Begin Falling Backwards
SPLASH IMPACT
4.
3.
SPLASH SUBSIDES AS FIGURE SINKS
5.
Figure Straight on Parallel to Camera as he hits water
FIGURE SUBMERGED ON BOTTOM with Wavy Disturbance
6.

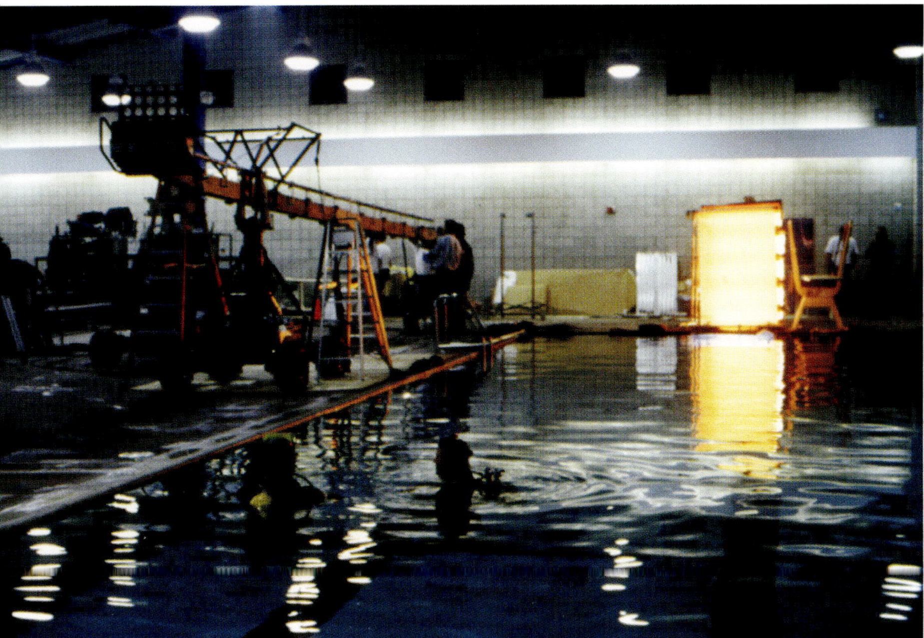

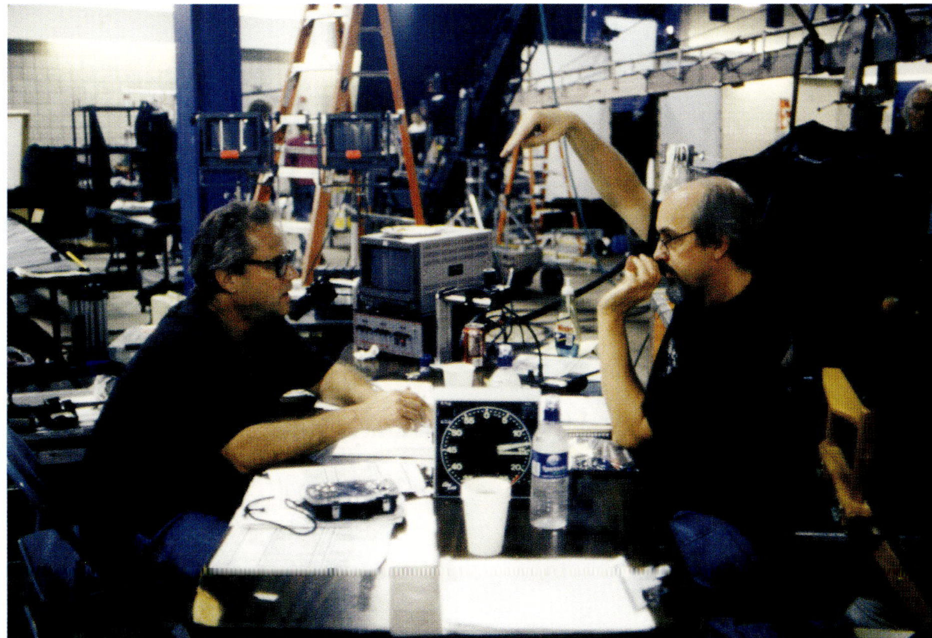

Opposite *Five Angels for the Millennium* (2001), drawing, *c.* 1999

Above Bill Viola and director of photography Harry Dawson on the set of *Five Angels for the Millennium* (2001), Martin Luther King Jr. Park Pool, Long Beach, CA, September 1999

Following four pages *Five Angels for the Millennium* (2001)

the larger view of a life bound to the cycles of nature."[7] The parallel depiction of different segments of time in the same space recomposes the timeless in a linear fashion. The use of the predella format establishes the work's connection to classical modes of expression. In the small, intimate screen of each panel, routine tasks are revealed and the simple gestures of daily activity are captured through the medium of the moving image.

Five Angels for the Millennium (2001) is one of the most powerful works of art of our time. Each of the five video channels projected onto the walls of the exhibition space is accompanied by stereo sound that enfolds the viewer in a rapturous celebration of the "act of Becoming."[8] Experienced together, the individual channels—"Departing Angel", "Birth Angel", "Fire Angel", "Ascending Angel," and "Creation Angel"—compose a visual whole, the five "bodies of light" appearing through an auditory and visual crescendo of water.[9] Harry Dawson was the project's director of photography. In his essay on the "Passions" series, John Walsh notes that there were "five different setups, each of which ran 30–40 seconds, including the preliminary stillness, the plunge, and the sinking (and also, in some cases, rising) of the man. Each sequence was slowed down, corrected for color, reframed and extended or accelerated as necessary, and then programmed so that the explosions would occur at the intervals Viola wanted. The five channels are not synchronized, so there is an element of randomness."[10] In his notes on *Five Angels*, Viola describes the work as "another form of the Passions, an unframed vs. a framed experience, an enveloping emotional experience like that of church."[11] It is this sense of an architecture of feeling that comes to life as the anonymous forms plunging through light and water become an all-embracing presence. Each of the angels occupies a place in our imagination and affirms a passion for life.

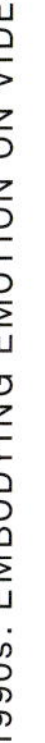

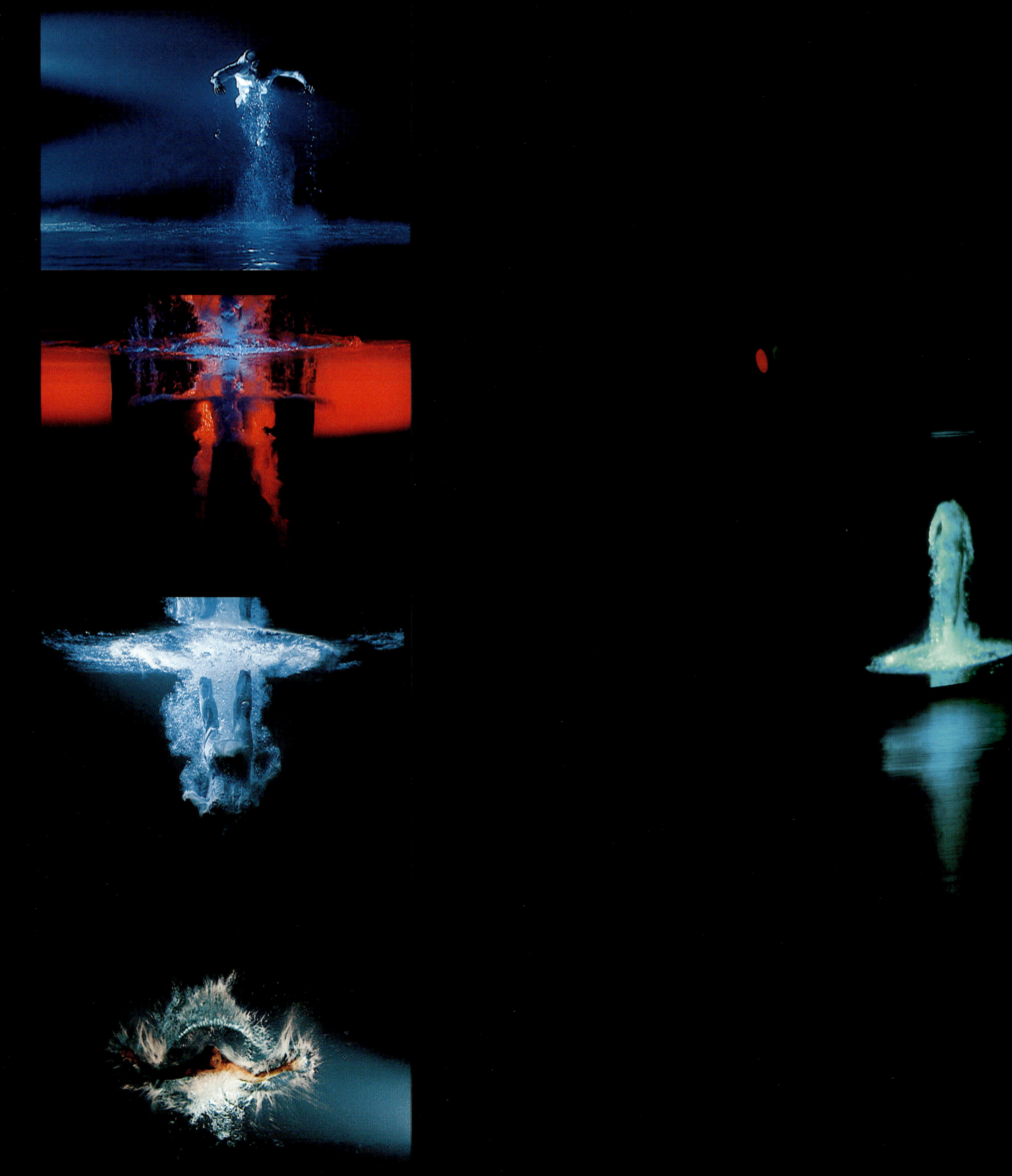

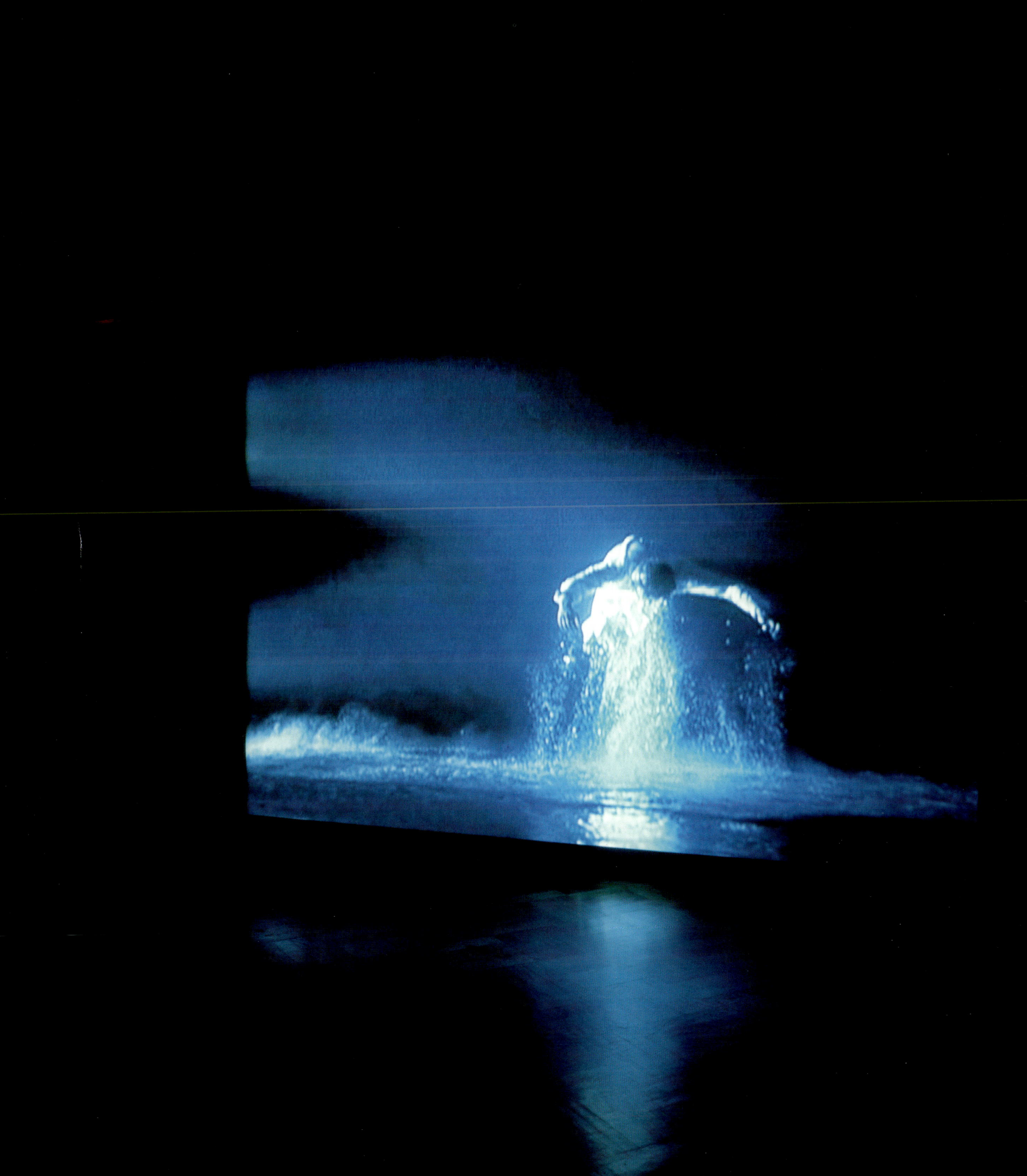

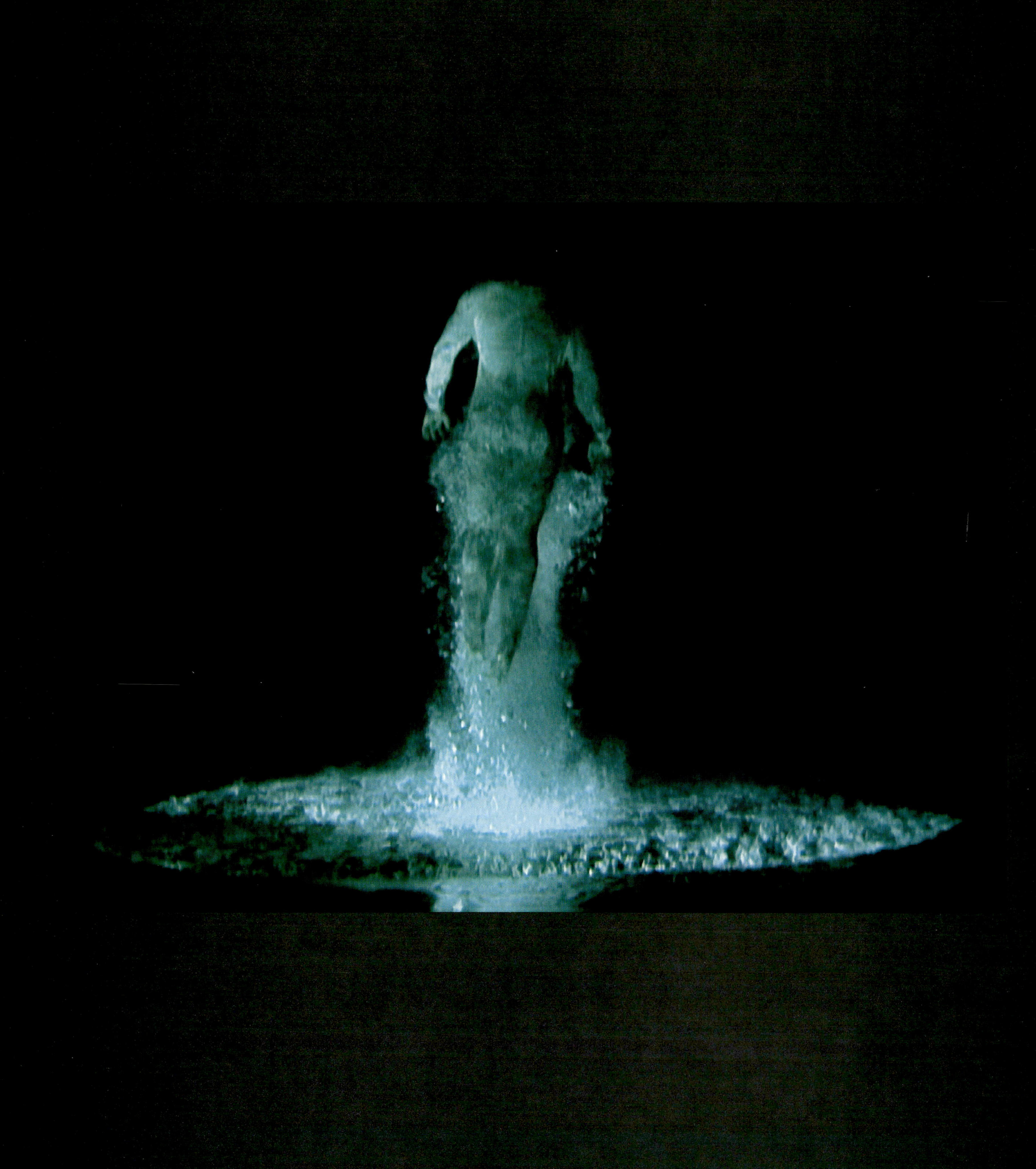

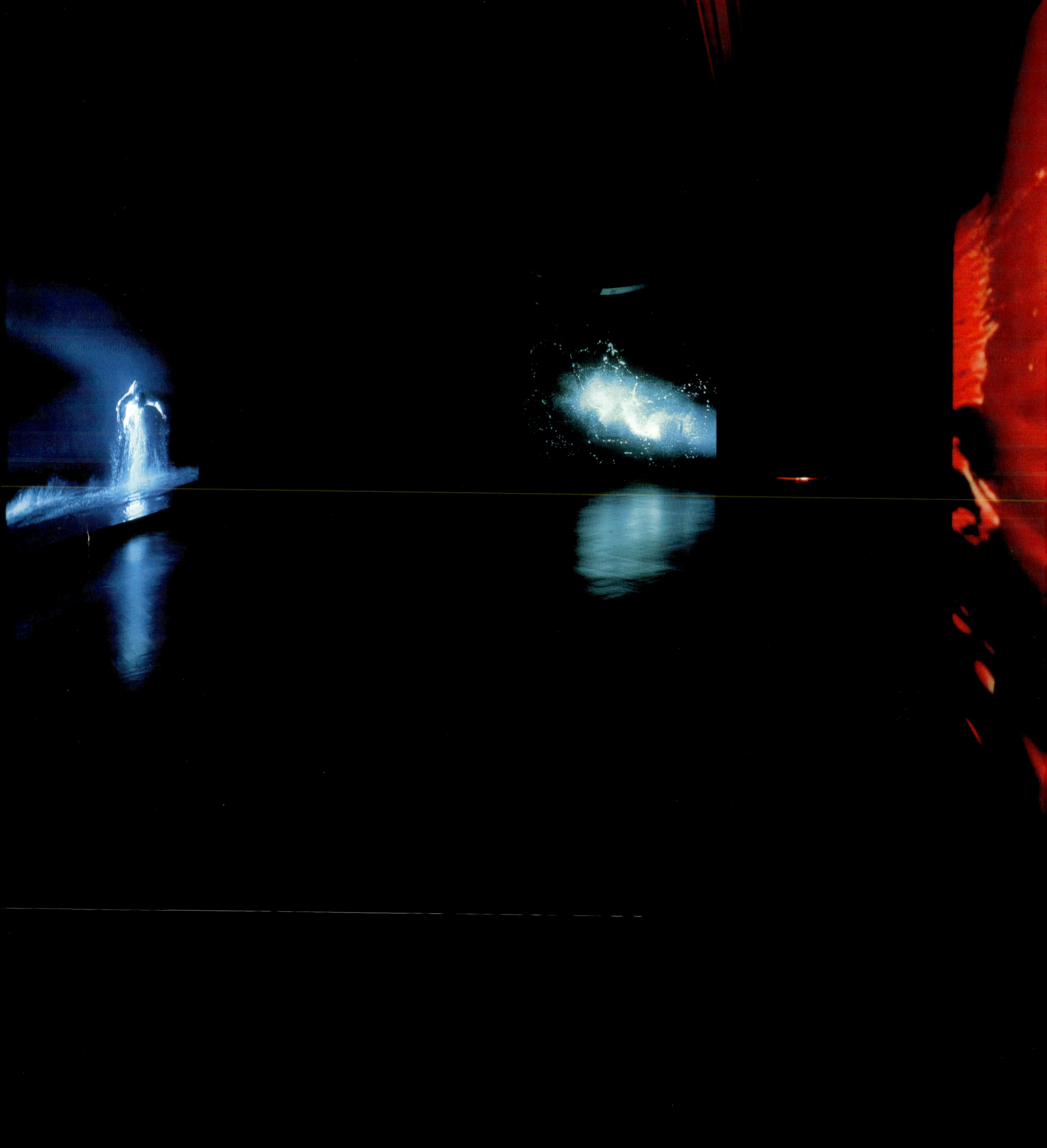

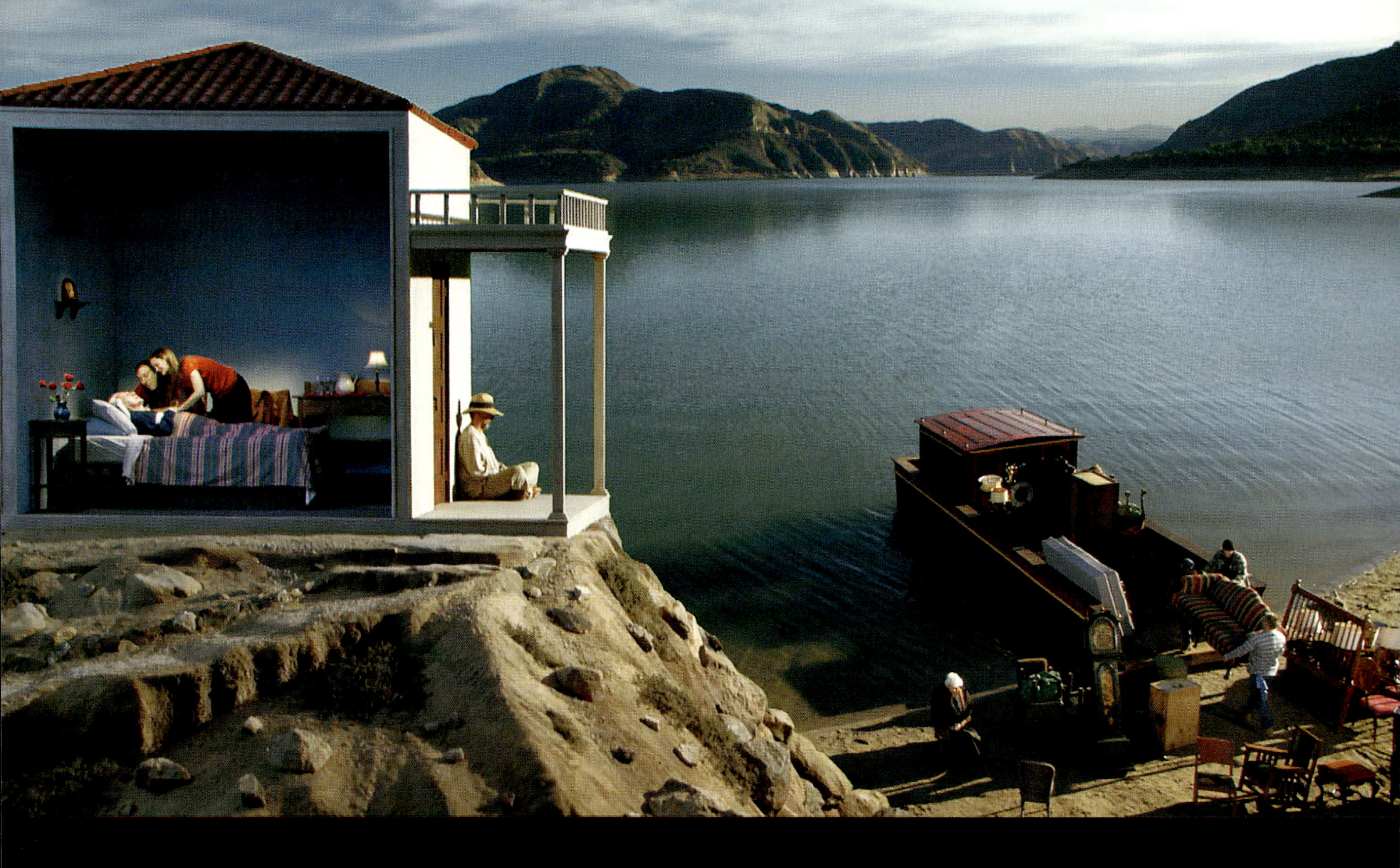

CHAPTER SIX

2000s: A HUMANISM FOR OUR TIMES

There is literally a world within every grain of sand, within every reflection on every object.

—Bill Viola, Italy, 1975

At the beginning of the new millennium, Viola embarked on a series of works that recognized the importance of acknowledging who we are in the world and of understanding the challenge of redefining who we are to one another. All of the philosophical issues and formal techniques that we have seen being developed in Viola's work came into play: the phenomenological address of the eye and consciousness; the use of the figure as an enactment of emotion; the representation of gesture and movement through an evocative treatment of time; the acknowledgment of the electronic moving image as something other than the cinema while keeping in view the history of that medium; the formal treatment of the tropes of genre painting and the attendant theories of spiritual enactment that attach to such tropes; and the exercises that maintain a spiritual life. All of these came together in his work, along with a startling return to the cinematic and a moving image that demanded of us a return to a caring and loving embrace of our world.

This is clearly expressed in the sublime power of *Going Forth By Day* (2002). Five projected scenes unfold like murals painted directly onto the walls of the exhibition space. Rather than providing the illusion of three-dimensional depth, the work enfolds the viewer into the moving image, since the narrative is projected directly onto the four walls. Originally commissioned for the Deutsche Guggenheim Berlin, the work received its North American premiere at the Solomon R. Guggenheim Museum

"The Voyage," panel 4 from *Going Forth By Day* (2002)

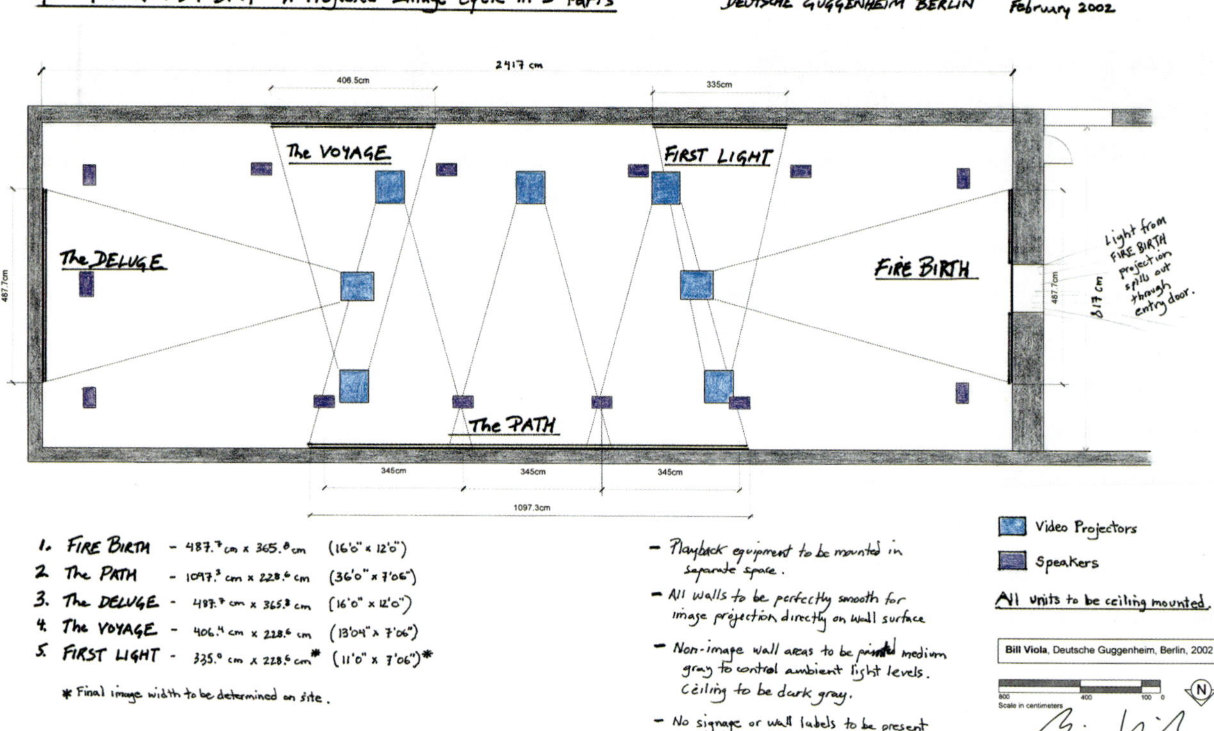

in New York on September 21, 2002; with the terrorist attacks of the year before still fresh in people's minds, the installation welcomed the viewer into a space of contemplation and thought. What follows is a combination of Viola's general account of the work (here, the first and last paragraphs) and (in between) the descriptions of each of the five projections that he wrote for the exhibition:

Going Forth By Day **is a five-part projected digital image cycle that explores themes of human existence: individuality, society, death, rebirth. The work is experienced architecturally, with all five image sequences playing simultaneously in one large gallery. To enter the space, visitors must literally step into the light of the first image. Once inside, they stand at the center of an image-sound world with projections on every wall.**[1]

> **Fire Birth: A Human form emerges from a dim submerged world. The body swims in the fluid of an unconscious state between death and rebirth. Orange rays of light penetrate the surface of the water, coming from the previous world, which ended in fire. Now illuminated by the light of prior destruction, the human essence searches for a way through the new underwater realm. It seeks the material form and substance necessary for its rebirth.**

Above Floor plan of *Going Forth By Day*, for Deutsche Guggenheim Berlin, February 2002

Opposite "Fire Birth," panel 1 from *Going Forth By Day* (2002)

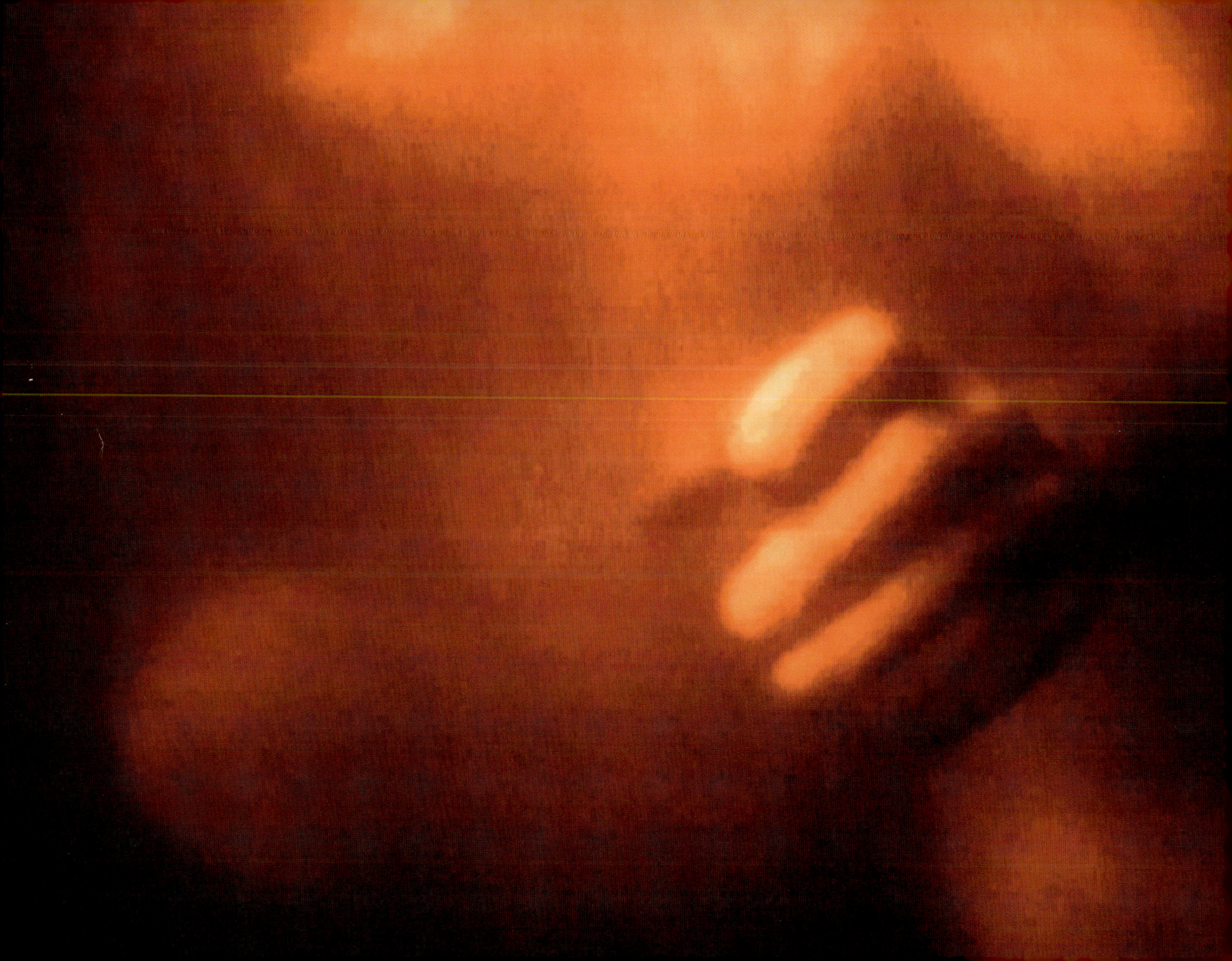

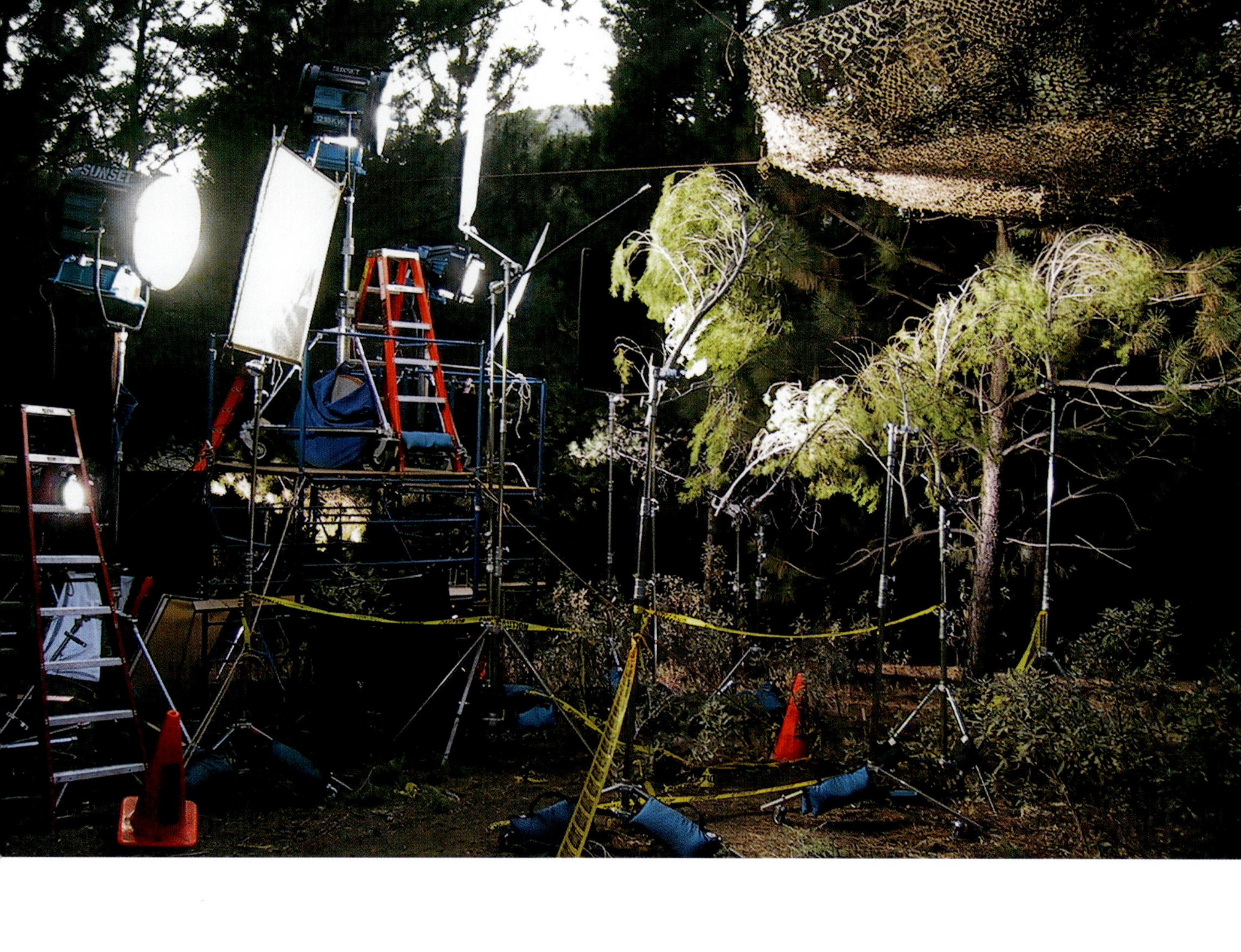

The Path: It is the time of the summer solstice high in the mountains. The early morning light reveals a steady stream of people moving along a path through the forest. They come from all walks of life, each traveling the path at their own pace in their unique way. There is no beginning or end to the procession of individuals—they have been walking long before we see them here, and they will be walking long after they leave our view. The constant flow of people suggests no apparent order or sequence. As travelers on the road, they move in the intermediate space between two worlds. A small marker in the forest grants them safe passage through this vulnerable state.

Above On location for "The Path" from *Going Forth By Day* (2002), Angeles National Forest, CA, October 2001

Opposite Drawing indicating three-camera alignment for "The Path," July 2001 (top); Bill Viola on location counting pixels to verify alignment, October 2001 (bottom)

2. The PATH

OVERLAP ZONES

① ② ③

3 Cameras - simultaneous record

NODAL VIEW - All cameras equi-distant to path.

① LEFT | ② CENTER | ③ RIGHT

FINAL PANORAMA PROJECTION - with digital edge blending

LOCATION

- Orientation - N E S W
- How long PATH?
- Size of people in frame?

DURATION - Action
- Screen

Slo Mo Needed?

OUTDOORS - 2 takes per day
- Weather
- Nature ('real')

INDOORS - Sets, Props
- Controlled Lighting
- Background/Depth?

SCENE - ~~Burned out~~? Verdant

TIME/LIGHT - AM, PM?

TREES

TALENT - Number of People? Dispersal?
- SAG, Non-SAG?
- Extras, Actors.
- Wardrobe
- Rehearsals staging Action
- Time Score of Action

PANORAMA

- 1 Camera / Multi camera?
- Source Format 35mm / HD?

Tech.

- Final Res - HD Resolution?
  - SXGA - 4 panels?
  - VGA - 4 panels? (recommended by PANORAM)
- Editing - 4:3 component frames, DVD or MPEG Player NTSC?
  - 16:9 component frames?

Panoramic System:

- Panoram Systems?
- Other? (incl. IN PROJECTOR)

TESTS/QUESTIONS

- Length of Path
- ARC OK? or angeled
- Focal Length
- Number of People
- Clothes, Details

Edge Blending:

- How to align the 3 cameras in the field?
- Physical grid system required in overlap zones?

- CUSTOM DESIGN Cam. mount for 3 Cameras.

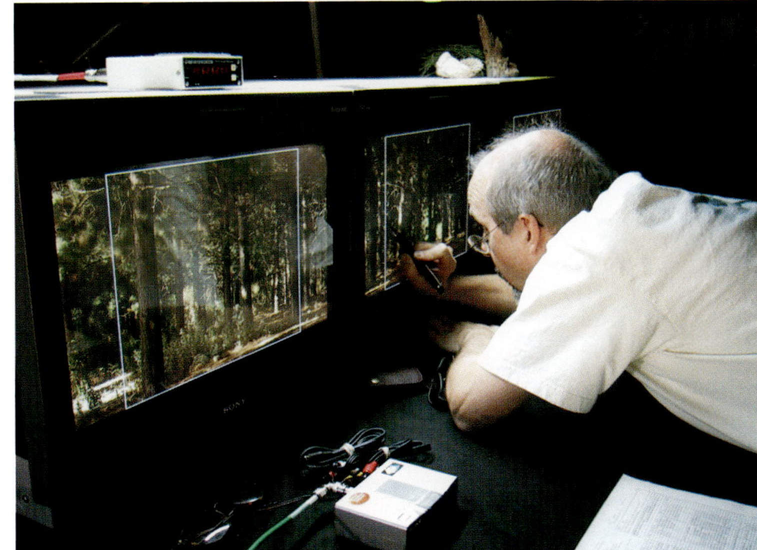

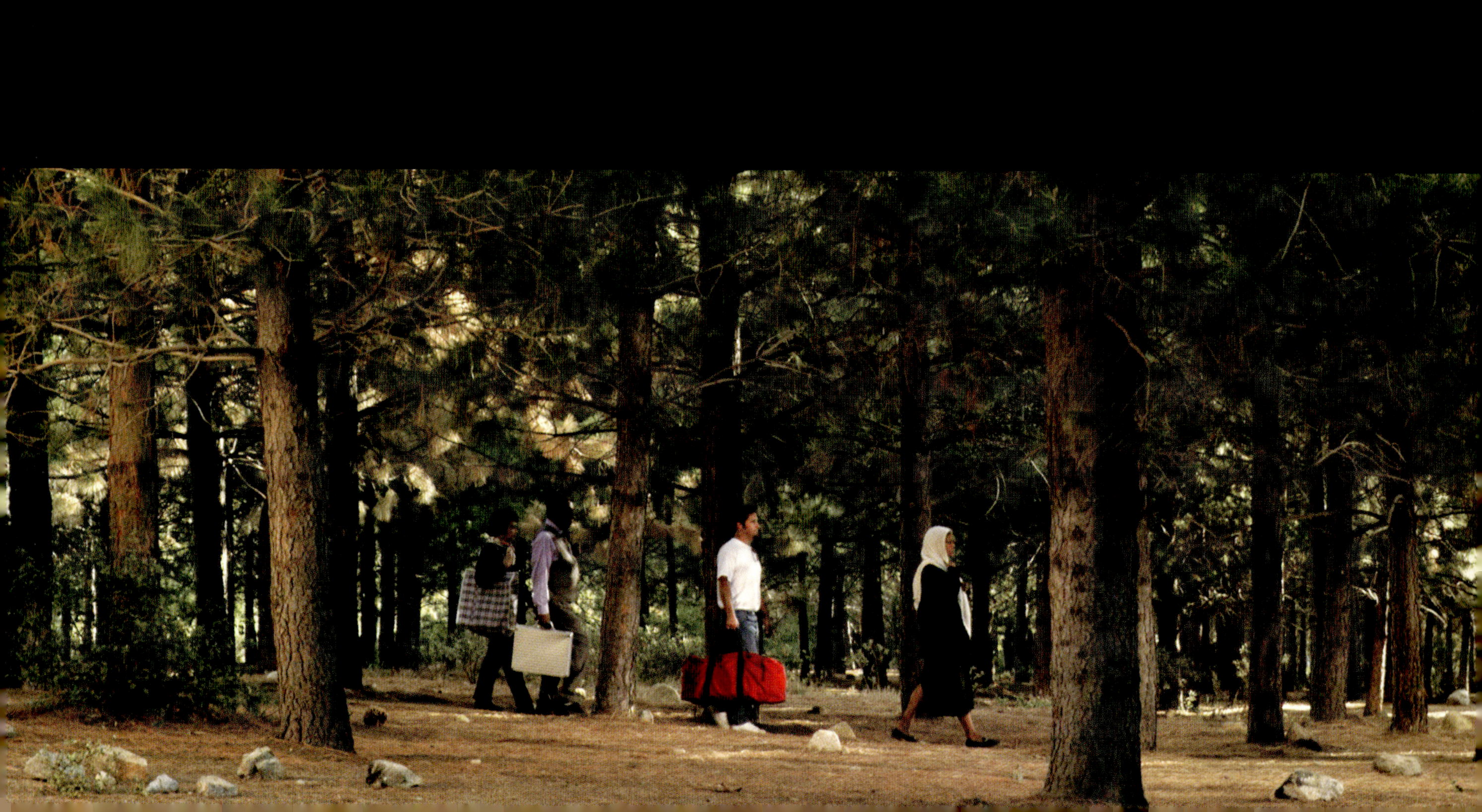

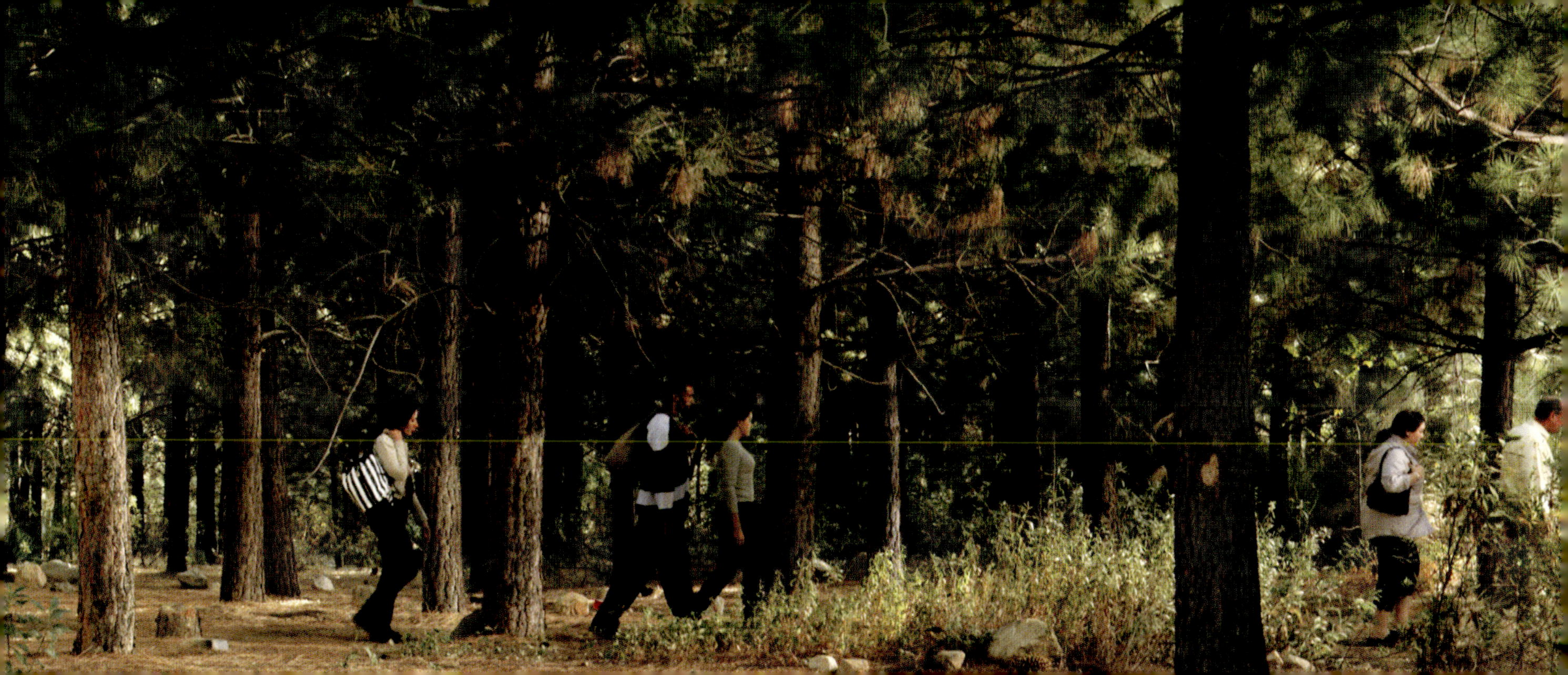

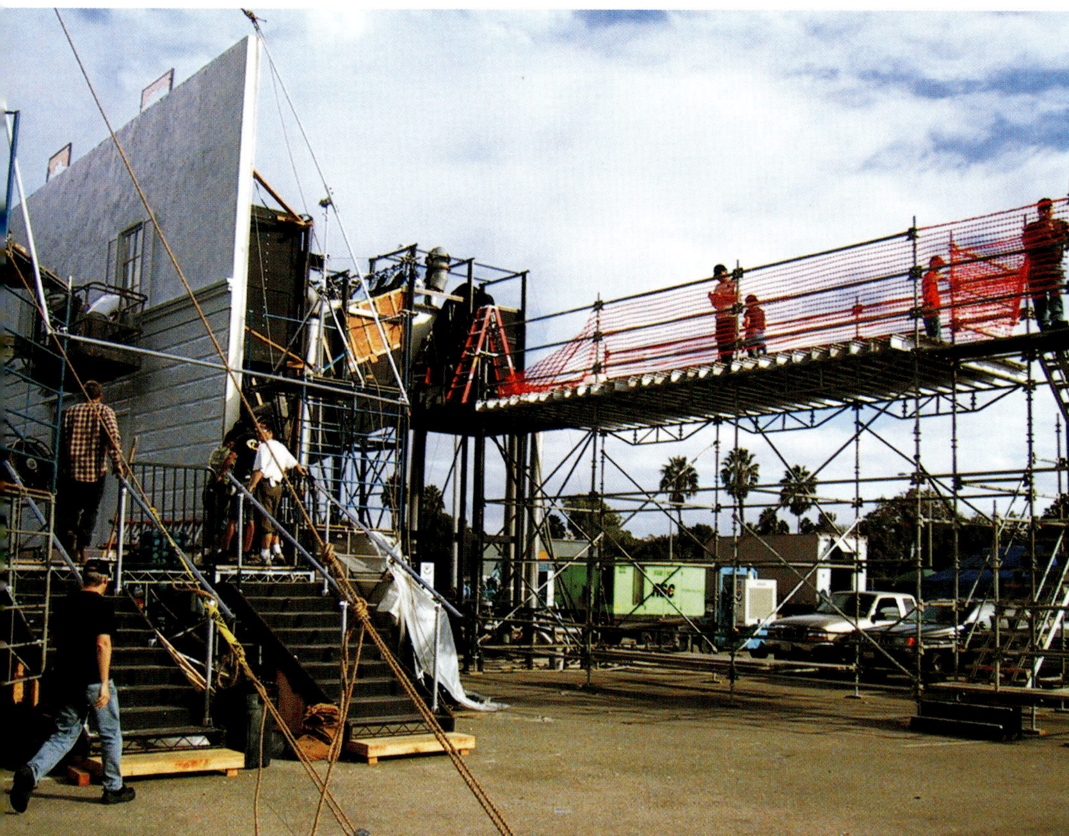

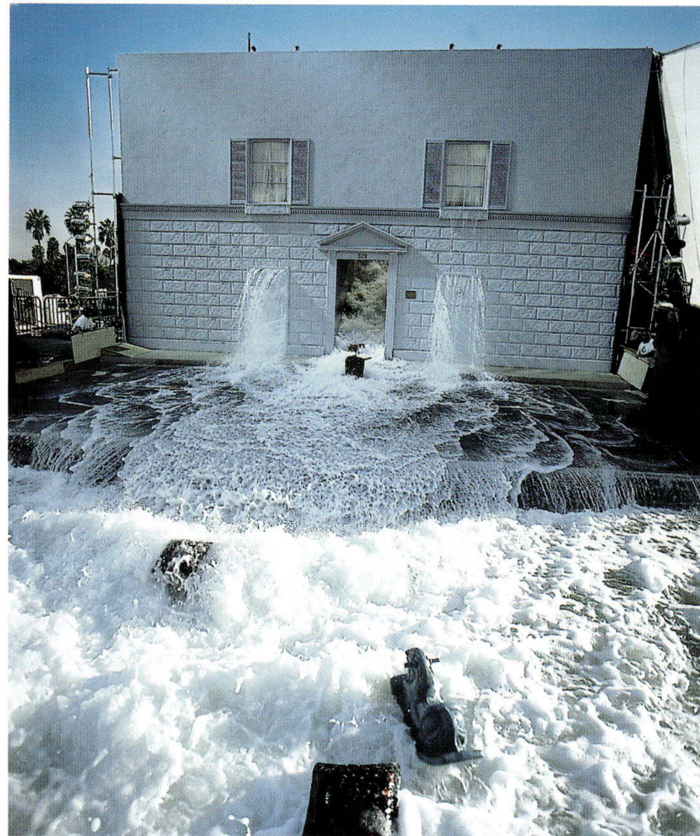

The Deluge: A stone building, newly restored, stands in the clear light of the autumnal equinox. People move along the street immersed in the flow of day-to-day events. Small incidents play out, affecting individual lives. Families are leaving their homes, people on the street are carrying personal possessions, and all actions become colored by an increasing tension in the community. Moments of compassion and kindness circulate within a mounting concern for individual survival. A final moment of panic ensues as individuals rush to save themselves. The last ones, in denial of the inevitable, have waited too long in the security of their own homes. Now they must run for their lives as the deluge strikes with full force at the very heart of their private world. They rush out of the building when it is suddenly flooded from within by a raging torrent of water. Individual lives and personal possessions are arbitrarily chosen to be lost in the process. Finally, the violence and fury subside as the surging water slowly recedes, leaving the building unharmed and the street washed clean. The empty sidewalk glistens in the midday sun.

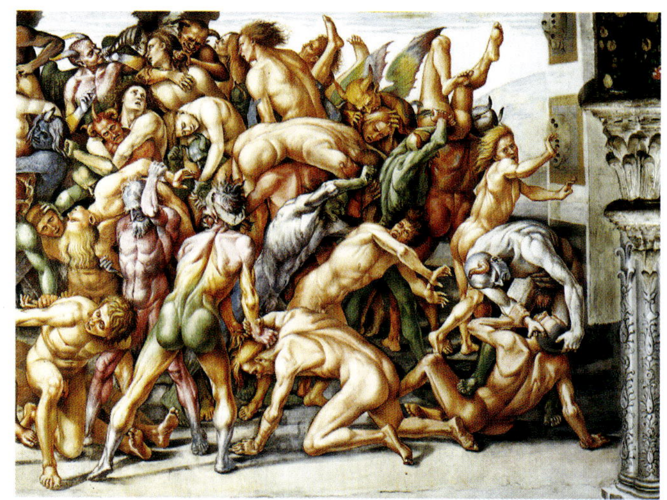

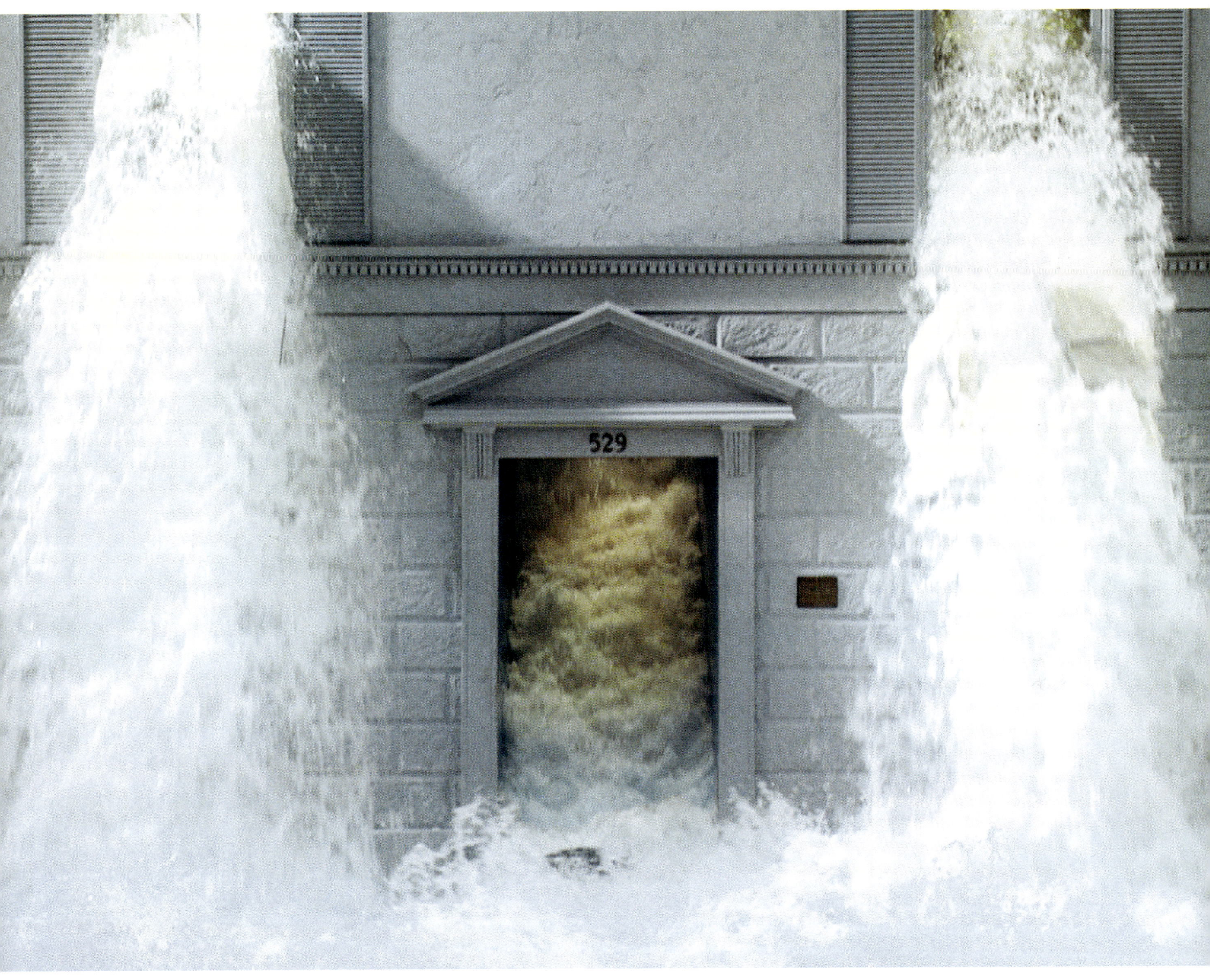

Opposite, top On the set of "The Deluge" from *Going Forth By Day* (2002), parking lot, Long Beach Airport, CA, November 2001

Opposite, bottom Luca Signorelli, *The Damned Cast into Hell* (1499–1504), detail, fresco, San Brizio Chapel, Orvieto Cathedral, Italy

Above "The Deluge," panel 3 from *Going Forth By Day* (2002)

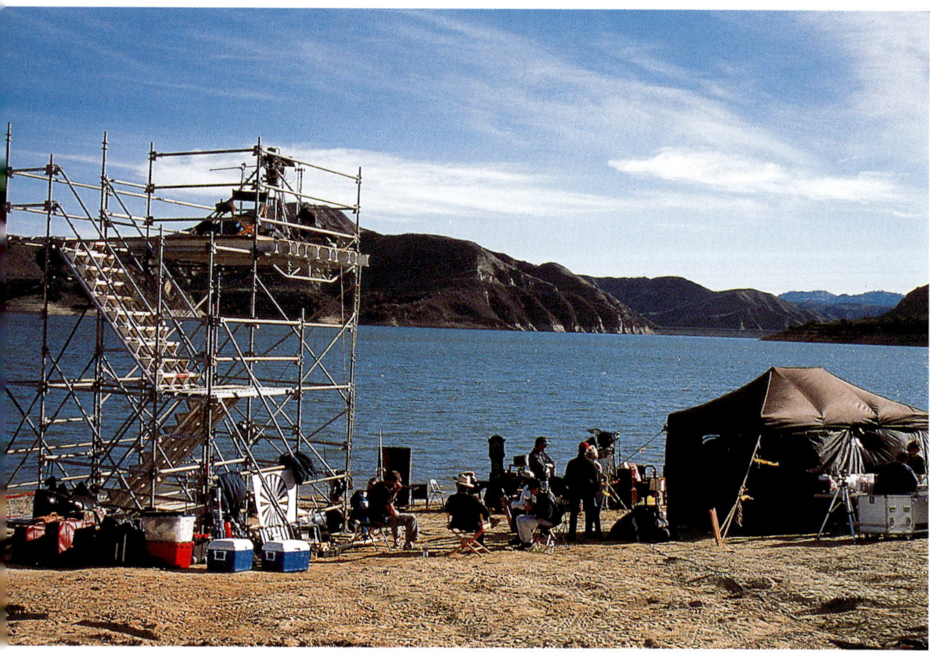

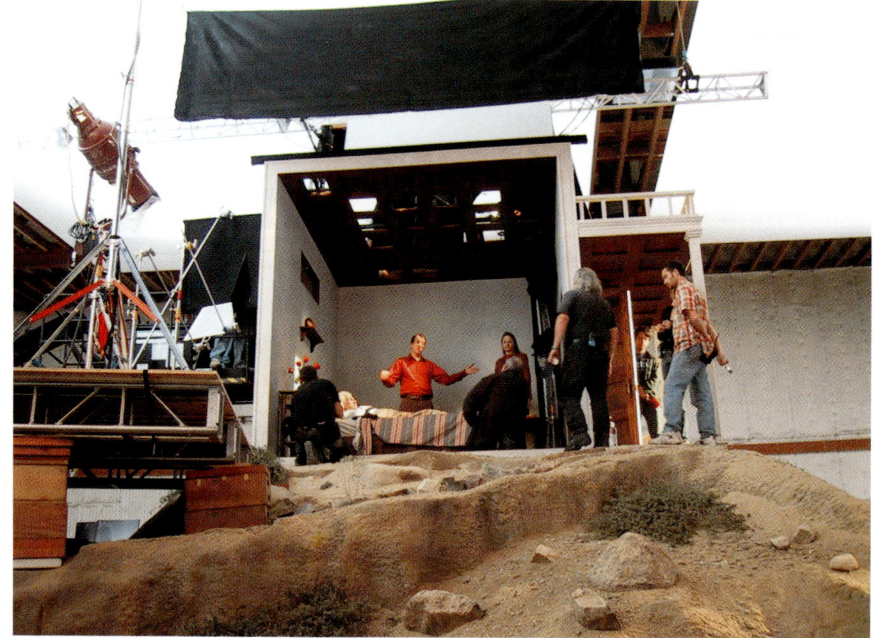

The Voyage: It is late afternoon at the time of the winter solstice. A small house stands on a hill overlooking the inland sea. Inside, an old man lies ill on a bed, attended by his son and daughter-in-law. Outside, another man sits by the door keeping vigil. Down by the shore, a boat is slowly being loaded with the personal possessions from the dying man's home. An old woman waits patiently nearby. After some time, the son and daughter-in-law must depart, leaving the old man alone with his dreams and fading breath. His house, container of lives and memories, is closed and locked. Soon after, the old man reappears on the shore and is greeted by his wife, who has been waiting for his arrival. The two board the boat, which departs, carrying them and their belongings to the distant Isles of the Blessed. Meanwhile, the son and daughter-in-law return to the house. Distraught, the son knocks frantically at the locked door, but there is no answer. Finally, accepting the inevitable, he and his wife once again leave and walk away together down the hill.

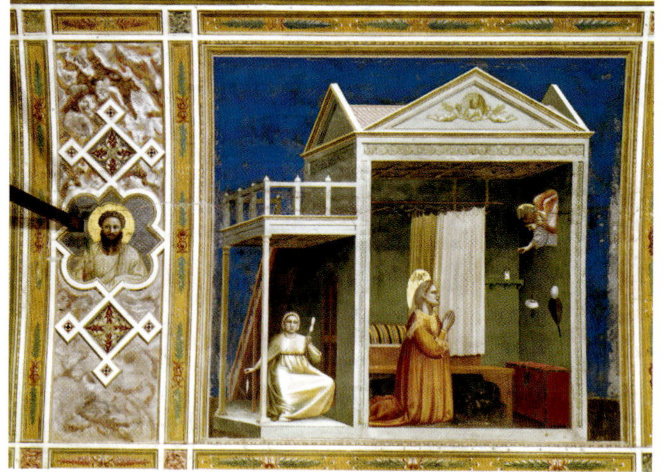

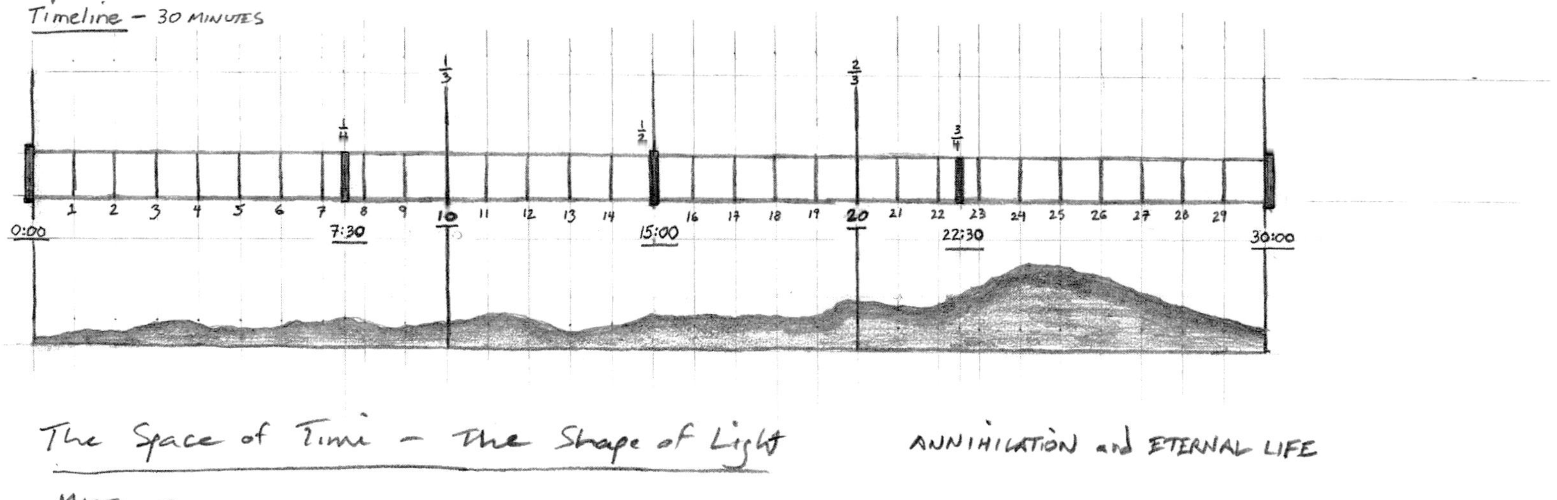

Opposite, top On location for "The Voyage" from *Going Forth By Day* (2002), Lake Piru, CA, December 2001 (left); on the set of "The Voyage," Raleigh Studios, Los Angeles, CA, December 2001 (right)

Opposite, bottom Giotto, *Scenes from the Life of Joachim: Annunciation to St. Anne* (1304–6), fresco, Cappella Scrovegni, Padua, Italy

Above Timeline for 30-minute sunrise for "First Light" from *Going Forth By Day* (2002), July 2001

First Light: It is dawn on the morning of the vernal equinox. A team of rescue workers has been laboring all night to save people caught in a massive flash flood in the desert. Exhausted and physically drained, they slowly pack up their equipment as the dawn light gradually builds and the emotional impact of the night's events deepens. A woman stands on the shore, looking off into the flooded valley where her friends and neighbors once lived. She silently waits, filled with fear and fading hope for the fate of her loved one, her son, who will never return. Eventually, the exhaustion and distress take their toll and, one by one, the four remaining individuals drop off to sleep. All is still and calm. Then, a disturbance appears on the surface of the water and a young man's face emerges. He rises up, limp and dripping wet, and floats into the sky. The drips falling off his body turn to rain, waking the sleeping people. Unaware of what occurred, they move to gather their things in the downpour. The light of the rising sun breaks through the rain as they walk off toward the main road. The rain subsides and the light of a new day shines brightly onto the rocks and hills.[2]

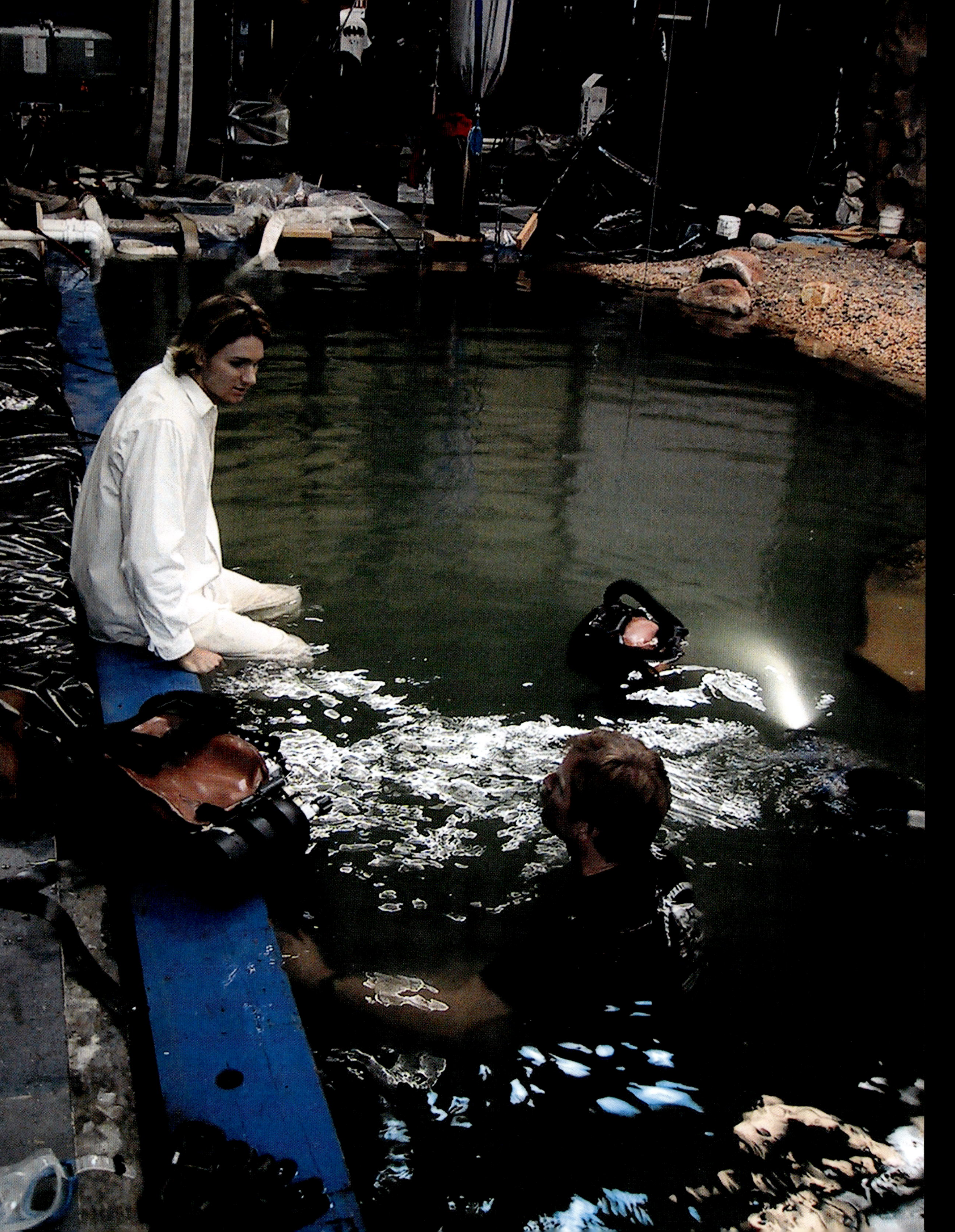

The story told by each panel is embedded within the larger narrative cycle of the room. Viewers are free to move around the space and watch each image panel individually or to stand back and experience the piece as a whole. The five image sequences are each approximately 35 minutes in length and play in synchronization on a continuous loop. Sound from each panel mixes freely in the space, creating an overall acoustic ambience. The images are projected directly onto the walls—without screens or framed support—as in Italian Renaissance frescoes, where the paint was applied directly into the plaster surface of the walls. The title of the work derives from a literal translation of the title of the Egyptian Book of the Dead, "The Ghost Going Forth by Day"—a guide for the soul once it is freed from the darkness of the body to finally "go forth by the light of day."[3]

Going Forth By Day is, by any measure, an epic work, both in the ambition of its scale and in terms of the issues it seeks to engage. At the time the Guggenheim commissioning the piece, I met with Viola regularly to discuss his plans for the installation. He noted at one point that he wanted to create an experience that was like "entering into a movie."[4] In being surrounded by the large-scale projections, the viewer enters a narrative that unfolds all at once, creating a visual experience that plays with the relationship of the projections to murals and to the cinematic experience. Viola's strategy here recalls *The City of Man* (1989), a piece the artist sees as "more connected than any of my other work to *Going Forth By Day*. *The City of Man* was the first time I used nonstandard aspect ratio in my work, something that's been a part of the normal repertoire for painters. I mounted the projectors sideways to maximize the resolution, and this also created the strange quality of having the video scan lines run vertically instead of horizontally in the images."[5] In addition, *Going Forth By Day* is in dialogue with the narrative dimension of the landscape tradition in painting. "It's the large-scale view," commented Viola, "the place of man in the natural environment and in the cosmos—no close-ups, no central characters. It's on the scale of society, not the individual. In this aspect *The City of Man* is more connected to *Going Forth By Day* than almost any other work of mine that references historical painting."[6]

In *Going Forth By Day* the spectator is encouraged to move about, sit on the carpeted floor, and follow the action as it unfolds, reaches closure, and starts again. As such the viewer is actively engaged in a complex transaction with expectation and the multiple-part narrative of the five projections. The formal elements of the installation and the mise-en-scène of the projections create a dialogue on multiple planes—with art history and theology, as well as with the theater and the cinema. Here, Perov describes the sources for the work:

On the set of "First Light" from *Going Forth By Day* (2002), performer John Hay, Santa Clarita Studios, CA, October 2001

Bill was deeply affected and inspired by Early Renaissance and Renaissance Italian frescoes, in particular those of Giotto and Luca Signorelli. After opening the U.S. Pavilion in Venice in 1995, we rewarded ourselves with a journey to Padua to see Giotto's Scrovegni Chapel, a fresco cycle of the life of Mary and of Christ with images that cover the entire interior of the chapel. It was overwhelming to be inside this extraordinary installation that unfolds in time and movement with the recounting of two sustained and highly detailed narratives. For *Going Forth By Day*, Bill later took a trip to Tuscany, and in Orvieto he saw the Luca Signorelli frescoes, in particular *The Last Judgment* in the cathedral, that influenced "The Deluge" and, later, *The Raft* (2004).[7]

Each shot in *Going Forth By Day* is richly composed, with many details in the scenic design, lighting, location, and special digital effects. The changes to the images that such effects enabled, the combining of elements filmed in one place and digitally placed in another, all unite to create a subtle treatment of the moving image. Just as a painter will erase and build up his or her composition and texture on the surface of the canvas, the digital imagery allowed Viola to treat every detail of the moving image he sought to create and to capture the humanistic ideals of the history of art in his own cinematic language. This is a very different work from, for example, *Hatsu-Yume*, which benefited from access to new technology but was realized on a much smaller scale of production, recorded solely by Viola and Perov out in the field. In *Going Forth By Day*, Viola drew on the professionalism and capabilities of the Hollywood film industry, renting sound stages and using stunt actors and cinematographers. Here we can see the artist's studio as made up of skilled specialists, including aerial artists, managing producers, special effects teams, grips, set designers, costumers, and lighting technicians.

Presiding over this creative team is Perov, who, as executive producer, shapes as well as informs the production process and realization of Viola's work. She recalls the making of *Going Forth By Day*:

For six months we were in production for the largest piece we had ever created, for the first time using the new high-definition cameras that would allow for good detail in the large projections Bill had imagined. For "The Deluge" it took one month to construct the building façade surrounded by a water catchment pool, adding enough huge water pipes behind the building that could deliver the kind of forceful flood that was required. For "The Path," director of photography Harry Dawson and his team developed a way of linking three high-definition cameras side by side to record the long pathway through the trees for a projection that is 36 feet wide. Both of these works required 150 extras to populate the scenes, a complex

"First Light," panel 5 from *Going Forth By Day* (2002)

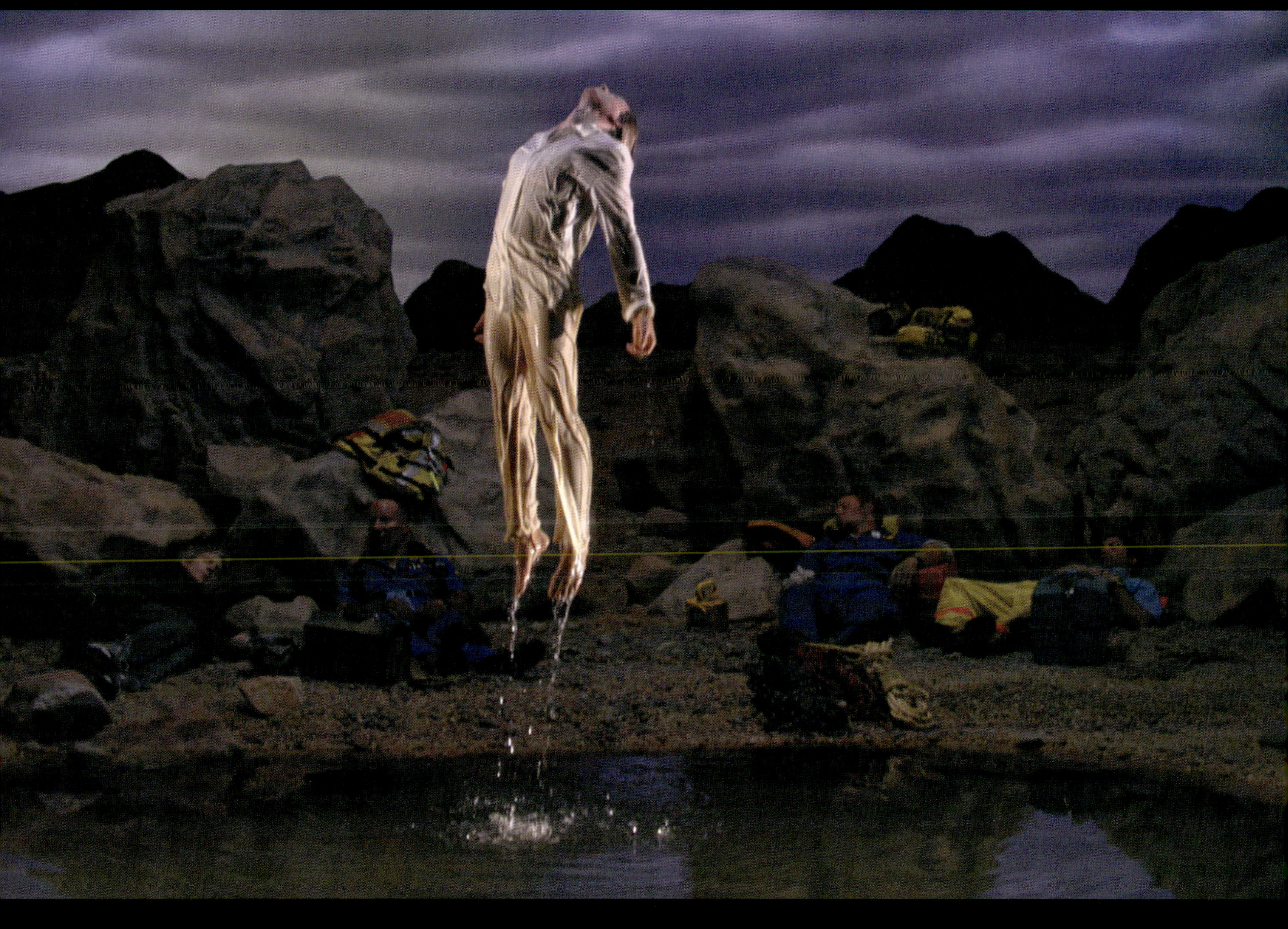

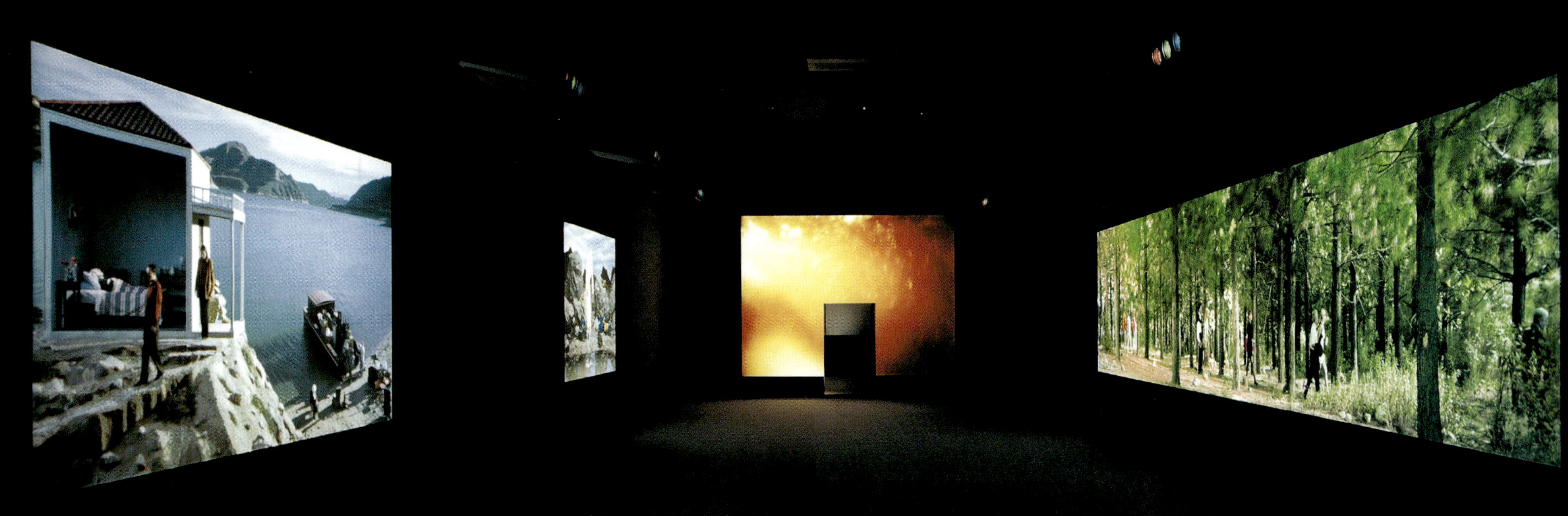

Going Forth By Day (2002), installation views, Deutsche Guggenheim Berlin

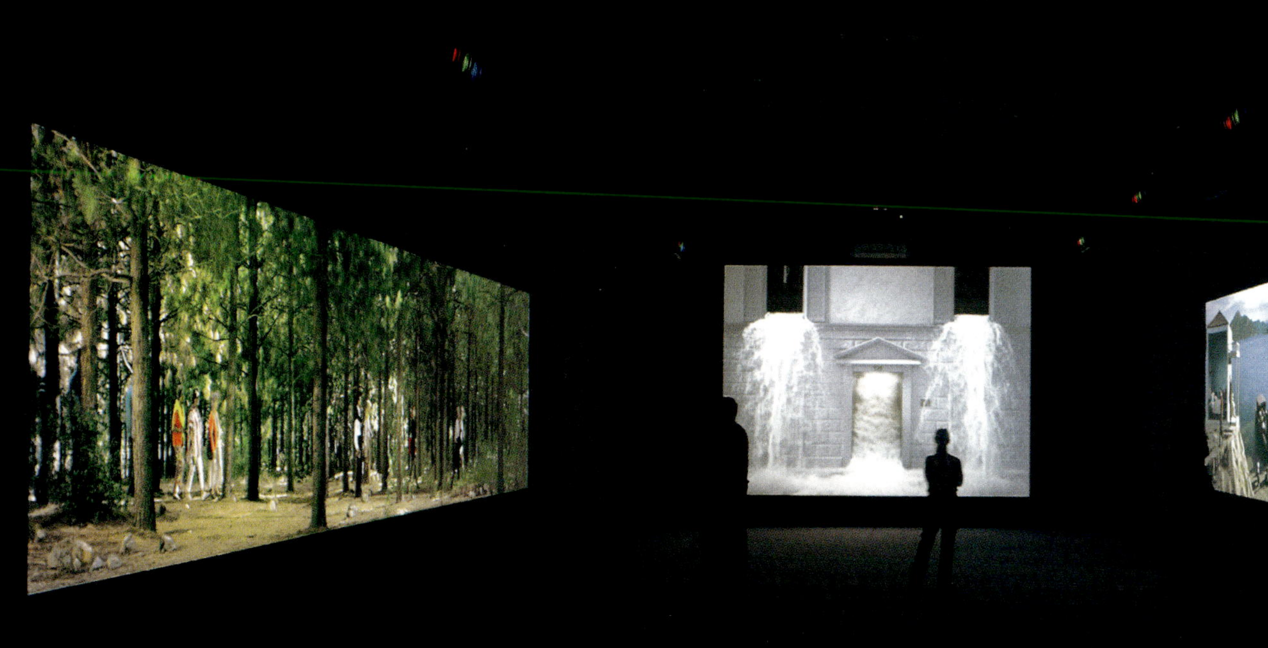
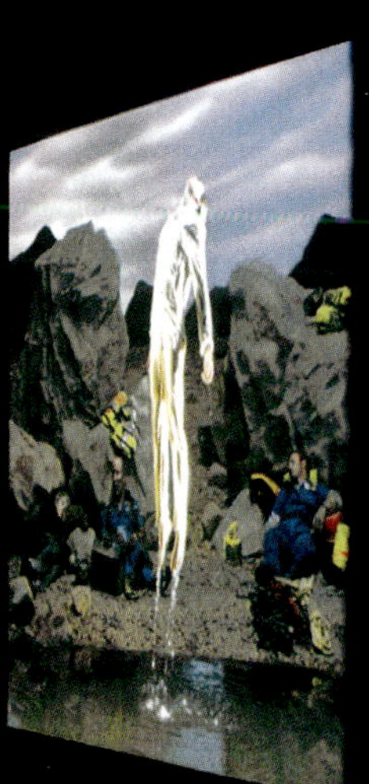

logistical feat on its own. Very capably coordinating the project were Hollywood video producer S. Tobin Kirk together with assistant director Kenny Bowers. "The Voyage" was recorded in two locations, the lake where the boat was loading the furniture, and the green-screened house on the hill (a nod to Giotto) shot in a studio and then combined in post-production. "First Light" was intended to be shot in the desert, but we needed full control of all elements so we brought them all into the studio, the boulders, the sand, the small lake, the rain shower, and a lighting board that could create a 36-minute sunrise. Three of these pieces were developed as a narrative, and for the first time in all of his art-making, Bill was telling a story.[8]

Viola has recreated and reimagined the world that he observed with the camera early on in his career. His language in describing *Going Forth By Day* returns to the themes of birth and death, which first took on significance with the birth of his sons and the death of his mother and, later, his father. Those subjects now inform a larger narrative that draws not on what the camera sees and reveals but on what Viola can create in front of the camera. Such constructions, like the theater and the cinema, are imaginary mise-en-scènes that allow for a retelling of the different stories from the different religious traditions that inform Viola's imagination.

The idea of the stage as a setting for both opera and cinema provides the link between Viola's opera project *Tristan und Isolde* (2004–5) and his *Ocean Without a Shore* (2007), an elaborate sculpture installation. In 2004 Viola began work on "The Tristan Project." Perov relates:

The 2004/5 season would be Gerard Mortier's first as general director of the Opéra National de Paris and, desiring a radical opener, he invited opera director Peter Sellars, conductor Esa-Pekka Salonen, and Bill to collaborate on a new production of *Tristan und Isolde* by Richard Wagner—yes, a nineteenth-century German romantic opera! This would be produced in partnership with the Los Angeles Philharmonic (in Los Angeles it was titled "The Tristan Project" since the three acts were to be presented, semi-staged, on three consecutive evenings) and the Lincoln Center [for the Performing Arts, New York]. It was hard to say no, so production began for another huge project that would take six months, once again using all the resources available from Hollywood and from our archive to create four hours of video, the length of the opera. All kinds of recording media were used: high-definition cameras, 35mm high-speed film, our old "Grainy Cam" that produces mysterious grainy images, and a handheld camcorder that Bill shot with on his own with no crew. The ideas for various scenes came from his notebooks of pieces that were already written down, so after the opera was completed, these pieces were reedited, some with added sound and others silent, to form the "Tristan" series of installations, including

Opposite and following two pages Peter Sellars' production of Richard Wagner's *Tristan und Isolde*, with 4-hour video by Bill Viola, premiere performance, Opéra National de Paris, April 12, 2005

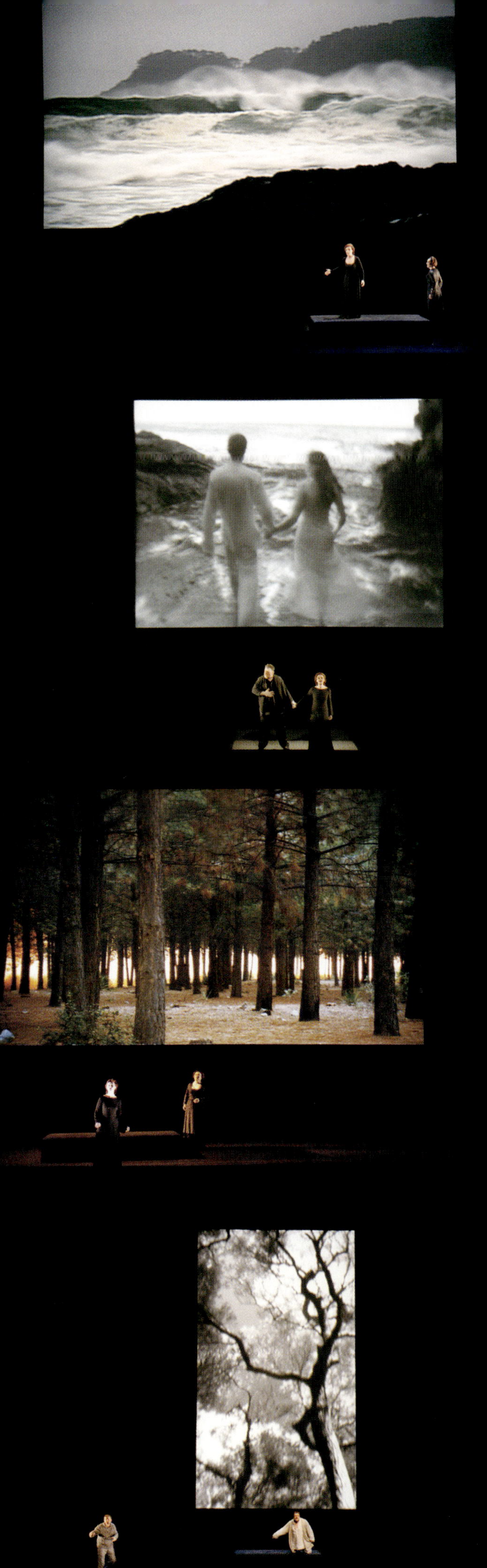

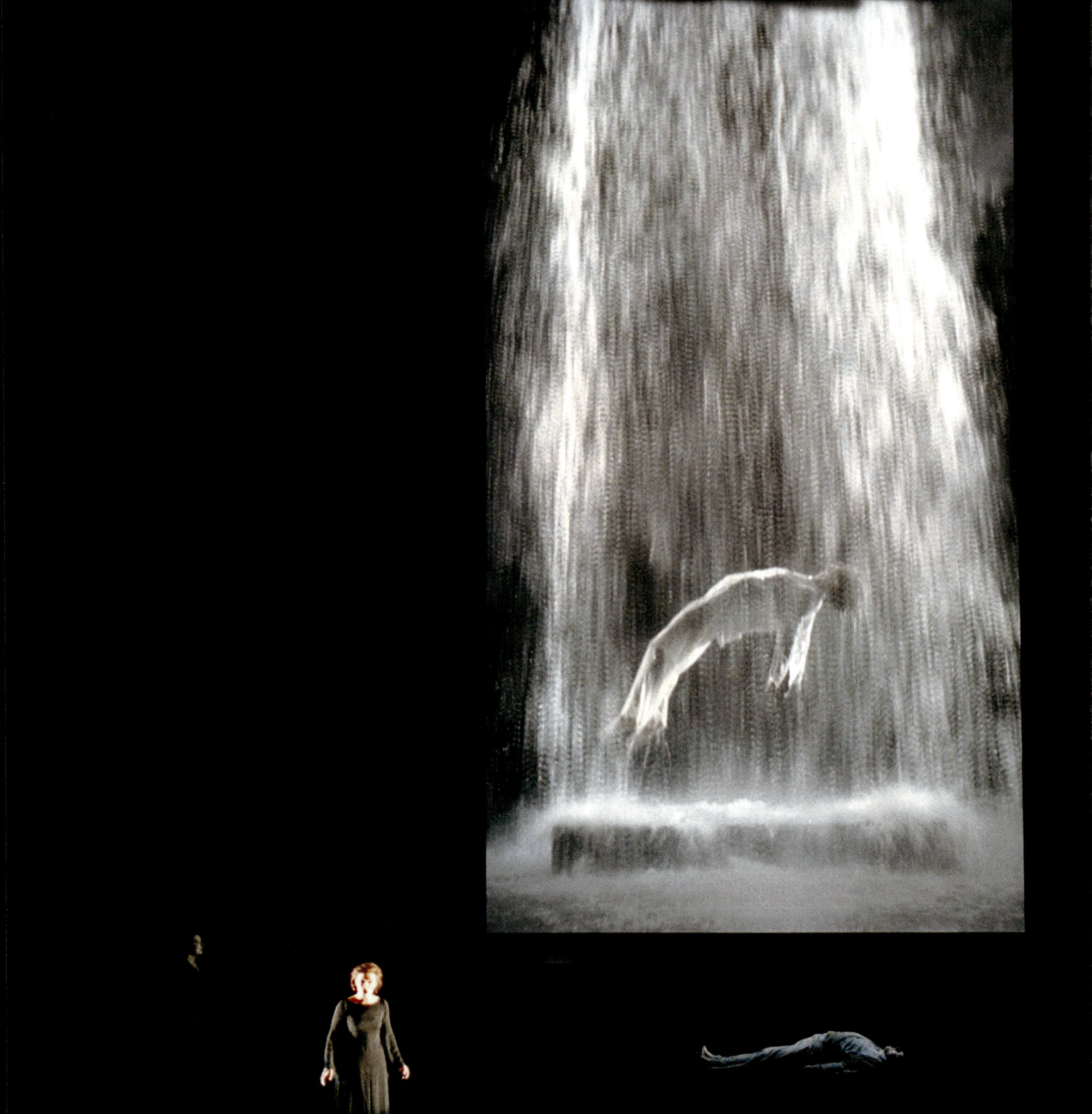

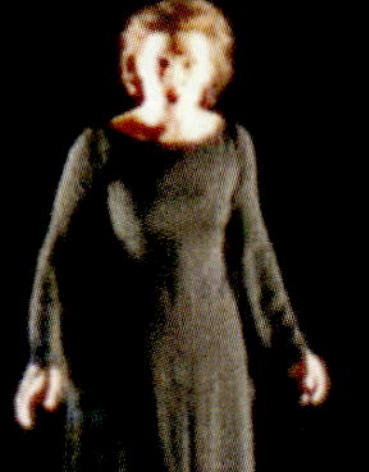

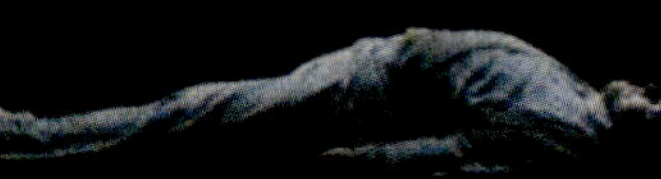

Following two pages On the set of *Tristan's Ascension* (2005), Bill Viola instructing stunt coordinator Tom Ficke and performer John Hay; and *Fire Woman* (2005), Tom Ficke testing the heat of the gas flames, Downey Studios, CA, July 2004

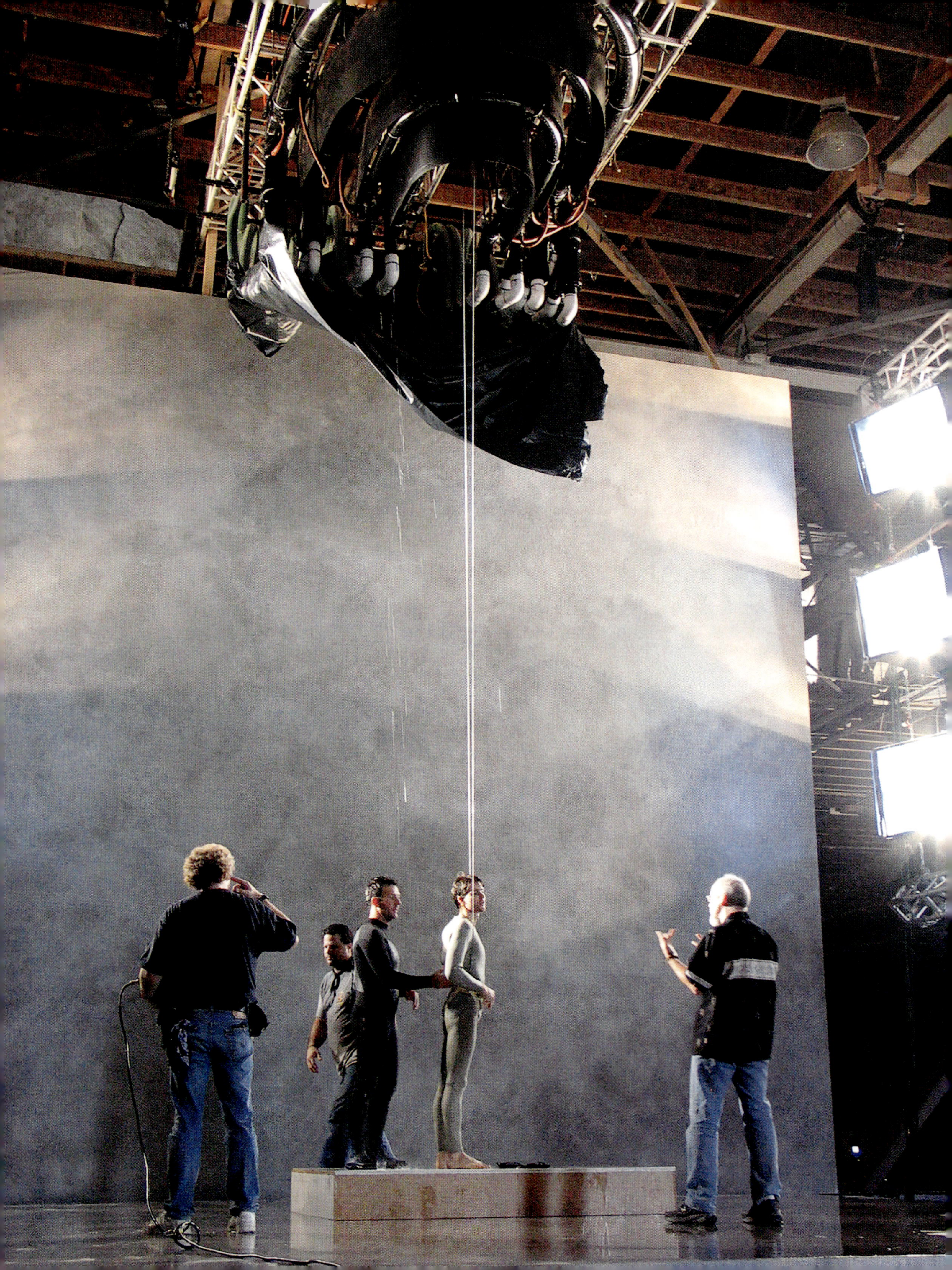

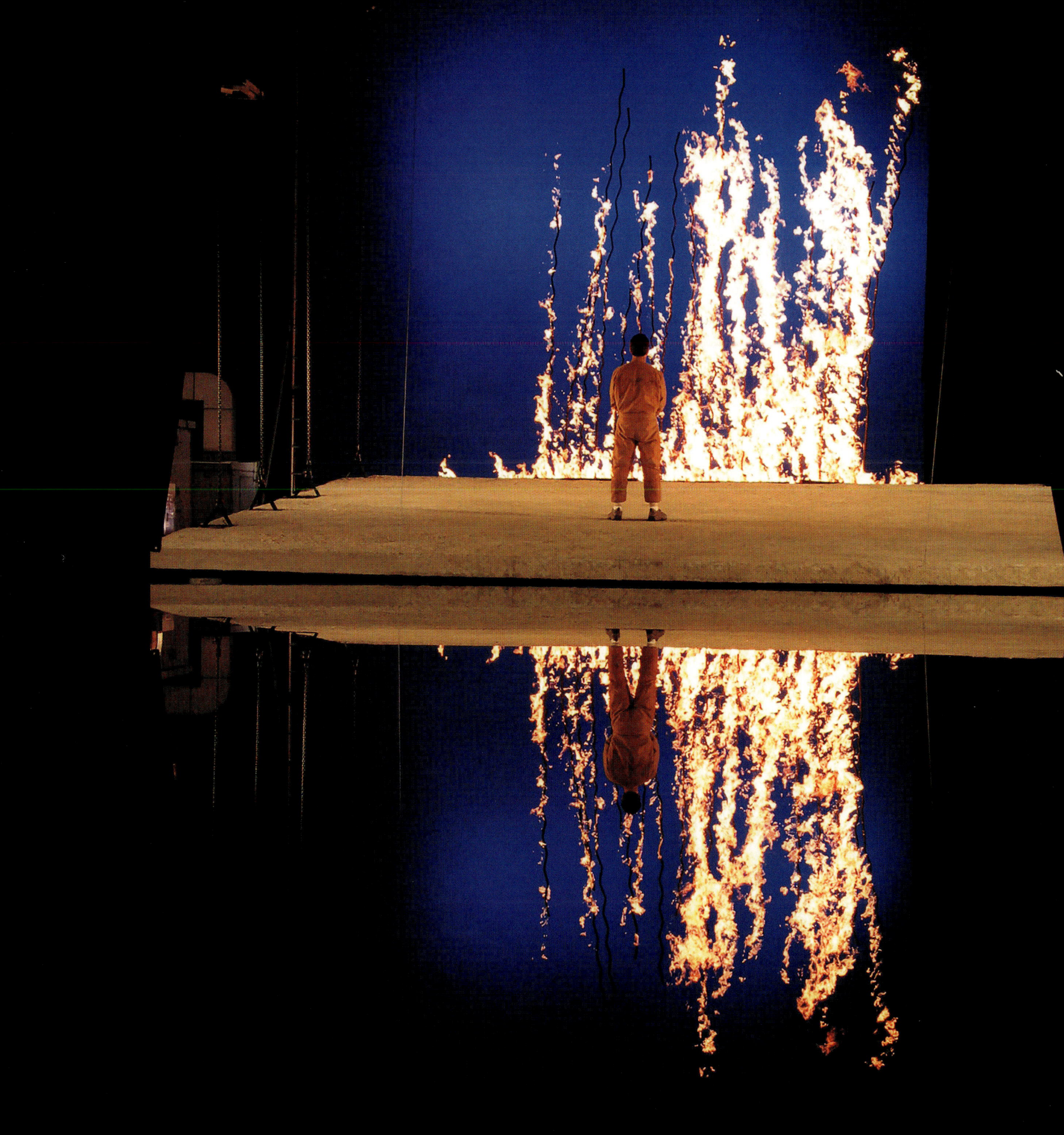

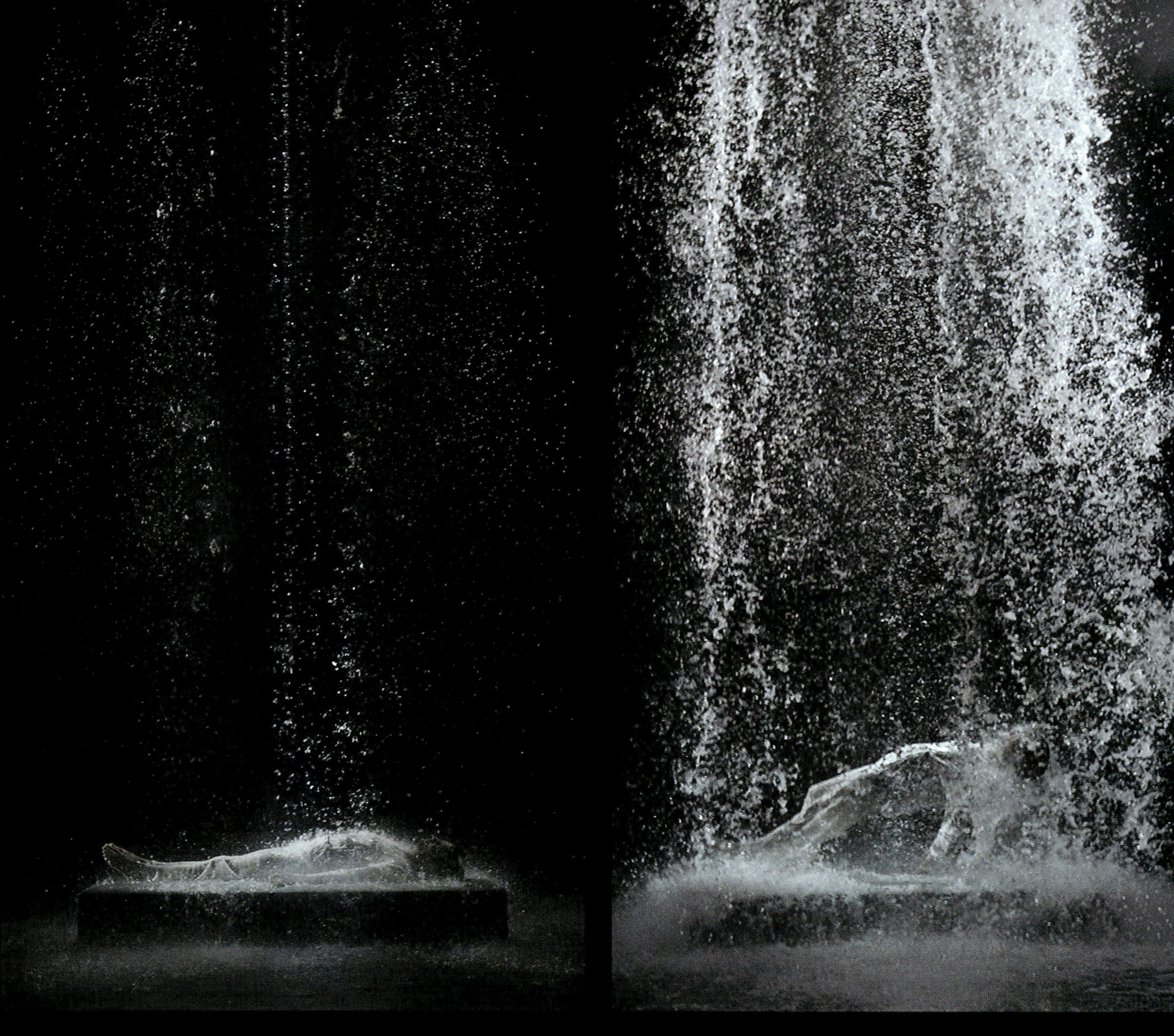

Tristan's Ascension (The Sound of a Mountain Under a Waterfall) (2005)

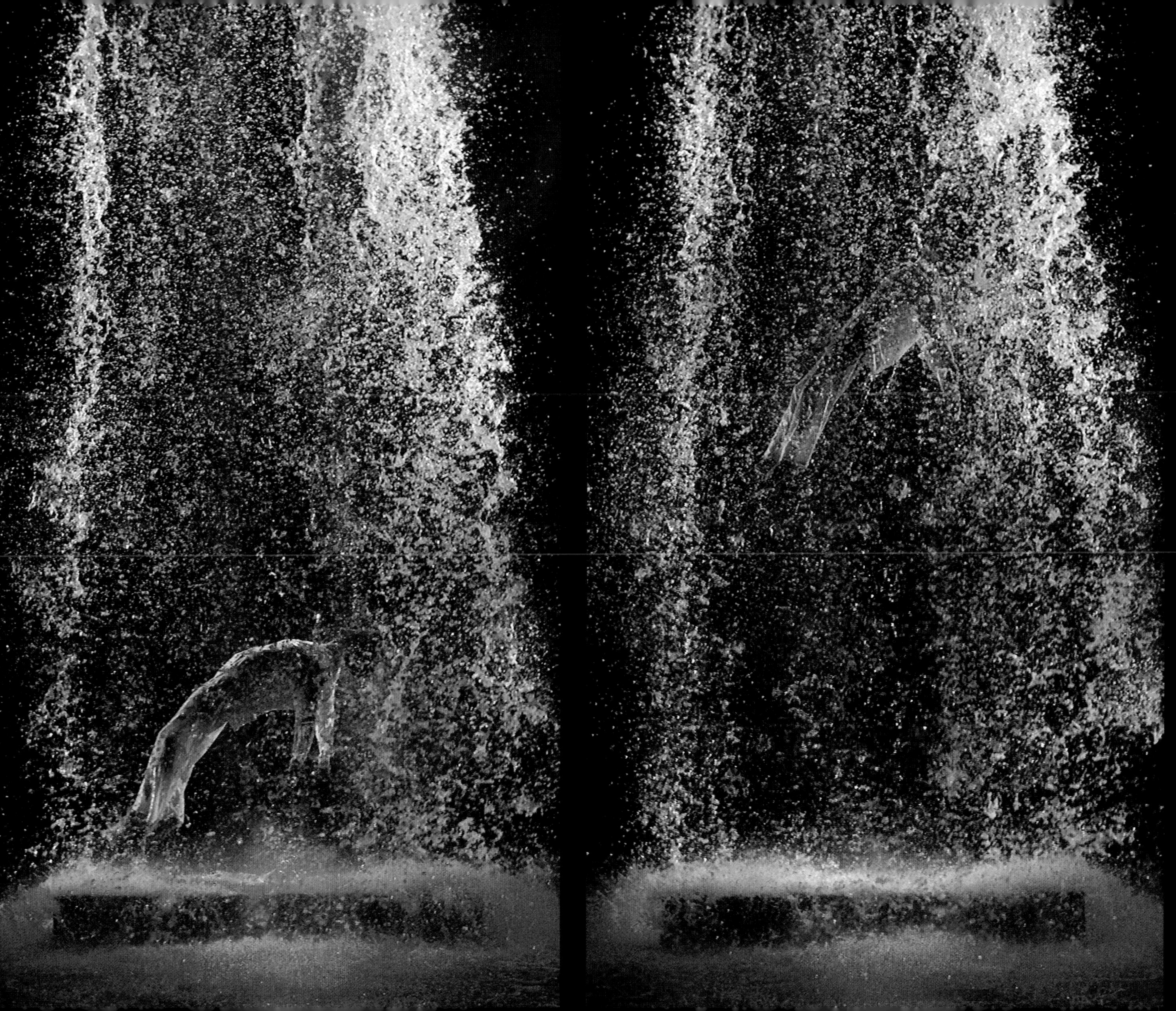

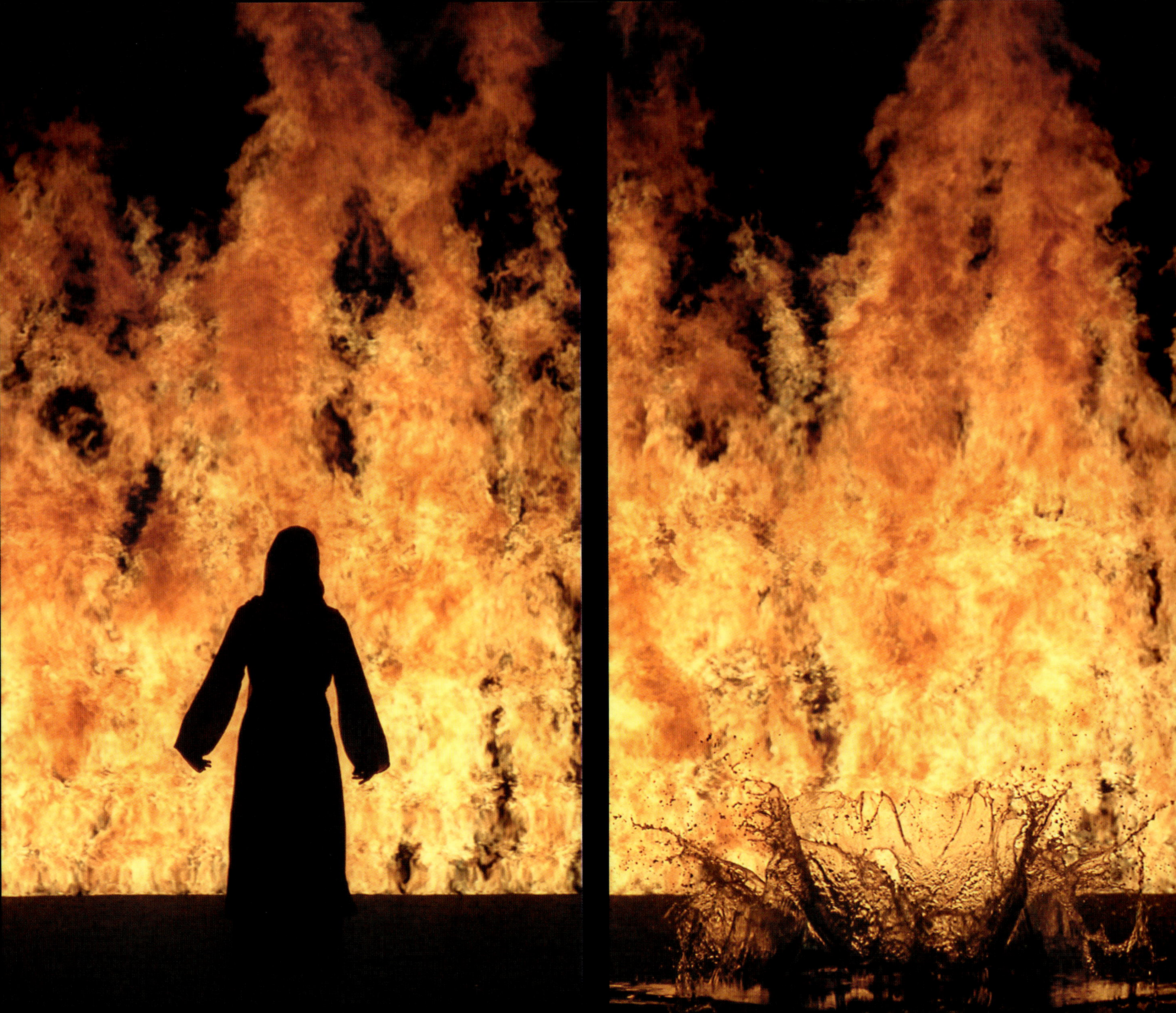

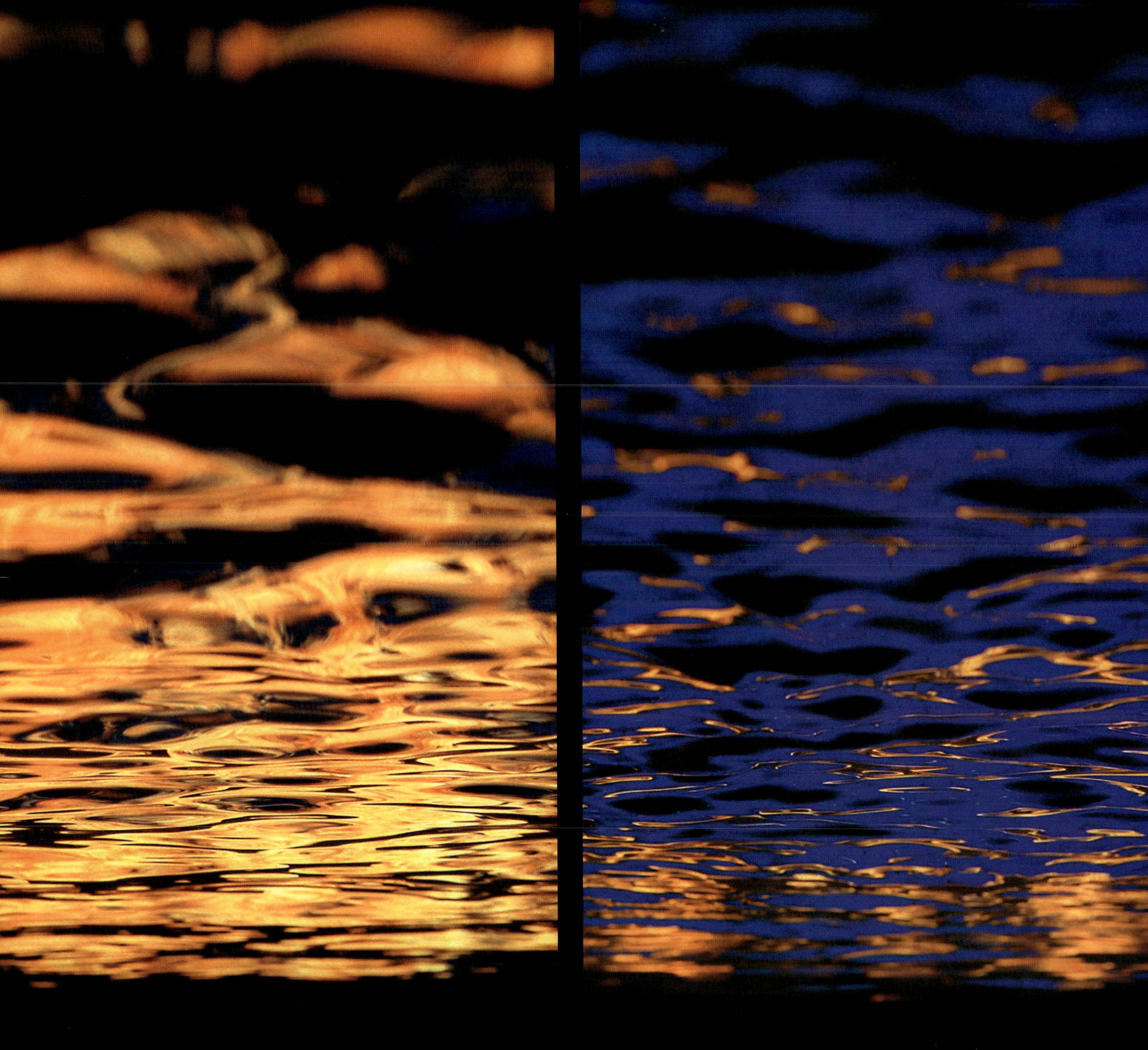

Tristan's Ascension and _Fire Woman_. For the performances of the opera, we developed a dual video system, coordinated by Alex MacInnis, where the sequences can run on longer or be cut shorter according to the tempo of the conductor and singers, so in fact the video is actually "performed live" with the music. The premiere in Paris in 2005 was brilliant and controversial, and the production continues to be presented to sold-out theaters in its concert hall version as well as in its fully staged form in world class opera houses.[9]

In a revealing paragraph on his approach to the *Tristan und Isolde* project, taken from his program notes for the Paris staging of the opera, Viola writes:

I first listened to various versions of the music and then worked primarily from the libretto to visualize an image world flowing within and without the dramatic storyline being enacted on stage. Moving images live in a domain somewhere between the temporal urgency of music and the material certainty of painting, and so are well suited to link the practical elements of stage design with the living dynamics of performance. I knew from the start that I did not want the images to illustrate or represent the story directly. Instead I wanted to create an image world that existed in parallel to the action on the stage, in the same way that a more subtle poetic narrative mediates the hidden dimension of our inner lives.[10]

Viola treats the music and libretto in relation to his video images much like an installation. In *Room for St. John of the Cross* (1983), for example, the spoken text plays against the two videos inside the small room and projected large on the rear wall of the exhibition space. The moving images become an extension of the spoken text and provide a context for the language of St. John's poetic reveries. They place the viewer in the turmoil of his incarceration and state of mind. In *Tristan und Isolde*, above the singers and the orchestra playing the music, the floating video world engages the audience in another experiential sphere. This enriches the complex narrative of the opera by picking up key images of immolation and transcendence of the body "in an image world that exists in parallel to the actions on the stage, intended to function as 'reflections of the spiritual world seen in the material and the temporal,' as the great Islamic scholar Seyyed Hossein Nasr has described."[11]

Created for the 52nd Venice Biennale, *Ocean Without a Shore*, a "Transfigurations" series piece, was first shown in the small fifteenth-century Church of the Oratorio San Gallo, near the Piazza San Marco. As Perov recalls, "Although the church had been deconsecrated, its three ornate stone altars were still intact. A large screen was positioned on the central altar, with two smaller screens placed on the side altars. They fit almost perfectly. Up high in the corners hung sculptures of saints, while bas-relief and

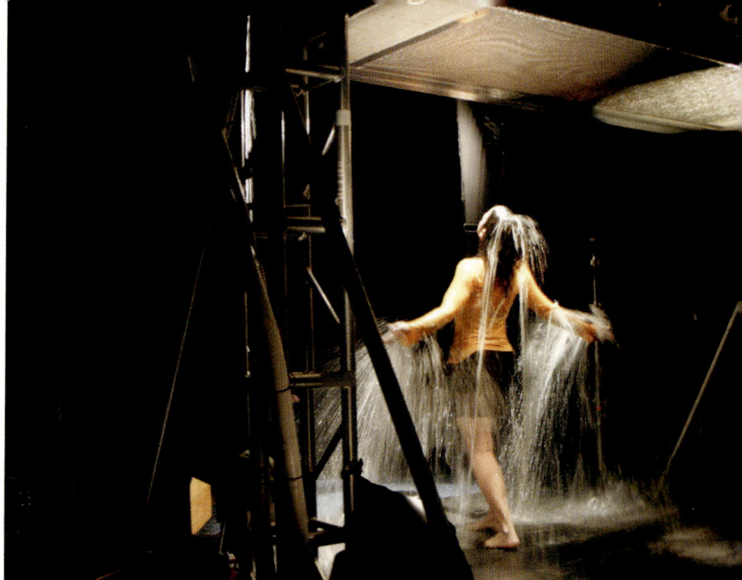

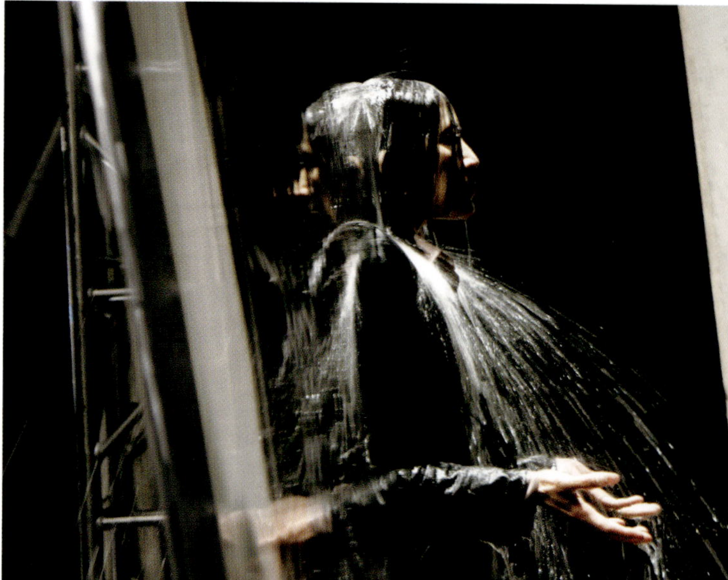

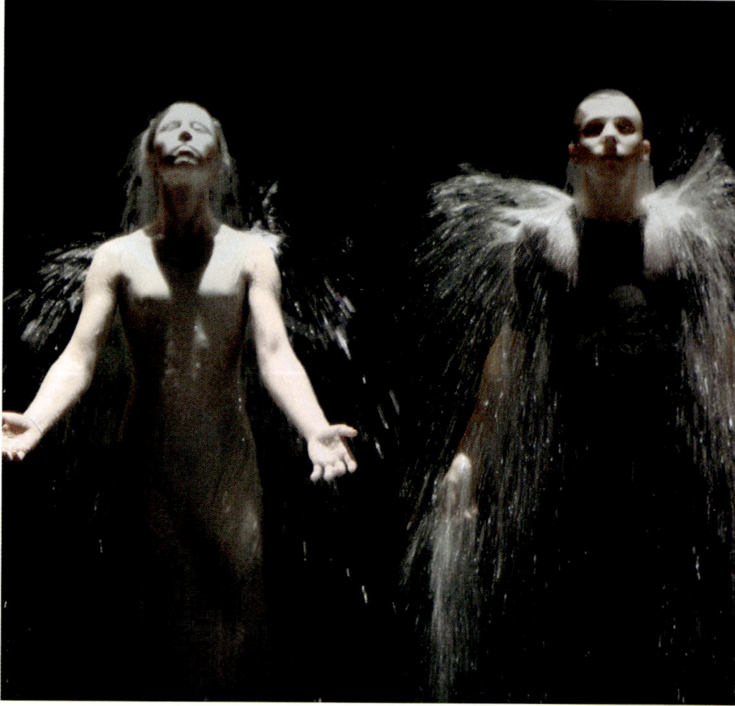

Top and center On the set for *Ocean Without a Shore*, Bill Viola Studio, Signal Hill, CA, March 2007

San Gallo project – Venice

Transition Zones

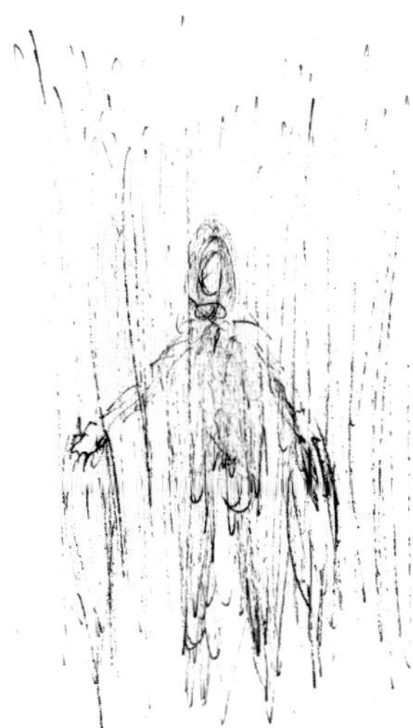

Water Sheet

Walking through a Sheet of Water

Camera

Can the water be smoothed so it reads as an image disturbance before the figure enters?

Water Sheet

Figure

Trough to prevent splash back

Space, distant Room?

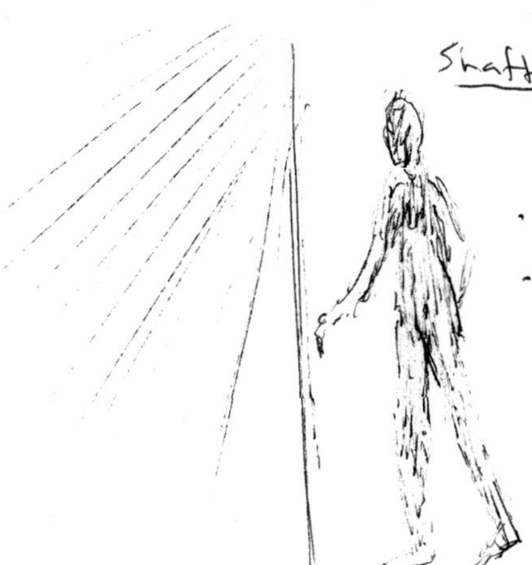

Shaft of High Intensity Light

. from B+W to color
- from dim/grainy to bright color
- from textured/abstract to
. high resolution colored clarity

VEIL

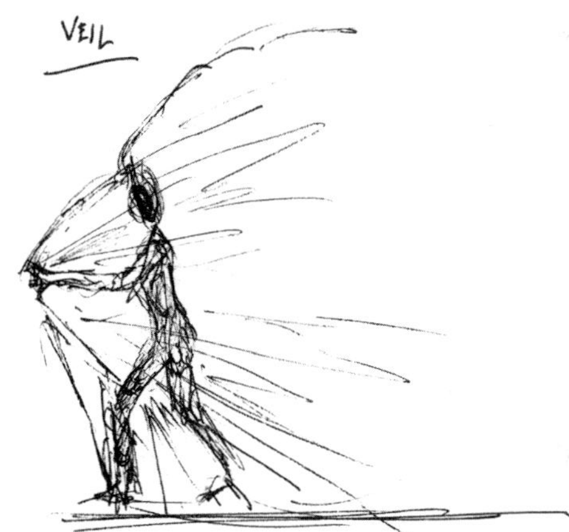

Gauze Sheer Fabric, stretched and pulled to the breaking point. Figure tears through.

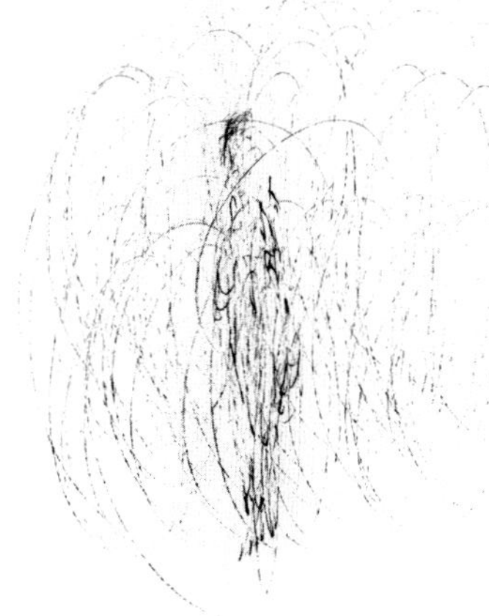

FOG

Cloud of dense smoke –
Figure approaches, clarifies . . .
passes through the fog into harsh clarity.

Lighting effects can produce multiple figures, shadows and silhouettes ■.

Feb 17, 2007

Opposite, bottom *The Innocents* (2007), a diptych from the "Transfigurations" series

Above Drawings for *Ocean Without a Shore*, Sketchpad, February 17, 2007

Friday 9 Feb. Misty, translucent day – coming into focus.

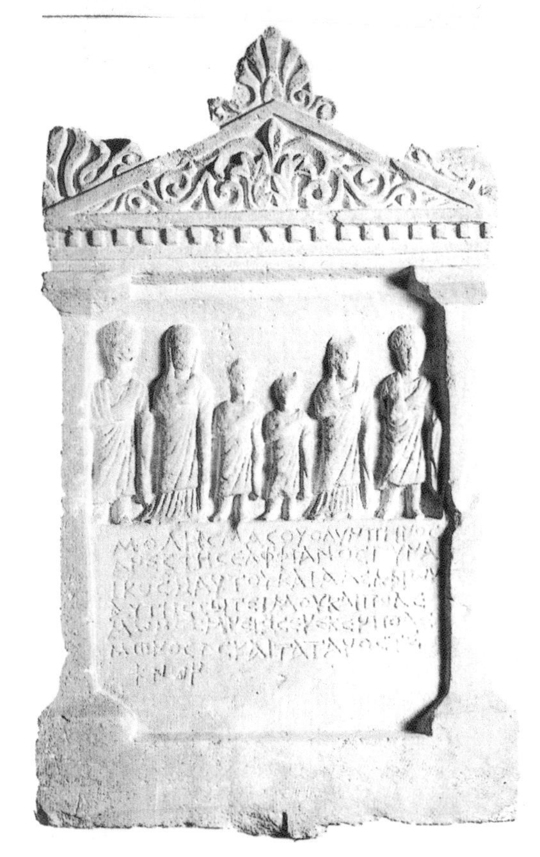

Late Roman –
Inscribed funerary
Pedimented Stele
ARCHEOLOGICAL MUSEUM
of RHODES

Figures trying to break out of their tombs. At certain rare junctures, stone becomes porous and transparent, allowing for effortless passage in both directions between the land of the dead and the land of the living. I need to recreate these moments.

VOTIVE RELIEF

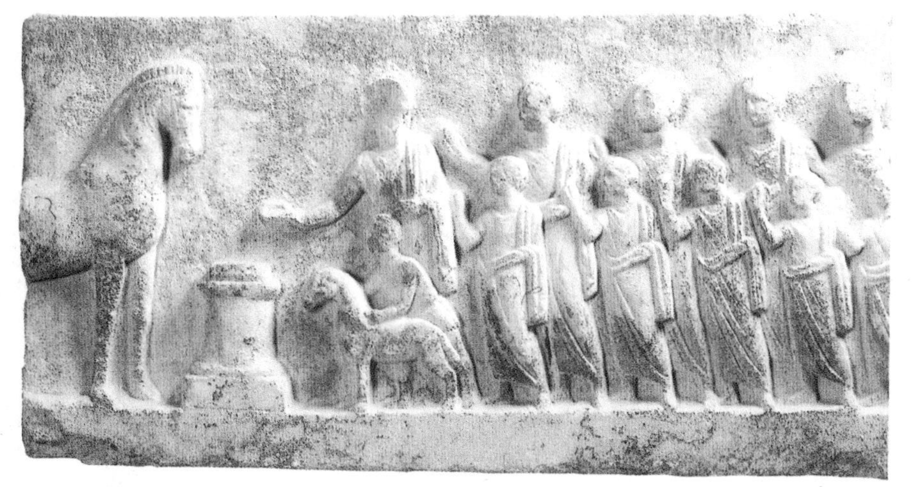

Right arms of 5 men and 5 children raised in blessing
Small child leads a lamb before a cylindrical altar

Hearing things more than beings,
Listening to the voice of fire,
the voice of water.
Hearing in wind the weeping bushes,
sighs of our forefathers.

The dead are never gone:
They are in the shadows.
The dead are not in earth:
They're in the rustling tree,
the groaning wood,
water that runs,
water that sleeps,
they're in the hut, in the crowd,
the dead are not dead.

The dead are never gone,
they're in the breast of a woman,
they're in the crying of a child,
in the flaming torch.
The dead are not in earth:
They're in the dying fire,
the weeping grasses,
whimpering rocks
they're in the forest, they're in the house,
the dead are not dead.

-Birago Diop Senegalese Poet and Storyteller

Opposite Page of taped photographs and notes for *Ocean Without a Shore*, San Gallo Project Book, February 9, 2007

Above Poem by Birago Diop transcribed by Bill Viola, 2007

marbles still decorated the walls."[12] Inspired by the writings of the Senegalese poet Birago Diop, *Ocean Without a Shore* takes its title from the philosophy of the thirteenth-century Andalusian Sufi mystic Ibn Arabi, who wrote, "The Self is an ocean without a shore. Gazing upon it has no beginning or end, in this world and the next."[13] Viola describes the work as "a series of encounters at the intersection between life and death." "The video sequence," he explains, "documents a succession of individuals slowly approaching out of darkness and moving into the light in order to pass into the physical world. Once incarnate, however, all beings realize that their presence is finite and so they must eventually turn away from material existence to return from where they came. The cycle repeats without end."[14] The passage from one world to another is represented by the act of moving through a clear "sheet" of falling water. On each screen, in the far distance,

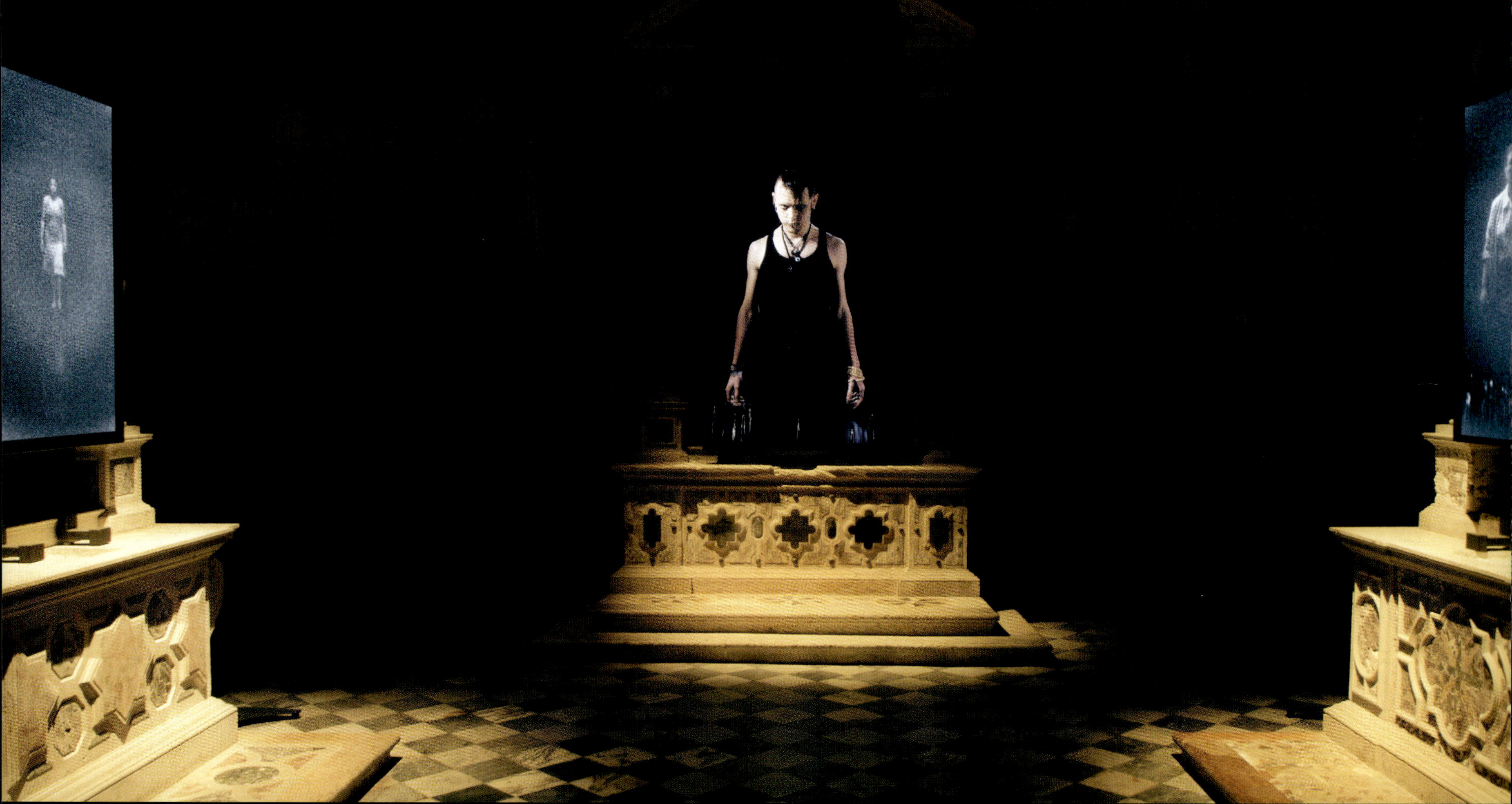

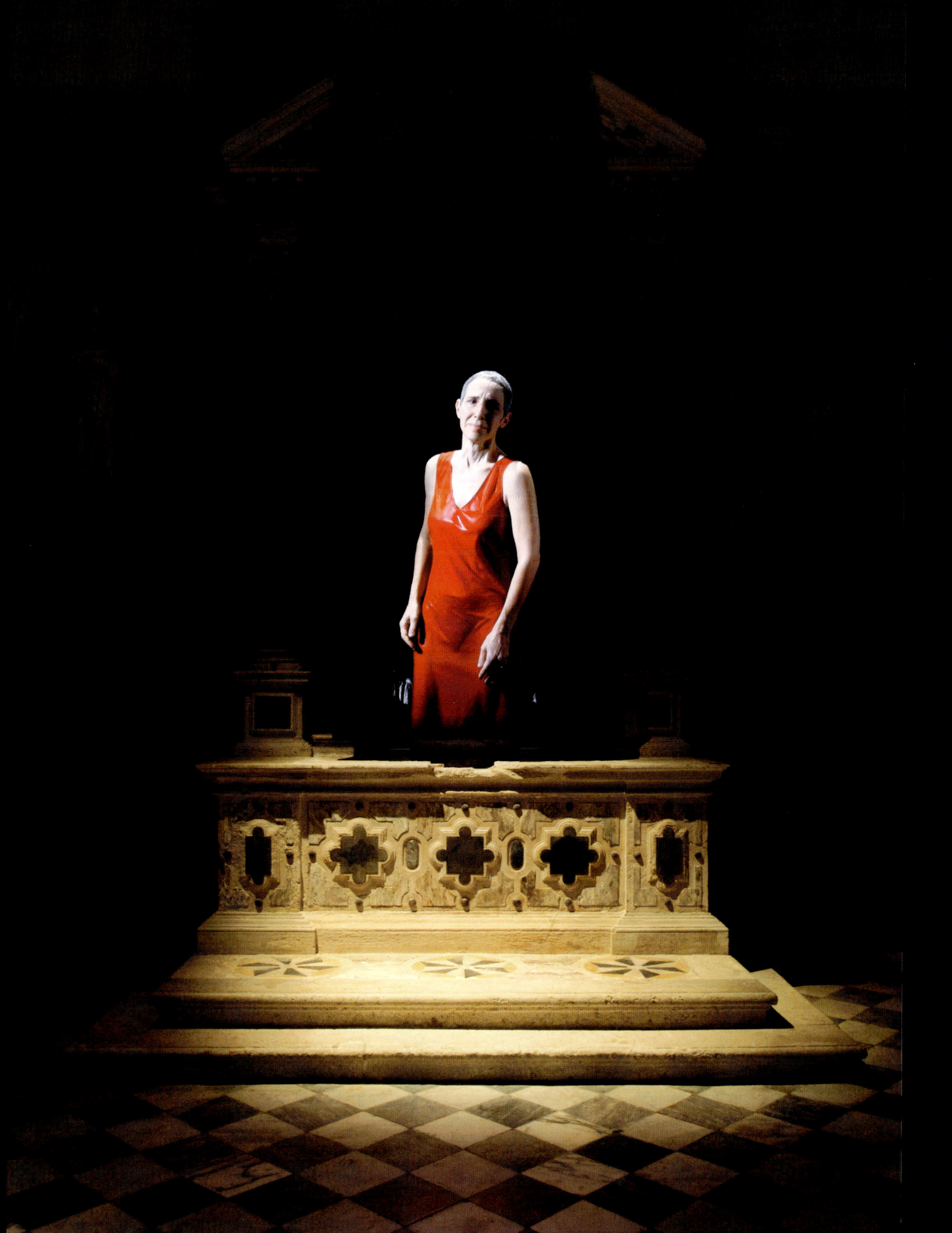

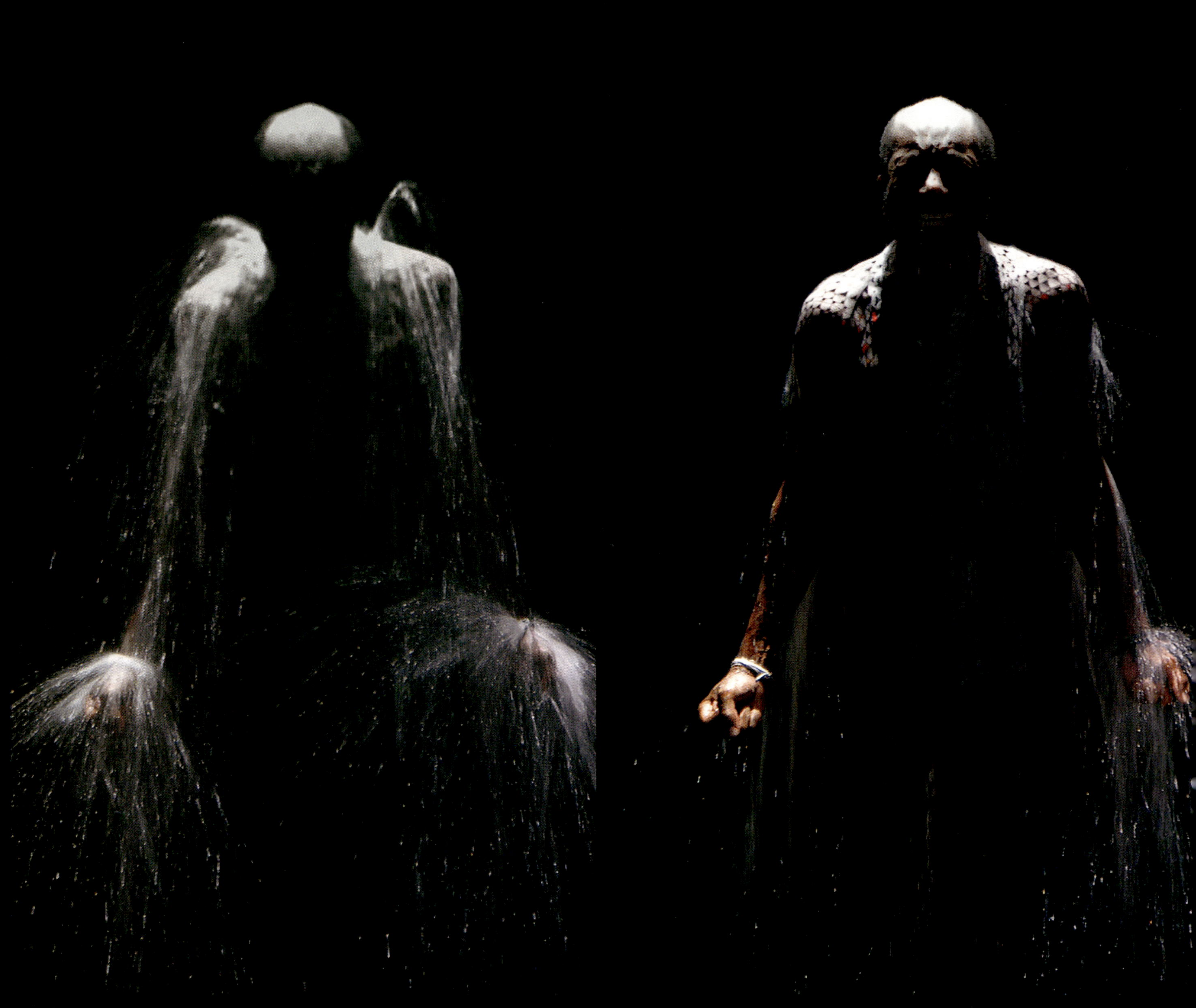

Ocean Without a Shore (2007)

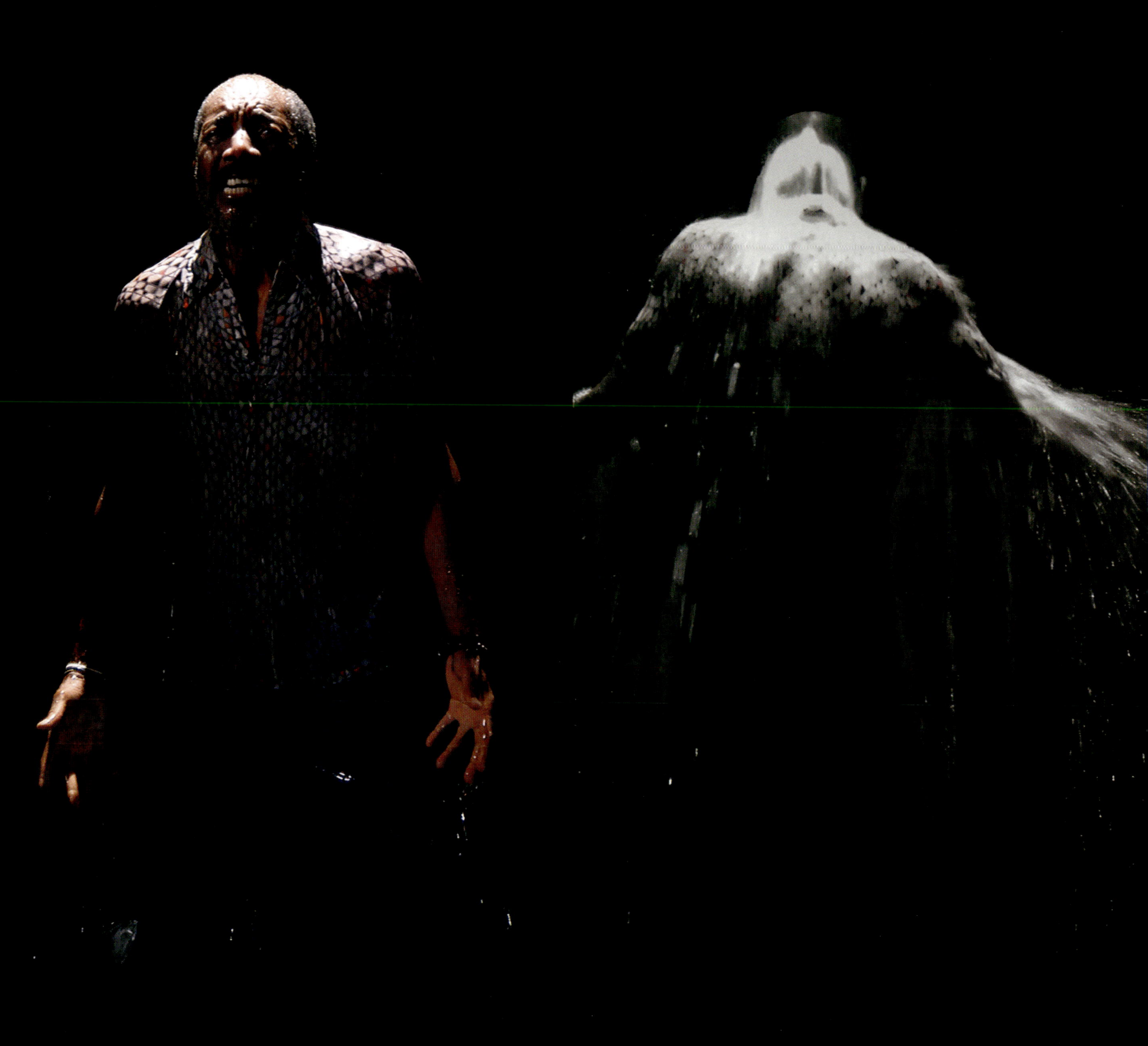

a figure appears and begins walking toward the viewer. The figures are seen in black and white and appear ghostly, coming from another world. As their bodies penetrate the film of water they emerge in color. Revealed to us, they look at us, and then return to where they came from, into the void, to reappear as the cycle begins again. The astonishing power of this installation lies in the simplicity and elegance of the individual characters and their performance as they approach, emerge, and return through the sheet of water. The sound of the water fills the space. The water itself becomes both material and immaterial, a thin veil that conveys not only the presence of water but also its power. Here, we are reminded of Viola's use of the river as a symbol of continuity and change.

An important influence on Viola for *Ocean Without a Shore* came from an untitled poem by Birago Diop, a powerful reflection on life and death. As I was reading it and experiencing Viola's artwork I was reminded of other artists and philosophers who have grappled with the passage between life and death. The celebrated opening of Goethe's *Faust* came to mind: "Wavering forms, you come again; / once long ago you passed before my clouded / sight."[15] As did the passage in the *Inferno* in which Dante follows the poet Virgil into an abyss: "It was full of vapor, dark and deep. / Straining my eyes toward the bottom, / I could see nothing. / 'Now let us descend into the blind world / down there,' began the poet, gone pale. / 'I will be first and you will come after.'"[16] These lines capture that moment of change and danger, and the stakes that are held in a life, and the hopes of a life remembered. The finitude of life is sustained in the hereafter in Dante's *Inferno* and the presumption of science rendered as magic in the Faustian bargain of Goethe's poem. The philosopher Samuel Scheffler has written that we live with the knowledge of those who will follow.[17] The cycles of life and death are their own proof of the perseverance of life. It is the quest for meaning in life and death that is foundational to Viola's art.

In 2012 Viola and Perov continued their exploration of the phenomenon of mirages. As Perov recalls:

A large commission brought us back to the desert once again to record the effects of mirages and heat waves on our perception of the landscape and the people who inhabit it. We were shooting in the Mojave Desert in California in July at the hottest time of the year in order to get the best effects. We had a whole tent city installed with our performers and crew on the El Mirage dry lake, which is ten kilometers in length. *Crossroads* (2014), for the Hamad International Airport in Doha, Qatar, is installed on hundreds of LED screens 25 meters wide and 5 meters high. The piece uses the edge of the mirage as the threshold between clarity and illusion, as nineteen people of different ages, race, gender, and ethnicity walk toward the viewer one by one in various stages of their journey and the entire length of the

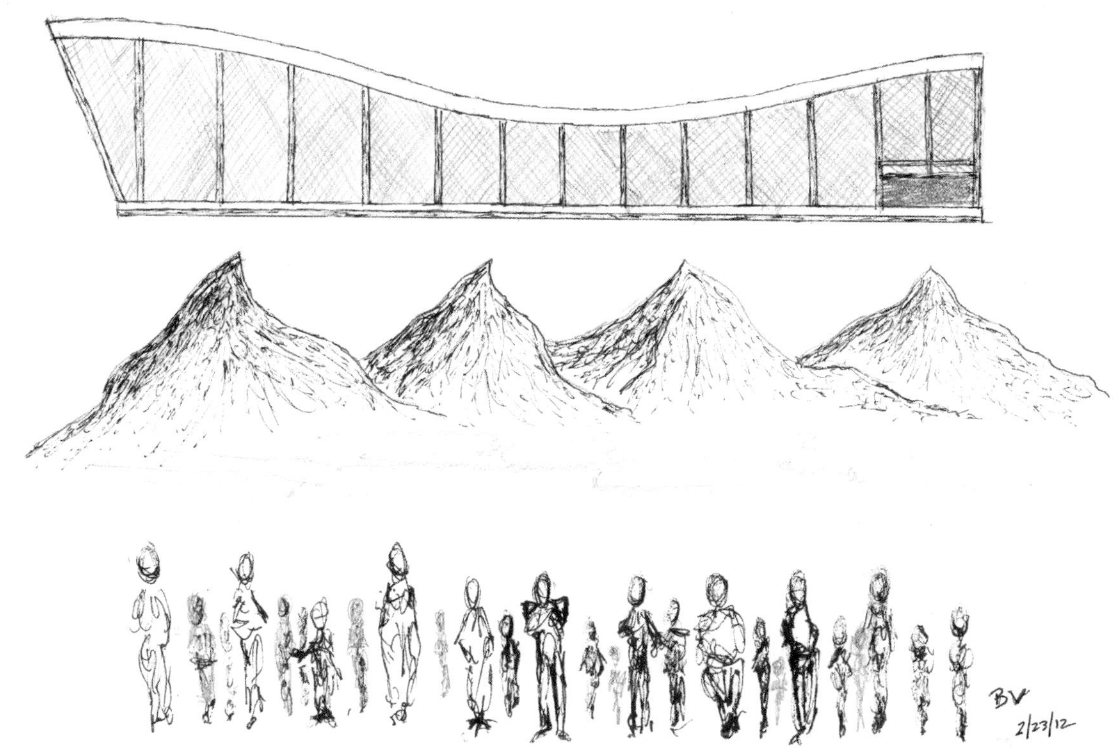

Crossroads (2014), drawing for proposal to Qatar Museums Authority for Hamad International Airport, Doha, February 23, 2012

screen is filled with the shimmering light of their dance of life. The group of works we recorded at the same time as *Crossroads* and later in October we title the "Mirage" series and includes *Inner Passage*.[18]

Inner Passage (2013), a vertical plasma-screen piece, stands with *I Do Not Know What It Is I Am Like* (1986) as one of the purest statements of the passage through human consciousness to our perception of the world around us. "*Inner Passage* chronicles a brief moment in one man's solitary journey into the Mojave Desert of Southern California," writes Viola. "It is an inner as well as an outer journey. In this landscape, the physical body confronts extremes of endurance in the form of scorching heat, numbing cold, blinding light, impenetrable darkness, infinite distance, and forced confinement. It is also where the metaphysical extremes of loneliness, isolation, stress, anxiety, and fear meet the forces of overwhelming beauty, mystery, wonder, and ecstasy. Between these two states lies the present moment, with all its uncertainty and promise."[19] Viola's description continues: "A man appears as a faint dot on the distant desert floor, and proceeds to move in a straight line toward us. As he gets closer he walks directly into the camera, blacking out the image. The screen goes dark, but it soon comes to life in an intense, jumbled cascade of images and fragmented sounds, that builds in intensity and frequency. When these begin to fade, the solitary light

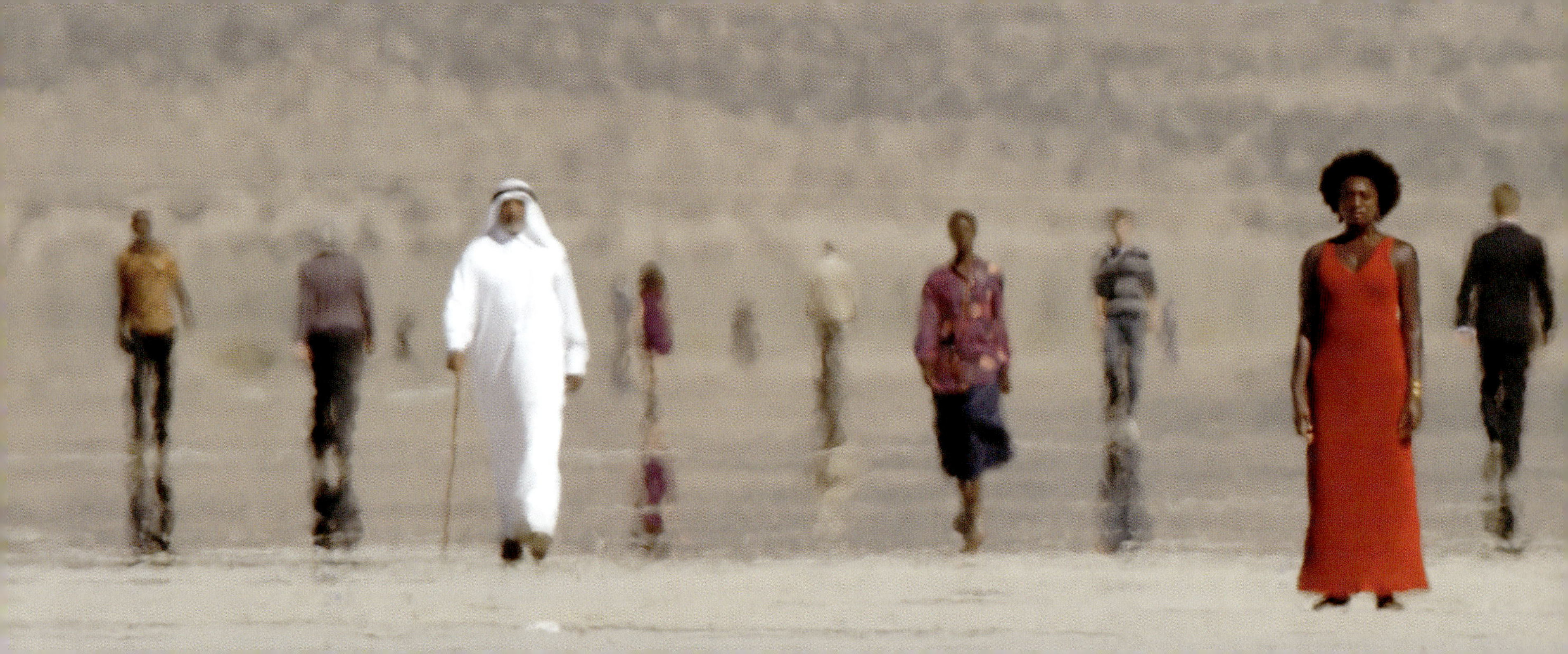

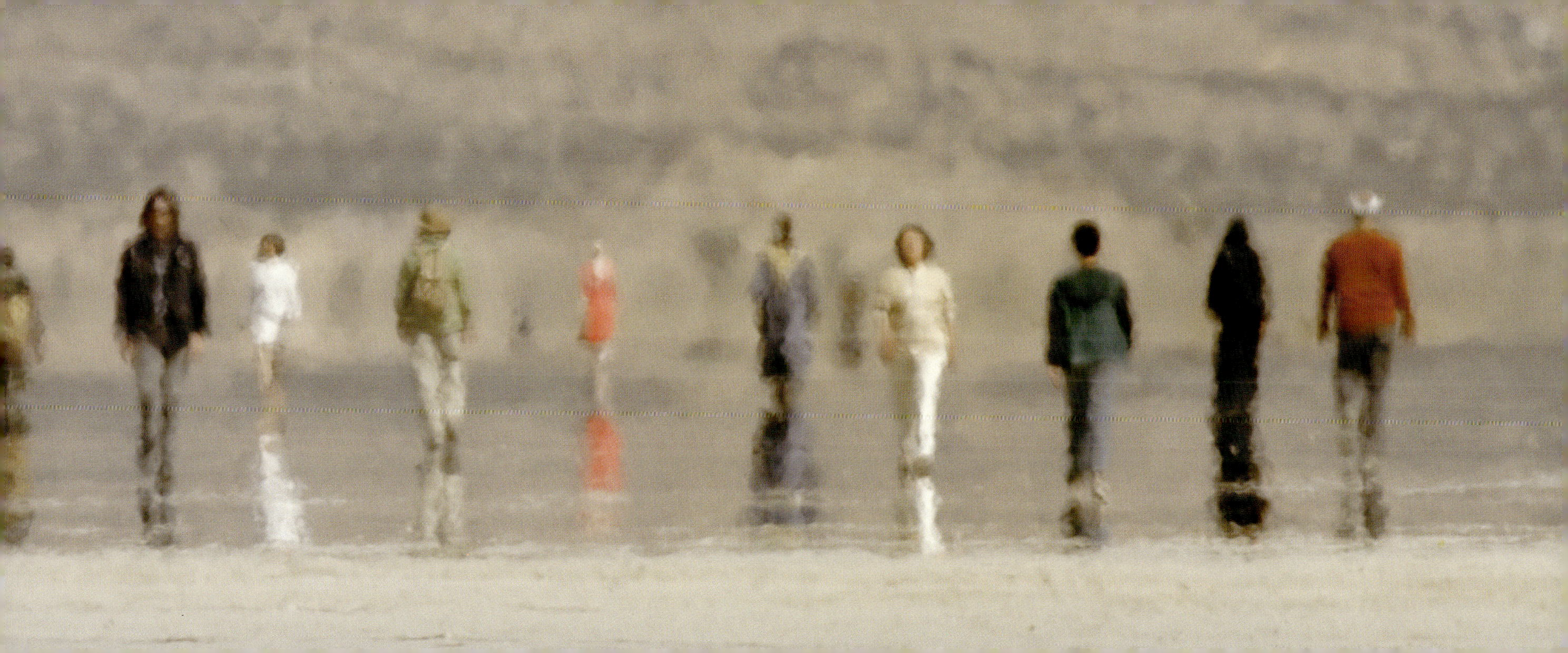

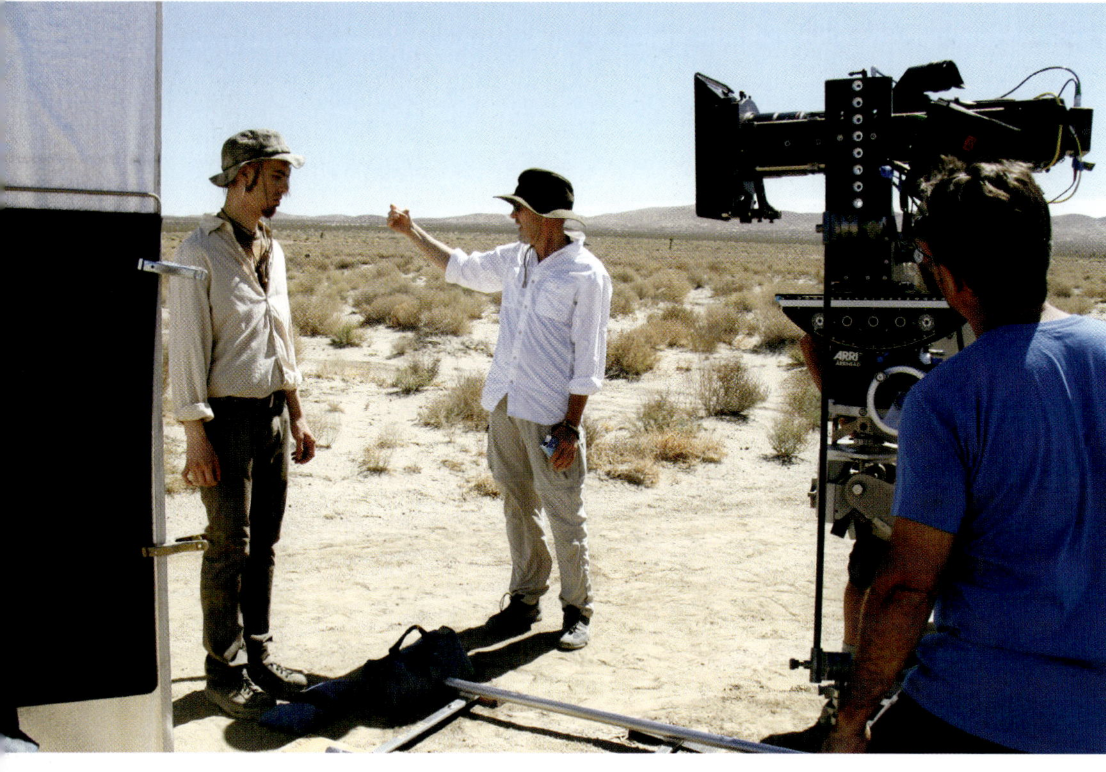

illuminates the path and the man finally emerges from the darkness into the light. He walks away and out into the desert floor once more, eventually disappearing into the far distance."[20]

Inner Passage is a homage to the British land artist Richard Long, whose art-making incorporates elements from the landscape and involves walking in rural and remote areas of the world. This tribute to man in nature is another step in Viola's quest to understand humankind. It also recalls Henry David Thoreau's essay on walking, in which he writes, "We should go forth on the shortest walk, perchance, in the spirit of undying adventure, never to return,—prepared to send back our embalmed hearts only as relics of our desolate kingdoms. If you are ready to leave father and mother, and brother and sister, and wife and child and friends, and never see them again,—if you have paid your debts, and made your will, and settled all your affairs, and are a free man, then you are ready for a walk."[21] Here, the act of walking into the world becomes a statement of no attachments and a purifying gesture toward freedom. However, Viola's work contains an epistemological representation of the memories that cascade through the free walker's mind, a state of being that is never a release into death or freedom. For we never leave, as Thoreau suggests, everyone and everything behind. They remain in our consciousness, and so we are never "ready for a walk" to leave, but always to return.

Viola's description of *The Dreamers* (2013), part of the "Water Portraits" series, belies the work's melancholy homage to death: "*The Dreamers* is a room-sized installation containing seven large plasma

Above Bill Viola directing Blake Viola for *Inner Passage* (2013), El Mirage Dry Lake, Mojave Desert, CA, July 2012

Opposite and following two pages *Inner Passage* (2013)

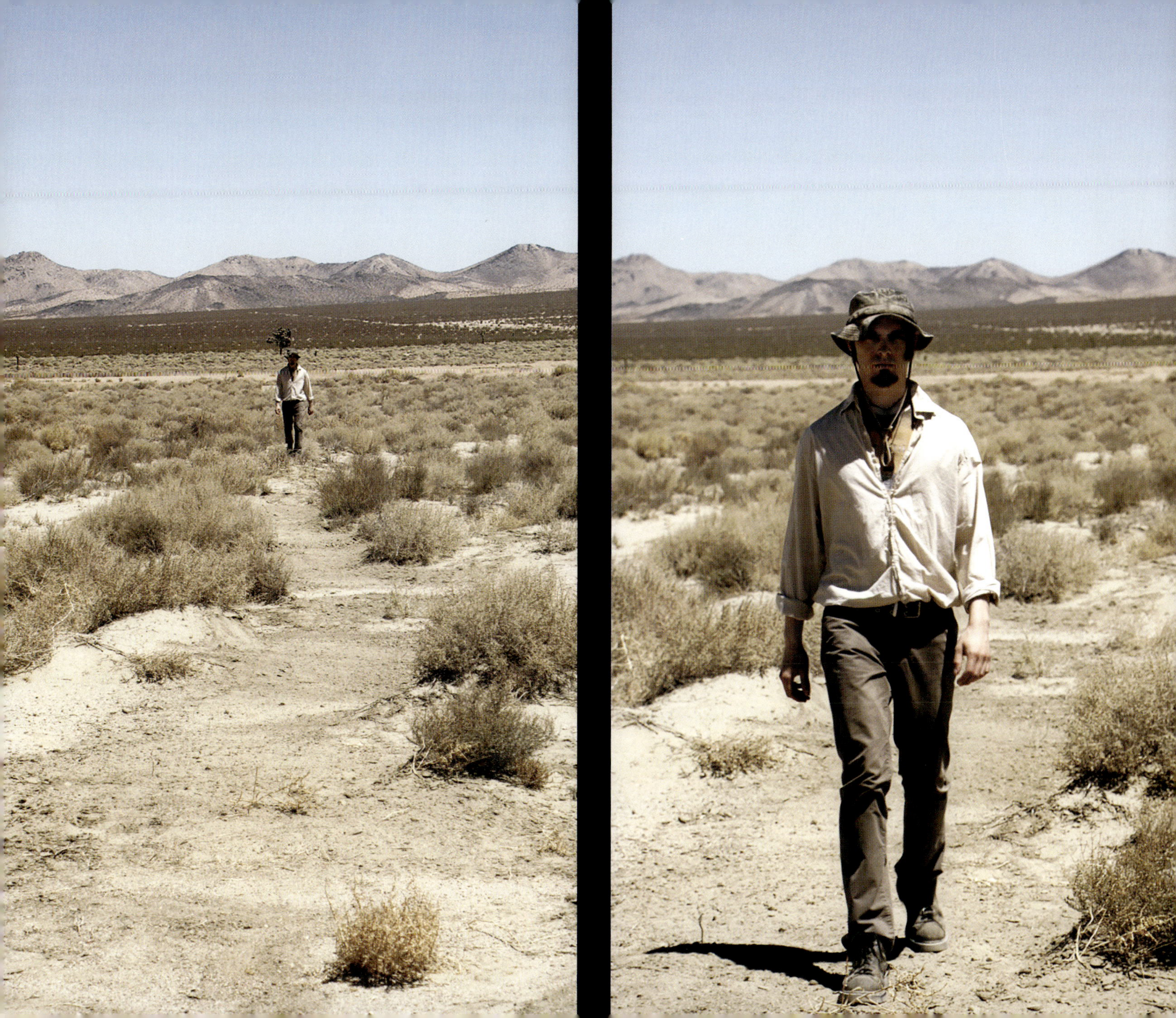

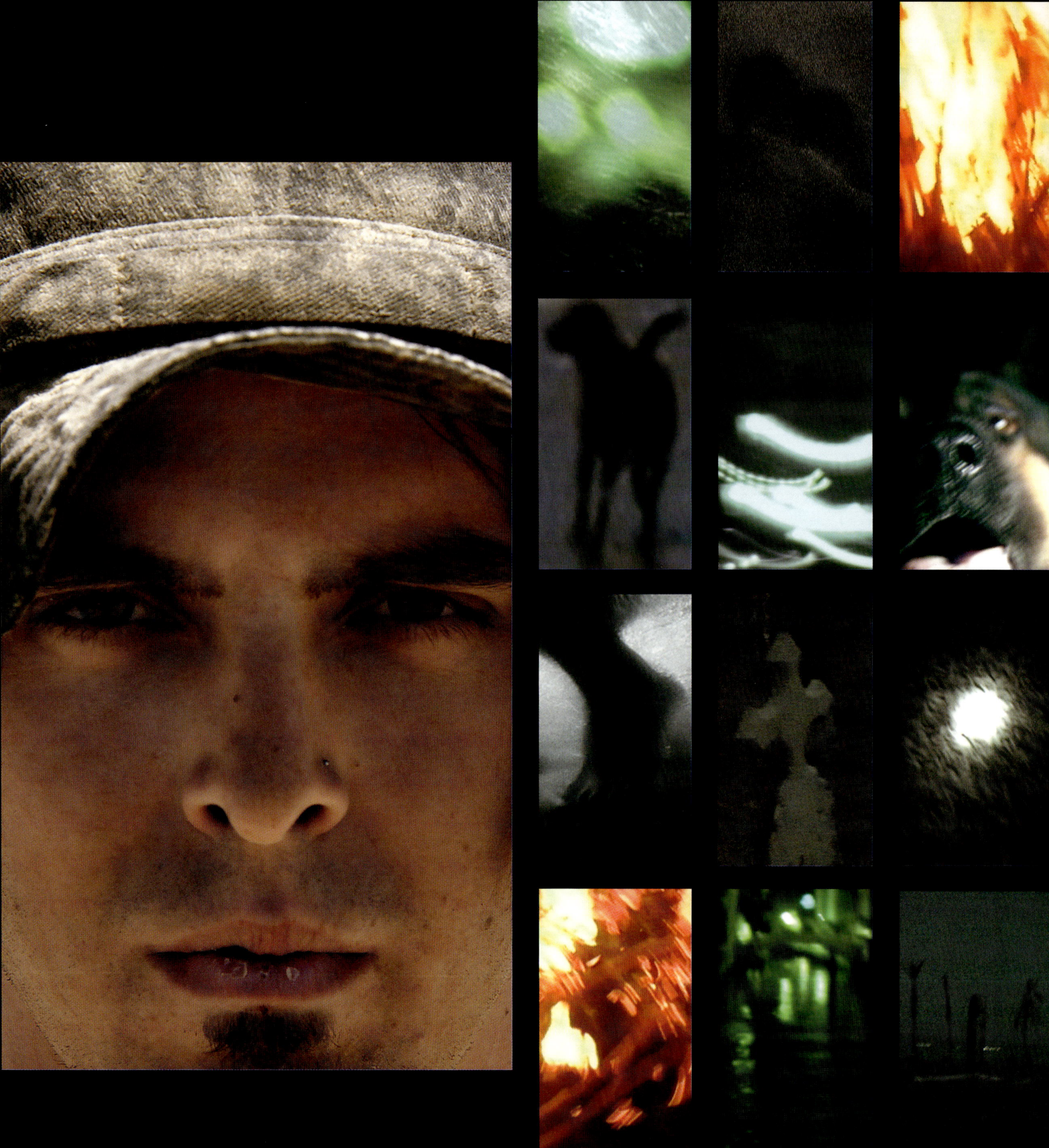

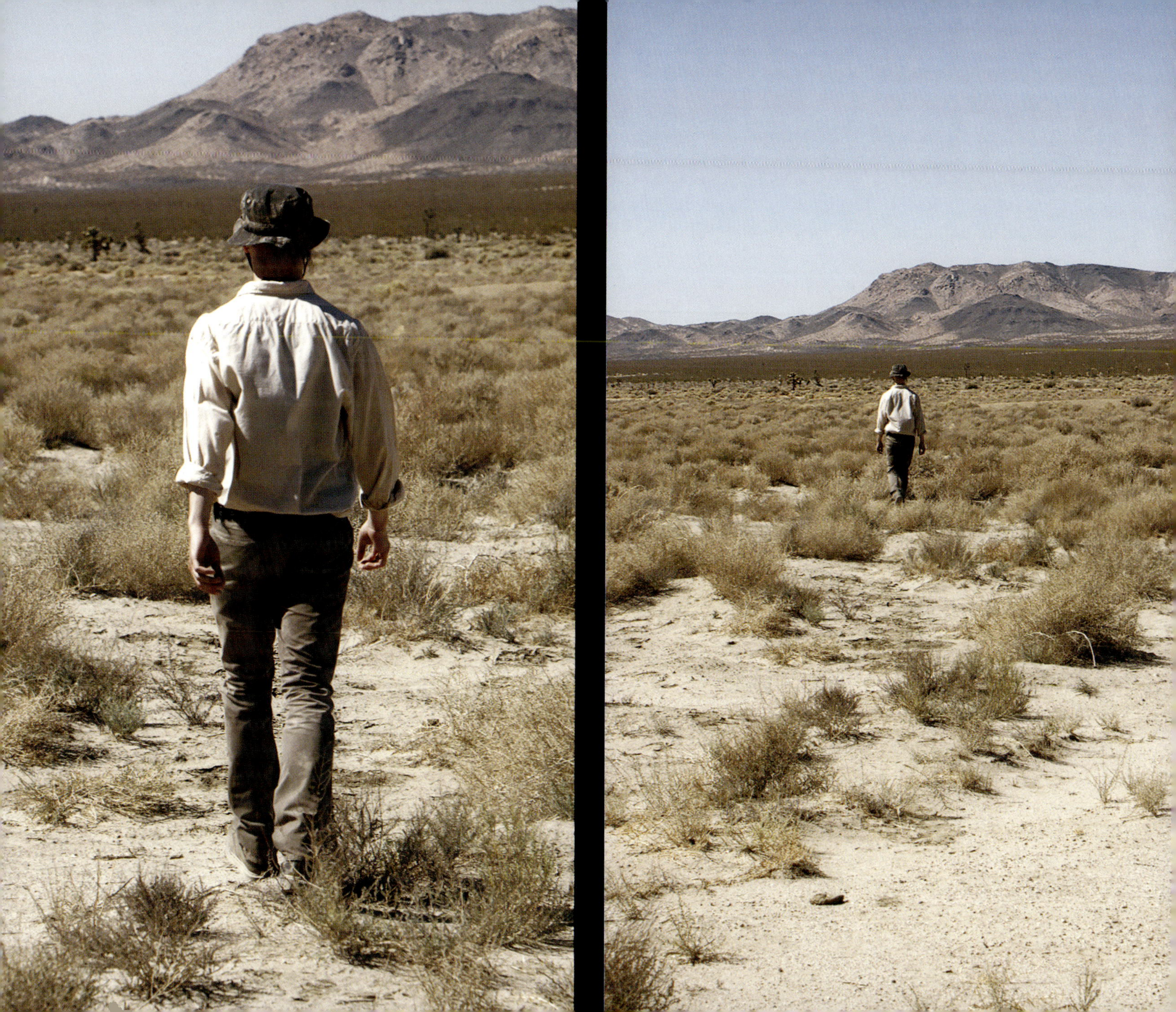

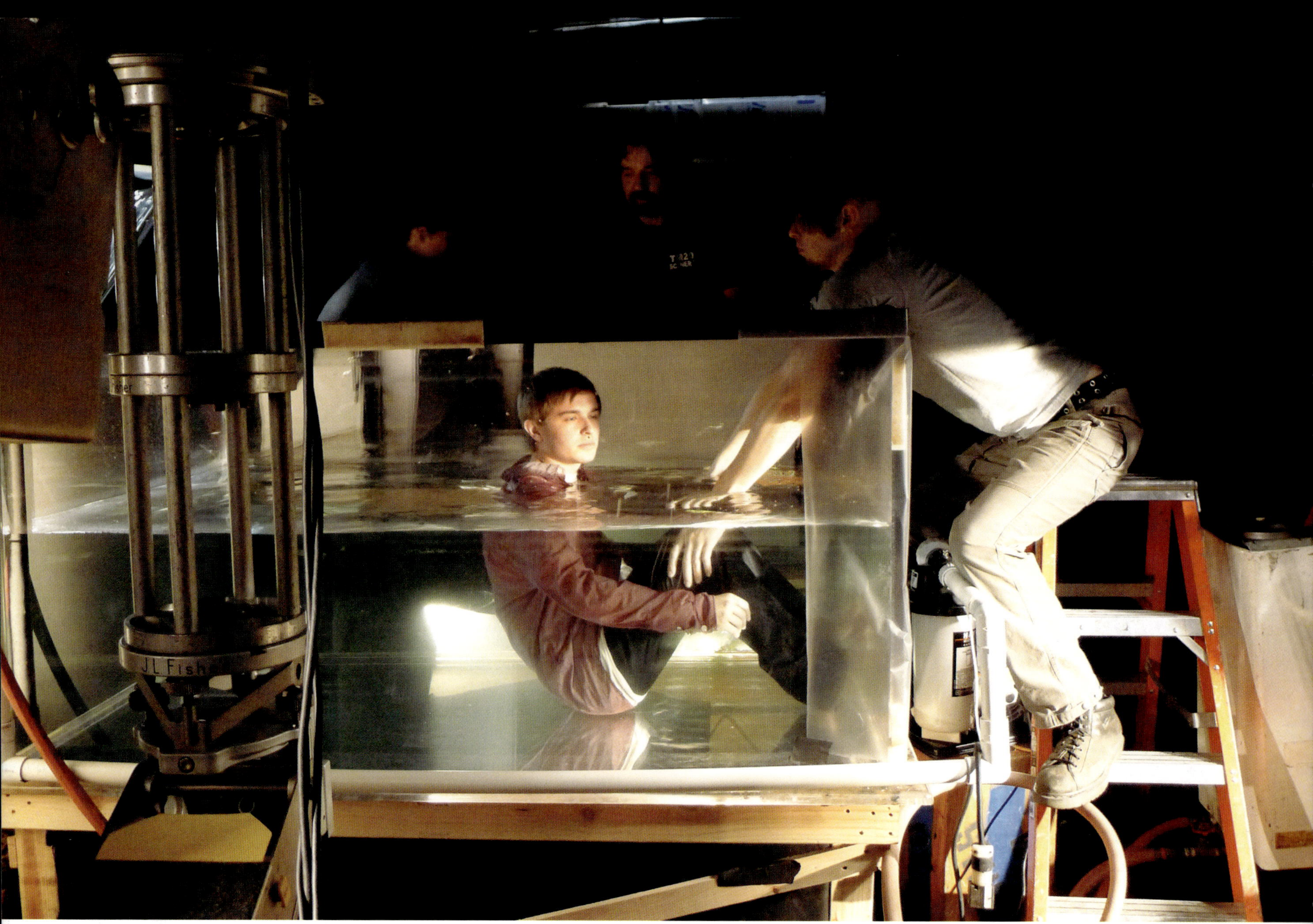

screens that depict seven individuals submerged under water at the bottom of a streambed. Their eyes are closed and they appear to be at peace. Water ripples across their bodies, subtly animating their movements. The sound of water permeates the space as dreams filter through the room."[22] The moving images recall photographs of the dead, the kind that were used in the nineteenth century as memorials to loved ones who had passed away. The look of *The Dreamers*, and how we receive the work, has much to do with the selection of performers and the choice of costume, as well as the direction and timing, all of which was determined by Perov, a reflection of the close collaboration between her and Viola in these and other artworks.

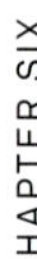

Throughout Viola's work, water plays a key role in his representations of the body's movement in space, as well as serving as a metaphor for birth and renewal. To quote Ralph Waldo Emerson: "The circulation of the water

Above On the set of *The Dreamers* (2013), performer Christian Vincent, Bill Viola Studio, Signal Hill, CA, November 29, 2012

Opposite and the following four pages *The Dreamers* (2013)

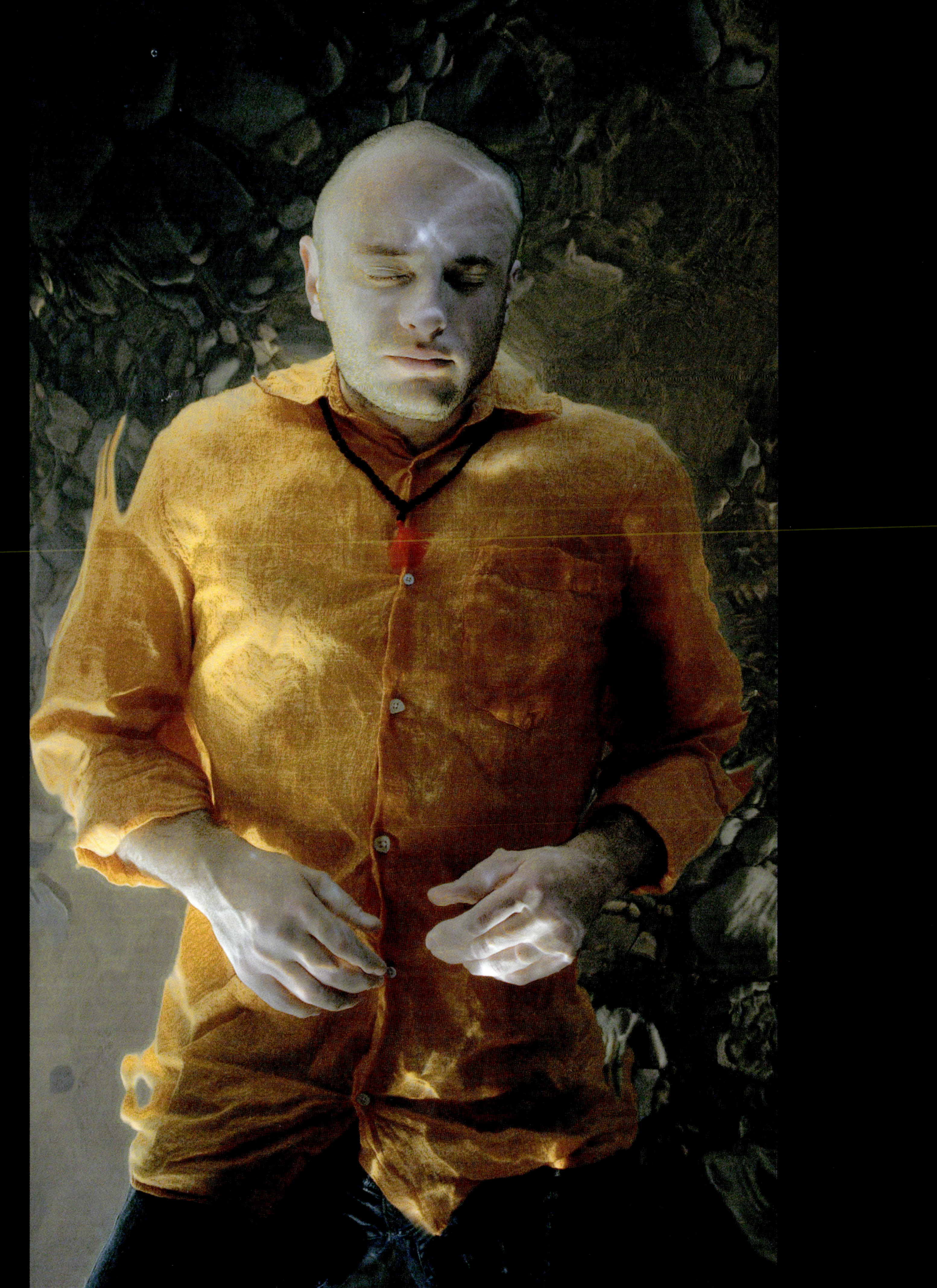

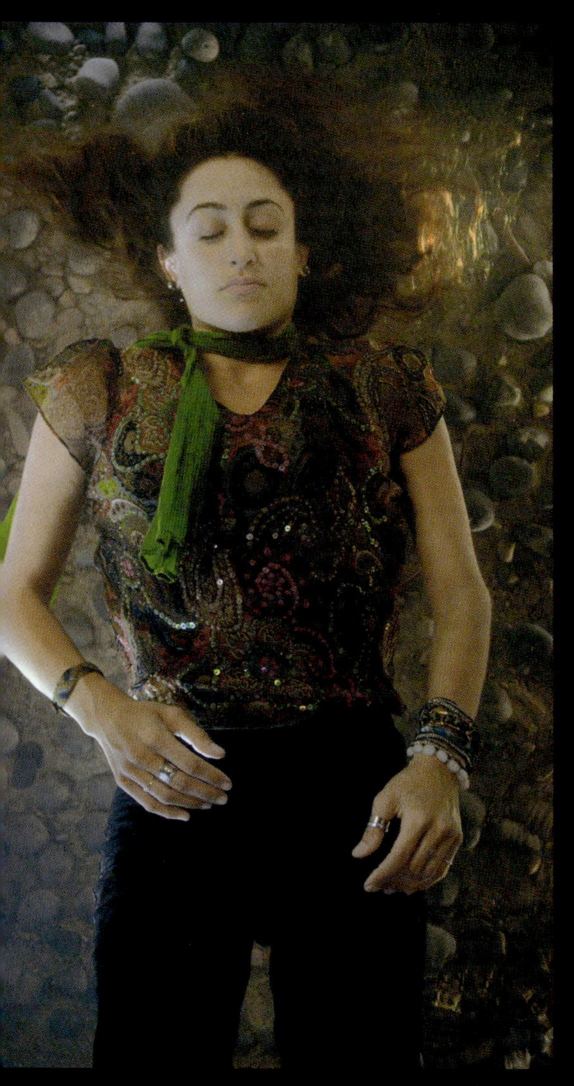
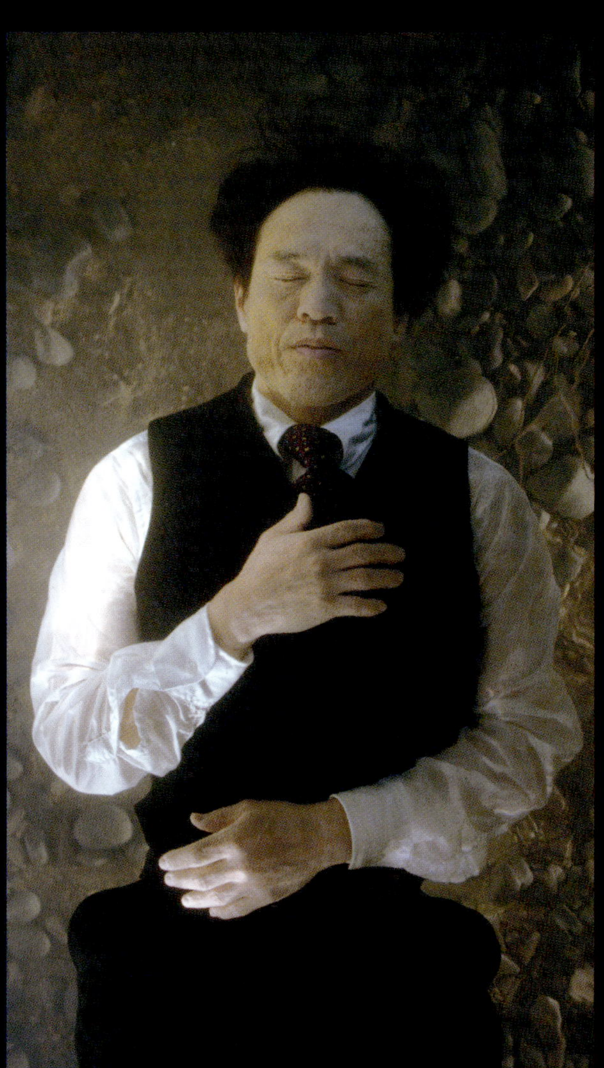
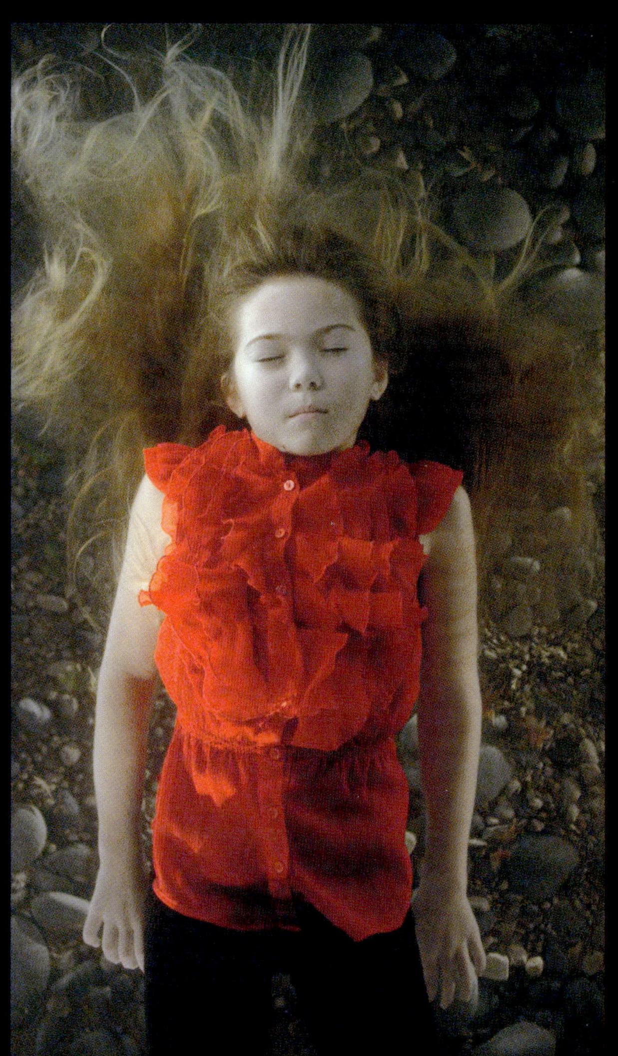

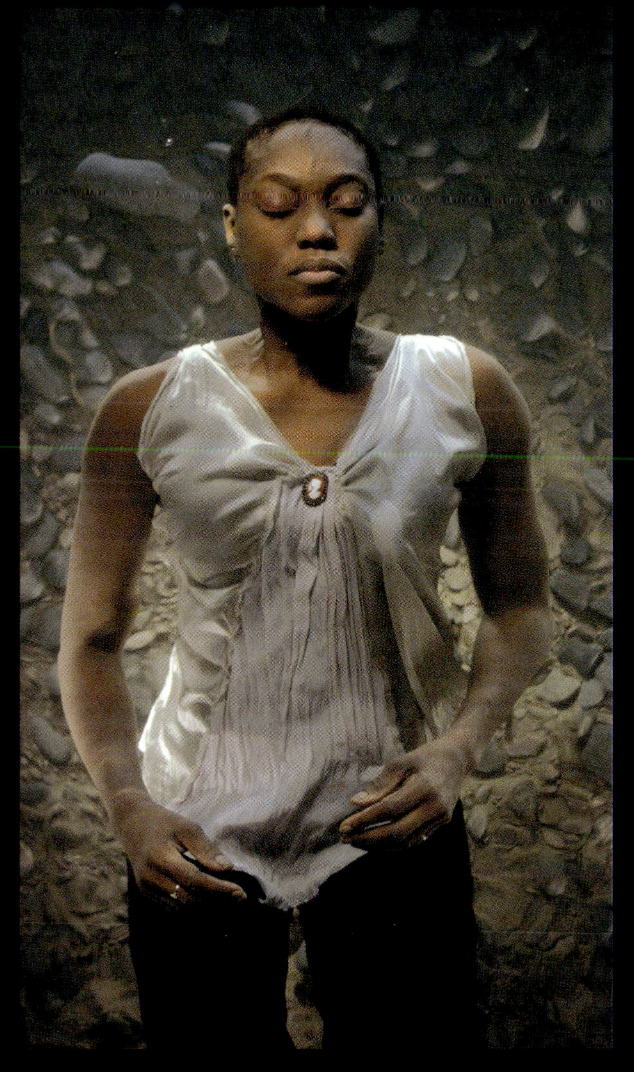
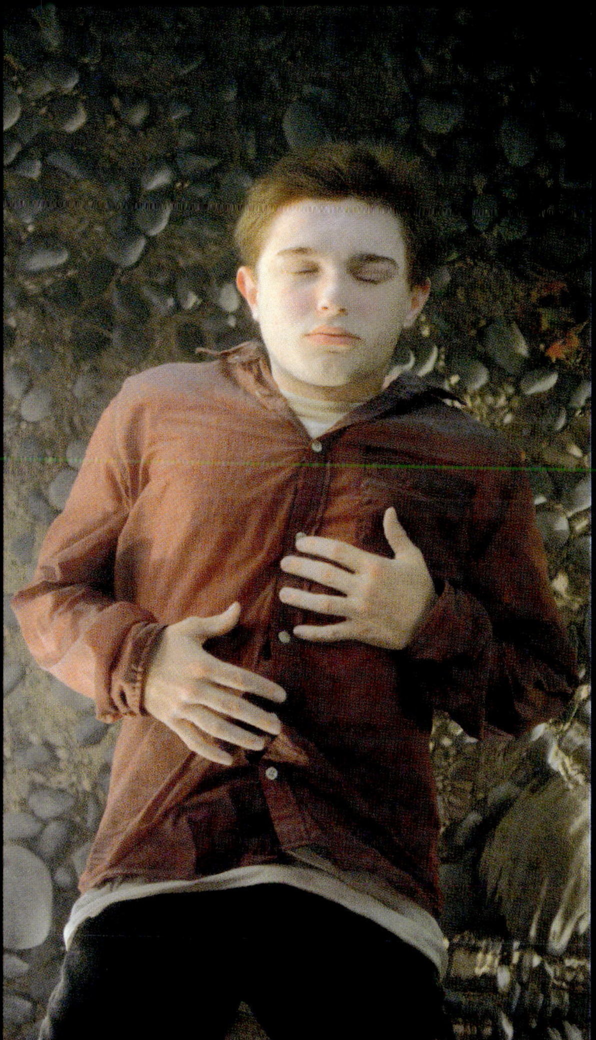
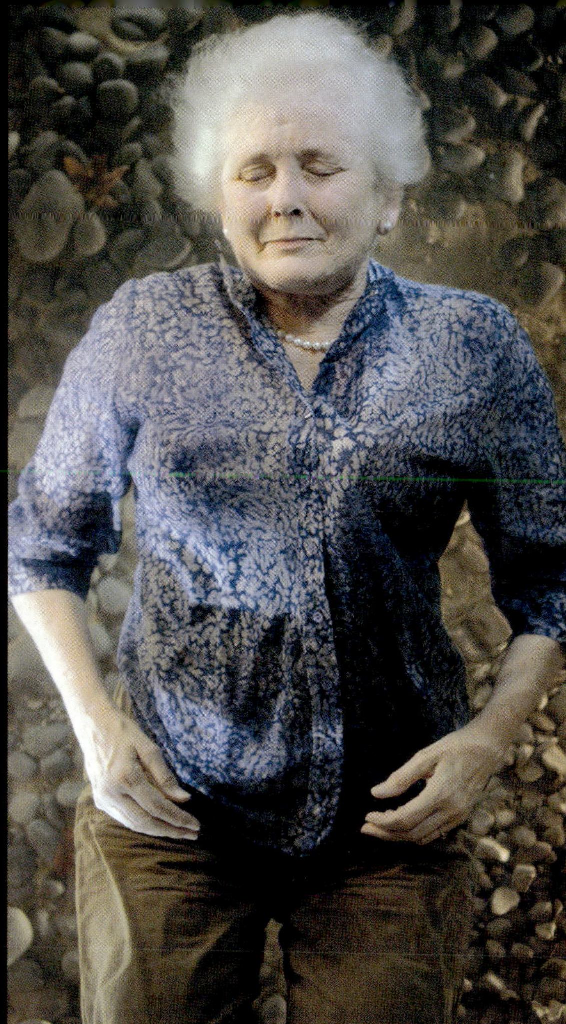

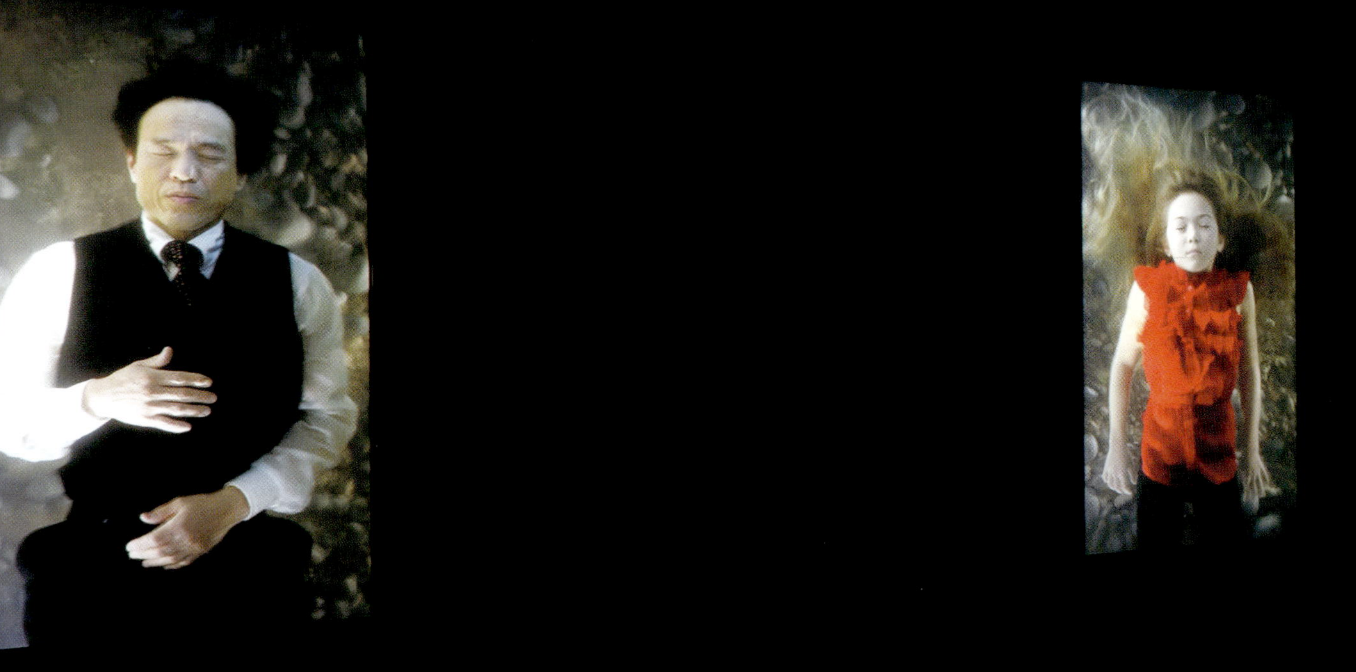

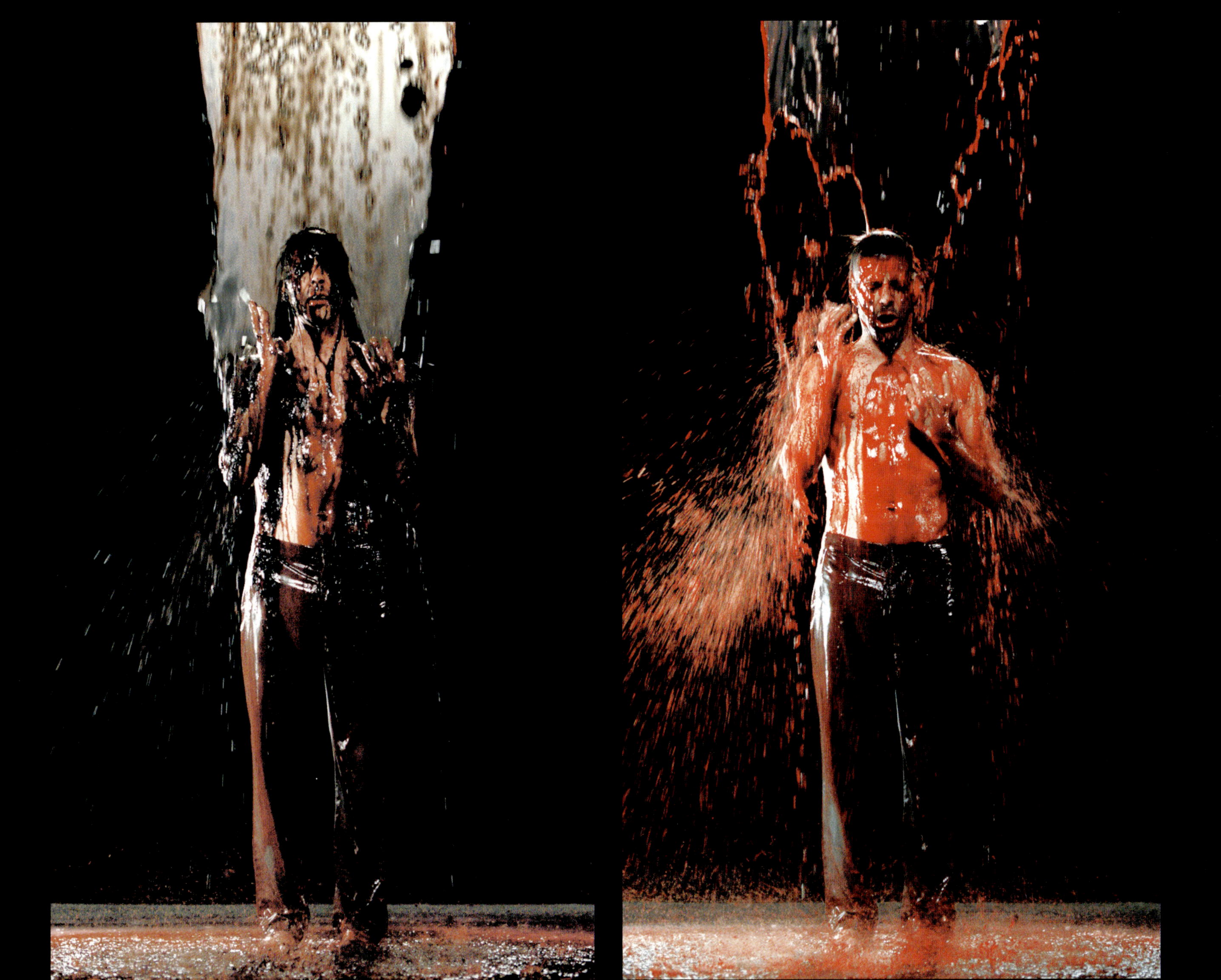

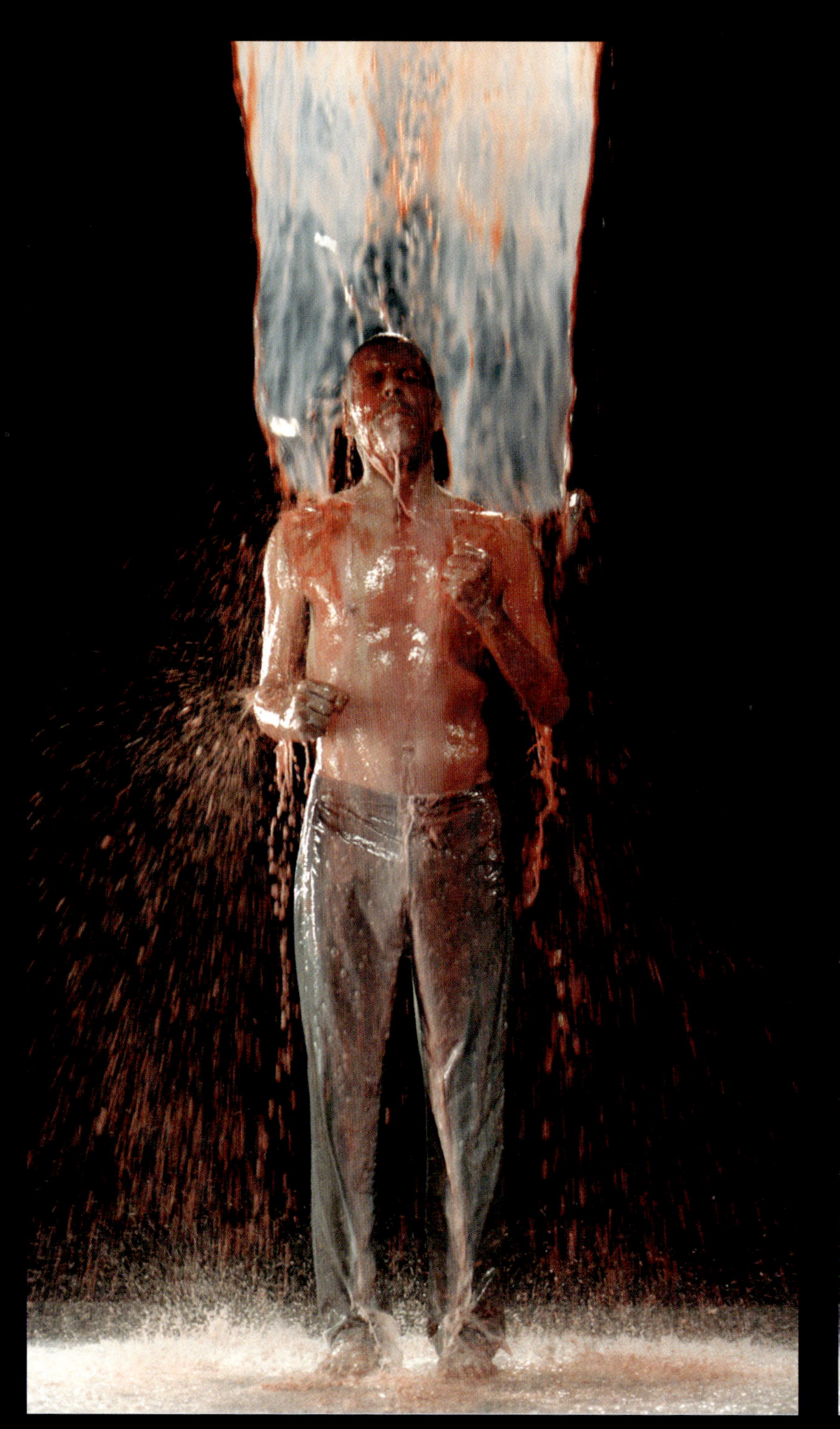

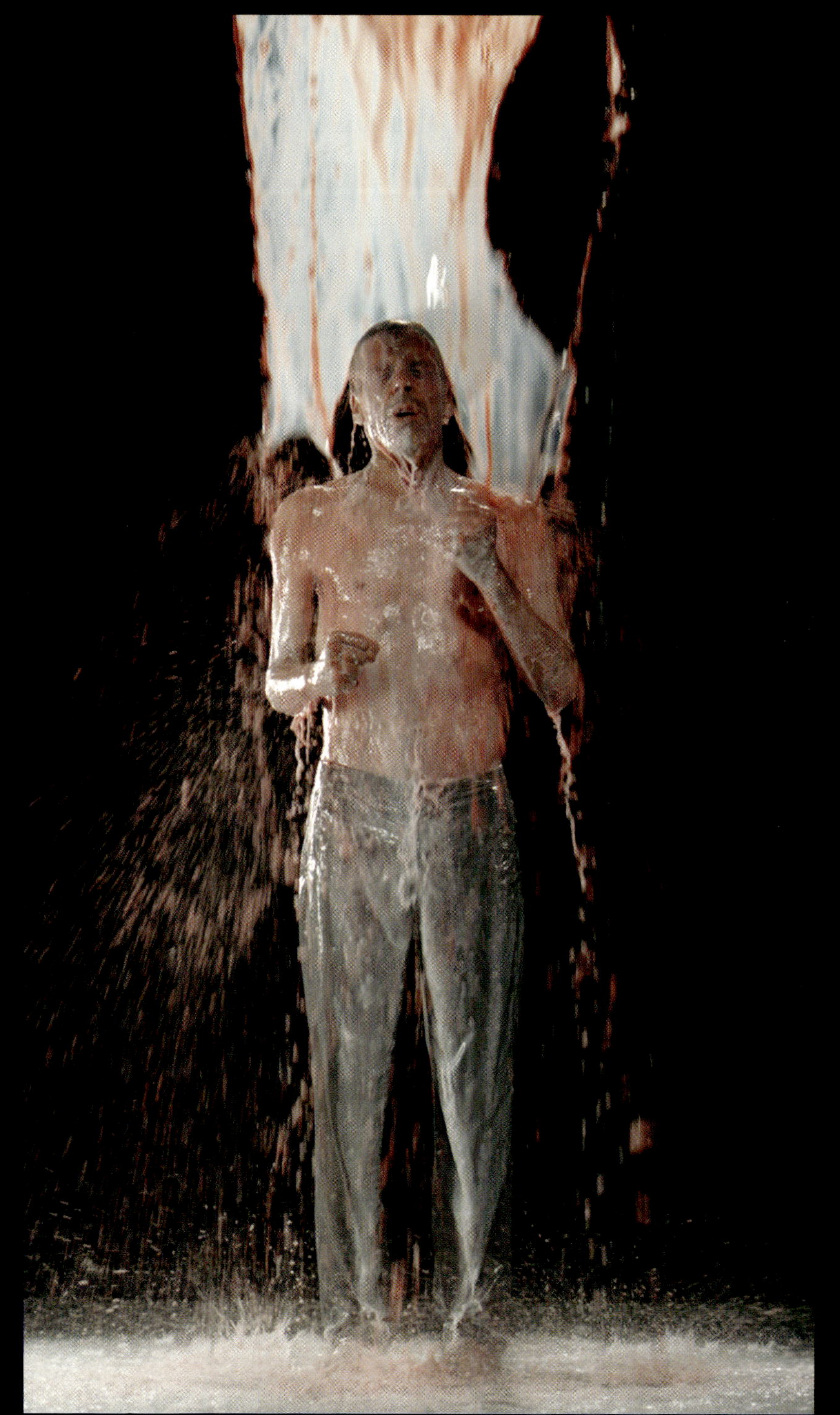

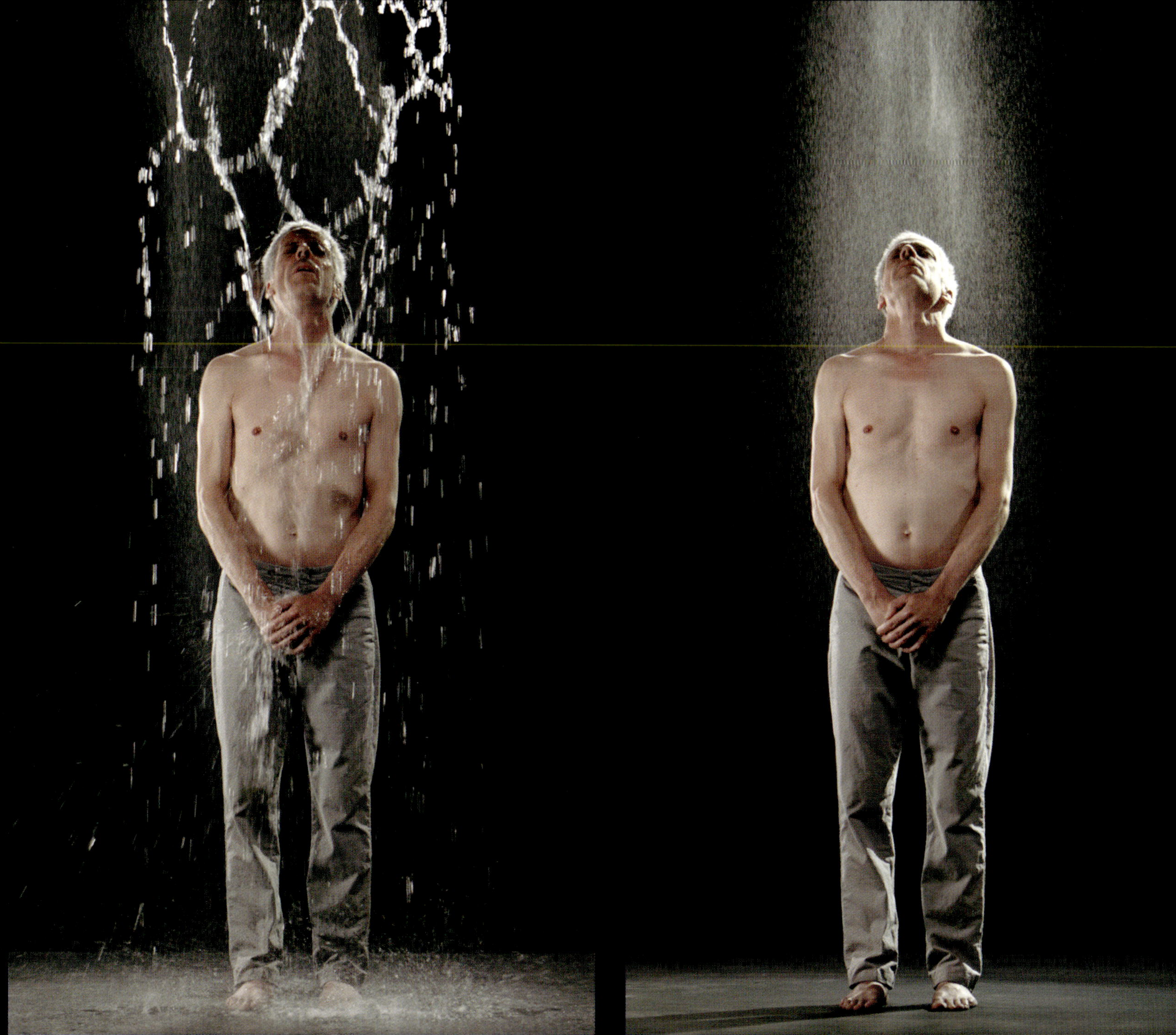

CODA

THE MARTYRS

I began this essay by identifying the art of Bill Viola as embodying a process of self-reflection, a quest for a renewal of the human spirit through art. That journey began with his early reflections on the medium as a means to look deeper into the movements of the body, and it became, over the years, a means to convey a poetics of human expression. In 2014, his work reached a sublime point with the completion of *Martyrs (Earth, Air, Fire, Water)*, commissioned for St. Paul's Cathedral in London. Opened in May 2014, the installation was created in close collaboration with Perov, whose creative input has steadily expanded over her years of working with Viola. The project with St. Paul's, which will see *Martyrs* being joined by a companion work, *Mary*, in 2016, has been more than ten years in discussion and planning. *Martyrs* serves as the pinnacle to a body of work that stands as one of the great achievements in contemporary art, and it offers a look forward to Viola and Perov's future work.

Martyrs is distinguished by its context, St. Paul's Cathedral, and by the times in which we live. The martyr in all religions serves as a profound expression of the believer's resilience in the face of intolerance, repression, and violence. The visual representation of Christian martyrdom is a significant part of the history of Western art. The martyr's story becomes, in the words of the American theologian Elizabeth A. Castelli, a "usable past" and a "living tradition" for Christian communities.[1] The iconic scenes of tortured saints embody the dignity of the human spirit as it overcomes and transcends physical humiliation and torture. Across the centuries and around the world, people have faced persecution for both their religious and their political beliefs. During Evensong when the work was first presented to the public, the chancellor of St. Paul's, Mark Oakley, asked, "Is there anything we, witnessing *Martyrs* and looking at our own lives, would die for: faith, justice, conscience, people we love?" "It is my hope," noted Viola, "that the imagery and themes of these works, as inscribed in the contemporary language of video, will not only give people an interesting visual experience during their visit to the cathedral, but afford them greater access to subject matter of utmost relevance and urgency in today's world."[2]

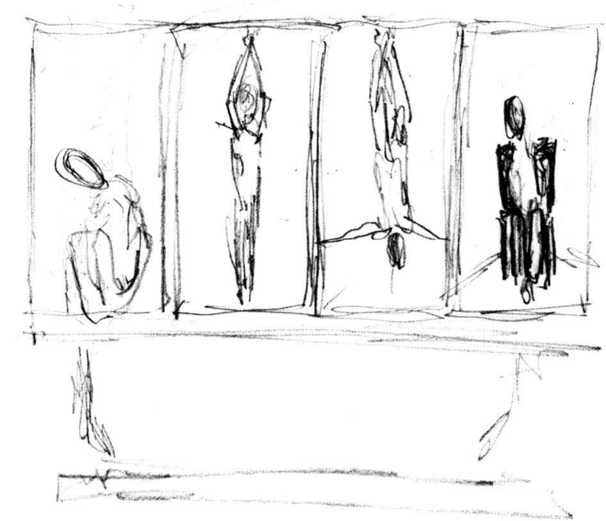

St. PAUL'S – S. Quire Aisle MARTYRS

Above Drawing for *Martyrs (Earth, Air, Fire, Water)* (2014), for proposal to St. Paul's Cathedral, 2010

Opposite *Martyrs (Earth, Air, Fire, Water)*, installation view, St. Paul's Cathedral, 2014

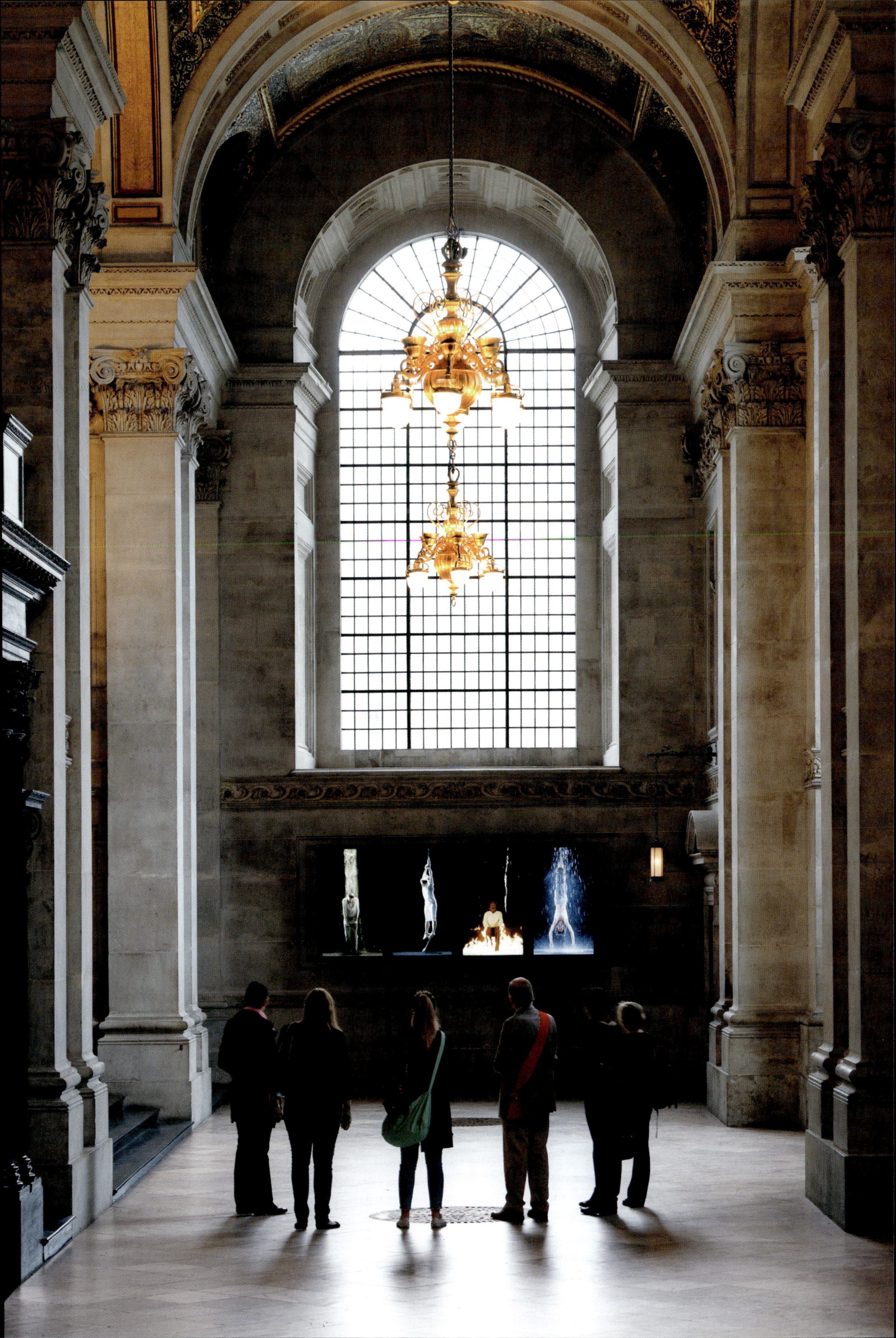

The four panels that comprise *Martyrs* are installed in the South Quire of the cathedral, in order, according to Viola, to "invoke in people the feeling that the further they proceed down the aisle the deeper they are engaging in the space that requires a different, more reflective mode of behavior."[3] It is important not to see the imagery, to quote Castelli, as an "overprivileging of the self-sacrificial dimensions of the 'martyr,'" which would result "in a flattening out, the dangerous eclipsing of the possibility of recognizing the suffering of others."[4] Perov's use of the four elements of earth, air, fire, and water as protagonists helped to resolve the symbolism that was needed to depict "the darkest hour of the martyr's passage through death into the light."[5] The use of these elements also serves to create a universal statement of suffering and transcendence that is relevant to all cultures and beliefs. In each of the work's four panels, a solitary figure is under attack: the first is covered in earth, the second buffeted by wind, the third assaulted by fire, and the fourth engulfed in water. They endure their suffering silently, achieving redemption as they are released—untouched by the attack—through the strength of their beliefs.

Sited as they are in Sir Christopher Wren's sacred space, Viola and Perov's moving images do not attempt to remake the iconography of graphic violence from the Middle Ages; rather, they remind us of the redemptive power of an aesthetics of belief. Viola recovers the role of sacrifice in the human imagination by making it a path toward human transformation. The compelling attraction of *Martyrs* lies in its composition and in its unfolding over time as moving images. In the distillation of their stories, the moving images represent not a specific event but a retelling that speaks to everyone in its essential embodiment of transcendence. With the sensitive use of lighting that details and models, each panel reveals over time the changing human figure. The dark background lends clarity to the dynamic visualization of the action, while the clothing and objects are designed to highlight the figure and the changes over the cycle of the scene. The digital manipulation of the images controls each detail; in the "Air" panel, for example, we see the woman's hands break out of the rope that binds them, and she is suspended in space, free. Viola's mastery of the medium and his treatment of color and movement of the earth, flame, and water, and the materialization of wind buffeting the individual martyr all add dramatic tension, and the sacrifice we witness in each panel ultimately becomes a release and a renewal of life.

Martyrs is composed so that time becomes a tangible presence in this timeless cathedral. The martyrdom that unfolds on the screens breathes life into each figure as the viewer contemplates and absorbs actions that suggest an openness to revelation. As in Viola's *Three Women* (2008), in which the figures move through a veil of water from darkness into a present of color and then back again, *Martyrs* is not frozen in time but

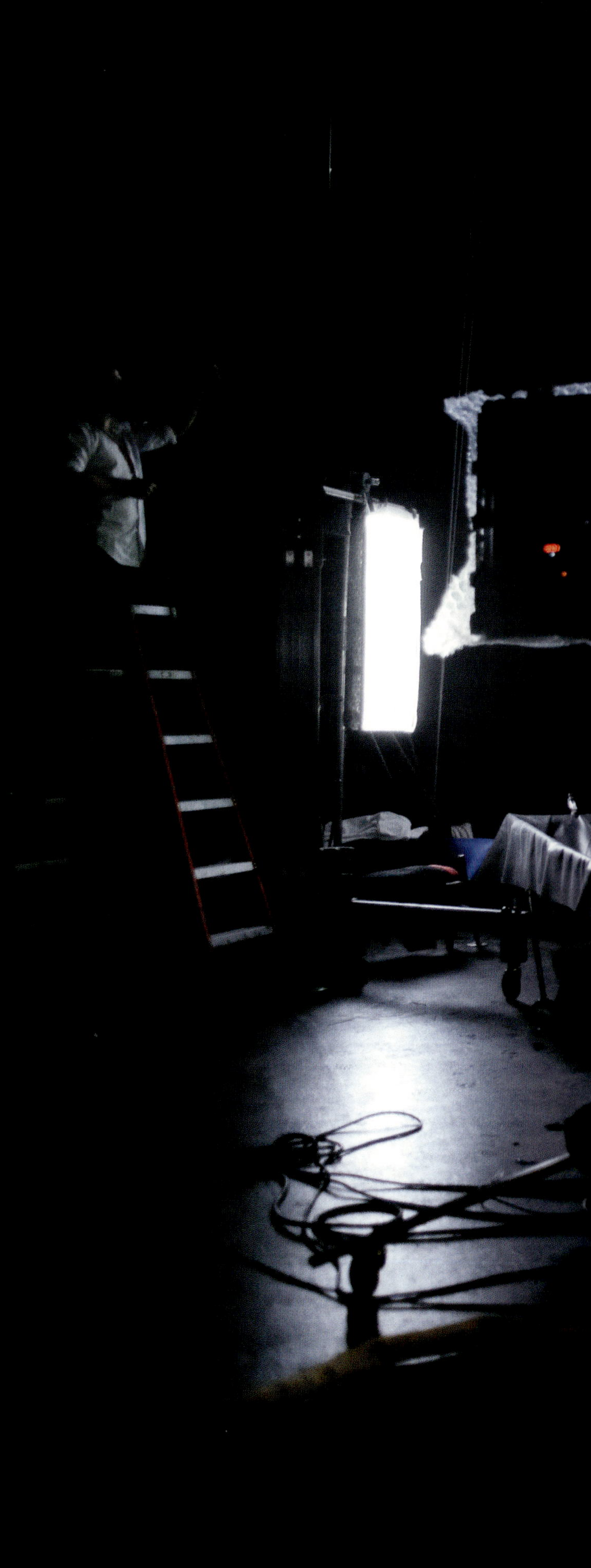

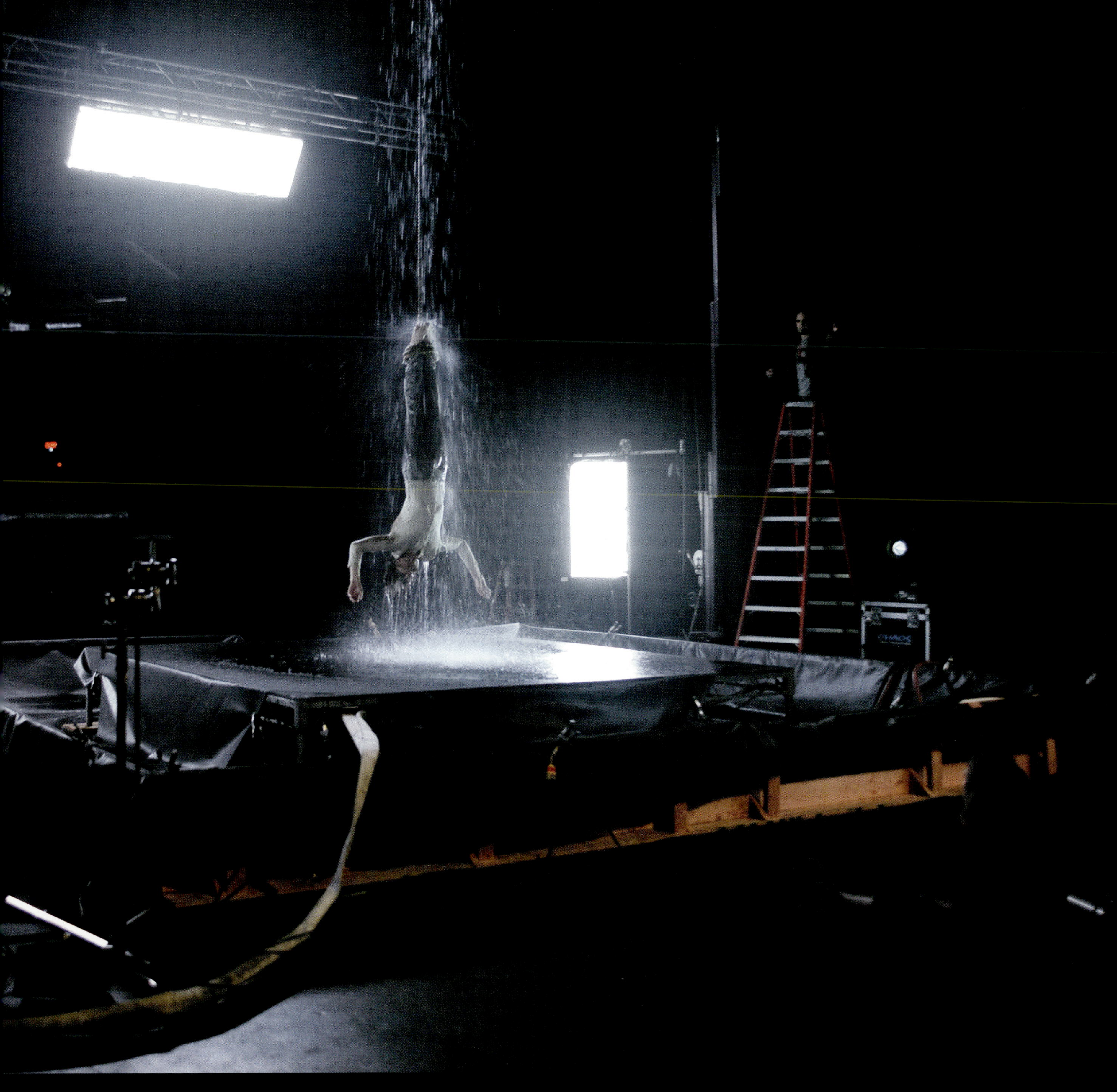

On the set of "Water Martyr," panel 4 from *Martyrs (Earth, Air, Fire, Water)* (2014), performer John Hay, Red Studios, Los Angeles, CA, October 11, 2013

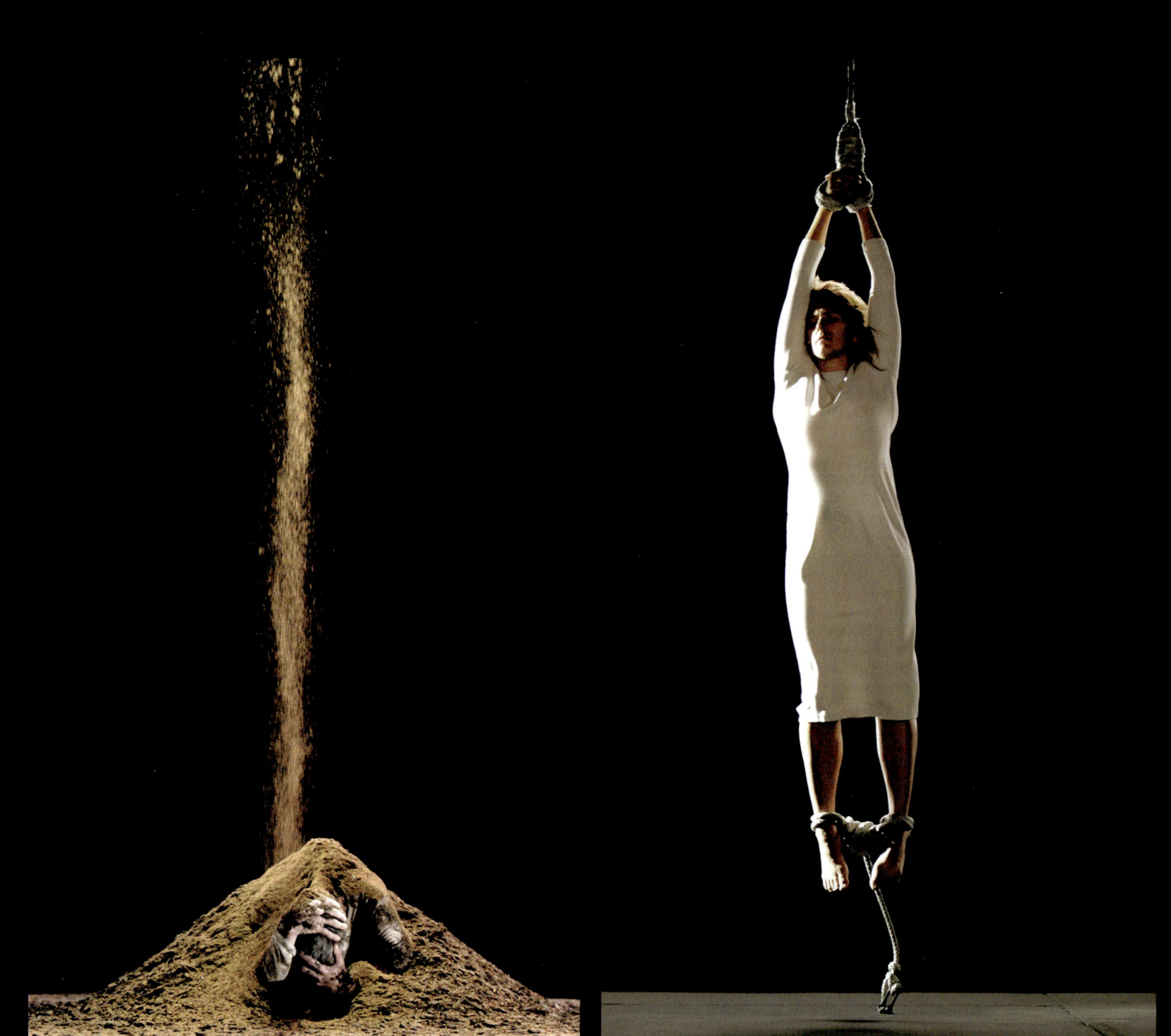

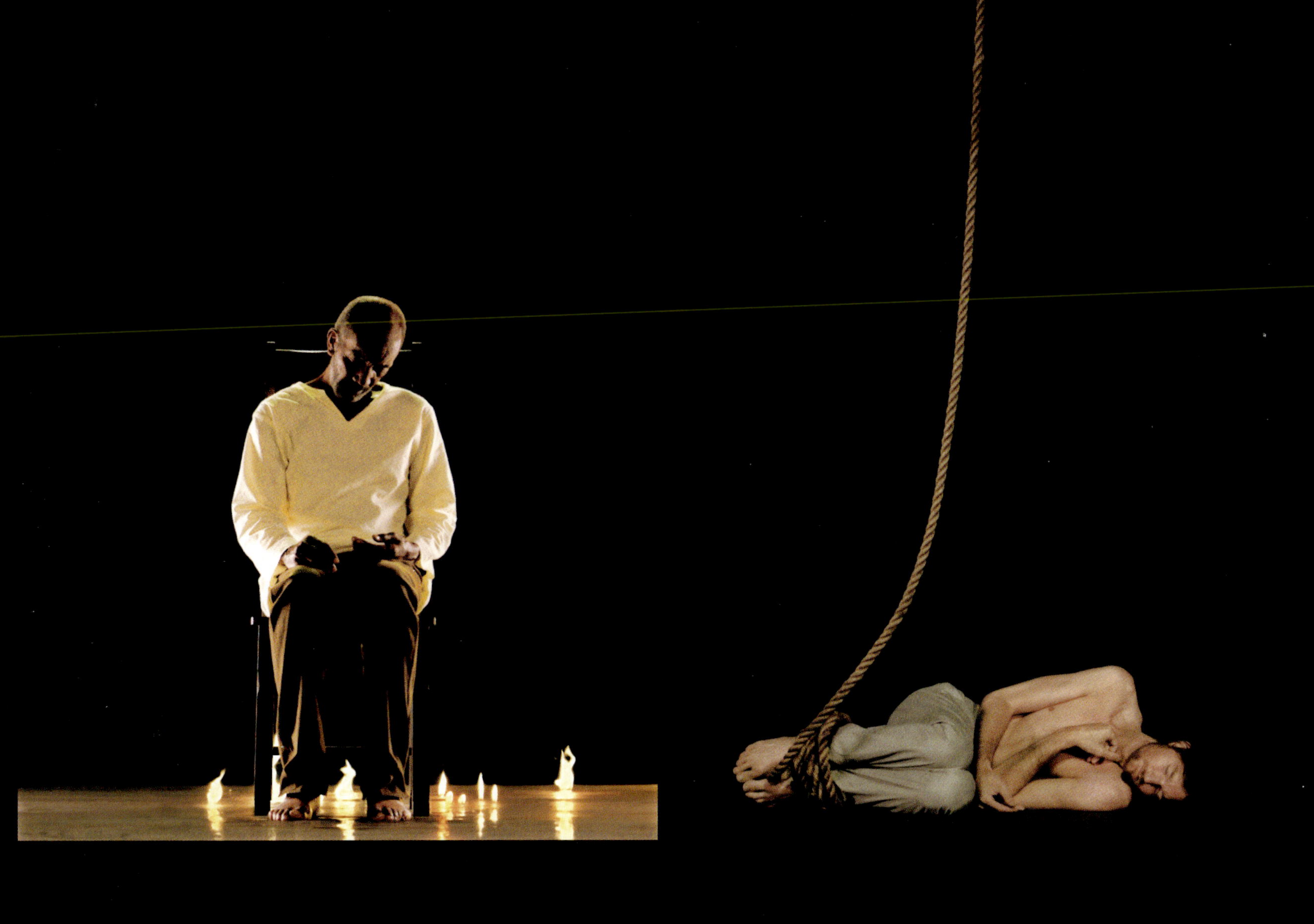

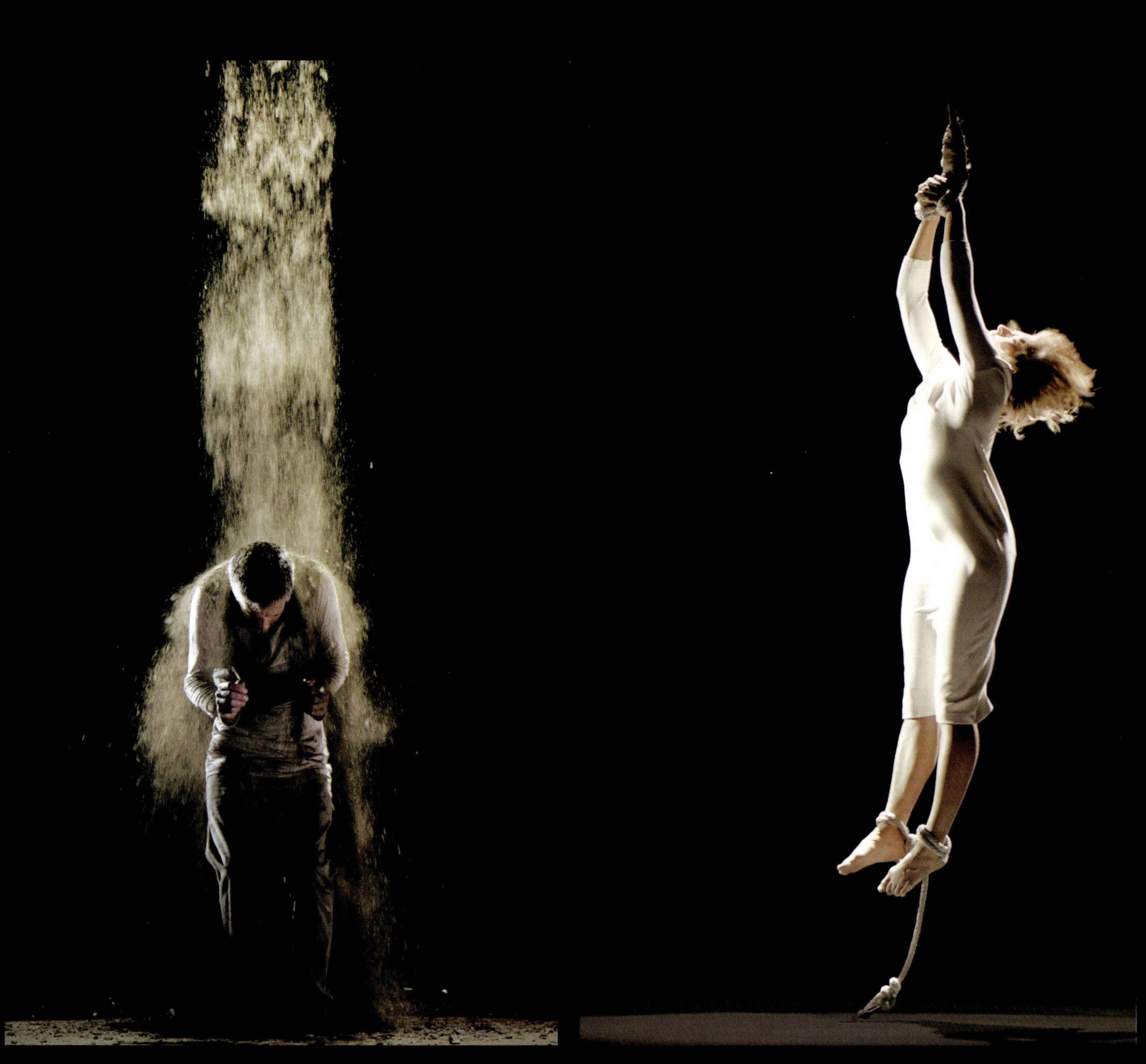

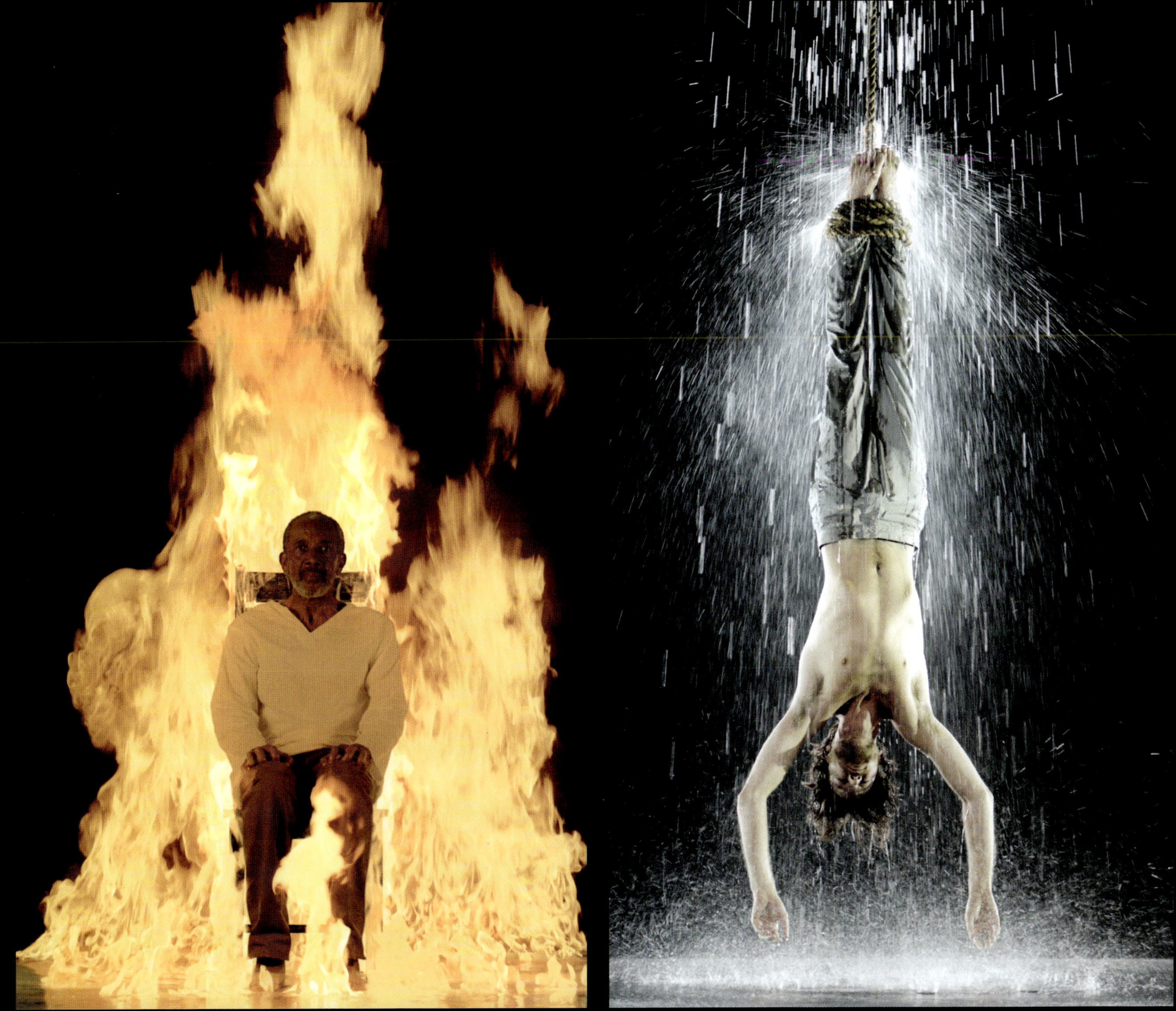

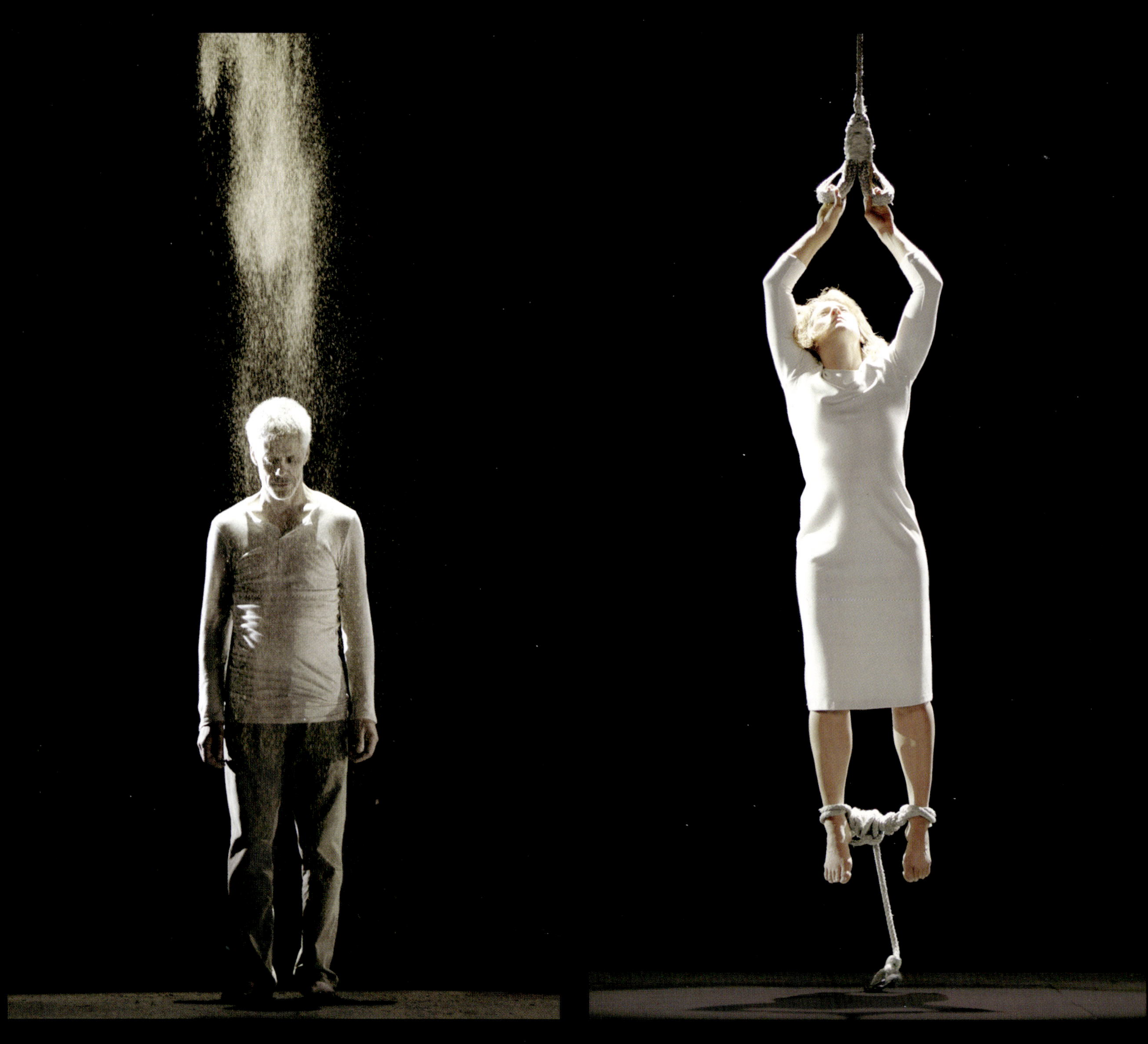

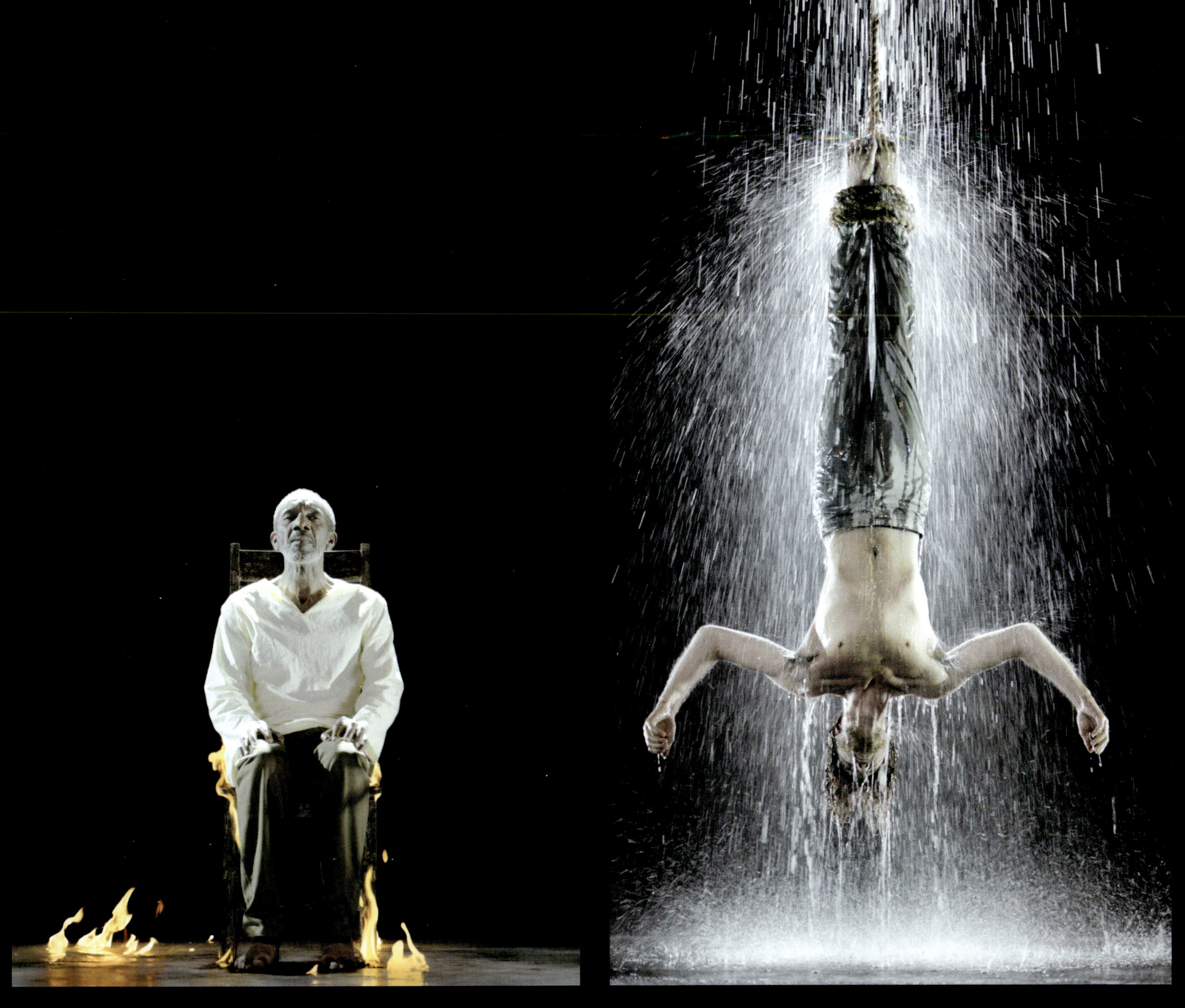

plays out in a constant *present*. Its power is revealed in the dignity of the individual and a community made up of many beliefs. As noted in St. Paul's second letter to the Corinthians, which was quoted in the inauguration of *Martyrs*:

But we have this treasure in clay vessels, that the exceeding greatness of the power may be of God, and not from ourselves. We are pressed on every side, yet not crushed; perplexed, yet not to despair; pursued, yet not forsaken; struck down, yet not destroyed; always carrying in the body the putting to death of the Lord Jesus, that the life of Jesus may also be revealed in our body... For our light affliction, which is for the moment, works for us more and more exceedingly an eternal weight of glory; while we don't look at the things which are seen, but at the things which are not seen. For the things which are seen are temporal, but the things which are not seen are eternal.[6]

The figures in the *Martyrs* say, "We are pressed... but not crushed." They endure the actions taken on their bodies "which are seen as temporal," and illuminated on the screen, which speaks to Being and to the fact that the "things which are not seen are eternal." The expression of the ineffable, the "things not seen," is realized through Viola's poetics of time, which give expression through the body to the power of sacrifice.

Martyrs was celebrated at its opening as a collaboration between "two poets of the visible," Bill Viola and Kira Perov, acknowledging "these two very remarkable human beings" and their ongoing project of creative inquiry and expression begun by Viola more than forty years earlier.[7] It is a shared artistic vision that acknowledges beauty and the spiritual in its quest to give hope in a time of growing challenges to planetary coexistence and life.

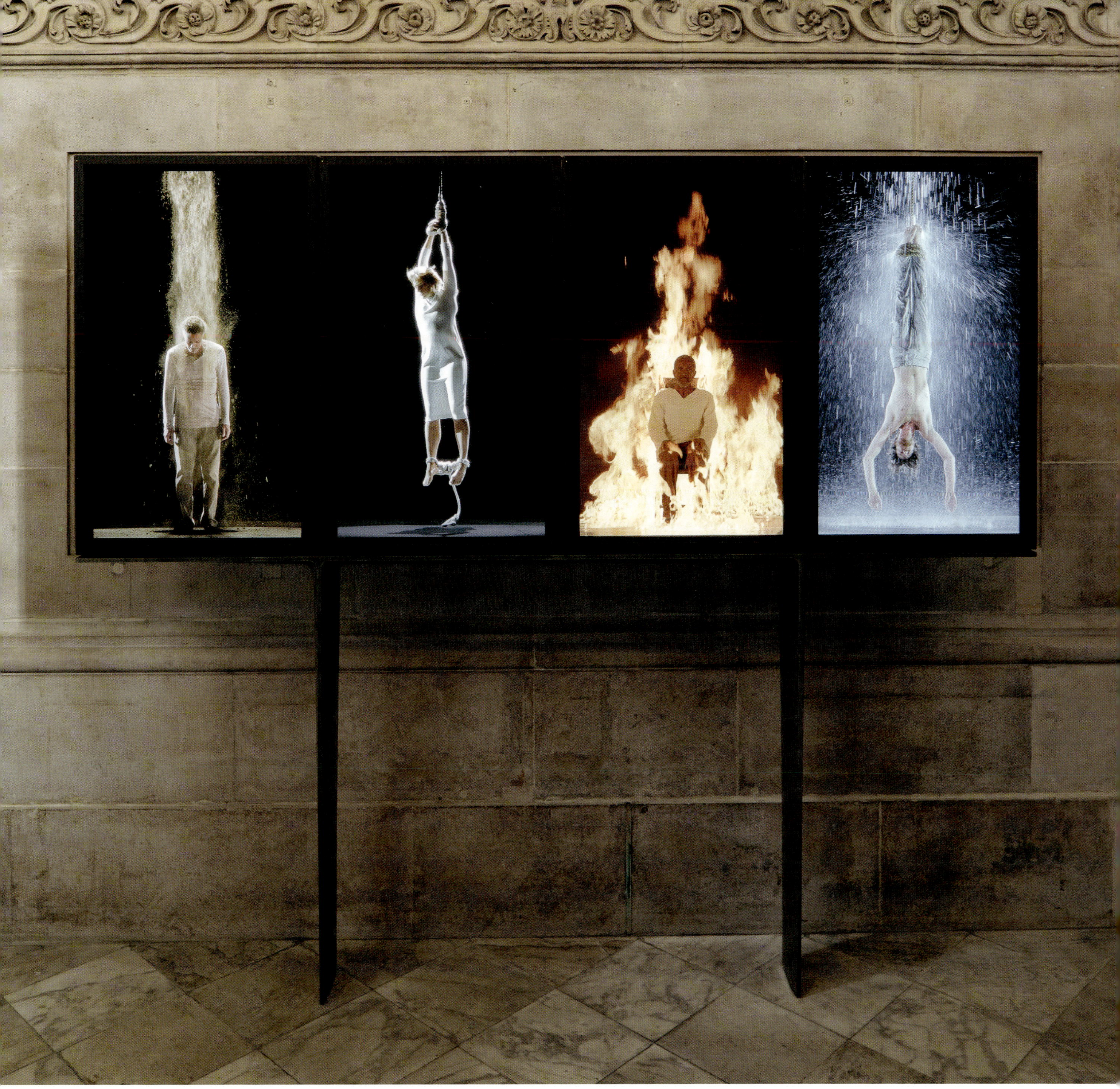

Martyrs (Earth, Air, Fire, Water) (2014)

Notes

Introduction

1. Rumi, quoted in Bill Viola, Notebook entry, March 2, 1977 (Notebook, March 2, 1977 – January 29, 1978), reproduced (incorrectly dated) in Robert Violette with Bill Viola (eds), *Bill Viola, Reasons for Knocking at an Empty House: Writings 1973–1994*, London: Thames & Hudson in association with Anthony d'Offay Gallery, 1995, p. 27; capitalization in original.
2. Bill Viola, "Presence and Absence: Vision and the Invisible in the Media Age," Tanner Lecture on Human Values, The University of Utah, March 7, 2007, transcript, p. 21.
3. Bill Viola, interview with the author, Long Beach, CA, August 9, 2013.
4. Bill Viola, in *Bill Viola: Going Forth By Day* (exh. cat.), Berlin and New York: Deutsche Bank and The Solomon R. Guggenheim Foundation, 2002, p. 100.
5. Pierre Hadot, *Philosophy as a Way of Life: Spiritual Exercises from Socrates to Foucault*, ed. Arnold I. Davidson, trans. Michael Chase, Oxford: Blackwell, 1995, p. 85; emphasis in original.
6. *Ibid.*, p. 83.
7. S. H. Nasr, "Traditional Art as a Fountain of Knowledge and Grace," in *Knowledge and the Sacred*, Albany, NY: State University of New York Press, 1989, p. 262.

Chapter One

1. Fred Camper, quoted in Paul S. Arthur, "3. 1959–1963," in *A History of the American Avant-Garde Cinema* (exh. cat.), New York: American Federation of the Arts, 1976, pp. 99–107.
2. Bill Viola, in Lewis Hyde *et al.*, *Bill Viola* (exh. cat.), New York: Whitney Museum of American Art, 1997, p. 40.
3. Bill Viola, in Robert Violette with Bill Viola (eds), *Bill Viola, Reasons for Knocking at an Empty House: Writings 1973–1994*, London: Thames & Hudson in association with Anthony d'Offay Gallery, 1995, p. 44.
4. *Ibid.*, p. 54.
5. Kira Perov, in Kira Perov (ed.), *Bill Viola: Visioni interiori* (exh. cat.), Florence: Giunti, 2008, p. 11.
6. Bill Viola, interview with the author, Long Beach, CA, August 9, 2013.
7. *Ibid.*
8. *Ibid.*
9. *Ibid.*
10. Bill Viola, unpublished description of *Localization* (1973).
11. Bill Viola, interview with the author, Long Beach, CA, August 9, 2013.
12. *Ibid.*
13. *Ibid.*
14. *Ibid.*
15. *Ibid.*
16. *Ibid.*
17. Bill Viola, in "A Conversation: Hans Belting and Bill Viola," in John Walsh (ed.), *Bill Viola: The Passions* (exh. cat.), Los Angeles: Getty Publications, 2003, p. 219.
18. *Ibid.*
19. Bill Viola, in Hyde *et al.*, *Bill Viola*, p. 60.

Chapter Two

1. Bill Viola, in Robert Violette with Bill Viola (eds), *Bill Viola, Reasons for Knocking at an Empty House: Writings 1973–1994*, London: Thames & Hudson in association with Anthony d'Offay Gallery, 1995, p. 30.
2. *Ibid.*, p. 38.
3. *Ibid.*, p. 42.
4. Rumi, quoted in Bill Viola's statement on *He Weeps for You 1976*, in Violette with Viola, *Reasons for Knocking at an Empty House*, p. 42.
5. Zentrum für Kunst und Medientechnologie, "Bill Viola: The Tree of Knowledge," http://on1.zkm.de/zkm/e/werke/TheTreeofKnowledge (accessed April 2015).
6. Bill Viola, in Violette with Viola, *Reasons for Knocking at an Empty House*, p. 56.
7. Bill Viola, in Anna Bernardini (ed.), *Bill Viola: Reflections* (exh. cat.), Milan: Silvana Editoriale, 2012, p. 90.
8. Bill Viola, in Lori Zippay (ed.), *Electronic Arts Intermix: Video—A Catalogue of the Artists' Videotape Distribution Service of EAI*, New York: Electronic Arts Intermix, 1991, p. 197.
9. Bill Viola, in Lewis Hyde *et al.*, *Bill Viola* (exh. cat.), New York: Whitney Museum of American Art, 1997, p. 50.
10. Bill Viola, in Zippay, *Electronic Arts Intermix: Video*, p. 199.
11. Karl Rahner, *Encounters with Silence*, trans. James M. Demske, South Bend, IN: St. Augustine's Press, 1999, p. 25; emphasis added.
12. Bill Viola, in Zippay, *Electronic Arts Intermix: Video*, p. 199.
13. Saint Augustine, quoted in Bruno Forte, *The Portal of Beauty: Towards a Theology of Aesthetics*, trans. David Glenday and Paul McPartlan, Grand Rapids, MI: W. B. Eerdmans, 2008, p. 4.
14. Jean-Luc Marion, *The Crossing of the Visible*, trans. James K. A. Smith, Stanford, CA: Stanford University Press, 2004, p. 1.

Chapter Three

1. See Mary Jacobus, *Romantic Things: A Tree, a Rock, a Cloud*, Chicago: The University of Chicago Press, 2012.
2. André du Bouchet, quoted in Jean-Louis Chrétien, *The Unforgettable and the Unhoped For*, trans. Jeffrey Bloechl, New York: Fordham University Press, 2002, p. 40.
3. Bill Viola, in Lewis Hyde *et al.*, *Bill Viola* (exh. cat.), New York: Whitney Museum of American Art, 1997, p. 68; emphasis added.
4. Kira Perov, e-mail correspondence with the author, September 3–18, 2014.
5. Bill Viola, in Hyde *et al.*, *Bill Viola*, p. 72.
6. *Ibid.*
7. Kira Perov, e-mail correspondence with the author, September 3–18, 2014.
8. *Ibid.*
9. Bill Viola, in Hyde *et al.*, *Bill Viola*, p. 76.
10. St. John of the Cross, quoted in Robert Violette with Bill Viola (eds), *Bill Viola, Reasons for Knocking at an Empty House: Writings 1973–1994*, London: Thames & Hudson in association with Anthony d'Offay Gallery, 1995, p. 117.
11. St. John of the Cross, quoted in Bernard McGinn, *The Essential Writings of Christian Mysticism*, New York: The Modern Library, 2006, p. 386.
12. *Ibid.*, p. 358.
13. Bill Viola, in Hyde *et al.*, *Bill Viola*, p. 83.
14. *Ibid.*, p. 84.
15. Bill Viola, in Violette with Viola, *Reasons for Knocking at an Empty House*, pp. 142–3.
16. Kira Perov, e-mail correspondence with the author, September 3–18, 2014.
17. Bill Viola, in Hyde *et al.*, *Bill Viola*, p. 86.
18. *Ibid.*
19. Kira Perov, e-mail correspondence with the author, September 3–18, 2014.
20. Bill Viola, in Hyde *et al.*, *Bill Viola*, p. 89.
21. Sigmund Freud, quoted in Leonard Barkan, *Mute Poetry, Speaking Pictures*, Princeton, NJ: Princeton University Press, 2013, p. xiv.

Chapter Four

1. Kathleen Stewart, *Ordinary Affects*, Durham, NC: Duke University Press, 2007, p. 21.
2. *Ibid.*
3. Bill Viola, in Lewis Hyde *et al.*, *Bill Viola* (exh. cat.), New York: Whitney Museum of American Art, 1997, p. 94.
4. *Ibid.*
5. Takuan Sōhō, *The Unfettered Mind: Writings of the Zen Master to the Sword Master*, trans. William Scott Wilson, New York: Kodansha, p. 3; emphasis in original.
6. Bill Viola, in Hyde *et al.*, *Bill Viola*, p. 45.
7. *Ibid.*, p. 94.
8. Cage tells this story on camera in Nam June Paik's single-channel videotape *Global Groove* (1973).
9. Niko Kolodny, "Introduction," in Samuel Scheffler, *Death and the Afterlife*, Oxford: Oxford University Press, 2013, p. 11.
10. *Ibid.*; emphasis in original.
11. Kira Perov, e-mail correspondence with the author, September 3–18, 2014.
12. Bill Viola, in Hyde *et al.*, *Bill Viola*, p. 96.
13. Kira Perov, e-mail correspondence with the author, September 3–18, 2014.
14. *Ibid.*
15. Bill Viola, in Robert Violette with Bill Viola (eds), *Bill Viola, Reasons for Knocking at an Empty House: Writings 1973–1994*, London: Thames & Hudson in association with Anthony d'Offay Gallery, 1995, p. 232.

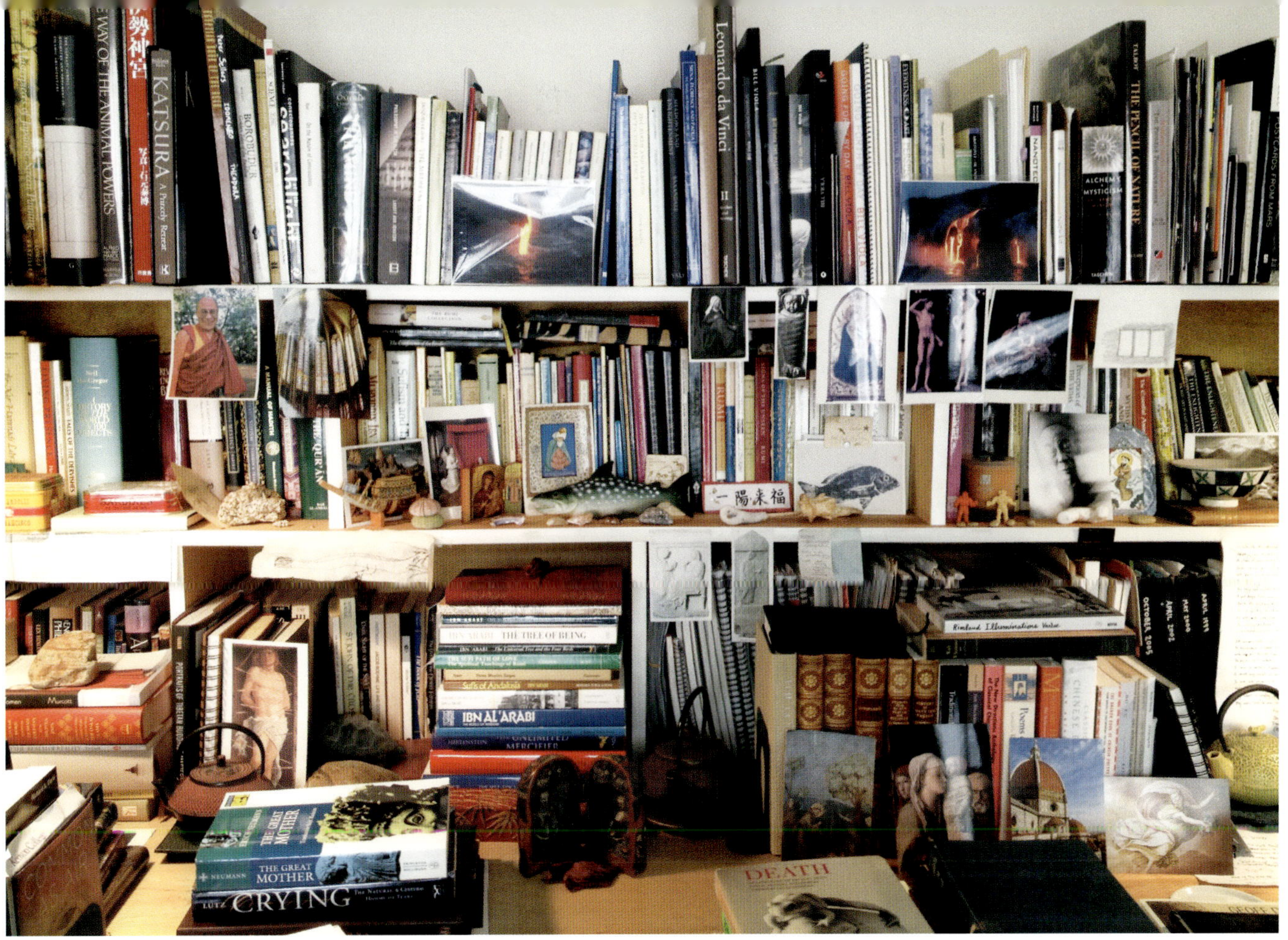

Study of Bill Viola, Long Beach, CA, May 2012

16. Bill Viola, in Hyde *et al.*, *Bill Viola*, pp. 54–5.
17. Bill Viola, in Violette with Viola, *Reasons for Knocking at an Empty House*, pp. 226–7.
18. Michel Foucault, quoted in Hilary M. Schor, *Curious Subjects: Women and the Trials of Realism*, Oxford: Oxford University Press, 2013, p. 1.
19. Martin Heidegger, *Hölderlin's Hymn "The Ister,"* trans. William McNeill and Julia Davis, Bloomington, IN: Indiana University Press, 1996, p. 44.
20. Bill Viola, in Hyde *et al.*, *Bill Viola*, p. 112.
21. Martin Seel, *Aesthetics of Appearing*, trans. John Farrell, Stanford, CA: Stanford University Press, 2005, p. 92.
22. *Ibid.*
23. Bill Viola, in Hyde *et al.*, *Bill Viola*, p. 110.
24. *Ibid.*
25. Aristotle, *Physics*, trans. Robin Waterfield, Oxford: Oxford University Press, 1996, pp. 153–4.
26. Bill Viola, in Hyde *et al.*, *Bill Viola*, p. 121.
27. John Sellars, *The Art of Living: The Stoics on Nature and the Function of Philosophy*, 2nd edn, London: Bristol Classical Press, 2009, p. 124.
28. *Ibid.*
29. *Ibid.*, p. 125.
30. Denis Donoghue, *Speaking of Beauty*, New Haven, CT: Yale University Press, 2003, pp. 53–4.

Chapter Five

1. Kira Perov, e-mail correspondence with the author, September 3–18, 2014.
2. Bill Viola, in Lewis Hyde *et al.*, *Bill Viola* (exh. cat.), New York: Whitney Museum of American Art, 1997, p. 122.
3. *Ibid.*, p. 124.
4. *Ibid.*, p. 126.
5. Bill Viola, in "A Conversation: Hans Belting and Bill Viola," in John Walsh (ed.), *Bill Viola: The Passions* (exh. cat.), Los Angeles: Getty Publications, 2003, p. 203.
6. *Ibid.*, p. 72.
7. *Ibid.*, p. 118.
8. Bill Viola, modified version of Notebook entry dated March 3, 1998 (Notebook, March 3, 1998 – April 5, 1999), reproduced in Walsh, *The Passions*, p. 226.
9. "Bodies of Light" is the title of Peter Sellars' essay in Walsh, *The Passions*.
10. John Walsh, "Emotions in Extreme Time: Bill Viola's Passions Project," in Walsh, *The Passions*, p. 49.
11. Bill Viola, quoted in *ibid.*, p. 48.

Chapter Six

1. Bill Viola, in *Bill Viola: Going Forth By Day* (exh. cat.), Berlin and New York: Deutsche Bank and the Solomon R. Guggenheim Foundation, 2002, p. 68.
2. *Ibid.*, pp. 15 ("Fire Birth"), 24 ("The Path"), 38 ("The Deluge"), 48 ("The Voyage"), 58 ("First Light").
3. *Ibid.*, p. 68.
4. Bill Viola, in conversation with the author, July 2001.
5. Bill Viola, in *Going Forth By Day*, p. 95.
6. *Ibid.*
7. Kira Perov, e-mail correspondence with the author, September 3–18, 2014.
8. *Ibid.*
9. *Ibid.*
10. Bill Viola, program notes, *Tristan und Isolde*, Opéra National de Paris, 2004–5, p. 38.
11. Bill Viola, e-mail interview with Concha Barrigós, Agencia EFE, December 17, 2013.
12. Kira Perov, e-mail correspondence with the author, September 3–18, 2014.
13. Ibn Arabi, quoted in David Anfam, *Bill Viola: Ocean Without a Shore* (exh. brochure), 52nd Venice Biennale, collateral event, 2007, n.p.
14. Bill Viola, quoted in *ibid.*
15. Johann Wolfgang von Goethe, *Faust*, rev. edn., trans. Peter Salm, New York: Bantam Books, 2007 (reissue; first published 1985), p. 3.
16. Dante Alighieri, *The Inferno*, trans. Robert and Jean Hollander, New York: Doubleday, 2000, p. 28.
17. Samuel Scheffler, *Death and the Afterlife*, Oxford: Oxford University Press, 2013, p. 45.
18. Kira Perov, e-mail correspondence with the author, September 3–18, 2014.
19. Bill Viola, in Kira Perov (ed.), *Bill Viola: Frustrated Actions and Futile Gestures* (exh. cat.), London: Blain|Southern, 2013, p. 48.
20. *Ibid.*
21. Henry David Thoreau, "Walking," quoted in Branka Arsić, *On Leaving: A Reading in Emerson*, Cambridge, MA: Harvard University Press, 2010, p. vi.
22. Bill Viola, in Perov, *Frustrated Actions*, p. 108.
23. Ralph Waldo Emerson, "Water," quoted in Arsić, *On Leaving*, p. 4.
24. Bill Viola, e-mail correspondence with the author, January 18, 2015.

Coda

1. Elizabeth A. Castelli, *Martyrdom and Memory: Early Christian Culture Making*, New York: Columbia University Press, 2004, p. 32.
2. Statement from dedication of *Martyrs* at St. Paul's Cathedral, London, May 21, 2014.
3. *Ibid.*
4. Castelli, *Martyrdom and Memory*, p. 203.
5. Statement from dedication of *Martyrs*.
6. 2 Cor. 4:7–10, 17–18.
7. Statement from dedication of *Martyrs*.

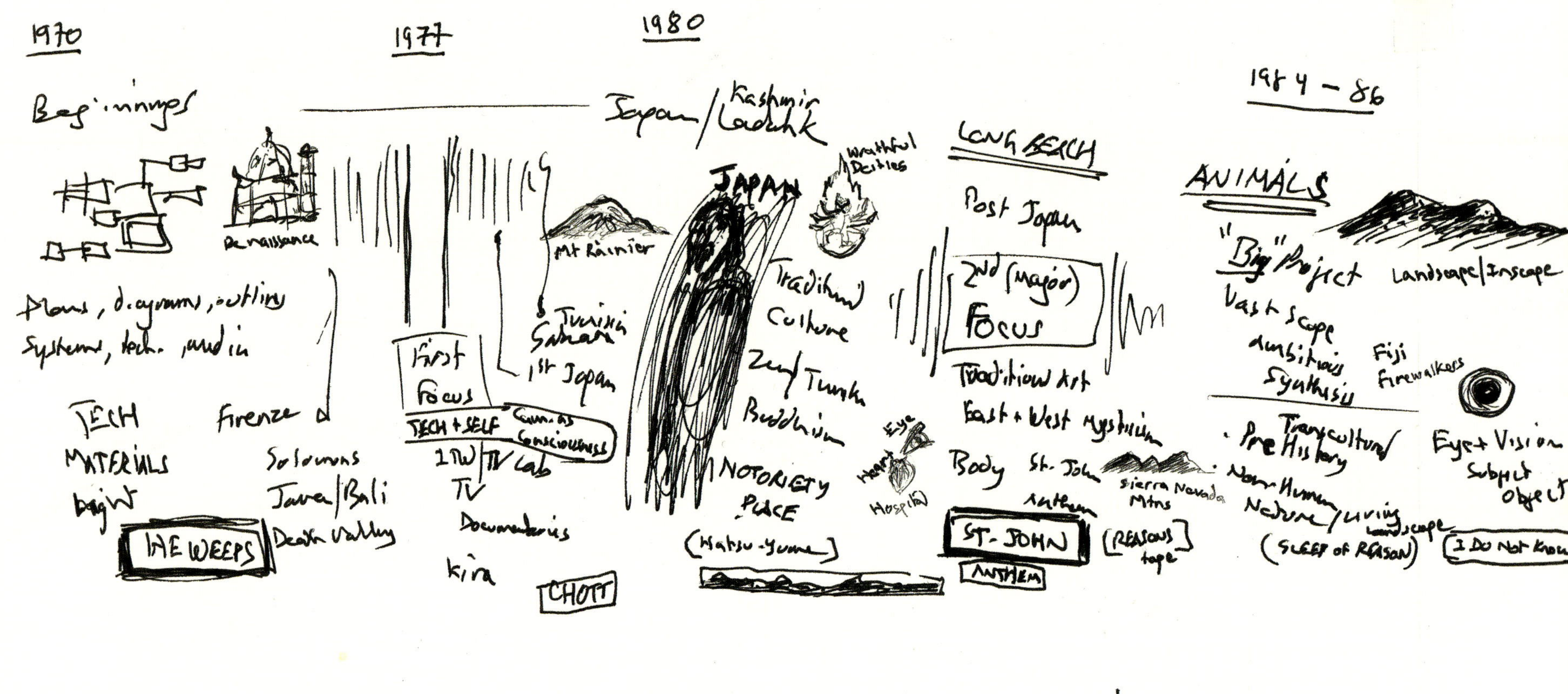

Timeline drawing of highlights of work, 1970–1997,
for Whitney Museum of American Art exhibition research, 1997

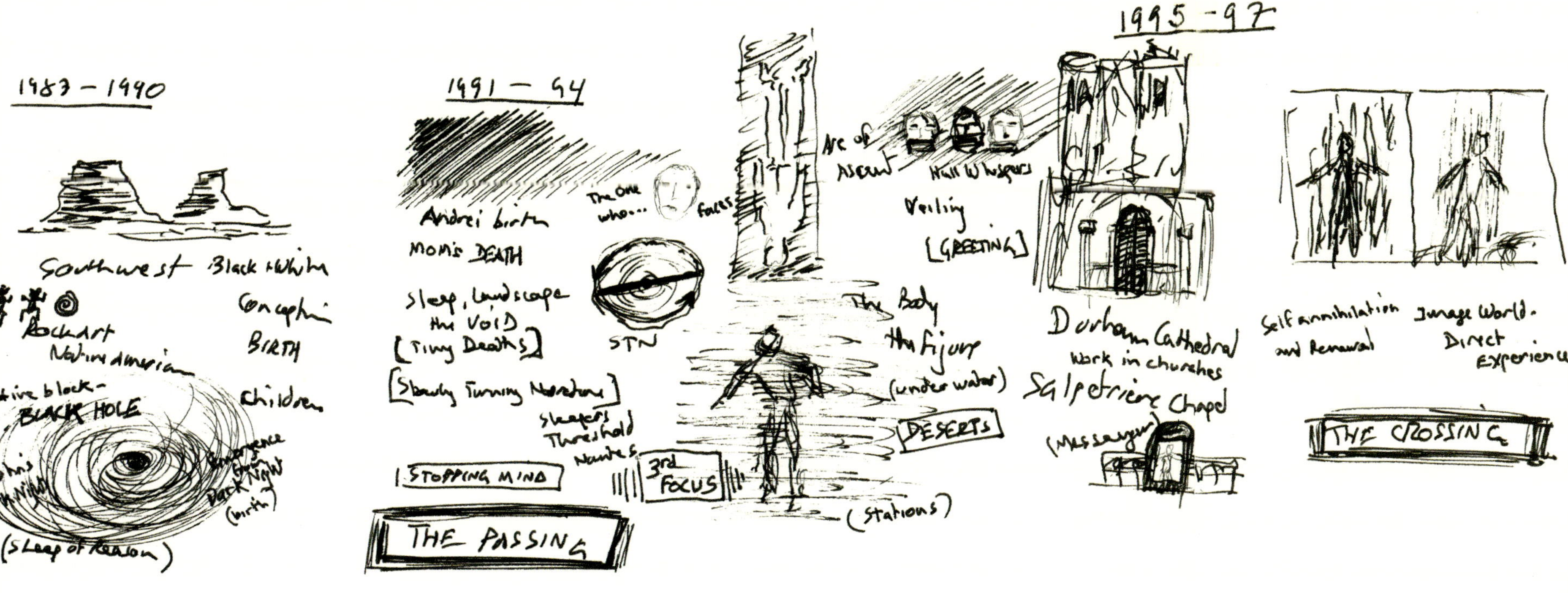

E PASSING | POST-PASSING – PRESENT

Chronology

1951
Born in Flushing, Queens, New York.

1960
Captain of the "TV Squad," PS 20 elementary school, Queens, New York.

1969
Enrolls in the art school at Syracuse University, Syracuse, New York, where he studies painting and electronic music, and encounters video at the university student center. Plays drums in a local rock band.

1971
Transfers to the Experimental Studios program, and studies under Professor Jack Nelson, who becomes a lasting influence. Founding member of the Synapse video group, installing and operating a cable TV system and color studio in the Syracuse student center.

1972
Creates first videotapes, including *Tape I*. Works as video preparator at the Everson Museum of Art, Syracuse (1972–4), under David Ross, curator of video art, assisting Nam June Paik, Peter Campus, Frank Gillette, and other artists. First public exhibition of videotape work (*Wild Horses*) in the group exhibition "St. Jude International" at the de Saisset Museum, Santa Clara University, California.

1973
Graduates with a BFA in Experimental Studios from the College of Visual and Performing Arts, Syracuse University. Enrolls in summer workshop in New Music in Chocorua, New Hampshire, and studies with David Tudor, beginning a lifelong relationship with him, performing in his *Rainforest* project, and becoming a member of Composers Inside Electronics, a group formed by Tudor in 1974. First exhibition of installations and videotapes: "New Video Works" at the Everson Museum. First public performance of Tudor's *Rainforest IV* at the Everson Museum. Initiates and instructs two courses in video/sound media for College of Visual and Performing Arts, Syracuse University (1973–4).

1974
Technical director of production at art/tapes/22, a video-art studio in Florence, Italy (1974–6). Meets and works with such established European and American artists as Giulio Paolini, Jannis Kounellis, Mario Merz, Vito Acconci, Joan Jonas, and Terry Fox. Travels to Death Valley in the Mojave Desert, California; this first encounter with the desert landscape profoundly influences future work. One-person exhibition of video and sound installations at The Kitchen, New York.

1975
Meets audio engineer and sound designer Bob Bielecki; they work on first collaborative project, an underwater soundscape, while Viola is artist-in-residence at ZBS Media, Fort Edward, New York. First exhibition of major installation in Europe: *Il Vapore* at Zona, Florence, Italy.

1976
Artist-in-residence at WNET/Thirteen Television Laboratory, New York (1976–81), where he first works with cutting-edge broadcast technology, including newly developed computer editing system; produces the videotape collection *Four Songs*. Creates *He Weeps for You*, an installation with live camera magnifying an image within a drop of water. Travels to the Solomon Islands in the South Pacific to record traditional music and dance, and to document the Moro Movement. First visit to Japan. Tours with Tudor's Composers Inside Electronics group, performing works by Tudor, John Cage, Takehisa Kosugi, and others at Festival d'Automne à Paris.

1977
Visits Java and Bali, Indonesia, to record traditional music and performing arts, working with resident ethno-musicologist Alex Dea. Travels to Melbourne, Australia, for exhibition "Video Spectrum," at invitation of director of cultural activities at La Trobe University, Kira Perov, Viola's future wife and collaborator. Presents video installation at Documenta 6, Kassel, West Germany (*He Weeps for You*).

1978
For the first presentation of his work in Japan, participates in symposium with a new performance titled *Olfaction*, at "X International Open Encounter on Video Tokyo 78," organized by Centro de Arte y Communication and Japan Video Committee Tokyo, Sogetsu Kaikan, Tokyo. Perov moves to New York, and she and Viola begin a lifelong collaboration, working and traveling together. Perov also begins to document with photographs the work and production process.

1979
Visits Saskatchewan, Canada, to record the winter prairie landscape, and then, with Perov, the Sahara Desert in Tunisia to videotape mirages (*Chott el-Djerid (A Portrait in Light and Heat)*) using telephoto lenses adapted for video. Exhibits installation, *He Weeps for You*, at the Museum of Modern Art, New York, as part of the "Projects" series. Artist-in-residence at WXXI TV, Rochester, New York. Viola and Perov record most of *The Reflecting Pool—Collected Work 1977–80*, an anthology of five videotape pieces.

1980
Perov and Viola marry. Viola receives Japan/US Creative Arts Fellowship, and he and Perov live in Japan for eighteen months to study traditional culture and advanced video technology. They study with Zen master and painter Daien Tanaka, who becomes a lifelong teacher. Perov has three exhibitions of photographs, in Tokyo, Sapporo, and Nagoya, and Viola shows "Selected Work 1976–1980" in the first video gallery in Japan, run by Fujiko Nakaya, and gives the gallery the name of SCAN. Sound performance (*Tunings from the Mountain*) composed for *Fog Sculpture Kawaji*, an outdoor work created by Nakaya for "A Fog, Sound, and Light Festival," Kawaji Onsen.

1981
Artist-in-residence at Sony Corporation's Atsugi research laboratories. Further develops work with precisely controlled time structures and computer-editing techniques (*Ancient of Days*), collaborating with Sony engineer Yasuo Shinohara; completes *The Reflecting Pool* collection. Awarded the Grand Prix for *Chott el-Djerid* at "International Video Art Festival, Portopia '81," Kobe. Travels with Perov throughout rural Honshu, Japan, with state-of-the-art video camera, recording images for *Hatsu-Yume (First Dream)*, and completes the work in the Sony labs in Atsugi. Perov and Viola move to Long Beach, California.

1982
Travels with Perov to the Ladakh region of the Himalayas in Northern India to observe religious art and ritual in Tibetan Buddhist monasteries. The Whitney Museum of American Art, New York, presents retrospective of videotapes.

1983
Artist-in-residence at Memorial Medical Center, Long Beach, where he gathers images and researches imaging technologies of the human body (*Anthem*). Utilizes Sony 1-inch tape machine with computer editor that can dial up the speed of the image from a stopped position to a very high rate (*Science of the Heart*). Creates the installation *Room for St. John of the Cross* based on the life of the sixteenth-century Spanish poet and mystic. Instructor in Advanced Video at the California Institute for the Arts, Valencia. Perov completes a book for the Long Beach Museum of Art that documents ten years of its video exhibition and production program (*Video: A Retrospective, 1974–1984*).

1984
Begins long-term project on animal consciousness, spending three weeks with a herd of bison in Wind Cave National Park, South Dakota, and becomes artist-in-residence at San Diego Zoo, California. Perov and Viola travel to Fiji to observe and videotape Hindu fire-walking ceremonies.

1985
The Theater of Memory, commissioned by John Hanhardt for the Whitney Biennial, integrates a 35-foot-long (10.5 meters) dead tree and fifty randomly blinking lanterns into a large video installation. The first time media work is installed alongside paintings and sculpture at a biennial.

1986
Completes first feature-length videotape, *I Do Not Know What It Is I Am Like*, a study of animal consciousness and human transcendence. The Museum of Contemporary Art, Los Angeles, acquires *Room for St. John of the Cross*, Viola's first room-size installation to be sold.

1987
Receives a grant from "Das kleine Fernsehspiel," a program produced by ZDF Television, Mainz, Germany, to create a desert landscape videotape piece (*The Passing*, 1991). Travels with Perov throughout the southwestern United States for five months to make nocturnal recordings of the desert landscape and to study ancient Native American archeological sites and rock art, one of Perov's interests. Works exclusively in black and white for the ZDF project, using a range of specially modified equipment, and recording images at the threshold of visibility with image intensifiers and infrared sensitive video cameras. "Bill Viola: Installations and Videotapes," presented at the Museum of Modern Art, New York, includes MoMA-commissioned *Passage*, an installation with 23-minute densely edited video played back at 1/16 speed so that the piece stretches to 7½ hours and plays once during the day.

1988
First child, Blake, is born to Perov and Viola. Begins working with computer-controlled self-generating time structures in installations (*The Sleep of Reason*).

1989
Initiates work with altered aspect ratios and the traditional triptych form in projected-image pieces (*The City of Man*). Begins to use video laserdisc technology as a programmed playback medium in multi-channel installations. Viola and Perov return to Japan for an exhibition of five installations at Fukui Fine Arts Museum, part of Third Fukui International Video Biennale. Receives a five-year fellowship from the John D. and Catherine T. MacArthur Foundation. Records the childbirth process, leading to a long-term exploration of the universal themes of the human condition.

1991

Mother dies in February. Perov and Viola's second son, Andrei, is born in November. Completes *The Passing* for ZDF Television, a personal meditation on birth, death, and the desert landscape. Moves into first large studio space for production and fabrication. For the inaugural exhibition of the new Museum für Moderne Kunst (MMK), Frankfurt, Germany, Viola creates *The Stopping Mind*, a complex video and sound installation that continues explorations begun in 1988 of self-generating time structures. The work is on continuous display at MMK for ten years.

1992

Produces a series of installations that focus on the themes of sleep, death, birth, and mortality. Makes his first work using 35mm high-speed film (*The Arc of Ascent*); it is also his first project with director of photography Harry Dawson, whose collaboration continues to the present. Creates a 24-hour continuous window projection (*To Pray Without Ceasing*), and produces a projected triptych altarpiece for a seventeenth-century church, the Chapelle de l'Oratoire, with the Musée des Beaux-Arts de Nantes, France (*Nantes Triptych*). First private gallery exhibitions at Donald Young Gallery, Seattle, and Anthony d'Offay Gallery, London. Perov organizes, with Marie Louise Syring of the Kunsthalle Düsseldorf, Germany, the first major tour of Viola's work, taking in six European venues. Ambitious for its time, the exhibition includes seven installations and a program of videotapes.

1993

Awarded the first Medienkunstpreis in Germany, presented jointly by Zentrum für Kunst und Medientechnologie, Karlshruhe, and Siemens Kulturprogramm. Receives the Skowhegan Award for video installation, New York. "Bill Viola," exhibition of six installations, Musée d'Art Contemporain de Montréal, Canada. Explores the edge of perception in such works as *Tiny Deaths* and *Pneuma* (1994) by recording images that are barely perceptible using low light and infrared cameras.

1994

Invited by the Ensemble Modern, Frankfurt, to create a new work based on the composition *Déserts* by Edgard Varèse for concert performance (*Déserts*); production uses full film crew, a constructed set, an actor, and 35mm high-speed film in combination with video segments. *Stations*, a five-channel installation with five large reflective black granite slabs and silky hanging scrims, is created for the inaugural exhibition at the American Center, Paris. Travels to Brazil for "Bill Viola: Território do Invisível/Site of the Unseen," Centro Cultural Banco do Brasil, Rio de Janeiro.

1995

Receives honorary degree of Doctor of Fine Arts from Syracuse University. Represents the United States at the 46th Venice Biennale, creating "Buried Secrets," five new installations on the themes of broken communication and sacred conversation. The show includes *The Greeting*, inspired by the sixteenth-century painting *Visitation* by the Italian Mannerist Pontormo. Collected writings published: *Bill Viola, Reasons for Knocking at an Empty House: Writings 1973–1994,* edited by Robert Violette with Bill Viola and Kira Perov.

1996

Commissioned by the Chaplaincy to the Arts and Recreation in North East England (Bill Hall, Senior Chaplain) to create an installation for the 900-year-old Durham Cathedral (*The Messenger*); the work is the first video installation to be acquired by a religious institution, the Church of England. Produces *The Crossing*, a large-scale projection installation depicting the transformation of the human form by the elements of fire and water. Both works feature in the exhibition "Bill Viola: Trilogy: Fire, Water, Breath," Chapelle Saint-Louis de la Salpêtrière, Festival d'Automne à Paris. First video installation of Viola's shown in Russia (*Science of the Heart*, 1983), Marble Palace, St. Petersburg. In March, Bobby Jablonski joins the team as studio director and becomes an invaluable member of Bill Viola Studio, creating exhibition plans and supervising all fabrications and installations of the work worldwide, continuing her collaboration through to the present.

1997

Creates his first interactive computer-graphics piece, the installation *The Tree of Knowledge*, collaborating with programmer Bernd Lintermann, Zentrum für Kunst und Medientechnolgie, Karlsruhe, Germany. "Bill Viola," a twenty-five-year survey exhibition organized by the Whitney Museum of American Art, New York, curated by David A. Ross and Peter Sellars, with Kira Perov, consisting of sixteen large-scale installation pieces and videotape works, launches at the Los Angeles County Museum of Art in November; first time digital video grabs of the work are used by Perov to represent video works in a catalogue. Receives honorary Doctor of Fine Arts degree from the School of the Art Institute of Chicago.

1998

Scholar-in-residence at the Getty Research Institute, Los Angeles, where the subject for that year is "Representing the Passions." He begins studying the depiction of extreme emotional states in medieval and Renaissance art, a theme that he will continue to develop in the coming years. Survey exhibition travels to the Whitney Museum of American Art, New York, and the Stedelijk Museum, Amsterdam.

1999
Father dies in January. Survey exhibition continues, opening at the Museum für Moderne Kunst and Schirn Kunsthalle in Frankfurt, and traveling to the San Francisco Museum of Modern Art. The last venue of the tour opens in October at the Art Institute of Chicago. Begins extended project with actors, especially Weba Garretson, who is central to many productions, in what becomes known as the "Passions" series. Director of photography, Harry Dawson, is a key collaborator for lighting and high-speed film recording.

2000
Exhibits *The Quintet of the Astonished*, the first work on the theme of the passions, at the National Gallery in London for the group exhibition "Encounters: New Art from Old." Works with Trent Reznor of Nine Inch Nails to create video interpretations of three songs for the band's U.S. "Fragility v2.0" tour. First gallery exhibition in New York, at James Cohan Gallery, features pieces from the "Passions" series and includes first works created for digital flat-panel and plasma displays. Opening of *The World of Appearances*, commissioned by Helaba Bank, first public permanently installed work, lobby, Main Tower, Frankfurt, Germany.

2001
Second group of "Passions" pieces are presented, at Anthony d'Offay Gallery, London, including the flat-panel predella sequence, *Catherine's Room* with Weba Garretson, as well as the large-scale, five-channel projection installation *Five Angels for the Millennium*. The Metropolitan Museum of Art in New York acquires *The Quintet of Remembrance*, the first video installation in its collection. Travels in Tuscany, studying narrative fresco cycles of the late Middle Ages and Renaissance. Viola and Perov, with studio producer S. Tobin Kirk, begin six-month production on largest project to date, *Going Forth By Day*, a projected digital fresco cycle in five parts created for the new medium of High-Definition video and involving a team of 125 technicians, special effects experts, stunt performers, full-scale construction sets, and more than 200 extras.

2002
Going Forth By Day premieres in February at the Deutsche Guggenheim Berlin; travels to the Solomon R. Guggenheim Museum, New York, in September. Two new works in High-Definition video, *Emergence* and *Observance*, created for an exhibition at the J. Paul Getty Museum, Los Angeles. *Five Angels for the Millennium* exhibited in "The Power of Art" at the Hyogo Prefectural Museum of Art, Kobe, Japan.

2003
"Bill Viola: The Passions" opens at the J. Paul Getty Museum, Los Angeles, and travels to the National Gallery, London; first solo exhibition in the main temporary galleries of both museums by a contemporary artist. New techniques employed by Perov to represent the work in the Getty *Passions* book, using digital grabs from High-Definition video and working closely with a printer who uses a new method of stochastic screening to achieve a photographic quality for each image. Viola completes *Living Witness (The Shortest Distance Between Two Points)*, a work recorded in the Mojave Desert near Lone Pine, California, commissioned for new E.ON AG headquarters, Düsseldorf, Germany. Enlarged version of *Five Angels for the Millennium* (2001) is installed in Gasometer Oberhausen, Germany, as part of Ruhrtriennale (festival director, Gerard Mortier). First solo exhibition in an Asian gallery, Kukje Gallery in Seoul, South Korea, includes "Passions" pieces and *The Veiling* (1995).

2004
Begins collaboration with director Peter Sellars, conductor Esa-Pekka Salonen, and executive producer Kira Perov to create a new production of Richard Wagner's opera *Tristan und Isolde*. Viola's accompanying 4-hour video is created in eight months with the assistance of director of photography Harry Dawson, producer S. Tobin Kirk, special effects supervisor Robbie Knott, performers John Hay, Jeff Mills, Lisa Rhoden, Sarah Steben, and Robin Bonaccorsi, live-performance video editor Alex MacInnis, and High-Definition editor Brian Pete. Premieres in project form as "The Tristan Project," by the Los Angeles Philharmonic, in December. "Bill Viola: Temporality and Transcendence," an exhibition of large installations including *Going Forth By Day*, Guggenheim Bilbao, Spain. Three video works are shown in "Lonely Planet," Contemporary Art Gallery, Art Tower Mito, Mito-City, Ibaraki, Japan.

2005
Production of the completed *Tristan und Isolde* receives its world premiere at Opéra National de Paris, Bastille, in sold-out run in April and November (the production continues to be performed, in its concert version and fully staged). "Bill Viola: Visions," ARoS Aarhus Kunstmuseum, Aarhus, Denmark, includes *Going Forth By Day* and, from its own collection, *Five Angels for the Millennium*. The Getty "Passions" exhibition travels to Fundación la Caixa, Madrid, Spain, and the National Gallery of Art, Canberra, Australia. "Tristan" series installation and video works are shown at the James Cohan Gallery in New York. Viola and Perov travel with sons Blake and Andrei to Dharamsala, northern India, to visit this mountaintop home of Tibetan refugees, to see monasteries, and to learn about Tibetan religion and culture. They are granted a private audience with H. H. Dalai Lama and

record a prayer for "The Missing Peace: Artists Consider the Dalai Lama," an exhibition organized by the Committee of 100 and the Dalai Lama Foundation that opens at the Fowler Museum of Cultural History, UCLA, Los Angeles, in June 2006. Viola also creates a new work for this show, *Bodies of Light*.

2006

"Bill Viola—Video," four installations exhibited at Kunsthalle Bremen; Viola receives NORD/Landesbank Art Prize in connection with the exhibition. Eleven "Tristan" series pieces are edited for exhibition in London at Haunch of Venison gallery and St. Olave's, a former school. The works range from a small LCD-panel triptych to plasma-screen diptychs, and to 18-foot-high (5.5 meters) projections. One of the largest exhibitions of Viola's installations to date, and the first large Asian retrospective, "Bill Viola: Hatsu-Yume (First Dream)," features sixteen works and attracts more than 340,000 visitors to the Mori Art Museum in Tokyo. Awarded Commander of the Order of Arts and Letters by the French government.

2007

Five installations are shown in "Bill Viola: Las Horas Invisibles," Museo de Bellas Artes de Granada, Palacio de Carlos V (Alhambra), Granada, Spain, on the occasion of the renovation of the Palacio de Carlos V. Viola's work is shown for the first time in Poland; the Zachęta National Gallery of Art, Warsaw, presents nine installations in an exhibition titled "Bill Viola." Uses new technical device allowing for the simultaneous recording of an event with two cameras, developed for the production of a new three-screen video/sound installation for the Venice Biennale, *Ocean Without a Shore*. Created for the fifteenth-century Church of the Oratorio San Gallo, the installation's theme "is about the presence of the dead in our lives." Additional recordings using the new technical system produce the "Transfigurations" series.

2008

"Bill Viola: The Tristan Project" features one installation at the Art Gallery of New South Wales, and two "Tristan" works projected onto a large vertical screen in front of the altar in St. Saviour's Church, Sydney, Australia. Exhibition at Kukje Gallery, Seoul, titled "Bill Viola: Transfigurations" includes six new works from the "Transfigurations" series and four earlier installations. "Bill Viola: Visioni interiori," the largest exhibition of Viola's work in Italy to date (sixteen video installations), is curated by Perov at the Palazzo delle Esposizioni in Rome; Perov also edits the accompanying catalogue.

2009

"Bill Viola: Installations and Screenings" at Haunch of Venison, Berlin; "Screenings," part of Forum Expanded, 59th Berlinale. Four installations shown in "Being Time," part of the ARTIST ROOMS tour, at the Pier Arts Centre, Stromness, Orkney, Scotland. Using a row of small, identical rooms that had previously been used for wool sorting, fourteen small video installations are shown at the De Pont Museum of Contemporary Art, Tilburg, the Netherlands, for the exhibition "Bill Viola: The Intimate Work." Exhibition at James Cohan Gallery, New York, titled "Bill Viola: Bodies of Light," includes a reworking of a 1994 installation, *Pneuma*. Receives Eugene McDermott Award in the Arts from MIT and XXI Catalonia International Prize from the government of Catalonia, Spain.

2010

"Bill Viola: The Tristan Project" features a large projection of two works in front of the altar of St. Carthage's Church as a Kaldor Public Project presented at the Melbourne Festival, Australia. To commemorate the 400th anniversary of the death of Caravaggio, six video installations are exhibited in "Bill Viola per Capodimonte" at the Museo di Capodimonte in Naples, Italy. *Emergence* is installed alongside Michelangelo's *David* at the Galleria dell'Accademia in Florence, Italy, on the occasion of the restoration of the *Palestrina Pietà*, originally attributed to Michelangelo.

2011

"Bill Viola: Transformations," exhibition at Gallery Koyanagi, Tokyo, featuring seven works. *Ocean Without a Shore* opens as a permanent installation at Pennsylvania Academy of the Fine Arts in Philadelphia, Pennsylvania. The first exhibition of Viola's work in the Canary Islands, "Bill Viola: Liber Insularum," is shown in Tenerife at Sala de Arte Contemporaneo del Gobierno de Canarias, and includes ten video installations; an expanded version travels to the Museum of Contemporary Art North Miami, Florida (2012). Receives the Arents Award for distinguished alumni from Syracuse University, Syracuse, New York. Awarded the Praemium Imperiale in Painting from the Japan Art Association, Tokyo.

2012

Returns with Perov to an exploration of mirages (light and heat). In two shoots at El Mirage, Mojave Desert, California, they complete the "Mirage" series and record *Crossroads*, a 16 ½ × 82-foot (5 × 25-meter) installation (finished in 2014) for the Hamad International Airport, Doha, Qatar. "Bill Viola: Reflections" exhibition featuring eleven video works is installed at Villa di Panza, Varese, Italy. James Cohan Gallery in Shanghai, China, presents "Bill Viola: Unspoken." Installed as a member of the National Academy, New York, making him one of the first media artists to be admitted into the academy.

2013

At the end of 2012 into 2013, Viola and Perov continue working in the studio and at nearby locations to produce two more series. The "Frustrated Actions" series includes *Chapel of Frustrated Actions and Futile Gestures*, a grid of nine 42-inch plasma screens, each with different video and audio. In the "Water Portraits" series, the performers are submerged in a Plexiglas tank filled with water (*The Dreamers*; seven 65-inch plasma screens surround the viewer and audio fills the space). "Frustrated Actions and Futile Gestures" solo exhibition at Blain|Southern in London includes nine works from Viola's three most recent series. Receives National Artist Award from Anderson Ranch, Aspen, Colorado, and the Aurora Award from the Aurora Picture Show in Houston, Texas. *Self Portrait, Submerged* is completed for the self-portrait collection in the Vasari Corridor, Uffizi Gallery, Florence. Perov and Viola work for five weeks with their twenty-four-member production team in a Hollywood studio to produce *Martyrs (Earth, Air, Fire, Water)* and *Inverted Birth*.

2014

Five small video works are installed among classical paintings at Real Academia de Bellas Artes de San Fernando, Madrid, in a break with the museum's tradition. *Tristan und Isolde* is staged in Madrid at the Teatro Real, and also in Paris at the Opéra National. "Bill Viola" at the Grand Palais, Paris, curated by Jérôme Neutres and Perov, the largest exhibition to date with twenty installations on view, attracts almost 300,000 visitors and 987 press reviews. Bern Cathedral installs five plasma works accompanied by a selection of videotapes on view at the Kunstmuseum Bern. Viola and Perov complete four-channel plasma screen piece *Martyrs (Earth, Air, Fire, Water)*, which is unveiled during evensong at St. Paul's Cathedral, London, and is the first permanent video installation in a Church of England cathedral. Premiere of *Inverted Birth* at the Faurschou Foundation in Beijing, shown as part of the solo exhibition "Transformation."

2015

Seven installations, most based on the theme of fire and water, are featured across three venues in the Adelaide Festival of Arts, Australia. An exhibition of seven works is exhibited at the Kukje Gallery, Seoul. The Yorkshire Sculpture Park in West Yorkshire, UK, presents a large exhibition of installations in its chapel and galleries.

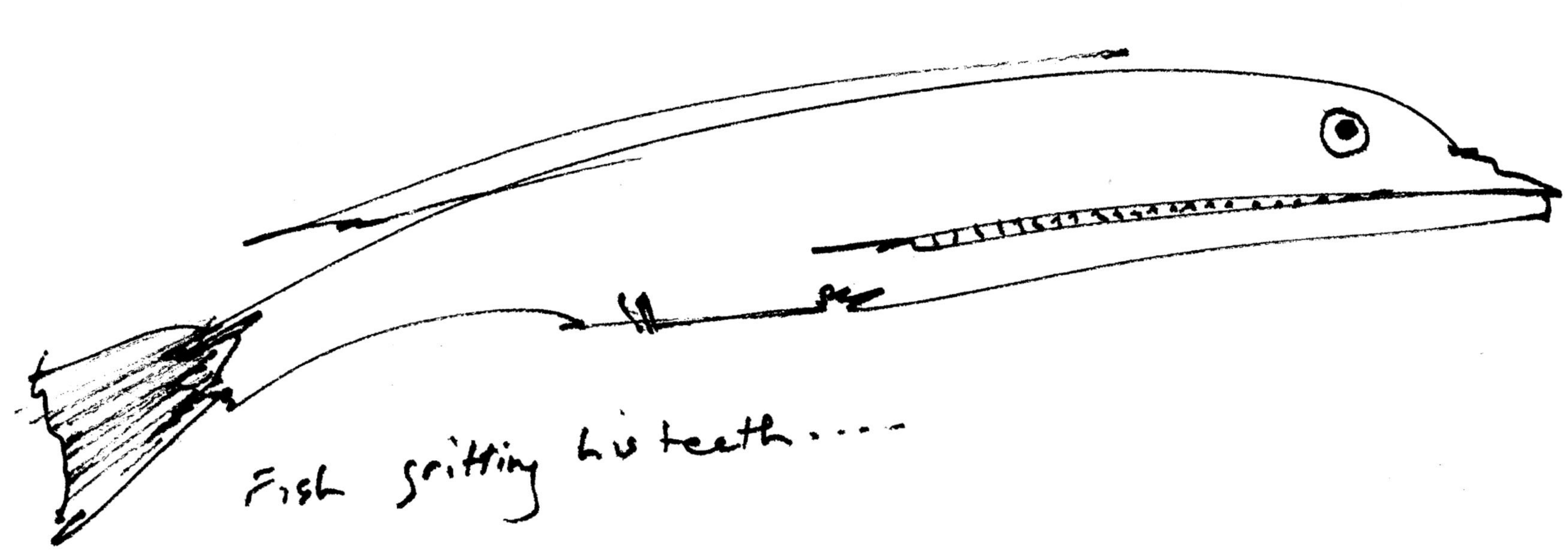

Drawing, February 12, 1995

in evidenza

SETTEMBRE

26

SS. Cosma de D.

MERCOLEDI

9 FORMAL STUDY ■, CRITICISMS, AND CONCERNS MUST
ALWAYS ■ REMAIN SECONDARY to the ARTISTIC
10 ENDEAVOR. IN the GENERAL SCHEME of THINGS,
FORMALISM is ~~always~~ A MINOR ASPECT IN
11 ~~SUBORDINATE~~ ALL WORK, of INTEREST MAINLY to
A SMALL GROUP of SPECIALISTS. ART TECHNIQUE
12 ALWAYS REMAINS SUBORDINATE to the ARTISTIC
VISION — IT IS the VISION, the CREATIVE SPIRIT
13 At the CENTER WHICH WILL IMPART A LONG AFTER LIFE.
"IN the HEARTS of MEN" ART IS the COMPREHENSION APPREHENSION
14 of LIFE. IS NOT FORMAL STUDY the STUDY of
the MECHANISMS of THAT WHICH IS ATTEMPTING
15 to DECIPHER LIFE? IT IS the STUDY of the
SHADOWS of the REAL. CRITICS STUDY ARTISTS.
16 ARTISTS STUDY GOD.

17

18

19

20

Above Notebook entry, Florence Notebook, April 1980

Opposite Bill Viola, Saskatoon, SK, Canada, July 26, 1979

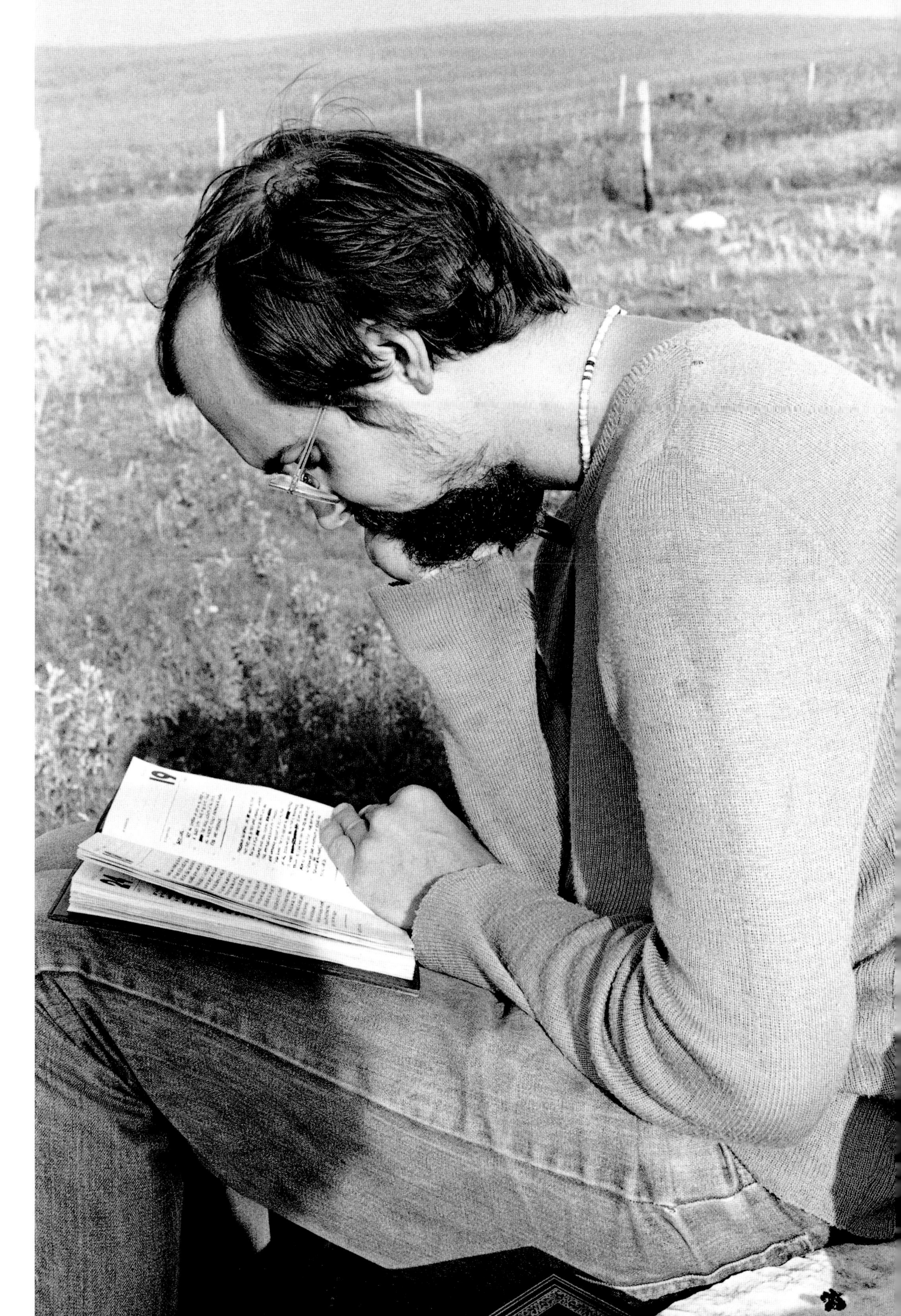

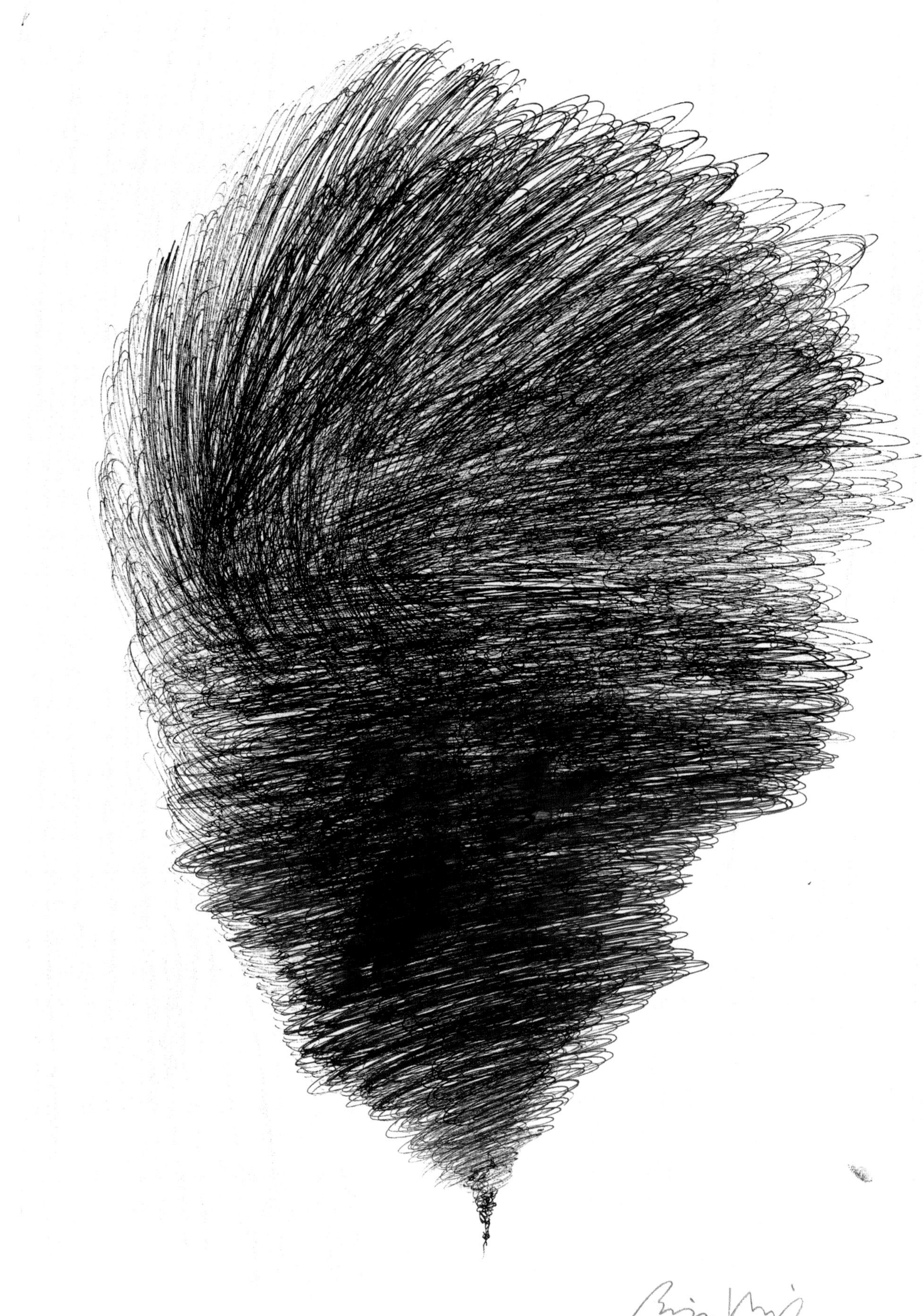

Exhibition History and Bibliography

SOLO EXHIBITIONS (SELECTED)

1973
"New Video Work," Everson Museum of Art, Syracuse, NY, USA

1974
"Bill Viola: Video and Sound Installations," The Kitchen, New York, NY, USA
"Bill Viola Videotapes," de Saisset Museum at Santa Clara University, CA, USA
"Bank Image Bank," Lincoln First Bank, Rochester, NY, USA

1975
"Il Vapore," one-day exhibition, part of "Per Conoscenza," Zona, Florence, Italy
"Rain—Three Interlocking Systems," Everson Museum of Art, Syracuse, NY, USA
"Bill Viola: Videotapes," Long Beach Museum of Art, Long Beach, CA, USA
"Origins of Thought," Vehicule Art, Montreal, Canada

1977
"William Viola: Video Installation and Tapes," The Kitchen, New York, NY, USA

1979
"Projects: Bill Viola," The Museum of Modern Art, New York, NY, USA
"Bill Viola: New Video Installation," Media/Study Buffalo, NY, USA

1980
"A Fog, Sound, and Light Festival," collaboration with Fujiko Nakaya, creating sound for a performance with her fog sculpture, Kawaji Onsen, Japan

1981
"Bill Viola," Vancouver Art Gallery, Vancouver, Canada

1982
"Bill Viola: Videotapes," Whitney Museum of American Art, New York, NY, USA

1983
"Bill Viola," ARC, Musée d'Art Moderne de la Ville de Paris, France

1985
"Bill Viola," Moderna Museet, Stockholm, Sweden
"Summer 1985," Museum of Contemporary Art, Los Angeles, CA, USA
"Bill Viola: Heaven and Hell," San Francisco Museum of Modern Art, San Francisco, CA, USA

1987
"Bill Viola: Installations and Videotapes," The Museum of Modern Art, New York, NY, USA

1988
"Bill Viola: Survey of a Decade," Contemporary Arts Museum, Houston, TX, USA

1989
"Bill Viola," Fukui Prefectural Museum of Art, part of 3rd Fukui International Video Biennale, Fukui City, Japan
"Bill Viola: The City of Man," Brockton Art Museum/Fuller Memorial, Brockton, MA, USA
"Bill Viola," Douglas Hyde Gallery, Dublin, Ireland
"Bill Viola," Museo de Arte Contemporaneo de Sevilla, Seville, Spain
"Bill Viola," Centro de Arte Moderna, Fundação Calouste Gulbenkian, Lisbon, Portugal
"Bill Viola: Sanctuary," Capp Street Project, San Francisco, CA, USA

1990
"Bill Viola: The Sleep of Reason," Fondation Cartier pour l'Art Contemporain, Jouy-en-Josas, France
"Bill Viola: He Weeps for You," LA BOX, École Nationale des Beaux-Arts, Bourges, France

1992
"Bill Viola: Slowly Turning Narrative," Institute of Contemporary Art, Philadelphia, PA, and Virginia Museum of Fine Arts, Richmond, VA, USA. In 1993 travels to Musée d'Art Contemporain de Montréal, Canada; Indianapolis Museum of Art, Indianapolis, IN, USA; Museum of Contemporary Art, San Diego, CA, USA; in 1994: Center for the Fine Arts, Miami, FL, USA; Parrish Art Museum, Southampton, NY, USA
"Bill Viola: Unseen Images," Stadtische Kunsthalle Düsseldorf, Germany. In 1993 travels to Moderna Museet, Stockholm; Museo Nacional Centro de Arte Reina Sofia, Madrid, Spain; Musée Cantonal des Beaux-Arts, Lausanne, Switzerland; Whitechapel Art Gallery, London, UK; in 1994: Tel Aviv Museum of Art, Israel
"Bill Viola: Two Installations," Anthony d'Offay Gallery, London, UK
"Bill Viola," Donald Young Gallery, Seattle, WA, USA
"Bill Viola: Nantes Triptych," Chapelle de l'Oratoire, Musée des Beaux-Arts, Nantes, France
"Bill Viola: Videos 1976–1991," Cinema Quadrat, Mannheim, Germany

1993
"Bill Viola," Musée d'Art Contemporain de Montréal, Canada

1994
"Bill Viola: Território do Invisível/Site of the Unseen," Centro Cultural/Banco do Brazil, Rio de Janeiro, Brazil
Déserts (A film created for the composition *Déserts* by Edgard Varèse), a collaboration with the Ensemble Modern, conductor Peter Eötvös, premiere of live performance, Wien Modern, Konzerthaus, Vienna, Austria (ongoing performances)
"Bill Viola: Stations," American Center inaugural opening, Paris, France
"Bill Viola," Salzburger Kunstverein, Salzburg, Austria
"Bill Viola: Images and Spaces," Madison Art Center, Madison, WI, USA

1995
"Buried Secrets," United States Pavilion, 46th Venice Biennale, Italy, organized by Arizona State University Art Museum. Travels to Kestner-Gesellschaft, Hannover, Germany; in 1996: Arizona State University Art Museum, Tempe, AZ; Institute of Contemporary Art, Boston, MA, USA

1996
"Bill Viola: New Work," Savannah College of Art and Design, Savannah, GA, USA
"Bill Viola: Trilogy: Fire, Water, Breath," Chapelle Saint-Louis de la Salpêtrière, Festival d'Automne à Paris, France
"Bill Viola: The Messenger," Durham Cathedral, Visual Arts UK 1996, Durham, UK. Travels to South London Gallery, London, UK; Video Positiva-Moviola, Liverpool, UK; The Fruitmarket Gallery, Edinburgh, UK; Oriel Mostyn, Gwynedd, UK; in 1997: The Douglas Hyde Gallery, Dublin, Ireland
"Bill Viola: Stations," Württemberger Kunstverein Stuttgart, Germany

1997
"Bill Viola: Fire, Water, Breath," Guggenheim Museum (SoHo), New York, NY, USA
"Bill Viola: A 25-Year Survey," organized by the Whitney Museum of American Art. Travels to Los Angeles County Museum of Art, CA, USA; in 1998: Whitney Museum of American Art, New York, NY, USA; Stedelijk Museum, Amsterdam, the Netherlands; in 1999: Museum für Moderne Kunst and Schirn Kunsthalle, Frankfurt, Germany; San Francisco Museum of Modern Art, CA, USA; in 1999–2000: Art Institute of Chicago, IL, USA

2000
"Bill Viola: The Greeting," Église Saint-Eustache, Festival d'Automne à Paris, France
"Bill Viola: New Work," James Cohan Gallery, New York, NY, USA
"The World of Appearances," Helaba Main Tower, Frankfurt, Germany (permanent installation)
"Stations: Bill Viola," Museum für Neue Kunst, ZKM, Karlsruhe, Germany

2001
"Bill Viola: Five Angels for the Millennium," Anthony d'Offay Gallery, London, UK

Disturbance 3, drawing, October 20, 2013

2002

"Bill Viola: Going Forth By Day," Deutsche Guggenheim Berlin, Germany. Travels to the Solomon R. Guggenheim Museum, New York, NY, USA

2003

"Bill Viola: Five Angels for the Millennium," Ruhrtriennale, Gasometer Oberhausen, Germany

"Bill Viola," Kukje Gallery, Seoul, Korea

"Bill Viola: The Passions," The J. Paul Getty Museum, Los Angeles, CA, USA. Travels to the National Gallery, London, UK; in 2005: Fundación "la Caixa," Madrid, Spain; National Gallery of Australia, Canberra

2004

"The Tristan Project," premiere, 4-hour video for Peter Sellars' new production of Richard Wagner's opera *Tristan und Isolde* (concert version), Walt Disney Concert Hall, Los Angeles, CA, USA, Los Angeles Philharmonic, conductor Esa-Pekka Salonen. New York premiere, Avery Fisher Hall, Lincoln Center for the Performing Arts, New York, NY, USA (2007), Los Angeles Philharmonic, conductor Esa-Pekka Salonen (ongoing performances)

"Bill Viola: Temporality and Transcendence," Guggenheim Museum Bilbao, Spain

2005

Tristan und Isolde, premiere of fully staged Peter Sellars production, with 4-hour video, conductor Esa-Pekka Salonen, l'Opéra National de Paris, France (repeated in the next 2005 season, 2007, 2009, and 2014). Performances in Kobe (Hyogo Performing Arts Center) and Tokyo (Tokyo Orchard Hall), Japan, 2007. Productions in Toronto, Canada (Canadian Opera Company, Four Seasons Center for the Performing Arts, 2013), and Madrid, Spain (Teatro Real, 2014)

"Bill Viola," James Cohan Gallery, New York, NY, USA

"Bill Viola Visions," ARoS Aarhus Kunstmuseum, Aarhus, Denmark

2006

"Bill Viola: Hatsu-Yume (First Dream)," Mori Art Museum, Tokyo, Japan. Reduced version travels to Hyogo Prefectural Museum of Art, Kobe, Japan

"Bill Viola—Video," 2006 Recipient of the NORD/LB Art Prize, Kunsthalle Bremen, Germany

"LOVE/DEATH The Tristan Project," Haunch of Venison and former St Olave's College, London, UK

"Bill Viola: Night Journey," Església del Convent de Sant Domingo, Pollença, Spain

2007

"Bill Viola: Ocean Without a Shore," Chiesa di San Gallo, Collateral Event, 52nd Venice Biennale, Venice, Italy

"Bill Viola," Zachęta National Gallery of Art, Warsaw, Poland

"Bill Viola: Works from the Tristan Project," James Cohan Gallery, New York, NY, USA

"Bill Viola: Las Horas Invisibles," Museo de Bellas Artes de Granada, Palacio de Carlos V, La Alhambra, Spain

2008

"Bill Viola: Visioni interiori," Palazzo delle Esposizioni, Rome, Italy

"Bill Viola: Ocean Without a Shore," National Gallery Victoria, Melbourne, Australia

"Bill Viola: Transfigurations," Kukje Gallery, Seoul, Korea

"Bill Viola: Ocean Without a Shore," National Museum of Contemporary Art, Gwacheon, Korea

"Bill Viola: The Tristan Project" (installation exhibition), Art Gallery of New South Wales and St. Saviour's Church, Sydney, Australia, presented by Kaldor Art Projects

"Bill Viola: Study for the Path," Basilica di San Marco, Milan, Italy (permanent installation)

2009

"Bill Viola: Bodies of Light," James Cohan Gallery, New York, NY, USA

"Bill Viola: The Intimate Work," De Pont Museum of Contemporary Art, Tilburg, the Netherlands

"Bill Viola: Being Time," The Pier Arts Centre, Stromness, Orkney, UK

"Bill Viola: Installations and Screenings" (screenings part of Forum Expanded, 59th Berlinale), Haunch of Venison, Berlin, Germany

2010

"Bill Viola per Capodimonte," Museo di Capodimonte, Naples, Italy

"Bill Viola: The Quintet of the Astonished," Urban Video Project, Syracuse University, Syracuse, NY, USA

"Bill Viola: Visitation," St. Louis Art Museum, MO, USA

"Emergence: Bill Viola at the Accademia Gallery," Galleria dell'Accademia, Florence, Italy

"Bill Viola: Figurative Works," Museo Picasso Malaga, Spain

"Bill Viola: Fire Woman and Tristan's Ascension," St. Carthage's Church, Melbourne, presented by Kaldor Public Art Projects in association with the Melbourne International Arts Festival, Australia

"Bill Viola: The Raft," Australian Centre for the Moving Image, Melbourne, presented in association with the Melbourne International Arts Festival and Kaldor Public Art Projects

"Bill Viola: 10 opere video single channel 1976–1994," Les Rencontres Rossiniennes, 2010, Galleria Franca Mancini, Pesaro, Italy

2011

"Bill Viola: The Quintet of the Unseen," Blain|Southern, London, UK

"Bill Viola: Liber Insularum," Sala de Arte Contemporaneo del Gobierno de Canarias, Tenerife, Canary Islands, Spain. In 2012 expanded version travels to Museum of Contemporary Art North Miami, FL, USA

"Bill Viola: Transformations," Gallery Koyanagi, Tokyo, Japan

"Amore e Morte," Gucci Museum, Florence, Italy

"Ocean Without a Shore," Pennsylvania Academy of the Fine Arts, Philadelphia, PA, USA

2012

"Bill Viola: The Raft," Nelson-Atkins Museum, Kansas City, MO, USA

"Bill Viola: Unspoken," James Cohan Gallery, Shanghai, China

"Bill Viola: Submerged Spaces," Norfolk & Norwich Festival, Sainsbury Centre for Visual Arts, Norwich, UK

"Bill Viola: Reflections," Villa e Collezione Panza, Varese, Italy

"Bill Viola: Water," Nordic Watercolor Museum, Skärhamn, Sweden

2013

"Bill Viola: Ascension," Wadsworth Atheneum, Hartford, CT, USA

"Frustrated Actions and Futile Gestures," Blain|Southern, London, UK

"Point of Departure," Parque de la Memoria, Buenos Aires, Argentina

"La Casa degli Dei," Palazzo Te, Mantova, Italy

"Bill Viola: Self Portrait, Submerged," Vasari Corridor, Galleria degli Uffizi, Florence, Italy (permanent installation)

2014

"Bill Viola: In Dialogue," Real Academia de Bellas Artes de San Fernando, Madrid, Spain

"Renaissance," Espace Culturel Louis Vuitton, Paris, France

"Bill Viola," Galeries Nationales—Grand Palais, Paris, France

"Bill Viola: Passions," Cathedral of Berne and Kunstmuseum Bern, Switzerland

"Martyrs (Earth, Air, Fire, Water)," St. Paul's Cathedral, London, UK (permanent installation)

"Tiny Deaths," Tate Modern, London, UK

"Bill Viola: Capturing Spectacle and Passion," Indianapolis Museum of Art, IN, USA

"The Passing: An Homage to Bill Viola," EMST/National Museum of Contemporary Art, Athens, Greece

"Bill Viola: Transformation," Faurschou Foundation, Beijing, China

2015

"Bill Viola: Selected Works," Art Gallery of South Australia, St. Peter's Cathedral, and Queen's Theatre, organized by Adelaide Festival of Arts, Adelaide, Australia

"Masterpiece 2015: Bill Viola," De Nieuwe Kerk, Amsterdam, the Netherlands

"Bill Viola," Kukje Gallery, Seoul, Korea

"Bill Viola," Yorkshire Sculpture Park, Wakefield, West Yorkshire, UK

GROUP EXHIBITIONS (SELECTED)

1972

"St. Jude Invitational Exhibition," de Saisset Museum at Santa Clara University, CA, USA

1974

"Impact Art Video Art '74," Musée des Arts Décoratifs, Lausanne, Switzerland

"Art Now," Kennedy Center, Washington, D.C., USA

"Projekt '74," Wallraf-Richartz-Museum, Cologne, Kunsthalle Cologne, and Kölnischer Kunstverein, Cologne, Germany

1975

"Biennial Exhibition," Whitney Museum of American Art, New York, NY, USA

"Video Art," Institute of Contemporary Art, Philadelphia, PA, USA

"Americans in Florence, Europeans in Florence," Long Beach Museum of Art, CA, USA

"La Biennale de Paris," ARC, Musée d'Art Moderne de la Ville de Paris, France

1976

Rainforest IV by David Tudor, and other individual works by Composers Inside Electronics, Festival d'Automne à Paris, France

"Video Art: An Overview," San Francisco Museum of Modern Art, CA, USA

"Change: Beyond the Artist's Hand," Art Gallery, California State University, Long Beach, CA, USA

1977

"Documenta VI," Fridericianum, Kassel, Germany

1978

"Video Art '78," London Video Arts, London, UK

1981

"International Video Art Festival," Theme Pavillion, Portopia '81, Kobe, Japan

1982
"National Video Festival," American Film Institute, Los Angeles, CA, USA

1983
"Video as Attitude," Museum of Fine Arts, Museum of New Mexico, Santa Fe, NM, USA; and University Art Museum, University of New Mexico, Albuquerque, NM, USA
"Noel Harding and Bill Viola: Two Video Installations," Video Culture/Canada International Video Festival, The Art Gallery at Harbourfront, Toronto, Canada

1984
"Het lumineuze beeld/The Luminous Image," Stedelijk Museum, Amsterdam, the Netherlands

1985
"Biennial Exhibition," Whitney Museum of American Art, New York, NY, USA
"1ère Semaine Internationale de Video," Saint Gervais Center, Geneva, Switzerland

1986
"Où va la vidéo?," La Chartreuse, Villeneuve-lez-Avignon, France
"Networking," Corderie dell'Arsenale, 42nd Venice Biennale, Venice, Italy
"Festival Nacional de Video," Circulo de Bellas Artes, Madrid, Spain

1987
"Avant-Garde in the Eighties," Los Angeles County Museum of Art, CA, USA
"Ritratti: Greenaway, Marinis, Pirri, Viola," Taormina Arte 1987, Taormina, Sicily, Italy

1988
"American Landscape Video: The Electronic Grove," Carnegie Museum of Art, Pittsburgh, PA, USA. Travels to San Francisco Museum of Modern Art, CA, USA; Newport Harbor Art Museum, Newport Beach, CA, USA
"Carnegie International," Carnegie Museum of Art, Pittsburgh, PA, USA

1989
"Image World: Art and Media Culture," Whitney Museum of American Art, New York, NY, USA
"Video-Skulptur: Retrospectiv und Aktuell 1963–1989," Kölnischer Kunstverein, Cologne, Germany; Neuer Berliner Kunstverein, Berlin, Germany; Kunsthaus Zurich, Zurich, Switzerland
"Einleuchten," Deichtorhallen, Hamburg, Germany

1990
"Passages de l'image," Musée National d'Art Moderne, Centre Georges Pompidou, Paris, France. Travels to Centre Cultural de la Fundació Caixa de Pensions, Barcelona, Spain; Wexner Center for the Arts, Columbus, OH, USA; San Francisco Museum of Modern Art, CA, USA
"LIFE-SIZE: A Sense of the Real in Recent Art," The Israel Museum, Jerusalem, Israel

1991
"Eröffnungsausstellung/Opening Exhibition," Museum für Moderne Kunst, Frankfurt, Germany
"Metropolis," Martin-Gropius-Bau, Berlin, Germany

1992
"Documenta IX," Documenta-Halle, Kassel, Germany

1993
"American Art in the Twentieth Century: Painting and Sculpture, 1913–1993," Martin-Gropius-Bau, Berlin, Germany, and Royal Academy of Arts, London, UK
"New World Images," Louisiana Museum of Modern Art, Humlebaek, Denmark

1994
"Visions of America: Landscape as Metaphor in the Late Twentieth Century," Denver Art Museum, CO, USA, and Columbus Museum of Art, OH, USA

1995
"Video Spaces: Eight Installations," The Museum of Modern Art, New York, NY, USA
"Rites of Passage: Art for the End of the Century," Tate Gallery, London, UK
"3e Biennale d'art contemporain de Lyon," Musée d'Art Contemporain, Lyon, France

1996
"Along the Frontier: Ann Hamilton, Bruce Nauman, Francesc Torres, Bill Viola," organized by International Center of Photography, New York. Exhibited at the Russian Museum, St. Petersburg, Russia; Galerie Rudolfinum, Prague, Czech Republic; National Gallery of Contemporary Art, Warsaw, Poland; Soros Center for Contemporary Art, Ukrainian House Gallery, Kiev
"Being and Time: The Emergence of Video Projection," Albright-Knox Art Gallery, Buffalo, NY, USA. Travels to Cranbrook Art Museum, Bloomfield Hills, MI, USA; Portland Art Museum, OR, USA; Contemporary Arts Museum, Houston, TX, USA; Site Santa Fe, NM, USA

1997
"Changing Spaces," Fabric Workshop and Museum, Philadelphia, PA, USA, organizers. Exhibited at Miami Art Museum, FL, USA; Arts Festival of Atlanta, GA, USA; Detroit Institute of Arts, MI, USA; Vancouver Art Museum, Canada

1999
"The American Century: Art & Culture 1900–2000, Part II, 1950–2000," Whitney Museum of American Art, New York, NY, USA

2000
"Encounters: New Art from Old," National Gallery, London, UK
"Spectacular Bodies: The Art and Science of the Human Body from Leonardo to Now," Hayward Gallery, London, UK

2001
"Plateau of Humankind," 49th Venice Biennale, Italy
"Hieronymous Bosch," Museum Boijmans Van Beuningen, Rotterdam, the Netherlands
"Artcité: When Montreal Turns into a Museum," Musée d'Art Contemporain de Montréal, Canada

2002
"The Power of Art," Hyogo Prefecture Museum of Art, Kobe, Japan
"Synopsis II: Theologies at the National Museum of Contemporary Art," National Museum of Contemporary Art, Athens, Greece
"Video Acts: Single Channel Works from the Collections of Pamela and Richard Kramlich and New Art Trust," PS1, MoMA, Long Island, NY, USA

2003
"Painting Pictures," Kunstmuseum Wolfsburg, Germany
"The Body Transformed," National Gallery of Canada, Ottawa, Canada
"Passion for Art: 100 Treasures 100 Years," Dallas Museum of Art, TX, USA
"Happiness: A Survival Guide for Art and Life," Mori Art Museum, Tokyo, Japan

2004
"Presence," St. Paul's Cathedral, London, UK
"Self-Evidence: Identity in Contemporary Art," DeCordova Museum & Sculpture Park, Lincoln, MA, USA
"Pontormo, Bronzino, and the Medici: The Transformation of the Renaissance Portrait," Philadelphia Museum of Art, PA, USA

2005
"25 years of Deutsche Bank Collection," Deutsche Guggenheim Berlin, Germany
"Marking Time/Moving Images," Miami Art Museum, FL, USA
"Getting Emotional," Institute of Contemporary Art, Boston, MA, USA
"Water in Myth and Nature," Hypo-Kulturstiftung, Munich, Germany
"A Kind of Magic," Lucerne Museum of Art, Switzerland
"Out of Time," The Museum of Modern Art, New York, NY, USA
"Intramoenia Extra Art," Castel del Monte, Andria, Italy

2006
"Without Boundary: Seventeen Ways of Looking," The Museum of Modern Art, New York, NY, USA
"Los Angeles, 1955–1985," Centre Pompidou, Paris, France
"The Missing Peace: Artists Consider the Dalai Lama," Fowler Museum at UCLA, Los Angeles, CA, USA. Travels to ten other venues (2006–11)
"Out of Time," The Museum of Modern Art, New York, NY, USA

2007
"Centre Pompidou Video Art 1965–2005," Australian Centre for the Moving Image, Melbourne
"Passage du Temps (Passage of Time)," Collection François Pinault Foundation, part of Lille3000, Lille, France

2008
"California Video," J. Paul Getty Museum, Los Angeles, CA, USA

2009
"Collection: MOCA's First Thirty Years," Museum of Contemporary Art, Los Angeles, CA, USA
"After Darwin: Contemporary Expressions," Jerwood Gallery, Natural History Museum, London, UK
"Tears of Eros," Museo Thyssen-Bornemisza, Madrid, Spain
"Un Certain Etat du Monde? A Certain State of the World? Works from the François Pinault Foundation," Garage Center for Contemporary Culture, Moscow, Russia

2010
"Mortality," presented in association with the Melbourne International Arts Festival, Australian Centre for Contemporary Art, Melbourne, Australia
"17th Sydney Biennale," Museum of Contemporary Art, Sydney, Australia
"Space," Foundazione MAXXI, Rome, Italy
"The Artist's Museum," Museum of Contemporary Art, Los Angeles, CA, USA
"Thierry Kuntzel/Bill Viola: Deux éternités proches," Le Fresnoy, Tourcoing, France

2011

"Real Virtuality," Museum of the Moving Image, Astoria, NY, USA

"Blink! Light, Sound, and the Moving Image," Denver Art Museum, Denver, CO, USA

"John Kaldor Family Collection," Art Gallery of New South Wales, Sydney, Australia

"MMK 1991–2011: 20 Years of Presence," Museum für Moderne Kunst, Frankfurt, Germany

"Exchange Evolution," Long Beach Museum of Art, CA, USA

2012

"Video Vintage," Centre Pompidou, Paris, France

"Art and Emotions Through Five Centuries," National Museum Stockholm, Sweden

"The Best of Times, The Worst of Times," Kiev International Biennale of Contemporary Art, Ukraine

"Extra-Large: Monumental Works from the Collection of the Centre Pompidou," Grimaldi Forum, Monaco

"Voices of Images," Palazzo Grassi, Venice, Italy

2013

"Seismic Shifts," National Academy Museum, New York, NY, USA

"Imminent Sounds—Falls and Crossings," Taipei Fine Art Museum, Taipei, Taiwan

"Á Triple Tour," Conciergerie, Paris, France

"Mystery of Tears," Metropolitan Arts Centre, Belfast, UK

2014

"1st International Biennial of Contemporary Art of Cartagena de Indias," Cartagena, Colombia

"Pontormo & Rosso Fiorentino: Diverging Paths of Mannerism," Palazzo Strozzi, Florence, Italy (*The Greeting* shown as adjunct to the exhibition)

"Videoformes 2014," LA DIODE, Clermont-Ferrand, France

"Video Art: New Horizons," Gallerie Marsam 2, Casablanca, Morocco

"Man in the Mirror," Vanhaerents Art Collection, Brussels, Belgium

"Equilibrium," Salvatore Ferragamo Museum, Florence, Italy

"Five Centuries of Melancholia," University of Queensland Art Museum, Brisbane, Australia

"Pure Water: The Most Valuable Resource in the World," LENTOS Kuntzmuseum, Linz, Austria

"The Sea," Museum Brandts, Odense, Denmark

"The Sea—An Homage to Jan Hoet," Cinema Capitole, VZW De Zee, Oostende, Belgium

"Invitation au Voyage," Louvre Museum, Paris, France

2015

"Leonardo da Vinci's Leicester Codex and the Power of Observation," Phoenix Art Museum, AZ, USA. Travels to Minneapolis Museum of Art, MN, USA

"Belle Haleine—The Scent of Art," Museum Tinguely, Basel, Switzerland

"Mater, Maternity in Art," Palazzo del Governatore, in association with Fondazione DNArt, Parma, Italy

"Watch This! Revelations in Media Art," Smithsonian American Art Museum, Washington, D.C., USA

"Heartbreak Hotel," 56th Venice Biennale, collateral event organized by Vanhaerents Art Collection, Zeucca Projects Space, Giudecca, Italy

BOOKS, CATALOGUES, AND DOCUMENTARIES ON BILL VIOLA

1983

Bill Viola (exh. cat.). Curator Dany Bloch. Texts by Anne-Marie Duguet, John G. Hanhardt, Kathy Rae Huffman, Suzanne Page, and Bill Viola; interview with the artist by Deirdre Boyle. Paris: Musée d'Art Moderne de la Ville de Paris. In French and English.

1985

"Bill Viola: Statements by the Artist," in *Summer 1985* (exh. cat.). Curator Julia Brown. Texts by Bill Viola. Los Angeles: Museum of Contemporary Art.

1987

London, Barbara, ed. *Bill Viola: Installations and Videotapes* (exh. cat.). Texts by J. Hoberman, Donald Kuspit, Barbara London, and Bill Viola. New York: The Museum of Modern Art.

1988

Zeitlin, Marilyn A., ed. *Bill Viola: Survey of a Decade* (exh. cat.). Texts by Deirdre Boyle, Kathy Rae Huffman, Christopher Knight, Michael Nash, Joan Seeman Robinson, Gene Youngblood, Bill Viola, and Marilyn A. Zeitlin. Houston: Contemporary Arts Museum.

1989

Bill Viola: The City of Man (exh. brochure). Text by Catherine S. Mayes. Brockton, MA: Brockton Art Museum/Fuller Memorial.

Bill Viola: Razones Para Llamar a la Puerta de Una Casa Vacia (exh. brochure). Texts by Anne-Marie Duguet, Catherine Elwes, and Bill Viola. Seville: Junta de Andalucía/Museo de Arte Contemporáneo de Sevilla. In Spanish.

1990

Loisy, Jean de, ed. *Bill Viola: The Sleep of Reason* (exh. cat.). Texts by Jean de Loisy and Bill Viola. Jouy-en-Josas: Fondation Cartier pour l'Art Contemporain. In French.

1992

Syring, Marie Louise, ed. *Bill Viola: Unseen Images/Nie gesehene Bilder/Images jamais vues* (exh. cat.). Texts by Rolf Lauter, Marie Louise Syring, and Bill Viola; interview with the artist by Jörg Zutter. Düsseldorf: Kunsthalle Düsseldorf. In German, English, and French. Reprinted and expanded for Spanish edition as *Bill Viola: Más allá de la mirada (imágenes no vistas)*. Madrid: Museo Nacional Centro de Arte Reina Sofía.

Bill Viola: Slowly Turning Narrative (exh. cat.). Texts by Melissa E. Feldman, H. Ashley Kistler, and Bill Viola. Philadelphia: Institute of Contemporary Art; Richmond: Virginia Museum of Fine Arts.

Emmerling, Leonhard and Susanne Kaeppele, eds. *Bill Viola: Videos 1976–1991* (exh. cat.). Texts by Leonhard Emmerling and Christmut Prager. Mannheim: Cinema Quadrat e.V. In German.

1993

Valentini, Valentina, ed. *Bill Viola: Vedere con la mente e con il cuore*. Texts by Valentina Valentini and Bill Viola; interview with the artist by Jörg Zutter, and interview with David A. Ross by Gianfranco Mantegna. Rome: Gangemi Editore. In Italian.

Bélisle, Josée, ed. *Bill Viola* (exh. cat.). Texts by Josée Bélisle and Bill Viola. Montreal: Musée d'Art Contemporain de Montréal. In French and English.

1994

Pühringer, Alexander, ed. *Bill Viola* (exh. cat.). Texts by Friedemann Malsch, Celia Montolió, Otto Neumaier, and Bill Viola; interview with the artist by Otto Neumaier and Alexander Pühringer. Salzburg: Salzburger Kunstverein. In German and English.

Bill Viola: Images and Spaces (exh. cat.). Introduction by Toby Camps; texts by Tina Yapelli and Bill Viola. Madison, WI: Madison Art Center.

Bill Viola: Território do Invisível/Site of the Unseen (exh. cat.). Texts by Ivana Bentes, Marcello Dantas, Kathy Rae Huffman, and Bill Viola; interview with the artist by Jörg Zutter. Rio de Janeiro: Magnetoscópio/Centro Cultural Banco do Brasil. In Portuguese and English.

Dantas, Marcello and Carlos Nader, directors. *Bill Viola: Território do Invisível/Site of the Unseen* (documentary). New York: Electronic Arts Intermix (distr.). In Portuguese and English. 26 minutes.

1995

Zeitlin, Marilyn A., ed. *Bill Viola: Buried Secrets/Segreti sepolti* (exh. cat.). Texts by Bill Viola and Marilyn A. Zeitlin. Tempe: Arizona State University Art Museum. In English and Italian. Reprinted and expanded as *Bill Viola: Buried Secrets/Vergrabene Geheimnisse*. Texts by Carl Haenlein, Susie Kalil, Bill Viola, and Marilyn A. Zeitlin. Tempe: Arizona State University Art Museum; Hannover: Kestner-Gesellschaft. In English and German.

Bill Viola, Reasons for Knocking at an Empty House: Writings 1973–1994. Edited by Robert Violette with Bill Viola. London: Thames & Hudson/Anthony d'Offay Gallery; Cambridge, MA: MIT Press.

1996

Sparrow, Felicity, ed. *Bill Viola: The Messenger* (exh. cat.). Curator Bill Hall. Texts by David Jasper, Stuart Morgan, and Bill Viola. Durham: Chaplaincy to the Arts and Recreation in North East England.

Bill Viola: Stations (exh. cat). Texts by Martin Hentschel, Hannelore Paflik-Huber, and Bill Viola. Stuttgart: Württembergischer Kunstverein Stuttgart. In German and English.

1997

Bill Viola: A Twenty-Five-Year Survey (exh. cat.). Texts by David A. Ross and Bill Viola; conversation between Lewis Hyde and Bill Viola; visual documentation by Kira Perov. New York: Whitney Museum of American Art; Paris: Flammarion. Stuttgart: Cantz, 1999. In German.

1999

Lauter, Rolf, ed. *Bill Viola: Europäische Einsichten|European Insights, Werkbetrachtungen|Reflections on the Work of Bill Viola.* Introduction by Rolf Lauter; texts by Jean-Christophe Ammann *et al*. Munich, London, New York: Prestel. In German and English.

2000

Stations: Bill Viola (exh. cat.). Introduction by Götz Adriani; texts by Reto Krüger, Ralph Melcher, Bill Viola, and Dörte Zbikowski. Karlsruhe: Museum für Neue Kunst/ZKM. In German.

2002

Bill Viola: Going Forth By Day (exh. cat.). Curator John G. Hanhardt. Texts by Bill Viola; interview with the artist by John G. Hanhardt. Berlin: Deutsche Bank; New York: Solomon R. Guggenheim Foundation. Separate books in English and German.

2003

Bill Viola (exh. cat.). Texts by David A. Ross, Susan Kalil, and Bill Viola. Seoul: Kukje Gallery. In Korean and English.

Walsh, John, ed. *Bill Viola: The Passions* (exh.cat.). Texts by Peter Sellars, Bill Viola, and John Walsh; conversation between Hans Belting and Bill Viola; visual documentation by Kira Perov. Los Angeles: The J. Paul Getty Museum in association with the National Gallery, London. Madrid: Fundación "la Caixa," 2004. Spanish edition titled *Bill Viola: Las Pasiones.*

Kidel, Mark, director. *Bill Viola: The Eye of the Heart* (documentary). Bristol, UK: Calliope Media; Delft, the Netherlands: C&S Entertainment, 2005. 59 minutes.

Schmitz, Jeanette and Wolfgang Volz, eds. *Five Angels: Bill Viola im Gasometer*, *Ein Projekt der Ruhrtriennale* (exh. cat.). Texts by Söke Dinkla, Friedhelm Mennekes, Jeanette Schmitz, Peter Sellars, and Bill Viola. Essen: Klartext. In German and English.

2004

Tristan und Isolde (program, 2004/5 season). Texts by Peter Sellars *et al*. Paris: Opéra National de Paris. In French, English, German.

Townsend, Chris, ed. *The Art of Bill Viola.* Introduction by Chris Townsend; texts by Cynthia Freeland *et al*. London: Thames & Hudson. Milan: Bruno Mondadori, 2005. In Italian.

Weevers, Arent. *Spiritualiteit bij Bill Viola: Inleiding Mystieke Invloed Op Zijn Videokunst.* Hengelo: Arent Weevers. In Dutch.

2005

Fargier, Jean-Paul. *The Reflecting Pool de Bill Viola*. Crisnée: Éditions Yellow Now Côte films #2. In French. Rome: Bulzoni Editore, 2009. In Italian.

Krogh, Anna and Jens Erik Sorensen, eds. *Bill Viola: Visions* (exh. cat.). Texts by Anna Krogh *et al*. Aarhus: ARoS Aarhus Kunstmuseum. In Danish and English.

Jahnsen, Angeli. *Kunst sehen ist sich selbst sehen: Christian Boltanski, Bill Viola*. Berlin: Dietrich Reimer Verlag. In German.

2006

Bill Viola: Night Journey (exh. cat.). Texts by Piedad Solans and Bill Viola. Pollença, Majorca: Ajuntament de Pollença. In Catalan, Castilian, and English.

Bill Viola: Love/Death: The Tristan Project (exh. cat.). Texts by Simon Grant and Bill Viola. London: Haunch of Venison.

Elliott, David and Akio Obigane, eds. *Bill Viola: Hatsu-Yume (First Dream)* (exh. cat.). Texts by David Elliott, David A. Ross, Bill Viola, and John Walsh; interview with the artist and Kira Perov by Akio Obigane. Tokyo: Mori Art Museum and Tankosha Publishing Co., Ltd. In Japanese and English.

2007

Bill Viola: Las Horas Invisibles (exh. cat.). Curator José Lebrero Stals. Texts by David A. Ross, Bill Viola, and John Walsh; conversation between Bill Viola, Otto Neumaier, and Alexander Pühringer. Seville: Junta de Andalucía, Consejería de Cultura. In Spanish.

Brewinska, Maria, ed. *Bill Viola* (exh. cat.). Texts by Maria Brewinska, Benjamin Cope, Minoru Hatanaka, Jaroslaw Lubiak, and Bill Viola. Warsaw: Zachęta National Gallery of Art. In Polish and English.

2008

Bill Viola: Transfigurations (exh. cat.). Texts by Kelly Sidley and Bill Viola. Seoul: Kukje Gallery. In Korean and English.

Dufour, Sophie-Isabelle. *L'image vidéo d'Ovide à Bill Viola*. Paris: Archibooks. In French.

Garbini, Don Luigi. *Bill Viola: Study for The Path* (exh.cat.). Milan: Artache. In Italian and English.

Perov, Kira, ed. *Bill Viola: Visioni interiori* (exh. cat.). Texts by Maria Gloria Conti Bicocchi, Kira Perov, Salvatore Settis, Valentina Valentini, and Bill Viola. Rome: Palazzo delle Esposizioni; Florence: Giunti Arte Mostre Musei. In Italian.

2009

Perov, Kira, ed. *Bill Viola: Bodies of Light* (exh. cat.). Texts by James Cohan and Bill Viola. New York: James Cohan Gallery.

2010

Bill Viola per Capodimonte (exh. cat.). Texts by Maria Gloria Conti Bicocchi, Angela Tecce, Mariella Utili, Valentina Valentini, and Bill Viola. Naples: Museo di Capodimonte. In Italian.

Fleischer, Alain, ed. *Thierry Kuntzel—Bill Viola: Deux Éternités Proches/Two Close Eternities* (exh. cat.). Texts by Raymond Bellour *et al*. Tourcoing: Le Fresnoy, Studio National des Arts Contemporains. In French and English.

2011

Ferrari, Luigi, ed. *Bill Viola: 10 opere video single channel 1976–1994* (exh. cat.). Curator Franca Mancini. Texts by Bruno Cagli, Paolo Fabbri, David A. Ross, and Bill Viola. Pesaro: Galleria di Franca Mancini; Ravenna: Danilo Montanari Editore. In Italian and English.

Laseca, Roc, ed. *La isla violada: ejercicios de nesolectura en torno a Bill Viola/The Rapted Island: Neso-lecture Excercises on Bill Viola* (exh. cat.). Texts by Ramón Salas *et al*. Santa Cruz de Tenerife, Canary Islands: Gobierno de Canarias/Centros de Arte Contemporáneo. In Spanish and English

Riedmatten, Henri de. *Narcisse en eaux troubles: Francis Bacon, Bill Viola, Jeff Wall.* Rome: L'Erma di Bretschneider. In French. English edition titled *Narcissus in Troubled Waters: Francis Bacon, Bill Viola, Jeff Wall*, 2014.

Utrera, Federico. *Viola on Video.* Madrid: Universidad de Las Palmas de Gran Canaria/Hijos de Muley-Rubio.

2012

Nordal, Bera, ed. *Bill Viola: Water* (exh. cat.). Text by Joanna Persman. Skärhamn: Nordic Watercolor Museum. In Swedish and English.

Bernardini, Anna, ed. *Bill Viola: Reflections* (exh. cat.). Texts by Salvatore Settis, Maria Rosa Sossai, and Bill Viola. Milan: Silvana Editoriale. In Italian and English.

2013

Bill Viola: The Raft (exh. cat.). Texts by Nicola Sodano, Marco Tonelli, Valentina Valentini, and Bill Viola. Mantova: Publi Paolini. In Italian and English.

Perov, Kira, ed. *Bill Viola: Frustrated Actions and Futile Gestures* (exh. cat). Introduction by Mario Codognato; texts by Kira Perov and Bill Viola. London: Blain|Southern.

Bill Viola: Punto de Partida (exh. brochure). Texts by Marcello Dantas and Bill Viola. Buenos Aires: Parque de la Memoria/ Monumento a las Victimas del Terrorismo de Estado. In Spanish.

Fargier, Jean-Paul, director. *Bill Viola, Expérience de l'Infini/ Experience of the Infinite* (documentary). Paris: Réunion des Musées Nationaux—Grand Palais. In French and English. 52 minutes.

2014

Neutres, Jérôme and Kira Perov, eds. *Bill Viola* (exh. cat.). Texts by Jérôme Neutres and Anne-Marie Duguet; interview with the artist and Kira Perov by Jérôme Neutres. Paris: Réunion de Musées Nationaux—Grand Palais. In French. Abridged version without essays, *L'Album de l'Exposition*, in French and English.

Bill Viola: Passions (exh. brochure). Texts by Martin Brauen, Kathleen Bühler, and Bill Viola. Bern: Kunstmuseum Bern. Separate brochures in German and English.

Bernier, Ronald R. *The Unspeakable Art of Bill Viola: A Visual Theology.* Eugene, OR: Wipf and Stock.

Fargier, Jean-Paul. *Bill Viola: Au fil du temps*. Saint Vincent de Mercuze: De l'Incience Éditeur. In French.

2015

Bill Viola (exh. cat.). Texts by Jérôme Neutres and Bill Viola. Seoul: Kukje Gallery. Separate books in Korean and English.

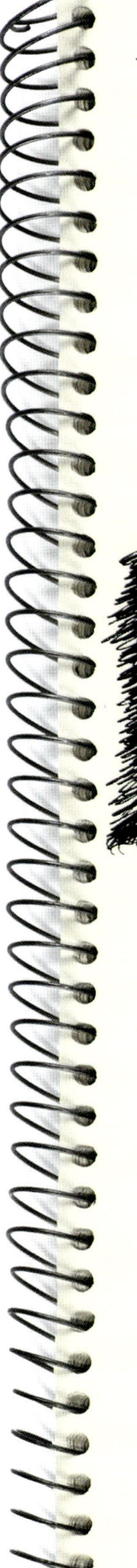

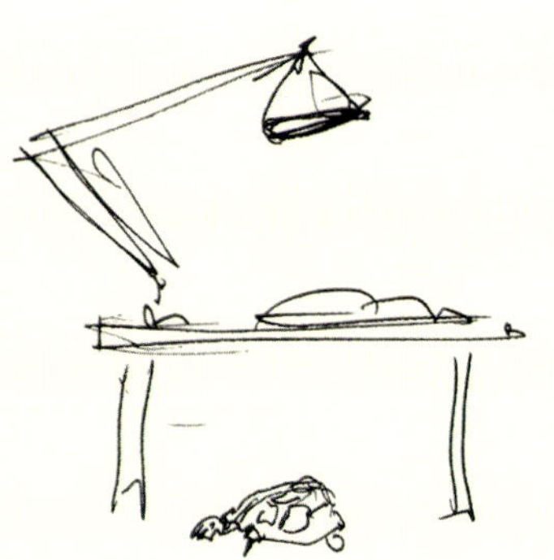

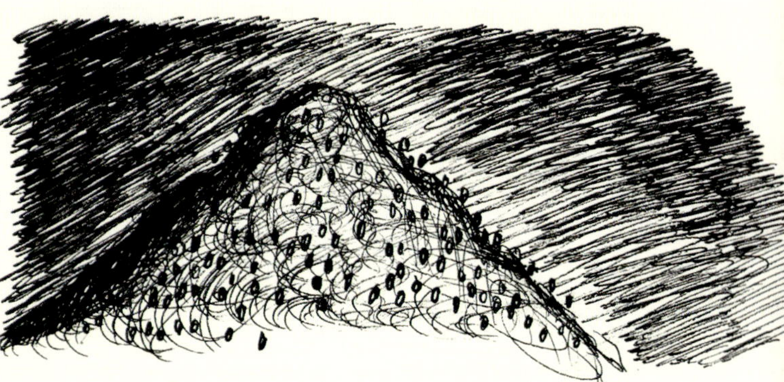

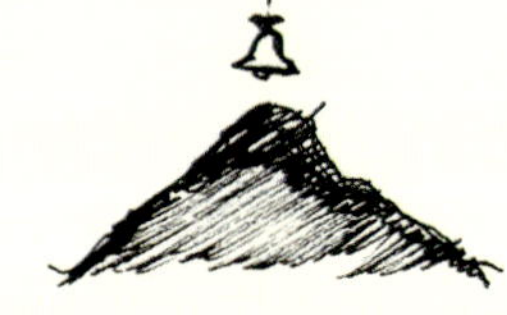

 Sketchbook drawings, April 18, 1988

The NAMING –

The Hall of Names

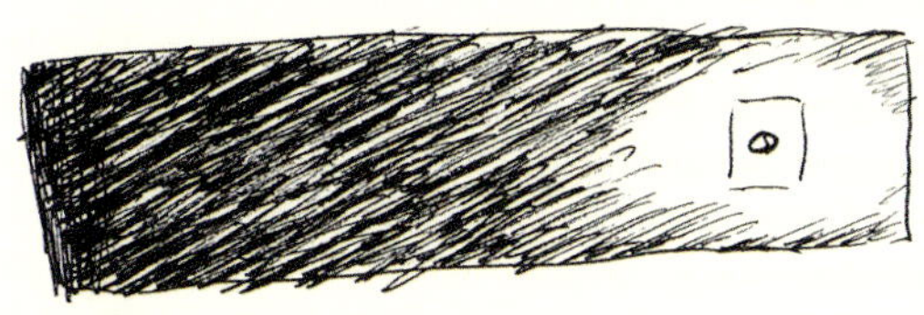

Names called out in the darkness
At the end of the hall, an object still life bathed in a strange blue light

The power of an individual's name and its attachment to their soul.

[work on the object still life more – there must be something else here. The piece needs an anchor, a weight. What are the objects? their significance? Is a vase on a wood table enough?]

Minimum 20 channels of sound (10 stereo auto reverse cassette tape machines)
Speakers (black) mounted in the walls and ceiling. Everything is painted black.
The voices seem to be calling out from everywhere, from all directions.
The observer feels submerged in a cloud of names. The objects at the end of the hall are lit with a deep blue light – They feel distant and detached – the first feeling is like witnessing a vision.
An important point is the identification with the names. The viewer should hear their own name being called out. There can be localized versions, or primary channels which play more often. These should be rotated depending on which country the piece is playing in.
Foreign names should be read in their original tongue.

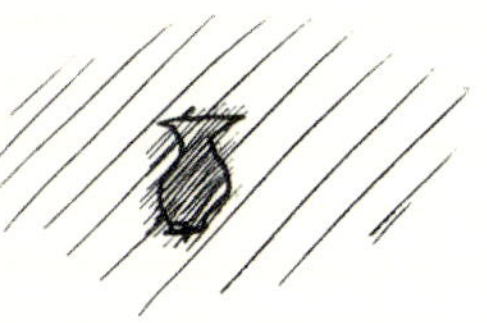

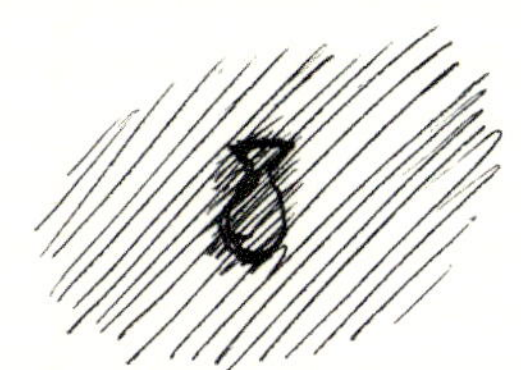

Objects at varying frequencies.
Finely tuned stroboscopic lights illuminate objects and situations. The frequency is subtly varied, or different frequency lamps illuminate the same scene, possibly creating beat frequencies and interference patterns.
or 2 objects side by side with different frequency illuminations.

- Projection vibration –

A film of a varying vibrating object – it starts subtley and builds to wild jittery patterns. The only light in the room is the projection of the object on itself.

with sound – a room of object projections. when the gong is struck they all vibrate wildly and slowly calm down to stability.

The Vortex – dual projection with overlap.

Umbra, Penumbra

Possibly inverted images of the same tape.

The anamorphic image-projection splayed down the walls at oblique angles.

Combined zooms, camera movements.
Other variations with multiple projections, non-overlap, overlap, non-oblique, etc.

The images:
The vanishing point. Perspective, Architecture.
Possibly the beginnings of the geometry piece. Anamorphic projections on specially constructed rooms.

or: possibly the electronic sign image panels – the image as architecture.....

Shoot with 2 cameras with calculated overlap zone.

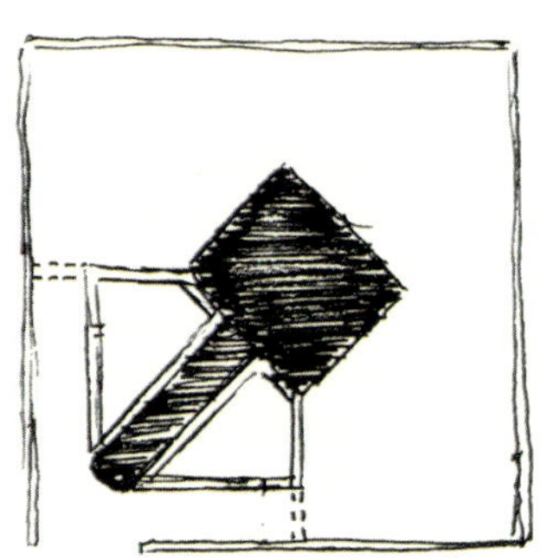

Diagonal structure –
Room of darkness
placed at an angle to
the space with 3
corridors converging on
the entrance space.

March 23

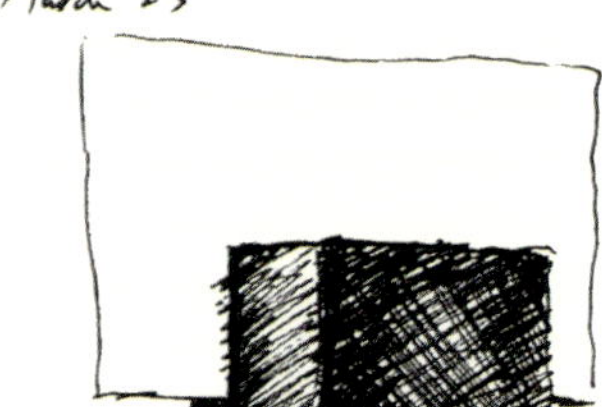

Slice out of Life

Screen embedded
in
Black stone
cubicle

The interior
of the cubicle is
accessible from a
separate entrance

It is cold and black,
but the portion of the
image cut is
visible, to scale, on
the screen inside
It is cut away, isolated
Separated from the outside
world and must answer to
the world of darkness.

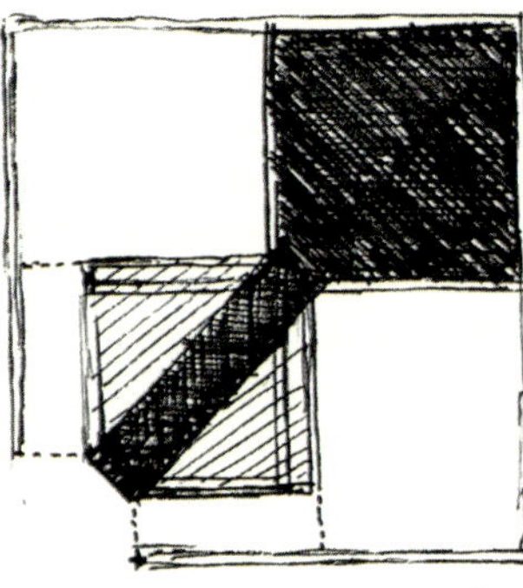

Trimorphic Protennoia

Tripartite construction:
3 corridors converge on
Main entrance.
Space divided up into
3 equal size rooms –
one black, the other two
of light.

Top View

(or it can
slice through
at an angle)

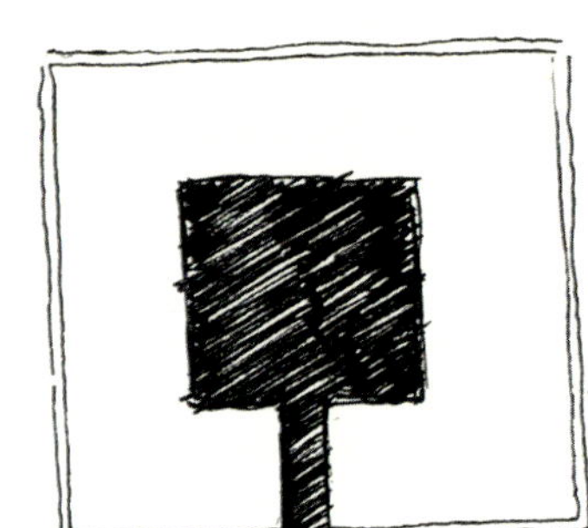

The Dark Room
Surrounded by
Light.

The Activity Without

There is a relationship between "the World of Darkness Surrounded by the World of Light" and the rotating screen piece "Eclipse" or "The Line of Division" with the black backed screen. They are the same idea – one is simultaneous and parallel, the other is sequential and serial.

Persons may only enter the inner dark room.
It is isolated from the main space, which
is painted white and illuminated by the
light of multiple video projectors.
A single channel of the Child's Mind
footage is projected on all walls.
Several projectors are aimed at the
central cubicle.
There are cracks and holes in the
walls of the cubicle. People
can peer out and see the large
images of the child's world looming –
mostly shot out of doors in nature.
Some of the projectors images fall into
the black room and can dimly be seen
on the walls. The sound of the outside
is loud and carries through to the black

More experiments with projections:
Develop small delicate floating images.
Make home made camera obscura
type projections

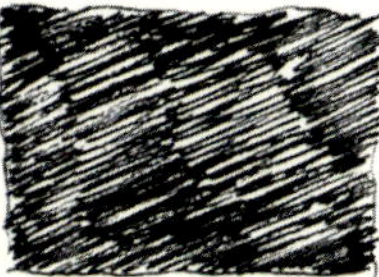

The Dark Wall –

One wall of dim room is black stone (slate?)

It has cracks and holes in it – behind which can be seen fragments of the whole image (the child's world)

Somehow design it so that the whole is present in the parts – ie. when someone goes up to the wall and looks through a crack or chink, they see the whole image in miniature, yet when they step back they can see the ~~whole~~ basic form of the whole image.

Sound penetrates the wall.

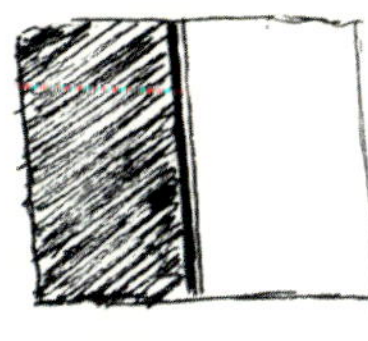

Adjacent room of darkness and room of light.

Seperation is the black wall, with cracks to see into each space. The light side contains the image, filling the space.

Viewers proceed into the dark space first and confront the black wall, then they move into the room of light.

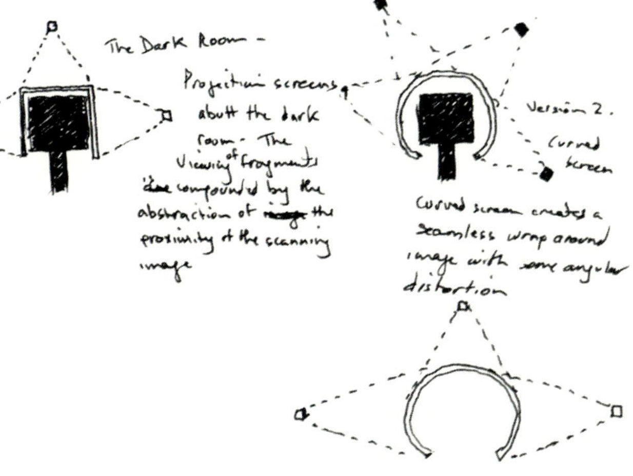

Version 2. Curved screen

Curved screen creates a seamless wrap around image with some angular distortion

Curved screen with 3 projectors. Registration controls can compensate for curved surface.

the connecting element.

Sketchbook drawings, March 23, 1990

List of Works and Illustrations

All works, drawings, and Notebook entries are by Bill Viola unless otherwise noted.
All photographs are by Kira Perov unless otherwise noted.

Dimensions are in feet and inches, followed by meters; height precedes width precedes depth. Where listed, room dimensions are ideal; where they are not listed they are variable. Video works that have no listed running time are looped for continuous playback.

Jacket, front
"Water Martyr," panel 4 from *Martyrs (Earth, Air, Fire, Water)* (2014)
Performer: John Hay
[for full description, see entry below for page 251]

Page 1
Notebook drawing, date on previous page, August 5, 1974 (Notebook, January 1973 – May 5, 1974)

Page 2
The Sleep of Reason (1988), detail
[for full description, see entry below for page 119]

Page 4
The Middens, drawing, January 1990, in Project Book for commission from Museum für Moderne Kunst, Frankfurt (January–April 25, 1990)

Page 7
Kira Perov and Bill Viola with equipment racks for *Slowly Turning Narrative*, Bill Viola Studio, Signal Hill, CA, August 1992

Page 8
Notebook entry, first page, *c.* January 1973 (Notebook, January 1973 – May 5, 1974)

Page 10
Kira Perov and Bill Viola on the set of *Five Angels for the Millennium* (2001), Martin Luther King Jr. Park Pool, Long Beach, CA, September 1999
Photo: Bill Viola Studio

Page 11
Notebook entry and drawing, February 14, 2007 (Notebook, October 25, 2005 – July 10, 2009)

Page 12, top
Bill Viola and David Tudor making pasta in Tudor's home in Stony Point, NY, August 20, 1979

Pages 12, bottom, and 13, bottom
Bill Viola and *Rainforest IV*, Drexel First National Bank Building, organized by Institute of Contemporary Art, Philadelphia, PA, April 1979
Photo page 13, bottom: Shigeo Anzai

Page 13, top
David Tudor, *Rainforest IV*. Bill Viola preparing for its first performance, New Music New Hampshire, Chocorua, NH, June 1973
Photo: Gordon Mumma

Page 14
The Talking Drum (1979)
Music composition (for Herman Heins)
Performer pounds large bass drum in an empty indoor swimming pool to excite and interact with room reverberations, with prerecorded natural sounds electronically gated by and concealed within the live drum beats. Composed for "Dry Pool Soundings," one-week acoustic research, and concert with three other composers, organized by Media/Study Buffalo, NY, May 1979; photo of July 1982 performance

Page 15, left
Drawing for sound installation *Eclipse*, *c.* 1973

Page 15, right
Notebook drawing for videotape *Eclipse*, November 1974 (Florence Notebook, November 1974 – July 1975)

Page 16
Drawing for sound installation *Hallway Nodes* (1973), drawing, 1972

Page 17
Drawing for sound installation *The Mysterious Virtue* (1974), drawing, 1973

Page 18
The Mysterious Virtue (1974)
Sound installation [original title: *River*]
Water-worn rocks, straw mat, heat lamp/spotlight, sine wave oscillator tuned to approximately 55hz
Photo: Bill Viola

Page 19, top
Main Sanctuary and West Treasure House, Inner Shrine (Naiku), at the Ise Shrine, Japan, photographed by Yoshio Watanabe in 1953
Collection Centre Canadien d'Architecture/Canadian Centre for Architecture, Montréal.

Page 19, bottom
Front and side view drawings of the Honden at the Ise Shrine, Japan
Published in *History of Japanese Architecture*, Katsukichi Hattori (1933)

Page 20
Proposal for *The Greeting* (1995) in L'église Saint-Eustache for Festival d'Automne à Paris, September 21, 2000

Page 21
Reasons for Knocking at an Empty House (1982)
Video/sound installation
Color video image on 25-in. monitor; wooden chair with amplified sound in attached stereo headphones; second amplified stereo sound source in room on two loudspeakers
Room dimensions: 12 × 18 × 25 ft (3.7 × 5.5 × 7.6 m)
(La Chartreuse, Villeneuve-lez-Avignon, France, July 1986)

Page 22
Bill Viola creating *Information*, Synapse, Syracuse University, Syracuse, NY, 1973
Photo: Phillip S. Block

Pages 24–5
Tape I (1972)
Videotape, black and white, mono sound; 6:50 minutes
Produced at Synapse, Syracuse University, Syracuse, NY

Pages 26–7
Migration (1976)
For Jack Nelson
Videotape, color, mono sound; 7:00 minutes
Produced at Synapse, Syracuse University, Syracuse, NY

Page 28
Jack Nelson and Bill Viola, Syracuse, NY, *c.* 1974

Page 29
Carol Huggler and Bill Viola recording Carl Geiger's *Multi-origination Dance Piece*, Syracuse University, Syracuse, New York, *c.* 1972; inflatable designed by Robert Charron
Photo: Robert Charron

Page 30, left
Cycles (1973)
Videotape, black and white, mono sound; 7:04 minutes
Produced at Synapse, Syracuse University, Syracuse, NY

Page 30, right
Level (1973)
Videotape, black and white, mono sound; 8:28 minutes
Produced at Synapse, Syracuse University, Syracuse, NY

Page 31, top
Russell Connor interviewing Bill Viola, Marge Monroe, and the Rainbow Video group, *First Half-Inch Video Festival Ever*, WGBH TV, Boston, MA, 1972

Page 31, bottom
Bill Viola and David Ross, working on the Whitney exhibition "Bill Viola: A 25-Year Survey," Long Beach, CA, March 1997

Page 32, top
Videofreex, *The Spaghetti City Video Manual* (1973)

Page 32, bottom
A Report on the Television Laboratory at WNET/Thirteen 1972–1978

Page 33, left
Peter Campus, *Shadow Projection* (1974)
Closed-circuit video installation
Courtesy of the Artist and Cristin Tierney Gallery, New York, NY

Page 33, right
Peter Campus, *Double Vision: Convergence* (1971)
Video, black and white, sound; 14:45 minutes
Courtesy of the Artist and Cristin Tierney Gallery, New York, NY

Page 34
Drawing for video installation *Localization*, 1973

Page 35
Localization (1973)
Video/sound installation
Live video and audio interchange between two indoor locations through two-way, black-and-white cable television system; two microphones, two speakers
(Watson Hall, Syracuse University, Syracuse, NY)
Photos: Bill Viola

Page 36
Drawing for video installation *Bank Image Bank* (1974), 1973

Page 37, top
Bill Viola installing *Bank Image Bank*, Lincoln First Bank, Rochester, NY, January 1974
Photo: Phillip S. Block

Page 37, bottom
Bank Image Bank (1974)
Video installation, site-specific work
Two banks of six monitors with eight black-and-white cameras in closed-circuit system with feedback; two escalators
(Lincoln First Bank, Rochester, NY, January 1974)
Photo: Phillip S. Block

Page 38, top
Olfaction (1976)
Video/sound installation
Black-and-white video projection of live camera mixed with previously recorded action; high-back easy chair with concealed speakers; brass bell
(The Art Galleries, California State University, Long Beach, CA, September 1976)
Photo: Peter Lu

Page 38, bottom
General system diagram for *Olfaction* (1976), drawing, 1974

Page 39
Rain (1975)
Video/sound installation in three parts
Amplified drop of water falling from ceiling onto metal tray reflecting optical wave patterns onto wall; black-and-white video projection of live camera mixed with previously recorded action; water-worn rocks with heterodyning sine tone and heat lamp
(installation views of exhibition "Rain—Three Interlocking Systems," Everson Museum of Art, Syracuse, NY, December 1975)
Photos: Robert Lorenz

Page 40, top
Palm Trees on the Moon (1977–8)
Videotape, color, mono sound; 26:06 minutes
Produced in association with International Television Workshop, New York, NY

Page 40, center
Memories of Ancestral Power (The Moro Movement in the Solomon Islands) (1977–8)
Videotape, color, mono sound; 35:19 minutes
Produced in association with International Television Workshop, New York, NY

Page 40, bottom
Bob Bielecki and Bill Viola in Java, Indonesia, December 1977
Photo: Alex Dea

Page 41
Polaroid documentation by Bill Viola of his performance *Tree Noise*, Syracuse, NY, 1973
Photos: Bill Viola

Page 43, top
Bill Viola, Muriel Olesen, and Gerald Minkoff in production, art/tapes/22, Florence, Italy, April 1975
Photo: Gianni Melotti

Page 43, bottom
Video artists and curators, EXPRMNTL, the Knokke Experimental Film Festival, Belgium, December 26, 1974
Left to right, front row: Wendy Clarke, Jean-Pierre Boyer; second row: Taka Imura, Woody Vasulka, Nam June Paik, Gerald O'Grady; third row: Bill Viola, Ed Emshwiller, Kit Galloway, Steina; back row: Walter Wright

Pages 44, 47–9
Information (1973)
Videotape, color, mono sound; 29:35 minutes
Produced at Synapse, Syracuse University, Syracuse, NY

Page 46
Nam June Paik, *Magnet TV* (1965)
Modified black-and-white television set and magnet
Overall 38 ¾ × 19 ¼ × 24 ½ in. (98.4 × 48.9 × 62.2 cm)
Whitney Museum of American Art, New York; purchase, with funds from Dieter Rosenkranz 86.60a-b. Reproduced by permission of the Estate of Nam June Paik

Page 50
Il Vapore (1975)
Video/sound Installation
Black-and-white videotape playback mixed with live camera on monitor in alcove; one channel of amplified sound; woven mat on platform; large metal pot of eucalyptus leaves boiling in water; live flame heating system
Room dimensions: 12 × 16 × 20 ft (3.7 × 4.9 × 6.1 m)
(Zona, Florence, June 1975)
Photo: Gianni Melotti

Page 51, top
Diagram for video installation *Walking into the Wall*, 1973

Page 51, bottom
Bruce Nauman, *Live-Taped Video Corridor* (1970)
Wallboard, video camera, two video monitors, videotape player, and videotape
Dimensions variable, approximately: (ceiling height) × 384 × 20 in. ([ceiling height] × 975.4 × 50.8 cm)

Page 52
Olfaction (1974)
Videotape, color, mono sound; 3:00 minutes
Produced in association with Synapse, Syracuse University, Syracuse, NY

Page 53
He Weeps for You, first description, Notebook (July 1975 – March 1977), October 7, 1975

Page 54
He Weeps for You, drawing, second description, January 1976

Page 55, top
He Weeps for You, first version, Watson Hall, Syracuse University, Syracuse, NY, May 1976
Photo: Bill Viola

Pages 55, bottom, and 56–7
He Weeps for You (1976)
Video/sound installation
Water drop from copper pipe; live color camera with macro lens; amplified drum; video projection in dark room
Projected image size: 7 ft 6 in. × 10 ft 2 in. (2.3 × 3.1 m)
Room dimensions: 12 × 20 × 26 ft (3.7 × 6.1 × 7.9 m)
(Museum of Modern Art, New York, NY, 1979)
Photo page 55, bottom: Shigeo Anzai

Page 59
Eternal Life, drawing, May 10, 2009, gifted to Gene Zazzaro

Pages 60–1
The Tree of Knowledge (1997), details
Interactive computer/video installation
33-ft-long (10 m) passageway opens out to large screen with color, computer-generated video projection; movement-sensing laser scanner
Projected image size: 10 ft 6 in. × 7 ft 10 in. (3.2 × 2.4 m)
Room dimensions: 10 ft 6 in. × 7 ft 10 in. × 52 ft 6 in. (3.2 × 2.4 × 16 m)
Tree animation sequence: Bernd Lintermann; tracking software: André Bernhard, ZKM, Karlsruhe, Germany

Pages 62–3
The Tree of Life (1977)
Sculpture event
High-powered searchlight illuminates a single large tree from afternoon to night; 5-hour, one-night event, Fort Edward, NY
Photos: Bob Bielecki and Greg Shefrin

Page 64
The Darker Side of Dawn (2005)
Color video projection on wall in dark room
Projected image size: 10 ft 8 in. × 19 ft (3.25 × 5.8 m)
60:00 minutes

Page 67
A Non-Dairy Creamer (1975)
Part of collection *Red Tape (Collected Works)* (1975)
Videotape, color, mono sound; 5:19 minutes
Produced in association with ZBS Media Art Center and Synapse, Syracuse University, Syracuse, NY

Page 68
In production for *The Semi-Circular Canals*, ZBS Media, Fort Edward, NY, September 1975
Photo: Bob Bielecki

Page 69
The Semi-Circular Canals (1975)
Part of collection *Red Tape (Collected Works)* (1975)
Videotape, color, mono sound; 8:51 minutes
Produced at ZBS Media Art Center and Synapse, Syracuse University, Syracuse, NY

Page 70
Bill Viola and Bob Bielecki, sound studio, ZBS Media, Fort Edward, NY, July 1982

Page 71
A Million Other Things (2) (1975)
Part of collection *Red Tape (Collected Works)* (1975)
Videotape, color, mono sound; 4:35 minutes
Produced at ZBS Media, Fort Edward, NY, and Inter-Media Art Center, Bayville, NY

Page 72
Return (1975)
Part of collection *Red Tape (Collected Works)* (1975)
Videotape, color, mono sound; 7:43 minutes
Produced at ZBS Media, Fort Edward, NY, and Inter-Media Art Center, Bayville, NY

Pages 74–5
The Reflecting Pool—Collected Work 1977–80
Videotape collection, color, stereo sound; 62 minutes total
Produced at WNET/Thirteen Television Laboratory, New York, and WXXI-TV Workshop, Rochester, NY

Consisting of the following five works:
The Reflecting Pool (1977–9) [page 74]
Videotape, color, mono sound; 7 minutes

[page 75, top to bottom]
Moonblood (1979–80) [corrected date]
For Kira
Videotape, color, stereo sound; 12:48 minutes
Silent Life (1979)
Videotape, color, stereo sound; 13:14 minutes
Ancient of Days (1979–81)
Videotape, color, stereo sound; 12:21 minutes
Vegetable Memory (1978–80)
Videotape, color, mono sound; 15:13 minutes

Pages 76–7
The Space Between the Teeth (1976)
Part of collection *Four Songs* (1976)
Videotape, color, mono sound; 9:10 minutes
Produced in association with WNET/Thirteen Television Laboratory, New York; portions produced at Synapse, Syracuse University, Syracuse, NY

Page 78
The Morning After the Night of Power (1977)
Part of collection *Memory Surfaces and Mental Prayers* (1977)
Videotape, color, mono sound; 10:44 minutes
Produced in association with WNET/Thirteen Television Laboratory, New York
Recorded at ZBS Media, Fort Edward, NY

Page 79
I Do Not Know What It Is I Am Like (1986)
Videotape, color, stereo sound; 89:00 minutes
Produced in association with the Contemporary Art Television Fund, Boston, MA, and ZDF, Mainz, Germany

Pages 80–1
Sweet Light (1977)
Part of collection *Memory Surfaces and Mental Prayers* (1977)
Videotape, color, mono sound; 9:08 minutes
Produced in association with WNET/Thirteen Television Laboratory, New York
Recorded at ZBS Media, Fort Edward, NY

Pages 82–3
On location for *Chott el-Djerid (A Portrait in Light and Heat)*, Chott el-Djerid salt lake, Tunisia, May 1979

Pages 84–7
Chott el-Djerid (A Portrait in Light and Heat) (1979)
Videotape, color, mono sound; 28:00 minutes
Produced at WNET/Thirteen Television Laboratory, New York

Pages 89, 91
Hatsu-Yume (First Dream) (1981)
For Daien Tanaka
Videotape, color, stereo sound; 56:00 minutes
Produced at Sony Corporation, Atsugi Plant, Japan, in association with WNET/Thirteen Television Laboratory, New York

Page 90
Bill Viola and sacred tree, on location for *Hatsu-Yume (First Dream)*, Tohoku, Honshu, Japan, April 1981

Page 92
Daien Tanaka at Abe family temple, Isu Peninsula, Japan, November 1980

Page 93
Kira Perov and Bill Viola on location for *Hatsu-Yume (First Dream)*, Tohoku, Honshu, Japan, April 1981

Page 94
Bill Viola, Mt Rainier coffee shop, WA, August 1979

Page 95
Proposal for *Room for St. John of the Cross*, for exhibition "Video as Attitude," Santa Fe, NM, May 1983

Pages 96–7, 99
Room for St. John of the Cross (1983)
Video/sound installation
In a large dark room, and black cubicle with window, the illuminated interior containing peat moss on the floor, a wooden table, glass with water, metal pitcher with water, color video image on 3.7-in. monitor, one-channel mono sound; black-and-white video projection on wall screen; amplified stereo sound
Projected image size: 8 ft 7 in. × 12 ft 8 in. (2.6 × 3.7 m)
Room dimensions: 14 × 24 × 30 ft (4.3 × 7.3 × 9.1 m)
Photo page 97: SQUIDDS & NUNNS and Kira Perov

Page 98
On location for *Room for St. John of the Cross*, recording Sierra Nevada mountains near Lone Pine, Owens Valley, CA, April 1983

Page 100
Proposal for installation *The Theater of Memory* to the Whitney Museum of American Art, New York, NY, 1985

Pages 101–5
The Theater of Memory (1985)
Video/sound installation
Color video projection on large wall screen; 35-ft (10.7-m) uprooted dead tree with fifty electric lanterns in dark room; wind chime; amplified stereo sound
Projected image size: 10 ft 6 in. × 14 ft (3.2 × 4.3 m)
Room dimensions: 14 × 23 × 31 ft (4.3 × 7 × 9.45 m)

Photo pages 102–3: SQUIDDS & NUNNS and Kira Perov

Page 106
Instant Breakfast (1974)
Videotape, color, mono sound; 5:05 minutes
Produced in association with Synapse, Syracuse University, Syracuse, NY

Pages 107, 108, right, 109–11
I Do Not Know What It Is I Am Like (1986)
Videotape, color, stereo sound; 89:00 minutes
Produced in association with the Contemporary Art Television Fund, Boston, MA, and ZDF, Mainz, Germany

Page 108, left
"Grazing as Pure Meditation," note, Animals Sketchbook (1984–6), 1986

Pages 112 and 113, bottom
On location for *Passage*, private home, Houston, TX, February 21, 1987

Page 113, top
Floor plan for *Passage*, 1987

Pages 114–17
Passage (1987)
Video/sound installation
Slow-motion color videotape playback, projection on large, wall-size rear screen, built into small room with a 21-ft (6.4-m) entrance corridor; amplified stereo sound
Projected image size: 11 ft 6 in. × 15 ft (3.51 × 4.6 m)
Room dimensions: 12 × 16 × 27 ft (3.7 × 4.9 × 8.2 m)
Approximately 7 hours 30 minutes

Page 118
Francisco de Goya y Lucientes, *The Sleep of Reason Produces Monsters*, plate 43 of "The Caprices (Los Caprichos)" (1799)
Etching, aquatint, drypoint, and burin
8 7/8 × 5 7/8 in. (21.5 × 15 cm)
Museo Nacional del Prado, Madrid

Pages 119–23
The Sleep of Reason (1988)
Video/sound installation
Color video images projected on three walls of a carpeted room; wooden chest with black-and-white video image on small monitor, vase with white artificial roses, table lamp with black shade, digital clock; monitor, room lights, and projections controlled by random timer; amplified stereo sound and one channel of audio from monitor
Projected image size: facing wall: 11 ft 4 in. × 15 ft 2 in. (3.5 × 4.62 m); side walls: 9 ft 9 in. × 13 ft (2.97 × 3.96 m)
Room dimensions: 14 × 27 × 31 ft (4.3 × 8.2 × 9.5 m)

Page 124
Proposal for *The Stopping Mind* (1991), for Museum für Moderne Kunst, Frankfurt, 1990

Page 127
Text for *The Stopping Mind*, transcribed from 1991 audio recording

Pages 128–30
The Stopping Mind (1991)
Video/sound installation
Four channels of color video projection, on four screens forming an open square suspended from ceiling of large dark room; computer-programmed random duration and freeze of image; five channels of amplified mono sound, using four loudspeakers, and one small focused speaker mounted in ceiling
Projected image size: 10 ft 6 in. × 14 ft (3.2 × 4.3 m), each screen
Room dimensions: 15 × 33 × 33 ft (4.6 × 10 × 10 m)

Pages 132–3
Bill Viola, Zabriskie Point, Death Valley, CA, May 1982

Page 134
Bill Viola and Kira Perov on five-month shooting trip for *The Passing* (1991), Valley of the Gods, UT, June 1987

Pages 135–7
The Passing (1991)
In memory of Wynne Lee Viola
Videotape, black and white, mono sound; 54:00 minutes
Produced in association with "Das kleine Fernsehspiel" (ZDF), Mainz, Germany

Pages 138–9
Nantes Triptych (1992)
Video/sound installation
Color video triptych; central panel front-projected onto 10 ft 6 in. × 13-ft (3.2 × 4-m) translucent scrim; two side panels rear-projected onto 10 ft 6 in. × 7 ft 7-in. (3.2 × 2.3-m) screens; mounted into wall in large, dark room; amplified stereo sound; two channels of amplified mono sound
Room dimensions: 18 × 40 × 21 ft (5.5 × 12.2 × 6.4 m)
29:46 minutes
Photo: Musée des Beaux-Arts de Nantes

Pages 140–1
The Sleepers (1992)
Video installation
Seven channels of black-and-white video images on seven small monitors, each submerged on the bottom of a 55-gallon white metal barrel filled with water; large dark room
Room dimensions: 12 × 20 × 25 ft (3.7 × 6.1 × 7.6 m)
Photo: Louis Lussier

Pages 142–5
Dot matrix printout of thirteen-page text for *Slowly Turning Narrative*, 1992 (condensed)

Page 145, right
Bill Viola with screen for *Slowly Turning Narrative*, Bill Viola Studio, Signal Hill, CA, August 1992

Page 146
The Rotating Screen: Image, Shadow, Mask, drawing, Brockton Triptych Project Book, *c.* July 1988

Pages 147–9
Slowly Turning Narrative (1992)
Video/sound installation
Central rotating screen, mirrored on one side; two channels of video projections at opposite ends of space, one color, one black and white, in large, dark room; amplified mono sound, one speaker; amplified mono sound, five speakers
Projected image size: 9 ft × 12 ft × 2 in. (2.75 × 3.7 × 0.05 m)
Room dimensions: 14 × 20 × 41 ft (4.3 × 6.1 × 12.5 m)
Photos pages 147, bottom, and 148: Gary McKinnis

Pages 150–1
Stations (1994), detail
Video/sound installation
Five channels of color video projections on five cloth screens, suspended from the ceiling of a large, darkened gallery; five slabs of black granite on floor in front of each screen; five channels of amplified mono sound
Scrim size: 9 ft 3 in. × 5 ft 10 in. (2.81 × 1.8 m) each
Room dimensions: 14 ft × 46 ft 6 in. × 45 ft 4 in. (4.3 × 14.2 × 13.8 m)
Performers: Cheri Gaulke, Claire Johnston, Gary Murphy, Griffith Stecyk, Jirayr Zorthian
Photo: Charles Duprat

Pages 152–5
Pneuma (1994/2009)
Video/sound installation
Three channels of black-and-white High-Definition video projected into three corners of a darkened, square space; three channels of amplified mono sound
Room dimensions: 14 × 20 × 20 ft (4.3 × 6.1 × 6.1 m)
Participants: Kira Perov, Andrei Viola, Bill Viola, Blake Viola

Page 157
Drawing for *The Veiling*, 1995

Pages 158–61
The Veiling (1995)
Two channels of color video projections from opposite sides of a large dark gallery through nine large scrims suspended from ceiling; two channels of amplified mono sound, four speakers
Scrim size: 8 ft 2 in. × 10 ft 10 in. (2.4 × 3.3 m) each
Room dimensions: 11 ft 6 in. × 24 ft 4 in. × 37 ft 10 in. (3.5 × 7.4 × 11.5 m)
30:00 minutes
Performers: Lora Stone, Gary Murphy
Photos pages 158–9: Roman Mensing

Page 162
Bill Viola with performers Angela Black, Suzanne Peters, and Bonnie Snyder on the set of *The Greeting*, Warner Drive Warehouse, Culver City, CA, April 1995

Page 164, top
Pontormo, *Visitation* (*c.* 1529)
Oil on panel
79 ½ × 61 ⅜ in. (202 × 156 cm)
Carmignano, Pieve di San Michele Arcangelo
Photo by Antonio Quattrone
Courtesy Palazzo Strozzi

Page 164, bottom
Bill Viola with Pontormo's *Visitation*, restoration studio of Daniele Rossi, Florence, Italy, December 15, 2013

Page 165
Drawing for stage design of *The Greeting* (view from above), 1995

Pages 166–7
On the set of *The Greeting*, Warner Drive Warehouse, Culver City, CA, April 1995

Pages 168–9
The Greeting (1995)
Video/sound installation (production stills)
Color video projection on large vertical screen mounted on wall in darkened space; amplified stereo sound
Projected image size: 9 ft 3 in. × 7 ft 11 in. (2.8 × 2.4 m)
Room dimensions: 14 × 22 × 25 ft (4.3 × 6.7 × 7.6 m)
10:22 minutes
Performers: Angela Black, Suzanne Peters, Bonnie Snyder

Page 170
On the set of *The Messenger*, performer Chad Walker, Belmont Olympic Pool, Long Beach, CA, August 1996

Pages 171–5
The Messenger (1996)
Video/sound installation
Color video projection on large vertical screen mounted on wall in darkened space; amplified stereo sound
Projected image size: 14 × 10 ft (4.3 × 3 m)
Room dimensions: 20 × 26 × 30 ft (6.1 × 7.9 × 9.1 m)
Performer: Chad Walker
(installation view, Durham Cathedral, Durham, UK; and details)
Photo page 171: Edward Woodman

Page 177
Drawing of "Man on Fire" for *The Crossing*, for Festival d'Automne à Paris, January 1996

Pages 178–9
The Crossing (1996)
Video/sound installation
Two channels of color video projections from opposite sides of a large dark gallery onto two large back-to-back screens suspended from ceiling and mounted to floor; four channels of amplified stereo sound, four speakers
Projected image size: 13 ft 2 in. × 9 ft 5 in. (4.01 × 2.86 m)
Room dimensions: 16 ft 5 in. × 26 ft × 60 ft (5 × 7.9 × 18.3 m)
10:57 minutes
Performer: Phil Esposito

Page 180
Hieronymus Bosch, *Christ Mocked (The Crowning with Thorns)* (*c.* 1490–1500)
Oil on oak
29 ¾ × 23 ¼ in. (73.5 × 59.1 cm)
The National Gallery, London

Pages 181–3
The Quintet of the Astonished (2000) (production stills)
Color video rear projection on screen mounted on wall in dark room
Projected image size: 55 × 95 in. (140 × 240 cm)
15:20 minutes
Performers: John Malpede, Weba Garretson, Tom Fitzpatrick, John Fleck, Dan Gerrity

Page 184, top
On the set of *Catherine's Room*, performer Weba Garretson, Bill Viola Studio, Signal Hill, CA, March 2001

Pages 184–5
Andrea di Bartolo Cini, Predella with *St. Catherine of Siena Praying*, from *St. Catherine of Siena and Blessed Dominican Women* (1393–4)
Tempera on panel
24 × 40 ½ in. (61 × 103 cm)
Gallerie dell'Accademia, Venice, Italy
Cameraphoto/Scala, Florence

Page 185, top
Drawing for *Catherine's Room*, 2001

Pages 186–7
Catherine's Room (2001)
Color video polyptych on five LCD flat panels mounted on wall
15 × 97 × 2 ¼ in. (38 × 246 × 5.7 cm)
18:39 minutes
Performer: Weba Garretson

Page 188
Drawing for *Five Angels for the Millennium* (2001), *c.* 1999

Page 189
Bill Viola and director of photography Harry Dawson on the set of *Five Angels for the Millennium* (2001), Martin Luther King Jr. Park Pool, Long Beach, CA, September 1999

Pages 190–3
Five Angels for the Millennium (2001)
Video/sound installation
i. "Departing Angel" [p. 190, third from top]
ii. "Birth Angel" [p. 192]
iii. "Fire Angel" [p. 190, second from top]
iv. "Ascending Angel" [p. 190, top]
v. "Creation Angel" [p. 190, bottom]
Five channels of color video projection on walls in large, dark room; stereo sound for each projection
Projected image size: 7 ft 10 in. × 10 ft 6 in. (2.4 × 3.2 m) each
Room dimensions: 12 × 50 × 60 ft (3.7 × 15.25 × 18.3 m)
Performers: Josh Coxx (panels i–iv), Andrew Tritz (panel v)
Photos pages 191, 193: Mike Bruce, courtesy Anthony d'Offay

Pages 194, 197, 200–1, 203, 209–11
Going Forth By Day (2002)
Video/sound installation
A projected image cycle in five parts
Five High-Definition color video channels projected onto walls in dark room; two channels of stereo sound for four panels; one panel with four channels of spatial quadraphonic sound
Room dimensions: 17 × 30 × 64 ft (5.2 × 9.15 × 19.5 m)
36:00 minutes

"Fire Birth" (panel 1) [p. 197]
Projected image size: 12 × 16 ft (3.7 × 4.88 m)

"The Path" (panel 2) [pp. 200–1]
Projected image size: 7 ft 6 in. × 36 ft (2.3 × 11 m)

"The Deluge" (panel 3) [p. 203]
Projected image size: 12 × 16 ft (3.7 × 4.88 m)

"The Voyage" (panel 4) [p. 194]
Projected image size: 7 ft 6 in. × 13 ft 4 in. (2.3 × 4 m)
Performers: John Fleck, Lois Stark, Ernie Charles, Butch Hammett, Willie Jackson, Valerie Spencer, Richard Stoble, Bill Viola

"First Light" (panel 5) [p. 209]
Projected image size: 7 ft 6 in. × 10 ft (2.3 × 3 m)
Performers: Melina Bielefelt, Hector Contreras, Weba Garretson, Dan Gerrity, John Hay, Michael Eric Strickland

Installation views [pp. 210–11]
Photos: Mathias Schormann

Page 196
Floor plan of *Going Forth By Day*, for Deutsche Guggenheim Berlin, February 2002

Page 198
On location for "The Path" from *Going Forth By Day* (2002), Angeles National Forest, CA, October 2001

Page 199, top
Drawing indicating three-camera alignment for "The Path," July 2001

Page 199, bottom
Bill Viola on location counting pixels to verify alignment of three cameras for "The Path," October 2001

Page 202, top, left and right
On the set of "The Deluge" from *Going Forth By Day* (2002), parking lot, Long Beach Airport, CA, November 2001
Photos: Darin Moran

Page 202, bottom
Luca Signorelli, *The Damned Cast into Hell* (1499–1504), detail
Fresco
c. 23 ft (7 m) wide
San Brizio Chapel, Orvieto Cathedral, Orvieto, Italy
Scala, Florence/courtesy Opera del Duomo of Orvieto

Page 204, top left
On location for "The Voyage" from *Going Forth By Day* (2002), Lake Piru, CA, December 2001

Page 204, top right
On the set of "The Voyage" from *Going Forth By Day* (2002), Raleigh Studios, Los Angeles, CA, December 2001

Page 204, bottom
Giotto, *Scenes from the Life of Joachim: Annunciation to St. Anne*, 1304–6
Fresco
78 ¾ × 72 ⅞ in. (200 × 185 cm)
Cappella Scrovegni (Arena Chapel), Padua, Italy
Scala, Florence

Page 205
Timeline for 30-minute sunrise for "First Light" from *Going Forth By Day* (2002), July 2001 [final sunrise timeline was 36 minutes]

Page 206
On the set of "First Light" from *Going Forth By Day* (2002), performer John Hay, Santa Clarita Studios, CA, October 2001

Pages 213–15
Tristan und Isolde, premiere performance, Opéra National de Paris, April 12, 2005
Conductor: Esa-Pekka Salonen; director: Peter Sellars; artist: Bill Viola
The video of *Tristan und Isolde* was produced by Bill Viola Studio in collaboration with the National Opera, Paris, the Los Angeles Philharmonic Association, the Lincoln Center for the Performing Arts, the James Cohan Gallery, New York, and Haunch of Venison London.
Photos: Ruth Walz

Page 216
On the set of *Tristan's Ascension (The Sound of a Mountain Under a Waterfall)* (2005), Bill Viola instructing stunt coordinator Tom Ficke and performer John Hay, Downey Studios, CA, July 2004

Page 217
On the set of *Fire Woman* (2005), Tom Ficke testing the heat of the gas flames, Downey Studios, CA, July 2004

Pages 218–19
Tristan's Ascension (The Sound of a Mountain Under a Waterfall) (2005)
Color High-Definition video projection; four channels of sound with subwoofer (4.1)
Projected image size: 19 ft × 10 ft 8 in. (5.8 × 3.25 m)
10:16 minutes
Performer: John Hay

Pages 220–1
Fire Woman (2005)
Color High-Definition video projection; four channels of sound with subwoofer (4.1)
Projected image size: 19 ft × 10 ft 8 in. (5.8 × 3.25 m)
11:12 minutes
Performer: Robin Bonaccorsi

Page 222, top and center
On the set of *Ocean Without a Shore*, Bill Viola Studio, Signal Hill, CA, March 2007
Performers: Melina Bielefelt, Page Leong
Photos: Matt Sersion

Page 222, bottom
The Innocents (2007)
From the "Transfigurations" series
Color High-Definition video diptych on plasma displays mounted on wall
36 × 44 × 4 in. (91.4 × 111.8 × 10.2 cm)
6:49 minutes
Performers: Anika Ballent, Andrei Viola

Page 223
Drawings for *Ocean Without a Shore*, Sketchpad, February 17, 2007

Page 224
Page of taped photographs and notes for *Ocean Without a Shore*, San Gallo Project Book, February 9, 2007

Page 225
Poem by Birago Diop transcribed by Bill Viola, an inspiration for *Ocean Without a Shore*, 2007

Pages 226–9
Ocean Without a Shore (2007)
High-Definition color video triptych, two 65-in. plasma screens, one 103-in. screen mounted vertically, six loudspeakers (three pairs, stereo sound)
Room dimensions: 14 ft 9 in. × 21 ft 4 in. × 34 ft 5 in. (4.5 × 6.5 × 10.5 m)
Performers: Luis Accinelli, Helena Ballent, Melina Bielefelt, Eugenia Care, Carlos Cervantes, Liisa Cohen, Addie Daddio, Jay Donahue, Howard Ferguson, Weba Garretson, Tamara Gorski, Darrow Igus, Page Leong, Richard Neil, Oguri, Larry Omaha, Kira Perov, Jean Rhodes, Chuck Roseberry, Lenny Steinburg, Julia Vera, Bill Viola, Blake Viola, Ellis Williams
(Church of San Gallo, Venice, Italy; pages 228–9, performer Darrow Igus)
Photos pages 226–7: Thierry Bal

Page 231
Drawing for proposal of *Crossroads* (2014) to Qatar Museums Authority for Hamad International Airport, Doha, February 23, 2012

Pages 232–3
Crossroads (2014)
Video installation
405 LED screens (arrayed 9 × 45); 22 ¾ × 22 ¾ × 5 in. (58 × 58 × 13 cm) each; total screen size: 16 ft 6 in. × 82 ft 8 in. (5.04 × 25.2 m)
Performers: Tina Ansah, Tomas Arceo, Barbara Bennet, Rick Cosnett, Kwesi Dei-Awuku, Sharon Ferguson, Dan Gerrity, John Hay, Lance Ho, Darrow Igus, Nandinee Iyengar, Chaim Jeraffi, Jacqueline Kim, Virginia Montero, Elizabeth Olin, Jy Prishkulnik, Andrei Viola, Michael Yama, Reha Zamani
Commissioned by Qatar Museums Authority for Hamad International Airport, Doha

Page 234
On location for *Inner Passage* (2013), Bill Viola directing Blake Viola, El Mirage Dry Lake, Mojave Desert, San Bernardino County, CA, July 2012

Pages 235–7
Inner Passage (2013)
Color High-Definition video on plasma display mounted vertically on wall; stereo sound
61 ¼ × 36 ⅜ × 5 in. (155.5 × 92.5 × 12.7 cm)
17:12 minutes
Performer: Blake Viola
(Homage to Richard Long)

Page 238
On the set of *The Dreamers* (2013), performer Christian Vincent, Bill Viola Studio, Signal Hill, CA, November 29, 2012

Pages 239–43
The Dreamers (2013)
Video/sound installation
Seven channels of color High-Definition video on seven plasma displays mounted vertically on wall in darkened room; four channels of stereo sound
Screen size: 61 ¼ × 36 ⅜ × 5 in. (155.5 × 92.5 × 12.7 cm) each
Room dimensions: 11 ft 6 in. × 21 ft 4 in. × 21 ft 4 in. (3.5 × 6.5 × 6.5 m)
Performers: Gleb Kaminer, Rebekah Rife, Mark Ofugi, Madison Corn, Sharon Ferguson, Christian Vincent, Katherine McKalip
Photo pages 242–3: Peter Mallet, courtesy Blain|Southern

Page 245
Drawing for *Inverted Birth* (2014), Project Book (St. Paul's London '07), October 20, 2013

Pages 246–9
Inverted Birth (2014)
Video/sound installation
Color High-Definition video projection on screen mounted vertically and anchored to floor in dark room
Projected image size: 16 ft 5 in. × 9 ft 3 in. (5 × 2.81 m)
8:22 minutes
Performer: Norman Scott

Page 250
Drawing for *Martyrs (Earth, Air, Fire, Water)* (2014), for proposal to St. Paul's Cathedral, 2010

Pages 251, 254–9, 261
Martyrs (Earth, Air, Fire, Water) (2014)
Color High-Definition video polyptych on four vertical plasma displays
55 × 133 × 4 in. (140 × 338 × 10 cm)
7:15 minutes
Performers: Norman Scott, Sarah Steben, Darrow Igus, John Hay
(permanent installation, St. Paul's Cathedral, London, on long-term loan from Tate)
Photos pages 251, 261: Peter Mallet, courtsey Blain|Southern

Pages 252–3
On the set of "Water Martyr," panel 4 from *Martyrs (Earth, Air, Fire, Water)* (2014), performer John Hay, Red Studios, Los Angeles, CA, October 11, 2013
Photo: Nicola Goode

Page 263
Study of Bill Viola, Long Beach, CA, May 2012
Photo: Bill Viola Studio

Pages 264–5
Timeline drawing of highlights of work, 1970–1997, for Whitney Museum of American Art exhibition research, 1997

Page 271
Drawing, February 12, 1995 (US Pavilion Venice Biennale Project Book, January 11 – May 15, 1995)

Page 272
Notebook entry, April 1980 (Florence Notebook, December 1978 – January 17, 1981)

Page 273
Bill Viola, Saskatoon, SK, Canada, July 26, 1979

Page 274
Disturbance 3, drawing, October 20, 2013

Pages 280–1
Drawings of ideas for works, April 18, 1988 (Sketchbook, January 1985 – February 10, 1991)

Pages 282–3
Drawings of ideas for works, March 23, 1990 (Sketchbook, January 1985 – February 10, 1991)

Page 293
Notebook entry, October 4, 2007 (Notebook, October 25, 2005 – July 10, 2009)

Page 294
Notebook entry, July 7, 2008 (Notebook, October 25, 2005 – July 10, 2009)

Page 295
Notebook entry, April 19, 2010 (Notebook, July 21, 2009 – December 1, 2014)

Page 296
Notebook drawing, January 12, 2010 (Notebook, July 21, 2009 – December 1, 2014)

Jacket, back
On the set of "Water Martyr," panel 4 from *Martyrs (Earth, Air, Fire, Water)* (2014), performer John Hay, Red Studios, Los Angeles, CA, October 11, 2013
Photo: Nicola Goode

Jacket, back flap
Kira Perov, John Hanhardt, and Bill Viola, first book discussions, Long Beach, CA, August 8, 2013
Photo: Bill Viola Studio

Acknowledgments

Kira Perov

It has been an amazing experience to look back and to trace the influences that a lifetime of mentors, collaborators, museum directors, curators, gallerists, collectors, and technology companies have had on the work: they have all had a part to play in the evolution, development, and expression of one person's vision. There are many people to whom we owe a large debt, and in gratitude we acknowledge some of them here. Their contributions have touched our lives and this body of work. In our studio, the installations would not go out into the world without the dedication and expertise of our studio director, Bobby Jablonski, an essential part of our team since 1996. Her knowledge and understanding of the work have been critical to achieving and maintaining a high standard in all our exhibitions. Marie Corboy, our financial manager since 1999, has diligently kept our accounting and contracts on track through all projects and exhibitions. In production, we are grateful to our invaluable long-term collaborators, including Harry Dawson (director of photography), S. Tobin Kirk and Genevieve Anderson (producers), Giuliano Fiumani (special effects), Wendy Samuels and David Michael Max (art direction), and Brian Pete (online editor).

There has never been a time when we have not been preparing for exhibitions or engaged in production. Fortunately, we have been partnered with some of the world's best **gallerists**, all of whom have actively supported the work: Anthony d'Offay, James and Jane Cohan, Graham Southern, Harry Blain, Stephanie Camu, Hyun Sook Lee, Tina Kim, Arthur Solway, and Donald Young. Our supporters have also include **distributors** of single-channel works: Lori Zippay, Bob Stein, Dick Lam, and Howard Wise, visionary early advocate of the media arts.

Many **directors and curators** dedicated to the moving image have given us opportunities to show the work, and we are grateful for their vision. The list is incomplete, so apologies to those not included. **USA and Canada**: David Ross, John Hanhardt, Gerald O'Grady, Steina, Woody Vasulka, Barbara London, Kathy Huffman, Lydia Modi Vitale, George Bolling, Deirdre Boyle, Jacky Kain, Marilyn Zeitlin, Josée Bélisle, Peggy Gale, Robin Reidy, Beau Takahara, Steve Seid, Bob Riley, Julie Lazar, Melissa Feldman, Ashley Kistler, Bill Judson, Tina Yapelli, Stephanie Barron, Howard Fox, John Walsh, James Rondeau, James Wood, Glenn Phillips, Julia Brown, Anne Strauss, Francesca Valente, Adam Weinberg, Elizabeth Armstrong, Lisa Dennison, Hugh Davies, Bonnie Clearwater. **Switzerland**: Jörg Zutter, André Iten, Martin Brauen, Kathleen Bühler. **Austria**: Alexander Püringer, Otto Neumaier. **Germany**: Jean-Christophe Ammann, Wulf Herzognerath, Ingrid Oppenheim, Marie Louise Syring, Heinrich Klotz, Peter Weibel, Jeffrey Shaw, Rolf Lauter, Carl Haenlein, Wolfgang Volz, Jeanette Schmitz, Juliana von Herz, Sara Bernshausen. **Scandinavia**: Monica Nickels, Anders Kold, Jens Erik Sorensen, Anna Krogh, Bera Nordal, Jens Faurschou. **The Netherlands**: Dorine Mignot, Hendrik Driessen. **Belgium**: Jan Hoet, Chris Dercon. **France**: Anne-Marie Duguet, Jean-Paul Fargier, Raymond Bellour, Alain Fleischer, Dany Bloch, Don Foresta, Jean de Loisy, Joséphine Markovits, Christine Van Assche, Hervé Chandès, Thierry Raspail, Caroline Bourgeois, Jean-Paul Cluzel, Jérôme Neutres. **Italy**: Maria Gloria Conti Bicocchi, Valentina Valentini, Salvatore Settis, Mario De Simoni, Franca Falletti, Elena Volpato, Mariella Utili, James Bradburne, Anna Bernardini. **UK**: Neil MacGregor, Nicholas Serota, Frances Morris, Bill Hall, Sandy Nairne, Mark Oakley, Martin Warner, Martin Stancliffe, Oliver Caroe, Clare Lilley, Robert Violette. **Japan**: Fujiko Nakaya, Akio Obigane, Mami Kataoka, Kenichi Kondo, Ko Nakajima. **Korea**: Hong Ra-hee, Hong Ra-young, Soonhoon Bae. **Spain**: Maria de Corral, Carlota Álvarez Basso, Marta Gili, Marta Canals, Víctor García de Gomar, José Lebrero Stals, Nerea and Idoia Fernández. **Australia**: Lucina Ward, Tony Bond, David Elliott, David Sefton, Lucy Askew, Frances Lindsay. **Russia**: Dr Mikhail Petrovsky, Elena Kolovskaya, Stella Kesaeva. **Other countries**: Maria Brewinska (Poland), Marcello Dantas (Brazil, Argentina), Anna Kafetsi (Greece), Roc Laseca (Canary Islands).

We also wish to express our gratitude to the following people: **Music**: David Tudor, John Driscoll, Linda Fisher, Alvin Lucier, Ensemble Modern, Andreas Mölich-Zebhauser, Peter Eötvös, Gerard Mortier, Esa-Pekka Salonen, Deborah Borda, Chad Smith, Jane Moss, Jon Nakagawa, Valery Gergiev, Trent Reznor. **Television, film, game projects**: Carol Brandenburg, Fred Barzyk, Susan Dowling, Carl-Ludwig Rettinger, Gabriele Faust, Mark Kidel, Gerald Fox, Kevin Teixeira, Scott Fisher, Tracy Fullerton, Kurosh Valanejad, Todd Furmanski. **Major private collectors and supporters**: François Pinault, Pamela and Richard Kramlich, John Kaldor, Naomi Milgrom, Maja Hoffman, Maja Oeri, Fred Henry, Toshio (Bing) Miyamoto, Lynn and Evelyn de Rothschild, Leonard Lauder, Ulrich Hartmann, Marion Stroud Swingle, Ana Vallés Blasco, Josephina Blasco Clemente, Julio Sorigué Zamorano, Elena and Norman Foster, John Studzinski, Sheikha Mayassa Al Thani, Susan and John Singer, Tor Dagfinn and Tone Veen, Gloria Von Thurn und Taxis, Christina and Pierre de Labouchere, Ella Fontanals Cisneros, Minoru and Yoshiko Mori, Sylvain Orebi, Frédéric Rouzaud. **Mentors and friends**: Jack Nelson, David Tudor, Nam June Paik, Peter Campus, Gene Youngblood, Russell Connor, Daien Tanaka, Thierry Kuntzel, Peter Sellars, Lewis Hyde, Hans Belting, Hunter Drohojowska-Philp, and Weba Garretson.

Grants, awards: We are thankful to have had the support of various government arts-funding bodies, foundations, corporate and private commissions, and television stations. In particular, we are grateful to the National Endowment for the Arts, New York State Council on the Arts, the Rockefeller Foundation, the Guggenheim Foundation, Japan/US Friendship Commission, MacArthur Foundation, Praemium Imperiale (Japan), and Catalonia International Prize (Spain).

Production

Over the forty years that Bill Viola has been creating his video works, he has had the production assistance of hundreds of people. The following list recognizes his principal collaborators, current and past. The performers are acknowledged in the List of Works and Illustrations (see page 284).

Executive producer: Kira Perov//Producers: Peter Kirby, Karin Stellwagen, S. Tobin Kirk, Genevieve Anderson//Director of photography: Harry Dawson//Camera technical adviser: Brian Garbellini//Assistant directors: Kenny Bowers, Nick Conroy//Technical director: Alex MacInnis//Stunt coordinator: Tom Ficke//Gaffers: Joey Alvarado, Bobby Wotherspoon//Key grips: Rick Petretti, Terry Wimmer, Kevin Erb, Chris Centrella, John Brunold//Underwater stunt coordinator: Greg Tash//Production designers: Dennis Kightley, Wendy Samuels, David Michael Max//Special effects coordinators: Mike Hill, Robbie Knott, Giuliano Fiumani//Wardrobe/stylists: Lizzy Gardiner, Lisa Grosso, Donna May, Christina Wright, Laurie Ellwood, Cassandre de le Fortrie, David Norbury//Post-production supervisor: Michael Hemingway//Online editors: Randy Lawder, Brian Pete//Digital artists, colorists: Brian Ross, Gino Panaro, Mike Sowa//Sound designers and mixers: Bob Bielecki, Mikael Sandgren, Becky Allen, John Chalfant, Tom Ozanich//*Crossroads* engineering and screen design: StandardVision, Adrian Velicescu, David Agnew//Other assistance: Lance Wisniewski, Henry Baker, John Sanborn, Kit Fitzgerald, Yasuo Shinohara, Joe Leonardi, John Lilly, Blake Viola//Installation management: 235 Media, Uwe Glaser, Ludger Hennig.

Bill Viola Studio

At the core of our busy operations is the very able and committed team at the studio.

Studio director: Bobby Jablonski//Financial manager: Marie Corboy//Curatorial assistants: Elizabeth Steele Basile, Christen Sperry-Garcia//Electronics engineer: Thomas Piglin (since 1982)//Video archivists: Astra Price, Alex McInnis//Playback systems: Benjamin Lien//Past curatorial assistants: Michelle Plochere, Jean Rasenburger, Diana Pescar, Dana Phan, Tracy Furan, Ann Doh, Dianna Santillano, Gene Zazzaro, McLean Fahnestock//Past studio assistants: Joseph Santarromana, Robert Campbell, Claire Johnston, Donna Matorin LePard, David Dalzell, Kimberli Meyer, Kenny Chey, John Sarmiento//Past financial: Deonne Lindley//Past archival: Meghan Cawley.

Galleries/distribution

Blain|Southern Gallery, London//James Cohan Gallery, New York//Kukje Gallery, Seoul//Electronic Arts Intermix, New York//C&S Entertainment, the Netherlands//Past galleries: Anthony d'Offay Gallery, London//Donald Young Gallery, Seattle/Chicago//Haunch of Venison, London//Gallery Koyanagi, Tokyo//The Voyager Company, Los Angeles

Index

Page references to illustrations are in *italics*. All works are Bill Viola's unless otherwise stated.

Kill the fear of making mistakes,
of Right or Wrong. There is no right or wrong in Death

Designed by Lorraine Wild and Amy Fortunato,
Green Dragon Office, Los Angeles

First published in 2015 in hardcover in the United States of America by Thames & Hudson Inc., 500 Fifth Avenue, New York, New York 10110

thamesandhudsonusa.com

Library of Congress Catalog Card Number 2015932479

ISBN 978-0-500-09392-4

Printed in Malaysia

Page 1 Notebook drawing, *c.* August 5, 1974

Page 2 *The Sleep of Reason* (1988), detail

Page 4 *The Middens*, drawing, Project Book, January 1990

Page 294 Notebook entry, July 7, 2008

Page 295 Notebook entry, April 19, 2010

Page 296 Notebook drawing, January 12, 2010

Notebook entry, October 4, 2007

July 7 2008

Does God cry?

The five rivers that separate HADES from the Land of the Living:

ACHERON - the river of Woe
COCYTOS - the river of lamentation
PHLEGETHON - the river of Fire
LETHE - the river of Forgetfulness
STYX - the river of Hate

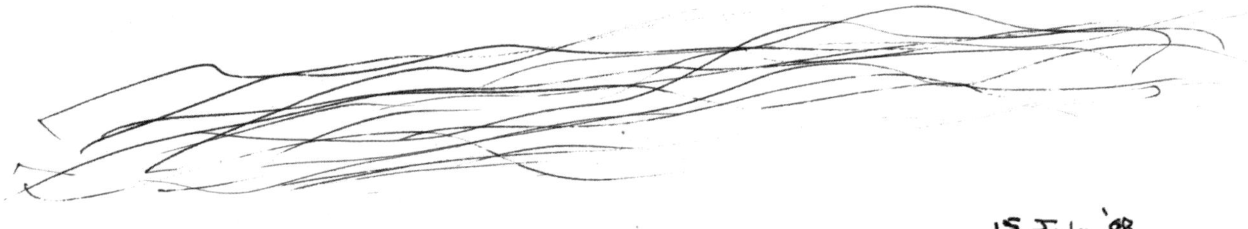

15 July '08

"Empty yourself, so that you may be filled.
Learn not to love so that you may learn how to love.
Draw back, so that you may be approached."

St. Augustine
Narration on Psalm 30:30.

April 19 Afternoon

Inner Voices

Voice of the BLOOD - Tells where you've come from, determines where you'll go along the migration of souls.

Voice of the MIND - Analyzes, Organizes, Plans, Calculates, Conceives, Deceives

VOICE of the HEART - Discerns the difference between right and wrong, good and bad, truth and falsehood, compassion and indifference.

VOICE of the FLESH Connects the spirit to the Earth, to the material realm, to form and substance and temporality.

VOICE of the ANGEL - Lives outside the body, a messenger from the light of the stars. Connects the spirit/self to the ethereal realm of the heavens and eternity.

BV

Hard Rain/
Brain Drain

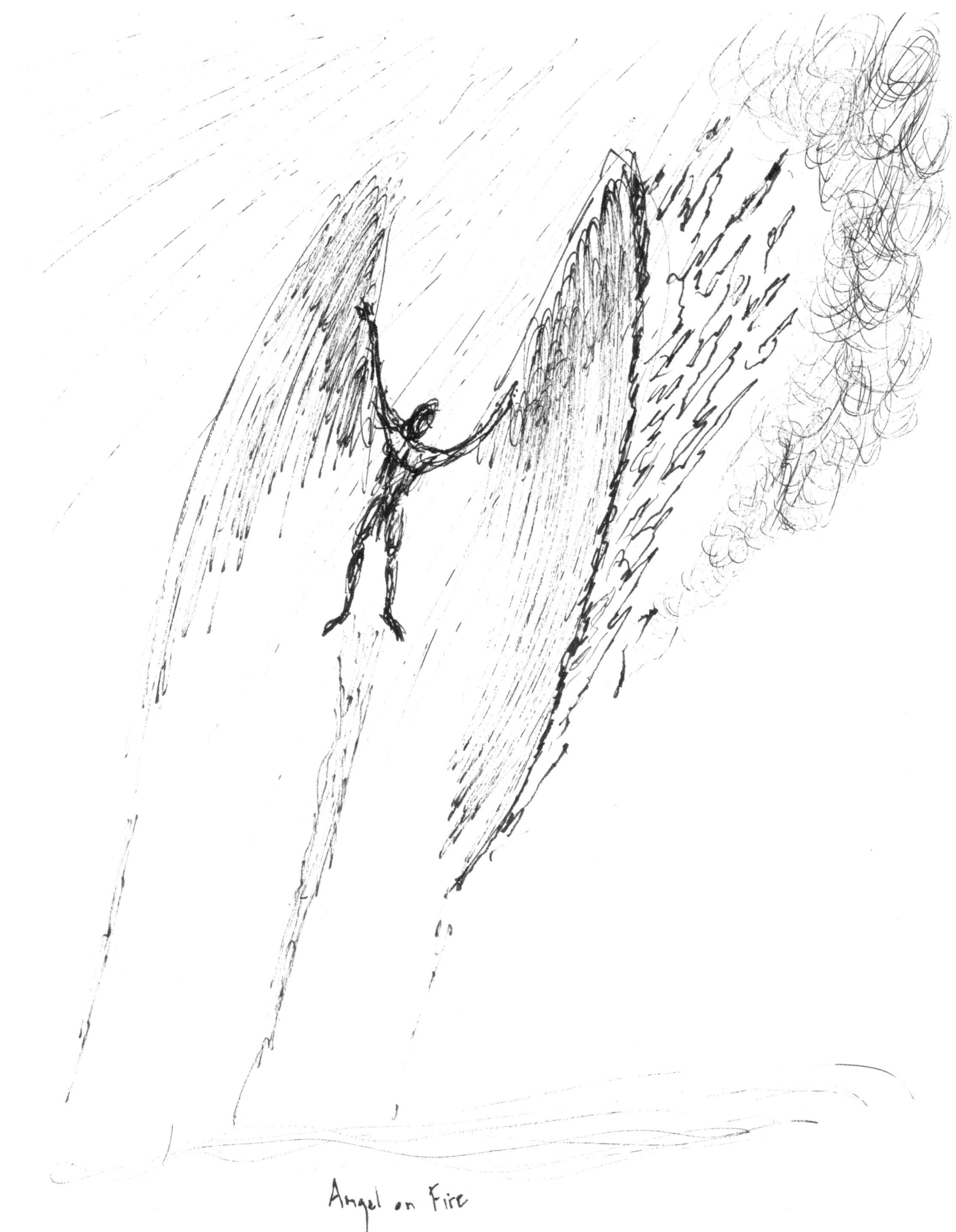

Angel on Fire